MÎZÂN

Studien zur Literatur in der islamischen Welt

Herausgegeben von
Catharina Dufft, Börte Sagaster,
Stephan Guth und Roxane Haag-Higuchi

Band 17

Essays in Arabic Literary Biography

General Editor: Roger Allen

Teil 1

2011
Harrassowitz Verlag · Wiesbaden

Essays in Arabic Literary Biography 925–1350

Edited by
Terri DeYoung and Mary St. Germain

2011
Harrassowitz Verlag · Wiesbaden

The signet on the cover was designed by Anwārī al Ḥusaynī and symbolizes a scale.

Cover: Courtyard of the Bayt Suhaym in Cairo, Egypt by Jere Bacharach.

Bibliografische Information der Deutschen Nationalbibliothek
Die Deutsche Nationalbibliothek verzeichnet diese Publikation in der Deutschen Nationalbibliografie; detaillierte bibliografische Daten sind im Internet über http://dnb.d-nb.de abrufbar.

Bibliographic information published by the Deutsche Nationalbibliothek
The Deutsche Nationalbibliothek lists this publication in the Deutsche Nationalbibliografie; detailed bibliographic data are available in the internet at http://dnb.d-nb.de.

For further information about our publishing program consult our website http://www.harrassowitz-verlag.de

Printed on permanent/durable paper.
Printing and binding: Hubert & Co., Göttingen
Printed in Germany

ISSN 0938-9024
ISBN 978-3-447-06598-6

Contents

Introduction to Volume 1 of Arabic Literature and Culture

TERRI DEYOUNG and MARY ST. GERMAIN
University of Washington

The subject of this volume is the period of Arabic literature beginning with 313 A.H./925 C.E. and lasting until 751/1350, or what sometimes has been called, in handbooks dealing with the era, "the late Abbasid period." This term is, of course, a misnomer for numerous reasons that have been ably recounted in critical studies from the last two decades. Most cogently, it is a purely chronological designation that has little descriptive relevance to the sorts of literary works produced within its confines. But, as long as the periodization and characterization of Arabic literature still constitutes a "work-in-progress," subject to many revisionary pressures, this label may do as well as any other for the nonce. It could in fact be seen as a useful reminder that many of the literary works—especially the poems—of these four centuries are deeply indebted to earlier models. They continue to employ features that achieved their initial mature form under the patronage of the first century of Abbasid caliphs in Baghdad (as well of as their provincial governors and other representatives in far-flung regions of the new Islamic polity bordering the shores of the Mediterranean).

It should be noted that for most of this "late" period, the Abbasid court, exercising but a shadow of its previous political power, was at the margins of literary activity, and by the end of it had faded completely from view. Most of the members of the immediate royal family were massacred during the Mongol invasion in 1258. But long before that horrific event, Baghdad would be replaced as cultural capital by an array of widely scattered regional centers. Other large cities in Iraq and Iran, like Rayy and Shiraz, would attain equal importance. Beyond the heartlands of the old Abbasid realm, Aleppo in Syria (seat of the Ḥamdānid dynasty) and Cordoba in Andalus (seat of the Umayyads) would shine. Curiously, Cairo in Egypt, though founded in 973 as the capital of the powerful and wealthy Fatimid caliphate, seems never to have generated a literary dynamism to match its political dominance of the southeast Mediterranean until late in this period, when it played host to major poets like **Usāmah ibn Munqidh** (1095-1188), his close friend **Ṭalā'ī' ibn Ruzzīk**, last of the significant Fatimid viziers, and the courtier and admirer of strophic poetry who composed an influential anthology of *muwashshaḥāt*, **Ibn Sanā' al-Mulk**. In the ensuing century, Cairo would be the home residence of two major religious poets, **Ibn al-Fāriḍ** (1181-1235) and **al-Būṣīrī** (1212-1294), whose appearance presaged a cultural renaissance of sorts in Egypt. But prior to that time, this area was intellectually in the hinterland.

As the 10th century dawned, however, all these centripetal forces were but a distant shadow on the horizon. The Abbasids had recovered much of the territory they had lost to independent governors in the previous fifty years. By 905, they again controlled Egypt, as well as most of the Tigris and Euphrates heartland. Only Andalus in the far west, and the far eastern territories of the Sāmānids maintained true independence. But, by the middle of the 10th century, this would all change. Even the capital of Baghdad would be controlled by a new dynasty, the Buwayhids, who would reduce the Abbasid caliph to one of their retainers, useful for commanding the allegiance of some of the inhabitants of Baghdad and its environs, but no more powerful than the head of the Shiite community in the same city. The long-term impact of the cultural institutions the Abbasids sponsored and shaped, however, would be more lasting.

The Arabic Language

In the preceding centuries, an outgrowth of the impact of the *Qur'ān* (Islam's scriptural text) on cultural life had been to focus an immense outburst of erudition on the codification of the Arabic language in which it had been revealed. Added to this was a newfound secular interest in a language that had led a fugitive and marginal existence in the Mediterranean basin until the Umayyad caliph ʿAbd al-Malik had decreed in 697 that all official government documents must be written in Arabic. The old imperial languages—Greek, Latin, Aramaic and Pahlavi—were thus no longer of practical importance to the large cadre of functionaries who ran the bureaucratic departments of the government. To get ahead at this time in the Islamic world, one had to know Arabic and know it well. This had an immense impact on the fortunes of the language and the literature that gave it vitality.

As the ninth century drew to a close, the major intellectual voices illustrated well the most pressing issues that had driven literary production in the preceding two centuries. In the area of language study, for example, two schools of thought had begun to emerge, one tracing its origins back to the Iraqi garrison city of Basra and the other to Kufa. The polemic over grammatical issues was still somewhat unsystematic, but its outlines can be traced in the works of the chief representative of the Basran school, Muḥammad ibn Yazīd al-Mubarrad (826-898), and his Kufan counterpart, Aḥmad ibn Yaḥyā Tha'lab (815-904), who both ended their careers in Baghdad—a portent of the fact that in the ensuing century the capital would become the new center of Arabic language studies. Though the common identification of both these figures as "grammarians" or "linguists" illustrates the new professionalization and specialization of intellectual activity, a quick review of their extant written works also shows the limits of this compartmentalization, since they both also composed a number of well-known treatises in several disciplines, including poetry. Their followers would continue to pursue an eclectic range of interests into the next century. Ibn Jinnī (d. 1002), for example, the foremost grammarian of his day, was also a close friend of the greatest poet of the age, **al-Mutanabbī** (915-965), was considered an expert on his work, and eventually became the teacher of the most widely admired poet in Baghdad at the turn of the eleventh century, **al-Sharīf al-Raḍī** (970-1016), who in turn led the Shiite community there for many years.

Probably the most important innovation that grammarians (primarily those of the Basran school) focused on in the tenth century was the question of whether it was possible to approach study of the language from a theoretical point of view. That is, would it be possible, primarily on the basis of analogy, to formulate general principles about the language, or would one necessarily always have to rely on precedent or proof text? This controversy would have a profound effect on approaches to religion and Islamic law (as can be seen in the position of someone like the Andalusian scholar **Ibn Ḥazm** (994-1064), who thoroughly rejected analogy, or *qiyās*). This had a residual effect even on conservative disciplines like poetry, where the growing concern with a theoretical understanding of figurative language—and especially metaphor—can be seen as owing something to arguments over the validity of analogy.

The Development of Arabic Poetry

In the course of the ninth century, poetry—on the pattern of what was happening with the study of language—also exhibited an emerging awareness of its past and its practitioners were increasingly willing to engage in a return to that past and re-examine it. Poetry had been the preeminent Arabic literary genre since before the rise of Islam. Most pressingly for linguistic reasons, students of the language and of the *Qur'ān* had preserved these *jāhiliyyah* (Preislamic) poems, finally committing them to writing (primarily in anthologies) in the early to mid-700s.

*Qaṣīdah*s from this period were often considered of the highest value among the subsequent generations of Muslim scholars as illustrations of the usage of Arabic vocabulary items also found in the *Qur'ān*.

Taken as poems, these *qaṣīdahs* not only had true quantitative syllabic metrical patterns, with rhythms that were easily perceived, but were monorhymed—features that distinguished them markedly from the poetry found in surrounding cultures. In Greek, for example, poetry had never featured systematic rhyme, and the earlier quantitative metrical system had increasingly evolved away from its earliest form as Late Antiquity progressed. It was slowly being replaced by a stress-accent system of regulation (possibly under the pressure of the composition of hymnic works that had become enormously popular since the consolidation of Christianity as an "official" religion), but this was a lengthy process, with many fits and starts, and there is currently no scholarly consensus as to when and where the new system can be said to begin and the old one end. Syriac (the widespread Aramaic dialect of Eastern Christians that would have been familiar to at least some Arabic speakers before the rise of Islam) exhibits characteristics similar to Greek, even though they do not belong to the same language family. When Syriac poetry begins to emerge in the fourth century, it is mostly in the form of Christian hymns (that probably were influential on the Greek ones, that only began to appear roughly a century later) that can be seen as having stress-accent meters, but no systematic rhyme. These Syriac hymns may, in turn, have been influenced by the Post-exilic Hebrew *piyyutim*, or liturgical songs, that formed part of the worship service of the synagogue, which again had no clearly marked rhyme and only slowly adopted a stress-accent patterning in its meter. Biblical Hebrew poetry seems to have had no identifiable formal features that incontestably set it apart from prose. We know very little for certain about Pahlavi (Old Persian) versification, but the available evidence seems to indicate that the principles were similar to Greek, which is related linguistically to Pahlavi.

Further differentiating Arabic poetry from Greek or Persian or Syriac compositions, many (though not all) *qaṣīdahs* had a tripartite thematic pattern rooted in the experience of the desert tribesman who had first composed them, one that became increasingly unfamiliar to later generations. By the time of Ibn Qutaybah (828-889), the great educator and polymath, a need had emerged to explain this structure explicitly. Ibn Qutaybah did precisely this in his introduction to his *Kitāb al-shi'r wa 'l-shu'arā'* (The Book of Poetry and Poets), the first attempt in Arabic to systematically discuss poetry as a literary genre and compile an authoritative list of canonical poets. There, he tells us that the first section of a *qaṣīdah*, the *naṣīb*, should speak of love, because everyone finds this subject attractive. But in the *qaṣīdah*, this should not be just any experience of love. Ideally, it should be occasioned by an incident where the (Bedouin) poet happens upon an old, now deserted, campsite, where he and his relations had settled briefly during their wanderings in search of pasture for their animals. During his earlier sojourn in this spot, he had met a woman from a group similarly encamped in the area—perhaps related to him and his family—and he had fallen in love with her. Then, when the groups had separated, the attachment was broken. Thus, the love affair is always represented in a retrospective light (though Ibn Qutaybah does not emphasize the point), and the poet's response to it, as memorialized in the poem, provides a field ripe for reflection on the tragic nature of human experience subject to the exigencies of time, and the tension between remembering and forgetting that is conventionally resolved (and so Ibn Qutaybah describes it) by the poet re-mounting his riding beast and leaving the deserted campsite behind.

The second section of the Preislamic *qaṣīdah*, the *raḥīl*, comprises a recollection by the poet of his subsequent journey through the desert, often accompanied by a detailed description of the animal he is riding on, and the ones he encounters along the way. Like the evocation of the beloved in the *naṣīb*, this section provides an opportunity for meditation on themes of more universal import. In the case of the *raḥīl*, these would have been those traditionally associated with the quest in the literature of Antiquity, like the opportunity afforded by observation of the things surrounding the questor for increased self-knowledge, or the transformative value of suffering as he struggles to complete the journey.

The third element in Ibn Qutaybah's schematic is the *madīḥ*, or panegyric section. The poet, exhausted by the rigors of his journey, arrives at the residence of a potential patron—the chieftain of a tribe or a client prince—who promises to alleviate the poet's sufferings, both material and emotional, by the offering of a reward, for which generosity he should be praised. Though generosity (*karam* or *jūd*) was the pre-eminent virtue of a *jāhiliyyah* patron, he could also be (and was) praised for virtues that echoed the traditional ones of Hellenistic culture (and perhaps Sassanian society as well): wisdom, courage, temperance and justness, although the former two were perhaps more commonly invoked than the latter.

It has been frequently noted by scholars and historians that the last section of the *qaṣīdah*, panegyric, was the most unstable in Preislamic poetry, often replaced by any number of other themes. But there is some justice in Ibn Qutaybah's taxonomy, because in his own time, when this kind of poem was revived (though it had never been completely abandoned), it was in a courtly context where panegyric was the *sine qua non* of the poetic profession. In fact the evidence would seem to support the contention that the other two themes, the *naṣīb* especially, are reformulated to complement a panegyric mode. The *naṣīb*, for example, becomes the place where the poet explores—in a process that flirts with allegory (though never quite adopting it wholeheartedly)—the complex emotional relationship that binds him to his patron: dwelling, not infrequently, on his wish to be free of such an allegiance, unless he could reasonably look forward to some reward in consequence of it. The poetry of **Abū Firās al-Ḥamdānī** (932-968) illustrates particularly well the emotional convolutions of this dynamic, since much of his poetry celebrates the reign of his cousin, the Aleppan prince Sayf al-Dawlah, who at one point cruelly abandoned Abū Firās to many years of captivity at the hands of the Byzantines. Al-Mutanabbī's poems composed in praise of the same Sayf al-Dawlah often evidence similar ambivalence.

Not surprisingly, however, immediately after the rise of Islam, when poetry must suddenly adjust to a new cultural context, the traditional Preislamic *qaṣīdah* suffers a temporary eclipse. It is replaced in its cultural centrality by shorter, less complex poems in a range of different thematic genres, of which the most striking and frequently cultivated are wine poems (*khamriyyāt*), which flout the Islamic prohibition against consumption of alcohol, and love poems (*ghazal*) that—like European courtly love lyrics—celebrate the very feelings of hopelessness and obsessive compulsion with the beloved object so soundly rejected by the aesthetics of the *naṣīb*. Both genres freely utilize religious language and imagery, but in contexts that are difficult to reconcile with the tenets of Islam. At their best, they represent a kind of earnest critique of the complacencies of unthinking religious conformity. At their least valuable, they appear to celebrate a kind of simple antiauthoritarian impulse to invert the values of the established order, without providing any guiding ethical framework independent of it that might be calculated to inform a renewed model for social behavior.

By the beginning of the ninth century, however, the model of the Preislamic *qaṣīdah* had been revived with a new emphasis on adapting it to a courtly environment. Coupled with this—and perhaps not unrelated to it—there is also a new emphasis on conscious manipulation of the language in which these poems are couched. The poets who dominate the century—Abū Tammām (796 or 804-842/843 or 845/846), first, and then the more "natural" poets, al-Buḥturī (821-897) and Ibn al-Rūmī (836-896) later on—crystallize in their work, and the subsequent reactions to it, the same tensions inherent in the new grammatical theories being developed using the principle of analogy as their basis. These new grammatical theories focus on deriving general rules about the structure of the language, without necessarily referring to actual linguistic usage. Similarly, the *badī'* (rhetorical) style of the poetry (and increasingly, the prose) focuses on the morphological and phonetic properties of individual words in the poetic line—and how they interact with one another—sometimes to the neglect of the relationship of the poetry to the lived reality that produced it.

It is then perhaps no accident that Ibn al-Rūmī, as one of the major poets of the period, emphasizes the fact that he spent some time in his youth as a pupil of the great Basran grammarian al-Mubarrad (ca. 815-898). Al-Mubarrad—along with his competitor from the Kufan school al-Tha'lab—also surfaces as the teacher of Ibn al-Mu'tazz (862-908), the most influential poet at the end of the ninth century, whose interests, significantly enough, combined poetic composition and literary criticism. Certainly, the close relationships between the poet al-Mutanabbī, the primary representative of the *badī'* style in the tenth century, the grammarian Ibn Jinnī, and his pupil al-Sharīf al-Raḍī, the dominant poetic voice supporting the traditional *qaṣīdah* form in the late tenth and early eleventh century, demonstrate the continuation of this lively convergence between the concerns of grammar and poetry that continues well beyond the period this volume covers.

One should not, however, leave ninth-century poetry without exploring in somewhat more detail the career of the poet at the Abbasid court whose work in many ways heralds the re-emergence of concern with the genres that had displaced the *qaṣīdah* in the first two Islamic centuries. This was Ibn al-Mu'tazz, son of the thirteenth Abbasid caliph, who was killed attempting to usurp his ineffective cousin al-Muqtadir at the end of 908. His political legacy was negligible, but his cultural impact was enormous.

In his youth, Ibn al-Mu'tazz had been a great admirer of al-Buḥturī, the foremost "natural" poet of the century. His own work, however, often harked back more to the wine and love poets active during the late Umayyad and early Abbasid periods. Nevertheless, he drew on al-Buḥturī's fondness for descriptive set pieces in establishing the *waṣf* (descriptive) poem as an important and independent genre. His intense, compact, almost elliptical descriptions of objects like fruit and flowers nicely anticipate the floral poetry of **al-Sanawbarī** (886?—945), as well as the character of the *nawriyyah* (floral) sections shortly to become common in Andalusian *qaṣīdahs*. **Ibn al-Khafājah** (1058 or 1059-1138 or 1139), was thus a disciple of both Ibn al-Mu'tazz and al-Sanawbarī. These early ninth-century masters can also be seen as providing a template for the vogue in "riddle" poems that would emerge throughout the Islamic world after the turn of the millennium, which are preserved in the *dīwāns* (collected works) of poets as distant from one another as **Mihyār al-Daylamī** (ca. 977–1037) in Baghdad and **Ibn Zaydūn** (ca. 1003-May 1071) in Seville.

In addition, Ibn al-Mu'tazz's interest in rhetoric and literary criticism led him to compose the *Kitāb al-badī'* (The Book of Tropes), one of the earliest Arabic examples of this sort of analytical composition about literature, whose major themes will be picked up by later authors. It could be seen as having an instrumental influence both on anthologies like **Abū 'l-Faraj al-Iṣbahānī**'s (897– ca. 972) monumental *Kitāb al-aghānī* (Book of Songs), and on the host of literary critical works, often of considerable insight and originality, which appear in the immediate wake of his *Kitāb al-badī'*. The study of figurative language in general, as inaugurated by Ibn al-Mu'tazz, receives an astonishingly original extension on the theory of metaphor in the subsequent century by the Ash'arī theologian, **'Abd al-Qāhir al-Jurjānī** (d. ca. 1081). As the entry on al-Jurjānī, his work on rhetoric and the inimitability (*al-i'jāz*) of the *Qur'ān* aptly illustrates how productive new insights were generated by the intense focus on the nature of the Arabic language inaugurated by scholarly engagements of this period with the impact of the new divine revelation on shaping the role of cultural institutions in Islamic society.

At roughly the same time, a work much influenced by Aristotelian ideas, *Naqd al-shi'r*, appears, written by **Qudāmah ibn Ja'far** (ca. 873or 874–948), whose initial impact is registered as far away as the writings of Ibn Ḥazm in al-Andalus and resonates down into modern times. Finally, this was the period that witnessed the subtle and impressive work of the premier theorist of tropes on both poetry and prose, **Abū Hilāl al-'Askarī** (d. after 1009), in his *Kitāb al-sina'ātayn* (Book of the Two Arts). Probably less directly influenced by Ibn al-Mu'tazz, but nevertheless produced in the same orbit, are two works that famously evaluate the poetry of earlier authors. The first of these is *al-Muwāzanah bayna Abī Tammām wa 'l-Buḥturī* (The Comparative Weighing of Abū Tammām and al-Buḥturī), by the otherwise very little known bureaucrat from Basra, Abū al-Qāsim al-Āmidī (d. 987). Al-Amidī, in the course of his comparison between the "artificiality" of Abū Tammām and the "naturalism" of al-Buḥturī (mostly to the detriment of Abū Tammām's poetry), manages to take several very telling swipes at some of Qudāmah's attempts to introduce Aristotelian standards into the evaluation of Arabic poetry. Somewhat more relevant to the concerns of this book, at about the same time as al-Āmidī, the respected legal scholar **al-Qāḍī al-Jurjānī** (ca. 902 or 928–976 or 1002) composes a work, *al-Wasātah bayna 'l-Mutanabbī wa-khusūmih* (The Mediation Between al-Mutanabbī and His Opponents) defending the ornate rhetorical style of al-Mutanabbī in his poetry. This work is treated at some length in the entry on al-Qāḍī al-Jurjānī in this volume, where the principles behind the Qāḍī's evaluative standards are helpfully laid out, so that their relevance takes on a sharper focus.

Religious Poetry

The spiritual impulses activated by the emergence of Islam in the seventh century were only slowly integrated into the structure of Arabic poetry. Panegyrists contemporary to Muḥammad, like his court poet Ḥassān ibn Thābit (d 674), or Ka'b ibn Zuhayr (d. ca. 645), who composed a famous poem seeking Muḥammad's forgiveness for slandering Islam, addressed the Prophet as they would any other tribal chieftain. The small amount of poetry that incorporates religious sentiments preserved from the first two centuries of Islam chiefly stresses either the importance of fighting bravely in support of the new religion or renunciation of worldly concerns to better prepare for the final judgment in the Hereafter. Sometimes, as in the poems produced by the Khārijite sect, it does both.

In the late 800s, with the increasing systematization of Sufi mysticism as an institution within Islam, a new sort of religious poetry comes to the fore. These are short lyrics, focusing on the emotional intensity experienced by their authors when encountering intimations of the Divine presence, and stressing the love of God over fear of Him. These poems are attributed to icons of the Sufi historical narrative like Rābi'ah al-'Adawiyyah (d. 801) or Abū 'l-Mughīth al-Ḥallāj (857-922)—as well as others—but they do not appear in written, attributed form until much later than their putative authors' lifetimes. Rābi'ah's poems, for example, are first recorded by the Persian mystic Farīd al-Dīn 'Aṭṭār (d. ca. 1230) in his biographical work, *Tazkirat al-awliyā'* (Reminiscences of the Friends of God). Similarly, although the outlines of al-Ḥallāj's life can be easily traced in contemporary historical chronicles, his poetry only has been collected by **Rūzbihān Baqlī** (1128-1209) long after his death. Baqlī was, moreover, accused by contemporaries of having added verses to al-Ḥallāj's *oeuvre*, but this kind of charge can more easily be placed in proper perspective when it is evaluated in the context of Baqlī's own very impressive original literary achievements.

The period following 925 was thus crucial for the formation of Arabic religious poetry, which is often of mystical orientation. Not only was this a time of consolidation, when verses of earlier poets were decisively attributed to their authors, but important new figures emerged. The most prolific of these was the Andalusian **Ibn al-'Arabī** (1165-1240), who traveled the length of the Arab world and ended up dying in Damascus, where his famous gravesite can still be visited. Many of his poems incorporate the traditional structure of the Preislamic *qaṣīdah*, but in his case the object of his desire and love is not a human woman, but God Himself. His achievements (and influence) are rivaled by the Egyptian poet **Ibn al-Fāriḍ** (1181-1235), who composes, like Ibn al-'Arabī, delicate and elaborate *qaṣīdahs* intended to express the author's veneration and longing for God.

Following Ibn al-'Arabī and Ibn al-Fāriḍ, the dominant strain in the religious impulse turns from charting direct encounters with the Divine to an intense concentration on the experience of the Prophet Muḥammad as a model for the spiritual quest most relevant to the individual believer. Considerable emphasis is also placed on the Prophet's role as intercessor with God for humankind. This turn in Arabic religious poetry was inaugurated by a humble Egyptian Sufi and governmental functionary, Sharaf al-Dīn al-Būṣīrī. His composition (popularly called the Burdah poem in reference to a dream al-Būṣīrī has in which he is enveloped in the Prophet's mantle (*burdah*) and is cured of a paralytic illness he had contracted), has—through the centuries—become one of the most influential Arabic works found in the Islamic tradition. The popularity of al-Būṣīrī's poem as a model, and the sort of inspiration it gave rise to, is illustrated by the example of one of his early imitators, the Iraqī poet **Ṣafī al-Dīn al-Ḥillī** (1278-ca. 1339). Al-Ḥillī combines his pious impulse, inspired by al-Būṣīrī, with an interest in Arabic rhetoric, producing a 154-line poem where every line illustrates a different rhetorical figure. This poem, in turn, inspired many imitators, down to modern times. Thus, the period from the eleventh to fourteenth centuries provides subsequent generations with several productive patterns for religious poetry, whose influence on Arabic—as well as other Islamic literatures—remains pervasively powerful until well into the nineteenth century.

The Development of Arabic Prose

The history of belletristic prose as a cultivated art begins in Arabic considerably later than poetry—after the decree by ʿAbd al-Malik that Arabic should be the sole official language in the caliphal chancery. But, once begun, its development was nothing short of meteoric and it had established a clearly individual character by the latter half of the ninth century. It is difficult to explain its antecedents entirely, as there is no trace in the surviving Arabic works of Roman or Byzantine models. It may owe something of its style to pre-Islamic specimens of oratory, or even to the chancery style of the late Sassanian empire (virtually all examples of which have been lost), since most of these who formed its canons in the early period came from Persian backgrounds.

Arabic secular prose certainly owes something to the inspiration of the *Qur'ān*, if only because the practice of quotation from the scripture in these works became widespread relatively early. But the *Qur'ān* was the direct word of God, with its own unique, inimitable, oracular style—a principle that was articulated early in the history of Islam—based on features that would make it ill-adapted to serve as a source of inspiration for the many of the mundane tasks of the government secretarial class who used it. Nor do the features that came to characterize the "secretarial style" seem to be directly traceable to specifically *Qur'ānic* origins.

We do find, by the middle of the eighth century, a major fictional prose work produced at the hands of Ibn al-Muqaffaʿ, a secretary of Persian descent who translated (with major changes and additions) the Indian fables of Bidpai from a (now lost) Pahlavi (Old Persian) version. But this book, *Kalīlah wa-Dimnah* (its title taken from the names of the two jackals who are its main characters), stands *sui generis* in the history of Arabic prose. There are no other major fictional works in the prose genre until the invention, by **Badīʿ al-Zamān al-Hamadhānī**, of the *maqāmah* in the late tenth century.

Instead, Arab prose writers initially take their cue from other compositions produced by Ibn al-Muqaffaʿ (and his contemporaries). Known as *rasā'il* (singular *risālah*)—the same word used for "letters," "messages" in Arabic—their closest counterparts would be the essays cultivated by late Renaissance European writers like Montaigne or Bacon. Their subject matter could be loosely described as *adab*, the range of topics (drawn from ethics, politics, philosophy, science, or religion) appropriate to the education of an aspiring "gentleman" or functionary with the Islamic state. The origins of the *risālah* form can be found as early as Ibn al-Muqaffaʿ's predecessor, ʿAbd al-Ḥamīd ibn Yaḥyā in his *Risālah ilā 'l-kuttāb* (Epistle to the Secretaries) and *Risālah fī naṣīhat walī 'l-'ahd* (Epistle of Advice to the Crown Prince). Ibn al-Muqaffaʿ (who was probably personally acquainted with ʿAbd al-Ḥamīd) is equally famous for his major efforts in the genre, *al-Adab al-kabīr* (The Greater Adab) and *al-Risālah fī 'l-ṣaḥābah* (The Epistle on Companions). But the form would be brought to its peak in the work of two authors from the next century, al-Jāḥiẓ (d. 869) and Ibn Qutaybah.

Al-Jāḥiẓ is reported to have been the descendent of African slaves, born in Basra in the most humble of circumstances, who eventually rose to become the intimate of the Abbasids and their ministers. His *Rasā'il*, which for the most part found their inspiration in the informal conversational tone of the personal letter, are famous for their digressive style, but the language (like ʿAbd al-Ḥamīd's and Ibn al-Muqaffaʿ's) is still relatively straightforward, lacking for the most part the adornment of *saj'* (rhymed prose) that would become increasingly ubiquitous by the eleventh century. Even at this early stage, prose and poetry (in the form of quotations) was intermixed in these compositions, but it was used more sparingly than it would later be. The titles of his signature works, *Kitāb al-ḥayawān* (The Book of Animals), *Kitāb al-bukhalā'* (The Book of Misers), *al-Bayān wa 'l-tabyīn* (Eloquence and How It is Shown) give evidence of the wide range of his interests and his lively intellect.

Ibn Qutaybah traveled in some of the same literary circles as al-Jāḥiẓ, but he was born when the latter was over fifty. Later generations would see him as the champion of Sunni Islam, in contrast to al-Jāḥiẓ, who was a Muʿtazilite, but one should perhaps be careful in applying these labels too strictly in this early period.

In a literary sense, Ibn Qutaybah can best be approached as more of a systematizer, even a pedagogue, than an idiosyncratically brilliant stylist like al-Jāḥiẓ. His encyclopedic works like the *Adab al-kātib* (The Adab of the Secretary), *Kitāb al-shi'r wa 'l-shu'arā'* (Book of Poetry and Poets), and above all the *'Uyūn al-akhbār* (Choice Anecdotes), nevertheless can be seen as inspiring the compositions of major authors in succeeding generations, like the Andalusian **Ibn ʿAbd Rabbih**'s *'Iqd al-farīd* (The Unique Necklace) or Abū 'l-Faraj al-Iṣbahānī's *Kitāb al-aghānī* (Book of Songs). In his writings, we can see the consistent employment of structural features that would later form the core of instruction in schools. The preamble, for example, that invokes God—often accompanied by a request to bless the Prophet Muḥammad and members of his family—is already securely in place in Ibn Qutaybah's writing, as is an opening exordium describing in detail the subject of the work. Such features can, of course, be found in al-Jāḥiẓ and earlier authors, but the key difference is in the consistency and regularity with which Ibn Qutaybah employs them, and how he subordinates all the elements of his writing to the production of an overall impression.

Ibn Qutaybah utilizes with dexterity all the several methods of supporting his argument and persuading his readers that he had inherited from earlier authors. Quotations from the *Qur'ān* and the *ḥadīth* occupy, naturally, the position of highest authority, appealing as they do respectively to the words of God, or the practice of the Prophet. Next would be statements from, or anecdotes about, wise individuals from the past (including the Preislamic past). Named individuals from the Islamic cultural tradition, of course, carry the greatest weight, but very often the authority is characterized simply as "one of the wise men (*al-ḥukamā'*)," and this is a signal that the person may be a denizen of the pagan (either Greek or Sassanian) world. Ibn Qutaybah is careful to limit himself mostly to Muslim authorities, but other authors, depending on their proclivities, may favor non-Muslims more, even placing them first sometimes in the list of the citations. Later, all such sources in a given prose work will be collectively called "traditional," "inherited," "transmitted" (*manqūl*), and the acquisition of information about these authorities will be the focus of much scholarly effort.

Complementing this transmitted material, an author like Ibn Qutaybah would rely on the description and analysis of his material through arguments based on his own reasoning and observations. In the beginning of his works, especially, Ibn Qutaybah generally devotes some effort to demonstrating the importance of the chosen topic and its major features, often through a description justifying the section/chapter divisions he has chosen for his presentation. Later, the techniques and areas of study that helped an author develop the skills necessary to construct such argument and taxonomies were collectively referred to as "rational," "logical," "discerning" (*ma'qūl*). To gain a reputation as a master of prose, then, one had to be well-acquainted with both the *manqūl* and *ma'qūl* branches of learning, and Ibn Qutaybah's works can be seen as an important milestone in the development of this educational philosophy, which would be brought to much higher level of refinement in the succeeding centuries.

We also see in Ibn Qutaybah's works the final component of a composition in the *adab* genre, which is the incorporation of poetic quotation into the prose framework, a phenomenon that is sometimes referred to (on the analogy of Classical Greek and Latin precedents, although works are in many ways dissimilar) as prosimetrum. In Arabic works, like Ibn Qutaybah's compositions, poetic citations are most often employed as proof texts for the arguments being made by the author, not to indicate different points of view or to underscore instances of heightened emotion or feeling, as was the case with many European examples of this prosimetrum form.

Ibn Qutaybah's interest in writing works directed toward the courtly world of the secretaries was complemented by an equal attentiveness to the *Qur'ān* and religious topics, and he also composed a number of treatises on these subjects. In many ways, this encyclopedic (and pedagogic) bent on Ibn Qutaybah's part paved the way for the last of the great intellectual figures of the ninth and early tenth century, whose work also laid out models for later writers, Muḥammad ibn Jarīr al-Tabarī. Al-Tabarī was born in 839 in the province of Tabaristan and began his education with the study of the religious sciences, specializing particularly in the field of *ḥadīth* (stories about the Prophet Muḥammad's sayings, doings, or the occasions when he witnessed certain incidents and either approved or disapproved of them). In order to perfect his preparations in this area, al-Tabarī traveled in his youth, first to Baghdad and then as far as Egypt, to study with acknowledged masters in the field.

But when al-Tabarī returned to Baghdad at the turn of the tenth century he went beyond his training to compose two multi-volume works that were unprecedented and had an incalculable impact on the course of subsequent scholarship. The first was a commentary on the *Qur'ān*, *al-Jāmi' fī al-bayān*, which was organized by verse and exceeded all other studies of the *Qur'ān* in its comprehensiveness and the depth of its explanation of every word and line of the holy text. The fame of this commentary quickly spread as far as al-Andalus and was extensively cited by later scholars. It later gave birth to many such commentaries, continuing on down to the present day.

The second work al-Tabarī produced was a universal history, going far beyond a mere chronicle of Islamic times to relate stories known to Muslims of earlier cultures and societies, though the treatment was somewhat selective. Al-Tabarī covers, for example, the history of the Hebrew Bible patriarchs and prophets extensively, but spends far less time on New Testament events. His history, however, was the first work that demonstrated the special genius Muslims would continue to demonstrate for writing history (as opposed to fictional tales). The importance for Muslims of historiography can probably be traced to the end of Sūrah 12 (Yūsuf), which justifies the narrative form of that *Qur'ānic* chapter on the basis of its truthfulness:

> In their stories is a lesson for those who
> have discernment. It is not a tale | con-
> trived, but a verification (*tasdīq*) of that
> which is before [you], a detailed | elabo-
> ration of every thing, and a guidance and
> mercy to a people who believe.

Al-Tabarī, however, was the first author to exploit that injunction by producing a lengthy, consistent, true and verifiable historical narrative work. His example—both in the *Qur'ānic* commentary and the history—spawned many imitators in subsequent decades. We can see the results of this trend in works like al-Masʿūdī's history, the commentaries of Zamakhsharī, al-Baydāwī and al-Qurṭubī, and even the trend toward comprehensive literary anthologies, like Abū al-Faraj al-Iṣbahānī's *Kitāb al-aghānī*, or Ibn Bassām's *al-Dhakhīrah fī maḥāsin ahl al-Jazīrah*.

Developments During the Tenth Through the Fourteenth Centuries

As noted at the beginning of this introduction "continuity," is an important keynote in these centuries. By the beginning of the tenth century, conversion to Islam in the areas controlled by the Abbasids was substantially complete and other religious groups (with other cultural traditions to draw on) were increasingly shrinking minorities. It would have been clear to any observer that Islam had come to stay, and in this century (before the renaissance of Persian, and the emergence of Turkish as a literary language) the expression of Islamic cultural ideas and attitudes was in Arabic, which by this time had created a substantial tradition to draw upon, in both poetry and prose.

Yet, beneath the surface of continuity, there were substantial currents of change. In some ways one can see this most clearly in the impact of Greek thought—particularly philosophy—on the entire intellectual system in the Islamic world. Part of this impact was seen in a reaction against Greek ideas (or at least attempts to make them conform to an Islamic worldview), but even in relatively conservative genres, like poetry, the influence of new vocabulary—and the concepts these words represented—could be found. This was because didactic works, like the Aristotelian corpus on logic and argumentation (the *Organon*) had a profound effect on the tenth-century educational system in the Islamic world, and this was increasingly the common training ground for all who aspired to elite status and were equipped to compose and appreciate poems. The immense variety and intellectual sophistication forming a background to these activities in this time period is superlatively well illustrated by the *Fihrist* (Catalogue) of the Baghdad bookseller **Ibn al-Nadīm** (d. 990), a unique and invaluable record of the books circulating during the author's lifetime, including many items translated from Greek, or influenced by Greek thought.

Yet, at the same time, a new openness to popular forms also developed, even in poetry. The effects of this were not so noticeable in the tenth century, but by the eleventh and especially in the twelfth century, they had begun to snowball. Not surprisingly, they seem to have first become apparent on the margins of the Islamic world in Spain in the far west and (a little later) on the boundary with what is today Iran.

Andalus (the Arabic name for the territories conquered by Muslims on the Iberian peninsula.) was for several centuries considered a backward province, with little of interest to offer more sophisticated circles of intellectuals farther east. This would change as the strophic forms of poetry, the *zajal* and *muwashshaḥah*, that appeared first in Andalus found a responsive chord as far east as Egypt and Syria, were enthusiastically adopted by poets like Ibn Sanā' al-Mulk and Ṣafī al-Dīn al-Ḥillī. Similarly, a form known as the *muzdawij* or *urjūzah* (that rhymed the hemistiches of lines rather than using monorhyme)—although examples can be found in earlier Arabic verse—became increasingly popular. It has close affinities with the Persian *mas̱navī* form and may very well have originated with oral poetic tradition in Persian. Notable examples are produced early in the tenth century by Ibn al-Muʿtazz and Abū Firās al-Ḥamdānī. It is testimony, however, to the ease of communication within the Islamic world at this time, that the form also became popular in Andalus by the middle of the tenth century, as is reflected in the work of Ibn ʿAbd Rabbih commemorating the exploits of the great Spanish Umayyad Caliph ʿAbd al-Raḥmān al-Nāṣir. This is not to speak of local popular forms of verse, like the *mawwāl*, the *band*, the *dubayt*, or the *kān wa-kān*, which were increasingly cultivated by elite poets in the latter half of this period. Ṣafī al-Dīn al-Ḥillī, one of the great poets of thirteenth-century Levant and Egypt, composed a detailed introduction to these non-standard genres of poetry that demonstrates their growing importance.

Prose, too, exhibits this same dichotomy of apparent continuity masking significant change. The *risālah* continued to be cultivated, and became the special province of secretaries and viziers, like **al-Ṣāḥib ibn ʿAbbād**, who, more and more, followed the conventions of *saj'* (rhymed prose), which often sacrificed clarity of meaning for euphony in sound. Yet, on the other hand, this period also saw the birth of a genre, the *maqāmah*, that depended on fictional narrative (for the first time since *Kalīlah wa-Dimnah*) albeit in elaborate *saj'*. The inventor of the genre was Badīʿ al-Zamān al-Hamadhānī in the tenth century. In the next century, he had two highly proficient students, **al-Ḥarīrī** in the East and **al-Saraqusṭī** in al-Andalus. They took the *maqāmah* to new heights of sophistication. Also paralleling poetry, popular forms of fiction (in colloquial Arabic) became increasingly widespread. The *Thousand and One Nights* is one such example whose fame has spread even in Europe and America, but this was also the heyday of *sīra*s (heroic tales) about the Banū Hilāl tribe, the Preislamic poet ʿAntarah, or the Mamlūk sultan of Egypt, Baybars. Although this was the age when these *sīra*s were first written down, they were never given the same recognition as popular forms of poetry, and they were rigidly excluded from the canon of high literature. Along with popular forms, literature incorporated vernacular usages of the mendicant classes. Al-Ṣāḥib ibn ʿAbbād was so fascinated with such language that he hosted particularly informative beggars at his court. Such language was often used in humorous writings mocking long established standards polite society and power structures. **Abū Ḥayyān al-Tawḥīdī** (ca. 922-ca. 1014) was an exceptional stylist and also exceedingly acerbic critic of leading individuals, particular of patrons who did not live up to his hopes. To supplement his income, **Ibn al-Ḥajjāj** (ca. 931–24 May 1001) who worked as an ordinary civil servant, wrote and sold voluminous quantities of obscene and scatological poetry. Reflecting the divergent values of the period, he also wrote excellent traditional poetry known for the sweetness of its expression.

This period was one of great creativity in many ways. It produced poets of tremendous importance as creative voices, like **Abū ʿAlāʾ al-Maʿarrī** and al-Mutanabbī. And the prose writers, like Badīʿ al-Zamān or al-Ḥarīrī or al-Tawḥīdī achieved fame that has resonated down to the present day, assuring them a prominent place in national school curricula all over the Arab world. The political fragmentation of the time—while fostering literary production by multiplying the sources of patronage—also took its toll on the reputations of many authors. The entire corpus of work from al-Andalus, for example, was largely forgotten until scholars in the twentieth century (both Arab and foreign) painstakingly retrieved it. Equally damaging to the appreciation of the achievements of these authors was the nineteenth-century dominance (both among European and Arab literary critics) of the Romantic aesthetic privileging originality and creativity over the value of subtlety, decorum, virtuosity and design. Understanding these authors takes more preparation and familiarity with their milieu than is the case with most literary figures, and this volume will have succeeded if it makes even a modest step in this direction.

Dating

Most Arabic literary histories dealing with this period use the Islamic "Hijrī" calendar, but at this time the dates when centuries begin are relatively close in both the Western and Hijrī calendars. Thus, the fourth Hijrī century begins in mid-912 C.E., the fifth century in August of 1009, the sixth century in mid-1106 and the seventh century in September of 1203. The Islamic eighth century coincides even more closely with the Western fourteenth century, beginning in 700 A.H. beginning on 16 September 1300.

Abū 'l-Faraj al-Iṣbahānī

(897– ca. 972)

GABRIEL SKOOG
University of Washington

WORKS

Maqātil al-ṭālibiyyīn (Unnatural Deaths of the Talibids);
al-Imā' al-shawā'ir (The Slave Poetesses);
Kitāb al-aghānī (The Book of Songs);
Adab al-ghurabā' (The Book of Strangers).

Editions

Maqātil al-ṭālibiyyīn (Unnatural Deaths of the Talibids), ed. Aḥmad Ṣaqr (Cairo: ʿĪsā 'l-Bābī 'l-Ḥalabī, 1949);
al-Imā' al-shawā'ir (The Slave Poetesses), ed. Nūrī Ḥammūdī Qaysī and Yūnus Aḥmad Sāmarrā'ī (Beirut: Maktabat al-Nahḍah al-ʿArabiyyah, 1984);

Kitāb al-aghānī (The Book of Songs) (Bulaq: al-Maṭbaʿah al-Amīriyyah, 1868); Fifth ed., with complete indexes, ed. Muḥammad Abū 'l-Faḍl Ibrāhīm, 24 vols. (Cairo: al-Hay'ah al-Miṣriyyah al-ʿĀmmah li 'l-Kitāb, 1992);
Adab al-ghurabā' (The Book of Strangers), ed. Ṣalāḥ al-Dīn al-Munajjid (Beirut: Dār al-Kitāb al-Jadīd, 1972).

Translations

Patricia Crone and Shmuel Moreh, *The Book of Strangers: Mediaeval Arabic Graffiti on the Theme of Nostalgia* (Princeton: Princeton University Press, 2000).

Abū 'l-Faraj ʿAlī ibn al-Ḥusayn ibn Muḥammad ibn Aḥmad ibn al-Haytham al-Umawī al-Iṣbahānī was born in 897, more than likely in or around Baghdad, the center of Abbasid power at that time. He was a member of the Prophet Muḥammad's Quraysh tribe and was a direct descendant of the Umayyad caliph Marwān ibn Muḥammad (d. 750), whose heirs had fled to Isfahan, which was then called Iṣbahān, after the fall of the Umayyad caliphate. At an unknown point Abū 'l-Faraj's branch of the family later moved to Baghdad. Many of Abū 'l-Faraj's relatives on both his father and mother's side were prominent administrative clerks, and it is not surprising that Abū 'l-Faraj also chose a clerical career.

Abū 'l-Faraj's greatest contribution to Arab literature was his enormous text *Kitāb al-aghānī* (The Book of Songs). At the core of the work is a collection of songs and poems from the Preislamic period through the Umayyad caliphate, ending in the early Abbasid era. What is singularly striking about the work is the wealth of contextual, historical, and biographical information included in its pages. Abū 'l-Faraj gives rich accounts of the lives of poets, composers, musicians, and other important figures associated with music at the time, and his text is a wonderful resource on subjects as diverse as the lives of Preislamic poets, ancient tribal conflicts, court intrigue, and musical humor. His work is still regularly consulted by scholars interested in topics ranging from history to musical performance practice to literature and has been a regularly cited resource since its completion over a millennia ago. Abū 'l-Faraj, following standard intellectual practice at the time, quotes earlier writers whose works have not come down to us, preserving texts that would have otherwise been lost. The *Kitāb al-aghānī* has maintained its honored position to the present day and will in all likelihood continue to be valuable resource well into the future. Four of the thirty works attributed to Abū 'l-Faraj are still extant today, and they are, in order of composition, *Maqātil al-ṭālibiyyīn*, *al-Imā' al-shawā'ir*, *Kitāb al-aghānī* and *Adab al-ghurabā'*.

Abū 'l-Faraj studied in two of the major intellectual centers of the period, Kufa and Baghdad. At the time, Kufa was a center for the study of the Arabian Preislamic period, and the overall tone of scholastic discourse there lent itself more to the study of grammar, aesthetics and the arts than to the more rarified, Greek influenced philosophical, rational and scientific pursuits. While there, Abū 'l-Faraj associated both with well-known scholars and with regional singers and entertainers.

Abū 'l-Faraj's mother was more than likely a member of the Shiite Banū Thawābah tribe, which would explain his personal Shiite convictions, at first surprising for someone of Umayyad descent, but ultimately understandable due to the fact that the development of Shiism was in great flux during his lifetime. The Banū Thawābah were a family of Christians, who, after conversion to Islam, rose to influential positions as clerks in the administration. Furthermore, Abū 'l-Faraj belonged to the Zaydī sub-set of the Shiah, which, as the Shiite tendency closest to Sunnism, may explain his comfort around both Sunni and Shiite companions. Little of his personal religious beliefs or sentiments are apparent in his extant writings, save in his first work, *Maqātil al-ṭālibiyyīn*, which shows a strong influence of Shiite scholarship in Kufa.

Maqātil al-ṭālibiyyīn (Unnatural Deaths of the Talibids), Abū 'l-Faraj's earliest extant work, was more than likely written while Abū 'l-Faraj was living and studying in Kufa. It relates the downfall of the descendants of the Prophet's uncle, Abū Ṭālib (ca. 540-ca. 619), from the Prophet's lifetime until 925, and as such could be considered a Shiite martyrology. Abū 'l-Faraj examines over 200 individuals, including in his definition of martyrdom not only those who were killed in battle, executed, or poisoned, but also those kept imprisoned for life, forced to live underground, or forced to flee to distant lands never to return.

Each entry is given in chronological order and follows a standard pattern of: name, genealogy, a profile sketch, events before the death, and the death itself. Variation occurs between the entries, with some entries including a poetic elegy or making mention of the subject being a *ḥadīth* transmitter. In addition, some Shiite uprisings are considered, and all the participants are listed in turn before the description of the event itself. The groupings of the sections are made in according to the caliph under whose reign the death occurred.

It is unclear when Abū 'l-Faraj made the transition from Kufa to Baghdad, but it was more than likely sometime after 912. At the time, Baghdad was the capital of the Abbasid caliphate and was developing into a major intellectual and artistic center, attracting some of the greatest artists and thinkers of the age. The roster of intellectuals under whom Abū 'l-Faraj studied in Baghdad is not exactly clear, but included the philologist and grammarian Abū Bakr ibn Durayd, the philologist, grammarian, *ḥadīth* and *Qur'ānic* science scholar Abū Bakr ibn al-Anbārī (885-940?), the narrator and grammarian ʿAlī ibn Sulaymān al-Akhfash (d. 927), the narrator and genealogist al-Faḍl ibn al-Ḥubāb al-Jumḥī, and the grammarian, biographer, and historian Ibrāhīm ibn Muḥammad ibn ʿArafah Niftawayh (858-935). Probably the best known of his teachers was the famous historian and *Qur'ān* commentator Muḥammad ibn Jarīr al-Ṭabarī (838?-923). Of Persian descent, al-Ṭabarī was renowned as a diligent historian, having produced the detailed and accurate *Tārīkh al-rusul wa 'l-mulūk* (History of the Prophets and Kings), translated into English as *The History of al-Tabari*, outlining the history of the Mediterranean region from creation until roughly 915. The influence of al-Ṭabarī's intellectual and historical rigor is apparent in the later work of Abū 'l-Faraj, particularly in the painstaking detail of the *Kitāb al-aghānī*.

Produced subsequent to his earlier work in Kufa, *al-Imā' al-shawā'ir* (The Slave Poetesses) is a collection of biographies about poetesses of the Abbasid period who had the status of personal slaves. These women were often highly educated and received extensive training in the musical arts, becoming part of the highest social circles and even the entourage of caliphs. Quickly compiled on the behest of Abū 'l-Faraj's patron, the vizier Abū Muḥammad al-

Ḥassan ibn Muḥammad al-Muhallabī (903-963), the text consists of a short introduction followed by 31 sections that altogether describe 33 women. Most of the selections are brief, with the three poetesses ʿInān, Fadl and ʿArīb, receiving extensive write-ups. The book is sub-divided into three sections, with each of the aforementioned poetesses' entries introducing a section. Overall Abū 'l-Faraj's work presents a rough sketch of the general contours of a slave singer's life in the Abbasid period, with particular attention paid to poetic competition, panegyric, and *ghazal* (love song). *Al-Imā' al-shawā'ir* was written before he started the *Kitāb al-aghānī* and can be interpreted as a sort of short exercise in biographical writing anticipating that later, more developed work.

Kitāb al-aghānī (The Book of Songs) is by far the most important and famous of Abū 'l-Faraj's work. Written over a period of fifty years, it is more than just an anthology of Arab poets, but in addition a grand treatise on Arabic music from the age before Islam to the early Abbasid period. Organized according to song, current printings have more than two-dozen volumes running to almost ten thousand pages in some editions. Never lost to obscurity, *Kitāb al-aghānī* has been highly regarded in the field of Arabic literature from its creation to modern times, currently having at least five different print editions and nine abridgments. It is a invaluable resource for scholars in myriad fields, and the information contained in its pages has enriched historical, literary, and musical studies, to name only a few.

Organized around a central core of song texts, the *Kitāb al-aghānī* mixes prose, poetry, anecdotes, statements of information, historical excerpts, jokes, and heroic tales, a conceptual hodgepodge characteristic of medieval Arabic compilations of *belles-lettres*. Additionally, Abū 'l-Faraj draws equally upon oral and written sources, documenting them according to the science of Muslim historiography *(isnād)*. This dizzying mixture of information and format can and often does leave modern readers disoriented. In reality, the work, while confusing, can be very systematic, and the author's overall aim is to report both songs and the various facts that are available concerning them. When the accounts disagree the author gives all of the different versions and a critical evaluation as to which is most likely true.

In his preface, Abū 'l-Faraj justifies the decision to arrange the book around a core set of song texts and mentions that the work was instigated at the request of an unknown patron, but contemporary scholarly consensus points to al-Muhallabī. Over a century earlier, the famous caliph Hārūn al-Rashīd (763 or 766-809) had ordered his court musicians Ibrāhīm al-Mawṣilī, Ismāʿīl ibn Jāmī, and Fulayh ibn al-ʿAwrā' to create a list of songs then popular at the court. This list was then again revised, and consequently attributed to, Isḥāq al-Mawṣilī (767-850). It is this list that served as a starting point for Abū 'l-Faraj's work. While Abū 'l-Faraj's unnamed patron only asked that he evaluate and revise the *Kitāb al-aghānī* attributed to Isḥāq al-Mawṣilī, the work eventually extended far beyond its original parameters. Abū 'l-Faraj is reported to have spent the better part of his life, in some accounts close to fifty years, working on the text.

The work is broken into three sections. The first section is primarily organized according to the top one hundred songs supposedly chosen by Isḥāq al-Mawṣilī, with additional songs beyond the top one hundred included under varying criteria such as composer or rhythmic mode. The second section consists of songs composed by caliphs and their descendants. Finally, the third section is a mixture of songs chosen by the author for inclusion, made up of a mixed bag of texts not subsumed under previous categories. One fact often overlooked by many is that the work itself is unfinished. The later entries become progressively more skeletal, until at the end only fragments are given.

In addition to documenting a song with the name of its poet, composer, rhythmic and melodic modes, Abū 'l-Faraj gave painstakingly detailed accounts of the context in which a song was composed and performed, the behavior of both musicians and audiences, the process of learning composition and change, the uses and functions of songs, and myriad aspects of textual and musical improvisation. The text was well received even during Abū 'l-Faraj's lifetime, and many apocryphal stories have grown up to illustrate this. For example, the vizier al-Ṣāḥib ibn ʿAbbād (938-995), a well rounded statesman, with a great interest in literature and poetry, is reported to have substituted the *Kitāb al-aghānī* for his normal traveling library of fifty camel loads of books, believing Abū 'l-Faraj's work to be a more than sufficient reference.

Some historical and intellectual influences are apparent Abū 'l-Faraj's work. As is clear from its history, he was influenced in particular by the early Abbasid musician and theorist Isḥāq al-Mawṣilī. Al-Mawṣilī and his father Ibrāhīm were of noble Persian descent and acted as court musicians and companions to the Abbasid caliphs Hārūn al-Rashīd and al-Ma'mūn (786-833). Isḥāq al-Mawṣilī is credited with creating the first Islamic theory of melodic modes and with writing over forty works on music that have since been lost to us. Abū 'l-Faraj based the *Kitāb al-aghānī* on a list of one hundred songs supposedly compiled by al-Mawṣīlī, and also used his modal system when referring to performance practice. As far as literary figures were concerned, Abū 'l-Faraj was also known to champion, among others, the works of the early Abbasid poet Abū Tammām (796 or 804-842/843 or 845/846) and the female slave singer ʿArīb.

While stories of multiple patrons abound, Abū 'l-Faraj's primary patron was the Buwayhid Muʿizz al-Dawlah's vizier Abū Muḥammad al-Ḥasan ibn Muḥammad ibn Hārūn al-Muhallabī. Born into a poor but well respected family, al-Muhallabī steadily built for himself a financial and political power base from very little. He was one of many viziers who, like al-Ṣāḥib ibn ʿAbbād a generation later, encouraged intellectual and artistic growth in the Buwayhid period, following the decline of the Abbasid caliphate. He established a reputation as a well-mannered and worldly patron of the arts and letters. His circle included *kātib*s, historians, judges, legal scholars, theologians, grammarians, lexicographers, philologists, literary critics, poets, and musical specialists such as Abū 'l-Faraj. Both *Kitāb al-aghānī* and *al-Imā' al-shawā'ir* were very likely commissioned by al-Muhallabī.

The chronology is unclear in many of the biographical records, but it is certain that Abū 'l-Faraj had students in his lifetime. He is recorded as a transmitter of *ḥadīth*, and the names of some who studied *Kitāb al-aghānī* with him have been preserved. In some biographical references Abū 'l-Faraj is reported to have given a copy of his *Kitāb al-aghānī* to the Ḥamdānid ruler Sayf al-Dawlah (915 or 916-967) (a sometime rival of the Buwayhids) in Aleppo, for which he was in return given the gift of a thousand *dīnārs*. Some sources go even further, stating that Abū 'l-Faraj spent time at the court in Aleppo. Recent scholarship by Hilary Kilpatrick has shed doubt on his spending an extended period in Aleppo, if he ever went there at all. Additionally, Abū 'l-Faraj is reported to have sent a copy of his *Kitāb al-aghānī* to the Umayyad court of al-Ḥakam II in al-Andalusia, a fact that has yet to be fully corroborated. Factual or not, Abū 'l-Faraj's supposed link to both Aleppo and Andalusia is illustrative of the high esteem with which his work has been regarded, with its profound impact seen as stretching across wide swaths of both time and space, encompassing much of the Arab world.

Abū 'l-Faraj's disheveled appearance, questionable hygiene, and uncouth manners are often commented upon by historical biographers, but his wit, intellect, and encyclopedic knowledge seems to have more than compensated for his coarse nature. Abū ʿAlī al-Muḥassin al-Tanūkhī (939 or 940/941-994), the Buwayhid literary figure who was known for harsh evaluations of his contemporaries, testified that Abū 'l-Faraj had memorized an extensive collection of poetry, songs, anecdotes, historical reports, authenticated *ḥadīth*, and genealogies, and was well informed on topics such as lexicography, grammar, fantastic stories, life histories, accounts of conquest, birds and animals of the hunt, veterinary science, medicine, astrology and drinks, all of which made him well suited as a boon companion, confidant, and advisor for any patron.

Next to nothing is known concerning Abū 'l-Faraj's career in administration. At one point he acted as a secretary to the Buwayhid ruler Rukn al-Dawlah (d. 976). It is clear that he often had to travel in order to prepare clerical reports; he mentions having visited Antioch, Ahwāz,

Raqqah, Mattūth, Daskarat al-Malik, Baṣra, Ḥiṣn Mahdī, Kūthā and Nahr al-Ubullah.

In 963 al-Muhallabī died on campaign near Baṣra shortly after arousing the ire of Muʿizz al-Dawlah (915 or 916-967). As a reprisal, Muʿizz al-Dawlah had his property seized and his family arrested. Many who were associated with the former vizier's household were subject to confiscation and arrest and, while there is no clear historical record of the time, it is very likely that Abū 'l-Faraj was not spared the aftershock of his patron's downfall. By now in his sixties, Abū 'l-Faraj was unable to find any new patron of significance and possibly turned to teaching for survival.

Adab al-ghurabā' (*The Book of Strangers*) is more than likely one of the last of Abū 'l-Faraj's works. Only recently discovered, it is a treatment on the subject of *ghurbah*, or absence from one's home and family and the emotions associated with this. Broken into over 70 sections of either prose or poetry, the overall tone of the work is one of melancholic loss, punctuated by moments of light-hearted optimism. Unlike Abū 'l-Faraj's other more meticulously documented works, the anecdote in *The Book of Strangers* are given with few sources. It is not organized chronologically or thematically, nor is there an overarching thematic core such as martyrs, songs, or slave singers. Many (but not all) of the texts quoted originated as graffiti, comments written upon walls by lonely travelers. The entries can be organized according to three basic themes: reflexive/philosophical, love and separation, and a mixed bag of lighter popular tales about treasure hunting or adventures at sea. Recent scholarship has thrown light on contradictions between the dating of the text and the known biography of Abū 'l-Faraj; in light of this, some researchers believe that the text was written by a different hand and only attributed to Abū 'l-Faraj, but the question has yet to be firmly decided on one side or the other.

With the removal of al-Muhallabī from power, Abū 'l-Faraj had a similar decline in fortune. After his patron's death the scholar gradually faded from the scene. He is said to have suffered a stroke and experienced mental confusion and dementia in his later years. His date of death is given from anywhere between 968 and 974, with 972 or 973 being the currently agreed upon date.

Of the thirty works Abū 'l-Faraj was reported to have written, copies exist only of the four mentioned above. Those worth mentioning from among his lost works include several genealogies reportedly sent to the Umayyad rulers of Spain and his *Ayyām al-'arab*, a collection of 1700 significant historical battle days. Additionally, brief fragments of Abū 'l-Faraj's *al-Qiyān* (The Singing Girls), *al-Diyārāt* (The Monasteries), and *Mujarrad al-aghānī* (Abstract of the Songs) have survived in the works of later authors. The first appears to have been a shorter work outlining the lives and accomplishments of famous singing girls, who were more than likely slaves. The second work seems to have been a description of a monastery, including its location, surrounding area, and appearance. The final work appears to have been a collection of song texts with performance indicators as to rhythm and melody.

REFERENCES

Hilary Kilpatrick, *Making the Great Book of Songs: Compilation and the Author's Craft in Abū l-Faraj al-Isbahani's Kitāb al-aghānī* (London and New York: Routledge Curzon, 2003);

George D. Sawa, *Music Performance Practice in the Early Abbasid Era* (Toronto: Pontifical Institute of Mediaeval Studies, 1989);

George D. Sawa, "The Status and Roles of the Secular Musicians in the Kitab al-Aghani (Book of Songs) of Abū 'l-Faraj al-Isbahani (D. 356 A.H./967 A.D.)," *Asian Music* 17,1 (1985): 69-82;

George D. Sawa, "Musical Humour in the Kitab al-Aghani" in *Logos Islamikos: Studia Islamica in honorem Georgii Michaelis Wickens*, ed. Roger M. Savory and Dionisius A. Agius (Toronto: Pontifical Institute of Mediaeval Studies, 1984), 30-50;

George D. Sawa, "The Survival of Some Aspects of Medieval Arabic Performance Practicem," *Ethnomusicology* 25,1 (1981): 73-86;

Fadlou Shehadi, *Philosophies of Music in Medieval Islam* (New York: E.J. Brill, 1995).

Abū Firās al-Ḥamdānī

(932-968)

TERRI DE YOUNG

University of Washington

WORKS

Dīwān (Collected Poems).

Editions

Dīwān, or Poetical Works (Beirut: al-Maṭba'ah al-Salīmiyyah, 1873);

Dīwān Abī Firās, 3 vols., ed. Sāmī Dahhān (Beirut: Institut français de Damas, 1944);

Dīwān al-amīr Abī Firās al-Ḥamdānī 'alā riwāyat Ibn Khālawayh wa-riwāyāt ukhar, ed. Muḥammad al-Tūnjī (Damascus: Manshūrāt al-Mustashāriyyah al-Thaqāfiyyah li 'l-Jumhūriyyah al-Islāmiyyah al-Īrāniyyah, 1987).

Translations

A.J. Arberry, *Arabic Poetry: A Primer for Students* (Cambridge: Cambridge University Press, 1965), 90-97.

Abū Firās ibn Sa'īd ibn Aḥmad ibn Ḥamdān al-Ḥamdānī was a skilled and talented poet whose particular circumstances and experiences combined to make his work especially memorable both for his own and subsequent generations of Arabic readers. His *qaṣīdahs*, especially the panegyrics and poems celebrating his exploits in battle and in the hunt, were much admired by contemporaries and have been influential among a select group of admirers down to the present day. He had the misfortune to find his work directly compared to that of the greatest poet many think the Arab world ever produced, Abū 'l-Ṭayyib al-Mutanabbī (915-965), but this should not detract from the value of his literary achievements. The poetry he wrote from Constantinople while a captive of the Byzantines, for example, introduced new themes into Arabic literature and provided him the opportunity for extended meditations on the complex relationship between poet and patron (in his case, his cousin Sayf al-Dawlah (915 or 916-967)). Even more importantly, his work consolidated the movement of Arabic poetry into a phase where revival of the panegyric in the grand tradition of the past loomed large. Although Abū Firās' poetry lacks some of the elegant design and crisp expression of his great rival, Abū Ṭayyib al-Mutanabbī, it has also been seen as making up for this deficiency in the authenticity and vividness of its presentation, conveying effectively the fact that Abū Firās actually was a soldier and leader in the heroic tradition. Thus his poetry has been seen as more genuinely reflecting the realities of life within the ruling class than that of many other poets of the time, al-Mutanabbī included. It is no surprise, then, that the greatest patron of Arabic literature in the tenth century, the Buwayhid vizier al-Ṣāḥib ibn 'Abbād (938-995), paid homage not long after Abū Firās' death to these retrospective aspects of his work when he said: "Arabic poetry began with a king [that is, Imru' al-Qays (497-545)] and ended with a king [that is, Abū Firās]." The value others have placed upon this judgment from a contemporary is reflected in the fact that Abū Firās has always been given a prominent place in the canon of Arabic literature, from his time to the present day.

Abū Firās was born into one of the most important governing families of the middle Abbasid period, the Ḥamdānids. Like their rivals, the Buwayhids (in western Iran and eastern Iraq) and the Ikhshidids (in Egypt and southern Syria), the Ḥamdānids capitalized on the weakness of the Abbasids to carve out personal domains in territories formerly controlled by the central government. Unlike the other dynastic families, however, they had a respectable tribal pedigree, going back to a Taghlibī origin, which they used to recruit soldiers and attract supporters in the area of northern Syria and Iraq where they established themselves. To count a talented poet like Abū Firās among their number was naturally helpful to them in this enterprise. This can be seen in the anecdote connected with the composition of Abū Firās' 225-line poem, known as the Ḥamdāniyyah, in which he glorifies his family's background and his ancestors' exploits. According to the sources, he composed it following a successful 956 expedition—led by his cousin Sayf al-Dawlah—against several rebellious tribes. The chieftain from one of these tribes, Abū Aḥmad ʿUbayd Allāh ibn Warqāʾ al-Shaybānī (himself a poet), while offering his submission to the victors, recited a poem in which he vaunted the deeds of his forefathers during the Preislamic and Islamic periods. In response, Abū Firās was able to compose his Ḥamdāniyyah, thus showing, in addition to his own poetic skills, the legitimacy of the Ḥamdānids' own claims to lordship and their leadership over the tribes living in the territory they aspired to rule.

Yet, while—as this anecdote shows—the Ḥamdānids were perfectly capable of presenting a united front to the outside world, things were not always so placid within the domestic relations of the family. In an incident illustrating the ruthlessness of their internal jockeying for position, Abū Firās' father Saʿīd lost his life when his son was only three years old. Saʿīd had accepted secret nomination to the governorship of Mosul from the weak caliph al-Raḍī (909-940), when this position had previously been held by his nephew Nāṣir al-Dawlah (d. 968, older brother to Sayf al-Dawlah). Nāṣir al-Dawlah decided to retake Mosul and, in the process of achieving that objective, treacherously attacked and slew his uncle, leaving the child Abū Firās and his mother (who was most likely originally a Byzantine captive) defenseless, without a protector in an unstable world.

Eventually, Sayf al-Dawlah (after his marriage to Abū Firās' sister and his conquest of a secure base of power in Aleppo in 944) took in the young Abū Firās, who came to regard his cousin as a second father, as can be seen in the first two lines of a short poem he addressed to his protector (*Dīwān*, ed. Tūnjī, 89):

How could eloquence, generosity
  and high aspiration avoid me?
Since you have been my lord, who raised and
    educated me,
  and my father was Saʿīd?

As the poem suggests, Abū Firās received his advanced education at his cousin's court, which already had a reputation as the most brilliant outside of Baghdad at the time. The philosopher al-Farābī (d. 950), the Arab grammarians Abū ʿAlī al-Fārisī (900-987) and his pupil Ibn Jinnī (d. 1002), and the influential orator Ibn Nubātah (d. 984 or 985) were at one time or another members of Sayf al-Dawlah's entourage in Aleppo. This does not include, of course, Abū Tayyib al-Mutanabbī who was, in the decade between 947 and 957, Sayf al-Dawlah's official panegyrist, as well as a good friend of al-Fārisī and Ibn Jinnī.

Abū Firās, however, appears to have been more closely associated with the grammarian Abū ʿAbd Allāh al-Ḥusayn Ibn Khālawayh (d. 980 or 981), editor of Abū Firās' *dīwān* after his death, and Abū Dharr, who had long served Sayf al-Dawlah's family and were the best known teachers of the Ḥamdānids. Abū Firās studied with them both, though we have little information about the exact curriculum he followed. What we do know is that Ibn Khalawayh, in particular, seems to have been often at variance with the faction of al-Fārisī and al-Mutanabbī, and that his pupil, Abū Firās, followed his lead.

But Abū Firās' rivalry with al-Mutanabbī would have become less pressing when Sayf al-Dawlah awarded his young cousin lands in the area of the town of Manbij—northwest of Aleppo—in 948. Soon after, Sayf al-Dawlah would make Abū Firās governor of Manbij and the surrounding territory, so the duties connected with that post would have taken him away from court for relatively long periods. Nevertheless, Abū Firās' work, as it matured, showed some of the same tendencies that we associate with the poetry of al-Mutanabbī. This would include a concern with language (including intricate wordplay, which unfortunately does not translate well) and a willingness to explore the emotional resonances of the relationship between poet and patron metaphorically through the love relationship traditionally described in the first section of the *qaṣīdah*, the *naṣīb*. We can see this latter aspect of Abū Firās' poetry developing in the series of early poems he addressed to another cousin, Abū Zuhayr ibn Naṣr, who died on an expedition in the company of Sayf al-Dawlah and Abū Firās in 339/950-51. In what is considered the earliest of these poems, from the beginning, he mixes the language of love and praise in addressing Abū Zuhayr (*Dīwān*, ed. Tūnjī, 161-62):

Truly, anyone who has come in the evening to see you has no need for the moon,
nor would he have need for raindrops, should he be in the place where you are.

Such a description, especially at the beginning of a poem, would normally be reserved for the beloved addressed in the naṣīb. Here, Abū Firās uses it to speak directly to his cousin, to indicate the intensity of his admiration for the older man. Later, in one of the examples from this series where Abū Firās reproaches his cousin for ignoring him, he would make it even more explicit that the feelings of love he expresses in the poem belong to the addressee, not to a separate female inamorata:

If I long for you, it is as an ardent lover longs for his intimate
even though he has behaved as an oppressive tyrant.

These accolades to Abū Zuhayr anticipate Abū Firās' later poetic strategies (similar to al-Mutanabbī's) with respect to his panegyrics for Sayf al-Dawlah himself.

The Ḥamdānids always had to struggle for military success in their respective territories, primarily because the military forces they could command were so much smaller than had been the case when the Abbasid dynasty ruled these lands and could recruit troops from a much vaster area beyond them. But in the early 950s, Sayf al-Dawlah entered a phase of relative success against both the Byzantines to the north and the tribal confederations around Aleppo. Abū Firās, despite his obligations in Manbij, joined his cousin on these campaigns, primarily the ones against the tribes in the area. This was probably the period when he composed his lengthy Ḥamdāniyyah. To this period we also owe several other poems more directly celebrating these victories. The most notable of them might be his poem that celebrates the defeat of several rebellious tribes, including the Banū Kaʿb belonging to the tribal confederation of Nizār, in 343/954-955. In an often quoted section of this *qaṣīdah*, Abū Firās sums up what he sees as the political principles followed by the Ḥamdānids (*Dīwān*, ed. Tūnjī, 29-30):

Have you not seen us as people who cherish our alliances with our neighbors,
who give them the maximum protection and make their lands flourish?
The mountains looking down on the Nizār [tribal lands] are ours,
we have settled in the uplands and hills above them.
All mankind prefers us, and we exclude no one,
the favors we do describe us, and we side with no one.
The clans of Rabīʿah, nay even Maʿadd, acknowledge that we
are the ones at the head of any column and the people who bring up the rear.
And when fools among those highly placed decided to act as tyrants,
we opened up a door for war between us,
We had granted them avenues to wealth; however,
when they committed outrages, we granted them spears.

Clearly, these lines celebrate traditional values, looking back to the Preislamic time period when tribal alliances held sway and determined the patterns of governance. This was no longer the case—as analyses of Ḥamdānid rule have shown—but Abū Firās' work had great value in perpetuating the illusion that past practices still held.

More consonant with the shifting allegiances of the time (since this has often been referred to as the Shiite century), Abū Firās wrote several poems celebrating the merits and accomplishments of ʿAlī ibn Abī Ṭālib (ca. 600-660), his son Ḥusayn (d. 680), and their descendants. These were not the first poems in this category, but Abū Firās was clearly influenced by ideas circulating in Shiite circles, and these poems are the clearest record of his religious inclinations. In these, he seems to have been following Shiite tendencies recorded among the Ḥamdānids as a whole, including Sayf al-Dawlah himself.

For instance, in a poem that Abū Firās begins with the reminiscence of a drinking party where he fell deeply in love with one of the participants, he suddenly shifts to an invocation of the sufferings of Ḥusayn on the day he was killed by Umayyad forces in the desert near the town of Karbala (*Dīwān*, ed. Tūnjī, 312-313):

I am forbidden to come close to him, just as Ḥusayn
  was forbidden water when he saw it,
When he said: "Give me something to quench my thirst!" he was given spears
  to drink, instead of the fresh water that would have satisfied him.
And then a head was hacked that had long been held sacrosanct
  because the fronts and backs of his grandfather's hands had held it close.
A day that had been in God's eye, or rather,
  God dictated it should be because of the tyranny of the tyrants.
Such it was. If only He had destroyed the enemies of the Prophet,
  the Possessor of the Throne, then the Prophet would not have known enemies.
A day when the morning sun changed to black
  and wept blood, on account of what the heavens saw.
There was no excuse for a soul not to break into tears,
  or for one weeping not to find those tears overflowing his eyes.
May a people perish who have followed their passions
  [on a course] whose outcome one day would lead them to evil.

Unlike others (most notably the leader of the Shiite community in Baghdad later in the century, al-Sharīf al-Raḍī (970-1016)), who chose to focus in their writings on ʿAlī and his association with the Prophet Muḥammad himself (d. 632), Abū Firās not only emphasizes the more typical Shiite theme of Ḥusayn's suffering, but also includes details (like the sun darkening and weeping blood) that will become common parlance in the later presentations of Ḥusayn's martyrdom. Such intense symbolism was not frequent in the poetry of this time sympathetic to the Shiite cause. Nevertheless, in assessing this aspect of Abū Firās' work, it should be noted that, in all, only four poems preserved in his dīwān have ʿAlid themes, and the longest (and most famous) of these is more clearly an indictment of the Abbasid dynasty and its tyranny than a celebration (or elegy) for any member of the house of ʿAlī.

Although in Sayf al-Dawlah's heyday, Abū Firās seems to have played only a small role in the wars against the Byzantines, this changed at the end of the 950s, when the Ḥamdānids suffered a series of reverses against this newly more formidable foe. The Ḥamdānid defeats seem to have stemmed, at least in part, from new leadership brought about by the appointment of Nicephorus Phocas (912-969) and his brother Leo as leaders of the Byzantine troops in 955. They replaced their father Bardas Phocas (d. 989), the old chief general (or Domestic of the Scholai, to give him his proper title), who had been a more cautious and defensive fighter than his sons. In 956, for example, Leo Phocas was able to capture Abū Firās' cousin Abū 'l-ʿAshā'ir in battle. Abū Firās addressed several poems to Abū 'l-ʿAshā'ir, encouraging him and telling him to be patient in the face of adversity, that help would soon come, but Abū 'l-ʿAshā'ir ended up dying several years later in captivity. The following year, in 957, the major fortress of Ḥadath was taken and sacked by the Byzantines, thus rendering the entire area around Manbij more vulnerable to attack.

In 962, Sayf al-Dawlah, whose health seems to have been failing, was struck with partial paralysis, or hemiplegia, at the same time that Abū Firās was captured by a Byzantine raiding party while out hunting with a small group of his soldiers. Abū Firās was very fond of the hunt, and wrote a long poem about it in the *muzdawij* or *urjūzah* form that had been popularized by another poet-prince, Ibn al-Muʿtazz (861-908, who had used it in a long poem celebrating the achievements of his own dynasty, the Abbasids). Abū Firās, perhaps to differentiate himself from Ibn al-Muʿtazz, did not adopt this form for his poem celebrating his own family (the Ḥamdāniyyah) but instead chose to use it as the framework for a lengthy poem celebrating his favorite pastime. Since the *muzdawij* does not use monorhyme, but only requires that the two half-lines of each verse rhyme, it is possible to extend the poem more easily than is the case with the *qasīdah* form, and Abū Firās exploited this flexibility to the fullest, producing a work that is 140 lines long.

Entirely apart from its unusual format, the *Ṭardiyyah* (Hunting) poem exhibits a freshness and immediacy that is striking, as this short excerpt from the beginning shows (*Dīwān*, ed. Tūnjī, 325):

Let me describe a day that passed in Syria,
the most enjoyable I have ever known.
I summoned the hawk master one day,
when I awoke at dawn from my sleep,
I said to him: "Pick seven older ones,
each a noble willing to drink the dust.
Two of them should be devoted to the rabbit
the other five set aside for gazelles.
Form the hunting dogs into two teams,
that you will send out two by two,
And do not keep back the tracking hounds
for they shall be the *coup de grace* of the gazelles [already wounded]."

Given his passion for the sport (as recorded here), it is perhaps not surprising that Abū Firās was out hunting on the day he was captured by the Byzantines in 962. He and a few retainers were surprised by a much larger Byzantine force scouting the road to Aleppo, where they were planning an attack. According to his own account, Abū Firās fought bravely against odds that he knew were insuperable (Dīwān, ed. Tūnjī, 144):

I was taken prisoner, though my companions were not unarmed in the tumult,
my horse was no gamboling colt, nor his master inexperienced,
But when a certain fate is decreed for a man,
then neither land nor sea will protect him.
My little companion said: "Flight or destruction [are our options]."
I said: "[Both are] matters [where] the sweeter of the two is bitter.
I will seek that which will not disgrace me,
but you should keep in mind that the better of them may be captivity."

Here, one sees a fatalistic attitude toward fighting and death that reaches back to the poetry of the Preislamic period, and has little to do with an Islamic world view.

Eventually, Abū Firās fell, badly wounded in the leg. The wound was serious enough that it took months to heal, but Abū Firās was not (at least at first) treated with great deference by his captors. Shortly after being taken prisoner, he was ordered to strip, which led him in a poem he later sent to Sayf al-Dawlah to boast (Dīw*ā*n, ed. Tūnjī, 45):

They wished me to take off my clothes, but rather
I was wearing clothes made of their blood, red.

Thus, he used the distancing power of rhetoric possible in poetry to aestheticize his suffering and make light of it. This is a fairly consistent feature of his poetic style.

From a fairly early period in his captivity, Abū Firās seems to have become enmeshed in disputations with the chief of his captors, Nicephoros Phocas, the Domestic of the Scholai. In one of these confrontations, Nicephoros ridiculed him and insulted his family (with their apparently well known penchant for literary patronage), by saying: "You are all clerks (*kuttāb*), and know nothing about war." To which Abū Firās replied: "Have we been tramping through your land for sixty years [carrying our] swords, or our pens?" He then composed a poem expressing in a more structured form the same idea (*Dīwān*, ed. Tūnjī, 34):

Do you claim, you with the double chin, that we
—lions of war—know nothing about spears,
Woe to you, who is an adherent of war, if we are not?

and who else will come and go on its behalf,
ever its companions?
Who else can wrap all the sides of an army up together?
who else led the center, and pushed back the other one?
Woe to you, who destroyed your brother at Marʿash?
Who has ever rained blows on your father's face with a sharp sword?

If nothing else, the anecdote shows us that Abū Firās and Nicephoros were able to communicate effectively with each other. This would not be surprising, given that Abū Firās' mother is assumed to have been captured from Byzantium in her youth, and (as he implies in another poem) that he had maternal uncles in Constantinople. But the anecdote also shows that they shared more than the ability to speak to one another in the same language. They also shared a common warrior code that meant more than the difference in religion or political allegiance. And it was through this common set of values that they communicated, despite any hostility they may have felt for one another.

What was probably more surprising to Abū Firās than the attitudes in the Byzantine court where he suddenly found himself was the puzzling lack of response by Sayf al-Dawlah to his plight. He seems to have assumed that he would quickly be ransomed by the ruler he had taken as a second father. This did not occur and it was a bitter blow to Abū Firās.

The delay was perhaps not surprising, given Sayf al-Dawlah's poor health. Also, barely a month after Abū Firās' capture, Nicephoros and the Byzantines besieged Aleppo, and Sayf al-Dawlah was forced to retire to his fortress of Mayyāfāriqīn beyond the Tigris river. Subsequent to this disaster, the Byzantines took many more Arab prisoners, and it has also been put forward that Sayf al-Dawlah was hesitant to ransom his own cousin, while leaving these other Muslims in Byzantine hands. So, in the end, Abū Firās remained a captive in Constantinople for four years, until shortly before Sayf al-Dawlah's own death in February 967.

During this time, however, Abū Firās did not remain incommunicado in Byzantine territory. He sent a series of poems to the Ḥamdānid court asking for assistance. These *Rūmiyyāt* (Byzantine Poems) were directly addressed to Sayf al-Dawlah and chart Abū Firās' growing disenchantment with his cousin's reputation as a beneficent patron, based on what he saw as Sayf al-Dawlah's unresponsiveness. He was also apparently in contact with his mother, who sought to intercede for her son, and her lack of success with her son-in-law (Sayf al-Dawlah, we should remember, was married to Abū Firās' sister) would also form an important subtext for Abū Firās' later *Rūmiyyāt.*

But at the beginning of his poetic correspondence, Abū Firās expresses a confident belief that Sayf al-Dawlah would soon ransom him, as we can see in this first poem he addressed to his cousin (Dīwān, ed. Tūnjī, 96):

I would disdain a death of humiliation in the land of exile
in the hands of the uncircumcised Christians, the death of a man bereft.
So do not leave the enemies around me to rejoice,
and do not cut off those asking questions about me, and be not uninvolved.
Do not abandon me, for the amount of my ransom has been set,
and you are not incapable of a generous act.
And how often you have supported me and granted me blessings
raising up my fate and making those who envied me many.
Attach to those another generous deed that you have omitted [to do before],
and stand up in rescuing me, true to your promise, and then rest.

The attitude expressed is very much an expectation that Sayf al-Dawlah will fulfill established precepts for a ruler (or someone charged with responsibility for another), and implicitly threatening him with loss of prestige if he does not. This threat is reinforced by the allusion in the next lines to a situation when the Zurayrah tribe did not pay a ransom they had promised to redeem one of their number and thus lost considerable standing with their peers.

One might argue that these lines project an almost overconfident and unrealistic expectation about the power of a ruler to respond to an individual supplicant, of which poets are simply the most articulate. In fact, the lines could be seen as contradicting a basic assumption that a traditional Arab leader must be able to stand above individual concerns and act for the good of the whole group (whether speaking of the member of a tribe, or a citizen of the community), something—as we have seen—for which Abū Firās earlier in his career praised the Ḥamdānids (and by implication Sayf al-Dawlah).

This contradiction between the needs of the individual and what will benefit the polity is something that al-Mutanabbī had already begun to explore in his own panegyrics (and satires) addressed to Sayf al-Dawlah and later to the Egyptian regent Kāfūr, once he had taken refuge at the latter's court in 957. The exploration of this question now begins to inform Abū Firās' work as well, and should be seen as an essential element in the convergence of the two poets' work that has been noted by some modern scholars as beginning in this period of Abū Firās' captivity.

To Abū Firās' concern with Sayf al-Dawlah as representative ruler, however, was added the parallel question of why Sayf al-Dawlah was not acting as a loyal kinsman, whose overriding obligation—as a cousin—was to take his relative's side. One can see this particular issue beginning to emerge as a central one in a poem that Abū Firās wrote after (as he himself says) he had been a prisoner in Constantinople for two years. Although he frames his rebuke in general terms and is careful not to attack Sayf al-Dawlah directly, Abū Firās here does register his disappointment specifically against his relatives, blaming them for his plight (*Dīwān*, ed. Tūnjī, 182):

Do I not have a single, solitary friend with lasting loyalty?
Who would devote himself to the one I do, guarding one who has always acted as a guard?
Why is there in every house a friend I feel affection for,
but when we part, I preserve [my friendship] while he wastes it away?
I have spent two years in the land of the Byzantines, not having seen
a single sad one among my people, nor [even] someone affecting such behavior
If I have feared my maternal uncles among the Byzantine once,
I have feared my Arab paternal uncles four times over.
And if one mark by my enemies has tormented me,
from loved ones I have encountered [things] far worse and more painful.

He is careful in this poem to hold back and limit his rebuke to his relatives in general. By his next composition, however, he turns more directly to Sayf al-Dawlah at the end of the poem (Dīwān, ed. Tūnjī, 40-41):

I do not claim to say what God knows is untrue:
the dwellings of [Sayf al-Dawlah] ʿAlī are wide open to those who call for aid.
His deeds, for those full of desire, are generous,
his wealth, for those who seek, are [like] spoils [to be taken away].
But he that was a sword upright in my hand has fallen from it;
in my eyes, a shooting star [that came] from him has turned dark.
He has been slow [to help] me, while the fates are swift,
and death has claws that have grown long, and teeth.
And even if there had not been a long-standing affection [between us] to be
taken into account, nor a close kinship among men,
It would still be the wisest course for the sake of Islam that he not neglect me,
for, on his behalf, [I have been] its guardian and deputy.

In this section, Abū Firās is working through the realization that his appeals to kinship have not been enough to encourage Sayf al-Dawlah to provide his ransom. Even though he has spoken earlier in this poem (and in all the Rūmiyyāt) about his patience and willingness to endure captivity, now he registers an even more powerful sense of urgency since death seems very close (as he says in line 4 above), which will scuttle any chance of return to his homeland.

To this urgency he counterpoises his final argument. If kinship ties are not enough to move Sayf al-Dawlah, then he should honor the precepts of Islam, which enjoin that a Muslim should help a fellow Muslim in need, regardless of their blood relationship. If he does not remember this imperative, then Sayf al-Dawlah risks imperiling his soul on the Judgment Day. Just as in the first of the *Rūmiyyāt*, Abū Firās has maneuvered Sayf al-Dawlah into a defensive position through an appeal to a wider, Islamic, set of ethical precepts. This time, however, the approach is much less direct, and this shows the increasing subtlety Abū Firās has come to command in composing his poetry during the enforced leisure of his imprisonment, much of which would have undoubtedly been devoted to composing and polishing his verses.

Despite the arguments he marshaled in pleading his cause, however, Abū Firās' captivity lasted for two more years. The case can be made that Abū Firās continued during this period to work on useful ways to channel his feelings, and express them in his poems, without making them so direct that Sayf al-Dawlah would simply refuse to listen to his entreaties and never ransom him. Thus, he focused more on the *naṣīb* portion of the poem as a way to express the power of his feelings, without moving to rebuke Sayf al-Dawlah more directly.

The results of this choice—very much in keeping with strategies pursued less consistently in his earlier poems—can be seen in what is probably the most famous of the *Rūmiyyāt* (adapted and set to music, for example, by the famous Egyptian singer Umm Kulthūm in the twentieth century). He says, addressing an individual who appears at first to be the beloved conventionally found in such passages (*Dīwān*, ed. Tūnjī, 142):

Truly I am one who longs, and in me pain burns
 but one like me, his secret is never divulged.
Night has injured me, where once I extended the hand of passion,
 my tears fall in curtains, characterized by greatness.
The fire between my ribs could be used to illuminate [the darkness],
 the intensity of love and thought have fanned it into flame.
My cherished hope was [but] a promise, and death [stands] before it,
 if I die thirsty, no drop [of rain] will fall [upon me].
I have preserved, and you have destroyed, the affection between us
 and [making] an excuse would have been better, considering the faithfulness [shown] to you
Our days are only sheets of paper, the letters on them scraped away
 by the hand of him who has written them.

Here, though he never mentions Sayf al-Dawlah explicitly, his lengthy treatment of his beloved's disdain for him contains all the emotions that he expressed more directly when speaking to his cousin in the previous poem. It is as though the catharsis that results from this intense focus on his emotions of both longing and of a sense of betrayal —really meant for Sayf al-Dawlah and not a female beloved—allows him to take a step backwards and move the poem to a different plane. Thus, at the end, the poem becomes an impersonal celebration of his family's glories (Dīwān, ed. Tūnjī, 145):

We are people among whom there is no middle ground
 we have the place of honor before the two worlds or the grave.
Our souls do not consider our [seeking] the heights a very great thing,
 and the one who engages himself to a beautiful woman [does not consider] any bride-price too high.
We are the mightiest of the sons of the world, the highest of the high,
 the most generous of those upon the soil [of the land], and this is no boast.

Such confident pride in his ancestry and the deeds of his own relations would not have drawn much notice in his poetry of the previous two decades. Here, however, it has a different tone, of greater introspection in some ways, because it is asserting an ideal that he hopes to retrieve solely by the power of his words. The key phrase in this effort becomes "one who engages himself to a beautiful woman [does not consider] any bride-price too high." This, of course, recalls the imagery of the naṣīb (with its indirect invocation of his ambivalent feelings for Sayf al-Dawlah). but here the bitterness of the disappointment in the object of his love, the pain of her rejection, that dogged the naṣīb is subsumed in the idea that a willingness to love at any cost and serve the beloved, no matter what the price, should be seen as part of his family's claim to nobility.

Besides Sayf al-Dawlah, the other person Abū Firās addresses frequently in the *Rūmiyyāt* is his mother. She was his greatest advocate at home, and attempted more than once to intercede—apparently unsuccessfully—for her son. Abū Firās made his gratitude for her activism known in several poems. But perhaps the most moving relic of his feelings for her was the elegy he composed upon hearing of her death while he was still in captivity.

From Preislamic times, elegies in Arabic generally included the convention of asking for rain to fall upon the grave of the dead person. This was a particularly effective image because it echoed the tears of the mourners and presaged symbolically the eventual return of new life to the deceased, as rain-fed grass and plants grew over the grave. References to this convention were most often used to conclude the elegy. Abū Firās, in contrast, opens his elegy for his mother with lines repeating such an invocation (*Dīwān*, ed. Tūnjī, 140):

Mother of the captive—may a strong rain slake your thirst—
  it was despite [what] you [did] that the prisoner met his fate.
Mother of the captive—may a strong rain slake your thirst—
  he is confused, neither able to stand up or move.
Mother of the captive—may a strong rain slake your thirst—
  to whom shall the bearer of good news bring tidings of the ransom?
Mother of the captive—may a strong rain slake your thirst—
  since you have gone before, for whom will the locks and hair [on the prisoner's head] be grown?

This passage illustrates one of the more unusual features of Abū Firās' poetic style (which also occurs elsewhere, in the Rūmiyyāt especially): his resort to repetition over several lines. This was a technique not encouraged in the Arabic poetry of the time. But one of the early Taghlibī tribal poets, Muhalhil, had been known for this device, and Abū Firās seems to have copied it as homage to his poetic ancestor. In his mother's elegy, the repetition is particularly effective, giving an indication of the intensity of the poet's emotion and recording his inability to move verbally (at least in part) beyond his initial reaction to the searing news of her death.

His mother's passing was followed not much later by Abū Firās' release from captivity in 966, which was in turn followed shortly by Sayf al-Dawlah's death. Though Sayf al-Dawlah's son (and Abū Firās' nephew), Abū 'l-Maʿālī, duly succeeded to his father's throne, his hold on it was not strong and he was only fifteen years old. Abū Firās raised a rebellion in Homs (though it is not clear whether the main force of the revolt was against Abū 'l-Maʿālī or his general, the Turk Farghawayh) and he was captured in a pitched battle before the city. Before he was put to death by Farghawayh, he was said to have addressed the following lines (a sort of self-elegy) to his daughter, awaiting his return (*Dīwān*, ed. Tūnjī, 29):

Daughter dear, do not show your sorrow,
  all human beings must prepare to go [from this earth].
Daughter dear, patience is beautiful
  for someone who would stand above being struck by misfortune.
Weep for your father, and mourn for him,
  but behind your curtain and your veil.
Say, when you call out to me
  and I can make no response:
"The ornament of youth, Abū Firās,
  did not have much joy in his [own] youth."

Thus ended the short but eventful life of Abū Firās. He was only thirty-six when he died. Although he was not otherwise known for his elegies, his poems for his mother and for himself became famous and show that death was never far from thoughts. And his success in composing these works at the end of his life add point and pathos to the poems he composed earlier as well.

REFERENCES

'Abd al-Jalīl Ḥasan 'Abd al-Mahdī, *Abū Firās al-Ḥamdānī: hayātuh wa-shi'ruh* (Amman: Maktabat al-Aqṣā, 1981);

Marius Canard, *Histoire de la Dynastie des Hamdanides de Jazîra et de Syrie* (Paris: Presses universitaires de France, 1953);

Hugh Kennedy, "The Hamdānids," in *Hugh Kennedy, The Prophet and the Age of the Caliphates* (London: Longman, 1986), 267-284;

James E. Montgomery, "Convention and Invention: Abū Firās' Poetic Correspondence with Abū Zuhayr," *Occasional Papers of the School of Abbasid Studies* 2 (1988): 1-14;

Abdullah el Tayib, "Abū Firās al-Ḥamdānī," in *'Abbasid Belles-Lettres*, ed. Julia Ashtiany, T.M. Johnstone, J.D. Latham, R.B. Serjeant and G. Rex Smith (Cambridge: Cambridge University Press, 1990), 315-327;

Aleksandr Vasiliev, *Byzance et les Arabes*, vol. 2, pt. 2, translated Henri Gregoire and Marius Canard (Brussels: Institute de philologie et d'histoire orientales, 1935), 349-370.

Abū Hilāl al-'Askarī

(d. after 400/d. after1009)

GEORGE J. KANAZI
University of Haifa

WORKS*

Dīwān al-'Askarī;

Dīwān al-ma'ānī;

al-Ḥathth 'alā ṭalab al-'ilm;

Jamharat al-amthāl;

Kitāb al-awā'il;

Kitāb faḍl al-'aṭā' 'alā 'l-'usr or Kitbāb al-kuramā';

Kitāb al-furūq al-lughawiyyah, or al-Farq bayna al-ma'ānī or (ma'rifat) al-furūq fī 'l-lughah;

Kitāb al-ṣinā'atayn;

al-Mu'jam fī baqiyyat al-ashyā';

al-Risālah al-māsa fī mā lam yuḍbaṭ min al-Ḥamāsa;

Sharḥ dīwān Abī Miḥjan;

al-Talkhīṣ fī 'l-lughah or Kitāb al-talkhīṣ fī ma'rifat asmā' 'al-ashyā'.

**Works are in alphabetical order, since the dates of their composition are unknown.*

Editions

Dīwān al-'Askarī, ed. George Kanazi (Damascus: Maṭbū'āt Majma' al-Lughah al-'Arabiyyah bi-Dimashq, 1979);

Dīwān al-ma'ānī (Cairo: Maktabat al-Qudsī, 1933); ed. Aḥmad Ḥasan Basaj (Beirut: Dār al-Kutub al-'Ilmiyyah, 1994); ed. al-Nabawī 'Abd al-Wāḥid Sha'lān, 3 vols. (Cairo: Mu'assasat al-'Alyā', 2008);

al-Faḍl al-'aṭā' 'alā 'l-'usr, ed. Maḥmūd Muḥammad Shākir (Cairo, 1934);

Hādhā kitāb jamharat al-amthāl (Bombay: al-Mīrzā Muḥammad Malik al-Kuttāb al-Shīrāzī, 1307/1889);

al-Ḥathth 'alā ṭalab al-'ilm, ed. Marwān Qabbānī (Beirut: al-Maktab al-Islāmī, 1986); ed.''Abd al-Majīd Diyāb (Cairo: Dār al-Faḍīlah li 'l-Nashr wa 'l-Tawzī' wa 'l-Taṣdīr, 1998);

Jamharat al-amthāl (Cairo: al-Maṭba'ah al-Khayriyyah, 1892); 2 vols., ed. Muḥammad Abū al-Faḍl Ibrāhīm and 'Abd al-Majīd Qaṭāmish (Cairo: al-Mu'assasah al-

ʿArabiyyah al-Hadīthah li 'l-Ṭabʿʿwa 'l-Nashr wa 'l-Tawzīʿ, 1964);
Kitāb al-awā'il, ed. Muḥammad al-Sayyid al-Wakīl (Asʿad Tarābizūnī al-Ḥusaynī, 1966); ed. Muḥammad al-Miṣrī and Walīd Qaṣṣāb, 2 vols. (Damascus: Wizārat al-Thaqāfah wa 'l-Irshād al-Qawmī, 1975);
Kitāb al-furūq al-lughawiyyah, 2 vols. (Cairo: al-Maṭbaʿah al-Salafiyyah, 1934 or 1935); 4th ed. (Beirut: Dār al-Āfāq al-Jadīdah, 1980);
Kitāb al-kuramā', ed. Mahmūd al-Jibālī (Cairo: al-Maṭbaʿah al-Shūrā, 1908);
Das Kitâb "al-mu'ğam fi baqîjati 'l-ešjâ," ed. Oskar Rescher (Berlin, 1915);
Kitāb al-ṣinā'atayn (Istanbūl: Maṭbaʿat Maḥmūd Bik, 1320/1902); (Cairo: M.A. al-Khānjī, 1320/1902); ed. ʿAlī Muḥammad al-Bajjāwī and Muḥammad Abū al-Faḍl Ibrāhīm (Cairo: Dār 'Iḥyā' al-Kutub al-ʿArabiyyah, 1952); 2nd ed., ed. ʿAlī Muḥammad al-Bajjāwī and Muḥammad Abū 'l-Faḍl Ibrāhīm (Cairo: ʿĪsā 'l-Bābī 'l-Ḥalabī, 1971);
Kitāb faḍl al-'aṭā' 'alā 'l-'usr, ed. Maḥmūd Muḥammad Shākir (Cairo: al-Maṭbaʿah al-Salafiyyah, 1934);
al-Mu'jam fī baqiyyat al-ashyā', ed. Ibrāhīm al-Abyārī andʿʿAbd al-Ḥafīẓ Shalabī (Cairo: Dār al-Kutub al-Miṣriyyah, 1934); 'ed. Aḥmad ʿAbd al-Tawwāb ʿAwaḍ (Cairo: Dār al-Faḍīlah, 1997);
al-Risālah al-māsah fīmā lam yuḍbaṭ min al-Ḥamāsah, ed. G. Kanazi, *Jerusalem Studies in Arabic and Islam*, 2 (1980): 97-163; ed. G. Kanazi (Haifa: Qism al-Lughah al-ʿArabiyyah wa-Ādābihā wa-Maʿhad Dirāsāt al-Sharq al-Awsāṭ fī Jāmiʿat Ḥayfā, 1991);
Sharḥ dīwān Abī Miḥjan (Cairo: Maṭbaʿat al-Azhār al-Bārūniyyah, ca. 1900); ed. Ṣalāḥ al-Dīn al-Munajjid (Beirut: Dār al-Kitāb al-Jadīd, 1970); in *Ṭuraf 'Arabiyyah*, collected by Carlo Landberg, 2 vols.(Leiden: E.J. Brill, 1885-1888) 1:55-75;
Shi'r Abī Hilāl al-'Askarī, collected and ed. Muḥsin Ghayāḍ (Beirut: Manshūrāt ʿUwaydāt, 1975);
al-Talkhīṣ fī 'l-lughah or Kitāb al-talkhīṣ fī ma'rifat asmā' 'al-ashyā', ed. ʿIzzat Ḥasan (Damascus: Maṭbūʿat Majmaʿʿal-Lughah al-ʿArabiyyah, 1960-1970); 2nd ed., ed. ʿIzzat Ḥasan (Bayrūt: Dār Ṣādir, 1993).

Abū Hilāl al-ʿAskarī was a prominent scholar in the 4th century A. H./10th century A. D. His full name, as recorded by his biographers, is al-Ḥasan ibn ʿAbdullāh ibn Sahl ibn Saʿīd ibn Yaḥyā ibn Mihrān. One source, Ismāʿīl al-Baghdādī (d. 1920 or 1921), in the 1951 Istanbul edition of his Hadiyyat al-ʿārifīn asmā' al-mu'allifīn wa-athār al-muṣannifīn min kashf al-ẓunūn (1:273) adds ibn Aḥmad al-Baghdādī. To distinguish him from his teacher Abū Aḥmad al-ʿAskarī (906-992), whose fuller name was Abū Aḥmad al-Ḥasan ibn ʿAbdallāh ibn Saʿīd, he was called al-adīb because of his interest in adab, while Abū Aḥmad was called al-muḥaddith because his expertise was in ḥadīth, the traditions of the Prophet Muḥammad (d. 632).

Abū Hilāl al-ʿAskarī was born in ʿAskar Mukram, a garrison city built during the Islamic conquests in Ahwāz, between Iraq and Persia. He seems to have been of Persian origin as the name of one of his ancestors, Mihrān, attests. Also, as found in his *Dīwān al-ma'ānī*, (1:85) he boasts of this heritage in his poetry. In addition, he was familiar with the Persian language. Still in his *Dīwān al-ma'ānī* (2:89) he compares Arabic and Persian proverbs, and in his *Kitāb al-ṣinā'atayn* (72-73, 253) he bases his explanation of some words found in Arabic poetry on their Persian etymologies.

Although little is known about Abū Hilāl's private life, it is known that he grew up in a family of learned men. He mentions his father as one source of information, and also al-Ḥasan ibn Saʿīd, the uncle of his father. He spent considerable time in the company of Abū Aḥmad al-ʿAskarī and learned a great deal from him. Yāqūt ibn ʿAbd Allāh al-Ḥamawī (1179?-1229), in his *Mu'jam al-udabā'* (8:263), mentions that this fact made some of Abū Hilāl's biographers conclude that he was Abū Aḥmad al-ʿAskarī's nephew, but this seems untrue.

From Abū Hilāl's poetry, we learn that he was married and had children, but more detailed information is not available. We also learn that he spent most of his life in 'Askar Mukram, the town where he was born, with the exclusion of short trips in its vicinity.

Abū Hilāl seems to have lived a reasonably comfortable life in spite of the fact that he complains in his poetry about having to "sit in the market" to earn his living. It is not evident whether he had an official job as a *kātib*, a position for which he was highly qualified, but he certainly had aspirations to hold such a job. He was in contact with the Buwayhid vizier al-Ṣāḥib ibn 'Abbād (938-995), who visited 'Askar Mukram specifically to meet Abū Aḥmad al-'Askarī, whom he venerated. Certainly Abū Hilāl was present at that meeting and later enjoyed the remuneration offered by the vizier to Abū Aḥmad and, after his death, to his students.

There is nothing in Abū Hilāl's books that reflects his religious views, but it seems that they were close to those of the *mu'tazilah*. Muḥsin al-Ḥusaynī al-'Āmilī (1865-1952), in his *A'yān al-Shī'ah* (22:155) considers him a Shiite without offering any decisive proof. However, two works by Muḥammad ibn Aḥmad al-Dhahabī, his *al-'Ibar fī khabar man ghabar* (1961, 3:208), and his *Tadhkirat al-ḥuffāz* (1957, 1121-1123), records that Abū Hilāl's teacher Abū Aḥmad was apparently a *Mu'tazilī,* and that one of the former's students, Abū Sa'd al-Sammān (d. 445/1053) was one of the leading scholars of the *mu'tazilah*. Abū Hilāl, in his *Kitāb al-awā'il* (2:138), seems a great admirer of Wāṣil ibn 'Aṭā' (699 or 700-748 or 749), the founder of the *Mu'tazilah* sect, and al-Ṣāḥib ibn 'Abbād (326-385/938-995), with whom he and his teacher were in contact, was also a prominent *Mu'tazilī*. Thus we might conclude that if not a *Mu'tazilī,* Abū Hilāl lived in a *Mu'tazilī* environment and certainly was a *Mu'tazilī* sympathizer.

The *Kitāb al-awā'il* was the last book dictated by Abū Hilāl in 395/1004. That year was taken by many of his biographers as the year of his death. Only''Alī ibn Yūsuf al-Qifṭī (1172 or 1173-1248), in his *Inbāh al-ruwāh 'alā anbāh al-nuḥāh*, (4:183) and al-Suyūṭī (1445-1505), in his *Ṭabaqāt al-mufassirīn*, stated that he lived "until after the year 400."

Abū Aḥmad's name starts almost every *isnād* (chain of transmitters) in Abū Hilāl's books, and therefore it is important to understand the areas of his influence in some detail. Abū Aḥmad al-Ḥasan ibn 'Abdallāh ibn Sa'īd ibn Zayd ibn Ḥakīm al-'Askarī (293-382/905-992) was famous for his thorough knowledge of philology, *ḥadīth*, or the traditions of the Prophet Muḥammad, and literature. He studied under widely known scholars such as Abū al-Qāsim al-Baghawī, Abū Bakr ibn Durayd and others. Abū Aḥmad lectured in 'Askar Mukram, Baṣra, Tustar and in other cities. Many of his students, such as Abū 'Abd al-Raḥmān al-Sulamī al-Ṣūfī (d. 412/1021), the well-known Bāqillānī (338-403/950-1013), the author of the *I'jāz al-Qur'ān*, and others, became famous. He was highly respected and his fame reached the Buwayhid vizier al-Ṣāḥib ibn 'Abbād, who made considerable efforts to attract him to his court, without success. He therefore resigned himself to visiting 'Askar Mukram to meet Abū Aḥmad, and he certainly seemed to have benefited greatly from him. That visit took place in 379/989. The vizier offered the scholar and his students valuable gifts, and, after the death of the master, continued to stay in contact with the students, among whom Abū Hilāl was prominent. When, in 382/992, al-Ṣāḥib heard the news of the death of Abū Aḥmad, he eulogized him in two lines of poetry that lamented the disappearance of the various branches of knowledge. In his book *al-Ḥathth 'alā ṭalab al-'ilm* (19-20), Abū Hilāl tells of another encounter between the vizier and Abū Aḥmad in Isfahan, when the latter was hurrying back to his home town from Rayy, where he had visited Abū al-Faḍl Ibn al-'Amīd (d. 360/970). When Abū Aḥmad reached Isfahan, the vizier made him stay in his company for a whole year in order to learn from him. There, we are told, Abū Aḥmad wrote a book entitled *Aqsām al-'Arab* and presented it to the vizier. This title is not mentioned by the biographers of Abū Aḥmad and nothing is known about it. The date of this meeting is not mentioned, but according to Yāqūt, in his *Mu'jam al-udabā'* (8:258), Abū Aḥmad visited Isfahan for the first time in 349/960, then in 354/965, as well as several other times.

Another unknown book by Abū Aḥmad is the *Kitāb rabī' al-abrār fī maḥāsin al-akhbār wa-'uyūn al-'ash'ār*. It is mentioned in Muḥibb al-Dīn Abu 'l-Faḍl Muḥammad Ibn al-Shiḥna's *al-Durr al-muntakhab fī tārīkh mamlakat Ḥalab*

(1984, 160). Yāqūt, in his *Mu'jam al-udabā'* (8:236) mentions another book that seems important, entitled *Ṣanā'at al-shi'r*, which seems not to have survived. Abū Hilāl, in his *Dīwān al-ma'ānī* (2:28), adds the *Kitāb al-waraqa*, of which nothing is known, and the biographers of Abū Aḥmad add additional titles of books authored by him which did not survive.

In one case a book was attributed to him, even though it is almost certain that he did not write it. The Dār al-Kutub in Cairo has a manuscript, *Zakiyyah* 297, on whose title page is written: *Hādhā Kitāb al-ḥikam wa 'l-amthāl li-Abī Aḥmad al-Ḥasan ibn 'Abdallāh al-'Askarī.* Kâtip Ç̧elebi (1609-1657), the author of *Kashf al-ẓunūn*, ascribed the book to him, also ascribes this book to him. Internal evidence, such as the chains of *isnād*, the quotations from people who lived after the death of Abū Aḥmad, and some other points, prove that the book must have been written long after his death in 382/992. This book was edited by M. Dabbūs, A. Mahdali and A. Imrān, revised by M. Mūsā, and published by al-Hay'ah al-Miṣriyyah al-ʿĀmmah li 'l-Kitāb, Cairo, 2006. This edition is far from being critical and is full of misleading information.

Only the following books authored by Abū Aḥmad have survived and have been published already. In *al-Maṣūn fī 'l-adab*, Abū Aḥmad discusses some points of literary criticism which, according to him must be based on literary taste. He points to beautiful similes, including a chapter on the similes of his contemporary, the poet Ibn al-Muʿtazz (246 or 247-296/862-908). He also deals with prose and quotes from eloquent people. It is an important early contribution to the classical Arabic literary criticism.

Regarding the *Kitāb sharḥ mā yaqa'u fīhi 'l-taṣḥīf wa 'l-taḥrīif*, the author's original plan was to write one book on the problems of *taṣḥīf* (a slip in writing or reading) and *taḥrīf* (alteration of a word), but then he divided it into two volumes. In this title, he discusses these problems in literature. The second part which deals with the *taṣḥīf* and *taḥrīf* in *ḥadīth* was printed under the title *Taṣḥīfāt al-muḥaddithīn* on the margin of Majd al-Dīn al-Mubārak ibn Muḥammad Ibn al-Athīr's (1149-1209) *al-Nihāyah fī gharīb al-ḥadīth*.

The *Risālah fī 'l-tafḍīl bayna balāghatay al-'Arab wa 'l-'ajam* is a short treatise--10 folios in manuscript 433 Aşir ef. in the Sülemaniye Kütüphanesi, Istanbul. It consists mainly of eloquent sayings of Arab orators, scribes and poets, and eloquent individuals from the ʻAjam, that is Greeks and Persians.

Even though the greater part of Abū Aḥmad's literary output did not survive, he greatly influenced his student Abū Hilāl and from the results of that influence, we can infer his views. Abū Aḥmad's influence on Abū Hilāl is indicated by the former's *Kitāb ṣinā'at al-shi'r* and by his attempts to introduce accurate readings of the poetry and names of poets into the *Ḥamāsa* of Abū Tammām. Abū Hilāl later wrote a chapter on Abū Tammām's *Ḥamāsa* in his *Kitāb sharḥ mā yaqa'u fīhi 'l-taṣḥīf wa 'l-taḥrīf.*

Abū Hilāl was a scholar with broad knowledge of language, *adab*, and general information, in addition to being a poet. Perhap because more of such works survived, he is widely known as a prominent critic and rhetorician of medieval Arabic literature. Although the biographers of Abū Hilāl mention a *dīwān*, or collection of his poetry, among his other books, it seems not to have survived. His extant poetry is scattered through his books and in general works or anthologies of classical Arabic poetry. So far, two attempts have been made to assemble his poetry. The first, by Muḥsin Ghayyāḍ, was entitled *Shi'r Abī Hilāl al-ʻAskarī.* It includes less than 1600 lines of poetry. The second attempt, by G. Kanazi, was published by the Academy of the Arabic Language in Damascus in 1979 and has 1600 lines. Neither edition collected all of Abū Hilāl's poetry. In a paper entitled "al-Mustadrak ʿalā shiʿr Abī Hilāl al-ʿAskarī," Ḥātim al-Ḍāmin added more lines, and other lines were added later by G. Kanazi in a paper entitled "Ziyādāt shiʿr al-ʿAskarī." Most of this poetry consists of short fragments or single lines. The longest passage consists of 16 lines in which Abū Hilāl describes winter and shows his preference for it over the other seasons. In his poetry he praises, derides, and boasts of himself, expresses certain ideas, and often describes nature, vegetables and fruits.

In addition to being a poet, Abū Hilāl wrote more than twenty books in the fields of rhetoric, literary criticism and general topics in Arabic culture. Although his fame was based mainly on his *Kitāb al-ṣinā'atayn*, which will be discussed later, his other books, which deal with language and linguistic issues, poetry, traditions and general information, are equally important. For the sake of clarity, they will be presented in three main categories.

The first category includes those books which deal with language and linguistic issues. Here are some details about three of them. The basic idea that led Abū Hilāl to write the *Kitāb al-furūq al-lughawiyyah*, also known as *al-Farq bayna al-ma'ānī* or *(Ma'rifat) al-furūq fī 'l-lughah*, is that different words or expressions that seem synonymous or nearly synonymous, actually have a small, inherent difference in denotation that one should know. He therefore takes words that seem to be synonyms and shows the nuances that make them different. For clarity and conciseness, he decided to concentrate on the diction of the *Qur'ān*, the words used by the *fuqahā',* or, scholars, and the general public. He intentionally discarded the *gharīb,* or, rarely used words, to keep the words between the high and the low standards of language, thus making it useful for both high and low classes. The words are organized into thirty chapters, according to categories, the last of which includes those words that were not included earlier. Thus, in chapter 18 he points to the difference between *dīn* and *milla*, *ṭā'a* and *ʽibāda*, *mubāḥ* and *ḥalāl*, *tawba* and *i'tidhār*, and so on. Here we rarely find quotations from poetry or from other material. The discussion is purely linguistic.

A part of the book was first published by R. Gosche in *Festgruss zur XXV Philologen Versamlung* Hall, 1864. The complete text was first published in Medina in 1966, then in Damascus in 1975 in two volumes, and a third edition appeared in Beirut in 1997.

Al-Talkhīṣ fī 'l-lughah, or *Kitāb al-talkhīṣ fī ma'rifat asmā' al-ashyā'* is a dictionary of concepts and attributes arranged in forty chapters. In each chapter the author puts together the concepts and attributes used in a certain field and explains pertinent meanings. The first chapter, for "names of the parts of human body, pregnancy, birth and related matters," contains the names and attributes of the head, the teeth, the nose, and the neck, etc. The second chapter deals with the manners and deeds of human beings, qualities for which one is praised or lampooned, types of maladies from which one suffers, love and the various names used to describe it according to its degree, nourishing new born babies, etc. By dividing the material into major subjects, he was able to put words together by field. Thus, he specifies one chapter for horses and all related matters, another for camels, one for the sky, sun, moon and stars, one for animals, one for birds, one for arts and crafts, and last chapter is left for things that he was unable to incorporate in the previous chapters.

The organization of this book by topic is important because it enabled the author to organize the material according to a certain logic. This aspect seems to have had an impact on ʽAlī ibn Ismāʽīl Ibn Sīdah, (1007-1066), who imitated the work in his huge dictionary *al-Mukhaṣṣaṣ*. In *al-Talkhīṣ fī 'l-lughah*, Abū Hilāl paid special attention to the Persian words that were arabicised (*mu'arrab*). This work was one of the main sources of Mawhūb ibn Aḥmad Jawālīqī's (d. 540/1145) *Kitāb al-mu'arrab*.

Al-Mu'jam fī baqiyyat al-ashyā' gives the names used in Arabic for the remnants of certain things and arranges them alphabetically. For example, *ramaq* denotes the very last sign of life in a dying person, and *su'r* is the small amount of water that remains in the cup after drinking all its contents.

To this category belong the following books, all of which were lost, and about which only their titles are known. *Mā yuktabu bi 'l-alif wa-mā yuktabu bi 'l-yā'*, *Sharḥ al-faṣīḥ*, which was apparently a commentary on the *Kitāb al-faṣīḥ* of ʽAbd al-Malik ibn Muḥammad al-Thaʽālibī (961 or 962-1037 or 1038), *Laḥn al-khaṣṣa*' and *al-Mudhakkar wa 'l-mu'annath. The Kitāb al-wujūh wa 'l-naẓā'ir* that was thought for long time to have been lost, is extant in two copies. One copy, titled *Taṣḥīḥ al-wujūh wa 'l-naẓā'ir*, from the year 480/1078 and in 194 folios, is in the al-Maʽhad al-Mawrītānī. The other, titled *al-Wujūh wa 'l-naẓā'ir*, in 57 folios, is from the year 547/1152 and is in the Central Library of Tehran.

The second category contains books that deal with literature. Among them, *Sharḥ dīwān Abī Miḥjan* was first published in Landberg's *Ṭuraf 'Arabiyya*, then in Cairo and in Beirut in 1970. It is a commentary on the poetry of Abū Miḥjan al-Thaqafī who lived in the first decades of Islam, and who was a wine drinker, but who expressed repentance and joined the early conquests of Islam. Abū Hilāl says that he intentionally chose to start with the *Dīwān* of Abū Miḥjan because others like Ibn al-Sikkīt (d. 857 or 858) and Abū Sa'īd al-Ḥasan ibn al-Ḥusayn al-Sukkarī (827 or 828-888 or 889) occupied themselves with the poetry of well-known and prolific poets. He therefore chose to collect the poetry of minor poets and started with Abū Miḥjan, promising to do the same with other poets.

After Abū Tammām compiled his *Ḥamāsa*, the anthology of classical Arabic poetry, several commentators interpreted it, and Abū Hilāl was one of them. He mentions his *Sharḥ al-Ḥamāsa*. in his *Jamharat* (1:407) and although many of his biographers also mention it, the book apparently did not survive. Yaḥyā ibn 'Alī Tibrīzī (d. 1109), in his own commentary on Abū Tammām, *Sharḥ dīwān al-Ḥamāsa*, (Cairo 1938, 1:142, 144, 155-156, 222, 294; 2:43, 56, 133, 155, etc.) quoted Abū Hilāl more than seventy times, considering him reliable for correct readings of certain lines of poetry or for the correct attribution of a certain passage of poetry to its true author.

Al-Risālah al-māsa fī mā lam yuḍbaṭ min al-Ḥamāsa is also referred to by the titles *al-Risālah fī ḍabṭ wa-taḥrīr mawāḍi' min dīwān al-Ḥamāsa li-Abī Tammām*, and *al-Risālah fī taḥqīq ba'ḍ abyāt al-Ḥamāsa*. It was first edited by G. Kanazi and published in Jerusalem Studies in Arabic and Islam, vol. II, 1980, pp. 97-163, and then in a separate book in *al-Karmil* publication series 4, Haifa 1991. It includes the author's comments on seventy cases in the Ḥamāsa of Abū Tammām, where he corrected the readings, the true attribution of a poem, or the true reading of the name of a poet.

Al-Ḥamāsa 'l-'Askariyya or *Ḥamāsat Abi Hilāl al-Ḥasan ibn 'Abdallāh ibn Sahl* was mentioned by Kâtip Çelebi (*Kashf* 693), Badr al-Dīn Maḥmūd ibn Aḥmad ibn Mūsā al-'Aynī (1361-1451) (*al-Maqāsid al-naḥwiyyah*, 4:598), Muḥammad ibn 'Abd al-Raḥmān 'Ubaydī (*al-Tadhkirah al-Sa'diyyah*, 42, 327, 557) and by the unknown author of *Majmū'at al-ma'ānī*, 133. This book, which did not survive, together with the two mentioned above, show that Abū Hilāl compiled an anthology of classical Arabic poetry following that of Abū Tammām, interpreted the *Ḥamāsa* of his predecessor and then added a shorter treatise on certain lines of Abū Tammām's *Ḥamāsa*.

It is easy to be confused by the *Dīwān al-ma'ānī*. Yāqūt (*Mu'jam al-udabā'* VIII. 263–264) mentions three different names: *Ma'ānī 'l-adab*, *A'lām al-ma'ānī fī ma'ānī 'l-shi'r*, and *al-Farq bayna 'l-ma'ānī*. Al-Baghdādī adds a fourth: *Dīwān al-Ma'ānī*. It seems that the first two titles mentioned by Yāqūt and that added by al-Baghdādī refer to the same book, while the third name mentioned by Yāqūt refers to *al-Furūq al-lughawiyyah*. This book is a good example of the *adab* in which Abū Hilāl was expert and for which he was called *al-adīb*. In its various chapters, many topics are introduced to cover poetry, prose, invocations, the sky and stars, kinds of food and wine, deserts and wild animals, in addition to short chapters on chess, the longing for one's homeland, etc. As a whole, the book is full of quotations from poetry and prose and reflects the author's fine taste and broad knowledge.

Literally, the title *Kitāb al-ṣinā'atayn* means "the book of the two arts," which are prose and poetry. This contradicts the author's concept that *kalām*, discourse, is in fact one basic phenomenon that has two main branches: *kitābah,* prose writing, and *shi'r*, or poetry. Consequently, the same rules for the art of writing apply to both branches, with the exception of meter, which is specific to poetry. The original title of the book seems to have been the *Kitāb ṣan'at al-kalām,* the book of the art of discourse. He mentions this title whenever he discusses rhetorical or literary criticism issues in his other books. The objectives of this book were to put together the arguments that support the dogma of the inimitability (*i'jāz)* of the *Qur'ān*, to outline the criteria for distinguishing between good and bad literary works, to show those who practice the art of writing how to avoid using the uncouth, to show the critic how to evaluate literary production, and to show the basis for choosing poetry for anthologies. Abū Hilāl depends substantially on earlier sources and follows a scholastic style via which he meant to teach students of rhetoric and literary criticism the basics of those arts. His contributions seem to have been arranging the material in a scholastic style, and introducing additional figures of speech, a trend which became widely accepted later.

Perhaps the most important aspect of the book is its discussion of plagiarism and devices of speech. With regard to plagiarism, al-ʿAskarī believes that *sariqah* (literally means theft), i.e. plagiarism, is inevitable and therefore he does not consider it negative. He even suggests the using the term *akhdh*, borrowing, instead. Consequently he points to methods of "borrowing," defined as a *ma'na*: an idea or a concept taken from one theme and transferred to another, or borrowed from prose and transferred to poetry, or visa versa, in order to conceal the source of ideas and thus look original and innovative. In his ninth chapter on *badī'*, figures of speech, he boasts of his own innovation by adding ten new figures that were not known previously. A close examination, however, proves that most of these devices were used by early poets even though the definitions of the devices were not properly formulated.

The *Kitāb al-ṣinā'atayn* was written around the end of the 4th century, a few decades after the appearance of Qudāma ibn Jaʿfar's (ca. 873or 874–948) book entitled *Naqd al-shi'r* (Leiden 1956), which presents a comprehensive theory on the evaluation of poetry. Qudāma's theory is based on Greek logic and attempts to set the Arabic theory of criticism in the framework of that logic. Critics contemporary with Qudāma turned against him and wrote several treatises to refute his book. Partly, this was due to a feeling at that time that Hellenistic influence was infiltrating Arabic literature and culture in order to change their nature. Modern Arab critics still argue that the implications inherent in Qudama's system limited the literary refinement of critics and disposed them toward excessive concern with formal aspects and the definition and classification of each point in the general framework of the theory. Abū Hilāl certainly knew his predecessor's book and was aware of the attitude of those who wanted to preserve Arab heritage from any foreign influence. In his *Kitāb al-ṣinā'atayn*, he made use of a good deal of material from Qudāma's book, but failed to accept the latter's highly organized system, that is, his four-element scheme and his various borrowings from Aristotle and other Greek philosophers.

In his *Geschichte der arabischen Litteratur* (G. I. 132), Brockelmann mentions a printed book of 170 pages entitled *Maḥāsin al-nathr wa 'l-naẓm min al-kitābah wa 'l-shi'r*. It is not another book by ʿAskarī, but simply the last two chapters of the *Kitāb al-ṣinā'atayn* printed separately.

The *Jamharat al-amthāl* contains about 2000 classical Arabic proverbs arranged alphabetically in 29 chapters, the number of the letters in the Arabic alphabet. Each chapter consists of two sections. The first gives the proverbs in alphabetic order and explains them or gives the story from which each was taken. The second lists the proverbs that start with verbal adjectives expressing the superlative *'f'alu min...* such as *ahwanu min namlah*, i.e., (he/it) is of no more value than an ant. The book is of great value because it contains so much information about Arab heritage and also because it quotes hundreds of lines of poetry. The author used anthologies of proverbs written before his time and tried to rid his book of their shortcomings.

Some biographers of Abū Hilāl include the *Kitāb al-maḥāsin fī tafsīr al-Qur'ān*, or *Tafsīr al-Qur'ān* or *Tafsīr al-'Askarī* in the list of his books. Fück even (*EI*, 2nd ed., s.v. al-ʿAskarī) assumes that the word "*maḥāsin*" in the title indicates that Abū Hilāl dealt mainly with the stylistic beauties of the *Qur'ān*. Brockelmann (*GAL*. S. I. 124) mentions that there are three manuscripts of this book, located in Mashhad, Tehran and Istanbul. Actually, this *Tafsīr* is that of *Imām* Ḥasan al-ʿAskarī and not of Abū Hilāl al-ʿAskarī.

The *Kitāb al-awā'il* is the last book that Abū Hilāl wrote. It was completed in the year 395/992, as he states at its end. This date was taken by many authors as the year in which Abū Hilāl died, but we have seen that this was not the case.

In this book, Abū Hilāl assembles the information that he said was scattered in various sources about people who were the first to do a certain thing, from the pre-Islamic period until his time. It is arranged in ten chapters and is justified by the fact that it not only brings together the material, but also arranges it in a useful way. The first chapter pulls together early information about the tribe of *Quraysh*. The second chapter discusses the first reference in the *Qur'ān* to the *Jāhiliyyah*, or the first man who said *'ammā ba'd'*. Abū Hilāl then moves on to the Muslim era and provides information about "the first emir who died in Basra, the first who crucified a man in Islam," etc.

The *Kitāb al-kuramā'* is a short treatise (43 pages) on generosity and philanthropy among the Arabs. It was first published in Cairo in 1326/1908, edited by Mahmūd Jabālī, and later, in 1934, edited by M. M. Shākir, under the title *Kitāb faḍl al-'aṭā' 'alā 'l-'usr*. This new title is taken from a phrase in the book itself (p. 29 of 1st ed.).

Al-Ḥathth 'alā ṭalab al-'ilm is a short treatise in which the author mentions the basic requirements for acquiring thorough knowledge. He specifies necessary seven qualities: an open mind, a long period of study, sufficient means to live, intensive work, a brilliant teacher, a real desire for knowledge, and finally a nature conducive to reason, which and makes such a program easier. It was published in Beirut-Damascus in 1986, and in Cairo 1412/1991, in a collection of similar treatises by several authors, entitled *al-Jāmi' fī 'l-ḥathth 'alā ṭalab al-'ilm*.

In this category too, we find names of books that did not survive, such as the *Kitāb al-dirham w'al-dīnār*, *al-Tabṣirah*, *Kitāb al-'umda*, *Kitāb al-'uzla*, *al-Watar* and *Man iḥtakam min al-khulafā' ila 'l-quḍāt*.

It becomes evident from the above survey of Abū Hilāl's efforts that he played an important role in the 4th/10th century in the sphere of rhetoric, criticism, proverbs and general information. In spite of the fact that almost half of his books did not survive, his extant books add much to our information about him as an active author and about the literary life of his time.

REFERENCES

Muḥsin al-Ḥusaynī al-ʻĀmilī, *A'yān al-Shī'ah* (Beirut: Maṭbaʻat al-Inṣāf, 1960-);

Ḥasan ibn ʻAbd Allāh al-ʻAskarī, *Kitāb al-taṣḥīf wa 'l-taḥrīf wa-sharḥ mā yaqa'u fīhi* (Cairo: Maṭbaʻat al-Ẓāhir, 1908-);

Ḥasan ibn ʻAbd Allāh al-ʻAskarī, *al-Maṣūn fī al-adab* (Kuwait: Dāʻirat al-Maṭbūʻāt wa 'l-Nashr, 1960);

Ḥasan ibn ʻAbd Allāh al-ʻAskarī, *Risālah fī 'l-tafḍīl bayna balāghatay al-'Arab wa'-'ajam* (Istanbul, 1884); (al-Khālidiyyah, al-Kuwayt: Kulliyyat al-Ādāb, Jāmiʻat al-Kuwayt, 2006);

Ḥasan ibn ʻAbd Allāh al-ʻAskarī, *Sharḥ mā yaqa'u fīhi 'l-taṣḥīf wa 'l-taḥrīf*, ed. al-Sayyid Muḥammad Yūsuf (Damascus: Majmaʻ al-Lughah al-ʻArabiyyah bi-Dimashq, 1981-);

Ḥasan ibn ʻAbd Allāh al-ʻAskarī, *Taṣḥīfāt al-muḥaddithīn*, ed. Aḥmad ʻAbd al-Shāfī (Beirut: Dār al-Kutub al-ʻIlmiyyah, 1988);

Badr al-Dīn Maḥmūd ibn Aḥmad ibn Mūsā al-ʻAynī, *al-Maqāsid al-naḥwiyyah fī sharḥ shawāhid shurūḥ al-Alfiyyah* (Beirut: Dār al-Kutub al-ʻIlmiyyah, 2005);

ʻAbd al-Qādir ibnʻʻUmar al-Baghdādī, *Khizānat al-adab wa lubb lūbab lisān al-'arab* (Cairo: Dār al-Kitāb al-ʻArabī li 'l-Ṭibāʻah wa 'l-Nashr, 1967-1986);

Ibn ʻAbd al-Majīd ʻAbīdī, *al-Tadhkirah al-sa'diyyah* (Baghdad: Yuṭlab min Maktabat al-Ahliyyah, 1972);

ʻAlī ibn al-Ḥasan Bākharzī, *Dumyat al-qaṣr wa-'asrat ahl al-'aṣr* (Cairo: Dār al-Fikr al-ʻArabī, 1968);

Ḥātim al-Ḍāmin, "al-Mustadrak ʻalā shiʻr Abī Hilāl al-ʻAskarī," *Majallat Majma' al-Lughah al-'Arabiyyah bi-Dimashq* 67, 1 (1992): 37-48;

Muḥammad ibn Aḥmad al-Dhahabī, *al-'Ibar fī khabar man ghabar* (Kuwait: Maṭbaʻat Ḥukūmat al-Kuwayt, 1961);

Muḥammad ibn Aḥmad al-Dhahabī, *Tadhkirat al-ḥuffāz* (Beirut: Dār al-Kutb al-ʻIlmiyyah, 1957);

Majd al-Dīn al-Mubārak ibn Muḥammad Ibn al-Athīr, *al-Nihāyah fī gharīb al-ḥadīth wa 'l-*

athar wa-ma'ahā fī 'l-ṣalb al-durr al-nathīr talkhīṣ nihāyat Ibn al-Athīr li-Jalāl al-Dīn al-Suyūṭī wa-bi 'l-hāmish kitābān aḥaduhumā Mufradāt al-Rāghib al-Isfahānī fī gharīb al-Qur'ān wa-thānīhumā taṣḥīfāt al-muḥaddithīn li 'l-Ḥāfiẓ Abī Aḥmad al-Ḥasan ibn 'Abd Allāh al-'Askarī (Cairo: al-Maṭbaʻah al-Khayriyyah, 1908); *al-Nihāyah fī gharīb al-ḥadīth wa 'l-athar*, ed. Ṭāhir Aḥmad al-Zāwī and Maḥmūd Muḥammad al-Ṭanāḥī (Cairo: Dār Iḥyā' al-Kutub al-ʻArabiyyah, 1990?);

Muḥibb al-Dīn Abu 'l-Faḍl Muḥammad Ibn al-Shiḥna, *al-Durr al-muntakhab fī tārīkh mamlakat Ḥalab* (Damascus, 1984);

Ibn Khallikān, *Wafayāt al-a'yān wa-anbā' abnā' al-zamān* (Cairo: Maktabat al-Nahḍah al-Miṣriyyah, 1948-1949);

George Kanazi, "al-ʻAskari's Attitude toward Poetry and Poets," *Journal of Semitic Studies* 20:1 (1975): 73-80;

G. Kanazi, "Murājʻa li-Kitāb *al-Hikam wa 'l-amthāl*, attributed to Abū Aḥmad al-ʻAskarī," *al-Karmil* (Dept. of Arabic Language and Literature, University of Haifa) 28 (2007): 229-243;

George Kanazi, "Organic Unity in the Kitāb as-Sināʻatayn of Abū Hilāl al-ʻAskarī," *Semitics* 3 (1973): 1-18;

George Kanazi, *Studies in the Kitāb al-Ṣina'ātayn of Abū Hilāl al-'Askarī* (Leiden: E.J. Brill, 1989);

George Kanazi, "The Works of Abū Hilāl al-ʻAskarī," *Arabica*: 22:1 (1975): 61-70;

George Kanazi, "Ziyādāt shiʻr al-ʻAskarī," *Majallat Majma' al-lughah al-'arabiyyah* (Damascus) 70:3 (1995): 568-581;

Kâtip Çelebi, *al-Mujallad al-thānī min kitāb Kashf al-ẓunūn "an asāmī al-kutub wa 'l-funūn* (Istanbul: Wikālat al-Maʻārif, 1943);

Amal al-Mashāyikh, *Abū Hilāl al-'Askarī nāqidan* (Amman: Wizārat al-Thaqāfah, 2001);

ʻAlī ibn Yūsuf Qifṭī, *Inbāh al-ruwāt "alā anbāh al-nuḥāt* (Cairo: Dār al-Kutub al-Miṣriyyah, 1950-1955);

Qudāma ibn Jaʻfar, *The Kitāb naqd al-ši'r of Qudāma b. Ġa'far al-Kātīb al-Baġdādī* (Leiden: E.J. Brill, 1956);

Rudolph Sellheim, *Die Klassische-arabischen Sprichwörtersammlungen: insbesondere die des Abū 'Ubaid* (s'Gravenhage: Mouton, 1954);

al-Suyūṭī, *Bughyat al-wu'āt fī ṭabaqāt al-lughawiyyīn wa 'l-nuḥah* (Cairo: Ṭubiʻa bi-Maṭbaʻat ʻĪsā 'l-Bābī 'l-Halabī, 1964-1965);

al-Suyūṭī, *Ṭabaqāt al-mufassirīn*, ed. A. Heursing, (1839);

al-Thʻālibī, *Kitāb tatimmat al-yatīmah* (Tehran: Maṭbaʻat Fardīn, 1353/1934);

al-Thʻālibī, *Yatīmat al-dahr* (Cairo, n.d.);

Muḥammad ibn ʻAbd al-Raḥmān ʻUbaydī, *al-Tadhkirah al-sa'diyyah* (Baghdad: Yuṭlab min Maktabat al-Ahliyyah, 1972);

G.J.H. Van Gelder, *Beyond the Line* (Leiden: E.J. Brill, 1983);

Yāqūt ibn ʻAbd Allāh al-Ḥamawī, *Mu'jam al-udabā'* (Cairo: Dār 'al-Maʻmūn, 1936-1938).

ʿAyn al-Qudāt al-Hamadhānī

(1096 or 1098-1131)

FIROOZEH PAPAN-MATIN
University of Washington

WORKS

Zubdat al-ḥaqā'iq;
Tamhīdāt;
Maktūbāt;
Musannafāt;
Shakwā 'l-gharīb 'an al-'awṭān ilā 'ulamā' al-buldān.

Editions

Zubdat al-ḥaqā'iq, ed. by ʿAfīf ʿUsayrān (Tehran: Tehran University Press, 1961);
Tamhīdāt. 4th ed., ed. with an introduction by ʿAfīf ʿUsayrān (Tehran: Manūchihrī, 1991);
Maktūbāt. 2d ed., ed. by ʿAfīf ʿUsayrān and ʿAlīnaqī Munẓavī, Vols. 1-2 (Tehran: Manūchihrī, 1983) ed. by ʿAlīnaqī Munẓavī, Vol. 3 (Tehran: Asātīr, 1998);
Musannafāt, ed. with an introduction by ʿAfīf ʿUsayrān (Tehran: Intishārāt-i Dānishgāh-i Tehran, 1962);
"Shakwā 'l-gharīb ʿan al-'awṭān ilā ʿulamā' al-buldān," in *Musannafāt*, ed. by ʿAfīf ʿUsayrān (Tehran: Intishārāt-i Dānishgāh-i Tehran, 1962).

Translations

"Šakwā-l-ġarīb ʿani l-'awṭān ila ʿulamā'-al-buldān," ed. and translated by Mohammed ben Abd el-Jalil. *Journal Asiatique*, 30, 1: 2-78; 30, 2:194-297;
Sufi Martyr: the 'Apology' of 'Ain al-Quḍāt al-Hamadhānī, translation and ed. by A.J. Arberry (London: George Allen and Unwin, 1969);
Les Tentations Métaphysiques (Tamhidât), translation and introduction by Christiane Tortel (Paris: Les Deux Océans, 1992.

Abū 'l-Maʿālī ʿAbd Allāh ibn Abī Bakr Muḥammad ibn ʿAlī ibn al-Ḥasan ibn ʿAlī 'l-Miyānajī, known as ʿAyn al-Qudāt al-Hamadhānī was a famous twelfth-century Persian mystic. He was born in Hamadan in A.D. 1096 or 1098 and was executed in the same town in 1131 on the charge of heresy. There are no biographical records from ʿAyn al-Qudāt's time that tell us about his personal life. The later sources on him are scant and limited to general remarks on his untimely death, his father, and his grandfather. Therefore, his writings are the most reliable source on his life and ideas. One of his personal letters makes a vague reference to a person named Aḥmad, who could had been his son; however, there is no reliable information that proves he was married and had any children. ʿAyn al-Qudāt came from a well-known family from Miyānj, a small town between Zanjān and Hamadan in Azerbaijan. We know that ʿAyn al-Qudāt was born in Hamadan but the exact date of his birth is open to dispute. Hamadan in northwest Iran, on the route connecting Baghdad and Khurāsān, was a major cultural center in medieval Persia. It took pride in having been home to the philosopher Avicenna (A.D. 980–1037) to whom ʿAyn al-Qudāt paid homage. ʿAyn al-Qudāt's acknowledgement of the philosophical tradition was uncharacteristic of the mysticism of his era, which was dominated by the teaching of Abū Ḥāmid ibn Muḥammad al-Ghazzālī (1058-1111) whose younger brother, Aḥmad (d. 1126) was ʿAyn al-Qudāt's teacher. ʿAyn al-Qudāt attributes his mystical enlightenment and the opening of his "inner sight" to the influence of Aḥmad al-Ghazzālī. The latter adhered to the teachings of al-Ḥusayn ibn Manṣūr al-Ḥallāj (858 or 859-922), especially in regard to his interpretation of

Satan. Inspired by their teachings, ʿAyn al-Quḍāt developed theoretical doctrines on Satan and his dark light as manifestations of God's attribute of majesty.

In his writings, ʿAyn al-Quḍāt never refers to himself by his name, ʿAbd Allāh, nor does he identify with his family's city of origin Miyānajī. He calls himself ʿAyn al-Quḍāt. I have not seen any biographer explain the etymology of ʿAyn al-Quḍāt's honorary name or explain in what sense this name applies to him, since we do not have any evidence that he held the position of a judge. This name seems to have some relation to the fact of his genealogy: both his father and grandfather were judges and it could mean he is the eye of the judges or the visionary (eye) who was born to these other judges. ʿAyn al-Quḍāt refers to himself by this name and expresses pride in his hometown of Hamadan. ʿAyn al-Quḍāt held lectures for his disciples and had a wide following in Hamadan and among some of the Saljuq court nobles. He was renowned for his exceptional intelligence and in depth knowledge of Islamic sciences. Nevertheless, his views on faith did not abide by the notional interpretations of Islam and the *Qur'ān*. He wrote about all religions as different paths that led one to God. During his short life he composed books and treatises on mystical subjects and other topics ranging from mathematics, natural sciences, to grammar and semantics, Arabic literature, jurisprudence, rhetoric, commentary on the *Qur'ān*, and the nature of prophecy. Most of these works were written in Arabic, the scholarly language of Islam. As a young man he wrote eleven books and treatises, none of which have survived. ʿAyn al-Quḍāt mentions these writings in his surviving texts, as well as in his defense treatise, as works he had completed in his youth, which, based on our reading of the texts means up to age twenty four. Only his works on mysticism survived the Mongol invasion of the thirteenth century. Among his major extant works are the following: (i) *Zubdat al-ḥaqā'iq*, a book in one hundred chapters written in Arabic (1123); (ii) his personal letters, known as the *Maktūbāt*; (iii) the *Tamhīdāt* (1127), written in Persian, is ʿAyn al-Quḍāt's principal work on mysticism; (iv) *Shakwā 'l-gharīb 'an al-awṭān ilā 'ulamā'al-buldān* (The Complaint of a Stranger Exiled from Home to the Scholars of the Lands), in Arabic, is his defense treatise which he completed during his imprisonment in Baghdad.

His personal letters, the *Maktūbāt*, follow the *masā'il wa-ajwibah* (question and answer) literary tradition of medieval times; they present the questions posed to ʿAyn al-Quḍāt by his associates and disciples. The letters provide insight into ʿAyn al-Quḍāt's immediate intellectual milieu and the nature of the issues and debates that concerned its members. The letters were produced as an extension of his teaching; they were duplicated and filed for reference. There is evidence that suggests there must had been a center in charge of handling ʿAyn al-Quḍāt's writings and his correspondence. *Zubdat al-ḥaqā'iq* is a major work that he completed in his early twenties. It includes topics on the essence and the attributes of God, prophethood, mysticism, the opening of the inner sight, and the ways of understanding the unseen and the afterlife. The *Tamhīdāt* is considered ʿAyn al-Quḍāt's most significant work because it is the most comprehensive. It consists of ten chapters on topics of mysticism and describes the wayfarer's visionary experiences and states of mind at different stages of the person's development. This work was esteemed highly by the early Chishtī scholars of India. In fact, the most important medieval commentary on a work by ʿAyn al-Quḍāt is by Khvājah Bandah Navāz Gīsūdarāz Chishtī (1321–1422) who analyzed the major themes in the *Tamhīdāt*. ʿAyn al-Quḍāt argues that all of creation is ultimately non-corporeal and our attachment to the body and matter is but a delusion. This gnosis enabled him to base his mystical arguments on the knowledge that everything is light. In this context, he represented Satan not as evil but as an obscure light that appeared in contrast with Muḥammad's luminosity. Moreover, he took issue with the perspective that interpreted faith through the teachings of the Sharia. He explained that Sharia promoted "habitude" (*'ādat*) and abiding by preconceived notions of the "unseen" (*'ālam al-ghayb*). The knowing wayfarer traveled the mystical path with the understanding that creation consists of different manifestations of God. This totality is the occasion for acquiring knowledge and approaching the unforeseen limits of understanding. Satan was a valuable teacher on this walk because he knew the way and was determined to bar the wayfarer from advancing on the path. The complexity of thought and expression encountered in ʿAyn al-Qudāt's writing poses a great challenge to the reader and requires careful analysis.

ʿAyn al-Qudāt completed his apology, *Shakwā 'l-gharīb 'an al-awtān ilā 'ulamā' al-buldān*, during his incarceration at the Tikrīt prison. He does not identify his adversaries but indicates that his enemies are motivated by envy toward him. His execution took place during the reign of the Saljuq king, Sultan Maḥmūd ibn Muḥammad ibn Malikshāh (1118–1131), whose vizier Qavām al-Dīn Nāṣir ibn ʿAlī Abī 'l-Qāsim al-Dargazīnī (d. 1133) was responsible for the arrest and execution of ʿAyn al-Qudāt. The *Shakwā 'l-gharīb* outlines the charges against him as follows: (1) his views on God as the all-encompassing Being with limited knowledge of the particulars, (2) his views on prophecy as a stage past the stage of reason and the stage of sainthood, (3) his views on the role of the spiritual leader (*imām*) in the life of the believer. ʿAyn al-Qudāt presents his case, arguing that his adversaries have distorted his views. We know he was executed on May 23, 1131 (23 Jumādā II, 525 A.H.) in Hamadan. He was executed at some point after his release from the Baghdad prison. He was put to death in a violent manner and his body was destroyed. According to the author of Tadhkarih-yi Riyvd al-ʿĀrifīn, ʿAyn al-Qudāt was killed in the courtyard of the school where he used to teach. The execution took place before Sultan Maḥmūd, who at the time was twenty–five years old. ʿAyn al-Qudāt's execution was turned into an spectacle for everyone to remember. The classical hagiographies do not mention any burial or grave for him, but the people of Hamadan identify a small ditch in the old cemetery of the city as the place where his remains were left. Considered to be a blessed place, this site is a memorandum of ʿAyn al-Qudāt's surviving memory in the folk culture of Hamadan.

REFERENCES

Henry Corbin, *En Islam Iranien, aspects spirituels et philosophiques*, Vols. 1–4 (Paris: Gallimard, 1972);

Hamid Dabashi, *Truth and Narrative: the Untimely Thoughts of 'Ayn al-Qudāt al-Hamadhānī* (Surrey: Curzon, 1999);

Louis Massignon, *La Passion de Husayn Ibn Mansûr Hallâj*, 4 v., (Paris: Gallimard, 1975)

Firoozeh Papan-Matin, *Beyond Death: Mystical Teachings of 'Ayn al-Qudāt al-Hamadhānī*, Islamic History and Civilization Studies and Texts Series (Leiden: E.J. Brill, in press, 2009).

Badīʿ al-Zamān Aḥmad ibn al-Ḥusayn al-Hamadhānī

(circa 358/969–398/1008)

JAAKO HÄMEEN-ANTTILA
University of Helsinki

WORKS

Maqāmāt;
Mulaḥ;
Rasā'il;
Dīwān.

Editions

Muḥammad Muḥyī al-Dīn ʿAbd al-Ḥamīd, *Sharḥ maqāmāt Badī' al-Zamān al-Hamadhānī* (Beirut: Dār al-Kutub al-ʿIlmiyyah, 1979);

Mulaḥ, in the margins of al-Hamadhānī, *Rasā'il*, 4th ed. (Cairo: Maṭbaʿat Hindiyyah bi 'l-Mūskī bi-Miṣr, 1346/1928), 293-331;

Ibrāhīm al-Aḥdab, *Kashf al-ma'ānī wa 'l-bayān 'an Rasā'il Badī' al-Zamān* (Beirut: al-Maṭbaʿah al-Kāthūlīkiyyah li 'l-Ābā' al-Yasūʿiyyīn, 1890);

Dīwān Badī' al-Zamān al-Hamadhānī, dirāsah wa-taḥqīq Yusrī ʿAbd al-Ghanī ʿAbd Allāh (Beirut: Dār al-Kutub al-ʿIlmiyyah, 1407/1987).

Translations

W.J. Prendergast, *The Maqāmāt of Badí' al-Zamān al-Hamadhānī* (London: Luzac & Co, 1915). Reprinted with foreword by C.E. Bosworth. (London: Curzon Press 1973).

The cognomen Badīʿ al-Zamān, which al-Hamadhānī received posthumously, shows how people saw him soon after his death: he had been the Wonder of His Age, due to an unusual talent for writing ornate prose, mainly literary letters and maqāmahs. Few authors in world literature can boast of having single-handedly originated a whole genre. The maqāmah, invented by al-Hamadhānī, was to survive for a millennium after him and in time it spread even into Hebrew, Syriac and Persian literature.

Al-Hamadhānī was born in Western Iran, in Hamadan, the ancient Ecbatana, into a family which seems to have claimed Arab descent and may well have been Arab. The literary culture of what today is Iran was still very much Arabic in character and language and although the situation was changing at the end of the tenth century, Arabs and Arabic literature still had a disproportionately great part to play in Iran. We do not quite know which was al-Hamadhānī's mother tongue, Arabic or Persian. It may have been Arabic, but he is said to have been fluent in Persian, too, although no writings by him in this language are known to have existed. The preserved, Arabic works of al-Hamadhānī do not, on the other hand, prove that his mother tongue would have been Arabic, since many non-Arab authors still used that language in literature, just like Latin was used in Europe. Irrespective of his mother tongue, al-Hamadhānī had to learn literary Arabic, as vernacular and literary Arabic had for centuries already been two completely different languages, and thus even native speakers of Arabic had to learn their written language.

Besides al-Hamadhānī himself, his family produced some scholars whom we know by name. They mainly worked in religious professions, but none of them made a reputation of his own. We know them from al-Hamadhānī's letters and the biographical sources primarily interested in al-Hamadhānī. His father may have been a man of learning: at least, some of his letters to his son, preserved among the latter's collected letters, would imply this. However, people almost contemporary to al-Hamadhānī were already expressing their doubt as to the genuineness of these letters, which makes it most uncertain whether they really are by the father or by the son. Al-Hamadhānī may well have forged these letters to cover his origins, if his father was in reality a less illustrious person, coming from outside literary circles. In any case, we have no articles on either his father or his other ancestors in the biographical literature.

The traditional date of al-Hamadhānī's birth, 358/969, may well have been derived by counting backwards from the date of his death, 398/1008; dates of birth were rarely given much attention in mediaeval Arabic culture, especially in a case involved social mobility: noble births were recorded but outside of the highest classes this was unusual. When he died, al-Hamadhānī is said to have been forty (lunar) years old. Forty is, however, a traditional expression for "a lot," similar to "dozens" or "hundreds" in English–a famous late example comes in Ali Baba and the forty thieves. In a man's life, forty marks the apogee of full manhood; the prophet Muḥammad (d. 632), for example, is said to have received his first revelation at that age. Saying that al-Hamadhānī died at age forty could be translated into our expression "as a middle-aged man." Thus, his year of birth has to be taken as only approximate.

Whatever the exact year of his birth, al-Hamadhānī received his first instruction in his home town from teachers of secondary importance. Among them only one, the philologist Aḥmad ibn Fāris (d. 395/1004), is generally considered a major figure. We also know the names of some of his other teachers, but they are all marginal, almost obscure characters of the tenth century. Al-Hamadhānī began his travels as a young man, and they continued almost up to his death. In some of his poems, al-Hamadhānī satirizes the good-for-nothing region of Hamadan, but this need not be the real reason for his setting out on journeys that took him into nearly every corner of the Iranian world, even up to Herat in modern Afghanistan, since invectives on cities were almost a *topos* in mediaeval Arabic literature.

Travelling was also considered a normal custom for scholars, and few *literati* remained in their native towns for the whole of their lives. It was common to go around in search of famous teachers and generous patrons. This also accelerated the spread of ideas, as well as new genres, which sometimes found their way within a couple of years to cities throughout the Islamic world, from Herat to Cordoba.

In his own town, al-Hamadhānī's studies must have been elementary and he starts to become visible only in Rayy, the ancient Rhagae, where he went in 380/990. Whether born in 358/969 or not, he was still a young man when he lived in Rayy. The city had become a major centre of learning because the influential vizier of the Buwayhids, al-Ṣāḥib ibn ʿAbbād (938-995), held his court there and did his best to combine courtly life with a literary salon.

Al-Ṣāḥib ibn ʿAbbād himself had ambitions in both literature and philology and he gathered around him a great number of scholars and writers. In addition, he had a marked predilection for the life of the lower classes: beggars, thieves and wanderers found refuge under his patronage, at least if they could tell him stories about lower-class life or, even better, write books about it. He was especially interested in the guile and jargon of beggars.

Later legends have it that the encounter between the mighty vizier and the young, aspiring al-Hamadhānī was a milestone in their lives: two leading intellectuals of the century meeting in one city. However, neither contemporary sources nor the works of either support this view. In reality, al-Hamadhānī was far too young to be noticed in a court full of already established intellectuals. The two may have met, but if so the meetings were in no way conspicuous. It is even possible that al-Hamadhānī was not directly attracted by Ibn ʿAbbād himself but rather, followed his teacher Ibn Fāris, who was invited to the court. In his teacher's entourage, al-Hamadhānī may, of course, have attended sessions at the court but hardly gained any prestige there. He would have been there to learn and to listen. None of the contemporary scholars mentions having met him at the court of Ibn ʿAbbād.

From Rayy, al-Hamadhānī soon continued his voyage to other cities. There is a well-known story explaining why he had to move on. He is said to have farted in the presence of the vizier and when trying to cover the incident by blaming the squeaking of his chair, the sharp-tongued vizier reportedly said that he would sooner believe that the sound was produced by al-Hamadhānī's backside (*taḥt*) than his chair (*takht*). The story, however, is originally told by al-Hamadhānī about another courtier, and was later misattributed to al-Hamadhānī himself. Al-Hamadhānī did not run away, ashamed, from the city but continued the usual "grand tour" of his age, moving on to meet new *literati* and find new patrons.

What he probably acquired at the court of Ibn ʿAbbād was an interest in lower classes and their lives. This subject matter, written in refined language and elegant style, produced literature that had an innate tension between the elevated form and the low content, or, to use the Greek terms, between *hupsos* and *bathos*.

We do not exactly know how long al-Hamadhānī stayed in Rayy, but in 382/992 he had already stayed a while in Jurjān on the Caspian Sea. In this city he was in contact with al-Ismāʿīliyyah, which, despite yet another legend, in this context does not refer to the Ismaili branch of Shiism but simply to the bourgeois Sunni family of al-Ismāʿīlī, some members of which became his patrons, especially al-Dihkhudā Abū Saʿd Muḥammad ibn Manṣūr al-Ismāʿīlī. Later biographers seem to have been confused by the name of the family, thereby surmising that al-Hamadhānī was an Ismaili, or was at least influenced by them. Some modern scholars have seen Ismaili tendencies in al-Hamadhānī's works, but they have probably exaggerated the importance of the few passages which could be interpreted in this way.

Al-Thaʿālibī (961 or 962-1037 or 1038), al-Hamadhānī's main biographer, who had actually met him and had access to his papers, mentions that in Jurjān, al-Hamadhānī had his first literary successes. Tellingly, he does not say anything about any success in Rayy, thus implying that in Rayy he had gone unnoticed. We do not know what al-Hamadhānī may have written in Jurjān, but what we do know is that his first works were favourably received there, and he may have written his first *maqāmahs* in Jurjān. Even though he had some success, he continued his travel in 382/992. He was not yet ready to settle down, but he aimed at higher and more influential patrons than the al-Ismāʿīlī family. Yet, in this case he does seem to have had a reason to leave town, since he had become involved in literary intrigues and seems to have made influential enemies. Such jealous quarrelling between scholars and writers was common, and the more ambitious a young scholar was, the more certainly he, sooner or later, found himself maligned to his patrons, for whose favour–and financial rewards–scholars competed.

Al-Hamadhānī may have started feeling uncomfortable in Jurjān, but he did not have to run away, since he had al-Dihkhudā's recommendations with him when he left for Nishapur, another cultural centre at that time. On the way he was attacked by robbers. Later he was again to undergo the same fate, so it is not surprising that he used the theme in his *maqāmahs*. Escaping the highwaymen, he managed to get to Nishapur alive, although with little more than the clothes he stood in.

There, his way to the court started with the established *arbiter elegantiae* of Nishapur, Abū Bakr al-Khwārizmī (d. 383/993), himself a poet, prosaist and, perhaps most importantly, the soul of the literary salon that had for some time dominated the literary life of the city. It was common for a young scholar to approach first a senior scholar and, in his entourage, to draw closer to more affluent patrons. Al-Khwārizmī was, though, not his only patron, since he soon found other supporters among prominent families.

The relations between al-Hamadhānī and the older al-Khwārizmī soon deteriorated, which may have been caused by the aspirations of a young man who had decided not to stay among the rank and file of the *literati* but to rise above his peers. Exactly what happened between the two is uncertain. Our main sources are the letters of al-Hamadhānī himself and his short biographies, written by men who admired him and were ready to accept al-Hamadhānī's version of the events.

According to al-Hamadhānī, the two became involved in a series of contests and debates in the salon and al-Hamadhānī was the victor. This led the older author to engage in backbiting against al-Hamadhānī, who tried to remain polite and unprovocative even in the face of these malicious attacks. Finally, the situation was resolved in yet another, and this time decisive, contest before an audience of the other *literati*. In this debate, al-Hamadhānī again proved superior in all fields of literary culture, the *adab*, including reciting poems by heart, composing literary letters and improvising poems. Al-Khwārizmī was so broken because of this final defeat that he soon died of grief, and the younger man inherited his place as the scholar supreme in the court.

This is al-Hamadhānī's version, but when it is compared to the few external references to the events and to the internal evidence provided by a careful analysis of al-Hamadhānī's letters, a different picture emerges. Al-Hamadhānī's problems in Jurjān–and perhaps in Rayy, too–mark him as no easier character than al-Khwārizmī and as at least as conceited as the older scholar, so one may presume that al-Hamadhānī was not the lovable and diplomatic person his version of events portrays him to have been. More probably al-Khwārizmī had some reason to deem him an arrogant upstart who did not want to waste time climbing to the top of the literary hierarchy.

Secondly, the letters, when carefully read, seem to refer to a long period of literary contests in which the "final debate" does not stand out as a definite end or finale. Instead of clearly-marked sessions ending in the victory of al-Hamadhānī, with the last one taking place due to al-Khwārizmī's inability to accept his initial defeats, we seem to have a series of small contests, presumably with varying success for both sides and perhaps culminating in a single, more memorable debate. They did not necessarily end with this--in some of his letters al-Hamadhānī alludes to further contests after the grand debate.

This debate, moreover, was probably more of a draw than a win for al-Hamadhānī. Al-Khwārizmī obviously remained a towering figure in Nishapur even after the debates, and when he died, there were no signs that al-Hamadhānī would have inherited his place at the top of the hierarchy. On the contrary, we soon find him moving on in search of new patrons, which he would probably not have done had he emerged clearly as the winner in the debates, thereby inheriting al-Khwārizmī's position. Such a position would have been a very satisfactory one for the young scholar and it would be inconceivable that he would have so easily and so soon given up such a position had he once achieved it.

What is important and incontestable in the debates, though, is that for the first time al-Hamadhānī's *maqāmahs* came to fore. According to one version, al-Khwārizmī admitted his competitor's mastery in dictating *maqāmahs* but claimed that that was the only thing al-Hamadhānī could do, whereas he, al-Khwārizmī, was prolific in all important genres. This may also be taken to imply that the genre which the younger scholar mastered was of his own invention, not one of the classical genres that should be mastered by contestants.

According to his main biographer, al-Thaʿālibī, al-Hamadhānī dictated 400 *maqāmahs* and his production was prolific in his first year during Nishapur, which implies that he had started already in Jurjān. Of the *maqāmahs*, 52 have been preserved (although in the commonly used, expurgated version, one of these has been excluded, giving support to the common misunderstanding that only 51 *maqāmas* by him are preserved). However, one should again emphasize that the number 400 is, like 40, a conventional number meaning roughly "very many" and one should not consider it exact. The preserved 52 *maqāmahs* most probably represent a majority of the *maqāmahs* which he had composed.

In later literature, the *maqāmahs* of Abū Muḥammad al-Ḥarīrī (1054-1122) are considered the exemplary model of the genre, which is, accordingly, often determined in terms which fit the Ḥarīrīan *maqāmah* but in fact misrepresent the earlier, Hamadhānīan *maqāmah*. The genre, as developed by al-Hamadhānī, consists of individual pieces of ornate prose, ranging in length from one to some ten pages. The features shared by all his *maqāmahs* include the use of *sajʿ*, or rhymed prose, almost throughout the text–except for the poems quoted in the *maqāmah*–and especially in descriptive passages. A second invariable characteristic is the use of a fictitious narrator on whose authority the piece is related. Arabic prose literature of the time usually claimed historicity, even when this was manifestly not true: anecdotes are usually told either of historical persons or anonymous types (a Bedouin, a slave girl, etc.) and in both cases the story claims to be a report of what had really happened. Al-Hamadhānī's narrator, ʿĪsā ibn Hishām, is, however, openly fictitious–although some authors were later misled into thinking he was a historical character. The strength of the convention of historicity was so strong that even the *maqāmahs* fell under suspicion of having been narrated by a real person.

Another common, although not ubiquitous, feature in Hamadhānīan *maqāmahs* is the comic hero, Abū 'l-Fatḥ al-Iskandarī, whose deeds the *maqāmahs* eternalize. In later examples of the genre, the hero usually remains the same throughout the collection, but it has to be emphasized that this is not the case for al-Hamadhānī, who prefers one hero, Abū 'l-Fatḥ, but in several *maqāmahs* uses other heroes, including the narrator, ʿĪsā ibn Hishām. In one *maqāmah* the hero is a historical character, the comic writer Abū 'l-ʿAnbas al-Ṣaymarī (213-275/828-888), although the story itself is fictitious in this *maqāmah*. Yet in all Hamadhānīan *maqāmahs* there is a comic hero, either Abū 'l-Fatḥ or someone else.

The hero is a chameleon, disguising himself now as an Arab, now a beggar, a preacher, anything that gives room for a comic plot and/or an exposition of superb oratory. Usually the story involves the meeting of the narrator and the hero in some part of the Islamic world, and the story often culminates in a recognition scene: the narrator realizes that the beggar, the trickster or the preacher he has been observing is his old friend and acquaintance, Abū 'l-Fatḥ. Sometimes, though, the two may be on the same side, adventuring together from the beginning. In one of the longer *maqāmahs*, the scene starts with the two having been robbed by highwaymen, an incident which, as mentioned earlier, al-Hamadhānī himself experienced twice in his adventurous life.

The scene of the plot varies, and the encounters take place around the Islamic world, thus widening the stage of the real travels of al-Hamadhānī to countries that he had never personally seen. This, however, is not crucial for the stories, since the scene usually receives very little attention, and the *maqāmahs* centre strictly on the persons involved: the narrator, the hero, and, usually, the gullible audience, whose leg the hero keeps pulling, time and again. The geographical setting has little importance, except for explaining the almost infinite repetition of the tricks. It allows al-Hamadhānī to evade the problem, common in serial literature, of presenting too many similar incidents at the same place (cf., e.g., the recurrent murders in Miss Marple's village–other detective stories evade this dilemma by making the solving of murders the hero's profession).

Likewise, other features that one might think constant in serial literature do, in fact, vary. The time of the encounters is usually the present time of al-Hamadhānī–a somewhat uncommon solution in the Arabic literature of the period, which tended to turn towards the past. But in some *maqāmahs* the narrator observes persons long since dead, like the poets Ghaylān ibn ʿUqbah Dhū 'l-Rummah (77-117/696-735) and al-Farazdaq (ca. 641-728): the hero and the narrator are at home equally well in the 8th as in the 10th century. Furthermore, the ages of the main characters vary from one *maqāmah* to another and, more importantly, they are not harmonized: the narrator is sometimes older, sometimes considerably younger than the hero. Al-Hamadhānī, obviously, did not aim at writing realistic and credible stories and did not try to hide the fictitious nature of his *maqāmahs*, but instead highlighted this quality, thus deliberately contrasting his *maqāmahs* with the historical or pseudohistorical prose literature of the day.

Although most of the Hamadhānīan *maqāmahs* contain a comic plot, there are also other variants or subgenres. Al-Hamadhānī's *maqāmahs* can be classified into six types, these being, in roughly descending order of importance in al-Hamadhānī's work: picaresque and comic *maqāmahs*; beggar *maqāmahs*; philological and aesthetic *maqāmahs*; exhortatory *maqāmahs*; panegyrical *maqāmahs*; and a residue group of a few uncategorizable *maqāmahs*. Later authors followed al-

Hamadhānī's example, although al-Ḥarīrī's preference for picaresque *maqāmahs* has made these the best known type.

The picaresque *maqāmah* contains a strong plot, often derived from earlier anecdotal literature. Most often it is the hero who makes the audience the laughing stock, but in one *maqāmah* (*al-Maḍīriyyah*) it is the hero himself who is the object of mirth. The beggar *maqāmahs* describe beggars and their tricks, often coming close to picaresque *maqāmahs*, but sometimes focusing not on the deeds of the beggars but on their words, thus sharing the interests of Ibn ʿAbbād in whose court the jargon of beggars had caught the attention of the mighty vizier. In philological and aesthetic *maqāmahs* this interest in language and in linguistic play dominates the *maqāmah*, but is now set on a literary level, manifesting itself in poetry and oratory. The exhortatory *maqāmah* also draws on earlier literature. In some comic *maqāmahs* a pseudo-preacher uses exhortation as a way to separate his gullible audience from their money, but in at least two *maqāmahs* in the collection there do not seem to be any comic overtones in the exhortation: mediaeval Arab authors were quite capable of sincerely religious, or philosophical, moments in their works, and comic aspects did not rule out serious aspects. Finally, the panygyrical *maqāmahs*, were written to please a patron and in them, the hero eulogized the generosity and wisdom of the patron whom the real author wanted to approach. Similar panegyrics were written in other prose genres and poetry.

All pieces of literature are written for a reason and they convey some message about the author and his attitude towards society. The significance of the *maqāmahs* has been a matter of some debate. They have been seen as the breakthrough of the bourgeoisie into literature, earlier dominated by the upper classes, or as a counter genre to more respectable literature. It has also been suggested that the author is actually speaking to his audience over the heads of his characters. By showing the underlying contradictions and absurdities in his characters–such as their varying ages, which form a non-logical sequence–and the incongruence between their words and deeds, the author wishes to turn their opinions upside down. If Abū 'l-Fatḥ-Fatḥ preaches something but does not reach his aims, one should give attention to the discrepancy and act accordingly, by disbelieving Abū 'l-Fatḥ and reading the hidden message of the author behind the hero's words. Working to the same effect, according to this line of thinking, is the initial mention of the (fictitious) narrator, which has a certain resemblance with the so-called *isnād* (witness chain) in the *ḥadīths*, the prophetic sayings on which Islam is to a great extent based. The purpose of the *isnād* is to prove the reliability and truth of the following short story about the Prophet. The openly fictitious "*isnād*" of the *maqāmahs* parodies, according to these scholars, the real *isnād* and hints at the unreliability of the protagonist and the story that follows. Thus read, the *maqāmahs* would be revealed to have a hidden philosophical or social message. Others, though, have remarked that the initial mention of the narrator is only distantly similar to the many-membered *isnād*, which lists many generations of narrators. In any case, the closest parallel to the use of an initial authority before a story comes from secular prose literature and philological works, not religious texts.

The question of potential underlying messages has not yet reached common agreement among scholars, and their attitutude towards such theories seems to depend on the literary theories they have adopted. Another bone of contention is the later influence of the *maqāmahs* outside the Islamic world, especially in Christian Spain. Generically, Arabic *maqāmahs* show clear and undeniable similarities with the Spanish picaresque novel, e.g. the anonymous *Lazarillo de Tormes*, but the question is more problematic if we try to show how and through what channels this influence was transmitted to Spanish literature. What is clear, though, is that if there was any such influence, it was not the *maqāmahs* of al-Hamadhānī which influenced the first picaresque novels, but later specimens of Andalusian *maqāmahs*.

Another matter which has caused much discussion is the question whether we should see in al-Hamadhānī the real originator of the genre or whether he had predecessors. This question now seems to be more or less settled. It seems clear that one cannot find any fully-developed *maqāmahs* before al-Hamadhānī, and the reports in mediaeval literature which would imply such are exaggerated and partly caused by misunderstandings.

Yet, obviously, al-Hamadhānī did not work in a literary vacuum. He was influenced by many genres or individual works, but the genre which he developed from these ingredients was something completely new and unheard-of. Among the works which influenced him were some pieces written by the philologist Muḥammad ibn al-Ḥasan Ibn Durayd (223-312/837 or 838-933). A misinterpreted passage from Abū Isḥāq Ibrāhīm ibn ʿAlī ibn Tamīm al-Ḥuṣrī's (d. 413/1022) *Zahr al-ādāb* set some scholars searching for a non-existent work by Ibn Durayd, which they believed was entitled "Forty Stories." Some stories in Arabic literature, transmitted on his authority, were, on rather superficial grounds, taken to be parts of this "lost" work. Although these efforts were fruitless, some other passages by Ibn Durayd, especially from his *Waṣf al-maṭar*, do resemble to a certain extent some of al-Hamadhānī's *maqāmahs*, but their similarities concern only the use of ornate prose and some technical features, and Ibn Durayd's stories are a far cry from the *maqāmahs*.

The name of the genre which was adopted, and perhaps invented, by al-Hamadhānī, may also owe something to the pious *maqām*, or exhortation. The similarity is further strengthened by the identical plurals of the two words, *maqāmāt*. The differences between the two genres are, however, obvious. The pious *maqāms* are always serious exhortation and they also claim historicity: they are presented as real records of encounters between real persons. The differences, however, did not hinder later *maqāmah* authors, such as Maḥmūd ibn ʿUmar al-Zamakhsharī (1075-1144), from bringing the two genres closer to each other, but the Hamadhānīan *maqāmah* falls rather far from these religious texts, except for the exhortatory *maqāmahs* which form a small minority of al-Hamadhānī's *maqāmahs*.

The plots, but not the style, of comic *maqāmahs* often resemble anecdotes, a term which in mediaeval Arabic literature refers to short, often comic prose stories which are collected in various anthologies and whose original author is usually unknown. Several plots used by al-Hamadhānī may be located in various anthologies and the similarities are compelling. Often the plot is, originally, rather simple and al-Hamadhānī has raised it to a much higher literary level by adopting it to his more complicated work and renaming the protagonists of the story.

One anonymous author of an anecdote, though, seems to have come especially close to developing something rather similar to the *maqāmahs*. This anecdote, probably originally dating from the 9th century, is usually known as the Weaver of Words (*Ḥā'ik al-kalām*), and half a dozen versions have been preserved. The story contains many of the basic features of the *maqāmahs*. Here the main difference seems to be that although this particular anecdote was well known, a tradition or genre of such anecdotes did not develop. The Weaver of Words remained a unique piece *sui generis*, and it was left to al-Hamadhānī to develop the idea into a new genre by systematically exploiting it and composing a series of such stories which changed an anomaly into a genre.

A further source for al-Hamadhānī was the various works on beggars, their jargon and their tricks (*kudya*). He may have become acquainted with some such works in the court of Ibn ʿAbbād, where he personally met one of the most famous beggars, Abū Dulaf. It is beyond doubt that the atmosphere of the court and the general interest in low life at the time gave an impetus for al-Hamadhānī to connect his literary abilities as a writer of ornate prose with the subject matter of thievery and begging, but it is also clear that the earlier beggar literature did not develop any clearly-defined genre of its own.

Further, there is an enigmatic work, *Ḥikāyat Abī 'l-Qāsim* by Abū 'l-Muṭahhar al-Azdī, where one finds many overall similarities with the *maqāmahs* and several passages which are identical, word for word. Here the problem is that the author, al-Azdī, is virtually unknown and can only be approximately dated, writing either just before or just after al-Hamadhānī. Thus, the direction of the borrowings cannot be known, although it seems that it is more probable that al-Hamadhānī borrowed from al-Azdī than *vice versa*, or that both borrowed from the same, unknown source. In any case, al-Hamadhānī seems to be in debt to some author, either al-Azdī or their common source, for some passages and perhaps he was also influenced more generally by the *Ḥikāyat Abī 'l-Qāsim*, if that work turns out to be the earlier of the two.

On a more general level, al-Hamadhānī was certainly influenced by the so-called *risālah* (letter) style, i.e., the use of ornate prose (*saj'*) with an ample use of rhymes, parallelism and literary quotations and allusions. Even though most literary letters are of descriptive content, some of them contain narrative elements which, although not exactly paralleling the contents and plots of the *maqāmahs*, certainly brought close the idea of narrating stories in rhymed prose with a subtle and elaborate style. On the other hand, animal tales, such as those of *Kalīlah wa-Dimnah*, prepared the way for the openly fictitious character of the *maqāmahs*, and as some versions of *Kalīlah wa-Dimnah* were written in an embellished style and they provide yet another parallel to the *maqāmahs*.

Finally, one must consider the possibility of sources in oral and popular literature. To assess their importance for al-Hamadhānī is difficult since we have very few provable traces of oral literature in the preserved, literary sources. There are some, rather ambiguous indications that al-Hamadhānī may have borrowed plots and story lines from this literature but it is difficult to prove conclusively. On the level of speculation, one has to consider these influences probable even though they remain unprovable, since the few traces of oral literature which were put down in written form date from the time after al-Hamadhānī and, thus, any similarities between *maqāmahs* and oral literature could be interpreted as traces of the influence of written literature on oral literature, not the other way round.

To sum up, it is obvious that al-Hamadhānī did not lack materials for his *maqāmahs* in earlier literature, but he did create a new and clearly-defined genre out of various materials. He even borrowed the term *maqāmah* for this new genre from older literature with, perhaps, an ironic reference to the word *majlis*. *Maqāmah* implies standing up (from Arabic *qāma* "to stand up") while *majlis* "session" is derived from *jalasa* "to sit down." The term *majlis* was used for serious sessions where scholars dictated their works on philology–or religious sciences–to their students, whereas the humorous stories of al-Hamadhānī were just the opposite, non-serious and perhaps to some extent subversive. Moreover, al-Hamadhānī, who was a minor scholar, is known to have dictated his *maqāmahs* to his students after such serious sessions, as a kind of light-hearted finale, following the prophetic dictum which advises one to refresh one's soul with lighter themes and topics so that one does not grow weary of studying serious matters.

The term may also refer to the encounters within the *maqāmahs*. Usually, the scene is set on street corners and public places and the hero performs–as a preacher, beggar or quack–standing up, and his audience listens to him likewise, whereas a scholar performed sitting down, as did his audience. *Maqāmah* would, thus, be a "standing-up session" in two senses: the scene is set in public places and the author and his audience ended their serious work with *maqāmahs* before standing up and leaving the place. The tension between *maqāmah* and *majlis*, frivolity and serenity, is alluded to in the choice of the term.

Al-Hamadhānī gave much freedom to the genre of *maqāmahs*, not wishing to draw the limits of the genre too narrowly and calling virtually all of his narrative pieces *maqāmahs*. Later, the limits of the genre were more strictly defined. Al-Hamadhānī parodied Bedouin romances and popular love tales, using well-known stories and setting his main characters in the place of the original *personae* of the anecdote. He used the *Qur'ān* as his intertext as well as created new stories *ex nihilo*, as far as we are able to deduce, for one has to remember that much of mediaeval Arabic literature has later been lost so that one can never with absolute certainty link a particular story to a certain author.

In the stories he ridiculed quacks and preachers as well as their gullible audience, admiring the tricks of his hero and laughing at those who were gulled by his guile. One must remember, however, that there are scholars who see here a double trick: the author making us laugh not at the audience of the hero but at the hero himself, who considers the ephemeral advantages he receives as something precious, while their real value is restricted. In the opinion of others, conversely, it is precisely this ephemerality that constitutes the hero's real gain: the *maqāmahs* are comic stories and when the hero, after his trick, runs away, laughing helplessly at the villagers, boors or city riffraff, he really has got what he wanted, a vagabond trickster hunting for a certain *joie-de-vivre*, refusing to settle down and die a respectable citizen–as some later *maqāmah* authors made their heroes do.

Al-Hamadhānī enjoys describing beggars' wiles and thieves' tricks and he is also ready to be vulgar and obscene. The limits of acceptable literature at his time were rather broad, and themes which in later literature, both Arabic and European, would have been deemed obscene and unsuitable, except for underground literature, were openly discussed at the time. Unfortunately, the standard editions used today, on which almost all translations in any European languages have been based, are bowdlerized, going ultimately back to the work of the late 19th-century theologian, philologist and philosopher Muḥammad ʿAbduh, who deemed it correct to excise from his edition one complete *maqāmah* and the latter half of another, so as not to corrupt the youngsters who were to read these *maqāmah,s* both for their edification and to learn impeccable classical Arabic. Putting it briefly, for ʿAbduh, the *maqāmahs* were valuable for their language and style and despite their content.

Although ʿAbduh openly admitted these changes in the preface of his edition, most scholars have not paid sufficient attention to this, but have worked on the bowdlerized but easily available version instead of turning to the older editions or the manuscripts. More seriously, ʿAbduh did not mention that throughout the text he made minor corrections to avoid embarrassing expressions and ideas that might corrupt readers. When a social upstart speaks in one *maqāmah* of his wife toiling in the kitchen–in itself a *faux pas* in the patriarchal Islamic culture–he mentions how she had an apron "around her arse" (*ist*) which the editor has tacitly changed to "around her waist" (*wasaṭ*).

Such changes have, in some *maqāmahs,* changed the tenor of the text: sexual innuendos and especially references to homosexuality have been diluted, and some of the cruder points have been eliminated either through changes or omissions. This makes the contrast between the elevated style and the low content less sharp. On the other hand, al-Hamadhānī was fond of allusions and many sexual or otherwise uncouth allusions are found even in the bowdlerized text since they are not openly obscene. Thus, when in the same *maqāmah* the upstart merchant mentions how twenty *cubits* of fine Jurjānian cloth were used for (literally: "went into") her wife's trousers, the text is seemingly innocent and has passed through the hands of the editor unharmed. Again, the lack of good breeding is shown by the mere mention of the wife and her clothes in a society where it was improper to speak of one's female relatives to male guests. Yet the joke acquires an edge when one remembers that the word cubit (*dhirāʿ*) was also used metaphorically or euphemistically for "penis": the bragging upstart turns out to be a cuckold by his own unwitting testimony.

Thus, when one reads the unbowdlerized text with an acute eye, one realizes that this whole *maqāmah* is built on sexual allusions which make the upstart merchant a ridiculous character who tries to impress his guest but who actually manages only to prove his own stupidity and uncivilized manners. An upstart remains an upstart despite all his efforts. If al-Hamadhānī himself worked his way up from lowly origins to eventually enter the court, this would give the text some added poignancy, but unfortunately we do not know for sure his social background.

Not all *maqāmahs* have such sexual overtones. Many, on the contrary, are harmless from this point of view, and a few of them (the philological *maqāmahs*) seem to aim mainly at showing off the superb linguistic talents of the hero–and through him, the author. It is somewhat difficult to appreciate these in translation, but read in the original the masterful use of language does have a charm of its own.

The *maqāmahs* seem to have been written as separate pieces but the audience must soon have become aware of the basic features of the genre, especially the recurrent appearance of the hero under various disguises. This seriality is emphasized in the present form of the text, which consists of 52 (51 in the bowdlerized version) *maqāmahs*. Much of the comic effect of the stories depends on this seriality: the reader's expectations are raised and the comic tension rises as the expected climax comes closer. In any analysis of the *maqāmahs*, this seriality has to be taken into account.

Today al-Hamadhānī's main work is seen to be his *maqāmahs*. Al-Khwārizmī's attitude, when the two had their debates in Nishapur implies that for the older scholar al-Hamadhānī's *maqāmahs* only showed the restricted nature of the young aspirant's talent. The debates, however, seem to have convinced the audience, perhaps even al-Khwārizmī himself, that al-Hamadhānī could do other things, too. In fact, al-Hamadhānī's early reputation seems to have been built on his literary letters, *rasā'il*, more than on the *maqāmahs*.

After the debate, al-Hamadhānī may have had some successes in Nishapur but he did not remain there, which implies that his victory, if such it was, was far from complete. When al-Khwārizmī died in 383/993, al-Hamadhānī was already on the move, visiting several cities in Iran. This part of his life becomes somewhat hazy, which may mean that he did not achieve any outstanding victories in these cities. Since his mediaeval biographies are closer to literary hagiography than critical study, one would suppose all major breakthroughs to have been reported in detail, whereas fruitless efforts to find patrons would be played down or not mentioned.

We do know that he tried to impress the mighty Maḥmūd al-Ghaznawī (d. 421/1030), who was busy conquering areas in Iran as well as in Afghanistan and India. Maḥmūd was also a major patron, but he was more interested in Persian literature than in Arabic–although the writer of Iran's national epic, Firdawsī, was discontented with the patronage he received. Whatever the cause, al-Hamadhānī found little support from Maḥmūd.

More important for him was the unscrupulous ruler of Zarang, Khalaf ibn Aḥmad, who was later forced to abdicate in 393/1003 and who had to leave his rule to Maḥmūd. Khalaf could be cruel when he wanted, but he did like courtiers and *literati* around him and he paid them well. Al-Hamadhānī approached him, writing some eulogical verses and dedicating six panegyrical *maqāmahs* to this ruler, which marked the beginning of the panegyrical subgenre of *maqāmahs*.

In mediaeval society, writers and poets had to earn their living within the entourage of wealthy patrons–there was no system of royalties, although some scholars did know how to make up for this by only allowing their works to be copied for a fee. This, however, was rare and usually authors earned their living by praising selected patrons and receiving a monthly stipend from them.

We do not know for sure whether al-Hamadhānī first wrote panegyrical prose passages and only later made *maqāmahs* out of them or not. It seems, though, probable that from the beginning panegyrical *maqāmahs* were composed as *maqāmahs*. If this is so, it would show that the genre, originated by al-Hamadhānī, had in a few years found favour among the lovers of Arabic literature in Persia. Rulers, in general, were not particularly innovative. They wanted to be praised in established and traditional patterns: revolutionary literary innovations are usually associated with revolutionary tendencies.

It is reported that al-Hamadhānī received the sum of 1,000 *dīnārs* from Khalaf. Why he left the court is not known. Perhaps he simply did not feel ready to settle down but wanted to continue his travels, perhaps in search of an even more appreciative and influential, or affluent, patron.

Whatever the reason, al-Hamadhānī continued his journeys but he did not have any great successes after this and again the details of his life become hazy. We know that he finally settled down in Būshanj near Herat, the present-day Afghanistan. He found his last patron in Abū ʿAlī al-Khushnāmī, a wealthy noble of restricted and strictly local influence, an obvious setback for the aspiring career of al-Hamadhānī.

He also married into the family of al-Khushnāmī and it seems that in settling down he also opted for a bourgeois life. He is known at this period of his life to have been involved in commerce, at least parttime, and in one letter he mentions the possibility of living as a *dihqān*, or landowner. It has been estimated that he lived in the Herat area for the last ten years of his life (ca. 388-398/998-1008) but very little is known about this period. He is said to have died insane. Later, his offspring lived in the same area and disseminated his poetry and, presumably, his *maqāmahs*.

Al-Hamadhānī's life seems to have ended in at least partial disappointment. Some of his letters take up the theme of the uselessness of culture in a world of merchants and money. This, of course, is a *topos* in Arabic literature, but the recurrent return to the theme as well as the bitterness with which he speaks of it, make it easy to believe that al-Hamadhānī is speaking of his own experience. It may also be that the reports about the success he had had, especially in Nishapur, are also to be seen against this background. The embittered and disappointed middle-aged al-Hamadhānī did not want to admit the ultimate disappointment of his career, but wanted to see his earlier career through rosy lenses.

He was not, however, completely forgotten, even though he could not translate his literary successes into material gain. The young al-Thaʿālibī, anthologist, biographer, poet and prosewriter in his own right, was presumably not the only one to admire al-Hamadhānī and his works. Al-Thaʿālibī came to meet al-Hamadhānī and received permission to copy materials from the master, and the article on al-Hamadhānī in al-Thaʿālibī's *Yatīmat al-dahr* is both extensive and unusually laudatory. What is worth noticing, though, is that he barely mentions the *maqāmahs*, instead concentrating on al-Hamadhānī's poems and his exemplary letters.

Modern scholars have been somewhat misled by the appreciative words which the most famous *maqāmah* author of all times, al-Ḥarīrī, wrote of his predecessor about a century later in the preface of his collection of *maqāmahs*. Al-Ḥarīrī's praise brought al-Hamadhānī's *maqāmahs* into the literary canon, although they seem to have been rather rarely read despite the lipservice that was paid to them: the relatively small number of preserved manuscripts, in comparison to the hundreds of manuscripts of al-Ḥarīrī's *maqāmahs*, makes this abundantly clear. It was the master of the genre, al-Ḥarīrī, whose collection was read and the words he wrote about al-Hamadhānī were copied unquestioningly into innumerable later biographies. Thus, modern scholars have through these come to the conclusion that al-Hamadhānī was, right from the beginning, greatly admired as a *maqāmah* writer. This notion has been further strengthened by the obvious narrative excellence of his *maqāmahs* which makes him, at least to Western taste, the greatest *maqāmah* author ever, although in the Arab world today he comes only second, after al-Ḥarīrī. More probably, his reputation was, in the beginning, limited to a few admirers–who gave him the name Badīʿ al-Zamān–and his canonization was due to al-Ḥarīrī who, at the same time, in practice eclipsed his predecessor.

When al-Hamadhānī died in 398/1008, he had not properly published a single work. His *maqāmahs* were collected soon after his death but at first they circulated in various forms. There was a collection of twenty *maqāmahs* as well as larger collections. The order of the *maqāmahs* also seems to have varied, which means that the present order, and number, of *maqāmahs*, does not originate with the author himself and should not be taken as the result of deliberation by the author. Thus, any conclusions drawn from the present order should be checked against manuscripts and read with due reservation.

It is also difficult to date individual *maqāmahs*. We may presume that al-Hamadhānī had started writing *maqāmahs* before arriving at Nishapur in 382/992, since he already seems to have established some kind of fame in writing in this novel genre when debating with al-Khwārizmī in 382-383/992-993. The only *maqāmah* which is dated in older sources is the *Ḥamdāniyyah*, dated by al-Ḥuṣrī to 385/995, and we know that the six panegyrical *maqāmahs* dedicated to Khalaf must date from between 383-390/993-1000. Although Khalaf was forced to abdicate only in 393/1003, he was rapidly losing authority from 390/1000, and al-Hamadhānī would probably not have tried his luck with a ruler who was obviously on his way out. During the final years of his life, there are no signs of al-Hamadhānī writing *maqāmahs*, and he may have stopped writing them after leaving Zaranj or soon after.

Unfortunately, we do not know who collected the *maqāmahs*. In around 1100, they had become established in roughly the present collection, although in the manuscripts the order of the *maqāmahs* may vary and there are even some omissions in some manuscripts. All this implies that his fame was rather restricted. This would not have been helped by his living his last years in Herat, far from the centers of Arabic literature where his works might have had more success. Provincial literature had serious difficulties in this period, and it was only in the major centres that authors could hope to become part of the literary canon during their life time.

The generations after al-Hamadhānī, but before al-Ḥarīrī, appreciated al-Hamadhānī's model letters (*Rasā'il*) more than his *maqāmahs*. The letters were collected and quoted extensively in various sources. Again, we know too little about their collection, although we do know that al-Hamadhānī himself did not make any final redaction of his own letters. We must also remember that when he died, he was about forty and probably had not seen any imminent reason to make a final collection–although he did keep at least some kind of a personal archive of them, and it was this archive that he gave to al-Thaʿālibī to be copied.

The letters seem to have been collected soon after his death by al-Ḥākim Abū Saʿīd ʿAbd al-Raḥmān ibn Muḥammad Ibn Dūst (d. 431/1040), but whether the preserved collection goes directly back to this Ibn Dūst or to some other collector is not known. It was to these letters that he mainly owed his fame before al-Ḥarīrī gave credit to his *maqāmahs* and even afterwards it was, perhaps somewhat surprisingly, the letters that were eagerly read, not so much the *maqāmahs*. The letters have a certain charm of their own but they are much more conformist than the *maqāmahs*. They followed earlier models and became standard references later but they exhibit few, if any, features that could be called innovative.

The lack of interest in al-Hamadhānī's *maqāmahs* may have been caused by general changes in literary taste. The time before and during al-Hamadhānī's activity saw an unusual amount of narrative literature being written, a kind of development that could have led to the birth of longer narrative genres and might have resulted in something like a novel. This did not happen, though, and the emphasis switched back from the plot more to the style, language and literary tropes in the centuries after al-Hamadhānī. His letters were masterful pieces of ornate prose, so they survived this change of taste, but his *maqāmahs* were less polished than those of al-Ḥarīrī and his imitators, and the reading audience lost interest in the simpler, although from a narrative point of view superior, *maqāmahs* of al-Hamadhānī and turned to the more elaborate *maqāmahs* of al-Ḥarīrī and other later writers.

Al-Hamadhānī's poems were likewise later copied as a *Dīwān*, a slim volume of no particular innovative merit: al-Hamadhānī had more talent as a prose writer. His poems are mediocre and would probably not have drawn any attention at all, had he not become famous in other fields.

Finally, we have, appended to one manuscript of his *maqāmahs*, a short collection of prose stories, or anecdotes, which find some parallels among the *maqāmahs*. These stories (*mulaḥ*, sg. *mulḥa*) are in themselves unremarkable, conforming to anecdote literature in general. They are not created by al-Hamadhānī, but merely transmitted by him: many of them may be traced back to earlier literature. What makes them interesting is that they show, at least partly, how al-Hamadhānī worked when writing his *maqāmahs*. Some of these *mulaḥ* contain stories which were later changed by al-Hamadhānī to *maqāmahs* by the addition of the fictitious narrator and some changes in the names of the protagonists and the settings of the stories. It is possible that these *mulaḥ* are actually al-Hamadhānī's reserve materials which he had been planning to turn into *maqāmahs* but which, except for a few cases, he finally had no time, or interest, to develop.

Finally, one must mention *al-Amālī*, which is attributed to al-Hamadhānī by the late bibliographer Kâtip Çelebi in his *Kashf.* Kâtip Çelebi's way of working is well known. He compiled his bibliographical work using both manuscripts which he had before him and references to texts that he found mentioned in other sources. Al-Hamadhānī's *al-Amālī* seem to belong to this second group and are probably caused by a misunderstanding. Many biographical sources mention the philological activity of al-Hamadhānī as a scholar who gave lessons to a small group of students. The lessons consisted of dictation (*imlā'*) of scholarly texts and fragments to students and when compiled, such sessions were usually called *Dictamina* (*al-Amālī*). The mention of al-Hamadhānī's scholarly activities seems to have led Kâtip Çelebi to presume the existence of such a text.

Al-Hamadhānī seems to have had a fate which many other major authors in world literature have shared. In his own time he received some fame but later fell into oblivion or at least his literary status became marginal. Later, he was mentioned by a writer, al-Ḥarīrī, who became one of the brightest stars in Arabic literature and this gave al-Hamadhānī a place among the greats, although he was never read as extensively as one might think. When he was rediscovered and edited in modern times, the interesting nature of his *maqāmahs* soon made him a favourite among both Arab and Western scholars and, posthumously, raised him to the highest top of the mediaval Parnassus. He was not deemed a major author during the Middle Ages. He should have been, though.

REFERENCES

A.F.L. Beeston, "The Genesis of the Maqāmāt Genre," *Journal of Arabic Literature* 2 (1971): 1-12;

Badīʿ al-Zamān al-Hamadhānī, *Maqāmāt (séances)*, trans. by Regis Blachère and Pierre Masnou, Études arabes et islamiques. Série 2, Textes et traductions, 2 (Paris: Klincksieck, 1957);

Clifford Edmund Bosworth, *The Mediaeval Islamic Underworld: the Banū Sāsān in Arabic Society and Literature*. 2 vol. (Leiden: E.J. Brill, 1976);

Johann Christoph Bürgel, "Gesellschaftskritik im Schelmengewand: Überlegungen zu den Makamen al-Hamadhanis und al-Hariris," *Asiatische Studien* 45 (1991): 228-256;

L.E. Goodman, "Hamadhānī, Schadenfreude, and Salvation through Sin," *Journal of Arabic Literature* 19 (1988): 27-39;

Jaakko Hämeen-Anttila, "The Author and His Sources: an Analysis of al-Maqāma al-Bishrīya," *Wiener Zeitschrift für die Kunde des Morgenlandes* 88 (1998): 143-164;

Jaakko Hämeen-Anttila, "The Maqāma of the Lion," *Arabic and Middle Eastern Literatures* 1:2 (1998): 141-152;

Jaakko Hämeen-Anttila, *Maqama: a History of a Genre*, Diskurse der Arabistik 5 (Harrassowitz: Wiesbaden 2002);

Abdelfattah Kilito, *Les Séances: récits et codes culturels chez Hamadhānī et Harīrī* (Paris: Sindbad, 1983);

Abdelfattah Kilito, *L' Auteur et ses doubles: essai sur la culture arabe classique*, Collection poétique (Paris: Éditions du Seuil, 1985);

Fedwa Malti-Douglas, "Maqāmāt and Adab: al-Maqāma al-Maḍīriyya of al-Hamadhānī," *Journal of the American Oriental Society* 105 (1985): 247-258;

John N. Mattock, "The Early History of the Maqāma," *Journal of Arabic Literature* 15 (1984): 1-18;

James T. Monroe, *The Art of Badī' az-Zamān al-Hamadhānī as Picaresque Narrative*, Papers of the Center for Arab and Middle East Studies 2 (Beirut: American University of Beirut, 1983);

Mohamed-Salah Omri, "There is a Jāḥiẓ for Every Age: Narrative Construction and Intertextuality in al-Hamadhānī's Maqāmāt," *Arabic and Middle Eastern Literatures* 1:1 (1998): 31-46;

Wadād al-Qāḍī, "Badīʿ az-Zamān al-Hamadhānī and his Social and Political Vision," in *Literary Heritage of Classical Islam: Arabic and Islamic Studies in Honor of James A. Bellamy*, ed. M. Mir (Princeton: The Darwin Press 1993), 197-223;

D.S. Richards, "The Maqāmāt of al-Hamadhānī: General Remarks and a Consideration of the Manuscripts," *Journal of Arabic Literature* 22 (1991): 89-99;
D.S. Richards, "The Rasā'il of Badī' al-Zamān al-Hamadhānī," in *Arabicus Felix: luminosus Britannicus: Essays in Honour of A.F.L. Beeston on his Eightieth Birthday*, ed. A. Jones, Oxford Oriental Institute Monographs 11 (Reading: Ithaca Press for the Faculty of Oriental Studies, Oxford University, 1991), 142-162;
Everett K. Rowson, "Religion and Politics in the Career of Badī' al-Zamān al-Hamadhānī," *Journal of the American Oriental Society* 107 (1987): 653-673;
Muṣṭafā 'l-Shak'ah, *Badī' al-Zamān al-Hamadhānī: rā'id al-qiṣṣah al-'arabiyyah wa 'l-maqālah al-ṣuḥufiyyah ma'a dirāsah li-ḥarakat al-adab al-'arabī fī- 'l-'Irāq al-'ajamī wa-Mā' warā' al-nahr* (Beirut: 'Ālam al-kutub 1403/1983);
Wendelin Wenzel-Teuber, *Die Maqamen des Hamadhani als Spiegel der islamischen Gesellschaft des 4. Jahrhunderts der Hidschra*, Zwische Orient und Okzident, hrsg. von der Rückert-Gesellschaft, Band 3 (Würzburg: ERGON Verlag, 1994);
Katia Zakharia, "al-Maqāma al-Bišriyya: une épopée mystique," *Arabica* 37 (1990): 251-290.

Rūzbihān Baqlī

(1128-1209)

FIROOZEH PAPAN-MATIN
University of Washington

WORKS

'Abhar al-'āshiqīn;
Kashf al-asrār;
Risālat al-quds;
Sayr al-arwāḥ.

Editions

'Abhar al-'āshiqīn, ed. Henry Corbin and Muḥammad Mu'īn (Tehran: Intishārāt-i Manūchihrī; Paris: Institut Français de Recherche en Iran, 1987).

Translations

Le jasmine des fidèles d'amour, ed. Henry Corbin and Muḥammad Mu'īn (Tehran: Intishārāt-i Manūchihrī; Paris: Institut Français de Recherche en Iran, 1987);
The Unveiling of Secrets: Diary of a Sufi Master. trans. Carl W. Ernst (Chapel Hill, NC: Parvardigar Press, 1997);
Le dévoilement des secrets et les apparitions des lumières: journal spirituel du maître de Shîrâz, trans. Paul Ballanfat (Paris: Le Seuil, 1997);
The Unveiling of Secrets Kashf al-Asrār: the Visionary Autobiography of Rūzbihān al-Baqlī (1128-1209 A.D.), ed, with critical introduction, Firoozeh Papan-Matin, in collaboration with Michael Fishbein, Islamic History and Civilization Studies and Texts Series, no. 59 (Leiden: Brill, 2006);
L'itineraire des espirits: suivi du Traite de la saintete, trans. Paul Ballanfat (Paris: Les Deux Oceans, 2001);
Quatre traités inèdits de Ruzbehân Baqlî Shîrâzî: textes arabes avec un commentaire, ed. Paul Ballanfat (Tehran: Institut Français de Recherche en Iran, 1998);
L'ennuagement du coeur: suivi de Les éclosions de la lumière de l'affirmation de l'unicité, trans. Paul Ballanfat (Paris: Le Seuil, 1998).

Rūzbihān Abū Muḥammad ibn Abī Naṣr al-Baqlī al-Fasawī (522/1128-606/1209) is a twelfth-century visionary mystic and scholar par excellence. Rūzbihān is known as a defining author of Islamic mysticism in Iran. A dominant theme in his mysticism is his contemplations of beauty, which he elaborates in his range of writings on *tafsīr* (interpretation), *ḥadīth* (traditions), *fiqh* (Islamic law), and commentary on the *Qur'ān*.

Rūzbihān was born in Fasī, a province in the south of Iran. In his autobiography, he explains that his spirituality is unrelated to his upbringing because he was born and raised in a family that was ignorant about God and was unable to understand Rūzbihān. He defines his call to mysticism in terms of his special relationship with God. His memories of this bond are as early as age three. At age fifteen, he was addressed by voices from the unseen world (*ghayb*) calling him a prophet. One day around this time, as he was leaving his shop for afternoon prayers, he heard an extraordinary voice and followed it to a nearby hill. There he saw a handsome shaykh telling him about God's oneness (*tawḥīd*). Rūzbihān describes this event as a turning point in his spiritual awakening. For the rest of his life, he experienced mystical states and secrets were disclosed to him.

Rūḥ al-jinān fī sīrat al-Shaykh Rūzbihān (The Spirit of the Gardens, on the Life of the Master Rūzbihān), and *Tuḥfat ahl al-'irfān fī dhikr Sayyid al-Aqṭāb Rūzbihān* (The Gift of the People of Gnosis, in Memory of the Chief Axis of the World Rūzbihān), are the titles of the hagiographies on Rūzbihān, which were composed by his grandsons ʿAbd al-Laṭīf ibn Ṣadr al-Dīn Abī Muḥammad Rūzbihān Thānī (d. A.D. 1305) and his brother Sharaf al-Dīn Ibrāhīm ibn Ṣadr al-Dīn Abī Muḥammad Rūzbihān Thānī (d. A.D. 1300). Sharaf al-Dīn in his *Tuḥfat ahl al-'irfān* (53, 64) gives Rūzbihān's lineage as Daylamite—a renowned tribe that had resided in Fārs for several centuries. Rūzbihān lived during the reign of the Saljuq dynasty, when the Salghurids, one of their vassal dynasties, held dominance over Fārs. The Salghurids' capital was in Shiraz, the city where Rūzbihān lived most of his life. Rūzbihān delivered sermons at the town's famous *'Aṭīq* mosque and enjoyed a large following in Shiraz among the townfolk as well as some of the local rulers such as *Atābak Sa'īd Abū Bakr Sa'd ibn Zangī* who is often discussed in Rūzbihān's hagiographies. This period witnessed much political unrest and rivalry among princes. Sharaf al-Dīn (63) also explains that the nobles of the town frequented Rūzbihān's hospice (*ribāt*) and at times extended their political feuds beyond its walls. Rūzbihān did not pay much heed to them. In fact, he ends *Kashf al-Asrār* (2006, 120-121) with a supplication to God to save him from dealing with these princes and their courts. The hagiographies on Rūzbihān, the *Tuḥfat ahl al-'irfān* (53, 65-65) and the *Rūḥ al-jinān* (224-226) provide enough evidence to indicate that the rulers of Shiraz were on good terms with the Shaykh and that some held him in high esteem and sought his blessing and advice.

Rūzbihān's writings are in Persian and in Arabic. According to the author of *Tuḥfat ahl al-'irfān* (18-19), he composed a total of sixty works, the majority of which were lost after his death. His writing describes the visionary events that constitute the life of the author and the knowledge that he acquired by these events. His famous extant work *Sharḥ-i shaṭḥīyāt* (An Exegesis of Ecstatic Sayings) is a classical reference on medieval Islamic mysticism. It is a compilation of sayings by entranced mystics as they were experiencing spiritual states. ʿAbhar al-ʿāshiqīn (The Jasmine of Lovers) is a masterpiece of Persian *belles lettres*. It provides a geography of love whence God's attributes of "might" (*jalāl*) and "beauty" (*jamāl*) come into view. Written in Arabic, with the exception of a few words and phrases in Persian, *Kashf al-asrār wa mukāshafāt al-anwār* (The Unveiling of Secrets and Disclosures of the Lights) is Rūzbihān's autobiographical account of his visionary life. He began writing the autobiography at age fifty-five, as an experienced mystic who could withstand the mysteries of the unseen. *Kashf al-asrār* is a unique document in the genre of Islamic autobiographies. Similar to many Islamic biographies and autobiographies, it concerns the inner spiritual life of the author/protagonist; but unlike most of them, its plot is not centered on the external events that advance the story of his life. In this respect, *Kashf al-asrār* differs from the works that constitute the canon in the medieval Islamic biographical and autobiographical literature. The

'Arā'is al-bayān fī ḥaqā'iq al-Qur'ān (The Brides of Clarity Concerning the Truths of the *Qur'ān*), as its name conveys, is an Arabic commentary on the *Qur'ān*, which Rūzbihān drafted in the tradition of Muḥammad ibn al-Ḥusayn al-Sulamī (937 or 942-1021) and ʿAbd al-Karīm ibn Hawāzin al-Qushayrī (986-1072). *Sharḥ al-ḥujub wa 'l-astār fī maqāmāt ahl al-anwār wa 'l-asrār* (The Description of the Veils and the Curtains in the Stations of People of the Lights and the Secrets) is a commentary on the separation of the soul from the unseen. *Manṭiq al-asrār* (The Utterance of the Secrets) written in Arabic, is the background to the Persian rendition of mystical ecstatic sayings that appear in the *Sharḥ-i shaṭḥīyāt*. *Mashrab al-arwāḥ* (The Spirits' Fount), *Risālat al-quds* (The Treatise on Sanctity), and *Ghalaṭāt al-sālikīn* (The Errors of the Wayfarers), are treatises on spiritual stations and states.

The *'Abhar al-'āshiqīn* relates that towards the end of his life, Rūzbihān was afflicted with paralysis. One of his disciples, who had recently traveled to Egypt, had brought him medicinal oil for his ailment. Rūzbihān refused the medicine, calling his condition an expression of the bonds of love between God and him. He then asked his disciple to rub the oil on a sick dog that was lying at their gate. Rūzbihān died in Shiraz, in the beginning of Muḥarram 606 A.H., or the middle of July 1209. In the *Shadd al-izār fī ḥaṭṭ al-awzār 'an zavvār al-mazār* (254), it is related that before his departure from this world, Rūzbihān is said to have predicted the death of Shaykh Abū 'l-Ḥasan al-Kardawiyyah and Shaykh ʿAlī 'l-Sarāj, his companion and brother-in-law; they died as predicted. Rūzbihān is buried in Shiraz but his tomb was abandoned for centuries until it was discovered by Ivanov (354) in 1928 and restored by the Iranian Ministry of Culture. At the time the local people did not have any memories of the Shaykh except that he was a Sunnite. This fact explains the neglect of his grave. This attitude changed after the restoration of his shrine, which is now an important pilgrimage site in Fārs.

REFERENCES

Rūzbihān Baqlī, *'Abhar al-'āshiqīn*, ed. Henry Corbin and Muhammad Muʿīn (Tehran: Kitābkhanah-i Manūchihrī, 1987);

Henry Corbin. "Les Fidèles d'amour Shîʿisme et soufisme," vol. 3 in *En Islam Iranien* (Paris: Gallimard, 1972);

Sharaf al-Dīn Ibrāhīm ibn Ṣadr al-Dīn Abū Muḥammad Rūzbihān Thānī, "Tuḥfat ahl al-ʿirfān fī dhikr Sayyid al-Aqtāb Rūzbihān," in *Rūzbihān Nāmah*, ed. Muḥammad Taqī Dānīsh'pazhūh (Tehran: Chāpkhānah-i Bahman, 1969), 1–149;

Shams al-Dīn ʿAbd al-Laṭīf ibn Ṣadr al-Dīn Abū Muḥammad Rūzbihān Thānī, "Rūḥ al-jinān fī sīrat al-Shaykh Rūzbihān," in *Rūzbihān Nāmah*, ed. Muḥammad Taqī Dānīsh'pazhūh (Tehran: Chāpkhānah-i Bahman, 1969), 152–370;

Carl W. Ernst, *Rūzbihān Baqlī: Mysticism and the Rhetoric of Sainthood in Persian Sufism* (Richmond: Curzon Press, 1996);

Alan Godlas, "The ʿArā'is al-bayān the Mystical Qur'ānic Exegesis of Ruzbihan al-Baqli" (Ph.D. diss., University of California, Berkeley, 1991);

W. Ivanov, "A Biography of Ruzbihan al-Baqli," *Journal and Proceedings of the Asiatic Society of Bengal*, n.s. 24 (1928);

Jāmī, *Nafahāt al-uns*, ed. Muʿīn al-Dīn Abū 'l-Qāsim Junayd Shīrāzī (Tehran: Majlis, 1328 [1949 or 1950), section 321, 291–292;

Louis Massignon, "La Vie et les œuvres de Rûzbehân Baqlî," in *Studia Orientalia Ioanni Pedersen Dicata* (Copenhagen: Munksgaard, 1953);

Mu'īn al-Dīn Abū 'l-Qāsim Junayd Shīrāzī, *Shadd al-izār fī ḥaṭṭ al-awzār 'an zavvār al-mazār*, ed. Muḥammad Qazvīnī and ʿAbbās Iqbāl (Tehran: Majlis, 1328 [1949 or 1950) section 177:254.

Sharaf al-Dīn Abū ʿAbd Allāh Muḥammad ibn Saʿīd al-Būṣīrī

(7 March 1212-1294 or 1297)

TERRI DE YOUNG
University of Washington

WORKS

Qaṣīdat al-burdah;
Dīwān.

Editions

Sharḥ al-Shaykh Khālid al-Azharī 'alā matn al-burdah (Cairo: Maṭbaʿah al-Khaṣṣah bi-Jamʿiyyat al-Maʿārif, 1869);

Dīwān al-Būṣīrī, ed. Muḥammad Sayyid Kīlānī (Cairo: Muṣṭafā 'l-Bābī 'l-Ḥalabī, 1955);

Dīwān al-Būṣīrī, ed. Aḥmad Ḥasan Basaj (Beirut: Dār al-Kutub al-ʿIlmiyyah, 1995).

Translations

Thoraya Mahdi Allam, *al-Buṣiri's Burda: the Prophet's Mantle*, revised by M. Mahdi Allam (Cairo: General Egyptian Book Organization, 1987);

R.A. Nicholson, "The Mantle Poem of al-Būṣīrī," in *A Reader on Islam*, ed. Arthur Jeffreys ('S-Gravenhage: Mouton and Co., 1962), 605-620;

Muhammad Riaz Qadiri, *Qasidah Burdah Sharif (The Mantle Ode)* (Gujranwala Pakistan: Abbasi Publications, 2002);

Stefan Sperl, "The Burda in Praise of the Prophet Muhammad," *in Qasida Poetry in Islamic Asia and Africa*, ed. Stefan Sperl and Christopher Shackle, vol. 2 (Leiden: E.J. Brill, 1996), 388-411.

Al-Būṣīrī was a government functionary (*kātib*) under the late Ayyubids and early Mamluk state in 13th-century Egypt. He held a number of minor posts and also composed a series of poems celebrating important occasions in his friends' and superiors' lives. But only one of these achieved lasting fame. This is the poem originally titled by the author "*al-Kawākib al-durriyyah fī madḥ khayr al-bariyyah*" (The Twinkling Stars Concerning Praise of the Best of Creation). Today it is popularly known as the *Burdah* poem, referring to the robe worn by the Prophet Muḥammad (d. 632) during his lifetime, that he bestowed on the poet Kaʿb ibn Zuhayr as the reward for a composition the latter recited before him. Al-Būṣīrī's *Burdah* was one of the earliest examples of the poetic genre devoted to praise of the Prophet Muḥammad and was considered by subsequent generations as the most perfect representative of this kind. It skillfully distilled beliefs about the Prophet that every Muslim could agree on, leaving aside more controversial subjects, such the Prophet's infallibility or whether he actually performed some of the more extraordinary miracles sometimes attributed to him by popular piety. The poem became extremely popular, the subject of innumerable commentaries, and up through the nineteenth century other poets translated it into all the languages of the Islamic world, even incorporating it into their own compositions. There even grew up a considerable lore about the curative powers belonging to verses from the poem when they were used as part of folk curative practices.

The sources give conflicting accounts about where exactly al-Būṣīrī was born, but it was somewhere in the vicinity of Abū Sīr, an ancient Egyptian town to the south of Cairo, near the cities of Fayyūm and Banī Suwayf. The village of Abū Sīr (or Būṣīr) was where his father originally hailed from, the family having ultimately migrated to Egypt from Morocco. His mother was from Dalās (or Dilās), a village near Abū Sīr, but we know little else about her with any certainty. We are equally uncertain about al-Būṣīrī's exact birth date. Dates from 1210 to 1214 have been recorded, but the most commonly accepted is the one given by the 15th-century historian Abū 'l-Maḥāsin Yūsuf Ibn Taghrībirdī (1411-1470) as 7 March 1212.

Sometime during his childhood, al-Būṣīrī went to Cairo to begin his formal education at the mosque school of Shaykh ʿAbd al-Ẓāhir. This was a very small establishment, and nothing else is known of it. It is likely, however, that al-Būṣīrī would have studied there the standard curriculum of the era: *Qur'ān*, *ḥadīth* and the linguistic disciplines like grammar, syntax and metrics. Traces of the jargons characteristic of these disciplines can all be found in his work. He almost certainly studied in addition arithmetic and calculation, because these were important subjects for any aspiring government employee to master, and this was the career he chose when he finished school. If his poetry is any evidence, he was far better at Arabic and literature than he was at mathematics. In one of his early compositions, from the period when he was employed in the small Delta town of Bulbays (also Bilbays), he lashes out at his fellow Christian clerks for accusing him of not knowing arithmetic well. He says, in a clear allusion to the Christian doctrine of the Trinity (*Dīwān*, ed. Basaj, 49):

And should one who considers three to be one
be thought more knowledgeable than I in arithmetic, and a better writer?

As can be seen from this passage, for a writer who would later become one of the most famous spiritual poets in Islam, in his early work, there is little reference to religion beyond conventional ones such as this. At one point in a panegyric to the governor of Bilbays, for example, he compares his patron to the Prophet Joseph, renowned in Islamic belief for his physical beauty as well as his uncompromising rectitude, but the conceit is not developed (*Dīwān,* ed. Basaj, 49). Most religious references in these poems are on the order of the satire of the Christian clerk mentioned above, or his complaint in another poem from the time he was in Bilbays (*Dīwān*, ed. Basaj, 189):

Bilbays encloses a band of thieves
I have turned from one of them, fatigued. . .
But how can offenders among the Christians be blamed,
when the [supposedly] upright one among the Muslims has acted treacherously?
The greater part of the people are treacherous,
though there are those who do not condone such things.

The lesson to be drawn from this early poetry is that al-Būṣīrī had a talent for satire and invective, which he cultivated assiduously, something one would not expect from a poet who would later become famous for his heartfelt expressions of deep religious feeling and spirituality.

The sources do not give an exact date, but probably some time in the late 1230s or early 1240s, al-Būṣīrī was dismissed from his post in Bilbays and returned to Cairo where he seems to have briefly opened a school for elementary pupils, but this initiative was not successful. After a time, he was able, through his contacts, to secure another government position in a larger Delta town, al-Maḥallah al-Kubrā. It may have been while he was there that he met the mystic Abū 'l-Ḥasan ʿAlī 'l-Shādhilī (ca. 1196-1258), who had settled in Alexandria as early as 1244 or as late as 1252. Originally from Morocco, al-Shādhilī became a highly regarded religious leader of his time and attracted a large group of followers when he ultimately settled in Egypt. His teachings would eventually become the basis for the Shādhilī order, one of the most widespread and influential Sufi brotherhoods during the Middle Ages in Egypt. It was most likely under al-Shādhilī's influence that al-Būṣīrī began to cultivate his poetic talents more actively in the service of Islam.

Al-Būṣīrī has a long poem mourning the death of al-Shādhilī (in Upper Egypt, while on pilgrimage) in 1258, and celebrating the installation of his second-in-command, the Andalusian mystic Aḥmad ibn ʿUmar Abū 'l-ʿAbbās Ahmad al-Mursī (d. 1287 or 1288), as his successor. It is clear from the poem that al-Būṣīrī thought of al-Mursī as his real guide in the study of Islam and his spiritual master. It is likely that al-Būṣīrī was acquainted by him with the works of another Andalusian, al-Qaḍī ʿIyād ibn Mūsā 'l-Yaḥṣubī (1083-1149). Al-Qaḍī ʿĪyād had composed a lengthy treatise on the virtues and merits of the Prophet Muḥammad, *al-Shifā' bi-ta'rīf ḥuqūq al-Muṣṭafā* (Gratification in Characterizing the Truths of the Chosen One), and as Suzanne Stetkevych has suggested (171), it is likely that al-Būṣīrī relied on this work for the details of his depiction of Muḥammad's life in the middle of the *Burdah* poem.

Al-Būṣīrī was well traveled in his youth, possible spending considerable time in Jerusalem as well as Mecca and Medina. But he also most likely performed the Pilgrimage again in the decade of the 1260s after al-Shādhilī's death. He describes portions of his journey in a long poem, originally entitled "*Umm al-qurā fī madḥ khayr al-warā*" (The Mother of Towns Concerning the Best of Mankind), but usually called the *Hamziyyah* (after its rhyming letter). The *Hamziyyah* is very much a companion piece to the *Burdah* and treats many of the same themes in a similar style, although at 457 lines, it is nearly four times as long. Nevertheless, they were very likely composed at about the same time.

The *Hamziyyah* has proved somewhat less popular than the *Burdah* over the centuries, but has attracted its own share of commentaries. Annemarie Schimmel (181) even praised it more highly than the *Burdah*. Both she and the more ancient commentators who devoted their attention to the *Hamziyyah* have remarked on the particular beauty of the initial lines of the poem, depicting the birth of the Prophet Muḥammad, in its skillful gradually intensified references to the light (*al-nūr al-Muḥammadiyyah*), said to have emanated from infant's body when he came into the world (*Dīwān*, ed. Basaj, 9-10):

Noble after noble {coming] from you
has graced existence, fathered by others!
A lineage the heights consider an adornment
and Gemini necklaced with stars.
How perfect the necklace of sovereignty and glory!
In this you are a white peerless [pearl].
And a countenance like the sun shines from you
before which a night blazing bright pales.
The night of a birth that was for the religion [of Islam]
a joy when it befell, and a shining splendor.

This atemporal beginning emphasizes the symbolism of light (opposed to darkness) that early on became associated in Islam with homage to the Prophet.

Then, however, the poem moves to recount in a more traditionally narrative fashion the childhood of Muḥammad (including the miraculous splitting of his chest and the washing of his heart by visiting angels), as well as chronicling his growing holiness and asceticism. It describes how his unshakeable integrity attracts the attention of the successful merchant Khadijah, who becomes his wife. The poem devotes considerable detail to her role in his life as his main support in the early period of his prophecy, as well as the growing opposition of leading Meccans to Muḥammad's message. Al-Būṣīrī in this poem does not neglect to enumerate many of the miracles attributed by popular piety to the Prophet in the period of his adulthood as well, including the *mi'raj*, or ascent to heaven to see God in person, which is also mentioned in the *Burdah* poem.

After this, the poem moves back briefly to a more chronological exposition, chronicling the dangers of the journey from Mecca to Medina when the Prophet agreed to act as arbiter of disputes among tribes in the latter city. In the process of describing Muḥammad's arrival in Medina and the growth of the Muslim community there, al-Būṣīrī interweaves extensive references to Prophetic miracles and praise of Muḥammad, in the process comparing him to earlier prophets and their experiences from the Jewish and Christian traditions. In essence he recapitulates and embroiders upon themes and motifs from earlier sections of the work. Then, very briefly, he alludes to the battles the Muslims fought against opposing forces from Mecca, a theme he will devote more attention to in the *Burdah*.

Enumerating the sites where these battles and raids took place recalls to al-Būṣīrī recollections from his own Pilgrimage (*Dīwān*, ed. Basaj, 24):

So I departed on [my camel] from Mecca,
the sun white in the heavens.
The place where [our] House, [the Kaʿbah] is located, where the Revelation

descended, the refuge of prophets, where the
lights are, the splendor is.
Where [we fulfill] the duty of circumambulation,
the running [of Hagar in search
of water], the shaving, the casting of the date-stones, and the presentation.
How perfect, how perfect are its abodes!
Every trace there is untouched by wear.

As this section continues, he depicts, in turn, the places the pilgrimage caravan passes through, and evokes the spiritual intensity experienced by his companions as they contemplate the sacred landscape around them.

Moving out of this transcendent moment, al-Būṣīrī re-anchors the poem in a historical framework, by describing at length the Prophet's family, his descendents and his Companions—those whose recollections of these events became the evidentiary basis for the narrative of Muḥammad's life, as preserved in the *ḥadīth*. It is in this section, as well, that al-Būṣīrī comes closest to acknowledging the generic antecedents of the *Hamziyyah* in Shiite poems enumerating the virtues and merits of the Prophet's family, the *Āl al-Bayt* (*Dīwān*, ed. Basaj, 26):

Then there was ʿAlī, whose eyes you anointed
with your saliva
when both of them together were sore.
So he was able to see with the gaze of an eagle
on a raid when [his banner] the Eagle led the way.
And with [his sons Ḥasan and Ḥusayn], the two
branches of sweet basil, whose
perfume comes from you, through your
daughter Fāṭimah. . . .
Two martyrs whose fallen bodies were not forgotten in my mind
because of al-Taff and Karbala. . . .
Family of the Prophet, you are so good, so panegyric
concerning you has become good to me, and
elegy has become good.
I have become the Ḥassān [ibn Thābit] of your
panegyric,
and if I mourn for you, I am al-Khansāʾ.

Here we can see both the influences of Shiite poetry on panegyrics for the Prophet—discussed extensively by Emil Homerin (83-84)—and its limitations. Undoubtedly al-Būṣīrī would have had some familiarity with these poems because the Shiite Fatimid dynasty that had ruled Egypt for several centuries before his birth had sponsored festivals where such poems were a staple. But, despite the clear honor given to the Prophet's relatives and descendents in the *Hamziyyah*—his cousin and son-in-law ʿAlī, his daughter Fāṭimah, his grandsons Ḥasan and Ḥusayn are mentioned—al-Būṣīrī consistently subordinates their accomplishments to the actions of the Prophet (he anoints ʿAlī's eyes, giving him his keen sight, he imparts sweetness to Ḥasan and Ḥusayn through the medium of his daughter Fāṭimah). But then al-Būṣīrī concludes this passage by aligning himself literarily to two early poets, to Ḥassān ibn Thābit (the Prophet's panegyrist during his lifetime) and al-Khansāʾ (the preeminent elegist among Preislamic poets, famous for her verses mourning the death of her brothers). Poets of the Shiah tradition are nowhere to be seen. At the end of the *Hamziyyah*, al-Būṣīrī again reverts to the encomiastic mode (the genre associated with Ḥassan ibn Thābit), beseeching the Prophet for blessings and praising one last time his fine qualities.

The most famous poem in al-Būṣīrī's *oeuvre*, the *Burdah* poem, contains many of the same elements as the *Hamziyyah*, but in the former the structure is much more purposeful and less diffuse. Traditionally, the commentators have divided the poem into ten sections:

Section 1: On Love and Complaint about Passion (lines 1-13)

Section 2: A Warning Against the Passions of the Soul (lines 14-28)

Section 3: Praising the Prophet (lines 29-61)

Section 4: On the Prophet's Birth (lines 62-74)

Section 5: On the Prophet's Miracles (lines 75-90)

Section 6: On the Glorious *Qur'ān* and Praise of It (lines 91-107)

Section 7: On the Prophet's Night Journey and Ascension (lines 108-120)

Section 8: On the *Jihād* of the Prophet (lines 121-142)

Section 9: [The Poet] Petitions the Prophet [for Protection] (lines 143-154)

Section 10: [The Poet] Seeks Communion and Presents [His] Needs to the Prophet (lines 155-164).

While these traditional divisions may not conform exactly to the actual treatment of the various thematic elements of the poem, which are interwoven more closely and reiterated more than the typology would suggest, they are in general an accurate guide to the poem's structure. As can be seen quite clearly from an examination of the order and content of the sections, the poem relies on a variety of envelope structure, in which six segments focusing on the Prophet Muḥammad and his life (sections 3-8) are flanked at the beginning and end of the poem by twin sections focused more on the poet as individual believer, exploring his personal reactions to the Prophet, both as somewhat distant object of reverent veneration, and object of a desire seeking a level of understanding and ultimately union with a beloved.

The parallel between a human erotic relationship and the religious believer's search for the presence of a divine being had already been well established in Arabic and Persian literature through Sufi mystical religious verse. In fact, al-Būṣīrī evokes (through contrafaction and allusion) that mystical tradition at the very beginning of the *Burdah*. It has long been recognized that the *Burdah* uses the same rhyme and meter as a well-known poem composed by the greatest mystical poet of the preceding generation, ʿUmar ibn ʿAlī Ibn al-Fāriḍ (1181 or 1182-1235). He had died in Cairo in 1235, when al-Būṣīrī was a young man in his twenties. The first section of the *Burdah* also mentions several of the same places in the Arabian peninsula as Ibn al-Fāriḍ's poem. That poem begins

Did Layla's fire shine at night above Dhū Salam,
or was it a lightning bolt that flashed over al-
Zawrāʾ and al-ʿAlam?

All these place names are mentioned at the beginning of al-Būṣīrī's poem.

This is not to say that al-Būṣīrī intended his work to be simply an imitation or copy of Ibn al-Fāriḍ's poem. They are very different. To name only the most glaring point of departure, Ibn al-Fāriḍ's verses are about his relationship to God, while al-Būṣīrī's poem is about his relationship to the holy and virtuous, but very human Prophet Muḥammad. It is as though al-Būṣīrī is dramatizing the distance between his own work and the Sufi tradition by invoking (and reminding the knowledgeable reader of) Ibn al-Fāriḍ's poem.

Nor is the Islamic mystical tradition the only antecedent invoked by al-Būṣīrī in the *Burdah*. There is a poem (also know as the *Burdah*, or "mantle" poem) by the early Islamic poet (and contemporary of Muḥammad) Kaʿb ibn Zuhayr, who only converted to Islam late in life. As the story goes Kaʿb's brother Bujayr became a Muslim and was rebuked by Kaʿb in a poem for abandoning the traditions of his ancestors. Bujayr persuaded his brother of the danger of remaining hostile to the new religion (both politically and in terms of the peril to his soul), and Kaʿb decided to adopt Islam. He then recited a poem before Muḥammad—using the style and idiom of Preislamic verse—praising him and his followers. Muḥammad responded by bestowing his mantle (*burdah*) on the repentant Kaʿb, showing his approval of the poetic tribute.

A story that was circulated—probably on the authority of al-Būṣīrī himself—connects the thirteenth-century *Burdah* poem to the much older tale about Kaʿb ibn Zuhayr. According to this anecdote, al-Būṣīrī was stricken by partial paralysis (hemiplegia) and composed the *Burdah* during his illness. Following the poem's completion, al-Būṣīrī had a dream where the Prophet appeared to him and covered him with his mantle, as he had done to Kaʿb. When he awoke, al-Būṣīrī found himself partially cured, a fact he attributed to Muḥammad's intercession on his behalf and his approval of the poem. The poem itself (perhaps understandably) makes no allusion to these events, but as Stefan Sperl has noted (2:470), it does "contain evidence of a spiritual crisis" that afflicted al-Būṣīrī prior to its composition. This very personal element (contained mainly in Sections 1-2, and 9-10, of the poem) differentiates it strongly from the *Hamziyyah* (as well as earlier poems praising Muḥammad and his family), which took a more strictly chronological approach, and may very well have contributed substantially to the popularity of the *Burdah*. Individual Muslims of many different levels of devotion could easily identify with the spiritual trial al-Būṣīrī describes.

Other Muslim authors—especially more modern figures—seem to have responded largely to the way that al-Būṣīrī selected from the Prophet's biography and chose to emphasize certain elements in Muḥammad's career in the middle sections of the poem. Throughout its long history, Arabic poetry had never emphasized chronological narrative in its elite poetry, thus there were no influential epic poems, as there had been in the Greek or Latin (or even Persian) traditions. Al-Būṣīrī's example gave inspiration to the nineteenth-century poets Maḥmūd Sāmī 'l-Bārūdī (1838-1904) and Aḥmad Shawqī (1868-1932), who composed their own *Burdah* poems that were very concerned with how the story of Muḥammad might become material for an epic-style treatment.

Even more consistently, throughout Arabic literary history, al-Būṣīrī's use of rhetorical figures in the *Burdah* has inspired poets who came after him. We find many contrafactions of the *Burdah*—like that of Ṣafī 'l-Dīn ʿAbd al-ʿAzīz al-Ḥillī (1278-ca. 1339)—that include a different rhetorical figure in every line. These frequently go by the collective name of *al-Badīʿīyāt*.

We know as little about the date and circumstances of al-Būṣīrī's death as we do about his birth, which indicates that he never achieved great fame as an individual during his lifetime. Nevertheless, the *Burdah* has a lasting impact on Arabic literature both popular and elite. Only in the twentieth century was its influence somewhat diminished, in the wake of the rise of Romantic and Modernist-influenced aesthetics, which did not value the traditionalism the *Burdah* represented. Similarly, the practices associated with its recitation have not been transferable to popular modern media. Yet even so, the poem has never been forgotten, and no study of the development of Arabic literature would be complete without taking its impact into account.

REFERENCES

Th. Emil Homerin, "Arabic Religious Poetry, 1200-1800," in *Arabic Literature in the Post-Classical Period*, ed. Roger Allen and D.S. Richards (Cambridge: Cambridge University Press, 2006), 74-86;

Zakī Mubārak, *al-Madāʾiḥ al-Nabawiyyah fī 'l-adab al-ʿarabī* (Cairo: Dār al-Kātib al-ʿArabī, 1967);

ʿAbd al-ʿAlīm al-Qabbānī, *al-Būṣīrī: ḥayātuh wa-shiʿruh* (Cairo: Dār al-Maʿārif, 1968);

Annemarie Schimmel, *And Muhammad Is His Messenger: the Veneration of the Prophet in Islamic Piety* (Chapel Hill: The University of North Carolina Press, 1985), 179-89 and *passim*;

Stefan Sperl, "Notes," in *Qasida Poetry in Islamic Asia and Africa*, vol. 2, ed. by Stefan Sperl and Christopher Shackle (Leiden: E.J. Brill, 1996), 470-76;

Suzanne Stetkevych, "From Text to Talisman: al-Būṣīrī's *Qaṣīdat al-Burdah (Mantle Ode)* and the Supplicatory Ode," *Journal of Arabic Literature* 37:2 (2006),146-189;

Suzanne Stetkevych, "From Sirah to Qasidah: Poetics and Polemics in al-Būṣīrī's *Qaṣīdat al-Burdah (Mantle Ode)*," *Journal of Arabic Literature* 38,1 (2007): 1-52.

Mihyār al-Daylamī

(ca. 977–1037)

TERRI DEYOUNG
University of Washington

WORKS

Dīwān (Collected Poems).

Editions

Dīwān, 4 vols., ed. with intro. by Aḥmad Nasīm (Cairo: Maṭbaʿat Dār al-Kutub al-Miṣriyyah, 1925).

Translations

A.J. Arberry, *Arabic Poetry: a Primer for Students* (Cambridge: Cambridge University Press, 1965), 106-111;

Stefan Sperl, *Mannerism in Arabic Poetry: a Structural Analysis of Selected Texts* (Cambridge: Cambridge University Press, 1989), 199-209.

Abū ʾl-Ḥusayn Mihyār ibn Marzawayh al-Daylamī was the most important author actively engaged in writing courtly poetry in Baghdad and Iraq in the first half of the eleventh century. It can be argued that his impact on the subsequent course of Arab and Islamic letters was not nearly so great as that of his close contemporaries, Abū ʾl-ʿAlāʾ al-Maʿarrī (973-1058) and Abū ʿAlī ʾl-Ḥusayn ibn ʿAbd Allāh ibn Sīnā (980-1037), who effected much more revolutionary transformations in their respective fields. But Mihyār's body of work gives us much deeper insight into the everyday workings of Arab court society—and the function of poetry within it—than that of any other poet in the late Buwayhid period.

His *dīwān* was carefully edited by an Egyptian scholar and Fatimid chancery clerk, ʿAlī ibn Munjib ibn al-Ṣayrafī (1071-1147), within a century of Mihyār's death, testifying to its wide and swift dissemination, as does a prominently placed assertion included in the introduction to the *dīwān* of the well known Andalusian poet, Ibrāhīm ibn Abī ʾl-Fatḥ Ibn al-Khafājah (1058 or 1059-1138 or 1139), affiliating himself proudly with the school of Mihyār and his teacher al-Sharīf al-Raḍī (970-1016). Similarly, the most famous Andalusian anthologist, Abū ʾl-Ḥasan ibn ʿAlī Ibn Bassām al-Shantarinī (d. 1147) devoted a whole chapter in the last volume of his work, *al-Dhakhīrah fī maḥāsin ahl al-Jazīrah* (The Treasury Containing the Virtues of the People of the Peninsula) to Mihyār's poetry.

Ṣayrafī's edition of the *Dīwān* included dates and commentary (possibly from Mihyār himself) on the poems, which added to its historical value. The actual text of this version of Mihyār's works disappeared from sight with the passage of time, but the manuscript from which the modern edition of the *Dīwān* was prepared is also Egyptian and has been dated by the editor to the twelfth century, which means that it likely contains material derived, directly or indirectly, from Ṣayrafī. The modern edition of Mihyār's *Dīwān* (in four volumes), edited in the early 1920s by Aḥmad Nasīm and never superseded, includes over four hundred poems, of which approximately three-quarters (over 300) are panegyrics. The rest are divided between elegies, love lyrics, versified epistles to friends (*ikhwāniyyāt*), and a relatively large number of undateable pieces in the format of riddles, which were probably recited at the social gatherings in the houses of Baghdad grandees that Mihyār would frequently have attended.

In the centuries immediately following Mihyār's death, his work was overshadowed by the prestige accorded to the poetry of his teacher al-Sharīf al-Raḍī. But in a somewhat surprising reversal, Mihyār's poetry has come to be received with increasing favor by posterity, especially in the twentieth century. Unlike many of the works by al-Sharīf al-Raḍī and his contemporaries, Mihyār's legacy is still actively invoked by modern creative writers. Most notably, the Syro-Lebanese poet Adūnīs (ʿAlī Aḥmad Saʿīd, 1930-)—himself of Shiite affiliation, like Mihyār—titled his most revolutionary and influential collection of modernist poems *Aghānī Mihyār al-Dimashqī* (Songs of Mihyār the Damascene; 1964), in direct homage to his predecessor. Earlier, the Egyptian dramatist and novelist Tawfīq al-Ḥakīm, had Muḥsin, the main character in his ground-breaking novel *'Awdat al-rūh* (*Return of the Spirit*; 1933) constantly carry around with him a copy of Mihyār's *Dīwān*, the love poetry of which he quoted in moments of high emotion. Mihyār's most famous short lyric, where he speaks of how he impressed his lady love Suʿād by the combination his noble Persian lineage and his intense Islamic piety, was even set to music in the mid-1940s and became a popular hit when recorded by the Egypt's greatest contemporary male singer, Muḥammad ʿAbd al-Wahhāb. Each of these instances reflects an aspect of how Mihyār has been perceived by a large group of admirers in modern times. For Adūnīs, he was a rebel against the prevailing political order in his vocal support of *Shu'ūbī* (pro-Persian) and Shiite views. By Ḥakīm, he was recognized as a consummate master of the poetic discourse of idealized longing and love. For ʿAbd al-Wahhāb and the musicians, his facility with language and the delicate yet powerful rhythms of his Arabic were the attractions.

More seriously, the selection of Mihyār's *Dīwān* for editing in modern and scholarly fashion was a project sponsored by the newly reorganized Egyptian National Library (Dār al-Kutub) in the 1920s, at least in part to demonstrate its credentials as an important institution worthy of international recognition. The interest generated by the success of this edited text led to the inclusion of Mihyār's work as the representative of his period in the Egyptian national school curriculum, which later on served as a model for educational curricula in other newly autonomous Arab countries.

For someone who lived his adult life in the public eye, and had many longstanding friendships among the Baghdad elite—by his own admission reaching back into his youth—we know remarkably little about Mihyār's early years. Even such mundane facts as the date of his birth or the exact form of his full name are matters for conjecture. Almost all the conclusions we can draw are based on scattered references in his poems, which of course are liable to exaggeration and manipulation for artistic purposes. Modern scholars tend to believe, for example, that he was born in 977 (or perhaps slightly earlier), because he refers in a dated poem in the *Dīwān* to being "a middle-aged man," and to being fifty years old, where subtraction would give us that date of birth. Again, the form of his honorific first name (*kunya*) is given by his biographers as either "Abū 'l-Ḥasan" or "Abū 'l-Ḥusayn"; in two poems he calls himself Abū 'l-Ḥasan, which would argue for the first option, but this does nothing to settle the matter, since the forms of names are frequently adjusted to meet the requirements of the poem's meter. His father, Marzawayh, is only a name (one that admittedly argues for a Persian origin and is consistent with his surname (*laqab*), the "Daylamite," Daylam being a region in modern Iran near the Caspian Sea). His mother's name and background are entirely unknown.

It is only in the late 990s, when he would have been around twenty years old, that he and the context of his work can be fixed with some reliability. According to notations in the *Dīwān*, he composed during this period a number of short lyrics on conventional subjects, especially love, as in his short eight-line poem describing a flock of doves that begins (*Dīwān* 1:345):

The ring-doves amongst the leafy branches
 wail as prisoners do,
Speaking about their hearts desolately broken
 as though they were speaking my mind.

He continues on to tell us that whether he travels to Najd, the desolate interior plateau of the Arabian Peninsula—like the birds—or remains in Baghdad, he knows he will not escape the feelings of desolation resulting from the loss of his beloved. There is nothing radically new here. Even though this poem later became famous, it is based on a traditional theme, familiar to countless generations both before and after Mihyār's time. But he does handle the transition from line to line and the rising emotional intensity with a certain adroitness, and the poem illustrates well what appears to have been a lifelong interest in combining urban settings with a nostalgic evocation of the desert tradition familiar to his educated audience, exposed from childhood to the classics of Preislamic Arabic poetry that glorified tribal life in the desert.

More cogently, this decade produced two major works, frequently studied, quoted and anthologized, that have made a sizable and long-lasting contribution to the perception of Mihyār as a Shuʿūbī (aficionado of Persian culture) and Shiite poet. The first, a poem rhyming in the consonant "m," (*mīmiyyah*) is dated in the *Dīwān* quite specifically to 997, and has been translated into English in A.J. Arberry's *Arabic Poetry*. It comprises what is easily the boldest statement of support for his fellow Persians that Mihyār ever made in his career. He begins the poem conventionally with a *naṣīb*, the traditional episode whereby the poet stops at an abandoned campsite and laments the unhappy end of a past love affair. In the course of this lament, he often addresses his absent beloved. But in the case of this poem, the beloved is no Arab tribeswoman. She is "the daughter of the non-Arabic speakers" (*a'ājim*), a term that early on in the history of the Islamic conquests in the East is applied specifically to Persians (in the West, it has been applied, often, to Berbers and Europeans). He tells her that others are blaming him for "his passion," which he then goes on to identify as—not the more usual love he might have for her or any other human woman—but his single-minded desire to emulate the great deeds of his ancestors, whom he compares to lions. Another word in Arabic for lion is *fāris* (beast of prey); thus anticipating his assertion in the fifth line of the poem, that Persia (*fāris*)—not the Arabs—planted the shade trees overgrowing this particular campsite, "whose branches have not bent pliantly to anyone seeking to test them (*'ājim*)."

This opening of the poem is clearly a tour-de-force whose effect is heightened by the complex interplay of words whose roots—*'a-j-m* and *f-r-s*—have primary meanings in Arabic associated with traditional Bedouin poetry, yet can also be used to refer to Persians and Persianness. He thus disposes of a complaint sometimes laid at the door of the Persians by their Arab conquerors—that they cannot use the language correctly or effectively (*a'jam* was originally used to refer to someone with a speech impediment)—and shows what a skillful manipulator of the language this humble non-Arab is.

Most of the ensuing verses glorify the poet more directly and relegate his Persian heritage to one aspect—though an important one—of his character. This is consistent with Mihyār's later Shuʿūbī poems, where Persian heritage is often combined with inventories of more general heroic virtues, as well as with Shiite religious affiliation. But this poem is unusual in the directness with which it insults the Arabs and particularly the Umayyad dynasty, which had made of a virtue of their Arab, Bedouin ancestry. He refers derogatorily to the dynasty in several lines, focusing especially on Yazīd, the Umayyad caliph held responsible for causing the death of the Prophet's grandson Ḥusayn, whom Shiites believe should have become ruler of the Islamic community. He ties his Shuʿūbism to this Shiite theme by asserting that the Persians, not the Arab tribesmen, have historically been the most loyal defenders of the Prophet's family (even though they were of Arab descent). The prominence of this theme is interesting at this juncture, because one of the few facts that Mihyār's biographers consistently mention is that he did not officially convert from Zoroastrianism to (Shiite) Islam until the year1003.

Giving voice to Shiite regret at the tragic history of the Prophet's descendents through the line of ʿAlī and Fāṭimah is also the focus of his second major poem of this period, his poem rhyming in the consonant "l" (*lāmiyyah*) that begins: "Let him who can do so, be consoled: Who, for us, can find a substitute? / And how can the last erase the first (*al-awwalā*)?" The poem belongs to a genre of works enumerating the virtues of ʿAlī and Fāṭimah, and their descendents (*manāqib āl al-bayt*) that were at this time becoming very popular at the public festivals of the Shiite community. On these occasions the events of Karbala, where Ḥusayn was killed, were recounted and the virtues of the Prophet's family enumerated in poetry and story. It would have been very lucrative for a young poet like Mihyār to produce these kinds of works, independent of whether he had actually converted to Islam. We certainly find them occurring rather frequently in his subsequent work.

Though he has begun here with a very general *naṣīb* lamenting the tyranny of time that brings all human endeavor to nothing, Mihyār quickly moves to relate this elegiac complaint to the specific example of the ʿAlids (*Dīwān* 3:48):

And I have a desire to publicly mourn the family of the Prophet
if poetry must make a *naṣīb* or speak of love.
In my soul dwell their stars, extinguished,
and righteousness will disdain to appear unless they are re-kindled.
In the uplands [of Najd] you can see their glowing bodies of light,
they fill it and give illumination to the open country.

This poem is a far more pedestrian work than the *mīmiyyah*. But both poems would have attracted the attention (if he did not directly commission them) of the man who would play a decisive role in Mihyār's life henceforward, becoming his teacher and patron, al-Sharīf al-Raḍī.

Al-Sharīf Abū 'l-Ḥasan al-Raḍī, a few years older than Mihyār, was (along with his elder brother al-Murtaḍā) heir to one of the most illustrious families of the time, which had had responsibility for leadership of the Shiite community in Baghdad and its environs for most of the Buwayhid period. By the 990s, he had taken over from his father the bulk of responsibility for the public functions of the community. In addition, al-Sharīf al-Raḍī had already begun to carve for himself a reputation as a formidable poet and scholar, as well as leader of a brilliant literary salon, whose poets followed his lead in producing a very nostalgic poetry that fully relied upon the traditional structure (*naṣīb*, *riḥlah*, *madīḥ*) and style of the Preislamic Arabic *qaṣīdah*, some of whose features (like the description of the camel journey or *riḥlah*) had gradually been abandoned as the setting of composition for poetry had moved from the desert to the more urban and cosmopolitan atmosphere of the Abbasid dynasty in the late seventh century. Both al-Raḍī and al-Murtaḍā would most likely have seen patronage and encouragement of this sort of poetry as useful buttressing of their own political, social and religious prestige, since they based their claims to power and leadership on descent from the Prophet's family, who—though their importance and appeal went far beyond such mundane matters—were fully fledged members of the Arabian tribal milieu.

As his *mīmiyyah* and *lāmiyyah* show, Mihyār fitted into al-Raḍī's circle well. Even if these poems were not commissioned by the Sharīf in the first place, but were conceived by Mihyār on his own, they had the potential to be seen as demonstrating remarkable consistency with the former's cultural agenda. Thus it is not surprising that Mihyār's next dateable major work is an elegy composed to commemorate the unexpected passing of the brothers' uncle in the year 1000. Given the pronounced Shiite-Shuʿūbī tone of the earlier works, this poem is surprising in its virtual lack of these elements. Nothing about it would make it unacceptable for mourning a Sunni Arab magnate of similar background, a position emphasized by Mihyār's focus on the uncle's martial capabilities.

After emphasizing the suddenness of the family's loss, Mihyār turns to the brothers, and emphasizes how their presence can compensate for—though not replace—their uncle. In so doing, he follows traditions that go back to the beginnings of the history of the elegy in Arabic, rather than breaking new ground. He also underscores his closeness to the brothers and his intimate emotional rapport with them.

Even in this early period of his career, however, Mihyār had begun to cultivate other patrons and develop relationships that would last his lifetime. Two, in particular, stand out. The first was the family of Abū 'l-Qāsim ibn ʿAbd al-Raḥīm (d. ca. 1030), who made their career as marshals (*nuqabāʾ*) of the Turkish units in the Buwayhid army (even though they themselves were of Persian origin). Mihyār wrote some of his last—as well as his first—panegyrics for members of this family, emphasizing the continuity of his relationship with them. In the many poems—over 30—that he wrote to or for Abū 'l-Qāsim, a number of them are in the form of versified letters (*ikhwāniyyāt*), rather than traditional panegyrics, and they reveal a much more informal stance than would be customary in later times between poet and patron.

The other frequent addressee in Mihyār's poems of this period is the administrator Abū 'Abbās ibn Ibrāhīm al-Dabbī, who, when he became one of the chief ministers to Fakhr al-Dawlah (ca. 952-997)—the senior Buwayhid prince headquartered in Rayy—was awarded the title of al-Kāfī 'l-Awḥad (the Singularly Sufficient One), by which he became generally known. Al-Kāfī 'l-Awḥad was a prominent member of the literary salon sponsored by Fakhr al-Dawlah's chief vizier, al-Ṣāḥib Ibn ʿAbbād (938-995). It is to this individual that Mihyār dedicates an important poem providing a highly nuanced picture of the spiritual and emotional impact of the most significant event that occurred in his life in this period: his conversion from Zoroastrianism to Islam in 1003 (*Dīwān* 1:12-14).

It is easy to view this event as primarily a career move, designed to make it easier to conform to the increasingly Islamized world of his patrons and the members of al-Sharīf al-Raḍī's circle. This would, indeed, seem to be the attitude projected by his most famous poem (the one set to music and sung by ʿAbd al-Wahhāb), probably also composed during this period (*Dīwān* 1:64):

Umm Saʿd was pleased with me among
  the circle of her kin, and she passed by, asking about me.
She was overjoyed by what she found out about my character,
  so she wanted to find out what my ancestry was.
Do not imagine it an ancestry that would diminish me
  I am the one who can satisfy you with respect to ancestry.
My kin have overpowered time with a young man
  and walked upon the heads of the ages.
They have turbaned the crowns of their heads with the sun
  and built their houses with shooting stars.
My father was Chosroes in his throne room
  and where—among the people—is a father like mine?
Spoiler among the kings of old is mine
  and sprung from the nobility of Islam and literature am I.
I have acquired glory from the best of fathers
  and acquired religion from the best of prophets,
And I have gathered up boasting along its edges
  with the sovereign power of the Persians and the religion of the Arabs.

Here, as in his earliest pieces, Islamic belief is not explored, but simply taken for granted, counted as part of the inventory of essential character traits for a successful courtier.

In his poem to al-Kāfī 'l-Awḥad, in contrast, Mihyār explores much more thoroughly his spiritual motivation for conversion, speaking (in the process of replying to those among his family who sought to keep him a Zoroastrian) of the need for repentance and acknowledgement of sin in order to arrive at a newfound level of spiritual awareness. Some have even, on the basis of this poem and others, seen a mystical, Sufi tendency in Mihyār's writing, though most of his work does not bear that sort of interpretation.

Thus, while it may be true, as one medieval biographer, Ibn Khallikān (1211-1282) has asserted, that this conversion took place "at the hands of al-Sharīf al-Raḍī" himself, there is no independent evidence in the poems to bear this out. Therefore, it would seem that Mihyār, in taking this step, was responding to something deeper and more meaningful to him than mere conformity to the prevailing trends, something that he wanted to share with a wider circle of his friends than simply the family of al-Raḍī.

It was nevertheless in response to a crisis within that family that we see the next notable deployment of Mihyār's poetic talent. In 1016 al-Sharīf al-Raḍī died suddenly and unexpectedly (of natural causes), and al-Murtaḍā commissioned Mihyār to join with him in producing the elegies for his brother's obsequies. The resulting work, which strives for a balanced picture of al-Sharīf al-Raḍī as both an intellectual and a man of action, established Mihyār even more thoroughly as the leading voice of the traditionalist school of poetry now that his mentor was gone. Mihyār's ability to serve as an effective spokesperson for continuing al-Raḍī's use of verse as a field for articulating a certain system of values representing an idealized code of conduct for the courtly class was tested by what happened following the funeral. Some of al-Sharīf's enemies spoke against Mihyār's mentor and challenged the picture he had drawn in his original elegy. So Mihyār compose a second, even more forceful poem delineating al-Sharīf's virtues and especially his ability to conciliate differing groups and to rise above the criticism of those who would oppose him, a trait in which Mihyār finds inspiration for continuing his own struggles. The reception of this poem apparently had the intended effect of reducing Mihyār's critics to silence and no doubt greatly enhanced his reputation as an independent poet.

Following al-Sharīf's death, Mihyār's talents were increasingly in demand to provide panegyrics for the administrators who formed the backbone of the secretarial class that kept the government functioning as the power of the Buwayhids began its disastrous decline in the second and third decades of the eleventh century. In fact, Mihyār personally was able to rise above these circumstances to maintain himself and his young family (he married late in life) by the fruits of his poetry alone. He maintained his old ties among the middle echelon of the bureaucracy, added new ones (such as his association with the chiefs of the Banū Mazyad tribal confederation who served the new Buwayhid ruler, Jalāl al-Dawlah (933 or 934-1044)), and even in the last years of his life composed panegyrics for the new Buwayhid prince and his most senior ministers, like members of the ʿUqaylid family and Abū 'l-Qāsim al-Ḥusayn al-Maghribī (981-1027). The latter, especially, sought to continue the reputation for intellectual largesse begun by the preceding generations of Buwayhid ministers like al-Muhallabī (903-963), Abū 'l-Faḍl Ibn al-ʿAmīd (d. 970) and al-Ṣāḥib Ibn ʿAbbād. A good example of the poems of this period is found in the panegyric to al-Maghribī translated into English in Stefan Sperl's *Mannerism in Arabic Poetry*.

The most serious crisis Mihyār faced in the last years of his life was an incident where he was accused of concealing and taking for his own use a large sum of money inadvertently left behind by a party of Muslim pilgrims who had stayed at a property he owned. Though he was briefly jailed by Jalāl al-Dawlah, he was soon found innocent and released, an outcome he commemorated in a graceful poem of thanks to the Buwayhid prince (*Dīwān* 3:193-200). Six years later he died peacefully in Baghdad, in comfortable circumstances, and with an intact reputation that had already begun to spread his fame among literary circles throughout the entire Arabic-speaking world.

REFERENCES

ʿIsām ʿAbd ʿAlī, *Mihyār al-Daylamī: ḥayātuh wa-shiʿruh* (Baghdad: Wizārat al-Iʿlām, 1976);

ʿAlī ʿAlī 'l-Fallāl, *Dirāsah taḥlīliyyah li-shiʿr Mihyār al-Daylamī* (Cairo: Dār al-Fikr al-ʿArabī, 1948, reprint 1960);

Ismāʿīl Ḥusayn, *Mihyār al-Daylamī: baḥth wa-naqd wa-taḥlīl* (Cairo: Maṭbaʿat al-ʿUlūm, 1931);

Abū 'l-Ḥasan ʿAlī Ibn Bassām al-Shantarinī, *al-Dhakhīrah fī maḥāsin ahl al-Jazīrah,* ed. Iḥsān ʿAbbās, 4 vols. (Beirut: Dār al-Thaqāfah, 1975).

Abū Muḥammad al-Qāsim al-Ḥarīrī

(446/1054 – 516/1122)

JAAKKO HÄMEEN-ANTTILA
University of Helsinki

WORKS

Durrat al-ghawwāṣ;
Mulḥat;
Maqāmāt;
al-Risālah al-shīniyyah;
al-Risālah al-sīniyyah.

Editions

Durrat al-Ġawwāṣ, von al-Ḥarīrī, ed. Heinrich Thorbecke = "Über die Verstösse von Gebildeten gegen die grammatischen Regeln," nebst *Kitâb al-malâḥin*: mit kurzer Einleitung und Anmerkungen = "Buch der doppelsinnigen Ausdrücke," von Ibn Duraid. (Leipzig, 1871; Heidelberg, 1882; repr. Amsterdam: APA – Oriental Press, 1981);

Aḥmad ibn ʿAbd al-Mu'min al-Qaysī 'l-Sharīshī, *Sharḥ Maqāmāt al-Ḥarīrī*, vol. I-IV, ed. Muḥammad ʿAbd al-Mu'min Khafājī (Beirut: al-Maktabah al-Thaqāfiyyah, s.a.);

Sharḥ Maqāmāt al-Ḥarīrī (Beirut: Dār al-Turāth, 1388/1968);

Sharḥ Mulḥat al-i'rāb, ed. Barakāt Yūsuf Habbūd (Ṣaydā; Beirut: al-Maktabah al-ʿAṣriyyah, 1418/1997);

"al-Risālah al-sīniyyah" and "al-Risālah al-shīniyyah," in *Sharḥ Maqāmāt al-Ḥarīrī* (Beirut: Dār al-Turāth, 1388/1968) 604-612.

Translations

Antoine Isaac Silvestre de Sacy, *Les Séances de Hariri publiées en arabe avec un commentaire choisi*, 2. éd. par Joseph Reinaud et Joseph Derenbourg (Paris, 1847-1853; repr. Amsterdam: Oriental Press 1968);

Makamat, or Rhetorical Anecdotes of Al Hariri of Basra, transl. T. Preston (1850; repr. London: Darf, 1986);

The Assemblies of al Harírí, Vol. I, transl. T. Chenery (1867), Vol. II, transl. P. Steingass (London: Oriental Translation Fund, 1898).

Al-Ḥarīrī is perhaps the most celebrated mediaeval Arab author. His collection of *maqāmahs* earned him the renown of an impeccable *littérateur* and it was imitated by generations of authors, up to our own time. On the other hand, out of his production only the *maqāmahs* became famous. His poems and literary letters are little known and even less read, and his other works fall outside the category of *belles lettres*.

Abū Muḥammad al-Qāsim al-Ḥarīrī is usually known by the name al-Ḥarīrī. In early sources, he is also called Ibn al-Ḥarīrī. The family name al-Ḥarīrī refers to silk (*ḥarīr*), presumably silk trade or manufacture, but there is no report that al-Ḥarīrī himself would have been working in silk. By his time the name had lost its original connotation and become a family name, as is also evident from the name form Ibn al-Ḥarīrī, "the Son of the Silk (Merchant/Manufacturer)."

Al-Ḥarīrī's family was of Arabian descent, deriving its ancestry from Rabīʿat al-Faras and living in al-Mashān, a village near Basra, where Basrans who had fallen out of favor were sent, to be out of harm's way. Not much is known of his ancestors, which implies that though the family was well-off, it had not distinguished itself by producing any scholars or other persons of note. Al-Ḥarīrī was born in about 446/1054 in al-Mashān. The date of his birth is not completely reliably known, as it seems to have been derived from counting backwards from his year of death, at which time he was said to have been 70 (lunar) years old, a suspiciously round figure.

He grew up in al-Mashān before leaving for Basra, which at that time was a major city in Iraq, although the capital, Baghdad, was where an aspiring poet or prosaist would have made his breakthrough. Yet Basra had a respectable past. Some three centuries before the birth of al-Ḥarīrī it had been, together with Kufa, the intellectual centre of the Arab world. By the time of al-Ḥarīrī, though, these times were gone by.

He received his education in Basra, but we know little of this period. Among his teachers was Abū 'l-Qāsim al-Faḍl ibn Muḥammad al-Qaṣabānī 'l-Baṣrī (d. 1052), who does not seem to have left many works behind him although in his own time he is said to have been a famous scholar and an authority in *adab*, or *belles lettres*. He seems to have written on both grammar and lexicography, as well as compiling a large anthology of poetry. In biographical sources, he is said to have died in 444/1052 during the reign of the Caliph al-Qā'im (ruled from 422/1031 to 467/1075). The date of his death must be wrong, as al-Ḥarīrī was not yet born in 444. In any case, he must have been an early teacher of al-Ḥarīrī, who cannot have been older than about 20 when al-Qaṣabānī died, if we accept the date of his death as during the reign of al-Qā'im. We also know that al-Ḥarīrī studied Islamic law, *fiqh*, and the science of division of inheritances, *'ilm al-farā'i'*, which would have given him a firm standing in Islamic law. Indeed, his literary work shows that he was well acquainted with these subjects. It may not be superfluous to add that after his death, one of his sons, ʿUbaydallāh, served as a *qāḍī 'l-quḍāt*, or supreme religious judge, in Basra, and such expertise tended to run in the family.

Otherwise we know precious little about al-Ḥarīrī's early years. He seems to have lived mainly in Basra, in the quarter of Banū Ḥarām (*maḥallat Banī Ḥarām*), which gave him the additional name al-Ḥarāmī, used in some sources. When he comes to light, he is a *ṣāḥib al-khabar* or a *ṣāḥib al-barīd* in the *dīwān* of the Caliph, posted in Basra and his native al-Mashān. In the role of *ṣāḥib al-khabar*, his duty was to keep informed of what was happening around him and to report to the Caliph's office in Baghdad, headed, at one time, by his patron-to-be Anūshirwān Ibn Khālid. He was something between an agent of the secret service and a local representative of the government. The same position was later held by his offspring until about 556/1160.

As the times were troubled, al-Ḥarīrī would have had much to report. Even in some of his poems, which were not part of the official correspondence, he reports the troubles in the area and pleads for royal intervention. The raids of the Crusaders did not reach southern Iraq, but looting Bedouins were an ever-growing threat to the civil society and the general situation was somewhat unstable.

Al-Ḥarīrī was rich. According to biographical sources, he had landed property in al-Mashān, amounting to some 18,000 date palms, which would have given him a fair income. Whether this was by inheritance or was acquired by him is not indicated in the sources. He also had a house in Basra and another in Baghdad, the latter with a garden that was to become famous as a *rendezvous* for his admirers. It was originally his job that took him to Baghdad, where he had to show up from time to time to report to his superiors. When he had achieved literary fame, he also came to the city in his role as a celebrated author, to read his works to an enthusiastic audience.

Al-Ḥarīrī does not seem to have been very likable, though. His biographers describe him as untidy in both his person and his clothes, as well as short and ugly. Moreover, he had a reputation of being a miser (*bakhīl*). What is even worse, he used to pluck his beard, which in mediaeval Arab culture was held to be shameful. Some of his biographers try to tone this down by saying that he merely played with it, which was bad manners, too. This he did, so they defend him, merely because he was so absorbed in his literary musings.

He seems to have written his first book when he was in his forties. The monograph *Durrat al-ghawwāṣ fī awhām al-khawāṣṣ* was probably written by 487/1094. It is a collection of linguistic mistakes made by contemporary or earlier authors, which al-Ḥarīrī corrects. The book belongs to the genre of *laḥn al-'āmmah*, commonly made mistakes, and it taps earlier sources such as ʿAbd Allāh ibn Muslim Ibn Qutaybah's (828-889) *Adab al-kātib*, besides picking fresh examples from contemporary writers. The book is usually considered a major contribution to the field, although one has to admit that it partly owes its reputation to its author's fame in another field.

Ten years later, al-Ḥarīrī finally found his genre. Badīʿ al-Zamān al-Hamadhānī (circa 358/969–398/1008) had a century earlier created a new genre, *maqāmah*, which was a brief and usually humorous story. These episodes were narrated in rhymed prose, with interwoven verses, and they had a fictitious, lower-class hero who performed his comic tricks throughout the Islamic world. Usually the hero either gained some money from his audience or had a good laugh at the expense of his gullible victims. The events were narrated by an equally fictitious narrator who met the usually disguised hero whom he recognized only after the trick had been performed. Part of the charm of the genre came from seriality: the individual episodes come one after the other and repeat certain patterns, which makes it possible for the reader to anticipate the events and to enjoy watching how the author handles the plot and guides it to its anticipated outcome. The genre had been in vogue during the century before al-Ḥarīrī, and about twenty authors are known to have written after al-Hamadhānī and before al-Ḥarīrī. It was probably in 495/1101 that al-Ḥarīrī started composing *maqāmahs*.

There are legends about his first *maqāmah*. In al-Ḥarīrī's *maqāmahs* there are, as is usual in the genre, two main characters, the comic hero and the narrator, in this case Abū Zayd al-Sarūjī and al-Ḥārith ibn Hammām al-Baṣrī. Both are fictitious, which in mediaeval Arabic literature was rare outside the genre of *maqāmahs*. According to an oft-repeated legend, traced in the sources back to al-Ḥarīrī himself, he began writing such stories after having met a real person in the mosque of Maḥallat Banī Ḥarām, an old but eloquent trickster named Abū Zayd al-Sarūjī. Here, though, a *caveat* is needed. The earliest sources are somewhat ambiguous as to whether that was the name under which the impostor introduced himself or whether it was a name given by al-Ḥarīrī to this curious person, who claimed to have been a fugitive from Sarūj, which had been under the Crusaders' attack.

The man duped his audience with his eloquence, just as *maqāmah* heroes tend to do. Having been an eyewitness, al-Ḥarīrī later spread the story, and this was to become *al-Maqāmah al-Ḥarāmiyyah*, the 48th *maqāmah* in his final collection. His story finding favor, he was encouraged to write more, and the real-life beggar was metamorphosed into a fictitious protagonist of a series of *maqāmahs*.

This story need not be true. Mediaeval Arabic literature is very uneasy with fictitious characters, and legends tend to be generated which explain away the fictitiousness. Thus, both the main hero and the narrator in al-Hamadhānī's *maqāmahs* have received a life of their own, and later authors speculated on their real identity and the circumstances under which al-Hamadhānī had met them.

The consensus on the narrator, however, is that he is a fictitious person, a *persona* created by al-Ḥarīrī. A Prophetic saying explains al-Ḥārith "the Tiller" and Hammām "the Worrier" to be the two most truthful names for a human who has to toil for and worry about his living. Thus, the name al-Ḥārith ibn Hammām can be equated with Everyman, and the *nisbah* al-Baṣrī hints at al-Ḥarīrī himself, who was an inhabitant of Basra. Roughly translated, the narrator's name would be "the Basran Everyman" or, Americanized, "John Doe."

Whether any real persons existed behind the characters or not is basically immaterial. Al-Ḥarīrī's hero and his narrator soon became literary figures and even if there had originally been a model for the hero or even the narrator in real life, the characters outgrew them.

There is also another, equally suspect story about the early phase of al-Ḥarīrī's literary production. According to one story, al-Ḥarīrī found favor with the mighty vizier Anūshirwān Ibn Khālid in Baghdad. At the instigation of Anūshirwān, al-Ḥarīrī wrote forty *maqāmahs*, or, in another version, he came to Anūshirwān with a completed collection of forty. These were admired by his patron, but they also aroused the jealousy of some people in the court. Backbiters started circulating a rumor that the ugly civil servant of Basra could not have composed the *maqāmahs* himself. He had stolen the stories from a stranger who had died in Basra and whose literary remains had fallen into the hands of the *ṣāḥib al-khabar*, as might be expected in such a case. In another version, it was a North African, Maghribī, who had been robbed by cut-throat Bedouins who sold their loot in Basra and the manuscript thus fell into al-Ḥarīrī's hands.

The legend goes on to tell that al-Ḥarīrī wanted to nip the rumor in the bud and volunteered to write another *maqāmah* in the same style, to prove his authorship. He retreated to his Baghdad house for forty days, but with little success. He was not inspired and could do nothing. As the legend, told by Yāqūt ibn ʿAbd Allāh al-Ḥamawī (1179?-1229), puts it, "he blackened a lot of paper but could not produce a thing." Defeated, he retired to Basra, and here his writer's block gave way to inspiration and he composed a new *maqāmah* with which he was able to return triumphantly to the capital. Incidentally, the story reminds one of the *fatra* of the Prophet Muḥammad (d. 632), who underwent a period when he received no new revelations. The story of al-Ḥarīrī may well have been modeled after the story of the *fatra*.

In another version of the same story, al-Ḥarīrī caught the attention of the Caliph himself. The Commander of the Believers invited him to his court and assigned him the task of writing an official letter to the Governor of Khurāsān. This he did to test whether he was sufficiently talented to write letters worthy of the Caliphal court–in Islamic culture, official letters were written with great care, using rhymed prose, occasional verse quotations and an extravagant style, far from the dry official letters of today. As in the other version, in this, too, al-Ḥarīrī remained impotent and dumbfounded, despite his efforts, because, ultimately, he had not mastered the official political jargon or terminology. He had to give up and was never appointed to the promising and well-paid post of Caliphal scribe. The failure astonished those who knew his literary talent. According to some biographers, al-Ḥarīrī later explained the failure by saying that he wanted to avoid the position which would have taken him permanently to Baghdad, since he could not have simply turned the offer down had it been offered to him by the Caliph.

In yet another version of the story, it was a vizier who wanted to test whether al-Ḥarīrī was the real author of the *maqāmahs*, forty at that time, or whether they were by a deceased Maghribī, wrongfully acclaimed by the *ṣāḥib al-khabar*. The vizier gave him the task of composing an official letter on a certain matter, and al-Ḥarīrī was unable to do this.

If there is any historical truth in these stories, they seem to imply that al-Ḥarīrī experienced an initial failure in Baghdad. He may have received some fame in provincial Basra but his entrée into the literary circles of Baghdad may not have gone smoothly at first. Whether the stories are historical or not, it took less than a decade for al-Ḥarīrī to achieve a breakthrough as a *maqāmah* author. Incidentally, it is an intriguing fact that a later biographer, Khalīl ibn Aybak al-Ṣafadī (ca. 1297-1363), deems his preserved letters so different from, and by implication inferior to, his *maqāmahs* that it was as if they had been written by two different persons. Whether inferior or not, though, this hardly justifies reviving the legend of a deceased Maghribī author.

According to all stories, the composition of *maqāmahs* took place in phases. In most versions, it is said to have been the vizier of the Caliph al-Mustarshid (ruled from 512/1118 to 529/1135), Anūshirwān Ibn Khālid, who spurred al-Ḥarīrī to write more *maqāmahs*, either after the very first one or after a set of forty already existed. Usually it is taken that the veiled reference to a mighty patron in the preface of the collection refers to this vizier, but there is a competing tradition in Ibn Khallikān's (1211-1282) biographical dictionary. Ibn Khallikān reports having seen, in Egypt, in 656, an autograph manuscript where al-Ḥarīrī explicitly dedicates the collection to another vizier of al-Mustarshid, Jalāl al-Dīn Ibn Ṣadaqah. Ibn Khallikān knows that this was a deviant tradition but he relies on the autograph. In either case, the viziers would have been sponsoring him before their tenure under the reign of al-Mustarshid, or their support must have come in the last phases of the *maqāmahs* which, by 512, would have been in their final shape. One might speculate that they were, or one of them was, his last patron(s), who in the stories and the dedications were substituted for the earlier ones.

In fact, there need not be any controversy between the stories. Rededicating extant works of art to new patrons was, in fact, rather common in mediaeval Arabic, and not only Arabic, culture. As there were no royalties, no bookshops selling thousands of copies, nor even scholarships, authors had to make a living as best they could and, when they found a new patron, they had to switch their loyalty from the older to the newer one and this sometimes led to rededications.

This phenomenon may explain why there is a rare tradition that it was the governor of Basra who first incited al-Ḥarīrī to compose more *maqāmahs*. An initial support from a parochial patron often led authors to the capital in search of wealthier, or more open-handed, patrons. The story that it was the Caliph al-Mustaẓhir himself (ruled from 487/1094 to 512/1118) who was instrumental in urging him to write more *maqāmahs* is, though, obviously exaggerated. Legends tend to escalate the story and to drag more and more eminent patrons into the picture. If al-Ḥarīrī later became the greatest author of Classical Arabic literature, certainly his patrons should have been the greatest luminaries of the time.

Another fundamentally unreliable story claims that al-Ḥarīrī wrote up to 200 *maqāmahs* before selecting the classical fifty into his collection. This is a topos in mediaeval Arabic literature. Almost all authors have, according to tradition, first produced huge volumes before condensing them into a more suitable size, if we are to believe all legends.

From the late 490s/early 1100s, there start to be indications to the effect that al-Ḥarīrī's fame was in ascendance. The earliest commentary to the work is ascribed to Ibn al-Simnānī, who is said to have died in 499/1105. The date of the death of this author is not definite and since the work has not been preserved, its attribution and even existence is not certain. If it really existed before 500, it would mean that even this early al-Ḥarīrī's *maqāmahs* had met with enough success to merit a commentary.

Another author, ʿAlī ibn Munjib Ibn al-Ṣayrafī (1071-1148 or 1155) mentions al-Ḥarīrī in a work, *Kitb al-afḍaliyyāt*, in a passage written between 487 and 515, and presumably closer to the earlier than to the later date. In this work, though, the author, who was in Egypt at the time, deems it necessary to explain who al-Ḥarīrī is, which shows that although al-Ḥarīrī was a rising star at the time he was not yet fully and internationally established. Another early author, al-Kāmil al-Khwārizmī (d. after 510/1117) is said in 502/1108 to have entitled one of his works *Kitāb al-riḥal*, "The Book of Travels," in imitation of the successful work by al-Ḥarīrī. This, though, may of course be later speculation.

By 504/1110 at the latest, al-Ḥarīrī started enjoying fame that was to last. At that date he probably read his work in public for the first time, which in a manuscript culture was not the same as the rather unimportant reading sessions in modern culture, but meant that the work was famous enough to entice people from various parts of the country to come and sit at the feet of the master. Among those who attended the sessions in his Baghdad garden were grandees, the list being headed by some sons of Caliphs, extending down to viziers and ordinary rich people. His success was extraordinary, with the author receiving ample recompense for his initial failure in the capital.

The lists of participants in this and various other readings have been preserved in manuscripts. During the last twelve years of his life, al-Ḥarīrī read his *maqāmahs* to enthusiastic audiences in al-Mashān and Basra, but his sessions in his garden in Baghdad became more celebrated than any other literary soirées. Though the report may be somewhat exaggerated, al-Ḥarīrī is said to have mentioned in 514, two years before his death, that he had authenticated 700 manuscripts of his *maqāmahs*. These were mainly transcripts of these sessions, where he read out the text, the audience copied it into their own manuscripts and the author signed them to prove their authenticity. Such soirées were held in series, as it took several nights before the work could be read and copied.

In the early twelfth century, 700 copies of one work was a huge number, equaling modern day world best sellers. Most books of the time have been preserved in a couple of copies, but al-Ḥarīrī's *maqāmahs* have been preserved in hundreds. He was a sensation, nothing less, even though the number of 700 authenticated manuscripts would turn out to be somewhat exaggerated.

The final collection consisted of fifty *maqāmahs*. This number was to remain canonical for all later collections. Earlier authors had written various numbers of *maqāmahs* and there does not seem to have been any standard number for the individual pieces in a collection. After al-Ḥarīrī, authors still continued to produce various numbers of *maqāmahs* but there was a clear sense that a full-fledged collection should consist of fifty *maqāmahs*. Shorter collections were deemed to be incomplete, and the few authors who wrote more than fifty clearly did this in order to outdo al-Ḥarīrī. Even the production of the originator of the genre, al-Hamadhānī, may have been fixed at about fifty–52 to be exact–only after the collection by al-Ḥarīrī had provided the standard for the genre.

What al-Ḥarīrī did with the genre was to give more it rigor. In the *maqāmahs* by al-Hamadhānī and other early authors, there was much variation. In one collection, there could be several heroes, and the subject matter varied from comic to serious, episodes being built, e.g., around speeches or sermons which could be taken as quite serious exhortation. Al-Ḥarīrī used only one hero, Abū Zayd al-Sarūjī, and almost all of his *maqāmahs* are picaresque, despite other materials being inserted into this frame.

Al-Ḥarīrī also made the relationship between the hero and the narrator more regular. In al-Hamadhānī's *maqāmahs*, the narrator could himself sometimes be the hero, or the two adventured together or, finally, the narrator could be the victim of the hero. In al-Ḥarīrī, the narrator does not take part in the tricks, except for a few occasions, such as *Tiflisiyyah* (33), where the narrator accompanies the hero for two years.

On the other hand, al-Ḥarīrī brought in the family members of the hero and let them be accomplices in the tricks. In al-Hamadhānī's *maqāmahs*, the "old woman" of the hero and their children had occasionally been mentioned but they had taken no active part in the plots.

As a collection, the *maqāmahs* have a wide range of topics. In this, the genre resembles the novel, which is able to fuse together various elements. In the *maqāmahs*, we have a similar array of materials but it is usually limited to one topic within one story. Al-Ḥarīrī himself says in his preface that "they contain Bedouin proverbs, learned witticisms, grammatical riddles, lexical quibbles (*fatāwā*), original letters, ornate speeches, sermons that cause tears and jokes that cause laughter"--in a word, all possible materials.

This led him to put long passages in the mouth of the hero so that he–the hero and through him the author–could show off his erudition. In earlier *maqāmahs*, eloquence and extemporized wit had been the sole *fortes* of the hero but from al-Ḥarīrī on, erudition takes its place besides eloquence.

Al-Ḥarīrī fixed the number of main characters in the *maqāmahs* to two, the hero and the narrator. Al-Ḥarīrī may also be credited with one structural innovation. The heroes of al-Hamadhānī had often remained at the scene of the crime–or trick–in order to have the last word. They either hid themselves and commented on what they saw resulting from their trick, or they imagined the scene from a safe distance.

This led to some awkwardness. Often the trick could be thought to have worked only if the trickster could get completely away from the scene before the comic climax. However, then it was difficult for him to have the last word or, at least, to have the victims hear it. Al-Ḥarīrī used a new device, a note, *ruq'a*, left for the victims to read after the hero had left and was safe from any revenge. The device of the *ruq'a* was frequently adopted by later authors.

Technically, there is a loose circular composition in many Harīrīan *maqāmahs*. The story line consists of an initial meeting of the hero and the narrator, followed by the climax of the episode and ending in the two separating from each other. In some *maqāmahs* there is a more strict circular composition but others lack any more detailed structures.

The collection as a whole also has a structure of its own, which was a novelty. Al-Hamadhānī's *maqāmahs* were written as separate pieces, and they received their final place in the collection only posthumously, by anonymous editors and, as it seems, rather randomly. They were not composed as chapters in a larger book. Al-Ḥarīrī, on the contrary, was very conscious of writing a set of episodes, not simply a collection of unrelated *maqāmahs*. In the main part this is not very pronounced, although in some subsequent *maqāmahs* a sort of fixed order may be seen, and in some the places mentioned seem to form a rough itinerary. The first and the last two *maqāmahs*, however, build up a basic story. In the first, the narrator meets the hero for the first time. After this, there come 47 *maqāmahs* which are not clearly structured as a whole. The penultimate *maqāmah* (49) gives the spiritual testament, *waṣiyyah*, of the hero to his son. Here the father gives up his profession of roguery but does not yet fully repent. On the contrary, he advises his son to take after him. In the last *maqāmah* (50) we finally meet a reformed rogue. When the narrator hears the hero exhorting people, both he and we, as readers, would by now expect the situation to end in some trick pulling the leg of the listeners. Nothing of this sort happens. Abū Zayd is a trickster no more and his exhortations spring up from a reformed heart.

This device was later adopted by many authors but they never developed it any further. No Arabic *maqāmah* collection took the final step towards the novel by setting all the stories in one collection into a frame in which one might see some progress in the characters and their life. *Maqāmah* collections never developed into a *Bildungsroman* nor even a picaresque novel. The first and the last *maqāmahs* often set a frame to the events but other pieces are not strictly interrelated with each other and the order could easily be changed.

Al-Ḥarīrī developed the language of the *maqāmah*. In comparison to al-Ḥarīrī, al-Hamadhānī's language sounds rather sober or poor, depending on the viewpoint. His use of rhymed prose, for example, is less rigid and less artistic than al-Ḥarīrī's. Al-Hamadhānī often narrates the transition from one scene to another in unrhymed prose, thus marking the transition passage as of secondary importance and directing the reader's attention to the next climax. Throughout the text, he also avoids excessive rhyming and literary tropes. Al-Ḥarīrī excels in ornate prose. His narration rarely, if ever, loses the rhyme, and there are few sentences completely without rhetorical devices. Letters avoiding certain consonants, or, on the contrary, using some consonant in each word, poems that can be read as palindromes from the end to the beginning, and other such feats of artistic prose abound in his text.

There is one device, though, which al-Ḥarīrī uses more rarely than his predecessors. Al-Hamadhānī and other early authors were very fond of inserting other poets' verses, or parts of them, into their own rhymed prose. In his preface, al-Ḥarīrī already remarks that all verses and rhymed prose of the *maqāmahs* are by him, except for two particular cases which he names. He was the writer of his text or, as he puts it, "my mind is the taker of its virginity'" (*abū 'udhrihi*). With this solution, however, he also lost something. Part of the charm of the Hamadhānīan *maqāmah* comes from its half-hidden intertextuality, which the perspicacious reader may take delight in noticing.

The transition from poetry to rhymed prose is also handled differently in the works of these two authors. Al-Ḥarīrī clearly marks the boundaries, inserting verses after rhymed prose passages with a link, such as "and then he recited." Al-Hamadhānī passes over this and often lets the syntax of the sentence continue from prose to verse and vice versa, which gives his text an additional flavor, due to the rhythm carrying over from the relatively free rhythm of prose to the bound rhythm of poetry and back again, with no stop at the transitions.

The rhymed prose of al-Ḥarīrī is more regular than al-Hamadhānī's. Al-Ḥarīrī prefers rhyming pairs (AABBCC), with only occasional triads or longer series, whereas al-Hamadhānī used pairs, triads and longer series rather freely, with unrhymed passages interspersed.

Al-Ḥarīrī's language is usually considered superb in comparison to that of earlier, as well as later, *maqāmah* authors. At least in the intricate difficulties woven into it, it certainly surpasses all earlier and most of the later *maqāmahs*. A later biographer, Yāqūt, is, rhetorically at least, ready to agree that inimitability, *i'jāz*, is found in al-Ḥarīrī's *maqāmahs*, which in Islamic language is a huge claim. The term *i'jāz* is used in reference to the *Qur'ān*, which is said to be inimitable and this inimitability is taken as proof of its divine origin. Claiming inimitability for the Harīarīan *maqāmah* is, technically, heretical, but it excellently describes the awe which later scholars felt when approaching al-Ḥarīrī's *oeuvre*.

The language and style of the Harīrīan *maqāmah* was its strongest point. The narratives themselves have for him less importance than their technical realization, and, in general, his plots are simpler than those of al-Hamadhānī. He gives less attention to creating the set-up and maintaining the tension, and he is far less accomplished as a comedian.

Al-Ḥarīrī wrote his *maqāmahs* fully cognizant of his predecessor, whom he mentions in the preface of his own collection. Some of his *maqāmahs* use those by al-Hamadhānī as their intertexts, in order to show his superiority by inviting the reader to compare the simpler style of al-Hamadhānī with his own more intricate one. Despite his polite words in the preface, al-Ḥarīrī obviously aimed at superseding al-Hamadhānī and, in the eyes of later generations, was able to do this.

The complex language of the *maqāmahs* have enticed philologists to write commentaries on them. More than sixty commentaries are known in Arabic before the nineteenth century, many of them preserved, and there are further commentaries and translations in Persian and Turkish.

Al-Ḥarīrī could never repeat this feat. His other production is meager, and it seems that he was content with the fame brought to him by the *maqāmahs*. He did write some poems but they are rather mediocre and they were only later collected into a *dīwān*, or collected poems. His letters, *rasā'il*, enjoyed some fame but it seems that the admiration they met with was mainly due to the author's *maqāmahs*; as mentioned above, al-Ṣafadī even said that it was as if two different persons had written the *maqāmahs*, on the one hand, and the letters and poems, on the other. Yet the majority thought that the writer of such superb *maqāmahs* must have been a good epistolographer, too. His letters were not collected during his lifetime, but by the time of Yāqūt, they seem to have existed as a collection, as the biographer mentions his collected letters (*Kitāb rasā'ilihi 'l-mudawwanah*). An earlier biographer, ʿImād al-Dīn Muḥammad ibn Muḥammad al-Kātib al-Iṣfahānī (1125-1201), had to collect the excerpts himself, which he inserted into his book.

Most of the letters circulated only in fragments. Only two of them became famous on their own and they were often copied together with the *maqāmahs*. These were *al-Risālah al-sīniyyah* and *al-Risālah al-shīniyyah*, "The Letter in S" and "The Letter in Sh," respectively. The gist in both is that each of the words in the rather long letters contains an S or, respectively, a Sh. This *tour-de-force* was later imitated by other writers but perhaps never superseded.

The letters of al-Ḥarīrī are written in the ornate language familiar from the *maqāmahs*. They are rather unsurprising and fall neatly within the tradition of literary letters. Most of them tell little of the real life of the author and several seem to have been written as exemplary letters, to show what could be written in a certain situation, and one may doubt whether all of them did ever have a real historical context in the life of al-Ḥarīrī.

The fame of al-Ḥarīrī after 504 seems to have been translated into some social advancement. He was accepted into high society in Basra and we meet him at the tables of the aristocracy there. Even in Baghdad high officials were ready to come to the garden of his house, to hear the author reading his *maqāmahs*. Some brought their little children with them, because it was an honor to receive an *ijāzah* from a well-known author. An *ijāzah* was originally a certificate and permission to teach the work of an author, but by al-Ḥarīrī's time the system had degenerated, and we meet little children brought by their fathers to attend the reading sessions so that they could receive the certificate of having heard the text from the author himself. A toddler of two was present in a session held in 512, and later he, Abū Ṭāhir al-Khushūʿī, was to become the last living person to have an *ijāzah* from the author himself. What he understood when attending the session was immaterial. What mattered was that he had a copy of the master's work and a certificate for having attended the sessions. The same al-Khushūʿī also transmitted the *Durrat al-ghawwāṣ* and he, or his father, seems thus to have been an al-Ḥarīrī enthusiast.

In his poems and letters, al-Ḥarīrī eulogized the high and mighty of his time, as was the custom. He sent poems to the vizier Anūshirwān Ibn Khālid, who, according to legend, received his *maqāmahs* favorably. One of the poems, though, seems to imply that he had first had little success, as it refers to letters the vizier had left unanswered. Yet if the legend is true, al-Ḥarīrī later struck gold with him. Less lucky was Saʿd al-Malik, the vizier of Muḥammad ibn Malikshāh. Saʿd al-Malik held tenure in the last years of the 490s but soon fell out of favor and was crucified in 500/1106. Al-Ḥarīrī's hopes of finding in him a patron were thus frustrated.

It seems that his last work was a short grammatical poem, *Mulḥat al-iʿrāb*, and the author's own commentary on it. This little poem was begun in 504/1110 and was perhaps completed in the same year or soon after. It was written at the instigation of his friend Abū 'l-Fatḥ Hibatallāh Ibn al-Tilmīdh, who asked the author to write a grammatical poem for beginners to learn by heart. The text is of little merit and, had its author not been famous due to the *maqāmahs*, it would probably have been forgotten centuries ago.

In addition to these, there are some works ascribed to al-Ḥarīrī but presumably misattributed. Thus, a late bibliographer, Kâtip Çelebi (1609-1657) knows a *Tawshīḥ al-bayān* by al-Ḥarīrī but little is known of this text and it is not mentioned in any of the earliest biographical sources. One also finds reference to a historical work, *Ṣudūr zamān al-futūr wa-futūr zamān al-ṣudūr*, but again there is little reason to accept the attribution.

The *maqāmahs* are often frivolous. This should not make us forget that they tell nothing of the author himself. In the mediaeval Arab tradition, frivolous poems were quite compatible with a serious and religious mind. Many a *qāḍī*, or religious judge, composed homosexual love poems, or lyrics celebrating the joys of wine. At least some, however, never tasted wine and were chaste in their real life. There is one story which implies that the same might hold true for al-Ḥarīrī, too. According to this story, he criticized a younger friend of his who had been drinking wine. When the culprit came to apologize, eating humble pie and promising never to drink wine again, al-Ḥarīrī further admonished him not even to sit with people who drink wine.

The story is, at least, told as a serious incident with no underlying hints at this being a joke. In some sources the same story is, though, told of one of al-Ḥarīrī's sons, Abū 'l-Qāsim ʿAbd Allāh, which makes it uncertain whether the ugly miser also held strict religious ideas. He might well have.

Al-Ḥarīrī died at his home in Basra on Rajab 6th, 516, equivalent to September 11th, 1122, at the age of seventy (lunar) years. In some sources, though, the date of the death is given differently. According to some he died a year earlier, in 515/1121, or even in 512/1118. He is usually said to have left two children, ʿAbd Allāh and ʿUbaydallāh, but there is also reference to a third one, Muḥammad.

According to some sources, this third son, Zayn al-Islām Abū 'l-ʿAbbās Muḥammad (d. 556/1160), kept the tradition alive in the family. After his father's death, he and some of the closest students of al-Ḥarīrī were the most authoritative transmitters of the text of the *maqāmahs*, and, e.g., the biographer al-ʿImād al-Iṣfahānī read the *maqāmahs* with him. There is also some confused information about a commentary written on the *maqāmahs* by a putative grandson, Muḥammad ibn Muḥammad al-Ḥarīrī, but this seems to be a later misunderstanding.

Al-Ḥarīrī's *maqāmahs* have remained in vogue ever since, and even today in Arab countries they are considered masterpieces of Arabic rhymed prose and eloquence. They belong to the very heart of the Arab literary canon. Together with Abū 'l-Ṭayyib al-Mutanabbī's (915-965) *Dīwān*, collected poems, and Ibn Nubāta's (d. 984 or 5) *Khuṭab*, sermons, al-Ḥarīrī's *maqāmahs* were often learnt by heart and copied in prestigious manuscripts. These three works and the *Qur'ān* form the supreme examples of Arabic language.

Outside of Arabic literature, al-Ḥarīrī's *maqāmahs* were translated into Hebrew by the Jewish author al-Judah ben Solomon Ḥarīzī (d. 622/1225) and imitated in Persian by Ḥamīd al-Dīn Abū Bakr ʿUmar ibn Maḥmūd Balkhī (d. 560/1164). They were also favored by miniaturists and some of the most vivid illustrations of mediaeval Arab literature come from the *maqāmah* manuscripts.

REFERENCES

A.F.L. Beeston, "The Genesis of the Maqāmāt Genre," *Journal of Arabic Literature* 2 (1971), 1-12;

Johann Christoph Bürgel, "Gesellschaftskritik im Schelmengewand–Überlegungen zu den Makamen al-Hamadhanis und al-Hariris," *Asiatische Studien* 45 (1991), 228-256;

Jaakko Hämeen-Anttila, *MAQAMA: a History of a Genre*, Diskurse der Arabistik 5 (Wiesbaden: Harrassowitz, 2002;

Abdelfattah Kilito, *L'auteur et ses doubles: essai sur la culture arabe classique*, Collection poétique. (Paris: Éditions du Seuil, 1985;.

Abdelfattah Kilito, *al-Ghā'ib: dirāsah fī maqāmah li 'l-Ḥarīrī* (Casablanca: Dār Tūbiqāl li 'l-nashr, 1987);

Abdelfattah Kilito, *Les Séances: récits et codes culturels chez Hamadhānī et Harīrī* (Paris: Sindbad, 1983);

Pierre MacKay, "Certificates of Transmission on a Manuscript of the Maqāmāt of Ḥarīrī," *Transactions of the American Philosophical Society*, n.s. 61 (1971), 4;

John N. Mattock, "The Early History of the Maqāma," *Journal of Arabic Literature* 15 (1984), 1-18;

Angelika Neuwirth, "Adab Standing Trial–Whose Norms Should Rule Society? The Case of al-Ḥarīrī's 'al-Maqāmah al-Ramlīyah'" in *Myths, Historical Archetypes and Symbolic Figures in Arabic Literature. Towards a New Hermeneutical Approach. Proceedings of the International Symposium in Beirut, June 25th–June 30th, 1996*, ed. Angelika Neuwirth et al., Beiruter Texte und Studien 64 (1999), 205-224;

Katia Zakharia, "Norme et fiction dans la genèse des maqāmāt d'al-Ḥarīrī," *Bulletin d'Études Orientales* 46 (1994), 217-231;

Katia Zakharia, "Les référénces coraniques dans les maqāmāt d'al-Ḥarīrī: éléments d'une lecture sémiologique," *Arabica* 34 (1987), 275-286;

Katia Zakharia, *Abū Zayd al-Sarūğī, imposteur et mystique: relire les Maqāmāt d'al-Ḥarīrī* (Damascus: Institut d'études arabes de Damas, 2000).

Ṣafī al-Dīn Abū 'l-Faḍl ʿAbd al-ʿAzīz ibn Sarāyā 'l-Sinbisī 'l-Ṭā'ī 'l-Ḥillī

(26 August 1278-ca. 1350)

TERRI DEYOUNG

University of Washington

WORKS

Dīwān (Complete Poems);

al-ʿĀṭil al-ḥālī wa 'l-murakhkhaṣ al-ghālī;

Dīwān al-mathālith wa-mathāni;

Sharḥ al-kāfiyyah wa 'l-badīʿiyyah fī 'l-madā'ih al-Nabawiyyah.

Editions

Dīwān (Damascus: Maṭbaʿat Ḥabīb Afandī Khālid, 1879-1883);

Dīwān (Beirut: Maktabat al-Maṭbaʿah al-Adabiyyah, 1892);

Dīwān, ed. Muḥammad ʿAlī 'l-Yaʿqūbī (Najaf: al-Maṭbaʿah al-ʿIlmiyyah, 1956); reprint. (Beirut: Dār al-ʿArabiyyah li 'l-Mawsūʿāt, 2005);

Dīwān, ed. Karam al-Bustānī (Beirut: Dār Ṣādir; Dār Bayrūt, 1962);

Dīwān, 3 vols., ed. Muḥammad Ḥuwar (Jordan: al-Mu'assasah al-ʿArabiyyah li 'l-Dirāsāt wa 'l-Nashr, 2000);

Dīwān al-mathālith wa 'l-mathānī fī 'l-maʿālī wa 'l-maʿānī, ed. Muḥammad Ṭāhir al-Ḥimṣī (Damascus: Dār Saʿd al-Dīn, 1998);

Sharḥ qasīdatihi al-badīʿiyyah, ed. Ibrāhīm ibn Muḥammad al-Safarjalānī (Cairo: n.p., 1899);

Sharḥ al-kāfiyyah al-badīʿiyyah fī ʿulūm al-balāghah wa-maḥāsin al-badīʿ, ed. Naṣīb Nashāwī (Damascus: Majmaʿ al-Lughah al-ʿArabiyyah bi-Dimashq, 1982);

al-Natāʾij al-almaʿiyyah fī sharḥ al-kāfiyyah al-badīʿiyyah, ed. Rashīd ʿAbd al-Raḥmān al-ʿUbaydī (Amman: Dār al-Bashīr, 2000);

Sharḥ al-kāfiyyah al-badīʿiyyah, ed. Rashīd ʿAbd al-Raḥmān al-ʿUbaydī (Baghdad: Markaz al-Buḥūth wa ’l-Dirāsāt al-Islāmiyyah, 2004);

al-Natāʾij al-ilāhiyyah fī sharḥ al-kāfiyyah al-badīʿiyyah, ed. ʿImād Ḥasan Marzūq (Kafr al-Dawwār [Egypt]: Maktabal Bustān al-Maʿrifah, 2007);

Die vulgärarabische Poetik: al-Kitāb al-ʿĀṭil al-ḥālī wa ’l-muraḫḫaṣ al-ġālī des Ṣafiyaddīn Ḥillī, ed. Wilhelm Hoenerbach (Wiesbaden: Franz Steiner Verlag, 1956);

al-ʿĀṭil al-ḥālī wa ’l-murakhkhaṣ al-ghālī, ed. Ḥusayn Naṣṣār (Cairo: al-Hay’ah al-Miṣriyyah al-ʿĀmmah li ’l-Kitāb, 1981);

“al-Qaṣīdah al-Sāsāniyyah (Arabic Text and English Translation),” in Clifford E. Bosworth, *The Medieval Islamic Underworld,* vol. 2 (Leiden: E.J. Brill, 1976): 295-345 and 43-83 (Arabic).

Ṣafī ’l-Dīn al-Ḥillī was a poet who attained considerable fame in the century following the Mongol conquest that ended the Abbasid caliphate in 1258. His contemporary, the influential literary critic Khalīl ibn Aybak al-Ṣafadī (ca. 1297-1363)—who knew him personally—considered him, for example, “the greatest poet of the age” (p. 69). Even Ṣafī ’l-Dīn’s only rival for that title, the great Egyptian poet Muḥammad ibn Muḥammad Ibn al-Nubātah (1287-1366)—who also knew him personally—evinced the greatest respect for him and his works. This regard was reciprocated (Dīwān, ed. Ḥuwar, vol. 1, 504-505 and Bauer, “Ibn Nubātah,” 192). In the century following his death, Ṣafī ’l-Dīn’s several biographers devoted lengthy entries enumerating his achievements and the authors who followed him often imitated his works.

In particular, the genre of poetry Ṣafī ’l-Dīn could claim to have invented, the so-called *badīʿiyyah* poem, whose subject was praise of the Prophet Muḥammad (d. 632), every line containing at least one variety of rhetorical figure, was frequently emulated by later poets. For example, Taqī ’l-Dīn Abū Bakr ibn ʿAlī Ibn Ḥijjah al-Ḥamāwī’s (d. 1434) influential compendium of Arabic literature, *Khizānat al-adab*, was really a commentary on his own *badīʿiyyah*, in which he deliberately set out to surpass al-Ḥillī’s earlier example. This trend continued even into the nineteenth century. As time went on, however, the admiration for al-Ḥillī’s verse became somewhat less enthusiastic. A harbinger of this can be seen in the biographical notice accorded al-Ḥillī in Muḥammad ibn ʿAlī al-Shawkānī’s (1759-1839) influential biographical work, *al-Badr al-ṭāliʿ bi-maḥāsin man baʿd al-qarn al-sābiʿ*, which is quite short and cursory, basically summarizing Aḥmad ibn ʿAlī Ibn Ḥajar al-ʿAsqalānī’s (1372-1449) more fulsome notice produced in the century after al-Ḥillī’s death, while implicitly treating al-Ḥillī’s compositions as having little merit. This attitude of dismissal was continued by Maḥmūd Sāmī al-Bārūdī (1838-1904), the great poet and influential Egyptian literary figure of the nineteenth and early twentieth centuries, who chose not to include a single example from al-Ḥillī’s poetry in his four-volume anthology of great medieval Arab poets, *al-Mukhtārāt al-Bārūdī* (1901). Similarly, the first systematic historian of Arabic literature writing in the nineteenth century, Jirjī Zaydān (1861-1914), had little to say about al-Ḥillī in *Tārīkh ādāb al-lughah al-ʿarabiyyah* (History of Literature in the Arabic Language) (1911), and did not treat him as a particularly important figure.

Since the beginning of the twentieth century this trend has largely continued. Al-Ḥillī has generally been admired more for his versatility than for the originality or emotional impact of his verse. His reputation suffered because he embraced and promoted styles of poetry that have been devalued as omens of the decline in Arabic poetic productivity in the later Middle Ages. A most prominent example of this concentration on form at the expense of content for many modern critics has been the twenty-nine poems he wrote early in his career praising the Artūqid ruler of Mardīn, al-Manṣūr Najm al-Dīn Ghāzī (r. 1294-1312). Each of these poems is twenty-nine lines long and uses as its rhyme a different letter from the twenty-nine composing the Arabic alphabet (*Dīwān*, ed. Ḥuwar, vol. 3, 1447-1533). In addition, each line in the poem begins and ends with the same alphabetical letter. Or one could point to the line quoted with much admiration by al-Ṣafadī (pp. 82-83, *Dīwān*, ed. Ḥuwar, vol. 3, 1189-1190), in which the words composing every clause can be read identically backwards and forwards. Such verses, it should be noted, comprise extreme cases in al-Ḥillī's writings and do not reflect the majority of his works, which are much more conventional and straightforward. This intermittently playful attitude to the poetic art, nevertheless, did not endear al-Ḥillī to modern authors and critics, most of whom promoted Romantic or Modernist values of poetic creativity and expressiveness. For them, poetry could only be considered successful if it sincerely expressed the poet's authentic experience in a direct way and this left little room for appreciation of al-Ḥillī's aesthetic, oriented as it is toward exploring the intricacies and ambiguity of language. So Ṣafī 'l-Dīn was, for much of the twentieth century, appreciated less as a source of poetic inspiration for current writers than as an often highly useful resource for better understanding certain trends and developments in the writing of his time. Balanced against this elite characterization of al-Ḥillī's work as superficial and largely irrelevant, however, one can juxtapose the fact that one of al-Ḥillī's *ghazal* (love) lyrics was set to music in the nineteen forties by the premier Egyptian singer-composer of the day, Mohammed Abdel Wahab (c. 1907-1991), and became an enormous popular success.

ʿAbd al-ʿAzīz ibn Sarāyā ibn ʿAlī ibn Abī 'l-Qāsim ibn Aḥmad ibn Naṣr ibn Abī 'l-ʿIzz ibn Sarāyā ibn Baqī ibn ʿAbd Allāh ibn al-ʿArīd al-Sinbisī al-Ṭā'ī al-Ḥillī, surnamed Ṣafī 'l-Dīn, was born in the town of Ḥilla in west central Iraq on the Euphrates River, on 16 August 1278, twenty years after the fall of Baghdad to the Mongols. Ḥilla had escaped, in those two decades, the worst of the unsettled conditions that followed the Mongol advance into Iraq and remained prosperous, substantially enhancing its reputation as a center of learning (especially of nascent Shiism) it would seem, ultimately, at the expense of Baghdad (Bosworth, vol. 1, 132-133). Al-Ḥillī's own family was Shiite, although this orientation did not leave readily discernible traces on most of his work. As with many poets of his and the previous generation, al-Ḥillī's ʿAlid sympathies were seldom overtly expressed. This would seem all the more difficult to explain in al-Ḥillī's case, however, since Shiite scholarship flourished in his birthplace during most of the thirteenth century, as can be seen in the pioneering work on Shiite legal theory carried out by Najm al-Dīn Jaʿfar ibn Ḥasan ibn Yaḥyā (1205-1277), known to posterity as Muḥaqqiq al-Ḥillī. Najm al-Dīn's nephew, Jamāl al-Dīn al-Ḥasan ibn Yūsuf ibn ʿAlī ibn Muṭahhar (1250-1325), known as ʿAllāmah al-Ḥillī (the sage of Ḥilla continued this scholarly tradition composing an important commentary on Naṣīr al-Dīn al-Ṭūsī's manual on logic, and producing in his own right the important basic texts on Shiite theology. None of these, however, seem to have had any noticeable impact on Ṣafī al-Dīn's poetry or prose works.

Later in his career, at the behest of the Naqīb al-Ashraf (head of the ʿAlid community in Iraq at the time) Ṣafī al-Dīn did write a refutation of Ibn al-Muʿtazz's (862-908) poem glorifying the Abbasid dynasty (*Dīwān*, ed. Ḥuwar, vol. 1, 167-170), but such an openly Shiite work was quite unusual for him. In fact—perhaps to anticipate any criticism this work might arouse—al-Ḥillī, in his arrangement of his *Dīwān*, placed two short poems praising the Companions of the Prophet and the first two caliphs, Abū Bakr (d. 634) and ʿUmar ibn al-Khaṭṭāb (d. 644) (traditionally considered hostile to ʿAlī ibn Abī Ṭālib (ca. 600-660)) next to his poem refuting Ibn al-Muʿtazz.

More noticeable, especially in his early output, is al-Ḥillī's glorification of his family's Arabian tribal origin. Many of his earliest poems celebrate his kin's achievements and seek to rally them after setbacks, especially in their struggles against their local rivals, the Abū Faḍl clan. In this, al-Ḥillī's early poetry resembles that of the tenth-century champions of Sayf al-Dawlah al-Ḥamdānī (916-967) (ruler of Aleppo): the Arab traditionalist poets Abū Firās ibn Saʿīd ibn Aḥmad ibn Ḥamdān al-Ḥamdānī (932-968), cousin of the prince, and al-Mutanabbī (915-965), the most famous of medieval Arab poets, who was Sayf al-Dawlah's chief panegyrist for many years. Al-Ḥillī seems to have consciously invited comparison with the latter, especially, and resemblances between the verses of the poets have been frequently remarked (see list in Alwash, 165-167, and *Dīwān*, ed. Ḥuwar, vol. 1, 110-112 and 171-177).

We have little information—especially in relation to his contemporaries—about al-Ḥillī's education: what books he read or what teachers he studied with. It is clear that he must have read the Jāhiliyyah poets (a number of whom he quotes or contrafacts in his own verses), especially those contained in the famous anthology al-Ḥamāsah by the early Abbasid poet Abū Tammām (796 or 804-842/843 or 845/846), as well as later canonical authors like al-Mutanabbī or Ibn al-Muʿtazz. But it is equally clear that he cultivated an air of mystery about exactly when he had encountered any particular work or how much he knew about it. Thus, when he refers in passing to the ancient Greek philosopher Plato (*Dīwān*, ed. Ḥuwar, vol. 1, 215) or invokes the *Rasā'il* (Treatises) of the Neoplatonic Ikhwān al-Safā' (fl. late 10th-early 11th centuries) in his verse (*Dīwān*, ed. Ḥuwar, vol. 2, 975), we have no way of knowing how seriously to consider these references as indicative of his educational background. Likewise, when he speaks (*Dīwān*, ed. Ḥuwar, vol. 3, 1421) of the well-known epistolary manual *al-Mathal al-sā'ir fī adab al-kātib wa 'l-shā'ir* by Ḍiyā 'l-Dīn Naṣr Allāh ibn Muḥammad Ibn al-Athīr (1163-1239) or quotes Abū Tammām's *al-Ḥamāsah* in his poetry (*Dīwān*, ed. Ḥuwar, vol. 1, 25-27, 60-61, 79-85 and 447) we cannot necessarily infer that al-Ḥillī was taught using these works early in life, although they were commonly used for educational purposes at the time. He himself only tells us (in the rhymed prose introduction to his *Dīwān*) that he excelled at composing poetry from an early age, and later undertook more formal instruction in the art.

Similarly, while the thoroughness of al-Ḥillī's background in classical Arabic language and literature is evident from even the most cursory glance at his *Dīwān*, little can be inferred from his work about his acquaintance with the other languages or literary traditions of the region, especially Persian or Turkish. Few foreign words appear in his collected poems—with the exception of his *Qaṣīdah Sāsāniyyah* (*Dīwān*, ed. Ḥuwar, vol. 3, 1264-1273)—and those are mostly place names. There are no references to major authors or works outside Arabic literature. On the other hand, he grew up with the colloquial Arabic of Iraq, which even at this time, would have been extensively Persianized, and he would certainly have had exposure to everyday Turkish as well, especially during the years he spent at the court of the Artūqid rulers of Mardīn, who were of Turkoman heritage. This polyglot background, however, might explain his interest, especially later in life, in the colloquial literature of the area, which found expression in the *Qaṣīdah Sāsāniyyah* and in his guide to the history and composition of colloquial poetry, *al-'Āṭil al-ḥālī wa 'l-murakhkhaṣ al-ghālī fī 'l-azjāl wa 'l-mawālī* (The Unadorned Decorated and the Cheapened Rendered Costly Concerning Zajals and Mawwals), which contains examples of his own efforts in these genres.

We are on somewhat firmer evaluative ground when we examine his background in the study of the *Qur'ān*, and religious literature like Sharaf al-Dīn Muḥammad ibn Saʿīd al-Būṣīrī's (1213?-1296?) *Burdah* poem. Here the influences are extensive and deep-seated, to a degree that can only be the product of lengthy acquaintance. He devotes an entire section of his dīwān to devotional poems, which remind us that his *badī'iyyah* poem (based on al-Būsīrī's *Burdah*) was not his only foray into this field. A good example of the kind of religious poetry he would compose throughout his entire life is the following short set of verses he was reputed to have recited upon the conclusion of a visit to the Prophet Muḥammad's tomb—probably in 1323 (*Dīwān*, vol. 1, ed. Ḥuwar, 157):

To you, Prophet of right guidance, anyone who is a friend,
affiliating himself to your love, is led.
There he obtains the wage of his mission
and is purified of any terror he has acquired.
He resorts to you seeking intercession:
to God belong the things He has connection to.
Ask God to make a way out for him
and provide him from whence he does not reckon.

The last line is an adaptation of verses 1 and 2 of Sūrat al-Ṭalāq (65): "God will furnish a way out for him who fears Him, and provide for him from whence he does not reckon." This *Qur'ānic* quotation, stressing the importance of absolute reliance on God, is seamlessly integrated into the poem, and provides an explicit religious framework that can highlight and enhance the intensity of the spiritual emotion portrayed by al-Ḥillī here. That he can so effortlessly adapt *Qur'ānic* wording into his work testifies to a great familiarity with the *Qur'ānic* text and turns of phrase that could only come through the process of an extensive and rigorous training begun, most likely, early in al-Ḥillī's life.

This pious streak in Hilli's work, however, contrasts with many of his later poems, which emphasize the enjoyment of extramarital love and wine, a subject matter expected from the ruler's nadīm, or boon companion, a role often filled by al-Ḥillī in the course of his career. A good example of this kind of work would be the following poem (*Dīwān*, ed. Ḥuwar, vol. 2, 719) that was adapted and sung by the renowned Egyptian recording artist Abdel Wahab in the mid-twentieth century, becoming a permanent and highly regarded part of his repertoire:

She said: "You have shadowed your eyelids with slumber."
I said: "As a result of wakeful waiting for your beautiful phantom."
She said: "You have sought to amuse yourself with diversions after our separation."
I said: "Abandoning my place of rest and peace of mind."
She said: "You have busied yourself with things other than our love."
I said: "With an excess of weeping and sadness."
She said: "You act as though you have forgotten." I said: "Give me strength!"
She said: "You have kept your distance." I said: "From my homeland."
She said: "You have absented yourself." I said: "Abandoning my ability to endure."
She said: "You have changed." I said: "[Only] in my body."
She said: "You have devoted yourself to everything but our friendship."
I said: "Weak and wayward where you are concerned."
She said: "You have divulged our secrets." I said to her:
"Passion for you has made my secret public knowledge."
She said: "You have given gladness to our enemies." I said to her:
"That is something, had you wished, would never have happened."
She said: "What do you want?" I said to her:
"A lucky hour spent trysting [with you] is all I need."
She said: "The spy's eye is watching us."
I said: "The [evil] eye is never far from me.
Your aversion to me has made me weak and thin, and
if death were not lying in wait for me, you would never have been able to see me."

The appropriateness of the recitation of this charming dialogue at an informal courtly gathering or feast, and the enthusiastic reception it would have received, can well be imagined. It is, however, not simply a spontaneous utterance, but deeply rooted in the literary tradition of Arabic ghazal, or love poetry, being an adaptation (using much of the same vocabulary and imagery) of an earlier lyric composed by al-Mutanabbī (*Sharh Dīwān al-Mutanabbī*, vol. 4, 317-319) where that poet describes himself as a long-suffering lover, the dying victim of a cruel, indifferent (and silent) beloved . In conclusion al-Mutanabbī describes himself as "a man [whose] body has been starved away: if it were not for the fact that I am speaking to you now, you would never have been able to see me." But the bite of al-Ḥillī's lyric depends not so much on any ingenious description of the encounter, or the participants, as on the dialogue between the lover and beloved with its unrelenting focus on the contest between them over who has suffered more as a result of their passion. Each time, the lover is able to deflate the beloved's verbose sallies with a brief well chosen reply that ultimately, however, takes a more serious turn as the lover acknowledges the imminence of his death.

This poem illustrates well the avoidance of overt sensuality or eroticism that is characteristic of much of Ṣafī 'l-Dīn's *ghazal* (as opposed to his wine (*khamriyyah*) or libertine (*mujūn*) poetry, which can be much more explicit). Instead, al-Ḥillī seems to be more intent on establishing a psychology of the lover (and beloved) that often devolves into the construction of a hierarchical framework suitable for examining the nuances of interchange (referencing the Islamized versions of Neoplatonism so much in fashion at the time) between the emotional vagaries of desire, which is depicted as transient and largely unproductive, vs. true love or lasting passion, which can take the lover to the heights of emotional self-awareness and, in contemplation of the beauty of the beloved, allow him to access a dynamic and enduring education in things either spiritual or philosophical or both. A fully realized example of this latter kind of *ghazal*, complex and almost drily theoretical in its construction, can be found in the following lines (*Dīwān*, ed. Ḥuwar, vol. 2, 708):

My two companions, how ignorant are those who go to extremes in passion,
and how little they know of the beauty found in every truly witty person!
They think that beauty can be grasped by the eye,
and that the secret nature of passion can be made apparent in a flash of lightning.
The aspirations of those who look will not be fulfilled at the time of seeing,
if the gaze of the heart does not know how to yearn.
Neither Jamīl, nor Kuthayyir, nor ʿUrwah the ʿUdhrī,
nor Ibn Dharīh, in their passion,
Were more knowledgeable than I in scrutinizing elegance,
and they did not incline to love, in even a small way, as I do.
Any intelligent person whose intelligence has been taken prisoner by beauty
will spend the night with a heart ulcerated by passion.
But if a true heart is [depicted as] free of passion,
then I am sure that the intellect [concerned] is not sound.

Here the complex interplay between "passion" (represented by the sensual quest for a sight of the beloved) and the more elevating perspective delivered by the experience of true "love" definitely suggests al-Ḥillī at some point in his youth received a thorough exposure to some form of philosophical thought (almost certainly influenced by Neoplatonism), a hypothesis that is supported by references in his poetry (*Dīwān*, ed. Ḥuwar, vol. 2, 975) to the *Rasā'il* (Treatises) of the *Ikhwān al-Safā'* (Brethren of Purity), works that are recognized as incorporating many Neoplatonic doctrines, as well as to individual philosophers from the Islamic tradition, like Ibn Sīnā (*Dīwān*, ed. Ḥuwar, vol. 3, 1417). The poem also indicates a thorough familiarity with the indigenous early Arabic love tradition (ʿUdhrī love)—that also stressed the spirituality and eternity of love—by mentioning its most important practitioners, the early Umayyad love poets Jamīl ibn ʿAbd Allāh al-ʿUdhrī (d. 701), Kuthayyir ʿAzzah ibn ʿAbd al-Raḥmān (d. 723), ʿUrwah (d. c. 650) and Qays ibn Dhāriḥ (d. 688). Thus, it should not be surprising, given the sophistication illustrated by the foregoing examples of al-Ḥillī's love poetry, to find that the poem recorded as the earliest product of his talent (*Dīwan*, ed. Ḥuwar, vol. 2, 809) is a *ghazal* poem, or that when the famous scholar

Muḥammad ibn Yaʿqūb al-Firūzābādī (1329-1415-16) meets al-Ḥillī late in the latter's life, during a stop in Baghdad; he contrasts the unkempt old man he encounters with the vision he had long nurtured of the author of those "*ghazal* more delicate than the breeze and more elegant than the most handsome countenance" and can scarcely believe that the disheveled individual standing before him "was the one who had composed those poems like pearls in the shell." Firūzabādī's description (passed on by other literary scholars like Ibn Ḥajar al-ʿAsqalānī (1372-1449)) suggests that, for his contemporaries at least, a large part of al-Ḥillī's genius lay in the *ghazal* he produced, perhaps even more than in the other genres he cultivated.

Whatever the nature of al-Ḥillī's youthful pursuits, and however much they did or did not incorporate the contemplative life or the enjoyment of worldly pleasures, they were rather abruptly interrupted in the year 1300 (when the poet was about eighteen). His maternal uncle, Ṣafī ’l-Dīn ibn Maḥāsin, was treacherously killed by members of the Abū Faḍl clan. At this point, al-Ḥillī, either fleeing Ḥilla in search of support for vengeance on behalf of his kinsman, or to avoid retribution for participating in revenge already carried out against the Abū Faḍl, deliberately sought aid from his family's traditional allies and overlords, the Artūqid dynasty reigning in the city of Mardīn, located in the northern Kurdish highland area of Iraqi Jazīrah (today within the southern boundaries of modern Turkey). That the ruling sultan, al-Manṣūr Najm al-Dīn Ghāzī, offered the young Ṣafī ’l-Dīn welcome hospitality and did receive his petition favorably can be seen in the verses al-Ḥillī sent to his kinfolk, via messenger, shortly after his arrival (*Dīwān*, ed. Ḥuwar, vol. 1, 239):

Please inform—once you have been led aright—the leader of my people
at Ḥilla in Bābil [province], upon arriving,
"Do not be vexed in your heart on account of how far away I am
for I am every day in abundance,
Because I have alighted in the sanctuary of kings,
in the pastures of their servants, in the refugee's cave.
Who would be the person to alight in the refuge of Kulayb,
when he could come, as I have, to the refuge of lions?

Despite the simplicity of its message and its lack of artistic pretension, it is interesting to see that al-Ḥillī cannot resist an allusion in the poem that is further evidence of the thoroughness and traditionalism of his literary education. Kulayb was a noted Preislamic tribal chieftain whose murder precipitated the War of Basūs, a tribal conflict that persisted for decades prior to the rise of Islam and inspired a considerable number of works by famous poets from this ancient period. Kulayb received his nickname (which means "little dog") for behavior that contradicted the norms of hospitality expected from leaders of the Bedouin tribes. If he found a location which he wanted to enjoy for himself, undisturbed, he would bring a defenseless young dog there and beat it until it howled and yelped in pain, thus frightening away (because of the ill-omened sound) anyone who might be tempted to go there. Al-Ḥillī contrasts, by introducing the reference to Kulayb, the place he has left (his hometown of Ḥilla), which—presumably because of the presence of the Abū Faḍl—would be like the "refuge of Kulayb" (where no one is welcome), with his new place of residence, Mardīn, inhabited by noble king-like lions (or, more prosaically, noble lion-like kings) who have given him refuge and will protect him from any intruders.

The time he spent in Mardīn at the court of the Artūqids seems, at least temporarily, to have given al-Ḥillī the opportunity to develop and hone his poetic talent in way he had not been able to do before. One important artifact from this period (or shortly before), which in many ways looks back to the tribal past he had abandoned when he had left Hilla, is the *fakhr* (boasting) poem that produced the single most memorable line from al-Ḥillī's entire body of work. This poem (*Dīwān*, ed. Ḥuwar, vol. 1, 51-54), composed to commemorate the success of the revenge taken by al-Ḥillī's kin against the Abū Faḍl, celebrates the might and determination of Ṣafī 'l-Dīn's family, and their ability to defend themselves against any outside attack:

Ask the spear hafts about our noble deeds
and demand to see the white [swords]: would hope miscarry among us?
And ask the Arabs and the Turks: What have their hands done
in the land where the grave of ʿUbayd Allāh [Ṣafī 'l-Dīn's maternal uncle] lies?
We have striven long and our determination has not wavered
with respect to our desires, and our efforts have never yet miscarried.

Many of the lines of this poem (such as the ones quoted above) can easily be married with the modern rhetoric of self-reliant nationalism, and it should probably be in this context that the enduring popularity of the following line (the twentieth of the poem) can best be understood:

White are our deeds, black are our battles,
green are our meadows, and red are our swords.

It had not been common for Arab poets, up to this point in time, to rely to any extent on complex color symbolism, and this is surely part of the reason for the impact this line has had on its readers. It also, however, does make effective use of a chain of metaphoric comparisons with gradually heightened intensity, a far more common strategy found among medieval Arab poets. This results in a perception of balance and fulfillment, as the four comparisons are enumerated and completed, but also of controlled tension, as the reader moves from the purity and impersonal calm of white deeds to the more active and stridently dynamic association between red (blood) and swords (the instrument of violence). The effect is heightened even more for the modern reader since the four colors themselves are now firmly associated in the popular imagination with the ceremonial colors of four dynasties that have successfully ruled the Arab world in the past: green was a color with historic ties to the Prophet Muḥammad and his descendents and thus to Islam itself, white was a color frequently used ceremonially by the Umayyads, black was the color of the battle flags of their rivals the Abbasids, and red the dynastic symbol of the Nasrids of Granada and their palace the Alhambra ("the red one" in Arabic). Al-Ḥillī's line marks the first instance when all four colors were brought together, in such symbolically charged fashion, in Arabic literature.

If the poem just quoted recalls the world of al-Ḥillī's youth and his tribal ancestry, the other major milestone of this period looks much more to Ṣafī 'l-Dīn's future as a sophisticated court poet. This is the group of twenty-nine poems known collectively as *Durar al-nuḥūr fī madā'ih al-Malik al-Manṣūr* (The Pearls on the Necks in Praise of King al-Manṣūr). The intricate alphabetical structure they follow was detailed at the beginning of this article. Internal references to this set of poems in a panegyric (*Dīwān*, ed. Ḥuwar, vol. 1, 193) al-Ḥillī also produced in this period to honor his patron indicate that the whole group was finished and presented fairly early during Ṣafī 'l-Dīn's residence in Mardīn. Thematically, the poems are quite conventional. They all contain the three themes traditional to the Arabic *qaṣīdah* form: *naṣīb* (depiction of a past love affair), *raḥīl* (description of a journey through the desert), and *madīḥ* (panegyric) that al-Ḥillī's audience would have expected. No treatment that al-Ḥillī includes of these themes cannot be found dozens of times over in the work of his predecessors. The poet shows his mastery of his art, rather, in his ability to search out appropriate rhyme words ending in the same alphabetical letter for twenty-nine lines, each time a different letter of the alphabet. As some letters of Arabic alphabet are considerably less common than others, this is a difficult task. Al-Ḥillī, nevertheless, carries it off with aplomb, thus indicating that he is no novice in the field of poetic composition.

Al-Ḥillī's other panegyrics for al-Manṣūr—while exhibiting considerable skill in structure and presentation of themes—are as conventional in content as his *Durar al-nuḥūr*. The following excerpt from the middle of the first such poem gives a good idea of their style (*Dīwān*, ed. Ḥuwar, vol. 1, 191):

A sky of glory has appeared there, embellished by a star
around which the stars on the horizon fall down.
He is a king for whom generosity has become part of his fingers,
and were he to try to force himself to abandon that generosity, he would not be able to,
He has returned the nights of destruction as morning, and how often his steeds
have run [so fast] they have shown us that the morning is like the dusk.
He scatters determination about him, along with his wealth,
his hands have not left any place for wealth to gather except at the point of dispersal.

To praise one's patron for his bravery, or his generosity and wealth, or to compare him in his nobility to a star in the sky, are all motifs common to many Arabic panegyric poems. Even the faint *Qur'ānic* echo of the story of Joseph (*Ṣūrah* 12), activated by the reference in the first line to the stars on the periphery of the heavens falling down in homage to the central one (as the stars bowed down in Joseph's dream) could hardly be considered particularly unconventional or daring in the context.

The other panegyrics al-Ḥillī produced during this period can be similarly seen to celebrate a successful weaving together of conventions into a seamless tapestry, designed to give greater support to the often shaky authority of the ruler, than an attempt to strike out on new ground. The closest we see to nonconformity in al-Ḥillī's compositions from this period is to be found in form rather than content: a handful of the panegyrics to al-Manṣūr are in *muwashshahah* (strophic) form, a new kind of structure that had only recently been introduced from Andalus (Muslim Spain). There, however, the muwashshahah had long been a staple of panegyric as well as lyric poetry, so it is not particularly noteworthy that al-Ḥillī used the form in such a way.

The few specimens of al-Ḥillī's prose that have been preserved from this period also show a preoccupation with issues that bear on the assimilation of conventional discourse and how it can be re-ordered (and thus reinterpreted) for a new generation of sophisticated literary connoisseurs. The first chronologically, *al-Risālah al-taw'amiyyah* (The Twinned Epistle), was produced at the beginning of his sojourn in Mardīn at the court of al-Manṣūr (*Dīwān*, n.e (1879), 513-15). According to the story that accompanies the text of the risālah, those present at a gathering in the palace of al-Manṣūr were discussing a poem by the great Arabic literary stylist of the twelfth century, Abū Muḥammad al-Ḥarīrī (1054-1122), who was famous for using word pairs with the same letter shapes but conveying different meanings through changes in the vocalization of the consonants or in the diacritical points placed on the letters. The assembled group expresses the opinion that no contemporary writer could equal al-Harīrī's masterstroke. Al-Ḥillī, who is present at the gathering (*majlis*) for the first time, takes up the challenge and produces *al-Taw'amiyyah*, a prose work of just a little over two pages that rigorously follows al-Ḥarīrī's example, and in addition, contains three short poems, all entirely made up of word pairs with the same skeletal consonantal structure conveying different meanings. The second risālah, *Ḥall al-manẓūm* (Prosification of a Verse Composition), presents a similar intellectual tour de force, this time using as its proof text the first seven lines of the "*Mu'allaqah*" of Imruʾ al-Qays, a touchstone of Preislamic poetry. Those present are asked to produce a prose composition using all the letters in the seven lines of poetry, and then to reassemble the letters in a new poem that echoes, but does not duplicate in any way, Imruʾ al-Qays' original work. Al-Ḥillī also succeeds in this task, thus showing himself adept at re-working an item from the canon into something new.

Although his relationship with al-Manṣūr remained cordial, as the first decade of the fourteenth century turned into the second, Ṣafī 'l-Dīn began gradually to strike out farther and farther from Mardīn in a series of journeys that combined mercantile pursuits with increasingly lengthy stays at other courts in the principalities that dotted the region. As early as 1302, al-Ḥillī visited Mosul and Karbala, and possibly also went to Mecca on pilgrimage. In 1312, when al-Manṣūr suddenly died, al-Ḥillī was in Baghdad and had to return to Mardīn for the funeral, missing the actual ceremony.

The close relationship that Ṣafī ’l-Dīn had cultivated with al-Manṣūr would, however, continue with the latter’s son and heir, Shams al-Dīn al-Ṣāliḥ, and last throughout the rest of al-Ḥillī’s life. Al-Ḥillī even felt free to criticize his overlord on occasion, as he did in *Risālat al-dār fī muhāwarāt al-fār* (*Dīwān*, n.e (1879), 484-91). This long *risālah*—more like a *maqāmah* by al-Ḥarīrī or Badīʿ al-Zamān Aḥmad ibn al-Ḥusayn al-Hamadhānī (circa 358/969–398/1008) than an essay—depicts a dialogue between the mice who live in al-Ḥillī’s house, next door to the citadel of al-Ṣāliḥ. In it, the mice complain of the stinginess of their neighbor, whose agent has refused to give their master enough money to keep sufficient food stocked in his house. Presumably, al-Ṣāliḥ remedied the situation, and al-Ḥillī resumed his stipend. In 1320, though, we find al-Ḥillī in Syria, perhaps his first visit to courts (in Damascus and Hama) that he would frequent more often as he aged.

By far the most important of the many journeys in these decades, however, was the one al-Ḥillī undertook in 1322, when he made a second pilgrimage to Mecca and eventually continued on to Cairo, the seat of the most powerful ruler of the age, the Mamlūk al-Nāṣir ibn Muḥammad ibn Qalāwūn (1285-1341). Al-Nāṣir had been sultan since 1294, but his rule had at first been precarious and he had twice been briefly deposed. He had come to the throne for the third time in 1309 and this time had assembled a court of capable administrators (*kuttāb*) and scholars, whose brilliance rivaled that of his fabled predecessor, Ṣalāḥ al-Dīn (r. 1171-1193). They included ʿAlā’ al-Dīn ibn Athīr (1281-1329), the Sultān’s confidential secretary, Shams al-Dīn ʿAbd al-Laṭīf (d. November 1330), a philosopher, historian and favorite of the Sultan, Ṣalāḥ al-Dīn Khalīl ibn Aybak al-Ṣafadī (ca. 1297-1363), the historian and scholar of Arabic literature, who produced one the most famous biographical works of the age, *A'yān al-'aṣr wa-a'wān al-naṣr* (The Important Persons of the Age), where Ṣafī ’l-Dīn was afforded a prominent place, and the poet Ibn al-Nubātah (1287-1366). All of these influential intellectuals developed close ties with al-Ḥillī and helped facilitate his entry into the world of the Mamlūk court. It is unclear exactly which of them was responsible, but one of the group introduced al-Ḥillī to al-Nāṣir Muḥammad himself, and the poet subsequently addressed several major panegyrics to him. Most notable of these was the first, a sixty-one line poem that contrafacts (uses the same rhyme and meter as) an early praise poem by al-Mutanabbī (*Sharḥ Dīwān al-Mutanabbī*, vol. 1, 250-60), addressed to an otherwise unknown ʿAlī ibn Manṣūr “the Chamberlain.” Al-Mutanabbī received only a single *dīnār* for his work, and the poem was subsequently called for this reason “*al-Dīnāriyyah.*” Al-Ḥillī undoubtedly sought here to out-do his predecessor and net a more substantial reward. We do not know how well he succeeded. But he went on to compose another poem (*Dīwān*, ed. Ḥuwar, vol. 1, 178-183) shortly thereafter, celebrating the annual ceremony where the breakwater containing the flooding Nile was broken and the water was allowed to inundate the area surrounding the city, which suggests that his initial efforts were not entirely ignored.

It was at this time certainly, and at the suggestion of al-Nāṣir Muḥammad himself, that al-Ḥillī first collected his poems into a Dīwān, arranging them in an unusual order with twelve chapters, each with number of different subheadings. They main divisions, in order, are: 1) “*fī ’l-fakhr wa ’l-ḥamāsah wa ’l-taḥrīḍ 'alā ’l-riyāsah*” (On self-praise, bravery and incitement to leadership); 2) “*fī ’l-madḥ wa ’l-thanā' wa ’l-shukr wa ’l-hanā'*” (On praise, commendation, thanks, and congratulation); 3) “*fī ’l-tardīyāt wa-anwā' al-sifāt*” (On hunting and various descriptive occasions); 4) “*fī ’l-ikhwānīyāt wa-ṣudūr al-murāsalāt*” (On friendship and poems prefaced to correspondence); 5) “*fī marāthī ’l-a'yān wa-ta'āzī ’l-ikhwān*” (On elegies for notable people and condolences for friends); 6) “*fī ’l-ghazal wa ’l-nasīb wa-tarā'if al-tashbīb*” (On love and remembrance of past amours, and exquisite examples of poems celebrating women); 7) "*fī 'l-khamrīyāt wa 'l-nubadh al-zahrīyāt*" (On wine poetry and choice selections of flower poetry); 8) "*fī 'l-shakwā wa 'l-'itāb wa-taqāḍī 'l-wa'd wa 'l-jawāb*" (On complaint, reproof, demand for fulfillment of a promise, and reply); 9) "*fī 'l-hadāyā wa 'l-i'tidhār wa 'l-isti'tāf wa 'l-istighfār*" (On poems for gifts, apologies, entreaties, and requests for forgiveness); 10) "*fī 'l-'awīs wa 'l-alghāz wa 'l-taqyīd bi 'l-i'jāz*" (On obscurities, riddles, and mnemonics); 11) "*fī 'l-mulaḥ wa 'l-ahājī wa 'l-iḥmād fī 'l-tanājī*" (On witticisms, lampoons and joking remarks about clandestine rendezvous); and 12) "*fī 'l-adab wa 'l-zuhdīyāt wa-nawādir mukhtalifāt*" (On didactics, renunciation of the world, and various oddities). To these chapters are appended the twenty-nine poems known as *Durar al-nuḥūr fī madā'ih al-Malik al-Manṣūr* and the one hundred forty-five line *qaṣīdah badī'iyyah* in praise of the Prophet Muḥammad. In all modern versions of the *Dīwān* (though not the manuscripts), the third section of Chapter 11, which really contains al-Ḥillī's *mujūn* (licentious) poetry, is omitted. Only in the first printing of the *Dīwān* (in Damascus in 1879-1883) is the section retained, though even here, it is removed from its place and relegated to an appendix at the end of the book.

There is no evidence of any overt rift occurring between al-Ḥillī and his new-found friends at court or with the Sultan. The last of the *rasā'il* preserved in the first edition of al-Ḥillī's *Dīwān* (n.e (1879), 511-513), *al-Risālah al-Muhmalah* (The Undotted Letter) does suggest, however, that something went amiss. Al-Ḥillī, in typically elegant fashion (every word in the essay is undotted), complains that one of the Sultan's agents has intercepted a gift that was destined for al-Ḥillī, who has yet to receive it. There is no record that he ever did.

What can definitely be said, however, is that Ṣafī 'l-Dīn left Egypt not too long after his arrival and returned to Iraq (though he may have come back to Egypt again as early as 1326). His pilgrimage to Mecca and his subsequent stay in Egypt, though, almost certainly paved the way for what was to become al-Ḥillī's most enduring and influential poem: the *badī'iyyah*, formally titled *al-Kāfiyyah al-badī'iyyah fī 'l-madā'ih al-Nabawiyyah* (The Complete Rhetorical Compendium in Praising the Prophet). From internal evidence, one should not conclude that the *Badī'iyyah* poem was composed during al-Ḥillī's time in Egypt, but it is unlikely that the one could have occurred without the other, which argues that the most probable date of composition was after Ṣafī 'l-Dīn left the Mamluk court.

When al-Ḥillī visited Egypt, Sharaf al-Dīn Muḥammad ibn Saʿīd al-Būṣīrī (1213?-1296?), the best known poet Egypt had produced in the last century, had been dead for less than thirty years. Undoubtedly, the impact of al-Būsīrī's poem praising the Prophet Muḥammad, the *Burdah* poem, was still fresh and strong in people's minds. Al-Būsīrī had widened the emphasis in Islamic religious poetry from a concentration on examining the poet's relationship with God (an attitude adopted by most early Sufi mystical poets)—an often difficult and ambiguous proposition, though always a tantalizing one—to an exploration in depth of the individual believer's relationship with the Prophet Muḥammad, a fellow human seeker (albeit an exemplary, or even infallible, one) on the road to spiritual understanding. So it should perhaps not be unexpected that al-Ḥillī, as someone with a reputation as a wordsmith unequaled in his age, should go one step further and combine al-Būsīrī's spiritual insight with his own aesthetic ideal of exploring the intricacies of language (and, after all, religious knowledge in the Islamic tradition was preeminently gained through the medium of words). Thus the *badī'iyyah* poem was born. Eventually, no less than thirty-five later authors (including some Christian Arabs) have been recorded as producing *badī'iyyah* poems modeled on al-Ḥillī's (Cachia, "*Badī'iyyāt,*" 124 and Ḥuwar, 67).

Al-Ḥillī undoubtedly intended that his own *badī'iyyah* should be seen as an extension of al-Būsīrī's *Burdah* (Stetkevych, 220). *Al-Kāfiyyah al-badī'iyyah* is in the same rhyme and meter as the earlier poem, is very nearly the same length, and uses allusions and imagery (especially at the beginning) that evocatively recall al-Būsīrī's work. Yet there are also significant differences. There is less narrative emphasis, more focus on the role of the Prophet as an intercessor and, of course, the imperative to include an order array of rhetorical devices (explicitly labeled as such with a label appended before each line), beginning with the *tajnīs* (paronomasia) that appears to be al-Ḥillī's favorite figure. All of this creates a more formal, and therefore more distancing, tone in the poem than al-Būṣīrī's.

This foray by al-Ḥillī, notable as it is, into the religious sphere cannot be seen as heralding a lasting change in the orientation of his literary focus. Once he settled again in Iraq and Syria, he adopted the same pattern of moving about from one small court to another, never staying in one place for long. He spent more time in Syria than before his Egyptian visit, most notably in Ḥāma, where he developed a close relationship with its ruler al-Mu'ayyad Ismāʿīl (a vassal of Egypt), and his son al-Afḍal. He does not abandon the Artūqids in Mardīn, but when al-Muʿayyad dies in 1332, al-Ḥillī composes a moving elegy (*Dīwān*, ed. Ḥuwar, vol. 2, 631-632) for him, contrafacting the Andalusian poet Aḥmad ibn ʿAbd Allāh Ibn Zaydūn (ca. 1003-May 1071)'s nūniyyah, which had celebrated his longstanding love for the Cordovan princess Wallādah. This elegy, unlike some of al-Ḥillī's other works in this genre, exhibits a real depth of feeling.

Sometime in the last two decades of his life, al-Ḥillī begins to spend longer and longer periods of his time in Baghdad, so it would not be inappropriate to locate his works that are more concerned with colloquial language and the life of the common people to this period. This supposition is supported by internal references in the works themselves. For example, the oldest manuscript of his exhaustive scholarly study of the four colloquial genres of poetry commonly found in the Arab East at this time (*zajal*, *mawwāl*, *kān wa-kān,* and *qūmā*), *al-'Āṭil al-ḥālī wa 'l-murakhkhaṣ al-ghālī* (The Unadorned Bejeweled and the Cheapened Given Value) was copied in Baghdad, 27 Ramadan 747/1346-1347, during the poet's lifetime. There are also considerable references in this work to other kinds of colloquial poetry found in Iraq before the dissemination of these types, and discussions of how Iraqis had adapted the importations from elsewhere into their own milieu (*al-'Āṭil*, 7 and 12 [Arabic text]).

Most of the book, however, is focused on the zajal, which reflects al-Ḥillī's interest in this genre and his admiration for its foremost practitioner, the Andalusian Abū Bakr ibn ʿAbd al-Malik Ibn Quzmān (1078 or 1080-1160). Al-Ḥillī tells us that he used to compose *azjāl* "in his youth" (*al-'Āṭil*, 99 [Arabic text]). But his interest in learning more about the form seems to have been piqued when he visited Cairo. There, he apprenticed himself to a teacher of *zajal* technique, but he did more than that. He obtained a collection of *azjāl*, containing poems by Ibn Quzmān, his successor Mudghalīs, and various other authors (*al-'Āṭil*, 97 [Arabic text]). But it was copied in the Maghribī script, and al-Ḥillī had great difficulty reading the poems. When he returned from Cairo, he was able to find in Aleppo a master copyist and connoisseur of the *zajal* form, Taqī al-Dīn Ibrāhīm Ibn al-Darīr, who was able to help him with problems in the manuscript and, along with his friends, answer many of al-Ḥillī's questions about the history of the genre and the rules pertaining to its composition in Syria and Iraq at the time (*al-'Āṭil*, 97-98 [Arabic text]). It is probably to these sources that al-Ḥillī owes much of the information contained in his book.

Al-Ḥillī is well acquainted with the issues about *zajal* composition raised by Ibn Quzmān in the introduction to his *Dīwān*, and he quotes from it (*al-'Āṭil*, 12-13 and 16 [Arabic text]). He agrees with many of the principles Ibn Quzmān elucidates, but he is more flexible as concerns admitting words that include case endings (*i'rāb*). Much of his discussion focuses on the proper and improper uses of contractions and additions to words found in the colloquial, but he does address the issue of meter at several points in the text (most notably *al-'Āṭil*, 26 and 52-55 [Arabic text]), where he acknowledges that irregular meters and even rhythms unknown to the traditional Khalilian system are found regularly in *azjāl*. But his judgment ultimately relates to the issue of performance, which he seems to believe has a decisive influence on how the rhythm of the poem is perceived. He illustrates the application of his rules with extensive quotation from earlier *zajal* poets, as well as his own compositions.

The sections on the other types of colloquial composition are much more cursory and tentative. Al-Ḥillī, however, gives us more samples of his own poetry in these sections than he does in the zajal section. The subject matter covered seems to be as varied (from formal panegyrics to wine poems and love lyrics) as in his *Dīwān* of formal poetry, and it is clear that to completely assess his body of work, it would not be possible to omit or neglect al-Ḥillī's colloquial poetry.

Similarly, no assessment of al-Ḥillī's literary career would be complete without some mention of the poem now known as the *Qaṣīdah Sāsāniyyah* (Beggars' Poem). It may have been written at any time in al-Ḥillī's career and at any place, but its context suggests Baghdad more than Damascus or Cairo. Its origins are very mysterious, even for Hillī's poetry. In the oldest manuscripts of the *Dīwān* (ed. Ḥuwar, vol. 3, 1264) the poem is prefaced simply with the statement that the poem was composed at the behest "of a friend of his, who had asked him to gather together [an account of] the language, the arts and the stratagems used by vagabonds (*ghurabā'*) in their daily life, and attribute it to him so that he could ingratiate himself with some of them, for some purpose he had." In the earliest published version of the Dīwān a further preface has been added, in rhymed prose (*saj'*), which would seem to indicate that the poem dates from the end of al-Ḥillī's life, when he "had let loose the reins of [his] travels" (*Dīwān*, n.e (1879), 444). But the authenticity of this preface would seem to be questionable and needs further investigation.

The poem was translated in its entirety in a critical edition by Clifford Edmund Bosworth in his book *The Medieval Islamic Underworld*, an introduction to the literature about popular culture in the period between the tenth and fourteenth centuries that has been widely, and justly, lauded by scholars ever since it was published in 1976. But Ibrāhīm Ḥuwar's rendering of the poem (which differs substantially from Bosworth's at some points), and additional research that has been conducted by other scholars on the period since the publication of Bosworth's study, would undoubtedly shed important new light on the literary and social context of the poem. Certainly, even within the context of Ṣafī 'l-Dīn's own poetry, additional study would be helpful that could provide a more overarching framework for interpreting his work, one that could comfortably accommodate under one umbrella the aesthetic principles guiding the composition of religious verse like the *Qaṣīdah Badī'iyyah* and its polar opposite the *Qaṣīdah Sāsāniyyah*, which is nothing if not skeptical toward the practices enshrined by popular piety. In the meantime, one can only stress the importance of Ṣafī 'l-Dīn al-Ḥillī as a transitional figure in the development of Arabic literature, and emphasize how well his work illustrates the popular Arabic saying: "*li-kulli maqām maqāl*" (every situation has its [appropriate] way of speaking).

Ṣafī 'l-Dīn al-Ḥillī died in Baghdad, in obscure circumstances, sometime around 1350. His medieval biographers differ by as much as five years about his death date. Certainly, the epidemic of plague that struck Baghdad in 1348-1349 (Bauer, "Ibn al-Nubātah," 198) could easily have carried the old man away. Or he may have survived as late as 1352 (Ṣafadī, 70, Ibn Ḥajar al-ʿAsqalānī (1372-1449) and Bosworth, vol. 1, 138, n. 26).

REFERENCES

Abū 'l-Ṭayyib al-Mutanabbī, *Sharḥ Dīwān al-Mutanabbī*, ed. ʿAbd al-Raḥmān al-Barqūqī, 4 vols. (Cairo: al-Maktabah al-Tijāriyyah al-Kubrā [196-?]);

Jawād Aḥmad ʿAlwash, *Shi'r Ṣafī 'l-Dīn al-Ḥillī* (Baghdad: Maṭbaʿat al-Maʿārif, 1959);

Thomas Bauer, "Mamluk Literature: Misunderstandings and New Approaches," *Mamluk Studies Review*, 9:2 (2005): 105-132;

Thomas Bauer, "Jamāl al-Dīn Ibn Nubātah," in *Essays in Arabic Literary Biography: 1350-1850*, ed. Joseph E. Lowry and Devin J. Stewart (Wiesbaden: Harrassowitz Verlag, 2009), 184-202;

Clifford Edmund Bosworth, *The Medieval Islamic Underworld*, vol. 1 (Leiden: E.J. Brill, 1976);

Pierre Cachia, “Badīʿiyyāt,” *Encyclopedia of Arabic Literature*, ed. Julie Scott Meisami and Paul Starkey (London: Routledge, 1998);

Pierre Cachia, “From Sound to Echo in Late Badīʿ Literature,” *Journal of the American Oriental Society*, 108:2 (April-June 1988): 219-225;

Ibrāhīm Ḥuwar, *Ṣafī ’l-Dīn al-Ḥillī: hayātuh wa-āthāruh wa-shi'ruh* (Damascus: Dār al-Fikr al-Muʿāṣir, 1990);

Ibn Ḥajar al-ʿAsqalānī, “Ṣafī al-Dīn al-Ḥillī,” in *al-Durar al-kāminah fī a'yān al-mi'ah al-thāminah*, ed. ʿAbd al-Wahhāb al-Bukhārī, vol. 3 (Hyderabad: Da’irat al-Maʿārif al-ʿUthmaniyyah, 1972), 65-168;

Wolfhart Heinrichs, “Ṣafī al-Dīn ʿAbd al-ʿAzīz b. Sharāyā al-Ḥillī al-Ta’ī al-Sinbisī,” *Encyclopedia of Islam*, Second Edition, ed. by P. Bearman, Th. Bianquis, C.E. Bosworth, E. van Donzel, and W.P. Heinrichs (Leiden: E.J. Brill,);

Salma Khadra Jayyusi, “Arabic Poetry in the Post-Classical Age,” in *Arabic Literature in the Post-Classical Period*, ed. Roger Allen (Cambridge: Cambridge University Press, 2006), 51-54;

Muḥammad Kurd ʿAlī, “Risālatān li-Ṣafī al-Dīn al-Ḥillī,” *Revue de l'Académie arabe de Damas* 4 (1924): 210-220;

Muḥammad ibn Shākir al-Kutubī, “al-Ṣafī al-Ḥillī,” in *Fawāt al-wafayāt*, vol. 2, ed. Iḥsān ʿAbbās (Beirut: Dār al-Thaqāfah, 1973), 335-350;

George Makdisi, “Notes on Ḥilla and the Mazyadids in Medieval Islam,” *Journal of the American Oriental Society* 74:1 (October-December 1954: 249-262;

Diyā’ al-Dīn Rayyis, “Ṣafī al-Dīn al-Ḥillī,” *al-Risālah* 2:27 (8 January 1934): 24-25 and 2:28 (15 January 1934), 27-29;

Everett Rowson, “al-Ṣafadī,” in *Essays in Arabic Literary Biography: 1350-1850*, ed. Joseph E. Lowry and Devin J. Stewart (Wiesbaden: Harrassowitz Verlag, 2009), 341-357;

Ṣalāḥ al-Dīn Khalīl ibn Aybak al-Ṣafadī, *A'yān al-'aṣr wa-a'wān al-Naṣr*, vol. 3 (Beirut: Dār al-Fikr al-Muʿāsir, 1998), 68-99;

Ṣalāḥ al-Dīn Khalīl ibn Aybak al-Ṣafadī, *Ṣafī ’l-Dīn al-Ḥillī*, ed. ʿAdnān Darwīsh (Damascus: Manshūrāt Wizārat al-Thaqāfah, 1995);

Ṣalāḥ al-Dīn Khalīl ibn Aybak al-Ṣafadī, *al-Wāfī bi ’l-Wafayāt*, vol. 18, ed. Ayman Fu’ād Sayyid (Wiesbaden: Franz Steiner, 1988), 481-510;

Maḥmūd Rizq Salīm, *Ṣafī ’l-Dīn al-Ḥillī* (Cairo: Dār al-Maʿārif, 1960);

Maḥmūd Rizq Salīm, *'Aṣr salāṭīn al-mamālīk wa-natājih al-'ilmī wa ’l-adabī*, vol. 8 (Cairo: Maktabat al-Ādāb, 1965);

Muḥammad ibn ʿAlī ’l-Shawkānī, *al-Badr al-ṭāli' bi-maḥāsin man ba'da ’l-qarn al-sābi'* (Beirut: Dār al-Fikr al-Muʿāṣir, 1998), 365-366;

Suzanne Stetkevych, “From Jahiliyya to Badiʿiyya,” *Oral Tradition* 25:1 (March 2010): 211-230;

Jurjī Zaydān, “Ṣafī al-Dīn al-Ḥillī,” in *Tārīkh ādāb al-lughah al-'arabiyyah*, vol. 3. ed. Shawqī Ḍayf (Cairo: Dār al-Hilāl, 1957), 139-40.

Ibn ʿAbd Rabbih

(860-940)

BRYAN AVERBUCH
Harvard University

WORKS

al-ʿIqd al-farīd (The Unique Necklace);
Dīwān (Collected Poems).

Editions

al-ʿIqd al-farīd wa-bi-hāmishihi Zahr al-ādāb wa-thamar al-albāb li-Abī Isḥaq Ibrāhīm ibn ʿAlī ʾl-maʿrūf bi ʾl-Ḥuṣrī ʾl-Qayrawānī ʾl-Māliki (Būlāq: al-Maṭbaʿah al-ʿĀmirah, 1876);

Kitāb al-ʿIqd al-farīd, ed. Aḥmad Amīn, Aḥmad al-Zayn and Ibrāhīm al-Ibyārī (Cairo: Maṭbaʿat Lajnat al-Taʾlīf wa-Tarjamah wa ʾl-Nashr, 1940-1949);

al-ʿIqd al-farīd, ed. Muḥammad Saʿīd al-ʿIryān (Cairo: Maṭbaʿat al-Istiqāmah, 1953); ed. Mufīd Muḥammad Qumayḥah (Beirut: Dār al-Kutub al-ʿIlmiyyah, 1997);

Shiʿr Ibn ʿAbd Rabbih, ed. Muḥammad ibn Tāwīt Tanjī (Casablanca: Dār al-Maghrib li ʾl-Taʾlīf wa ʾl-Tarjamah wa ʾl-Nashr, 1978).

Dīwān Ibn ʿAbd Rabbih, ed. Muḥammad Riḍwān Dāyah (Beirut: Muʾassasat al-Risālah, 1979).

Translations

The Unique Necklace = al-ʿIqd al-farīd, ed. Issa J. Boullata (Reading, U.K.: Garnet Publishing, 2006-);

James Monroe, *Hispano-Arabic Poetry: a Student Anthology* (Berkeley: University of California Press, 1974), 74-129;

Henry George Farmer, *Music: the Priceless Jewel, from the Kitāb al-ʿIqd al-farīd of Ibn ʿAbd Rabbihi* (Bearsden, Scotland.: H.G. Farmer, 1942).

Abū ʿUmar Aḥmad ibn Muḥammad ibn ʿAbd Rabbih was a tenth-century writer and poet, widely considered to be the first prose writer from Islamic Iberia (al-Andalus) to have had a major impact on the wider Islamic world. Inasmuch as a great deal of Ibn ʿAbd Rabbih's verse has been lost, it is difficult to make a balanced assessment of his qualities as a poet. Much of what survives is included in his prose composition, *al-ʿIqd al-farīd*, or "*The Unique Necklace*," and thus cannot be assessed without consideration of the intent of the work in which his verses are embedded. Several scholars have nevertheless studied and discussed the relative merits of his surviving poetry (see references below). His reputation in modern times is due to his composition of the compilation known as *al-ʿIqd al-farīd.* This voluminous work, as of yet un-translated in its entirety, stands as a pinnacle of the *adab* genre in medieval Arabic literature. Drawing almost entirely on materials from eastern authors, Ibn ʿAbd Rabbih attempted to systematically present a sampling of the general knowledge that he thought a gentleman of his day should possess.

Ibn ʿAbd Rabbih was born in Cordoba in 860, and died there in 940. His great-grandfather had apparently come to Spain as a *mawlā* of the Umayyad caliph in Spain, ʿAbd al-Raḥmān I (731-787 or 788). The young Ibn ʿAbd Rabbih was raised and educated in Cordoba by scholars steeped in the literary and scholarly traditions of the eastern Islamic world, although he is not known to have ever traveled outside of the Iberian peninsula. Apart from this, and some remarks by later authors on his personal temperament and the names of his teachers, very little biographical information on Ibn ʿAbd Rabbih has survived. It seems that Ibn ʿAbd Rabbih was, for at least part of his life, a court panegyrist for the Spanish Umayyads, and it was in this capacity that his magnum opus, *al-'Iqd al-farīd*, was written.

Typologically, *al-'Iqd al-farīd* was part of the *adab* genre of Arabic literature, which had flourished since the eighth century, and which had been developed further by prominent eighth and ninth-century authors such as ʿAbd Allāh Ibn al-Muqaffaʿ (d. ca. 760), Abū ʿUthmān ʿAmr ibn Baḥr al-Jāḥiẓ (d. 868 or 869), and ʿAbd Allāh ibn Muslim Ibn Qutaybah (828-889), all of whom lived and worked in Iraq. *Adab* represented, in medieval Islamic society, the general knowledge which social elites were expected to possess. Forms of address, administrative and literary conventions, religious topics, history, poetry, music, proverbs, anecdotes, and even jokes fell within the domain of *adab*. Earlier ninth-century works on *adab*, such as the *'Uyūn al-akhbār* of Ibn Qutaybah, are first and foremost anthologies of accumulated knowledge, although they may contain original contributions by the compiler. In addition, it is important to note that the first works of *adab* developed in the eastern domains of the Abbasid caliphate, and that they reflect, in both form and content, the literary concerns and social milieu of elites in the Islamic East (*al-Mashriq*). *Al-'Iqd al-farīd*, with its anthology format reminiscent of *'Uyūn al-akhbār*, is dependent on and follows the already-established *adab* genre. In terms of content, *al-'Iqd al-farīd* is essentially a compilation of knowledge derived from the eastern Islamic world, and it contributes practically no *adab* knowledge from sources apart from those originating in the Abbasid caliphate. However, as we shall see, Ibn ʿAbd Rabbih included in his work a panegyric chronicling the military campaigns of his then patron, the Umayyad Spanish Caliph ʿAbd al-Raḥmān III (891-961), which gives *al-'Iqd al-farīd*, in content if not in form, a certain amount of local character. It is in this sense that Ibn ʿAbd Rabbih's work represents a preliminary stage in the development of a native Andalusian literary tradition. The *ʿIqd* is divided into twenty-five books or chapters. Each chapter is named after a precious stone or metal ornament. These gemstones come together to form the *ʿIqd,* or necklace, hence the book's title. Taken together, these "gems" formed the most comprehensive anthology of *adab* to date in the Islamic world. The chapters comprising *al-'Iqd al-farīd* have been described in detail by a number of authors, notable Anwar G. Chejne and Issa Boullatta, who differ somewhat in their translations of the book titles. Nevertheless, a very brief resume of their contents may be useful here.

Chapter One: on rulers and government
Chapter Two: on warfare
Chapter Three: on generosity, favors, and gift-giving
Chapter Four: on holding royal audiences
Chapter Five: on the ways in which rulers should be addressed
Chapter Six: on religious knowledge (*'ilm*), *adab*, and scholarship
Chapter Seven: on sayings and proverbs
Chapter Eight: on preaching and ascetics
Chapter Nine: on eulogies and oratory
Chapter Ten: on the lineage and qualities of the Arabs
Chapter Eleven: on Arabic proverbs and orations
Chapter Twelve: on how to conduct conversations
Chapter Thirteen: on famous speeches
Chapter Fourteen: on writing and government scribes
Chapter Fifteen: on the lives of Muḥammad, the first Caliphs, and the Umayyads of Damascus and Spain, followed by a panegyric poem celebrating the campaigns of Ibn ʿAbd Rabbih's patron, the then-reigning Umayyad Caliph ʿAbd al-Raḥmān III.
Chapter Sixteen: on the histories of prominent governors and administrators
Chapter Seventeen: on the inter-tribal wars and exploits of the Arabs before Islam
Chapter Eighteen: On the virtues of poetry
Chapter Nineteen: On versification and meter
Chapter Twenty: On singing, and on the detractors and supporters of song
Chapter Twenty-One: On the virtues and vices of women
Chapter Twenty-Two: On humorous anecdotes regarding pseudo-prophets, misers, and lunatics
Chapter Twenty-Three: On the virtues of various lands, and on the characteristics of different peoples and animals. Diverse topics

such as sorcery, poisons, geography, and angelology are also discussed.

Chapter Twenty-Four: On foods and beverages, diet and nutrition

Chapter Twenty-Five: On jokes, riddles, and amusing anecdotes

As a work of *adab*, *al-'Iqd al-farīd* represents an attempt to dissimulate knowledge to the elites of tenth-century Islamic Spain, knowledge that in the Eastern Islamic world would have been considered marks of a refined and educated member of society. There is also a markedly political dimension to *al-'Iqd al-farīd*, namely, its role as a vehicle of dynastic propaganda. Ibn ʿAbd Rabbih included in chapter fifteen, as noted above, an original panegyric *urjūzah*, or poem in rhyming couplets, on the military exploits of Ibn ʿAbd Rabbih's patron, the Umayyad Spanish Caliph ʿAbd al-Raḥmān III, who styled himself "*al-Nāṣir li-Dīn Allāh*," "the Victor for God's Religion." This ruler, who would declare himself Caliph of the Islamic world in 928, was lionized by later Muslim historians dealing with Islamic Spain, such as Abū Marwān Ḥayyān ibn Khalaf Ibn Ḥayyān (987 or 988-1076) and Ibn Khaldūn (1332-1406), who tended to lavish praise upon the accomplishments of ʿAbd al-Raḥmān III. These written testimonies, along with impressive architectural monuments like the great mosque of Cordoba and the palace complex of Madīnat al-Zahrā', have caused many modern historians to evaluate ʿAbd al-Raḥmān III in a favorable light. Indeed, the medieval Arabic testimonies of ʿAbd al-Raḥmān III's promoters remain, together with archaeology, among our only substantial sources for his reign. It is a mark not only of the effectiveness of the Caliph but of the skill of the poets and chroniclers who extolled his virtues that the tenth century is remembered as a high point of Islamic civilization in Spain, with Cordoba as its most brilliant city, and ʿAbd al-Raḥmān as its greatest ruler. Richard Fletcher noted that the claims of the medieval authors about ʿAbd al-Raḥmān III can seldom be correlated with any other sources, and that "We must be prepared to take their claims with a pinch of salt–sometimes a generous one (54)." One of these sources, Ibn ʿAbd Rabbih's panegyric *urjūzah*, is calculated precisely to promote such a positive view of the Caliph. The inclusion of this poem in *al-'Iqd al-farīd*, is far from coincidental. ʿAbd al-Raḥmān III, ruling a comparatively small kingdom on the periphery of the Islamic world, is made out to be the rightful inheritor of the Prophet and the first Caliphs. Whoever read *al-'Iqd al-farīd*, whether in Spain or in the wider Islamic world, would presumably read the panegyric celebration of ʿAbd al-Raḥmān III's political and military prowess be persuaded by it. And it is in this light that the work can be read as not merely a compilation of facts meant to assist in the education and refinement of elite society in Islamic Spain, but as part of a broader political agenda that sought to bolster support for ʿAbd al-Raḥmān III's claims to legitimacy, both in Spain and in the wider Islamic world.

Although *al-'Iqd al-farīd* is widely seen as a derivative work relying on eastern sources, the *urjūzah* is, in several respects, a distinctly Iberian literary production. The *urjūzah* seems to have been a comparatively rare form in early Arabic literature. Like the *adab* contents of *al-'Iqd al-farīd*, the *urjūzah* is an import from the Abbasid world. As James Monroe has shown, *urjūzah* compositions seem to have enjoyed a certain popularity in Islamic Spain, and various locally-composed *urjūzah*s were certainly circulating in ninth and tenth-century Iberia. Ibn ʿAbd Rabbih's work is one of the earliest to have survived extant, because of its inclusion in *al-'Iqd al-farīd.* In terms of content, as well, Ibn ʿAbd Rabbih's *urjūzah* is a local product. The setting is al-Andalus, the protagonists and antagonists are Iberian, whether Muslims or otherwise, and the conflict is a Spanish one, arising, in the words of Fletcher, out of the geographical peculiarities that led to "the great difficulty that a single political authority has always had in enforcing its will over the entire peninsula (13)."

After a fairly conventional opening praise of God, which contains an orthodox defense of the intellect as the best means of perceiving the Creator, (as opposed to the reliance of mystics on the imagination or the senses), the poet sets the scene by writing "We were in a time of dark nights, and a civil war like scum deluged by the flood….when hypocrisy (*al-nafāq*) prevailed, and apostasy and oath-breaking was rife (Monroe, *Hispano-Arabic*, 74-77)." The inhabitants of the realm cannot celebrate the holiday of *ʿīd* (traditionally a period of truce) without armed men to protect them. Into this misery, then, strides ʿAbd al-Raḥmān III, the protagonist. This ruler is said to have had "Piety (*al-taqwā*) on his forehead, and the religion and the world lay in his right hand." He is "foremost of the Marwānids," (a branch of the Umayyad house). These attributes, aside from being traditional, also seem to answer specific problems associated with the ʿAbd al-Raḥmān. The challenges to his secular authority from Berber chieftains, Spanish Muslim leaders, disaffected Arab tribesman, and the incipient Christian kingdoms to the north notwithstanding, the rival Shiite Fatimid Caliph of North Africa, operating from his base at Qayrawan, posed a greater and possibly existential threat to the Umayyads of Spain. The assertion of religious authority is a recurring theme of the poem. The proclamation of his preeminence amongst the Banū Marwān is likewise interesting, inasmuch as ʿAbd al-Raḥmān was described by the French historian Evariste Lévi-Provençal as blue-eyed, with reddish hair and fair skin. He was the product of multiple unions with hostages and slaves from the Pyrenees. In a milieu preoccupied (although theoretically inimical to Islam) with lineage and birth, ʿAbd al-Raḥmān was apparently in the habit of dyeing his hair black in order to appear more of an Arab. Likewise, the poet asserts the legitimacy of his master's line at the beginning of the panegyric, while hypocritically mocking Ḥabīb, the rebel governor of Carmona, as being the descendent of a black woman (Ibn ʿUmar Ibn Sawādah). The 445 lines of the poem are mainly preoccupied with rampant warfare, the consistent theme being ʿAbd al-Raḥmān's inexorable rise to power by defeating and conciliating rebels and infidels. As one would imagine, the victories of the Caliph are the victories of God and his partisans against unbelievers. Enemies are slandered repeatedly. Ibn ʿAbd Rabbih repeatedly refers to the rebel Ibn Ḥafsūn as a pig. His followers and sons are the followers of Satan (*ʿiṣābah min shīʿah al-shayṭan*). Sancho I Garcés (ca. 860-925), King of Pamplona, and Ordoño II of Galicia (ca. 873-924), known as "*al-banbalūnī*" and "*al-jilīqī*," are a pair of "barbarians" (*ʿiljāni*). Other enemies are referred to as dogs, vipers, or serpents. The city of Pamplona is referred to as damned (*al-madīnah al-malʿūnah*). It is interesting to note some of the similarities in the descriptions of Ibn ʿAbd Rabbih, and those used by the ninth-century Abbasid poet Abū Tammām (796 or 804-842/843 or 845/846), when he described the downfall of the general Khaydār b. Kāvūs Afshīn (d. 941). In both cases, a protagonist is "the lion of the thicket," although their lexicon is different (*asad al-ʿarīn* in the former, *layth al-ghīl* in the latter), further evidence, as noted above, of the author's heavy reliance on the literary heritage of the *Mashriq*. At any rate, the heavy-handed rhetoric and sharp-tongued insults of Ibn ʿAbd Rabbih, a man described by the modern literary historian Iḥsān ʿAbbās as being hot-tempered and quick to mockery would seem to fit in well with the needs of the Umayyad ruler, namely to legitimize his struggles against rebels and opponents by degrading them, and to legitimize himself by being portrayed as the Caliph of God (*khalīfat Allāh*). Just as important to the Caliph's image, however, was the portrait of a merciful and moderate ruler, ready to negotiate and to grant clemency to any who applied. His coming to terms on multiple occasions with rebels like Ibn Ḥafsūn is proudly noted, as is a similar occasion with the Emir of Toledo, Yaḥyā Ibn Dhī 'l-Nūn. In both cases, the *Imām* forgives the offenses of his enemies and accepts their submission, reconfirming in the latter case the governorship of the former rebel over his district. In 934, according to the poem, the Caliph receives the "Dame of the Basques" (*rabbah al-bashāqiṣ*, i.e. Queen Theuda of Navarre), who uses her leverage as a blood relative of the Caliph to secure peace. The Caliph withdraws from her lands and grants her safe-conduct after a prisoner exchange. That these qualities should be alluded to proudly in a war poem goes beyond the desire to portray the ʿAbd al-Raḥmān as a pious Islamic ruler, of whom mercy and clemency were expected. Ibn ʿAbd Rabbih was "spinning" the situation, framing as clemency and mercy the pressing need of a relatively weak central ruler to compromise with his enemies, in a terrain and era that favored regionalism and secession. He seems to have succeeded in his aim, for the Caliph emerges in the poem as both ruthless and compassionate, the crucifier of Ibn Ḥafṣūn's sons on one hand, the gentle pardoner of Yaḥyā and Theuda on the other.

Whether fighting or negotiating, the Caliph is always victorious in these encounters, even if his generals are not always. It was perhaps fortunate for Ibn ʿAbd Rabbih that he ended his poem in the year 935, four years prior the Caliph's humiliating and personal defeat at the hands of Ramiro II, King of León (ca. 900-951) at the battle of Simancas, about a year before the poet's death. The same was not true for chroniclers, to whom the task fell of explaining this embarrassing event.

The reputation of early Andalusian dynasties for a general tolerance of confessional communities has been championed by a number of modern authors. It is interesting to see that this early picture of inter-confessional warfare takes on a rather different tone, even in the centuries before crusading zeal or Almoravid/Almohad intolerance had appeared on the scene. When in combat with Christian enemies in the North, the churches are not spared, in fact, Ibn ʿAbd Rabbih celebrates their destruction in these terms:

Fa mā baqā min janabāti dawri
  min bīʿatin li-rāhibin aw dayri
Illā wa qad sayyarahā habbaʿā
  ka-an-nāri idh wāfaqat al-abaʿā
Wa zʿazaʿat katāʿib aṣ-ṣulṭāni
  li-kulli mā fīhā min al-bunyāni

Not a parish church or monastery remained for
  the monks,
For he incinerated them as would the fire that
  reaches dry grass,
While the ranks of the Sultan tore down all the
  buildings within…

While allowing for obvious poetic exaggeration, there appears to be ample evidence supporting targeted attacks on churches and monasteries by Islamic armies of al-Andalus during the 10th century, as noted by Fletcher. What is perhaps as criticized by both contemporaries and later scholars as a wholly imitative work, Ibn ʿAbd Rabbih's encyclopedic work became an important repository of *adab* knowledge for later authors in the wider Islamic world. Additionally,

important is the fact that a poet of Cordoba, such as Ibn ʿAbd Rabbih, would be moved to describe this attack in celebratory terms. Viewed alongside the poet's disdain for the lords of Galicia and Pamplona, and the delegation of Queen Theuda, it is a fine illustration of the limits of *convivencia* during the Caliphal period in the Iberian Peninsula. Tolerance was for those who submitted, however nominally, to Cordoba. The poem makes it clear that this applied to Muslims no less than to Christians. It is the failure to acknowledge ʿAbd al-Raḥmān as an overlord, not confessional identity, which makes people heretical in Ibn ʿAbd Rabbih's poem. This underscores one of the central purposes of the poem: to give the impression to its audience that disobedience is tantamount to disbelief. At the same time, however, it reassures transgressors that they can still be forgiven for their errors, and even come away with favorable terms, if they will only negotiate. It is a carrot-and-stick policy that Ibn ʿAbd Rabbih is displaying for future readers of *al-ʿIqd al-farīd*, i.e., the educated upper classes of Islamic Spain, precisely the people most likely to lead a rebellion, whatever the composition of its rank-and-file.

A number of observations on the milieu in which Ibn ʿAbd Rabbih wrote thus emerge from a critical reading of his *urjūzah*. Firstly, his poem was carefully framed to support the grand strategy of his patron, and to develop an image of that patron that would promote the latter's pretensions to the title of Caliph. Secondly, he did this by adapting certain conventions of *mashriqī* Arabic laudatory poetry to a local and Iberian context.

To conclude, although the paucity of the sources makes a traditional biographical sketch of Ibn ʿAbd Rabbih difficult, reading his works gives us a clear picture of the political and social context in which he wrote, the sources from which he drew inspiration, and, perhaps most importantly, a basis for discussing the purposes of his composition of *al-ʿIqd al-farīd*. Although

his composition of a panegyric concerned wholly with Iberian politics, within the decidedly imitative *al-ʿIqd al-farīd,* marks an important step in the evolution of an independent literary tradition in al-Andalus.

REFERENCES

Iḥsān ʿAbbās, *Tārīkh al-adab al-Andalusī: 'aṣr sīyādat Qurṭubah*, 2d ed. (Beirut: Dār al-Thaqāfah, 1969);

Ibn ʿAbd Rabbih, *The Unique Necklace = al-'Iqd al-farīd,* trans. by Issa J. Boullata (Reading, U.K.: Garnet Publishing, 2006-);

Carl Brockelmann, "Ibn ʿAbd Rabbih," in *Encyclopaedia of Islam, Second Edition*, ed. by: P. Bearman, Th. Bianquis, C.E. Bosworth, E. van Donzel and W.P. Heinrichs. (Leiden: Brill, 2008), Brill Online. http://www.brillonline.nl/subscriber/entry?entry=islam_SIM-3031;

Anwar Chejne, *Muslim Spain* (Minneapolis: University of Minnesota Press, 1974), 202-209;

Richard Fletcher, *Moorish Spain* (London: Weidenfeld and Nicolson, 1992);

Abū Marwān Ḥayyān ibn Khalaf Ibn Ḥayyān, *Crónica del califa 'Abdarraḥmān III An-Nāṣir entre los años 912 y 942,* trans. by Ma. Jesús Viguera and Federico Corriente (Zaragoza: Anubar: Instituto Hispano-Arabe de Cultura, 1981);

Evariste Lévi-Provençal, *Histoire de l'Espagne Musulmane*, vol. 2. Le Califat Umaiyade de Cordue, 912-1031 (Paris: G.P. Maisonneuve, 1950);

James T. Monroe, *Hispano-Arabic Poetry: a Student Anthology* (Berkley: University of California Press, 1970), 75-129;

James T. Monroe, "The Historical Arjūza of ibn ʿAbd Rabbihi, a Tenth-Century Hispano-Arabic Epic Poem," *Journal of the American Oriental Society* 91:1 (Jan.-Mar., 1971): 67-95.

Ibn al-ʿArabī

(560/1165-638/1240)

JANE CLARK

Senior Research Fellow, Muhyiddin Ibn 'Arabī Society, Oxford

WORKS

Kitāb mashāhid al-asrār al-qudsiyyah wa-maṭāli' al-anwār al-ilāhiyyah;
Kitāb al-tadbīrāt al-ilāhiyyah fī iṣlāḥ al-mamlakah al-insāniyyah;
Kitāb al-isrā ilā'l-maqām al-asrā;
Mawāqi' al-nujūm;
Kitāb 'anqā' mughrib fī ma'rifat khatm al-awliyā' wa-shams al-mughrib;
Risālat al-ittiḥād al-kawnī;
Kitāb inshā' al-dawā'ir;
Kitāb ḥilyat al-abdāl;
Kitāb rūḥ al-quds fī munāṣaḥat al-nafs/al-Durrah al-fākhirah;
Kitāb al-tanazzulāt al-Mawṣiliyyah;
Risālat al-anwār (Kitāb Asrār al-khalwah);
Kitāb al-isfār 'an natā'ij al-asfār;
Kitāb al-tajalliyāt al-ilāhiyyah;
Tarjumān al-ashwāq/Kitāb al-dhakhā'ir wa'l-a'lāq;
Kitāb al-'abādilah;
Fuṣūṣ al-ḥikam;
al-Dīwān al-kabīr;
al-Futūḥāt al-Makkiyyah.

Editions

Kitāb mashāhid al-asrār al-qudsiyyah wa-maṭāli' al-anwār al-ilāhiyyah, ed. Suad Hakim y Pablo Beneito in *Las contemplaciones de los misterios* (Murcia: Editora Regional de Murcia, 1996);

Kitāb al-tadbīrāt al-ilāhiyyah fī iṣlāḥ al-mamlakah al-insāniyyah in *Kleinere Schriften des Ibn al-'Arabī*, ed. H.S. Nyberg (Leiden: E.J. Brill, 1919), 101-240, Arabic section;

al-Isrā ilā 'l-maqām al-asrā, aw, Kitāb al-Mi'rāj, ed. Suʿād al-Ḥakīm (Beirut: Dandarah li'l-Ṭibāʿah wa'l-Nashr, 1988);
Kitāb mawāqi' al-nujūm wa-maṭāliʿ ahillat al-asrār wa'l-'ulūm, ed. Muḥammad Badr al-Dīn al-Naʿsānī (Cairo: Maṭbaʿat al-Saʿādah, 1907);
Kitāb 'anqā' mughrib fī ma'rifat khatm al-awliyā' wa-shams al-mughrib (Cairo, 1934); (Cairo: Yuṭlabu min Maktabat wa-Maṭbaʿat Muḥammad ʿAlī Ṣubayḥ, 1954?); ed. Saʿīd ʿAbd al-Fatāḥ, in *Rasā'il Ibn 'Arabī*, vol. 4 (Beirut: Mu'assasat al-Intishār al-ʿArabī, 2001);
Kitābt al-ittiḥād al-kawnī in *L'Arbre et les quatre oiseaux*, ed. Denis Gril (Paris: Les Deux Océans, 1984);
Kitāb inshā' al-dawā'ir in *Kleinere Schriften des Ibn al-'Arabī*, ed. H.S. Nyberg (Leiden: E.J. Brill, 1919), 1-38, Arabic section;
Kitāb inshā' al-dawā'ir in *La Production des cercles = Kitâb inshâ ad-dawâ'ir al-ihâtiyya*, ed. H.S. Nyberg (Paris: Editions de l'Eclat, c1996);
Ḥilyat al-abdāl in *The Four Pillars of Spiritual Transformation: the Adornment of the Spirituality Transformed (Ḥilyat al-abdāl)*, ed. Stephen Hirtenstein (Oxford: Anqa, 2008);
Risālat rūḥ al-quds, ed. ʿAbd al-Raḥmān Ḥasan Muḥammad (Cairo: ʿĀlam al-Fikr, 1989);
Sharḥ Risālat rūḥ al-quds fī muḥāsabat al-nafs, ed. Maḥmūd Maḥmūd Ghurāb (Dimashq: M. M. al-Ghurāb, 1987);
Kitāb al-tanazzulāt al-Mawṣiliyyah, ed. Saʿīd ʿAbd al-Fattāḥ in *Rasā'il Ibn 'Arabī*, vol. 6 (Beirut: Mu'assasat al-Intishār al-ʿArabī, 2001-2004);
Risālat al-anwār (Kitāb Asrār al-khalwah) in *Rasā'il Ibn al-'Arabī* (Hyderabad: Maṭbaʿat Jamiyyat Dā'irat al-Maʿārif al-ʿUthmāniyyah, 1938); (Hyderabad: Maṭbaʿat Jamiyyat Dā'irat al-Maʿārif al-ʿUthmāniyyah, 1948); ed. Saʿīd ʿAbd al-Fattāḥ in *Rasā'il Ibn 'Arabī*, vol. 6 (Beirut: Mu'assasat al-Intishār al-ʿArabī, 2001-2004);
Kitāb al-isfār 'an natā'ij al-asfār in *Le dévoilement des effets du voyage*, ed. Denis Gril (Paris: Editions de l'Eclat, c1994);
al-Tajalliyāt al-ilāhiyyah, ed. ʿUthmān Ismāʿīl Yaḥyā (Ṭihrān: Markaz-i Nashr-i Dānishgāhī, 1988);
The Tarjumán al-ashwáq: a Collection of Mystical Odes, ed. Reynold A. Nicholson, Oriental translation fund, n.s., v. 20 (London: Royal Asiatic Society, 1911);
al-'Abādilah, ed. ʿAbd al-Qādir Aḥmad ʿAtā (Cairo: Maktabah al-Qāhirah, 1969);
Fuṣūṣ al-ḥikam, ed. Abū ʿAlā ʿAfīfī (Beirut, al-Nashr Dār al-Kitāb al-ʿArabī, 1966);
al-Dīwān al-akbar (Cairo: Būlāq, 1855);
Kitāb al-futūḥāt al-Makkiyyah, 4 vols. (Cairo: Dār al-Kutub al-ʿʿArabiyyah al-Kubrā, 1911); ed. Aḥmad Shams al-Dīn, 9 vols. (Beirut: Dār al-Kutub al-ʿIlmiyyah, 1999); ed. ʿUthmān Yaḥyā (Cairo: al-Hay'ah al-Miṣriyyah al-ʿĀmmah li'l-Kitāb, 1972-).

Translations

Suad Hakim y Pablo Beneito, *Las contemplaciones de los misterios* (Murcia: Editora Regional de Murcia, 1996);
Cecilia Twinch and Pablo Beneito, *Contemplation of the Holy Mysteries* (Oxford: ʿAnqa Publishing, 2001);
Tosun Bayrak, *Divine Governance of the Human Kingdom* (Louisville: Fons Vitae, 1997);
Gerald T. Elmore, *Islamic Sainthood in the Fullness of Time: Ibn al-'Arabī's Book of the Fabulous Gryphon*, Islamic Philosophy, Theology, and Science; v. 32 (Leiden: E.J. Brill, 1999);
Denis Gril, *L'Arbre et les quatre oiseaux* (Paris: Les Deux Océans, 1984);
Angela Jaffray, *The Universal Tree and the Four Birds: Treatise on Unification (al-Ittiḥād al-kawnī)* (Oxford: Anqa Pub., 2006);
Paul B. Fenton and Maurice Gloton, The Book of the Description of the Encompassing Circles (al-Inshâ' ad-Dawâ'ir) in *Muhyiddin ibn 'Arabi: a Commemorative volume*, ed. Stephen Hirtenstein and Michael Tiernan (Shaftsbury, Dorset: Element, 1993), 12-43;
Paul Fenton and Maurice Gloton, trans., *La Production des cercles = Kitâb inshâ ad-dawâ'ir al-ihâtiyya* (Paris: Editions de l'Eclat, c1996);
Stephen Hirtenstein, *The Four Pillars of Spiritual Transformation: the Adornment of*

the Spirituality Transformed (Ḥilyat al-abdāl) (Oxford: Anqa, 2008);
R. W. J. Austin, *Sufis of Andalusia: the 'Rūh al-quds' and 'al-Durrat al-fākhirah' of Ibn 'Arabī* (London, Allen and Unwin, 1971); (Sherborne: Beshara Publications, 1988); (Roberton: Beshara Publications, 2002);
Roger Boase and Farid Sahnoun, "Excerpts from the Epistle on the Spirit of Holiness" in *Muhyiddin ibn 'Arabi: a Commemorative Volume*, ed. Stephen Hirtenstein and Michael Tiernan (Shaftsbury, Dorset: Element, 1993), 44-72;
Rabia Terri Harris, *Journey to the Lord of Power: a Sufi Manual on Retreat* (London: East West Publications, 1981);
Bernd Radtke, *Neue kritische Gänge = New Critical Essays: on the Present State and Future tasks of the study of Sufism* (Utrecht: Houtsma Stichting, 2005);
Denis Gril, *Le dévoilement des effets du voyage* (Paris: Editions de l'Eclat, c1994);
Angela Jaffray, *The Unveiling from the Effects of the Voyages* (Oxford: Anqa Pub., 2011) forthcoming;
Stéphane Ruspoli, *Le livre des théophanies d'Ibn Arabî: introduction philosophique, commentaire et traduction annotée du Kitâb al-tajalliyât* (Paris: Cerf, 2000);
Reynold A. Nicholson, *The Tarjumán al-ashwáq: a Collection of Mystical Odes*, Oriental translation fund, n.s., v. 20 (London: Royal Asiatic Society, 1911);
Michael A. Sells, *Stations of Desire: Love Elegies from Ibn 'Arabi and New Poems* (Jerusalem: Ibis Editions, c2000);
Maurice Gloton, *L'interprète des désirs = Turjumân al-ashwâq*, Spiritualités vivantes (Paris: Albin Michel, c1996);
Titus Burckhardt and Angela Culme-Seymour, *The Wisdom of the Prophets = Fusus al-hikam* (Aldsworth, Eng.: Beshara, c1975);
R.W. J. Austin, *The Bezels of Wisdom*, The Classics of Western spirituality (New York: Paulist Press, c1980);
Caner K. Dagli, *The Ringstones of Wisdom: Fuṣūṣ al-ḥikam* (Chicago: Distributed by Kazi Publications, c2004);
Charles-André Gilis, *Le livre des chatons de sagesse* (Beirut: al-Bouraq, 1997);
Federico Corriente and Ed Emery, *Twenty-seven Muwashshahaat and One Zajal* (London, 2004);
Michel Chodkiewicz, *The Meccan Revelations*, 2 vols. (New York: Pir Press, 2002-2004);
William C. Chittick, *The Self-Disclosure of God: Principles of Ibn al-'Arabī's Cosmology*, SUNY Series in Islam (Albany: State University of New York Press, c1998);
William C. Chittick, *The Sufi Path of Knowledge: Ibn al-'Arabi's Metaphysics of Imagination* (Albany, N.Y.: State University of New York Press, c1989);
Aisha Abdurrahman Bewley, *Ibn al-Arabi on the Mysteries of Bearing Witness to the Oneness of God and Prophethood of Muhammad* (Chicago: Great Books of the Islamic World, c2002);
Aisha Abdurrahman Bewley, *Ibn al-Arabi on the Mysteries of Fasting from the Futūḥāt al-Makkīyah (Meccan Revelations)* (Chicago: Great Books of the Islamic World, 2009);
Aisha Abdurrahman Bewley, *Ibn al-Arabi on the Mysteries of the Pilgrimage from the Futūḥāt al-Makkīyah (Meccan Revelations)* (Chicago: Great Books of the Islamic World, 2009);
Aisha Abdurrahman Bewley, *Ibn al-Arabi on the Mysteries of Purification and Formal Prayer from the Futūḥāt al-Makkīyah (Meccan Revelations)* (Chicago: Great Books of the Islamic World, 2000);
Aisha Abdurrahman Bewley, *Ibn al-Arabi on the Mysteries of the Purifying Alms from the Futūḥāt al-Makkīyah (Meccan Revelations)* (Chicago: Great Books of the Islamic World, 2009).

Muḥyī'l-Dīn Ibn al-ʿArabī (560/1165-638/1240) is one of the most important intellectual forces in Islamic culture. Living at a pivotal moment in Islamic history, when the *Dar al-Islam* and its culture was under threat from the Mongol invasions in the East and the Franks in the centre and West, his writings synthesized the rich and highly sophisticated heritage of the previous six hundred years into a coherent and unified spiritual vision. His vision brought together the experiential knowledge of Sufism with the highly developed understandings of philosophy and *kalām,* and the theological traditions of *ḥadīth* and *Qur'ānic* commentary. During the 14th-18th centuries, his works and those of his followers such as Muḥammad ibn Isḥāq Ṣadr al-Dīn al-Qūnawī (d. 1273 or 4), Muḥammad ibn Ḥamzah Fanārī (1350 or 51-1430 or 31), also called Mulla Fanārī, and ʿAbd al-Karīm ibn Ibrāhīm al-Jīlī (b. 1365 or 6) were disseminated to every corner of the Islamic world. They became highly influential not only spiritually, within the increasingly important and powerful Sufi orders, but also upon the political, literary and artistic culture of the great empires of the post-Mongol era. For instance, Ibn al-ʿArabī was revered within the Ottoman Empire as the *Shaykh al-akbar* (the greatest teacher) and studied by many of the emperors and grand viziers, whilst the Mughal Emperor Akbar (1542-1605) and his immediate successors in India are known to have been influenced by his ideas of religious tolerance and human perfectibility; it has been suggested that the design of the Taj Mahal is based upon a diagram in *al-Futūḥāt al-Makkiyyah.* In literary spheres, his works inspired the works of poets such as Fakhr al-Dīn Ibrāhīm al-ʿIrāqī (d. 1289?), Maḥmūd ibn ʿAbd al-Karīm Shabistarī (d. ca. 1320), Jāmī (1414-1492) and subsequently the great traditions of Ottoman, Iranian and Indian poetry down to the present day.

One of the unique features of Ibn al-ʿArabī's legacy is that it is largely embodied in written works. Unlike contemporary spiritual teachers, such as Nazhmiddin Kubro (1145 or 6-1221), or Jalāl al-Dīn Rūmī (1207-1273), his ideas were not transmitted through an institutionalized Sufi order, as no such order was ever established by his family or followers. Rather, his ideas were set down in texts which were subsequently studied in a wide variety of cultural and geographical settings. The exact number of his compositions is not known. The Egyptian scholar ʿUthman Yahyā, who published a comprehensive bibliography entitled *Histoire et Classification de l'Oeuvre d'Ibn 'Arabī* in 1964 noted that more than 800 works have been attributed to him. But it is now widely acknowledged that this is far too high a figure, as many of the works listed have subsequently been shown to be misattributed, or, having no extant manuscripts, their existence has been deduced from secondary sources and is therefore speculative. Most scholars now accept a figure of 2-300 based on two lists which Ibn al-ʿArabī himself drew up during his lifetime. However, recent research based on the earliest and most authenticated copies indicate that the number may be much lower; only 83 surviving works can be attributed without any doubt to Ibn al-ʿArabī, with a further 12 which have a high probability of being authentic. Of course, some works have not survived to the present day—there are no extant manuscripts of well-attested works such as his *Tafsīr al-Qurʾān*. But it seems unlikely, given the care with which his heritage was treated by his immediate followers, that less than half of the original *corpus* has survived. The explanation for the discrepancy, we would suggest, is that many smaller works became part of his masterwork *al-Futūḥāt al-Makkiyyah,* finalized in the last ten years of his life, and so were not perpetuated as self-standing works by later copyists.

Even if the number of separate books is nearer to 100 than 300, the written heritage is still enormous. Many of the works are quite short—a few pages dashed off in a day in answer to a question by a student—but *al-Futūḥāt al-Makkiyyah* is a lifetime's work in itself, running to 37 volumes (over 9,000 pages) in the autograph copy—over 2,700 pages in the standard printed edition (Dār al-Ṣādir, nd). In addition, there are eight other major works, carefully constructed and comprehensive in their scope, of 100-200 pages in manuscript, several of 50-100 pages, and a *Dīwān* of more than 800 poems. One of the striking features of the *opus* is the number of manuscripts which have survived from Ibn al-ʿArabī's lifetime; there are 24 known works copied out in his own hand, including the final version of *al-Futūḥāt* (now in the Museum of Turkish and Islamic Art in Istanbul), and a further 25 which were written by disciples in his lifetime, presumably under his supervision. The extraordinary high number of historical texts contrasts sharply with the legacy of contemporaries such ʿUmar ʿAlī Ibn al-Fāriḍ (1181 or 1182-1235) for whom the earliest surviving manuscript is some 30 years after his death. This exceptional wealth seems to be due partly to the care taken by his spiritual heir, Muḥammad ibn Isḥāq Ṣadr al-Dīn al-Qūnawī (d. 1273 or 4), who set up a special *waqf* for the preservation of Ibn al-ʿArabī's books, partly to the particular situation in the regions where his close disciples lived—such as Konya and Aleppo—which escaped being sacked by the Mongols, and partly to the interest of the early Ottoman state in his work.

Given the size of the manuscript heritage and Ibn al-ʿArabī's importance in classical Islamic culture, it is surprising that it is only in the last forty years that there has been extensive study and translation of his work in English. The first English edition of his work was R. A. Nicholson's translation of his mystical love poems, *Tarjumān al-ashwāq* (*Interpreter of Desires*), published by the Theosophical Society in 1911. Nicholson also wrote introductions to his metaphysics (*Studies in Islamic Mysticism*, 1921; *Mystics of Islam*, 1914), particularly outlining the idea of the *insān al-kāmil* (perfected human being), but the baton was not picked up by English or American orientalists for several decades. The next major works did not appear until the 1970s when translations of *Fuṣūṣ al-ḥikam* by Titus Burckhardt and Angela Culme-Seymour (*The Wisdom of the Prophets*, 1975) and Dr. R. W. J Austin (*The Bezels of Wisdom*, 1980) were published, as well as Henry Corbin's seminal study, *Creative Imagination in the Sufism of Ibn 'Arabi* (1969).

In the intervening years, there was important scholarship taking place in France and Spain, led by figures such as Titus Burckhardt, Michel Valsan and Miguel Asín Palacios, and this in turn led to the emergence of a new generation of scholars who began to work specifically on Ibn al-ʿArabī's legacy. Since the 1980s, figures such as Michel Chodkiewicz, Denis Gril, Charles-André Gilis, Claude Addas and Pablo Beneito have produced translations and highly influential studies which have been translated into many languages, including English, whilst within the English-speaking world scholars such as Toshihiko Izutsu, William Chittick, Michael Sells and James Morris have brought Ibn al-ʿArabī's ideas into a contemporary context. In the last decade, scholarship has begun to blossom, but nevertheless, only 18 of the 95 works we have identified as authentic have yet been fully brought into English. The picture is slightly skewed by the existence of *al-Futūḥāt al-Makkiyyah* because of its length and the comprehensive nature of its content, as much of the recent translation work has been concentrated upon this *magnum opus*. But even here, only a small fraction of the book has yet been thoroughly studied, and it will be many years before anything like a complete translation is achieved.

The concentration on *al-Futūḥāt* and *Fuṣūṣ al-ḥikam* has also tended to skew understanding of the overall nature of Ibn al-ʿArabī's writing. Early writers tended to see him primarily as a philosopher and concentrated on the metaphysics. For example, Izutsu's *Sufism and Taoism* (1984) and Affifi's earlier study, *The Mystical Philosophy of Muḥyid Dīn-Ibnul 'Arabī* (1939), approached him largely as a neo-Platonist, emphasizing the principle of *waḥdat al-wujūd* (oneness of being) as a metaphysical principle, whilst more recently, William Chittick's *The Sufi Path of Knowledge* (1989) and *The Self-Disclosure of God* (1998) have attempted to systematize the metaphysics in a form compatible with contemporary philosophical approaches. Even when considering a major poetic work such as *Tarjumān al-ashwāq*, Anne Marie Schimmel (see *As Through a Veil* (1982, pp. 37-41)), considered the poetry, whilst "charming," to be subservient to the metaphysics, whilst Nicholson felt that Ibn al-ʿArabī should be seen as "a great theosophist rather than a great poet (Nicholson, *Studies*, 124)." However, as a greater number of texts have come into print, other, more literary, aspects of Ibn al-ʿArabī's expression have become evident. Many of his early works, for instance, are visionary in nature, written in dense symbolic language with long sections in rhymed prose (*sājʿ*), which are quite unlike a philosophical treatise and show great mastery of words and written forms. Similarly, it is now known that poetry is interspersed throughout all of his work—for instance, each of the 560 chapters of *al-Futūḥāt* begins with a poem which encapsulates the main theme of the chapter. Claude Addas's seminal article *The Ship of Stone,* which cannot be recommended highly enough, has drawn attention to the importance he himself gave to poetical expressions of mystical truth, and it becomes increasingly clear that Ibn al-ʿArabī should be regarded as an important literary figure as well as a spiritual and philosophical master.

The blossoming of scholarship in Europe and America has been paralleled by rising interest in the Arabic-speaking world. One of the reasons for the neglect of Ibn al-ʿArabī by early 20th century orientalists was the decline of interest in his work in the Islamic world. He has been a controversial figure since his lifetime, or at least from the 14th century when he attracted the criticism of both Aḥmad ibn ʿAbd al-Ḥalīm Ibn Taymiyyah (1263-1328) and Ibn Khaldūn (1332-1406) for his radical interpretations of religion and the relationship between man and God. With the rise of the *salafiyyah* groups in the 19th century, and the corresponding eclipse of the Sufi orders, Ibn al-ʿArabī's ideas became discredited in many quarters; even in the present day, there are sections of the Islamic community who regard him as a heretical thinker. There were some early publications; *Fuṣūṣ al-ḥikam* was one of the first major works to appear in an Arabic printed edition, produced by the famous Būlāq Press in 1252/1837, followed by editions of the *Dīwān* (1271/1855) and *al-Futūḥāt al-Makkiyyah* (1274/1857), whilst an important collection of 29 short works, the *Rasā'il*, appeared in 1361/1944 in Hyderabad-Deccan. But it is only in the past 10-20 years that publication has really taken off. This is to some degree because of the increased attention paid by western scholars, but it is also due to the pioneering work by Arabic scholars such as Abū'l-ʿAlā ʿAfīfī and Suʿād Ḥakīm and Turkish scholars such as Mustafa Tahralı, Mahmut Kiliç and Ekrem Demirli. New Arabic editions of works are now appearing regularly. However, many of these (including the Hyderabad *Rasā'il*) are poorly edited, taken from late and inaccurate copies of manuscripts, or they are merely reproductions of previous poor editions in which errors are compounded. Therefore, despite a seeming wealth, finding a good edition for translation or analysis is not always easy or even possible, and the best translators are still working from manuscript. But there are a growing number of critical editions which have been rigorously put together by western or western-trained scholars, and where possible these have been cited for the works considered in this article.

Given the immense wealth of material available, this article limits itself to outlining just twenty major works, which are representative of Ibn al-ʿArabī's *oeuvre*. The criteria for selecting these include: the length and importance of the work in the context of the whole opus; the quality of work which has been done in terms of Arabic editions, and the availability of English translations. In some cases all three criteria are met, but in others, only one or two. For instance, it would be impossible to exclude the *Dīwān* from consideration here, even though only a few fragments have appeared in English translation and there is not even a major published study.

Ibn al-ʿArabī was born in Murcia, in Andalusia, in 560/1165 and died in Damascus in 638/1240; to this day his tomb, housed in the mosque built for it by Sultan Selim I (1470-1520), is a centre for worship and pilgrimage in the district called Muhyiddin at the foot of Mount Qāsiyūn. His life has an extraordinary symmetry to it; about 36 years in the western regions of the Islamic empire—Andalusia and North Africa—and about 36 years in the eastern regions, with a period of 2-3 years in Mecca in the middle. For the purposes of this article, his life will be divided into three parts; firstly, his upbringing and spiritual education in the west, culminating in his arrival in Mecca in 600; secondly the period 602-20, when he was constantly travelling between the major cities of Syria, Egypt, Anatolia and Iraq, teaching and establishing groups of disciples, and thirdly, the final twelve years when he settled in Damascus and concentrated upon teaching and writing, producing his long major works.

We know quite a lot about his life from his own accounts. His writing constantly weaves elements of autobiographical material into the exposition, mentioning people he has met, experiences he himself had, and teachings delivered to him by the many masters he encountered. The early years in the Maghrib are especially well documented because he wrote an account of his spiritual education at the hands of some 70 masters in *Rūḥ al-quds fī munāṣaḥat al-nafs*, which will be discussed below. It is said that he wrote a similar account of his eastern teachers called *Tartīb al-riḥlah*, but no manuscript has survived. For exact dates and places in the later years biographers have therefore had to rely upon notes on manuscripts, of which, as we have already mentioned, there is fortunately an exceptional number. Drawing together the information from all these sources, there are now two excellent biographies available: Claude Addas's *Quest for the Red Sulphur* (1993) (translated from the French original) and Stephen Hirtenstein's *The Unlimited Mercifier* (1999).

It seems that Ibn al-ʿArabī's father was a military man, and at the time of Ibn al-ʿArabī's birth was serving in the army of Ibn Mardanīsh, a local prince. He moved to Seville to serve at the court of the new Almohad rulers when Ibn al-ʿArabī was around seven years old. Seville at that time was a busy, cosmopolitan city where the most important ideas of the day were fluent; it was a melting pot of different cultures and races where poetry and music as well philosophy and science flourished. The Almohads represented the last flowering of the unique culture of Moorish Spain, where the three cultures of Islam, Christianity and Judaism had co-existed fruitfully. Although they had been founded as a religious reform movement and were less sympathetic than previous rulers to their non-Islamic subjects, the Caliphs nevertheless had wide cultural interests and ran a lively court. They are known to have introduced the ideas of Abū Ḥāmid ibn Muḥammad al-Ghazzālī (1058-1111) to Andalusia, and Ibn Rushd (1126-1198), the great Aristotelian philosopher who was so influential on medieval Europe, was a member of the court and became a friend of Ibn al-ʿArabī's father; in *al-Futūḥāt*, Ibn al-ʿArabī describes meeting him in Cordoba when he was a 'beardless youth.'

In this environment, Ibn al-ʿArabī received his early education. There is no indication that this had a particularly religious bent, but as the son of a Muslim family of good standing it would have included study of the *Qur'ān* alongside poetry, literature and *fiqh*. He also seems to have been interested in physical pursuits such as hunting and horsemanship, and followed his father into the army for a short period. Then, in his teens (the date is not known; the evidence would seem to indicate that he was about sixteen) he had a sudden and dramatic conversion to the way of God when he was interrupted by a Divine command in the midst of feasting, and went away into seclusion in a local graveyard. There he received a series of revelations which set the course of his life. In his later writings, he mentioned one particular vision where he saw the three prophets of the monotheistic traditions—Moses, Jesus and Muhammad (d. 632)–and was given instructions by each one. This unique receiving from all three traditions gives an indication of the inclusive nature of the knowledge which he was to express so prolifically. Jesus spoke to him of renunciation, and it was under his influence, not through the intermediary of any physical master, that in Safar 580H/May 1185 he formally entered upon the Sufi path, renouncing his possessions in favour of his father.

There followed a period of spiritual instruction, which is relatively well documented to the extent that Ibn al-ʿArabī gives us a detailed account of his many Sufi masters in Seville and throughout Andalusia and North Africa. Amongst them were many followers of the important Maghribī teacher, Abū Madyan (d. 1197 or 8), "the great master of the West," whom Ibn al-ʿArabī came to regard as his principal teacher, although they never met in the flesh. Ibn al-ʿArabī also includes four women in his list, two of whom, Nūnah Fātima bint Ibn al-Muthannā in Seville and a woman he calls "Shams, Mother of the Poor (Umm al-fuqarāʾ)," clearly had a major influence upon him. It seems that the presence of female Sufi masters was not unusual during this period but their lives are not well documented in the literature, and Ibn al-ʿArabī was exceptional in mentioning them. As we shall see later, his vision lays particular emphasis upon the feminine aspect of the Divine revelation, and he expresses a startlingly modern attitude towards women in his writings, maintaining their complete equality with men in intellectual and spiritual matters.

This period of outer instruction was accompanied by continued interior instruction in the form of revelations in dreams and visions which he received directly in his heart. Of particular note was a vision he had in the great mosque in Cordoba in 586/1190, when he saw all the prophets and messengers, from Adam to Muhammad, and their secret spiritual realities were revealed to him. This understanding of the prophets as representatives of Divine wisdom was to become a characteristic of his mode of expression, coming up again and again in his writings, forming not only the explicit structure of many of his major works such as *Kitāb al-isrā, Fuṣūṣ al-ḥikam* and *Kitāb al-'abādilah*, but also constituting a founding principle of the metaphysical vision which underlies all his mature works.

Shortly after this experience, in 589/1193, he left Andalusia for the first time and crossed over to North Africa with the intention of visiting some of the disciples of Abū Madyan. He spent nearly a year in Tunis, and formed in particular a strong relationship of friendship with a master called ʿAbd al-Azīz al-Mahdawī and his circle of followers. It is here that we hear of his first recorded composition, which was a poem which he recited at one of their gatherings, later included in *al-Futūḥāt.* On his return to Andalusia in 590/1194, he wrote the first book of which we have knowledge, *Kitāb mashāhid al-asrār al-qudsiyyah* (Contemplation of the Holy Mysteries), dedicating it to the companions al-Mahdawī. This is a series of 14 "contemplations" in the first person, written in the form of dialogue between the Real and the aspirant; in its tone and form it is evidently inspired by the *Mawāqif* (Books of Spiritual Stayings) of Muḥammad ibn ʿAbd al-Jabbār al-Niffarī (d. 965), one of his predecessors in the Sufi tradition. Each contemplation has a title in the form "Contemplation of the Light of Existence as the Star of Direct Vision rises"; "Contemplation of the Light of Taking as the Star of Affirmation rises," etc. and like the work of his predecessor, is full of paradoxes, metaphors and allusions to mysteries. Such was the enigmatic nature of the work that it attracted a number of later commentaries; in particular, one by Ibn al-ʿArabī's close companion in his later years, Ismāʿīl ibn Sūdkīn al-Nūrī (1192 or 3-1248 or 9) who was most probably recording notes from study of the text with the author himself, and another very long *sharḥ*, unique in Sufi literature, written after his death by a female mystic Sitt ʿAjam Bint al-Nafīs (d. ca. 685/1288) who took her inspiration from a dream image of Ibn al-ʿArabī. These two commentaries were used by Pablo Beneito and Suʿād Ḥakīm to produce a good critical edition of the text alongside a translation into Spanish (*Las Contemplaciones de los Misterios*) in 1994, and this in turn was used by Cecilia Twinch to produce a clear and fully annotated English translation (*Contemplation of the Holy Mysteries*) published in 2001. To give a taste, here is an extract from Contemplation 5 (*Contemplations*, 55):

> The Real made me contemplate the light of silence as the star of negation rose, and He made me speechless. However, there did not remain a single place in the whole universe where my word was not inscribed, nor was there any writing which did not come from my substance and my dictation… "Then He said to me, "I created you with speech which is the essential reality of your silence, so that, although you speak, you are silent. Through you I speak, through you I give, through you I take, through you I expand, through you I contract…

Around the same time (the exact date is not known), Ibn al-ʿArabī also produced a rather different kind of work entitled *al-Tadbīrāt al-ilāhiyyah* (Divine Governance of the Human Kingdom), which he describes as being prompted by seeing a philosophical work called *Sirr al-asrār* (The Secret of Secrets, purportedly written by Aristotle for his pupil Alexander the Great as advice on how to rule the world) at the house of one of his Andalusian masters, Abū Muḥammad al-Mawrūrī. Ibn al-ʿArabī describes how he wrote *al-Tadbīrāt al-ilāhiyyah* in less than four days, producing a book of 21 chapters which amounts to an esoteric, Sufi interpretation of the classical philosophical correlation, as in *The Republic*, between the city/kingdom and the human constitution. The exposition is centred around the position of the human being as the *khalīfah* or viceregent of God, ruled by the soul with the intellect *('aql)* acting as prime-minister and the other faculties as his ministers and servants; the metaphor is developed in some detail to include the role of, for instance, the armed forces, the scribe and the tax collector. There is still no totally reliable critical edition of *al-Tadbīrāt al-ilāhiyyah*, despite there being some good manuscripts dating from Ibn al-ʿArabī's lifetime; the early edition by H. S. Nyberg (*Kleinere Schriften des Ibn al-'Arabī*, 1919), is probably still the best. There is an English version by Tosun Bayrak (*Divine Governance of the Human Kingdom*, 1997), but this is an "interpretation" rather than a fully annotated translation and is based upon an Ottoman (therefore late) manuscript.

The exposition in *al-Tadbīrāt al-ilāhiyyah* is typical in many ways of Islamic philosophical writing, whose aim was generally to "Islamicise" the philosophical heritage of the ancient Greeks. What is not clear is the source of Ibn al-ʿArabī's knowledge of either the genre or of the ideas he discusses in such an accomplished manner, as we have no record of any philosophical instruction. We know that he was familiar with the works of al-Ghazzālī, which, as we have mentioned, had become known in al-Andalūs during the reign of the Almohads, and some people have suggested an influence by the *Ikhwān al-Safā*ʾ. In addition, Andalusia had, by the 12th century, developed its own unique culture of what might be termed "mystical philosophy" developing from writers such as Muḥammad ibn ʿAbd Allāh Ibn Masarrah (882 or 3-931), ʿAbd al-Salām ibn ʿAbd al-Raḥmān ibn Muḥammad Ibn Barrajān (d. 535/1141) and Ibn Bājjah, also known as Avempace (d. 1138), and these ideas would have been common currency. Therefore, although he confesses to no formal education in philosophy or theology (*kalām*), Ibn al-ʿArabī, rather like Shakespeare in Elizabethan England, seems to spring up spontaneously as the voice of the highly developed culture which nurtured him, demonstrating from the very beginning of his writing career remarkable knowledge and scope.

The speed with which he wrote *al-Tadbīrāt al-ilāhiyyah* is also characteristic; he wrote many of his major works in astonishingly short times, in what would appear to be a kind of fever of inspiration. He said later of his own writing methods (*al-Futūḥāt al-Makkiyyah* 1:59; *Unlimited Mercifier*, 232)

> Our writings do not follow the course of ordinary compositions... Every [other] writer acts according to the dictates of their own choice and free-will, or according to the knowledge which is specifically being promulgated... We, on the other hand, write in the following fashion: the heart clings devotedly to the door of the Divine Presence, watchful for what unfolds when the door is opened, in poverty and need, empty of all knowledge... Whatever comes to it from behind that Divine curtain, the heart hastens to obey and sets it down according to the measure appointed in the [divine] command.

Between 590/1194 and 593/1197, Ibn al-ʿArabī travelled to North Africa again, this time visiting the ancient city of Fez, which was a great spiritual centre as well as the political and cultural capital of the Almohads. Here he encountered many great saints and knowers of God, including a man he identified as the "pole" (*quṭb*) of the age, and continued to receive extraordinary interior revelations. These culminated, during his second visit, in an experience of ascension (*mi'rāj*) which mirrored that of the Prophet Muhammad on the Night Journey. He describes being taken, like Muhammad but in the imaginal world only, first on a horizontal journey across the earth to Jerusalem and then on a vertical journey through all the cosmic realms until he reached the furthest point possible, the "lote tree of the extreme limit" where he was "enveloped in lights until I became wholly light" (*al-Futūḥāt al-Makkiyyah* 3:350). In each of the heavenly spheres he encountered one of the prophets, from Adam in the sphere of the moon to Abraham in the sphere of Saturn, and had a conversation with them, through which was imparted the wisdom unique to that prophet.

There are several accounts of this journey; the first, *Kitāb al-isrā* (Book of the Night Journey) was written in 594/1198 within days of the experience, in a complex form of rhyming prose interspersed with long poetic interludes (critical edition by Suʿād Ḥakīm entitled *Kitāb al-Isrā*, 1988 but no translations). He also describes the experience twice in *al-Futūḥāt*; once in an autobiographical manner in Chapter 367 and again in the much more metaphysical and dense Chapter 167, entitled *Concerning the Mystical Knowledge of the Alchemy of True Happiness*, where the reality of the journey as inner transformation is made explicit. The image of the spiritual path as travel through the celestial spheres was also the central *motif* of the works that followed in the final years of the western period. In these, we find an increasingly detailed and comprehensive symbology which encompasses not only the planetary spheres and their correspondences or affinities (*munāsabah*) with things of the world (metals, colours, etc), but also integrates these with both the human, spiritual hierarchy of the prophets and saints, and the science of the Divine Names, i.e. the Names of God found in the *Qur'ān*.

Thus in 595H/1199 after he returned to Andalusia, whilst visiting Almeria, the home of the great Sufi school founded by Aḥmad ibn Muḥammad Ibn al-ʿArīf (1088-1141), he wrote *Mawāqi' al-nujūm* (The twilight of the stars and the rising of the crescent moons of secrets and sciences). This is a complex description of ascent as a cyclical process in which the journey passes through three spheres, each marked by the phases of twilight (signifying the end of one phase) and the dawn of the first and last crescent moons which mark a new lunar cycle (signifying a new possibility of human perfection). This important book, whose symbolism is a radical departure from the classical Sufi treatments of the *mi'rāj*, is not yet published in either an Arabic critical edition or a translation into any European language, but Denis Gril's preliminary study (*Journal of the Muhyddin Ibn 'Arabī Society Volume 40*, 2006) gives a broad outline of its form and purpose. It was also the first of many books which were written specifically for his disciple Badr al-Ḥabashī (d. 618/1220), who had been with him since his second visit to Fez and who was to remain with him for more than 20 years.

Also written in Almeria, according to Gerald Elmore, in the following year, is *Kitāb 'anqā' mughrib* (The Book of the Fabulous Gryphon concerning the Seal of the Saints and the Sun (rising) in the West). In this Ibn al-ʿArabī refers back to *al-Tadbīrāt al-ilāhiyyah*, saying that in this earlier work he had omitted to mention certain "secret functions." This second book, written again in rhymed prose (*sājʿ*), is thus devoted to bringing out the role of the *mahdī*—the "rightly guided leader"—and the Seal of the Saints (whom he identifies with Jesus), discussing both a prophetic aspect which looks to the unfolding of their functions in time, and a mystical aspect which understands them as realities which can be realised in the heart of the complete human being. It has been rigorously translated into English by Gerald Elmore in a thoroughly annotated version based upon the earliest manuscripts as *Islamic Sainthood in the Fullness of Time* (1999), although as yet no critical Arabic edition has appeared.

The ascension also forms the implicit background of a short work *Risālat al-ittiḥād al-kawnī,* which is believed to have been written in this pre-Meccan period although we have no definite information on its composition. This is a beautiful, lyrical and allusive work, reminiscent of the visionary fables of writers such as Avicenna (980–1037), Yaḥyā ibn Ḥabash Suhrawardī (1152 or 3-1191) and Farīd al-Dīn ʿAttār (d. ca. 1230). Written again in a mixture of prose, verse and rhyming prose, it fully displays Ibn al-ʿArabī's love of the Arabic language and his mastery of it. Angela Jaffray, who has translated *al-Ittiḥād* into English (*The Universal Tree and the Four Birds*, 2006, based upon Denis Gril's critical edition of the text) writes in her introduction of both the pleasure and the difficulty which his works pose for the translator (*The Universal Tree*, 19):

> Drawing from nearly all the disciplines of his time—the traditional Islamic sciences, mysticism, theology, philosophy and even alchemy and magic—Ibn al-ʿArabī's language is astoundingly rich. Anchoring himself in the (primarily) tri-consonantal Arabic root, he leaves his imagination free to explore a complex world of interpenetrating meanings and associations attainable by

> acceptable morphological permutations. Although this approach generally produces a scintillating multifaceted gem whose surfaces delight and whose deep hues attract, the reader is often at a loss when trying to fathom the seemingly endless potential meanings, both lexicographical and symbolic, of any given word or phrase.

The text itself describes a *mir'āj* experience, culminating with his arrival at the extreme limit of the cosmos/himself where the author encounters the Universal Tree and four birds—the eagle, the ringdove, the fabulous ʿAnqā' and the jet-black crow (representing intellect, soul, prime-matter, body)—who each speak to him. To give a brief taste, this is from the speech of the Universal Tree as rendered by Jaffray (*Universal Tree*, 36):

> I am the Tree of light, of speech and the eye-balm of Moses… The fruits of my garden are near at hand and my bough sways loftily as if intoxicated. It bestows grace and tenderness upon all living creatures. My branches always offer frankincense to the spirits of the Guarded Tablet and my foliage is a protection for them against the diurnal rays. My shade extends over those whom God envelops in his solicitude and my wings are spread over the people of sainthood. The spirit winds blow on me from many directions and disarrange the order of my branches. From this entanglement one hears such melodious sounds. They enrapture the supreme intellects in the utmost heights and set them running on the course inscribed upon their scroll. I am the music of wisdom that removes care through the beauty of its rhythmic song…

The final lines here would seem to be clear reference to poetic modes of expression. It is clear that Ibn al-ʿArabī produced numerous verses in this first period, both singly and as part of longer works, and many of these were later collected into *al-Futūḥāt* and the *Dīwān*. Claude Addas also mentions several visionary experiences which Ibn al-ʿArabī had during these early years which indicate that not only was the composition of poetry given to him as a particular gift; he also regarded it as the most appropriate mode for expressing the ineffable mysteries of the essential revelation given to the saints. For instance, in Bejaïa, now in Algeria, in 597/1201, whilst travelling to Mecca, he saw himself in nuptial union with each of the stars of the sky and each of the letters of the Arabic alphabet, and describes how (*Ship of Stone*, 15-16):

> God had me hear the screeching of the styluses [that record human actions]; it was a melody in double or triple time, depending on whether they were adding or taking away. "What is that refrain?," I asked. "What you are hearing is poetry" was the reply. "And what has poetry to do with me?" "It is the origin (*aṣl*) of all the following: poetic language is the permanent principle (*al-jawhar al-thābit*), while prose is the immutable consequence (*al-far' al-thābit*)."

Later, in the introduction to his *Dīwān,* he recounts that after another experience he "uttered verses that came forth from no reflection and no intellectual process whatsoever. Since that time, this inspiration has never ceased." In so upholding the value of poetry, Ibn al-ʿArabī was running counter to current theological opinion, based on the interpretation of the *Qur'ān*: 26:224 that poetry was a deviant art. This opinion he directly challenged in his introduction to his *Dīwān*, maintaining that (*Dīwān*, see *Ship of Stone,* 19):

> The Prophet was not forbidden from using poetry because of its being contemptible, degrading or in any way inferior, but rather because of its basis in allusions (*ishârât*) and symbols (*rumûz*), since poetry springs forth from subtle knowledge (*shu'ûr*). It is incumbent upon the Prophet to be clear for everyone and to use expressions as straightforward as possible.

Through this argument, repeated later in *al-Futūḥāt,* Ibn al-ʿArabī laid a metaphysical foundation for the flourishing of mystical poetry that was to play such an important role in the akbarian tradition in the centuries after his death. This was pertinent not only to his own poetical works and the direct influence they had on the later tradition, but to other poets such as Fakhr al-Dīn Ibrāhīm al-ʿIrāqī, Shabistarī, Jāmī, Fuzulī (1495?-1556) and Şeyh Galip (1757 or 8-1799) who were explicitly inspired by his ideas. These hugely popular works were one of the most important vehicles for the dissemination of Ibn al-ʿArabī's unique vision throughout the whole Islamic world in the centuries after his death (see Clark *Early Bestsellers in the Akbarian Tradition*).

In 597/1201, Ibn al-ʿArabī left Andalusia, after receiving instruction from God, to make the *ḥajj* and never returned to his native land. He travelled through Morocco and Algeria, making his farewells, and on to Tunis where he spent almost a full year with al-Mahdawī before continuing on to Cairo, Hebron and finally Mecca. We do not know the situation regarding the original texts of his first works, as there are no extant manuscripts from this period. The earliest copy we have is of *'Anqā' mughrib* (Berlin Oct. 3266) written in Fez in 1201 in a beautiful Maghribī hand by an unknown scribe, containing fragments of Ibn al-ʿArabī's own writing. All surviving copies of the other Maghribī works were written much later, opening up the question of whether they were amended in the process. From 1201 onwards, however, the situation is very different, with most of the major works mentioned below having at least one copy which can be traced to the presence of the author or one of his closest disciples.

The first work of this period that we know is a short cosmological treatise entitled *Inshā' al-dawā'ir* (The Description of the Encompassing Circles) which was written during his last stay in Tunis. This makes explicit the complex system of cosmological connections between heaven and earth which underlies all Ibn al-ʿArabī's work, and is distinguished by the inclusion of several diagrams and tables which synthesize his vision. A critical edition based on six manuscripts was produced by Nyberg in *Kleinere Schriften des Ibn al-'Arabî* (1919), and this is still probably the best Arabic text. It is reprinted alongside a good French translation by Paul Fenton and Maurice Gloton as *The Production of Circles* (1996), with an English translation in *Muhyiddin Ibn 'Arabī: a Commemorative Volume* (1993).

The two or three years Ibn al-ʿArabī spent in Mecca in 1202-1203 were a pivotal period for him, marked by a series of major spiritual experiences which confirmed his rank as a great teacher and master. The first of these happened soon after his arrival in 1201, in which, whilst circumambulating the Kaʿbah he encountered an imaginal youth (*fatā*) whom he understood to be the very embodiment of Divine Wisdom (*al-Futūḥāt* 1:47, *Unlimited* 151-2): "both speaker and silent, neither alive nor dead, both complex and simple, encompassed and encompassing." This youth communicated only in symbols, and instructed Ibn al-ʿArabī to (*al-Futūḥāt* 1:47, *Unlimited* 151-2):

> … circumambulate in my footsteps, and observe me in the light of my moon, so that you may take from my constitution that which you write in your book and transmit it to your readers.

This book was *al-Futūḥāt al-Makkiyyah,* which was begun in the first Meccan period, although it was not completed until thirty years later; it will be discussed in detail in the last section, below. In this same time period Ibn al-ʿArabī also encountered another embodiment of Divine Wisdom and Beauty in the form of a young girl, Niẓām, the daughter of a Shaykh with whom he studied *ḥadīth*. It was to her that the famous series of mystical love poems *Tarjumān al-ashwāq* was addressed. It seems that this, like *al-Futūḥāt,* was begun in Mecca, but completed some years later, as we will see. This experience of love appears to have marked the beginning of a new phase of Ibn al-ʿArabī's life, for it was in Mecca that he married for the first time and became a father.

Of works actually composed at Mecca, we have two important and subsequently very popular treatises based upon the forms of Sufi manuals, and therefore, unlike the earlier works, written in more or less straight prose. *Ḥilyat al-abdāl* (The Visible Qualities of the Substitutes) is a very short treatise written in 1202 for two of his growing group of followers concerning the four pillars of spiritual practice—seclusion, silence, hunger and vigilance. Here Ibn al-ʿArabī produces an interpretation of these principles which goes beyond the mere outward practice and looks to the most interior, essential understanding; seclusion, for instance, he defines as "having no contact with created things in one's heart." This penetration to the most essential principle was to become a characteristic of his many writings on the nature of the spiritual path in *al-Futūḥāt* and elsewhere. *Ḥilyat* has been published in a critical edition with an English translation by Stephen Hirtenstein as *Four Pillars of Spiritual Transformation* (2008).

Shortly afterwards he produced a much longer work concerning the Sufi path, *Rūḥ al-quds fī munāṣaḥat al-nafs* (The Holy Spirit in the Counselling of the Soul) which was composed in 1203, according to the prologue in response to a remark overheard in a Cairene *khanaqah* dismissing the spiritual attainments of the masters of the Maghrib. Based loosely upon the form of the classical manuals of al-Qushayrī and al-Muḥāsibī, the book can be divided into three sections, each of which describes a different aspect of "counselling." The longest, middle part is a testament to the 70-odd masters with whom he had studied in Andalusia and North Africa. This has been translated by Ralph Austin, along with selections from another autobiographical work, *al-Durrah al-fākhirah*, as a stand-alone book entitled *Sufis of Andalusia* (1971), and is one of Ibn al-ʿArabī's most accessible available works in the English language. The first part is also concerned with Ibn al-ʿArabī's own education, but in the form of a remarkably honest, internal dialogue between himself and his soul, by which he brings her into conformity with the Divine will, whilst the last concerns the cosmic function of the soul as the vice-regent of God, including a section on what Ibn al-ʿArabī calls "my non-human masters":

> [There was] gutter in the city of Fez, on a wall—it poured the water off a terrace like the gutter of the Ka'abah. I had gnosis of its adoration and was at pains to imitate it. There was also the shadow which stretches away from my body; from it I learned the two forms of adoration which it was practising. We also have shaykhs among the animals. Among those in whom I found support, there was the horse, whose adoration is astonishing, the falcon, cat, dog, the cheetah, the bee and others …

There is as yet no complete translation into any European language of the first and last sections, although there is a partial translation of the first by Roger Boase and Farid Sahnoun in *Muhyiddin Ibn 'Arabī: a Commemorative Volume* (1993, ed. Hirtenstein and Tiernan) and a summary of the whole text by Denis Gril (see *Saint et sainteté dans le christianisme et l'islam, 2007).* Neither is there a good critical edition of the Arabic text; the best source is probably the Cairo 1989 edition, and the text with commentary edited by M. al-Ghurāb (1987). Austin worked directly from manuscript, there being a very good text with an authentification by Ibn al-ʿArabī himself (Istanbul University 79).

In 1205, Ibn al-ʿArabī left Mecca and travelled East with his new family and faithful companion al-Ḥabashī. Although we know much less about this phase of his life from his own writing, there are a great many extant manuscripts which contain notes about the writing of the texts and the communal readings which took place with his groups of followers, which increased in both size and number throughout the period. It is clear that for the next twelve years he was constantly on the move between Egypt, Syria, Palestine, Iraq and Anatolia, teaching and writing. He also became an advisor to, and received patronage from, many of the local princes and rulers of the region. In this latter, which was a radical departure from his behaviour towards rulers in Andalusia, he was aided by a close friendship with Majd al-Dīn Isḥāq b. Yūsuf, a man of both spiritual and social standing whom he met in Mecca. Majd al-Dīn was a member of the court of the Seljūks of Rūm, and also one of the leaders of the Abbasid caliph's programme of Islamic revival. He invited Ibn al-ʿArabī to

Anatolia, where he consequently became an advisor to the Seljūk caliphs Giyaseddin Keyhüsrev I (1164-1211) and İzzeddin Keykâvus I (d. 1220), settling his growing family (we know of at least two sons, who are buried with him in Damascus, and a daughter who died) in Malatya. In Anatolia, he also came into contact with other important figures from the Iranian spiritual tradition which was to play such an important role in the later dissemination of his thought; he did not have direct contact with the family of Jalāl al-Dīn Rūmī as far as we know (although there are a number of stories in the oral tradition), but he did form a friendship with the great master Awḥad al-Dīn Kirmānī (d. 1238), who was also well-known as a poet (see *The Heart's Witness: the Sufi Quatrains of Awḥaduddīn Kirmānī,* trans. Bernard Weischer and Peter Lamborn Wilson, 1978).

This was an immensely fruitful phase for his writing, and many of the medium-length and shorter works (20 and 30 at an estimate, although many of these texts are undated) were written as he criss-crossed his way between the major cultural centres of the central region. Often they were composed under the power of revelation or at the request of a student. In 1205, for instance, during a stay in Mosul which lasted less than a month, he composed at least three works: two short pieces (*Kitāb al-jalāl wa'l-jamāl* (The Book of Majesty and Beauty), *Kitāb al-kunh mā budd li'l-murīd minhu* (What is essential for the seeker) and a major work entitled *al-Tanazzulāt al-Mawṣiliyyah* (Descents of the Revelation at Mosul). This last is a substantial text of 90 pages in the autograph manuscript (Murad Bukhari 162), consisting of 55 chapters concerning the esoteric significance of the acts of daily worship such as ablution and prayer, correlating these with the celestial spheres and those who dwell in them. According to Addas (*Red Sulphur*, 221) it is one of the works whose inspired nature is most evident, with several of the middle chapters (46 to 54) being highly reminiscent of *Kitāb al-Isrā.* There is also evidence that Ibn al-ʿArabī at this time was having to take precautions against the religious authorities, for he says in the introduction that he wrote the text in "enigmatic and symbolic language" so as to "frustrate and punish the exoteric scholars." There is no critical edition of the Arabic text, despite there being a number of very good early manuscripts, nor any translation into a European language. There are a number of Arabic editions, of which the latest is in *Rasā'il Ibn 'Arabī,* Volume 6, ed. Saʿīd ʿAbd al-Fattāḥ, 2001, which also gathers together many of the shorter treatises and *rasā'il.*

It is not possible to mention all the important works of this period, as they are so numerous. Of special interest because of the existence of two good English translations is *Risālat al-anwār* (Treatise of Lights) which was composed in Konya in 1206 at the request of a friend who asked that Ibn al-ʿArabī should explain the journey of ascension to the Lord of Power and the return to the creatures. Rabia Terri Harris's translation of this text *Journey to the Lord of Power* (1981), including material from the later commentator ʿAbd al-Karīm al-Jīlī, gives a general rendering, whilst a more scholarly version by Radtke and O'Kane in *New Critical Essays: on the Present State and Future Tasks of the Study of Sufism* (2005) also includes a new German translation, plus a French rendering by Michel Chodkiewicz and a critical edition of the Arabic text in transcription.

Also worthy of mention is *Kitāb al-tajalliyāt al* (Book of Theophanies) composed some time before 1209 in Aleppo. This describes a number of theophanic visions on subjects such as perfection, generosity and compassion, with the distinctive feature of assuming the form of dialogues between the author and the great Sufis of the past such as Abū al-Qāsim Junayd ibn Muḥammad (d. 910), Sahl ibn ʿAbd Allāh al-Tustarī (818 or 19-896?), al-Ḥusayn ibn Manṣūr al-Ḥallāj (857-922), etc. There is a good critical edition of this text prepared by ʿUthmān Yaḥyā (1988) with a commentary alongside it by one of Ibn al-ʿArabī's most important followers in these later years, Ismāʿīl ibn Sūdkīn al-Nūrī. There is as yet no English translation, although there is a French version by Stephan Ruspoli (*Le Livre des Théophanies d'Ibn 'Arabī*, 2000), but from it has emerged one of Ibn al-ʿArabī's most famous texts in the English-speaking world, *The Theophany of Perfection,* as rendered into verse form by Henry Corbin. It begins (*Creative Imagination*, p. 174-175):

Listen, O dearly beloved!
I am the reality of the world, the centre of the circumference,
I am the parts and the whole.
I am the will established between Heaven and Earth,
I have created perception in you only in order to be the object of My Perception.

If then you perceive Me, you perceive yourself.
But you cannot perceive Me through yourself.
It is through My Eyes that you see Me and see yourself,
Through your eyes you cannot see Me.

Dearly beloved! I have called you so often and you have not heard Me.
I have shown Myself to you so often and you have not seen Me.
I have made Myself fragrance so often, and you have not smelled Me,
Savorous food, and you have not tasted Me.
Why can you not reach Me through the object you touch
Or breathe Me through sweet perfumes? Why do you not see Me?
Why do you not hear Me?
Why? Why? Why?...

Perhaps the best known work of this period is the already-mentioned, *Tarjumān al-ashwāq* (Interpreter of Desires), which was composed during a return visit to Mecca in 1214. Dedicated to a living woman, the work takes the form of a cycle of 61 love poems based upon the form of the classical Arabic *qaṣīdah*, using pre-Islamic motifs of remembrance of the beloved *(naṣīb)*, and especially the theme of the *za'n*, the journey of the beloved and her female companions away from the poet. Ibn al-ʿArabī develops the form, however, to integrate both post-Islamic imagery and the language of mystical experience. As Michael Sells, the main modern commentator on *Tarjumān al-ashwāq,* has explained (Sells, Poem 18):

> Throughout the *Tarjumān,* Ibn al-ʿArabī constructs two parallel worlds of stations: the stations of the classical Arabic poetic tradition and the stations of the Islamic *ḥajj*. ... The language of the *ḥajj* is a major motif throughout the *Tarjumān,* with continual references to the Kaʿbah, the circumambulation *(ṭawāf)* of the Kaʿbah, and stations along the *ḥajj* route, such as the station of Mina. Indeed, when the *Tarjumān*'s sensual love-lyricism in the pre-Islamic style of the remembrance of the beloved raised suspicions that Ibn al-ʿArabī was writing profane verse, Ibn al-ʿArabī defended it with the justification that it was simply an account of his own *ḥajj.*

The poems have become famous in two particular respects. Firstly, for their depiction of the Divine feminine, with the image of the beloved (Niẓām) becoming the very embodiment of the Divine Sophia in a way which is almost unique within Islamic literature. This is aptly shown by this extract from the middle of Poem 2 where he compares her to Bilqīs (Queen of Sheba) (Nicholson, 49):

When she walks on the glass pavement, thou seest a sun on a celestial sphere in the bosom of Idris.
When she kills with her glances, her speech restores to life, as though she, in giving life, were Jesus.
The smooth surface of her legs is [like] the Torah in brightness, and I follow it and tread in its footsteps as though I were Moses.
She is a bishopess, one of the daughters of Rome, unadorned; thou seest in her a radiant goodness.
Wild is she, none can make her his friend; she has gotten in her solitary chamber a mausoleum for remembrance.
She has baffled everyone who is learned in our religion, every student of the psalms of David, every Jewish doctor and every Christian priest.
If with a gesture she demands the Gospels, thou would deem us to be priests and patriarchs and deacons...

Secondly, the poems are famous for the ending of Poem 11 which lines are perhaps the most famous in Sufi literature, widely used to show the breath and tolerance of the Sufi approach to spirituality (Sells, *Longing and Belonging*):

Marvel, a garden among the flames!
My heart can take on any form: a meadow for gazelles, a cloister for monks,
For the idols, sacred ground, Kaʿbah for the circling pilgrim, the tables of the Torah, the scrolls of the *Qur'ān*.
I profess the religion of love; wherever its caravan turns along the way, that is the belief, the faith I keep.

It is perhaps surprising, given the power of these poems, that there has been so little work done on them. The only complete translation remains that of Nicholson in the 1911 edition, which also includes a critical edition of the text. Michael Sells has written some very helpful commentaries upon the major poems, and himself produced a set of translations in *Stations of Desire* (2000). As he intimates in the extract above, the poems attracted criticism when they were written, and Ibn al-ʿArabī was prevailed upon by his main disciples al-Ḥabashī and Ismāʿīl ibn Sūdkīn al-Nūrī to write a commentary to explain their spiritual meaning. This he seems to have done in a great hurry in Aleppo in the same year, adding a new preface to the work at the same time, and it became customary to publish the resulting work, entitled *Dhakhā'ir al-a'lāq* alongside the poems themselves. There is not yet a full translation of *Dhakhā'ir* in English—Nicholson's, printed alongside the poems in the 1911 edition, is only a selective translation—but there is a good complete version of both texts in French by Maurice Gloton (*L'interprète des desires*, 1996).

The writing of the commentary founded a whole new genre of mystical writing, and it became the custom in the akbarian tradition as it unfolded over the following centuries to write metaphysical commentaries upon mystical poems by other writers. Thus there is a tradition in particular of producing commentaries upon Ibn al-Fārid's two famous poems, *The Poem of the Way* and *The Wine Song,* which began with the early followers of Ibn al-ʿArabī such as Ṣadr al-Dīn al-Qūnawī and al-Farghānī (d.699/1299) and continued into the 18th century, with a famous commentary being produced by the Damascene follower ʿAbd al-Ghanī ibn Ismāʿīl Nābulusī (d. 1731). Within the Ottoman tradition, a tradition grew up of commentary upon Rūmī's *Mathnawī,* the most famous of which is that of al-Anqarawī (d.1041/1631).

The last work which should be mentioned in this middle period is the short-medium length *Kitāb al-isfār 'an natā'ij al-asfār* (The Unveiling of the Effects of the Voyages). This is a meditation on the meaning of the spiritual journey in general, and on the inner meanings of various prophetic journeys, such as the ascension of Muhammad, the fall of Adam, and the journeys of Idris/Enoch, Noah, Abraham, Lot, Jacob, Joseph and Moses in particular. This is available in a critical edition and translation by Denis Gril (*Le Dévoilement des Effets du Voyage*, 1994) and is soon to be available in an English translation by Angela Jaffray (forthcoming).

In 618/1221, a number of events occurred which loosened Ibn al-ʿArabī's ties with the Seljuk regime in Malatya and Konya. Firstly, his long-term companion al-Ḥabashī died and was buried in Malatya. Secondly, his friend Majd al-Dīn died, leaving his young son, then about eight years old, in the care of Ibn al-ʿArabī; this young boy, Ṣadr al-Dīn al-Qūnawī, was educated by Ibn al-ʿArabī and eventually became his spiritual and literary heir. Thirdly, the Seljuk sultan İzzeddin Keykâvus was succeeded by his brother Alâeddîn Keykubad I (d. 1237) with whom Ibn al-ʿArabī had no special connection. In 1223, Ibn al-ʿArabī moved to the Umayyad capital, Damascus, and settled there under the patronage of the Qādī Muḥyī'l-Dīn Ibn al-Zakī, who provided him with a house large enough for his now substantial household and his students. He remained there until his death, and as far as we know, ceased travelling, concentrating instead on consolidating his written heritage and teaching increasingly large groups—the final *samā'* on *al-Futūḥāt* in the last two or three years of his life list as many as 40 people, many of them from Iran and even further East.

He produced four of his most important and influential works during these final eighteen years. Firstly, the complex and as yet almost unpublished *Kitāb al-'abādilah* (Book of the Servants of God) which was composed sometime before 1229. This is a systematic work in which 117 "servants of God" *('abd Allāh)* are described according to the different character traits (*akhlāq*) of the Perfect Human Being, each *'abd Allāh* representing a spiritual modality symbolized by the association of a Divine Name and the name of a particular prophet or *waliyy*. There are as yet no translations at all of the work, and no reliable Arabic editions; the Cairo 1969 edition has only 96 chapters, for instance. But it deserves a mention because of length of the work (80 pages in the autograph manuscript, Yusuf Aga 4859) and because of the importance of its content, representing a mature synthesis of Ibn al-ʿArabī's understanding of the interior meaning of the prophetic heritage. It also displays an innovative literary form in which Ibn al-ʿArabī speaks in the voice of each servant, assuming different writing styles and characteristics for each one, a device later made famous by the 20th century Portuguese poet Fernando Pessoa who called it "heteronymy" ("On the Spiritual Typologies in Ibn al-ʿArabī's *Kitāb al-'abādilah*").

Secondly, the *Fuṣūṣ al-ḥikam* (The Ringstones of Wisdom) written in 1232 after a dream in which Ibn al-ʿArabī saw the book being handed to him by the Prophet Muhammad himself, is probably the best known work of the whole *opus*. It consists of 27 chapters, each dedicated to the spiritual meaning and wisdom of a particular prophet from Adam to Muhammad. Each prophet is considered to be like the ringstone of a signet ring, on which is engraved a divine wisdom, and between them they represent all the different communities of mankind. A dense and demanding text which is considered to contain the quintessence of Ibn al-ʿArabī's teaching, it combines between the different intellectual traditions of medieval Islam—philosophy, kalam and hadith—as well as including a number of verses. It is about eighty pages in length in the earliest manuscript (written by Ṣadr al-Dīn al-Qūnawī with an authorisation by Ibn al-ʿArabī himself (Evkaf Muzesi 1933)) and is relatively accessible due to its foundation in the stories of the *Qur'ān*. Thus it has been the most studied and discussed text in the centuries since Ibn al-ʿArabī's life, attracting a massive commentary tradition which began with the circle of immediate disciples (Ṣadr al-Dīn al-Qūnawī's *al-Fukūk*) and continued into the 20th century; unfortunately, this lies outside the scope of this article. To give a taste of the flavour of the book, and its perspective, one could probably not do better than the first few lines, from "The Divine Wisdom in the Word of Adam." (Burckhardt *The Wisdom of the Prophets,* 8)

> God (*al-ḥaqq*) wanted to see the essences of His most perfect Names, whose number is infinite—and if you like, you can equally well say: God wanted to see His own Essence in one global object which, having been blessed with existence, summarized the Divine Order, so that there He could manifest His mystery to Himself. For the vision that a being has of himself in himself is not the same as that which another reality procures for him, and which he uses for himself as a mirror. In this, he manifests himself to himself in the form which results from the 'place' of vision…

The *Fuṣūṣ al-ḥikam* has been the most widely translated of Ibn al-ʿArabī's works, and versions are currently available in at least 10 modern languages, including Persian, Hindi, Turkish and Serbo-Croatian. It is not surprising, therefore, that there are many translations into English. To mention just a few; the first to appear was a partial translation, consisting of twelve chapters, by Angela Culme-Seymour (*The Wisdom of the Prophets* (1975)), based upon the French translation by Titus Burckhardt. In the 1980s a full translation was done by Ralph Austin entitled *The Bezels of Wisdom* (1980), and more recently there has been a rendering by Caner K. Dagli with comprehensive notes as *The Ringstones of Wisdom* (2004), although the best translation into a European language probably remains Charles-André Gilis's two-volumed *Le Livre des Chatons des Sagesse* (1998) in French. There is a critical edition by Abū'l-ʿAlā ʿAfīfī (Beirut, no date), although he did not have access to the authenticated copy.

The third major work of this final period is the compilation of poetry, *al-Dīwān,* to which

Ibn al-ʿArabī devoted considerable energy in the last years of his life. A version of this was amongst the earliest of works to be published (Būlāq, Cairo, 1855) and this, reproduced in various forms using litho or digital printing, remains the principal source text. In recent years it has become clear that it represents only a part of the total poetic heritage; research into the manuscript base has revealed that there are many versions of the *Diwān* which include additional material, and in particular, Claude Addas has discovered a manuscript in Bibliothèque Nationale in Paris entitled *Dīwān al-ma'ārif al-ilāhiyyah,* comprising some 239 folios, which hardly overlaps at all with the Būlāq volume. It is evident that much more work needs to be done before the real extent of Ibn al-ʿArabī's poetic heritage is fully established.

However, as the Būlāq edition remains the only easily-available version in print, this article will concentrate upon that. Again, given the importance of the work, it is surprising how little scholarly attention it has received, and this is perhaps because unlike *Tarjumān al-ashwāq,* where the poems work together as a whole, it is much more difficult to perceive any unified structure within *al-Dīwān.* Also, it is here that Ibn al-ʿArabī's poetry appears at its most metaphysical and challenging; R. W. J. Austin, one of the few scholars to have worked on translations of these poems, contrasts him to other great figures such as Rūmī and Ibn al-Fāriḍ, saying that (Hirtenstein and Tiernan, *A Commemorative Volume,* p. 182):

> In the *Dīwān*, Ibn al-ʿArabī does indeed offer us a wide variety of poetic styles and topics, but the poetic genius of Ibn al-ʿArabī is much more razor-like and taut, revealing always to us the great teacher he must have been, the great creator of structured visions and the weaver of closely woven ontological tapestries. Thus, the overall impression of the poetry of the *Dīwān* is less that of a great mystical forest than that of a magnificently constructed and finely decorated and embellished castle or fortress of Sufi doctrine and experience.

Gerald Elmore's study of the text proposes (although he admits that the evidence is not conclusive) that the ordering of the poems is basically chronological, with the first 40 pages consisting of poems drawn from the early works *Kitāb al-isrā, Mawāqi' al-nujūm, Kitāb 'anqā' mughrib.* The middle section (40-218) seems to date from the period 1210-1221. It consists of many miscellaneous verses, but also several coherent groups devoted to particular themes; a group of 27 describing the initiation of students (mostly women) with a *khirqah;* another group ending with the rhyme *alif maqsūrah*; a major series of 114, unique as far as we know within Arabic literature, each dedicated to a *sūrah* of the *Qur'ān*, and a final group (218-32) of twenty-nine *mu'ashsharāt* (i.e. poems of ten lines) each devoted to one of the letters of the Arabic alphabet. Some of these groups may have been written originally as independent works—there are several extant manuscripts, for instance, of the *mu'ashsharāt.* By contrast, the remainder of the book (232-475) consisting of nearly 400 poems, seems to have been written in the last period of Ibn al-ʿArabī's life, in Damascus, and are not therefore to be found elsewhere. As such they constitute, Elmore suggests, a "veritable poetic journal of the Shaykh's thoughts, dreams and feelings during the last few years of his life."

Very few of these poems have been translated or studied. Both Austin and Elmore present translations of a few verses, but the only systematic translation is "Odes of Ibn al-ʿArabī: Twenty-seven *Muwashshahāt* and One *Zajal*" by Emery and Corriente which is an English and Spanish rendering of some of the strophic poems scattered throughout the *Dīwān.* The only long study in English known to me is an as-yet-unpublished PhD thesis by Denis McAuley "An Analysis of Selected Poems from Ibn al-ʿArabī's *Dīwān*" (Oxford 2007) which concentrates upon commentary and analysis of individual poems, taken particularly from the *mu'ashsharāt*, the *Qur'ān* series and a number of poems with specific rhymes, such as *ri'*. To give a taste of the style of the *Dīwān*, here are two examples which are in translation: the first an extract by Austin (Austin, *Translation*), showing Ibn al-ʿArabī's habit of moving from personal experience to metaphysical commentary, and the second a poem based upon a famous ode by Ḥallāj, in a rendering by McAuley (McAuley, p. 160)

With my own hands I laid my little daughter to rest because she is of my very flesh.
Thus I am constrained to submit to the rule of parting, so that my hand is now empty and contains nothing.
Bound to this moment we are all in, caught between the yesterday that has gone and the tomorrow that is yet to come.
This flesh of mine is pure silver, whilst my inner reality is as pure gold.
Like a bow have I grown, and my true posture is my rib.
My Lord it is who says he has created me in a state of suffering and loss.
How then can I possibly hope for any rest, dwelling as I do in such a place and state.
Were it not for that state I would be neither child nor parent…

****

When the secret appeared in my heart,
my being was effaced and my star disappeared.
My heart changed with the secret of my Lord,
And I became absent from the outline of my body's senses.
I came from Him, through Him to Him,
on a boat built from my shining determination.
I hoisted onto it the sails of my thought,
in the waves of my hidden knowledge.
The wind of my longing blew towards Him,
and the boat passed through the sea like an arrow.

I crossed the sea of proximity, until
I saw clearly the one I do not name.
So I said, "My heart has seen you,
and I will own a part in your love.
For you are my intimacy and my celebration,
my goal in love and my spoils."

The final work of this last period, and therefore of Ibn al-ʿArabī's life, is *al-Futūḥāt al-Makkiyyah*. Begun in 1202 in Mecca, Ibn al-ʿArabī completed the first version of the work more than thirty years later in 1233 in Damascus and almost immediately embarked upon re-writing it from beginning to end. The second recension was completed in 1239, and it is this text, in the author's own handwriting, which has survived to the present day. The evidence of more than 70 certificates indicates that it was read out, section by section, to groups of disciples, many of them quite large, between 1236 and 1240 at the Shaykh's house in Damascus, and that the reading was continued in Aleppo by a much smaller group lead by Ṣadr al-Dīn al-Qūnawī and Ismāʿīl ibn Sūdkīn al-Nūrī in 1240-1241, after Ibn al-ʿArabī's death, presumably honouring a task dear to their master's heart. There is as yet no complete critical edition of the text based upon this manuscript, although ʿUthmān Yaḥyā embarked upon the task, producing 14 out of an expected 30+ volumes before his death in 1997 (1972-1991). The standard version of the text, used by common consent for referencing, is the third Būlāq edition (1329/1911), subsequently cloned into many lithographed or digitized versions, which is based upon the second recension. In recent years a good nine-volume edition with an index has appeared which is also widely used (1999).

Although *al-Futūḥāt* is in some ways a *summa* that gathers together and adds detail and order to ideas that Ibn al-ʿArabī had dealt with in earlier works, Chodkiewicz argues that nevertheless it is evident "that a new spiritual inspiration is at work here, that a brighter light is shining over a landscape he had already noted and that it clarifies aspects of the landscape that theretofore had remained hidden" (see *Meccan Revelations 2*, p.7). One aspect of the coherence of the vision which underlies these "revelations" or "openings" is that the structure of the book, consisting of 560 chapters divided into six main sections (*fusūl*), each with its own prologue and *muqaddimah,* remains constant over the two recensions, indicating that Ibn al-ʿArabī adhered to the original imaginal form of the book given by the youth he encountered at the Kaʿbah. Each of these six sections has an over-riding theme, which Chodkiewicz outlines as follows:

Section 1 (Chapters 1-73)

Seventy-three chapters on "knowledge" giving the metaphysical and cosmological underpinning of the spiritual journey which the book constitutes.

Section 2 (Chapters 74-189)
One hundred and sixteen chapters on the Sufi "behaviours" (*mu'āmalāt*) such as repentance (*tawbah*), remembrance (*dhikr*), certainty (*yaqīn*) which Chodkiewicz has shown are based upon the virtues outlined in al-Qushayrī's famous *Risālah*—except that Ibn al-ʿArabī couples each virtue with a second chapter about its "abandonment"—*tark al-tawbah, tark al-dhikr*—in which any trace of duality is removed from the practice.

Section 3 (Chapters 190-269)
Eighty chapters on spiritual states (*aḥwāl*).

Section 4 (Chapters 270-383)
One hundred and fourteen chapters on "spiritual abodes" (*manāzil*) which Chodkiewicz has shown to correspond to the 114 *surāh*s of the *Qur'ān*.

Section 5 (Chapters 384-461)
Seventy-eight chapters on the "meeting places" (*munāzalāt*)—the half-way point at which God's descent towards the person and the person's ascent towards God coincide.

Section 6 (Chapters 462-560)
Ninety-nine chapters on the spiritual stations (*maqāmāt).*

Some of these chapters are quite short—a page or two—but some are long enough to have been books in their own right, and indeed are often found as independent works; Chapter 178, for instance, on Divine Love, Chapter 558 on the Divine Names or the lengthy final chapter, Chapter 560. As we have already mentioned, each chapter begins with a poem which encapsulates its message, and within the text Ibn al-ʿArabī weaves together metaphysics with biographical detail, stories and descriptions of his own spiritual experiences to make a complex narrative in which, as Jim Morris has said; "the heart of the fully realized human being is understood as the locus of every conceivable form and dimension of human experience, of all the infinite, ever-renewed divine 'signs' or theophanies that constitute the ever-renewed creation." (*The Reflective Heart*, p.2)

Only a fraction of *al-Futūḥāt* has been translated to date, and even complete translations of individual chapters are rare, most of the available publications combining study and translation because of the difficulty of the content. To mention just a few: *The Meccan Revelations, vol. 1 & 2* (2002 &2004) has an excellent introduction by Michel Chodkiewicz and translations and summaries of key chapters by some of the best scholars in the field. William Chittick's comprehensive summaries of Ibn al-ʿArabī's metaphysics in *The Sufi Path of Knowledge* and *The Self-Disclosure of God* (1989 & 1998) contain long passages of direct translation, whilst his *Imaginal Worlds* (1994) gives a complete rendering of Chapter 66. Jim Morris has written extensively not only on the content of *al-Futūḥāt* but also on how to approach it in a contemporary context (see *The Reflective Heart*, 2005). Finally, one of the very few extended translations has been undertaken by Aisha Bewley in the *Great Books of the Islamic World* series; she has produced a series of renderings, without notes or commentary, of the chapters concerned with the *shari'a* in Section 1 (Chapters 68-72). As we have already mentioned, the project of producing a full version of *al-Futūḥāt* is an enormous one, requiring not only great linguistic skills to cope with the complexity of Ibn al-ʿArabī's language, but also great insight into the meaning of the material.

This summary, relatively extensive as it is, gives only a taste of the vast heritage which Ibn al-ʿArabī has left us. It has focused upon giving an outline of the major long works and works with a literary bent which have English translations. Amongst the works omitted are more overtly religious works such as prayers and *ḥadīth* collections, and more directly Sufi works such as books of spiritual advice to students, even though good English translations have appeared in the last few years of some of the major works in these *genres*. Most of the shorter works in the Hyderbad *Rasā'il,* including the series of treatise on the letters of the Arabic alphabet, have also remained undiscussed. But it is hoped that the works which have been included give some idea of both the depth and breadth of Ibn al-ʿArabī's thought, and a taste of the richness of his language and forms of expression, thus beginning to re-instate—or even, one could say, "instate"—his reputation as a great literary genius as well as a master of metaphysics. Taking an overview of the whole *corpus* of editions and translations at this point, exactly 100 years since the publication of the first English translation of an Ibn al-ʿArabī work—Nicholson's *Tarjumān al-ashwāq*—also gives us a chance to appreciate the work of the pioneering scholars of the 20th century who have begun to establish an approach to the translation and understanding of these very demanding texts. There are now many people both in the West and within Islamic countries who are building upon these solid foundations, and it is hoped that in the 21st century we shall see much more of the vast heritage of this important and challenging figure brought into good editions and translations, thus opening up the treasury of his unique vision to contemporary readers.

REFERENCES

Claude Addas, *Quest for the Red Sulphur: the Life of Ibn 'Arabī*, Islamic Texts Society Golden palm series (Cambridge: Islamic Texts Society, 1993);

Claude Addas, "The Ship of Stone," *Journal of the Muhyiddin Ibn 'Arabī Society*, 19 (1996): 5-24;

A.E. Affifi, *The Mystical Philosophy of Muhyid Din Ibnul Arabi* (Cambridge: Cambridge University Press, 1964);

R.W.J. Austin, "Ibn al-ʿArabī, Poet of Divine Realities" in *Muhyiddin Ibn 'Arabī: a Commemorative Volume*, ed. Stephen Hirtenstein and Michael Tiernan (Oxford: Muhyiddin Ibn 'Arabī Society, 1993);

R.J.W. Austin, "Translation of Two Poems from the *Diwân* of Ibn 'Arabi," *Journal of the Muhyiddin Ibn 'Arabi Society,* 7 (1988): 1-16;

Pablo Beneito, "On the Spiritual Typologies in Ibn ʿArabī's *Kitāb al-Abādila*," Symposium of the Muhyddin Ibn ʿArabī Society, Oxford, May, 2011;

William C. Chittick, *Imaginal Worlds: Ibn al-'Arabī and the Problem of Religious Diversity*, SUNY Series in Islam (Albany: State University of New York Press, c1994);

William C. Chittick, *The Self-Disclosure of God: Principles of Ibn al-'Arabī's Cosmology*, SUNY Series in Islam (Albany: State University of New York Press, c1998);

William C. Chittick, *The Sufi Path of Knowledge: Ibn al-'Arabi's Metaphysics of Imagination* (Albany, N.Y.: State University of New York Press, c1989);

Jane Clark, "Early Bestsellers in the Akbarian Tradition," *Journal of the Mudhyiddin Ibn 'Arabī Society*, 33 (2003): 22-54;

Henry Corbin, *Creative Imagination in the Sufism of Ibn 'Arabī*, (Princeton: Princeton University Press, 1969);

Gerald Elmore, "The Būlāq Dīwān of Ibn ʿArabī: Addenda to a Tentative Description," *Journal of Arabic Literature,* 29, 3-4 (Oct-Dec. 1998): 136-166;

Denis Gril, "The Journey Through the Circles of Inner Being according to Ibn ʿArabī's *Mawāqi¡ al-nujūm,*" *Journal of the Muhyddin Ibn 'Arabī Society*, 40 (2006): 1-20;

Denis Gril, "Le saint et le maitre ou le sainteté comme science de l'Homme d'apres le *Rūh al-Quds* d'Ibn ʿArabī" in *Saint et sainteté dans le christinisme et l'islam,* ed. Denis Gril and Nelli Ami (Paris: Maisonneuve & Larose; Aix-en-Provence: Maison méditerranéenne des sciences de l'homme,2007);

Suad Hakim y Pablo Beneito, *Las contemplaciones de los misterios* (Murcia: Editora Regional de Murcia, 1996);

Stephen Hirtenstein, *The Unlimited Mercifier: the Spiritual Life and Thought of Ibn 'Arabī* (Oxford: Anqa Publishing; Ashland, Or.: White Cloud Press, 1999);

Toshihiko Izutsu, *Sufism and Taoism,* (Berkeley: University of California Press, 1994);

Awḥaduddīn Kirmānī, *The Heart's Witness: the Sufi quatrains of Awḥaduddīn Kirmānī*, ed. Bernd Manuel Weischer; trans, Bernard Weischer and Peter Lamborn Wilson (Tehran: Imperial Iranian Academy of Philosophy, 1978);

Denis E. McAuley, "An A to Z of Sufi Metaphysics: Ibn 'Arabi's *Mu'ashsharat*" in *The*

Meeting Place of British Middle Eastern Studies: Emerging Scholars, Emergent Research & Approaches, ed. Amanda Philips and Refqa Abu-Remaileh (Cambridge: Cambridge Scholars Publishing, 2009), 60-77;

Denis E. McAuley, "An Analysis of Selected Poems from Ibn al-ʿArabī's Dīwān" (Ph.D. diss. Oxford University, 2007);

Jim Morris, *The Reflective Heart: discovering spiritual intelligence in Ibn 'Arabi's "Meccan illuminations"* (Louisville: Fons Vitae, 2005);

Jim Morris, "Ibn ʿArabi's Rhetoric of Realisation: Keys to Reading and 'Translating' the *Meccan Illuminations, pt. 1-2,*" *Journal of the Muhyiddin Ibn 'Arabī Society*, 33 (2003): 54098, 34 (2003): 103-144;

Reynold Alleyne Nicholson, *Mystics of Islam* (London: G. Bell and Sons, 1914);

Reynold Alleyne Nicholson, *Studies in Islamic Mysticism*, (Cambridge: Cambridge University Press, 1921);

Michael A. Sells, "At the way stations, stay: Ibn ʿArabī's Poem 18 (*Qif bi 'l Manāzil)* from the *Translation of Desire,*" *Journal of the Muhyiddin Ibn 'Arabī Society*, 18 (1995): 41-57;

Michael A. Sells, "Longing, Belonging and Pilgrimage in Ibn ʿArabī's *Interpreter of Desires*" in *Languages of Power in Islamic Spain*, ed. Ross Brann. Occasional Publications of the Department of Near Eastern Studies and the Program of Jewish Studies, Cornell University, No 3 (New York: CDL Press, 1997), 178-96;

Michael A. Sells, *Stations of Desire: love elegies from Ibn 'Arabi and new poems* (Jerusalem: Ibis, 2000);

Anne Marie Schimmel, *As Through a Veil: mystical poetry in Islam* (New York: Columbia University Press, 1982); (Oxford: One World, 2001), 37-41;

Osman Yahya, *Histoire et Classification de l'Oeuvre d'Ibn 'Arabī: étude critique* (Damascus: Institut Français de Damasc, 1964).

.

ʿUmar ʿAlī Ibn al-Fāriḍ

(1181-1235)

TH. EMIL HOMERIN
University of Rochester

WORKS

Dīwān

Editions

Ibn al-Fāriḍ's collection of Arabic poetry, his *Dīwān*, has been published in a number of editions since the 19th century. By far the best and most critical edition is:

Dīwān of 'Umar Ibn al-Fāriḍ, ed. Giuseppe Scattolin (Cairo: Institut Français d'Archéologie Orientale, 2004).

Translations

The Mystical Poems of Ibn al-Fāriḍ, trans. and annotated by A.J. Arberry (Dublin: Emery Walker Ireland, Ltd., 1956);

The Poem of the Way, trans. A.J. Arberry (London: Emery Walker Ltd., 1952);

Th. Emil Homerin, *From Arab Poet to Muslim Saint: Ibn al-Fāriḍ, His Verse and His Shrine*, 2nd rev. ed. (Cairo: American University in Cairo Press, 2001);

Th. Emil Homerin, "Ibn al-Fāriḍ: Rubaʿiyat, Ghazal, Qasida," in *Windows on the House of Islam*, ed. John Renard (Berkeley: University of California Press, 1998), 194-201;

Th. Emil Homerin, "Ibn al-Fāriḍ, 'A Call to Remembrance,'" in *Night & Horses & the Desert: an Anthology of Classical Arabic Literature*, ed. Robert Irwin (New York: Overview Press, 1999), 331-333;

Th. Emil Homerin, "Mystical Improvisations: Ibn al-Fāriḍ Plays al-Mutanabbī," in *Ghazal as World Literature I*, ed. Thomas Bauer and Angelika Neuwirth (Beirut: Orient-Institut Beirut, 2005), 107-129;

Th. Emil Homerin, *'Umar Ibn al-Fāriḍ: Sufī Verse, Saintly Life* (New York: Paulist Press, 2001);

Th. Emil Homerin, *The Wine of Love and Life: Ibn al-Fāriḍ's al-Khamriyyah and al-Qaysarī's Quest for Meaning* (Chicago: University of Chicago Center for Middle Eastern Studies, 2005);

Martin Lings, *Sufi Poems: a Mediaeval Anthology* (Cambridge, UK: Islamic Texts Society, 2004);

R.A. Nicholson, *Studies in Islamic Mysticism* (Cambridge, UK: Cambridge University Press, 1921);

Stefan Sperl, "Qasida Form and Mystic Path in 13th Century Egypt: a Poem by Ibn al-Fāriḍ," in *Qasida Poetry in Islamic Asia and Africa*, ed. S. Sperl and C. Shackle (Leiden: E.J. Brill, 1996), 1:65-81; 2:106-111, 423-424;

Wheeler McIntosh Thackston, Jr., "*The Jīmīyah*," in *Introduction to Classical Arabic Literature, ed.* Ilse Lichtenstader (New York: Schocken Books, 1974), 312-314.

ʿUmar ʿAlī Ibn al-Fāriḍ (1181 or 1182-1235) is the most accomplished Arab poet within Islamic mysticism. He mastered the Arabic poetic tradition, composing verse in a number of forms including the quatrain, the *ghazal*, and the formal ode (*qaṣīdah*). Ibn al-Fāriḍ's verse is highly lyrical and often mannered, as he employed a variety of rhetorical devices to evoke religious themes and feelings involving the love between ephemeral creation and its eternal creator. Ibn al-Fāriḍ intimates a mystical view of life in which the human being may regain a lost union with the divine beloved. The mystical content of his poems, their intricate style, elegant beauty, and moving power have impressed generations of Arab poets, popular singers, and contemporary Egyptian writers, including the Nobel laureate Najīb Maḥfūẓ (1911-2006). As a result, for centuries, Ibn al-Fāriḍ has been admired and imitated as an Arab poet and venerated as a Muslim saint, and he continues to bear the title *sulṭān al-'āshshiqīn*, "the sultan of lovers."

At the time of his death in 1235, ʿUmar Ibn al-Fāriḍ was an established poet and a respected teacher, and several of his students left brief accounts of him. These earliest sources agree that ʿUmar was born in Cairo on the 4th of Dhū 'l-Qaʿdah 576/1181. He was the son of Abū 'l-Ḥasan ʿAlī ibn al-Murshid ibn ʿAlī, and a descendent of the Saʿd tribe of Preislamic Arabia. His father ʿAlī ibn al-Murshid migrated to Cairo from Ḥamāt prior to ʿUmar's birth, probably to serve in the judiciary under the Ayyubid dynasty, where he was a women's advocate (*fāriḍ*), thus ʿUmar's eventual title Ibn al-Fāriḍ, "son of the women's advocate." ʿAlī ibn al-Murshid was a member of the Shafiʿi law school and noted for his religious knowledge and scholarship.

ʿAlī ibn al-Murshid oversaw ʿUmar's education in the religious sciences and, especially, in Arabic language, literature, and poetry. ʿUmar also studied *ḥadīth*, the traditions of the prophet Muḥammad (d. 632), with the noted traditionalist of Damascus Abū Muḥammad al-Qāsim ibn ʿAlī al-ʿAsākirī (d. 527/1203). Early sources also note that Ibn al-Fāriḍ was a member of the Shafiʿi law school, and undertook the study and practice of Islamic mysticism, or Sufism, and composed Sufi poetry, but they do not give any information regarding mystical guides or guidebooks that he may have consulted. Ibn al-Fāriḍ's earliest biographers add that he went on pilgrimage to Mecca, where he lived and studied for a time, after which he returned to Cairo. There, he resided at the Azhar congregational mosque, supporting himself by teaching *ḥadīth* and poetry. ʿUmar Ibn al-Fāriḍ died on Jumādā I 632/1235, and was buried at the foot of Mt. Muqaṭṭam in the Qarāfah, the large cemetery north east of Cairo.

The early accounts of Ibn al-Fāriḍ's life by his students and younger contemporaries may be augmented by an important later source, the *Dībājah* ("The Adorned Proem") by the poet's grandson ʿAlī (d. ca. 1335). ʿAlī wrote this work as an introduction to the *Dīwān Ibn al-Fāriḍ*, the definitive collection that he made of his grandfather's verse. However, the *Dībājah* must be used with circumspection regarding material on Ibn al-Fāriḍ's life, for the work is clearly a hagiography praising a saintly life, not a factual biography. Nevertheless, ʿAlī does provide critical information, particularly regarding Ibn al-Fāriḍ's family. ʿAlī notes in the*Dībājah* that Ibn al-Fāriḍ was married and had at least two sons, Kamāl al-Dīn Muḥammad (d. 1290) and ʿAbd al-Raḥmān, and an unnamed daughter, who was ʿAlī's mother. For the most part, ʿAlī organizes his stories in such a way as to portray Ibn al-Fāriḍ's progression along the mystic path from a religiously naive youth to an enlightened Sufi master and divinely inspired poet. Not surprisingly, ʿAlī recounts many miraculous events involving his grandfather, including Ibn al-Fāriḍ's instantaneous travel over hundreds of miles, his talking with a lion, and his week-long trances followed by automatic recitation of scores of verses.

Yet, leaving aside such tales, ʿAlī may have based his narrative, if loosely, on Ibn al-Fāriḍ's life. According to the *Dībājah*, ʿUmar, as a youth, would accompany his father in court and teaching sessions. But growing restless, ʿUmar would go to the Muqaṭṭam Hills for spiritual retreat, where he met an old shaykh who instructed him to seek enlightenment in Mecca. ʿUmar followed this advice and went on pilgrimage to Mecca, where he stayed for fifteen years. Then, Ibn al-Fāriḍ returned to Cairo as a mature and educated religious scholar and a spiritually illumined poet. In Cairo, Ibn al-Fāriḍ was a member of the religious and cultural elite of his day, teaching at the Azhar mosque, and discussing poetry with colleagues. This is corroborated by the literary scholar Khalīl ibn Aybak al-Ṣafadī (ca. 1297-1363), who recounts an instance of Ibn al-Fāriḍ adjudicating a dispute between two poets who claimed to have composed the same poem.

In several other stories, ʿAlī underscores his grandfather's reputation as a venerated poet and religious figure in Cairo, where his verse was recited before the Ayyubid sultan Malik al-Kāmil Muḥammad (ruled 1218-1238). As a result, the sultan sent an emissary with a gift of money for the poet, which Ibn al-Fāriḍ flatly refused. The sultan and one of his amirs made similar offers on several later occasions, which Ibn al-Fāriḍ declined, with the clear moral being that Ibn al-Fāriḍ would not be tainted by money or power. Again, we can not verify the historical accuracy of these accounts, but it is significant that Ibn al-Fāriḍ's collected poems do not contain any panegyrics for rulers or their retainers. Moreover, the Ayyubid sultan Malik al-Kāmil is commemorated in the Christian tradition as venerating holy men, particularly St. Francis of Assisi (1182-1226), who was said to have gone to Egypt to put a stop to a bloody crusade.

ʿAlī mentions that Ibn al-Fāriḍ composed some of his poems in Mecca, although ʿAlī suggests that Ibn al-Fāriḍ composed much more of his verse in Cairo, including his famous poem *Naẓm al-sulūk* ("Poem of the Sufi Way"). ʿAlī apparently believed that this celebrated poem of over 750 verses was the product of Ibn al-Fāriḍ's overwhelming mystical experiences. ʿAlī states:

In most of his moments of inspiration, the Shaykh [Ibn al-Fāriḍ] was always perplexed, eyes fixed, hearing no one who spoke, nor even seeing them. Sometimes he would be standing, sometimes sitting, sometimes he would lie down on his side, and sometimes he would throw himself down on his back wrapped in a shroud like a dead man. Ten days, more or less, would pass while he was in this state, he neither eating, drinking, speaking, or moving... Then he would regain consciousness and come to, and his first words would be a dictation of what God had enlightened him with of the ode *Naẓm al-sulūk*. (Homerin, *'Umar Ibn al-Fāriḍ*, 313).

This account of Ibn al-Fāriḍ's trance has led many of his admirers to believe that Ibn al-Fāriḍ's verse was inspired by God. Overwhelmed by mystical love, Ibn al-Fāriḍ would recover and spontaneously recite verses for his most famous mystical poem, the *Naẓm al-sulūk*. Yet this depiction of Ibn al-Fāriḍ as an inspired oracle, so popular in the later Sufi tradition, deflects attention from the literary qualities of his verse. For Ibn al-Fāriḍ carefully crafted and polished his poems as is evident from his reuse and variations on key themes and language within his verse. Moreover, his poems often display antithesis, word play and other rhetorical elements, as well as occasional conscious imitations of verse by earlier Arab poets, especially the great Abū 'l-Ṭayyib al-Mutanabbī (915-965). In his poem *al-Dhāliyyah*, for instance, Ibn al-Fāriḍ used 17 of 18 rhyme words from a poem by al-Mutanabbī. Yet while the latter praised his patron's prowess on the battlefield, Ibn al-Fāriḍ commends the patience of a lover slain by love, thus transforming al-Mutanabbī's panegyric into a lament on love.

In addition to the *al-Dhāliyyah*, Ibn al-Fāriḍ composed about a dozen other poems, including love poems (*ghazal*), odes (*qaṣīdah*), wine odes (*khamriyyah*), and his massive *Naẓm al-sulūk*. He also composed a number of quatrains and riddles. Regardless of the genre, Ibn al-Fāriḍ usually speaks of love, longing, and the quest for union ("Ibn al-Fāriḍ: Rubaʿiyat," 196):

Pass round remembrance of one I desire, though that be to blame me,
for tales of the beloved are my wine.

Let my ear witness the one I love, though she be far away,
in blame's fantasy not the phantom dream of sleep.

For her memory is sweet to me in whatever form
even if those rebuking me mix it with bitter grief.

In these opening verses, Ibn al-Fāriḍ likens the memory of a lost love to wine that consoles the lover. Intoxication results from the remembrance of the beloved (*ḥabīb*), a term often used for the prophet Muḥammad, "the beloved" of God. Ibn al-Fāriḍ again alludes to Muḥammad with the phrase "tales of the beloved" (*aḥādīth al-ḥabībī*), a clear reference to the prophetic traditions (*aḥādīth*). Moreover, his use of the term *dhikr* ("remembrance," "recollection") suggests the Sufi *dhikr* ceremonies that produce ecstatic experiences. The lover of the poem goes on to claim that he has remained true to his beloved, no matter the cost:

My spirit be her ransom, in loving her I've lost it;
my fate was at hand before my day of death.

But because of her, my disgrace is good, and savory still
is being thrown and broken down from my high station (*maqām*).

Ibn al-Fāriḍ almost invariably describes the pain and torment that the lover must experience to eradicate selfishness and so purify his heart ("Ibn al-Fāriḍ: Rubaʿiyat," 196):

On the edge of night, my heart (*qalb*) is parched for passion,
while in morning light, my anguished eyes shed tears.

My heart and my eye: one is snared by her beauty's subtle sense (*manā*);
the other lured by her soft, supple stature.

The lover's body is emaciated by love, thereby revealing that his will and desires have been purged as well ("Ibn al-Fāriḍ: Rubaʿiyat," 197):

I was hidden, consumed, concealed even from consumption,
and, too, from my diseases' cure and the cooling of my burning thirst.

So I knew no one save passion who knew my place,
and my keeping the secrets to guard my honor.

All that love left of me (*yubqī*) was a heart broken
by grief, affliction, and boundless disorders.

Having undergone spiritual transformation, the lover appears as the archetypal lover encompassing all passion and every slain lover:

So in my every limb was every heart
hit by every arrow whenever she gazed with pleasure.

Had she unrolled my body, she would have seen in every essence
every heart holding every burning passion.

The lover has learned true humility by suffering patiently, and when he meets his beloved, he passes away in a timeless union ("Ibn al-Fāriḍ: Rubaʿiyat," 198):

I rubbed my cheek in the dust for her to step on,
so she said: "Good news for you, kiss my veil!"

But my soul would not have it, guarding me jealously
to keep my longing pure.

So we passed the night together as my command
willed over desires:
I saw kingship my kingdom and time my
slave.

In this and other poems, Ibn al-Fāriḍ often employs standard Sufi technical terms to refer to the lover's heart (*qalb*) and subtle essence (*ma'nā*), his mystical station (*maqām*) and rapture (*wajd*), as the lover passes away to abide (*yubqī*) in loving union (*waṣl*). Here and in several other poems, Ibn al-Fāriḍ declares the beloved to be the object of the lover's prayers and pilgrimage ("Ibn al-Fāriḍ: Rubaʿiyat," 196):

I pray and chant when I recite, in memory of her,
and I delight in the prayer-niche where she
leads my prayers before me;

On pilgrimage, purified I cry in her name: "I'm
here to serve!" (*labbayka*)
and I see my holding back from her to be like
the breaking of my fast.

A distinguishing feature of many of Ibn al-Fāriḍ's poems is their many place names referring to sites in Arabia located along the Cairo to Mecca pilgrimage route, a route Ibn al-Fāriḍ traveled several times ("Ibn al-Fāriḍ: Rubaʿiyat," 199):

Oh rider of the sturdy she-camel--may you be
protected from ruin--
if you cross the rugged hard ground or roll up
the wide-spread torrent beds

Traveling by Naʿmān al-Arāk, turn aside there
to a wide valley, which I knew well.

Then to the right of ʿAlamān, east of Naʿmān,
halt and head for its fragrant *arīn* blossoms.

In speaking these place names, Ibn al-Fāriḍ recollects his pilgrimage, and in memory, at least, joins his physical residence in Cairo with his spiritual home in sacred Mecca. In this way, Ibn al-Fāriḍ again intimates the spiritual nature of both his love and beloved. Ibn al-Fāriḍ's poems, then, may be read as hymns of love to God and His prophet Muḥammad.

This is clearly the case in two of his poems that are part of the canon of Islamic mystical literature, the *al-Khamriyyah* ("Wine Ode"), and the *Naẓm al-Sulūk* ("Poem of the Sufi Way"). Ibn al-Fāriḍ begins the *Wine Ode* by stating explicitly that his wine is not from earthly grapes (Homerin, *'Umar Ibn al-Fāriḍ*, 47):

In memory of the beloved, we drank a wine;
we were drunk with it, before creation of the
vine!

Ibn al-Fāriḍ's *Wine Ode* resembles classical Arabic poems praising earthly wine and human love. Yet, from this first verse, there is a persistent mystical quality to the poem, whose wine has been viewed as a symbol, a metaphor, and, perhaps, too, as an earthly manifestation of the divine love suffuse in all existence. Ibn al-Fāriḍ goes on to describe the wine's miraculous medicinal properties, which can cure all who are in some way spiritually or emotionally broken (Homerin, *'Umar Ibn al-Fāriḍ*, 48):

Could they sprinkle the wine on a dead man's
earth,
the spirit would return to him, his body revived.

Could they fling into the shadow of its trellised
vine
a sick man on the point of death, disease
would flee him;

Could they bring a cripple near its tavern, he
would walk,
and from mention of its flavor, the dumb
would talk.

Once again, in the *Wine Ode*, Ibn al-Fāriḍ links wine with *dhikr*, "memory," and the Muslim mystical practice of recollection. In addition, he claims to have been intoxicated by the wine prior to his earthly existence ("Ibn al-Fāriḍ: *Ruba'iyat*," 50):

The wine made me drunk before my birth,
abiding always with me though my bones be
worn away.

Here, Ibn al-Fāriḍ alludes to Sufi interpretations of the *Qur'ānic* passage 7:172:

> And when your Lord drew from the loins of the children of Adam, their progeny and made them bear witness against themselves, "Am I not your Lord?" They said: "Indeed, Yes! We so witness!" Lest they say on the Day of Resurrection: "Indeed, we were unaware of this!"

Like many other Sufis, Ibn al-Fāriḍ regarded this pre-eternal covenant as a love pact with God. In this light, the lover and his various companions in the *Wine Ode* could stand for all of the spirits of human beings prior to creation, while the vine represents the material world. Thus, the wine drunk before the vine's creation may be the wine of Paradise. This heavenly drink cleanses its drinkers of the stains of human volition, selfishness, and duality, and so renders them worthy of union ("Ibn al-Fāriḍ: Rubaʿiyat," 51):

Be drunk from it, if only for the life an hour,
and you will see time a willing slave under your command!

The underlying themes of the *Wine Ode* are the loving relationship between God and His worshippers, and the intoxicating effects of its recollection (*dhikr*). This leads to mystical union, when God annihilates His lover and assumes his senses, another key theme in Ibn al-Fāriḍ's verse. Ibn al-Fāriḍ elaborates on these and other aspects of Islamic mysticism in the 760 verses of his *Naẓm al-sulūk*, or *Poem of the Sufi Path*, one of the longest Arabic poems ever composed. The poem begins in the tavern, like the *Wine Ode*, but it quickly shifts to the lover's long lament for his sufferings on behalf of the beloved. However, in sharp contrast to classical Arabic poetry where women are usually seen but not heard, the beloved speaks to rebuke her pretentious suitor for being in love with himself, not her. This spurs the lover on to a genuine quest for love, which culminates with union near the Kaʿbah in pre-eternity ("Ibn al-Fāriḍ: Rubaʿiyat," 119-121):

I was given her protection on a day that was not a day
in my priority prior to her appearing to enjoin the pact.

So I gained love of her, but not by sound or sight,
not by fated acquisition, or tugging disposition,

And I burned with thirst for her in the World of the Command
where nothing was manifest, drunk before my creation.

Passion annihilated the attributes here between us
that had never abided there, so they passed away,

And I found what I had cast away from me
emerging to me, returning from me with more.

In my contemplation, I saw my soul with the attributes
that had veiled me from myself in my confining cloister;

I was without doubt she whom I had loved,
and for her, my soul had passed me on to me.

For my soul had burned for her unaware, but in my witnessing
it was not ignorant of the soul of the affair.

Here, after 167 verses, Ibn al-Fāriḍ abruptly informs his audience that it is now time to explain his long love poem. This leads him to address a number of mystical themes revolving around love, particularly that between human beings and God. Frequently, Ibn al-Fāriḍ assumes the poetic persona of a guide for the perplexed, as he offers advice on a range of matters including unselfish love, spiritual intoxication and illumination, the pains of separation from the beloved and the indescribable bliss of union. Throughout the poem, the individual is urged to pass away from a self-absorbed life to one of selfless love. Though always difficult, this progressive mystical transformation relies on the power of the love between God and His worshipper, that eternal love that underlies all of existence ("Ibn al-Fāriḍ: Rubaʿiyat," 149):

The beloveds and the lovers--and this is no suspect surmise--
are our manifestations to us, self-revelations in love and splendor.

So every hero in love am I and she
the beloved of every hero, all names of a disguise,

Names which named me truly as I appeared
to myself by a self that was hidden.

I was still her and she still me,
no separation, one essence in love.

At the conclusion of the *Poem of the Sufi Way*, the lover reaches his apotheosis as an embodiment of the all-embracing Light of Muḥammad, God's instrument of creation and revelation, and so he returns enlightened to his heavenly home ("Ibn al-Fāriḍ: Rubaʿiyat," 291):

My full moon never waned; my sun, it never set,
and all the blazing stars were led by means of me.

By my leave, in my realm my planets moved,
and my angels bowed down to my rule.

In the world of remembrance the soul has her ancient lore;
right guidance to it my students seek from me,

So hurry to my union old where I have found
the elders of the tribe as babes,

For my friends drink dregs I left behind,
while those before, ahead of me, their heady drink falls short of mine!

Ibn al-Fāriḍ's poems were admired and memorized during his lifetime, and they have been read, studied, and imitated for centuries. Occasionally, a few, more conservative, Muslims have censored Ibn al-Fāriḍ for his unitive vision of existence, for using a female beloved as a symbol of God, and for comparing God's love to an intoxicating wine, a drink that the *Qur'ān* prohibits. However, generations of Arab-speaking Muslims have admired Ibn al-Fāriḍ for his beautiful and moving love poems advising those who would travel the Sufi path. These poems and a grandson's reverent account of Ibn al-Fāriḍ's mystical life have inspired many Muslims to venerate Shaykh ʿUmar as a saint and make pilgrimage to his shrine, where they still bless his memory and grave in Egypt today.

REFERENCES

Ibn al-Fāriḍ, *The Mystical Poems of Ibn al-Fāriḍ*, trans. A.J. Arberry (Dublin: Emery Walker Ireland, Ltd., 1956);

Ibn al-Fāriḍ, *The Poem of the Way*, trans. A.J. Arberry (London: Emery Walker Ltd., 1952);

Issa J. Boullata, "Towards a Biography of Ibn al-Fāriḍ," *Arabica* 38(1981), 38-56;

Issa J. Boullata, "Verbal Arabesque and Mystical Union: a Study of Ibn al-Fāriḍ's 'Al-Ta'iyyah al-Kubrā'," *Arab Studies Quarterly* 3(1981), 152-169;

Emile Dermenghem, *L'Éloge du vin* (Paris: Les Éditions véga, 1931);

Ignazio Di Matteo, "Sulla mia interpretazione del poema mistico d'Ibn al-Fāriḍ," *Rivista degli studi orientali* 8(1919-1920): 479-500;

Ignazio Di Matteo, *Il gran poema mistico noto col nome di At-tâ'iyyah al-kubrá* (Rome: n.p., 1917);

Joseph von Hammer-Purgstall, *Das arabisch hohe Lied der Liebe* (Vienna: Kaiserl. konigl. Hofund staatsdrukerei, 1854);

Muḥammad Muṣṭafā Ḥilmī, *Ibn al-Fāriḍ: sultān al-'āshiqīn* (Cairo: Maṭbaʿat Miṣr, 1963);

Muḥammad Muṣṭafā Ḥilmī, *Ibn al-Fāriḍ wa 'l-ḥubb al-ilāhī*, 2nd ed. (Cairo: Dār al-Maʿārif, 1971);

Th. Emil Homerin, *From Arab Poet to Muslim Saint: Ibn al-Fāriḍ, His Verse and His Shrine*, 2nd rev. ed. (Cairo: American University in Cairo Press, 2001);

Th. Emil Homerin, "Ibn al-Fāriḍ: Rubaʿiyat, Ghazal, Qasida," in *Windows on the House of Islam*, ed. John Renard (Berkeley: University of California Press, 1998), 194-201;

Th. Emil Homerin, "Ibn al-Fāriḍ's Personal Dīwān," in *Le dévelopement du soufisme en Égypte à l'époque mamelouke*, ed. Richard McGregor and Adam Sabra (Cairo: Institut

Français d'Archéologie Orientale, 2006), 234-243;
Th. Emil Homerin, "Mystical Improvisations: Ibn al-Fāriḍ Plays al-Mutanabbī," in *Ghazal as World Literature I*, ed., Thomas Bauer and Angelika Neuwirth (Beirut: Orient-Institut Beirut, 2005), 107-129;
Th. Emil Homerin, *'Umar Ibn al-Fāriḍ: Sufi Verse, Saintly Life* (New York: Paulist Press, 2001);
Th. Emil Homerin, *The Wine of Love and Life: Ibn al-Fāriḍ's al-Khamrīyah and al-Qaysarī's Quest for Meaning* (Chicago: University of Chicago Center for Middle Eastern Studies, 2005);
Martin Lings, "Mystical Poetry," in *ʻAbbasid Belle-Lettres, ed.* Julia Ashtiany et al. (Cambridge: Cambridge University Press, 1990), 235-264;
ʻAbd al-Khāliq Maḥmūd, *Shi'r Ibn al-Fāriḍ* (Cairo: Dār al-Maʻārif, 1984);
Carlo A. Nallino, "Ancora su Ibn al-Fāriḍ e sulla mistica musulmana," *Rivista degli studi orientali* 8(1919-1920): 501-552;
Carlo A. Nallino, "Il poema mistico arabo d'Ibn al-Fāriḍ in una recente traduzione italiana," *Rivista degli studi orientali* 8(1919-1920): 1-106;
ʻĀṭif Jawdah Naṣr, *Shi'r Ibn al-Fāriḍ: dirāsah fī fann al-shi'r al-Sūfī* (Beirut: Dār al-Andalus, 1982);
R.A. Nicholson, *Studies in Islamic Mysticism* (Cambridge, UK: Cambridge University Press, 1921);
Giuseppe Scattolin, "al-Farghānī's Commentary on Ibn al-Fāriḍ's Mystical Poem *al-Tā'iyyat al-Kubrā*," *Mélanges* (Institut dominicain d'études orientales du Caire) 21(1993): 331-383;
Giuseppe Scattolin, *L'esperienza mistica di Ibn al-Fāriḍ attraverso il suo poema al-Tā'iyyat al-Kubrâ* (Rome: Pontificium Institutum Studiorum Arabicorum et Islamologiae, 1988);
Giuseppe Scattolin, "L'expérience mistique de Ibn al-Fāriḍ a travers son poèma al-Tā'iyyat al-Kubrā," *Mélanges* (Institut dominicain d'études orientales du Caire) 19(1989): 203-223;
Annemarie Schimmel, *As Through a Veil: Mystical Poetry in Islam* (New York: Columbia University Press, 1982).

Abū ʻAbd Allāh Ibn al-Ḥajjāj

(ca. 931–24 May 1001)

MARY ST. GERMAIN
University of Washington

WORKS

Dīwān (Collected Poems).

Editions

Durrat al-tāj min shi'r Ibn al-Ḥajjāj, 2 vols., selected by Badīʻ al-Zamān Hibat Allāh al-Asturlābī, ed. ʻAlī Jawād al-Ṭāhir (Kūlūniyya: Manshūrāt al-Jamal, 2009);

Taltīf al-mizāj min shi'r Ibn al-Ḥajjāj, selected by Jamāl al-Dīn Muḥammad ibn Nubātah; ed. Najm ʻAbd Allāh Muṣṭafā. (Sūsah: Dār al-Maʻārif li 'l-Ṭibāʻah wa 'l-Nashr, 2001);

Yatīmat al-dahr fī maḥāsin ahl al-'aṣr, selected by ʻAbd al-Malik Ibn Muḥammad al-Thaʻālibī (Beirut: Dār al-Kutub al-ʻIlmiyyah, 1983), 3:35-119.

Abū ʻAbd Allāh al-Ḥusayn ibn Aḥmad Ibn al-Ḥajjāj was one of the leading poets of the Buwayhid period. He spent most of his life in Baghdad and was a Shiite. After finishing his formal education he began a career in the Buwayhid bureaucracy. At this time he began to write formal poetry. He soon resigned his position to concentrate on his writing, having quickly found that he could earn considerably more by writing poetry in *mujūn* and *sukhf*, two styles particularly popular in his time. Both of these styles involve a high level of verbal obscenity and disregard for social mores. His *Dīwān* eventually filled ten volumes. Although Ibn al-Ḥajjāj received monetary rewards for his poetry from Buwayhid rulers, he is more closely associated with the viziers Abū Muḥammad al-Ḥasan ibn Muḥammad al-Muhallabī (903-963) and Abū 'l-Fatḥ ʿAlī ibn Muḥammad Ibn al-ʿAmīd, (948 or 949-ca. 977). On the basis of the good impression left by one of his poems, Ibn al-Ḥajjāj was appointed *muḥtasib*, or market inspector, of Baghdad. There was considerable disparity between the position's responsibility for upholding public morality and the obscenity of his poetry. Thus, it is perhaps not surprising that, due to another of his poems, he lost his position as *muḥtasib* and was sent to prison. Nevertheless, this interlude apparently did not ultimately harm his career, because he invested the earnings from his poetry in estates and died a wealthy man. Throughout his lifetime he participated in influential literary circles in Baghdad and was ranked among the most important poets of the period. When he died in 1001, he was buried in Baghdad at the feet of Mūsā 'l-Kāẓim (ca. 745–ca. 800), the seventh *Imām* of the Twelver Shiites.

Very little biographical information is available about Ibn al-Ḥajjāj. ʿAbd al-Malik ibn Muḥammad al-Thaʿālibī (961 or 962-1037 or 1038), another writer of the Buwayhid period, wrote prolifically about Arabic literature, culture and language and knew Ibn al-Ḥajjāj personally. Al-Thaʿālibī included a substantial section of Ibn al-Ḥajjāj's poetry and prose in his *Yatīmat al-dahr fī maḥāsin ahl al-'aṣr*, an anthology surveying major writers of the second half of the tenth century, but included only minimal biographical information. In the late twelfth or early thirteenth century, Yāqūt ibn ʿAbd Allāh al-Ḥamawī (1179?–1229), an Arab geographer and student of literature, gave some information about Ibn al-Ḥajjāj in his biographical dictionary of literary figures, the *Irshād al-arīb ilā ma'rifat al-adīb*. In the nineteenth century, Muḥsin al-Ḥusaynī 'l-ʿĀmilī (1865-1952) in his biographical dictionary of important Shiites, the *A'yān al-Shī'ah*, compiled a more thorough biography than is found in the earlier works and in his selection of Ibn al-Ḥajjāj's poetry, included some poems not found in the *Yatīmat al-dahr fī maḥāsin ahl al-'aṣr*.

Ibn al-Ḥajjāj's full name was Abū ʿAbd Allāh al-Ḥusayn ibn ʿAḥmad ibn Muḥammad ibn Jaʿfar al-Nīlī 'l-Baghdādī. He was born in Baghdad. In his *Tārīkh Baghdād*, Abū Bakr Aḥmad ibn ʿAlī Khatīb al-Baghdādī (1002-1071) specifies Ibn al-Ḥajjāj's year of birth as around 941. However, some of his poems refer to his age in a way that suggests an earlier birth date, around 931. Also, his 78-line poem praising Nāṣir al-Dawlah the Ḥamdānid (d. 968), an important member of the Syrian dynasty that included Sayf al-Dawlah (915 or 916-967), was written late in 947. It is highly unlikely that Ibn al-Ḥajjāj would have been in a position to write a serious praise poem at six or seven years of age.

Following a typical traditional education in Islam and Arabic language, Ibn al-Ḥajjāj became a student of Abū Isḥāq Ibrāhīm al-Ṣābī (925-994), who served as chief secretary to the early Buwayhid ruler, Muʿizz al-Dawlah (915 or 916–967). When senior secretaries such as al-Ṣābī took beginning secretaries like Ibn al-Ḥajjāj under their wing, they provided advanced training in appropriate styles of writing as well as guidance in the manners, clothing, behavior towards individuals of various ranks and other factors essential to the success of the "Renaissance" men of the Buwayhid period. Presumably, this was an important part of Ibn al-Ḥajjāj's education. Ibn al-Ḥajjāj's family had traditionally served in government service and as secretaries, so it is not surprising to find him in al-Ṣābī's entourage. Al-Ṣābī certainly encouraged Ibn al-Ḥajjāj in starting an administrative career, too. However, the latter soon noticed that he could earn more through his poetry and gave up his position in the bureaucracy.

Ibn al-Ḥajjāj is described at length by Ṣalāḥ al-Dīn Khalīl ibn Aybak al-Ṣafadī (ca. 1297-1363) in his biographical dictionary *al-Wāfī bi 'l-wafayāt*. This description dates from more than two hundred years after the subject's death and may therefore reflect some degree of literary and ethical conventions instead of being strictly factual. Nevertheless, it indicates that Ibn al-

Ḥajjāj espoused the dress and manners required for success at court. He was characterized as good looking, dignified, and devout, with fine clothes and good manners. He is portrayed as regularly praising kings, nobles, and amirs, as was expected of poets.

In his early career as a poet, Ibn al-Ḥajjāj first joined the court of al-Muhallabī, who was vizier to Muʿizz al-Dawlah from 950-963. Abū 'l-Ṭayyib al-Mutanabbī (915–965), another major poet, but one whose pride and sensitivity over "appropriate" recognition of his status frequently led to the loss of his patrons, spent some time in Baghdad attempting to develop a relationship with al-Muhallabī. The two did not get along and al-Muhallabī encouraged poets of his court to satirize al-Mutanabbī. Ibn al-Ḥajjāj produced one such poem.

After this period, Ibn al-Ḥajjāj joined the courts of the viziers Abū 'l-Faḍl al-ʿAbbās al-Shīrāzī and Abū 'l-ʿAbbās Muḥammad ibn al-ʿAbbās. Under the vizier Abū Ṭāhir Muḥammad Ibn Baqiyyah, who held that position from 973-977, he was appointed *muḥtasib*, often translated as "market inspector." A *muḥtasib*, however, held much wider responsibilities. As well as checking the weights and measures in the market and controlling disagreements, he was supposed to ensure adherence to acceptable public morals. Thus, his duties included such wide ranging responsibilities as controlling prostitution and other kinds of meetings between men and women, enforcing the prohibition on the use of alcohol, the prohibition on the use of a tomb owned by a different person, interdictions against the use of spells, prophecies, and talismans, destroying musical instruments, preventing public games of backgammon or chess, prevention of surgeons from performing castrations on men, upkeep of drains, ensuring legal methods of slaughter, and even conducting discussions of what constituted correct performance of religious practices such as *idhān* and prostration. Ibn al-Ḥajjāj lost this position when he was jailed because one of his poems offended a high-ranking individual.

Sometime during the same period, he was in contact with Abū 'l-Fatḥ ʿAlī ibn Muḥammad Ibn al-ʿAmid, (948 or 949–ca. 977), who was the son of the great vizier Abū 'l-Faḍl Ibn al-ʿAmīd (d. 970) and succeeded his father as vizier from 970 to around 977. Abū 'l-Fatḥ Ibn al-ʿAmid greatly admired Ibn al-Ḥajjāj's poetry. Abū 'l-Faḍl Ibn al-ʿAmīd eventually irritated his master, the Buwayhid ruler Mu'ayyad al-Dawlah (d. 984), and was executed. Al-Ṣāḥib Ibn ʿAbbād then succeeded him as vizier. He too apparently admired Ibn al-Ḥajjāj's poetry, since he provided him with a generous pension.

Ibn al-Ḥajjāj lived in a neighborhood of eastern Baghdad called Sūq al-Yaḥyā It was located between the main bridge at Bāb al-Ṭāq and the caliphal palaces on the eastern side Baghdad. Thus it was a wealthy district until riots from around 959 between the Sunnis and Shiites and civil unrest by the poor caused significant damage in Bāb al-Ṭāq and surrounding areas. Nevertheless, the area remained one of the leading districts throughout Ibn al-Ḥajjāj's life. Over the years, he earned a great deal of money from his poetry and invested it in property there and elsewhere. As a result, he eventually had estates in a variety of locations. One location was in the city of Wāsiṭ and another was in al-Nīl, another suburb of Baghdad.

Ibn al-Ḥajjāj's poetry was highly respected by his contemporaries. He wrote in two complete different styles: one was traditional Arabic poetry and the other emphasized *sukhf* and *mujūn*. Although neither *sukhf* nor *mujūn* has been studied sufficiently to determine a comprehensive definition, *mujūn* was said to employ a type of joking involving a combination of a frivolous attitude, obscenity, bad manners and impudence, and *sukhf* was said to involve a shallow wit, lack of concern for social consequences and obscenity. This second style contributed to his reputation for skill but there was also prejudice against a tendency toward obscenity and general rudeness in its subject matter, particularly among more religious or conservative individuals. In all fairness, *sukhf* and *mujūn* were more popular with the upper classes of the Buwayhid period than they had been in several preceding generations. Although the reasons behind this have not been determined, it is possible that it relates to the difference in traditional expectations versus actual experience. Since the rulers and upper eschelons of power could no longer support their staff and literary contributors the way earlier generations had, *sukhf*'s disrespect of authority may have resonated particularly well with its audience. In addition, with the tenuous economic conditions of the period, it was not too far a step down to poverty or even homelessness. Thus, there may have been a greater sympathy towards the down and out than in some other periods.

The continuing respect and admiration of succeeding generations for Ibn al-Ḥajjāj's work can be seen in the fact that Yāqūt, in his *Irshād,* reports that Abū ʿAbd Allāh was a poet of the same rank as Imrū' al-Qays and that no writer in between was quite like either one of them. His assessment seems to have been based on skill in the use of traditional techniques, plus their ability to introduce a new technique or topic smoothly. In Ibn al-Ḥajjāj's case, he was noted for the sweetness of his traditional poetry and his innovation was the insertion of *sukhf* and *mujūn* into this sweetness. Yāqūt stressed that no other poet before him had inserted such an extremity of *mujūn* into sweet pronunciation.

During Ibn al-Ḥajjāj's lifetime, his friend al-Sharīf al-Raḍī (970-1016)—who was the *naqīb*, or head, of the ʿAlids, and himself a highly respected Neoclassical poet—made a selection of Ibn al-Ḥajjāj's poems, excluding those with *sukhf* and *mujūn*. The collection was entitled *al-Nazīf min al-sakhīf*, but an extant copy has so far not been found. Close to a century later, Badīʿ al-Zamān Hibat Allāh al-Asṭurlābī (d. 1139 or 1140), a scholar, poet and astronomer critical in the development of the astrolabe, put together a collection, this time concentrating on his *sukhf* poetry. This work was entitled *Durrat al-tāj fī shiʿr Ibn al-Ḥajjāj.* That Ibn al-Ḥajjāj's poetry continued to be popular is evidenced by the appearance of yet another selected anthology. Nearly two centuries after his death, Muḥammad ibn Muḥammad Ibn Nubātah al-Miṣrī (1287-1366) would compile the *Laṭā'if al-taltīf*, later published as *Taltīf al-mizāj min shi'r Ibn al-Ḥajjāj*. It contains poetry both with and without *sukhf* and *mujūn*. Significant amounts of Ibn al-Ḥajjāj's poetry are also quoted in *al-Risālah al-Baghdādiyyah*. This work was published in an version minimally edited by Adam Mez and attributed to the unidentifiable author, Abū 'l-Muṭahhar Muḥammad b. Aḥmad al-Azdī. Al-Azdī is the name found on the manuscript. Another edition, edited by ʿAbbūd al-Shāljī, attributed to Abū Ḥayyān al-Tawḥīdī (ca. 922-ca. 1014), because of a significant quantity of quotations from his works.

Like Yāqūt, al-Thaʿālibī considered the strengths of Ibn al-Ḥajjāj's poetry to be the way he carefully arranged lines for both meaning and smoothness of pronunciation, the sweetness of the sound, its beauty, eloquence, and pure Arabic language. He considered its weaknesses to be the use of slang, cant, colloquial Arabic, local dialects, and its *sukhf* and *mujūn*. He noted that Ibn al-Ḥajjāj frequently used regional pronunciations, both Meccan and Khuldī.

Over the years, Ibn al-Ḥajjāj received a substantial stream of income from his poetry. He would write a poem praising an individual and present it to him in expectation of a substantial reward. If the reward was not forthcoming or not large enough, he would then write a satirical poem about the person. He received one thousand *dīnārs* for a poem praising an unnamed Fatimid. His *dīwān* eventually filled ten volumes. A copy would sell for between 50 and 70 *dīnārs*. He received these large amounts at a time when the vizier al-Ṣāḥib Ibn ʿAbbād—who was considered a generous patron—usually awarded from one hundred to five hundred *dirhams* for a single poem. There were a few periods during which Ibn al-Ḥajjāj was out of favor and reading his poetry was prohibited, such as around 977 when he was jailed because a poem offended an influential figure. Even during these periods, his *dīwān* continued to spread to remote areas of the Islamic empire.

During the Buwayhid period there was a large pool of highly skilled secretaries, but only a limited number of positions and most of them offered only a moderate living. There was great competition for a relatively small number of highly paid positions. Participation in intellectual groups was a way for an aspiring author to publicize skills and increase status. There were three main types of these groups. A school was a group of advanced students, who often lived with a high respected "master" scholar, but who worked fairly independently in a subject area of common interest to the group, instead of receiving formal lessons. Basically each member of the school contributed to the overall scholarly project rather than receiving formal lessons from the master. Circles, on the other hand, has less of a strictly didactic tone and were more fluid, being led by influential individuals such as rulers, high ranking officials or important scholars. Societies were formal associations based on a specific ideology. It was possible to participate in any combination of these settings and even for an individual to be the central figure of more than one type of group.

In addition to participating in the circles of the viziers with whom he was associated, Ibn al-Ḥajjāj was in demand in other settings. He frequently recited his *sukhf* and *mujūn* poetry for the individual who purchased it. He was also a core member of the circle of Abū ʿAbd Allāh al-Ḥusayn ibn Aḥmad Ibn Saʿdān (d. 984 or 985), another Buwayhid vizier. As was customary, Ibn Saʿdān chose individuals who were leaders in their fields for his circle. Some of them espoused beliefs or participated in activities that did not match the most conventional social standards. Although Ibn Saʿdān was sometimes criticized over who was included as members, associating with such a wide range of individuals provided him with information about minority groups within a very diverse society. Frankly, the traits for which some of them were criticized were not particularly objectionable in many sectors of Buwayhid society and were not widely considered significant in light of the accomplishments of these individuals. However, satirizing competitors and members of other groups was one way of attempting to decrease the status of other poets and groups while increasing one's own, and perhaps these criticisms should be viewed in that light.

One member of Ibn Saʿdān's circle was Abū Saʿd Bahrām ibn Ardashīr, a Mazdean, a religion considered heretical by Muslims. Yet he served as an envoy of the *amīr* ʿAḍud al-Dawlah (936-983) to other powerful rulers. Abū Bakr Ibn Shāhawayh was a Qarmatī, i.e. Carmathian, a sect of Islam that had attacked Mecca and had stolen the black stone from the Kaʿbah in 930. He was instrumental in having the Friday sermon said in the name of ʿAḍud al-Dawlah rather than his cousin and competitor, Bakhtiyār (d. 967 or 968) during their competition for control of Baghdad. Abū ʿAbd Allāh ibn Makīkhah was ʿAḍud al-Dawlah's treasurer and a Christian. Abū ʿAlī ʿĪsā ibn Zurʿah (943–1008) was a Christian and a philosopher interested in Aristotle's writings. He translated works, particularly those by Aristotle, and commentaries on Plato, from Syriac into Arabic. Then there was Abū 'l-Wafā' al-Būzjānī (940–998), a mathematician, probably of Persian descent. He introduced Abū Ḥayyān al-Tawḥīdī (ca. 922-ca. 1014), a prose writer, to Ibn Saʿdān. Abū Ḥayyān, too, became a member of the circle. Despite Abū Ḥayyān's social clumsiness, he found the kind of position he had always sought under Ibn Saʿdān's patronage. Aḥmad ibn Muḥammad Ibn Miskawayh (ca. 932-1030) was a philosopher and historian. Aṣbagh ibn Muḥammad Ibn al-Samḥ (980?-1035) was a mathematician and astronomer.

Ibn Saʿdān himself joked about members of his group, for example, by complaining that Abū 'l-Wafā' al-Būzjānī still had some mannerisms of his Khurāsānian heritage that were less elegant than Baghdādī mannerisms or by complaining that Ibn Miskawayh was a name dropper. Again the criticisms are relatively trivial and were made in a joking vein. Ibn Saʿdān strongly defended members of his circle and described them as vastly superior to those of other circles. As individuals rose and fell in rank and status, circles broke up or members joined other groups. Thus there was an ongoing changing pattern of interactions between intellectuals and considerable competition for status. Over his lifetime, Ibn al-Ḥajjāj was both criticized for, and nevertheless recruited into, groups such as this one because of the obscenity in his poetry.

These are some examples of Ibn al-Ḥajjāj's poetry containing *sukhf* and *mujūn*, which show his common usage of scatological language and how he employed it in his poetry. A particular trait of *sukhf* was the shock value of inappropriate language inserted in otherwise pleasant poetry. (Risālah, 27; variant *Yatīmat*, 3:37)

If my lord finds fault with what I say
  And maligns me badly behind my back
I will shit on the chapter 'Verb form *afʿaltu'*
  In the *Book of Pure Language*.

Another (*Yatīmat*, 3:39):

And this *qaṣīdah* is like a bridegroom
  A *muwashshaḥ* with a witty meaning
Without a breeze from an accidental fart
  And not a mustard's weight of shit.
And if it had been created as a Friday sermon
  It would have dissolved a marriage contract
They looked for a storehouse in winter
  And in summer [for] camphor stripped from farts

Ibn al-Ḥajjāj wrote love poetry. In many cases it too contained considerable elements of *sukhf* and *mujūn* (*Yatīmat*, 3:49):

For this (girl) only seduces me
  And that (girl) merely beguiles me,
Indeed among you is a youth who mourns for sobering up
  So he pours musk wine for me even if it is his shit.

Another (*Yatīmat*, 3:41):

I had observed you craving
  My nearness and inviting my presence
And I see the avoidance of fulfillment
  Like the silent farting after incense
O shitting because of underdone
  True lentils and unleavened bread!
In the center of a weak nature
  And the strength of a senior old man
He shits and it exits his ass
  Hand spans from the pain of a groan.
O silent farting after supper
  With egg and lots of yogurt
And the pastry is dough without
  Crushed salt or yeast
O farting of a respected old man
  Among the anxious ones who are present

Another (*Risālah*, 209-210):

For I see such as these
  Gathered together in the hermit's cell
That one: with an eye smeared with kohl
  And a glance as sharp as sword blades.
But then she raises her veil to reveal
  An old woman, (brightly) painted.
An old woman with a face
  Ravaged and pock marked,
A lass of ninety (years) by counting
  And of ten (more when) marked by writing.
In letting her cheat death, it is
  A grave that discards (the ten years)
And with a creased forehead
  And broken front teeth.
With saliva green like pond scum
  And a uvula as green as verdigris
And breath like the dung
  Of a poorly fed horse
And a pussy like an elephant's
  Ear shorn of its hair.

Ibn al-Ḥajjāj did not hesitate to describe even influential individuals according to the canons of *sukhf* and *mujūn* (*Risālah*, 59):

May Allah mount every stud alive today
  On the Head of the Dīwān's mother!
To me he is like a dog or like dog shit
  When it has dried up—the two are equivalent.

Ibn al-Ḥajjāj and another poet, Ḥusayn ibn Muḥammad Ibn Sukkarah (d. 1120 or 1121), did not like each other. They had both served the vizier al-Muhallabī. Both poets wrote *mujūn* poetry, but Ibn al-Ḥajjāj was much more successful and earned considerably more. Ibn al-Ḥajjāj also satirized Ibn Sukkarah. Over time hostility built up between the two. When asked the value of Ibn al-Ḥajjāj's *dīwān*, Ibn Sukkarah responded, "It has the value of a drainpipe." The following poem by Ibn al-Ḥajjāj shows his awareness of Ibn Sukkarah's comment (*Yatīmat*, 3:47).

A piece of shit after gurgling
  Among the last of the shit
It completed the night, all of it
  Inside of my stomach, fermenting
Then it wanted freedom
  And it came in the early morning, chattering
Then it set out like arrows
  From bows stretched taught
For it hit boldly
  The hollow of Ibn Sukkarah's chin

Not all of Ibn al-Ḥajjāj's poetry contained *sukhf* and *mujūn*. One category of the serious poetry he wrote emphasized his Shiite beliefs. He refers to ʻAlī ibn Ṭālib. Ghadīr Khumm is specifically the name of a pool between Mecca and Medina. Its significance is that during a rest stop on a journey, the prophet Muḥammad (d.

632) made a statement praising ʿAlī that Shiites believe indicated he intended ʿAlī to be his successor. During the late 10th and early 11th centuries, Fāṭimah (d. 632 or 633), Muḥammad's daughter and ʿAlī's wife, was sometimes referred to as the Virgin (*Risālah*, 54).

I am purer than any one who harbors treachery
 Against the pact of the Legatee on the day of Ghadīr
I am a follower of Muḥammad and ʿAlī
 And of the two *imāms*, Shabbar and Shabīr
I am truly a follower of the Virgin
 Without corruption, quibbling or falseness
I am a follower of one for whom the sun was held back
 And a follower of the partitioner of Hell fire
I am a follower of one by whom faith is
 Divided between permitted and forbidden
I am a follower of the one who spoke with the wolf
 In Babylon, among a group who were present with him
And of one whom the dead man's skull addressed
 In the land of Babylon, about various affairs
I am a follower of the one who spoke to the eagle in Kufa
 On the day of his famous beneficence
I am a follower of the one who will have the banner
 Of praise around his shoulders on the day of the Resurrection
I am the follower of the one who returned to battle on the day of Ḥunayn
 When the sword blades had lodged in the upper chests,
And spear points in armored hands
 Broke as they pierced breasts
In the din of a battle that would leave behind
 Only killed, fugitives or prisoners
I am the follower of the one through whom Islam conquered
 Two forts: Qurayẓa and al-Naḍīr
And of the one who shook the gate of Khaybar until
 All the people knew for sure of its destruction
And of the one who taught the widows
 Of the polytheists at Badr to crop their hair
The one whose victims, as the Night of Ḥarīr passed, were all
 Smitten by calls of "God is great" as if felled by pebbles

Although Ibn al-Ḥajjāj is primarily remembered for his vulgar poetry, and to a much lesser extent for poetry expounding his Shiite leaning, he did write a considerable amount of socially acceptable poetry (*Yatīmat*, 3:52).

People ransom you from necessity
 And I ransom you by choice
And one of them is in the vicinity of another
 And you until I die are my charge
So live on my bread and live on my water
 And live in my house and (with) the people of my house
O You who in his beauty attained
 The haughtiness of greatness and affluence
For today Qārūn in his wealth
 Is my slave and Khusraw is a follower of my house.

Ibn al-Ḥajjāj died in at his home in al-Nīl on May 24, 1001. His body was buried in northwest Baghdad at the feet of Mūsā 'l-Kāzim (ca. 745–ca. 800), the seventh Imam of the Twelver Shiites. His friend al-Sharīf al-Raḍī eulogized him in a *qaṣīdah*.

REFERENCES

Muḥsin al-Ḥusaynī 'l-ʿĀmilī, *A'yān al-Shī'ah*, 5th ed., ed. Ḥasan al-Amīn (Beirut: Dār al-Taʿaruf, 1998-);

Abū 'l-Muṭahhar Muḥammad b. Aḥmad al-Azdī, *Abulḳâsim, ein bagdâder Sittenbild = Ḥikāyat Abī al-Qāsim al-Baghdādī*, ed. Adam Mez (Heidelberg: Carl Winter's Universitätsbuchhandlung, 1902);

Abū 'l-Muṭahhar Muḥammad b. Aḥmad al-Azdī, *al-Risālah al-Baghdādiyyah*, ed. ʿAbbūd al-Shāljī (Beirut: Maṭbaʿat Dār al-Kutub, 1980);

Carl Brockelmann, *Geschichte der arabischen litteratur* (Leiden, E.J. Brill, 1943-1942), Supplement I, 130;

Dāirat al-ma'ārif, ed. Fu'ād Afrām Bustānī (Beirut, 1956-), 2:433-435;

Yāqūt ibn ʿAbd Allāh al-Ḥamawī, *Irshād al-arīb ilā ma'rifat al-adīb* (London: Luzac and Co.,

1923-1925) reprint, Cairo, Maṭbaʿah Hindiyyah, 1968, 6-16;
Joel L. Kraemer, *Humanism in the Renaissance of Islam: the Cultural Revival during the Buyid Age*. 2nd rev. ed. (Leiden: E.J. Brill, 1992);
Adam Mez, *The Renaissance of Islam* (London: Luzac and Co., 1937).

Abū 'l-Faraj Muḥammad ibn Isḥāq Ibn al-Nadīm

(d. 990)

DEVIN STEWART
Emory University

WORKS

al-Fihrist (The Catalogue), 987.

Lost Works

Kitāb fī 'l-awṣāf wa 'l-tashbīhāt (Book on Poetic Descriptions and Similes), before 987.

Editions

Kitāb al-Fihrist mit Anmerkungen, ed. Gustav Flügel and Johannes Roediger, 2 vols. (Leipzig: F.C.W. Vogel, 1871-1872; repr. Beirut: Maktabat Khayyāṭ, [1966]); *Kitāb al-Fihrist*, ed. Muṣṭafā Muḥammad (Cairo: al-Maṭbaʿah al-Raḥmāniyyah, 1929); *Kitāb al-Fihrist*, ed. Riḍā Tajaddud, ʿAlī ibn Zayn al-ʿĀbidīn Māzandarānī, 1st ed. (Tehran: Maṭbaʿah-i Dānishgāh, 1971); ed. Riḍā Tajaddud, 2nd edition, with introduction by Minovi (Tehran: Marvi Offset Press, 1973); ed. Riḍā Tajaddud, 3rd edition (Beirut: Dār al-Masīrah, 1988); ed. Ibrāhīm Ramaḍān (Beirut: Dār al-Maʿrifah, 1978); Yūsuf ʿAlī 'l-Ṭawīl (Beirut: Dār al-Kutub al-ʿIlmiyyah, 1996), with indices by Shams al-Dīn Aḥmad.

Translations

The Fihrist of al-Nadim: A Tenth-Century Survey of Muslim Culture, ed. and trans. Bayard Dodge, 2 vols. (New York: Columbia University Press, 1970; repr. Chicago: Kazi Publications, 1998);

Kitāb al-Fihrist, Persian trans. Riḍā Tajaddud (Tehran: Kitābkhānah-i Ibn Sīnā, 1964); (Tehran: Chāpkhānah-i Bank-i Bāzargānī-yi Iran, 1968); (Tehran: Amīr-i Kabīr, 1964, 1968, 1987, 2002);

al-Fihrist, Urdu trans. Muḥammad Isḥāq Bhatti and Muḥammad Ḥanīf Nadvi (Lahore: Idārah-yi Thaqāfat-i Islāmiyah, 1969).

Ibn al-Nadīm is the author of the *Fihrist* or "Catalogue," one of the most important sources for the intellectual history of the Middle East during the first four Islamic centuries. Completed in Baghdad in the late tenth century, the work is a carefully arranged presentation of all the Arabic books published in all fields that were known to Ibn al-Nadīm. Like a grand library catalogue of Baghdad, the greatest intellectual center of the Islamic world at the time, it contains over seven thousand book titles in fields ranging from poetry to theology to alchemy. It is at once an invaluable and frustrating source. It often provides a picture of the development of individual sciences in the Islamic world that is unavailable in other sources. At the same time, its long lists of authors and book titles is a constant reminder to the reader of the tremendous number of works from the first four Islamic centuries that have been lost to the ravages of time. Perhaps only two percent of the titles mentioned by Ibn al-Nadīm have been preserved. Unfortunately, no other works by Ibn al-Nadīm are extant, and biographical sources provide nearly no information about the man behind the *Fihrist*. With the exception of his death date, 990, all the information we have about him derives from the text of the *Fihrist* itself.

Ibn al-Nadīm's full name is Abū 'l-Faraj Muḥammad ibn Abī Ya'qūb Isḥāq ibn Muḥammad ibn Isḥāq. Ibn al-Nadīm, literally, "Son of the Boon Companion" appears to be his family name, and probably did not refer to him or his father in particular. The actual boon companion must have been a more remote ancestor. Ibn al-Nadīm's birth date is not known, but his birth must have taken place in the early decades of the tenth century. Since he died in 990, a birth date anywhere between 910 and 930 would appear within the realm of likelihood. The earliest date that he mentions in the *Fihrist* in connection with his own activities is 951-952, the year he met a Khārijī jurist and Muʿtazilī theologian by the name of Abū Bakr al-Bardaʿī. He asked this jurist about the works he had authored, and he lists them in the *Fihrist*. His description of this interchange suggests that he was an adult at the time, and probably already working as a book dealer. He also appears to have been collecting material for this *magnum opus*, even at this early date, nearly forty years before compiling the final copy of the *Fihrist*. One concludes from this report that it is unlikely that he was born any later than ca. 930.

Ibn al-Nadīm was probably born and raised in Mosul. This fact has often been overlooked, as he has been associated primarily with Baghdad, where he lived later in life and where he wrote the *Fihrist*. He associated with Khushkanānjah, an Ismaili secretary, in Mosul. In Mosul, he knew the relatives of a certain author on music, Yaḥyā Ibn Abī Manṣūr al-Mawṣilī. In Mosul as well, he examined a manuscript of Ismāʿīl Ibn al-Qāsim Abū 'l-ʿAtāhiyah's (747 or 748-826?) poetry in the handwriting of Ibn ʿAmmār, a well-known copyist. He met the tutor of one of the sons of the Ḥamdānid ruler Nāṣir al-Dawlah (d. 968), probably Abū Taghlib (940-979), Muḥammad ibn al-Layth al-Zajjāj, in Mosul. Ibn al-Nadīm was also personally acquainted with Abū 'l-Ḥasan ʿAlī ibn Muḥammad al-ʿAdawī 'l-Shimshāṭī (d. after 987), another tutor and then boon-companion of two of Nāṣir al-Dawlah's sons, Abū Taghlib and one of his brothers, presumably in Mosul as well. He mentions that he knew al-Shimshāṭī as a morally upright man *qadīman* "a long time ago, in the old days," suggesting that their association had occurred many decades before 987, when he was writing. When the monk and alchemist Iṣṭifan [Stephanos, not the famous Byzantine Stephanos of Alexandria who was at the court of Heraclius ca. 610-641] died at the Monastery of Michael in nearby Jazīrat ʿUmar, and his books appeared in Mosul, Ibn al-Nadīm examined some of them. In another passage Ibn al-Nadīm describes ʿAlī ibn Aḥmad al-ʿImrānī, a scholar of Mosul, as a great book collector and mathematician, adding that people traveled great distances to study with him. Ibn al-Nadīm saw a copy of the tenth Book of Euclid's *Elements* in the translation of Abū ʿUthmān al-Dimashqī (d. after 914) in al-ʿImrānī's library, presumably before al-ʿImrānī's death in 955-956. Ibn al-Nadīm reports that he met Abū ʿAbd Allāh Muḥammad ibn Aḥmad ibn ʿAbd Allāh ibn Quḍāʿah ibn Ṣafwān ibn Mahrān al-Jammāl al-Ṣafwānī in the year 957-958. Al-Ṣafwānī resided in Mosul, and Ibn al-Nadīm must have met him there. According to Muḥammad ibn al-Ḥasan al-Ṭūsī (995-1067), al-Ṣafwānī attended the court of Sayf al-Dawlah (915 or 916-967), where he debated and performed a mutual curse-ordeal (*mubāhalah*) with the judge of Mosul. The judge died the day after the ordeal, an indication that the ordeal had proved the Shiite al-Ṣafwānī correct. In this report, al-Ṭūsī must have confused Sayf al-Dawlah, the Ḥamdānid ruler of Aleppo 945-967, with his brother Nāṣir al-Dawlah, who ruled in Mosul 929-969. Otherwise, it is difficult to explain the reference to the judge of Mosul in the account. Presumably in Mosul as well, Ibn al-Nadīm met the famous Shiite poet Abū Bakr al-Khālidī (d. 990), a native of the nearby town of al-Khālidiyyah, writing of him, "I was amazed by the tremendous amount of the material he had memorized and the speed of his extemporaneous composition." He may have had contact with al-Khālidī's rival, another Shiite poet, Abū 'l-Ḥasan al-Sarī ibn Aḥmad al-Kindī 'l-Raffāʾ al-Mawṣilī (d. 972-973), in Mosul as well. Al-Sarī was born and raised in Mosul, and gained fame as a poet there. After traveling to the court of Sayf al-Dawlah in Aleppo in 956-957, he settled in Baghdad, where he praised the Buwayhid Vizier Abū Muḥammad al-Ḥasan ibn Muḥammad al-Muhallabī (903-963). Ibn al-Nadīm may therefore have had contact with him at a later date in

Baghdad as well. Ibn al-Nadīm probably spent his youth in Mosul and remained there at least until 957-958, when he met al-Ṣafwānī.

Ibn al-Nadīm was a Shiite and Muʿtazilī. He never says this explicitly, but it is evident from his presentation of material in the *Fihrist* itself. He uses the term *'āmmī* "the common people, the generality" to refer to Sunnis. He refers to the Twelver Imams frequently, and uses the typically Shiite blessing after their names, *'alayhi 'l-salām* "may peace be upon him," which Sunnis usually reserve for prophets. He calls Abū al-Ḥasan ʿAlī ibn Ismāʿīl al-Ashʿarī (873 or 874-935 or 936) and related theologians *mujbirah* "compulsionists" and Sunni *ḥadīth* scholars such as Aḥmad Ibn Ḥanbal (780-855) *ḥashwiyyah* "stuffers"; both are pejorative terms that indicate an extremely critical attitude toward them. One may also mention his references to al-Shāfiʿī's Shiite proclivities, to the prominent role he assigns to Shiites in the sections on *tafsīr*, theology, and law, and many other instances.

During these years in Mosul, Ibn al-Nadīm already had a profound interest in books. Ibn al-Nadīm appears to have been a *warrāq* or professional bookseller from a young age. This is evident from the numerous reports of having examined books or seen specific editions of books in private libraries, such as the library of al-ʿImrānī in Mosul, most likely before 955-956. Little is known about Ibn al-Nadīm's formal education. Poolson has characterized Ibn al-Nadīm as a simple bookseller who was not very accomplished as an academic but merely on the outskirts of scholarly activity because of his job. This characterization is a bit unfair, as a number of very important scholars were also *warrāqs*, that is, belonged to the profession of professional copyist, booksellers and publicists. They include the Christian philosopher Yaḥyā ibn ʿAdī, for example. Other *warrāqs* were very influential, such as those who worked for al-Jāḥiẓ, Dāwūd al-Iṣfahānī, and Muḥammad ibn Jarīr al-Ṭabarī. *Warrāqs* were important figures in the intellectual life of the ninth and tenth centuries. They were not only sellers and purveyors of books, but also copyists, publicists, and private librarians. Ibn al-Nadīm seems to have had a special interest in poetry as well as mathematics, and he may have written his work on poetic descriptions and similes during this period. He also had a wide circle of contacts from many different contemporary groups. He describes the Ismaili secretary Khushkanānjah, as "my friend and companion," and he met the Ismaili *dā'ī*. He had contacts with the Khārijī jurist and Muʿtazilī theologian al-Bardaʿī, as mentioned above, and also with many local Twelver Shiites and Christians.

The *Fihrist* mentions a few of Ibn al-Nadīm's teachers. He transmits material by *ijāzah* from the famous grammarian Abū Saʿīd al-Ḥasan ibn ʿAbd Allāh ibn al-Marzubān al-Sīrāfī (d. 979) and from the Shiite literary scholar and historian, Abū 'l-Faraj al-Iṣbahānī (897-ca. 972), the famous author of *Maqātil al-ṭālibiyyīn* and the *Kitāb al-aghānī*. Polosin corrects a misconception that goes back to Aḥmad ibn ʿAlī Ibn Ḥajar al-ʿAsqalānī's (1372-1449) work *Lisān al-mīzān*, resulting from a mis-reading of the text, that Ibn al-Nadīm studied with Ismāʿīl ibn Muḥammad al-Ṣaffār (861-952). Polosin argues convincingly that it was Ibn al-Nadīm's teacher al-Sīrāfī who studied with al-Ṣaffār and not Ibn al-Nadīm himself. I have argued that Ibn al-Nadīm studied with an Ismaili scholar in Baghdad, whose name he gives only as al-Ḥasanābādī. This list, however, is probably far from complete. The text of the *Fihrist* suggests that Ibn al-Nadīm was a Muʿtazilī theologian and was probably versed in the Greek sciences, such as mathematics, as well. However, he does not provide information about any of his teachers in these subjects.

While only the *Fihrist* survives, there is evidence that Ibn al-Nadīm wrote at least one other work. He mentions in one passage of the *Fihrist* a work that he had written on similes. The work was apparently an anthology of poetry; the specific chapter to which he refers had to do with similes regarding pens. It appears that a substantial passage devoted to pens and writing instruments in the first section of the Book I, on scripts and scripture, has been lifted or at least paraphrased from that early work. The date of the work's composition is not stated. It must of course be before 987, the date of the *Fihrist*, but it is probably much earlier, and Ibn al-Nadīm may have composed it while he was still in Mosul.

Ibn al-Nadīm is not known to have traveled outside Iraq. Gustav Flügel (1802-1870) had understood, erroneously, that he traveled to Constantinople in search of books, but Victor Rosen showed that this was based on a misunderstanding of the term Dār al-Rūm, which referred to the Greek quarter in Baghdad and not Byzantium. He did travel to the Iraqi city of al-Ḥadīthah in addition to Mosul and Baghdad. This not al-Ḥadīthah on the Euphrates, the best known town by that name, but instead Ḥadīthat al-Mawṣil, located at the confluence of the Greater Zāb and the Tigris, just south of Mosul. There Ibn al-Nadīm viewed the private library of a certain Shiite book-collector, Muḥammad ibn al-Ḥusayn, known as Ibn Abī Baʿrah, who kept his books hidden because he feared the Ḥamdānid rulers would confiscate them. The library was the most impressive Ibn al-Nadīm had ever seen, and included extremely rare manuscripts that Ibn Abī Baʿrah had received from an avid book collector from Kufa who gave them to him just before he passed away. Ibn al-Nadīm describes the contents of a 300-pound chest of manuscripts, including documents in the handwriting of ʿAlī ibn Abī Ṭālib (ca. 600-660) and his sons Ḥasan and Ḥusayn, as well as autograph works by early scholars such as ʿAmr ibn ʿUthmān Sībawayh the grammarian, Yaḥyā ibn Ziyād al-Farrāʾ al-Daylamī (761 or 762-822 or 823), Sufyān ibn Saʿīd al-Thawrī (d. 778?), ʿAbd al-Raḥmān ibn ʿAmr al-Awzāʿī (d. 773 or 774), and others. Ibn al-Nadīm reports that he visited this man a number of times, but that the books disappeared after he died. He is probably the same figure, termed Muḥammad ibn al-Ḥasan al-Warrāq, who transmitted to Ibn al-Nadīm reports about Abū Bakr Muḥammad ibn Zakariyyā ʾl-Rāzī (865?-925?) from an old man from Rayy. Ibn al-Nadīm's contact with Ibn Abī Baʿrah must have taken place while he was still living in Mosul. Ibn al-Nadīm also met a prominent Khārijī jurist named Abū ʾl-Qāsim al-Ḥadīthī. While he does not say where exactly he met this jurist, the *nisbah* al-Ḥadīthī may indicate that he lived in Ḥadīthat al-Mawṣil as well. In addition, one assumes that Ibn al-Nadīm would have traveled at least to the Shiite shrines in Sāmarrā, Najaf, and Karbala, and perhaps to the important city of Basra as well, though there is no explicit evidence that he did so.

Ibn al-Nadīm probably left Mosul and settled in Baghdad ca. 958-959. Polosin's estimate of Ibn al-Nadīm's years in Mosul, until the 350s A.H. (961-970) or 360s A.H. (970-980) is too late. The key piece of evidence is Ibn al-Nadīm's report that he heard Jaʿfar al-Khuldī, a well-known Baghdādī Sufi master who died in 959-960, in person. He states, "I read in the handwriting of Abū Muḥammad Jaʿfar ibn Muḥammad ibn Nāṣir al-Khuldī (d. 959) ... and I heard him say that which I had read in his handwriting." This reference suggests that Ibn al-Nadīm had left Mosul and settled in Baghdad ca. 958-959, that is, after his meeting with al-Ṣafwānī in 957-958 but before the death of al-Khuldī. In addition, in the section on Greek scripts, Ibn al-Nadīm mentions a doctor who "came to us" from Baʿlabakk in 959-960 and claimed to know the *sāmiyā* (*semeia*?) script, a type of shorthand. Ibn al-Nadīm tested him by dictating a text to him and having him read it back. This was presumably in Baghdad: by "he came to us" (*jāʾanā*), Ibn al-Nadīm does not likely mean "to Mosul," when he was writing in Baghdad. It was probably in Baghdad as well that Ibn al-Nadīm met Abū ʾl-Ḥasan ʿAlī ibn Hārūn Ibn al-Munajjim (890-963 or 964), before 963, when Ibn al-Munajjim died. Ibn al-Nadīm also associated with Ḥaydarah ibn ʿUmar (d. 968 or 969), the leading Ẓāhirī jurist in Baghdad during his day, of whom he remarks, "I saw him, and he was a friend of mine." Their association occurred before 968-969, the date of Ḥaydarah's death. While it is possible that Ibn al-Nadīm traveled back and forth between Mosul and Baghdad, the most probable interpretation is that he lived in Mosul until ca. 958-959, then relocated to Baghdad, where he remained for the next thirty-three years, until his death in 990.

Very soon after arriving in Baghdad, he must have attended the lectures of Abū Muḥammad Jaʿfar ibn Muḥammad ibn Nāṣir al-Khuldī, the famous Sufi teacher. He also heard the lectures of the well-known literary scholar and boon-companion of several caliphs Abū ʾl-Ḥasan ʿAlī ibn Hārūn ibn ʿAlī ibn Yaḥyā ʾl-Munajjim, who died in 963-964. Also early during his years there, he studied with al-Ḥasanābādhī, a Persian

Ismaili teacher. He mentions that he used to go attend al-Ḥasanābādhī's lectures with a group of his regular students. Also in Baghdad, Ibn al-Nadīm studied with the well-known grammarian and judge Abū Saʿīd al-Sīrāfī, presumably in grammar and related fields, and not in law, for al-Sīrāfī was a Ḥanafī jurist, and Ibn al-Nadīm does not seem to have any affiliation or special familiarity with the Ḥanafī *madhhab*. After Abū Saʿīd's death in 979, Ibn al-Nadīm derived information for his entry in the *Fihrist* directly from his son Abū Muḥammad Yūsuf ibn al-Ḥasan al-Sīrāfī (d. 995). Ibn al-Nadīm refers to the logician and philosopher Abū Sulaymān Muḥammad ibn Bahrām al-Manṭiqī 'l-Sijistānī (d. after 1000) as "our Master" (*shaykhunā*), indicating, in all likelihood, that he was Ibn al-Nadīm's teacher. Ibn al-Nadīm also has high praise for the literary critic and historian al-Marzubānī, Abū ʿAbd Allāh Muḥammad ibn ʿImrān ibn Mūsā, ibn Saʿīd ibn ʿAbd Allāh (d. 994), whom he describes as the last of the great writers of the age, and it appears that he attended his lectures, though it is not clear whether he studied under him.

Ibn al-Nadīm, beyond his goal of producing a comprehensive catalogue of extant knowledge written in Arabic, had a very lively intellectual curiosity and a drive to collect information from reliable sources. It is therefore evident from the *Fihrist* that made extensive efforts to locate, interview, and associate with representatives of many different academic specialties and others who had rare information that could not be found in other sources. This is particularly evident in his treatment of religious traditions. About Zoroastrianism, he consulted the contemporary Zoroastrian high priest of Iraq and Western Iran, Hêmît-î Asavahistân. About India, he consulted Misʿar ibn Muhalhil Abū Dulaf al-Yanbūʿī (d. ca. 1000), who had recently returned from extensive travels there. On the religions of China, he consulted a Nestorian priest who had just returned from a six-year sojourn there. About Christianity, he consulted a number of Christian acquaintances, including an informant whom he calls Yūnus the priest. About Judaism, he consulted a certain unnamed notable. Ibn al-Nadīm was very well informed about Ismaili Islam, though during his period Ismailis must have been very guarded in their dealings with people outside their group. He met the Ismaili *dāʿī* in Mosul, Ibn Ḥamdān, he was a close friend to an Ismaili secretary in Mosul, ʿAlī ibn Waṣīf Khushkanānjah, and he studied with an Ismaili teacher, al-Ḥasanābādī, in Baghdad. He reports that he knew a community of 300 Manichaeans in Baghdad during the reign of Muʿizz al-Dawlah (945-967), but that it had dwindled to less than five by the time he was writing, 987.

Ibn al-Nadīm presumably continued to ply his trade as a bookseller in Baghdad. He certainly associated with other *warrāq*s, including copyists and book-sellers in Baghdad, including Abū 'l-Ḥusayn ibn Abī Bakr Aḥmad ibn Naṣr and his son, whom he mentions as engaged in producing copies of the *Qur'ān*. He also mentions prominently the *warrāq* Abū 'l-Ḥasan ʿAli ibn Aḥmad al-Duraydī as a source for biographical information on his former client, Muḥammad ibn al-Ḥasan Ibn Durayd (837 or 838-933). Another famous *warrāq* with whom Ibn al-Nadīm had direct contact was the Christian philosopher Yaḥyā ibn ʿAdī. He also associated with Abū ʿAli Ibn Siwār al-Kātib, a famous bibliophile, scholar, secretary, and patron who had founded the public library in Basra. Abū ʿAlī provided Ibn al-Nadīm with bibliographies of several figures mentioned in the *Fihrist.*

In Baghdad, Ibn al-Nadīm presumably lived in the Shiite quarter of Karkh. This is probable in general because he was a Twelver Shiite and would have gravitated toward the area where most of them lived. Ibn al-Nadīm continued to associate with Twelver Shiites. He had direct contact with the leading Twelver Shiite jurist and theologian in Baghdad during his period, Abū ʿAbd Allāh ibn Muḥammad ibn al-Nuʿmān, known as Ibn al-Muʿallim or al-Shaykh al-Mufīd (d. 1023). He visited the house of a wealthy Shiite notable in Baghdad, Abū 'l-Qāsim ibn Abī 'l-Khaṭṭāb Muḥammad ibn Jaʿfar ibn Muḥammad Ibn al-Furāt. Abū 'l-Qāsim was member of the famous Shiite Ibn al-Furāt family, many of whom held high positions in the Abbasid administration, and nephew of Abū 'l-Ḥasan ʿAlī ibn Muḥammad Ibn al-Furāt (d. 924), who had served as vizier several times under the caliph al-Muqtadir. Ibn al-Nadīm examined at his residence an exemplar of book *Kitāb al-*

qabā'il al-kabīr wa 'l-ayyām by the philologist Muḥammad Ibn Ḥabīb (d. 860). Ibn al-Nadīm may have met the Shiite poet and traveler Abū Dulaf Misʿar ibn Muhalhil al-Khazrajī 'l-Yanbūʿī (d. ca. 961), the well-known Shiite traveler and poet, in Baghdad. It was probably in Baghdad as well that he studied with Abū 'l-Faraj ʿAlī ibn al-Ḥusayn ibn al-Haytham al-Iṣfahānī (897–c. 972), famous Shiite author of *Kitāb al-aghānī* and *Maqātil al-ṭālibiyyīn*. Enumerating Shiites little known to him, Ibn al-Nadīm reports that Abū 'l-Qāsim Būbash [Yūnus?] ibn al-Ḥasan informed him about the bibliography of a Shiite author who lived in Wāsiṭ, ʿUbayd Allāh ibn Aḥmad ibn Yaʿqūb al-Anbārī, stating that he had written one hundred forty books and treatises. Another possible Shiite contact is Abū 'l-Ḥasan Muḥammad ibn Yūsuf al-Nāqiṭ, whom Ibn al-Nadīm cites as an expert on the *Qur'ān* and with whom he may have studied.

Ibn al-Nadīm's circle also included important members of various Islamic legal schools. He knew Abū 'l-Faraj al-Muʿāfā ibn Zakariyyā 'l-Jarīrī 'l-Nahrawānī (ca. 917-1000), judge and leading jurist of the Jarīrī *madhhab* which had been founded by the famous jurist, historian, and *Qur'ān* commentator Muḥammad ibn Jarīr al-Ṭabarī. He was a close friend of Abū 'l-Ḥasan Ḥaydar ibn ʿUmar al-Ṣāghānī (d. 968), one of the leading Ẓāhirī jurists in Baghdad. As mentioned above, he had contact with Khārijī jurists as well.

Ibn al-Nadīm had many contacts with Christians, probably both in Mosul and in Baghdad. They resulted not only from Ibn al-Nadīm's interest in other religions but also, and perhaps primarily, from his interest in translation and the Greek sciences. The most famous of these was undoubtedly Abū Zakariyyā Yaḥyā ibn ʿAdī, Christian philosopher and also a fellow *warrāq*. Ibn al-Nadīm also refers to several other members of Yaḥyā ibn ʿAdī's circle, including his student Abū 'l-Khayr al-Ḥasan ibn Suwār ibn Bābā (942-1017), known as Ibn al-Khammār, a Nestorian Christian who was a physician, philosopher, and translator from Syriac into Arabic. Ibn al-Nadīm reports a discussion with him about the origin of philosophy at the *majlis* of ʿĪsā ibn ʿAlī (d. 1001) in Baghdad. Son of the famous "Good Vizier" ʿAlī ibn ʿĪsā, ʿĪsā ibn ʿAlī was also a disciple of Yaḥyā ibn ʿAdī and a patron of scholars interested in philosophy and the Greek sciences, including many Christians. Ibn al-Nadīm's Christian acquaintances also included the doctor Abū ʿAlī Naẓīf ibn Yumn (d. 990), who was a translator, translator of Greek works, Melchite priest, and doctor in Baghdad. He treated the Buwayhid ruler ʿAḍud al-Dawlah and was employed at the ʿAḍudī Hospital there. He informed Ibn al-Nadīm about rare manuscripts of Euclid's *Elements* that included more than the well-known versions of the work. In addition, Ibn al-Nadīm mentions a certain Yūnus the priest, who provided him information on Christian scriptures, and a Nestorian Christian monk who had traveled to China and whom he interviewed about Chinese religion shortly before writing the draft of the *Fihrist*. The Christian Abū Saʿīd Wahb ibn Ibrāhīm ibn Ṭāzādh al-Naṣrānī provided Ibn al-Nadīm with a calendar of the Sabians or Ḥarrānians. He was the secretary in the service of the Caliph al-Muṭīʿ (ruled 946-974) and the Daylamī commander Abū Jaʿfar Muḥammad ibn Yaḥyā Ibn Shīrzād. Ibn al-Nadīm knew another Christian secretary, Abū 'l-Ḥasan Ibn Naṣr, whom he reports died a few months before the compilation of the *Fihrist* in 987 and who had informed Ibn al-Nadīm about his unpublished works. Yet another Christian acquaintance of Ibn al-Nadīm is Abū Isḥāq ʿAbd Allāh Ibn Shahrām, who traveled to Constantinople in 981-982 on a diplomatic mission from the Buwayhid ruler ʿAḍud al-Dawlah to the Byzantine Emperor Basil II (976-1025) after the rebel general Bardas Skleros had taken refuge in Baghdad. At a gathering in Baghdad, Ibn al-Nadīm heard him describe an ancient temple containing a fabulous library in Byzantine territory. This lecture may have occurred after Ibn Shahrām's return from the famous mission to Basil II, but he reports that the incident in Byzantium occurred in the time of Sayf al-Dawlah, suggesting that it was on a much earlier mission.

Ibn al-Nadīm also had contact with an odd assortment of lesser known scholars, probably in Baghdad, including an indigent alchemist named Abū 'l-Ḥasan Aḥmad al-Khanshalīl and an exorcist of demons (*jinn*) named Abū ʿAmr ʿUthmān Ibn Abī Raṣṣāṣah, both of whom Ibn al-Nadīm questioned regarding the validity of their crafts. he also knew Abū 'l-Faraj Muḥammad ibn ʿUbayd Allāh al-Lajlāj (d. after 970), a famous chess player who left Baghdad to serve ʿAḍud al-Dawlah in Shiraz. Another friend of Ibn al-Nadīm was Abū Bakr Muḥammad ibn Ibrāhīm al-ʿAwwāmī, a judge and grammarian who, he reports, died after 961. This is perhaps a copyist's error for Abū Bakr Muḥammad ibn Ibrāhīm *ibn 'Imrān* al-Ḥawzī, a grammarian who died in 965-966. Regarding Turkish writing systems, Ibn al-Nadīm also consulted a certain Abū 'l-Ḥasan Muḥammad ibn al-Ḥasan ibn Ashnās, perhaps a descendant of the famous Turkish commander Ashnās, a prominent figure in the political history of the Abbasid caliphate in the mid-ninth century.

An overview of Ibn al-Nadīm's contacts in the *Fihrist* indicates that he had a tremendous intellectual curiosity and was very energetic in seeking out representatives of minority traditions, with a strong emphasis on Twelver and Ismaili Shiites and Christians. With regard to Islamic theological traditions, it is not evident that he had substantial contact with representatives of the Shāfiʿī, Mālikī, or Ḥanbalī legal traditions, or with theologians of the Ashʿarīs or traditionalist schools. This may be simply because, as majority traditions, he did not deem it necessary to explain how he retrieved his information. Jews get significantly less attention than Christians, though he mentions that he consulted "one of their notable men" about Jewish scripture, omitting a name. This predilection for Christians may have been due in part to his interest in Greek sciences and the translation movement from Greek and Syrian into Arabic, which was obviously very strong.

In the *Fihrist*, Ibn al-Nadīm set out to present the entire legacy of Arabic writing, from the beginning of Islam until his own time, including all the known sciences of the period. He arranged the work in ten large books (*maqālah*, pl. *maqālāt*), each containing one or more sections (*fann*, pl. *funūn*). His choice of the term *maqālah* rather than *kitāb* for the major divisions indicates that he was following for his own work the tradition of the Greek sciences, where this rubric was *de rigeur*, as opposed to the Islamic sciences such as law and *ḥadīth*, where the term *kitāb* was regularly used. He presents the ten books as follows:

I. Scripts, Jewish and Christian Scriptures, the *Qur'ān*.
II. Arabic Grammar.
III. History, Genealogy, etc.
IV. Poetry.
V. Theology.
VI. Law.
VII. Greek Sciences: Philosophy, Mathematics, Medicine.
VIII. Stories, Fables, Entertainment Literature.
IX. Other Religions.
X. Alchemy.

The *Fihrist* contains over 7,000 book titles, but it is not simply an amorphous grab-bag. It represents an attempt on the part of the author to provide a complete taxonomy of human knowledge, primarily as it has been recorded or transmitted in the Arabic language. Close examination of the structure of the work reveals that Ibn al-Nadīm arranged and articulated the entries, sections, and books of his work in order to make reasoned, ideological statements about the history of the sciences in Arabic writing.

Consideration of the topics of the ten books of the work suggests that they are arranged in the manner they appear for several reasons. "Foreign" material, Books VII-X, appears last, preceded by what is apparently "indigenous" material. The exceptions are the first two subsections of Book I, which treat various non-Arabic scripts and the scriptures of Jews and Christians. Chronology is one of the most important principles of organization in the *Fihrist* as a whole. The arrangement of the ten Books suggests that Ibn al-Nadīm viewed Arabic letters as beginning with the *Qur'ān*, and that the *Qur'ān* belongs to the tradition of monotheistic scripture known from Judaism and Christianity. This is not surprising. However, his arrangement makes explicit a strong link between script and scripture. For Ibn al-Nadīm, the two go hand in hand. The Jewish and Christian scriptures are, in his view, ancient, perhaps the oldest texts in existence, and the *Qur'ān* appears here because of its association with them.

The scripts Ibn al-Nadīm describes are the following: Arabic, including Himyarite (South Arabian); Syriac, including several types of script; Persian; Hebrew; Greek; Lombard and Saxon; Chinese; Manichaean; Soghdian; Indian scripts, which an informant told Ibn al-Nadīm number about 200; African scripts, including a Beja script which Ibn al-Nadīm has heard about but not seen, and Ethiopian, which Ibn al-Nadīm reports is similar to South Arabian script; Turkish; Russian; Latin; and Armenian. This section shows Ibn al-Nadīm's very strong interest in languages, scripts, writing instruments, types of paper, and the production of books. This section includes many valuable pieces of information, including an accurate description of Middle Persian ideograms, based on Aramaic, such as LḤMʾ for *nān* "bread," as well as a Russian system of writing that predates Cyrillic, involving notches carved into pieces of wood.

After Book I, Ibn al-Nadīm presents several chapters devoted to the Arabic sciences (Books II-IV). These are fields in which Arabs excelled, even before Islam, and were not borrowed from other cultures. Book II treats Arabic Grammar, and is divided into three sections, devoted to the Kufan grammarians, Basran grammarians, and grammarians of mixed school. Here as elsewhere, this division is chronological, based on the date when the schools in question were founded historically. Book III also contains three sections, the first devoted to historians and genealogists, the second devoted to secretaries and their writings, and the third devoted to court companions and the like. Book IV, on poetry, provides a clear example of the chronological arrangement of the sections, or *fann*s, within one book. It contains two chapters: the first devoted to ancient poets--essentially Preislamic and Umayyad poets--and the second devoted to modern poets—that is, poets of the Abbasid period.

Books V and VI present Islamic religious sciences: theology and law. Though the Islamic religious sciences, even by Ibn al-Nadīm's date, were many, he subsumes them under three great categories. The *Qur'ānic* sciences appear in Book I, Islamic theology in Book V, and Islamic law in Book VI. There is no separate book devoted to *ḥadīth*; most of the works in this field appear in the sixth section of Book VI, on law, devoted to the "legal school" of the traditionists. Nor is there a separate book devoted to Sufism or Islamic mysticism. Ibn al-Nadīm presents Sufism in the fifth section of Book V, as one of five theological schools.

The books on theology and law are constructed in such a way as to make an argument concerning the history of these fields. As in Books II and IV, they are in chronological order according to Ibn al-Nadīm's estimated date of foundation of the various schools.

Book V, on theology, is arranged in the following manner:

1. The Muʿtazilīs.
2. Imami and Zaydī Shiites.
3. Mujbirah and Ḥashwiyyah [Ashʿarīs, et al.].
4. Khārijīs.
5. Sufis, including the Ismailis.

Book VI, on law, is arranged in the following manner:

1. Mālikīs.
2. Ḥanafīs.
3. Shafiʿis.
4. Dāwūdīs [Ẓāhirīs].
5. Shiites [Imamis].
6. *Aṣḥāb al-ḥadīth* [Ḥanbalīs et al.].
7. Jarīrīs.
8. Khārijīs.

In both cases, these are not simply taxonomies of the fields in question, theology and law, showing the variety of opinion found within them, but a presentation of the historical development of the field, showing the relative dates of the foundation of each scholarly tradition.

Books VII-X, as mentioned above, are devoted to sciences of foreign origin—mainly Greek, Persian, and Indian—that have been adopted into Arabic. These Books are particularly important for an understanding of the translation movement—or movements—in the course of which hundreds of important works were translated from Greek, Syriac, Persian, and Sanskrit on many scientific and literary topics. They exerted a profound influence on Islamic intellectual history, and Ibn al-Nadīm provides many details about the works translated, the translators, and the dates of translation that are not available in other sources. The many foreign terms in these Books, however, have presented many problems for the textual criticism of the work.

Book VII treats the Greek sciences, and is divided into three sections. The first section treats philosophy, the second section treats mathematics and astronomy, and the third section treats medicine. In each section, Ibn al-Nadīm begins with the authors in the Greek tradition, then presents the writers from the Islamic period who have written on that science, until the present time; in the section on mathematics and astronomy, he includes a short intervening section on Indian authors in these fields.

Book VIII treats entertainment literature, a great deal of which was based on Persian and Indian models. It contains three sections, the first devoted to fables and other stories, the second devoted to exorcists, jugglers, and magicians, and the third devoted to miscellaneous anthologies of anecdotes and works devoted to such topics as horsemanship, falconry, dream interpretation, perfume, cooking, amulets, and so on.

Book IX is devoted to religions outside the Abrahamic tradition and is divided into two sections. The first section treats the Sabians, Manichaeans, and other religions. The second section treats the religions of India and China, including Hinduism and Buddhism and their varieties.

Book X is devoted to alchemy, which it connects with Hermes, the Babylonians, and the Egyptian pyramids, before treating the contributions of Greek scientists. He reports that the Umayyad prince Khālid ibn Yazīd (d. 704 or 708) was the first figure in the Islamic period who became interested in alchemy and patronized the translation of books on alchemy as well as medicine and astronomy. He then addresses the well-known but semi-legendary figures Jābir ibn Ḥayyān and Ibn al-Waḥshiyyah, before treating more recent alchemists.

Ibn al-Nadīm was also collecting material for the *Fihrist* over many years. He reports having met the Khārijī jurist al-Barda'ī already in 951-952, presumably in Mosul, and he made it a point of asking the man the titles of works that he had authored. It thus appears that Ibn al-Nadīm had an encyclopedic urge already as a youth, and it was this urge that kept him collecting information on books throughout his life. A note in the Chester Beatty manuscript of the work indicates that he was producing a fair copy in 987--the implication is that he had collected the material in draft form earlier. The format of the oldest manuscripts, which endeavor to follow that of the original autograph copy (*dustūr*) meticulously, suggests that he worked out a broad outline of ten books or *maqālah*s and devoted one blank *kurrāsah*, a quire or pamphlet, to each. Then he filled up each quire over time with material from notes and other sources, leaving blank spaces for material he had not yet gathered. The fair copy was produced over a fairly short time in 987, for the date is mentioned at several places in the work.

However, there is abundant evidence that Ibn al-Nadīm's fair copy, the one that was eventually copied and of which witnesses have come down to us, was far from complete. First, and most significantly, the earliest manuscripts, which follow the autograph quite closely, include many blank spaces for additional material, even entire pages. Ibn al-Nadīm left hundreds of blank spaces for additional information, including death dates of the subjects, their given names and genealogies, additional book titles, lists of chapter titles in named works, and entire entries.

In addition, the process of adding information to the work produced some anomalies in its organization. At several points, he remarks that a certain entry belongs elsewhere, e.g., *qabl hādhā 'l-mawḍi'* "before this passage." The explanation for such remarks is that he has put these entries where they are out of expedience, because the passages where they belong have run out of space. This is particularly clear in the fifth section of Book V, on theology, which purports to be devoted to ascetics and Sufis, but is organized as follows:

A. Ascetics and Sufis. (*Tajaddud*, 235-238)
B. Ismailis. (*Tajaddud*, 238-241)
C. al-Ḥallaj. (*Tajaddud*, 241-243)
D. Imami Shiites, eight entries. (*Tajaddud*, 243)
E. Zaydī Shiites, five entries. (*Tajaddud*, 244)

F. Imami Shiites, eleven entries. (*Tajaddud*, 244-247).

G. Shiites of unknown affiliation, two entries. (*Tajaddud*, 247).

Analysis of this chapter suggests that A, B, and C actually belong in this section, but that D, E, F, and G belong more properly in the second fann, devoted to Imami and Zaydī Shiite theology. That this is the case is corroborated by the fact that al-Shaykh al-Mufīd has been inadvertently devoted two entries in the *Fihrist*. One entry appears in the second *fann*, and one appears here, in the fifth. Ibn al-Nadīm cannot possibly be classifying all Shiites as mystics; the only plausible explanation for this odd arrangement is that he has placed the entries of D-G here out of expedience, because the space he allotted to the second *fann* is already full. If and when he produced another fair copy, he could then insert these entries in their proper place.

The *Fihrist* was dedicated to a patron whose identity remains a mystery. Ibn al-Nadīm refers to him in the introduction to the work in a fashion that reveals only that he was probably a *sayyid*, that is, a descendant of the prophet. In the absence of relevant sources, we can only speculate as to his identity. It is likely that the patron would have been, like Ibn al-Nadīm, an Imami Shiite and a Muʿtazilī theologian living in Baghdad; anyone inimical to Shiites or Muʿtazilīs would not have been pleased with the work. Perhaps the patron was Abū Aḥmad al-Ḥusayn ibn Mūsā 'l-Mūsawī, the father of al-Sharīf al-Raḍī (970-1016) and ʿAlam al-Hudā ʿAlī ibn al-Ḥusayn al-Sharīf al-Murtaḍā (966-1044) and *naqīb* of the ʿAlawī *sayyid*s intermittently from 965 until his death in 1009-1010. As one of the most prominent *sayyid*s and Imami Shiite scholars, as well as heir to a tremendous fortune, he seems a likely candidate for the dedication of Ibn al-Nadīm's work. Another possible candidate is ʿĪsā ibn ʿAlī, a patron of scholarship in the Greek sciences whose salon Ibn al-Nadīm is known to have attended.

In compiling the *Fihrist*, Ibn al-Nadīm relied on a large number of sources. Some of his information derived from direct contacts and the other sources one would expect him to have as someone involved in the book trade, such as examination of the books themselves. He frequently mentions that he has seen a certain book, or a particular recension of a book, or part of a book himself, in a private library. He, on occasion, notes as well that the books of a certain individual are not available to him directly but are known to be found in another region, such as Egypt or western Iran. In several cases, it is clear that he received some lists of publications orally from the authors themselves, as is the case with the Khārijī jurist al-Bardaʿī mentioned above. A reading of the *Fihrist* reveals that Ibn al-Nadīm was inquisitive and had a respect for specialization. When investigating topics, he sought out relevant experts and informants who could be presumed to know more than all others. On Persian script, he consulted the Zoroastrian *mobed* Hêmît-î Asavahistân. On Chinese religion, he consulted a Nestorian monk from the town of Najrān (in Iraq, not Arabia) who had just returned from a six-year trip to China. On Indian religion he consulted Abū Dulaf al-Yanbūʿī, who had traveled widely there. He derived much of his information about Ismaili beliefs from Ismaili contacts.

Many sources that Ibn al-Nadīm used, however, were not oral but written. One important category of these sources are bibliographies of individual authors, which had become an established genre of writing by the ninth century, and without which a work like Ibn al-Nadīm's would have been difficult to conceive of, let alone produce. Ibn al-Nadīm states that he is quoting verbatim the individual *fihrist*s of major authors such as the theologian and literary scholar al-Jāḥiẓ, the doctor Abū Bakr al-Rāzī, the alchemist Jābir ibn Ḥayyān (fl. 8th century), the jurists Muḥammad ibn Idrīs al-Shāfiʿī (767 or 768-820) and Abū Bakr Muḥammad ibn Dāwūd ibn Khalaf al-Iṣfahānī (868 or 869-909 or 910), the Shiite theologian and *Qur'ān* commentator from Abū 'l-Naḍr Muḥammad ibn Masʿūd ibn Muḥammad Ibn al-ʿAyyāshī 'l-Samarqandī (fl. 9th-10th century), the Ismaili leader ʿAbdān (d. 899), Theon's bibliography of Plato, and so on. In many other cases, he may be drawing on such individual *fihrist*s without saying so explicitly, as in the entries on Aristotle or Yaʿqūb ibn Isḥāq al-Kindī (d. ca. 873), which present extensive and systematically organized bibliographies.

Another major category of Ibn al-Nadīm's sources is that of biographical and bibliographical works. In some cases he names these sources when he quotes them. In many cases, he does not provide a title, but only an author, simply stating "I read in the handwriting of so-and-so ..." By such statements, Ibn al-Nadīm does not mean that he is reading from handwritten private missives or privately-circulate notes of a particular author but rather from published works. He has simply omitted the title of the work because, one supposes, he means to emphasize transmission from the individual in question. One of the works most frequently quoted in this fashion is a work by Abū 'l-Ḥasan ʿAlī ibn Muḥammad ibn ʿUbayd ibn al-Zubayr al-Asadī Ibn al-Kūfī (d. ca. 960), the title of which Ibn al-Nadīm does not give. J. Lippert suggested that this work was in essence the forerunner of the entire *Fihrist*, or a large part of it; Ibn al-Nadīm had only enlarged and expanded Ibn al-Kūfī's opus. But there are many other such works evident in the *Fihrist*. On grammarians, for example, Ibn al-Nadīm frequently quotes his professor Abū Saʿīd al-Ḥasan al-Sīrāfī. Polosin has shown that these quotations derive from al-Sīrāfī's work *Ṭabaqāt al-naḥwiyyīn al-baṣriyyīn*. On Sufis, Ibn al-Nadīm quotes a biographical work by the Baghdādī Sufi master Abū Jaʿfar al-Khuldī. In the section on poets, he derives a great deal from *Kitāb al-Waraqah* by the vizier Muḥammad ibn Dāwūd Ibn al-Jarrāḥ (857-908 or 909). Further bibliographical research and careful study of the text of the *Fihrist* itself may make it possible to identify many of the works Ibn al-Nadīm cites in this fashion. There are a number of outstanding puzzles, such as the history of Abū 'l-Qāsim al-Ḥijāzī from which he derives an account of the arrest of the famous jurist al-Shāfiʿī after participating in a rebellion in Arabia against the Abbasid caliph Hārūn al-Rashīd (763 or 766-809). In many other cases it appears that Ibn al-Nadīm is lifting or paraphrasing entire passages from earlier works without acknowledging a source.

The textual history of the *Fihrist* after Ibn al-Nadīm's death is complex. Two manuscripts, thought to be two halves of the same copy of the work, are believed to stand at one remove from Ibn al-Nadīm's autograph copy and to date from the early eleventh century. The first half of this copy is housed in the Chester Beatty Library in Dublin, and the second in the Şehid Ali Paşa Library in Istanbul. According to Polosin, they are the closest representation in the tradition of Ibn al-Nadīm's original work. He also claims that the copyist endeavored to mimic Ibn al-Nadīm's exact layout of the text and even his original handwriting. The main complication to the textual history occurred because al-Ḥusayn ibn ʿAlī 'l-Wazīr al-Maghribī (Abū 'l-Qāsim al-Ḥusayn ibn ʿAlī, d. 1027), had what was probably Ibn al-Nadīm's autograph, and added material to the *Fihrist*, directly into his copy. This copy was later consulted by Yāqūt ibn ʿAbd Allāh al-Ḥamawī (1179?-1229), and became the basis for many later copies of the *Fihrist*. The result was that Ibn al-Nadīm's original material and al-Wazīr al-Maghribī's interpolations became indistinguishable in later copies, which led to many confusions, when, for example, dates after the death of Ibn al-Nadīm appear in the text. The editors of the various editions of the *Fihrist* to date were not aware of this problem, though Dodge and Tajaddud did have the oldest manuscripts, which represent Ibn al-Nadīm's text more closely, at their disposal. For this reason, Polosin rightly argues that a complete, new edition of the *Fihrist* must be completed.

The new edition must be based on the Chester Beatty and Şehid Ali Paşa manuscripts. These provide a nearly complete version of the text, but a piece in the middle is missing from them. This part of the work is particularly important because it falls in the middle of the section on Muʿtazilī theology. Fortunately, a manuscript from Rajasthan was located which includes the missing material. Other than that, only a few folios are missing from the two halves of the oldest manuscript and will have to be supplied from other manuscripts, although it may yet be difficult to distinguish between Ibn al-Nadīm's original text and the interpolations of al-Wazīr al-Maghribī in those passages. Examination of the manuscripts, even the earliest ones, nevertheless reveals that there are many corruptions of the text that need to be remedied. Careful examination of the text and efforts to provide conjectural emendations at many points will be necessary to restore the original text to the greatest possible extent.

Polosin claims, somewhat hyperbolically, that the *Fihrist* fell into oblivion after he wrote it and was only "rediscovered" in the thirteenth century and later by such authors as Yāqūt al-Ḥamawī (d. 1229), ʿAlī ibn Yūsuf Ibn al-Qifṭī (1172 or 1173-1248), al-Ḥasan ibn Muḥammad al-Ṣāghānī (1181-1252 or 1253), Aḥmad ibn al-Qāsim Ibn Abī Uṣaybiʿah (d. 1270), Muḥammad ibn Aḥmad al-Dhahabī (1274-1348), Aḥmad ibn ʿAlī ʾl-Maqrīzī (1364-1441), and Aḥmad ibn ʿAlī Ibn Ḥajar al-ʿAsqalānī (1372-1449). This is not entirely accurate, because the work was obviously used extensively by al-Wazīr al-Maghribī as well as by the eleventh-century Shiite jurist al-Shaykh Muḥammad ibn al-Ḥasan al-Ṭūsī (995-1067), who drew on the *Fihrist* extensively for his own bibliographical work, *Fihrist kutub al-Shīʿah*. Examination of al-Ṭūsī's work suggests that he had access to original version of Ibn al-Nadīm's work, perhaps even Ibn al-Nadīm's autograph, without the interpolations of al-Wazīr al-Maghribī.

Ibn al-Nadīm will always remain a man of one work, but that work is one of the most important books in the history of Arabic letters, and it has revealed a great deal about the history of most known genres in Arabic writing in the course of the first four Islamic centuries. In some areas, such as the *Qurʾānic* sciences, Muʿtazilī theology, and Islamic law, it provides much information not found elsewhere. Ibn al-Nadīm's account of the beliefs of the Manichaeans is likewise of inestimable value. We owe a large portion of our understanding of the translation of scientific works from Greek into Arabic, sometimes via Syriac, less commonly via Persian, from Persian into Arabic, and from Sanskrit into Arabic to the *Fihrist*. The *Fihrist* also provides unique information on the translation of fables and wisdom literature from Persian into Arabic, including some of the earliest mentions of such books as the *Thousand and One Nights* and the legend of Sindbad.

In addition to descriptions of books and their transmission, the *Fihrist* includes choice accounts and anecdotes, such as the description of a dream the caliph al-Maʾmūn (786-833, ruled 813-833) had of Aristotle that caused him to patronize the translation of Greek philosophical works, or the account of a Chinese scholar who recording all the books of Galen in shorthand while Abū Bakr al-Rāzī and one of his students dictated. A critical edition of the *Fihrist* has yet to be produced, though the work of Polosin has explained how this should be done. Moreover, the contents of the *Fihrist* have yet to be fully exploited. The continual publication of other early sources makes it possible to check the information Ibn al-Nadīm provides against similar accounts, providing a better gauge of his accuracy and biases and at times correcting the text or throwing new light on it. Many passages remain obscure or unclear, and there is abundant evidence that many are corrupt and in need of emendation or have been interpreted incorrectly by scholars to date. It is hoped that scholars will take up both of these challenges in the near future.

Ibn al-Nadīm provided not only a bibliography but a map of human knowledge, and he therefore deserves more recognition as a thinker in his own right than has usually been accorded to him. From the pages of the *Fihrist* he emerges as relatively ecumenical and open-minded for a scholar of his day. Though he often reveals his opinion, he is careful to let other sources speak for themselves, often telling the reader that he cannot vouch for the validity of a certain text. The work as a whole shows that he had a well-developed intellectual curiosity that ranged far beyond his immediate surroundings, to other religious traditions such as Buddhism, Hinduism, Zoroastrianism, and Manichaeism, and to other languages such Russian, Latin, Soghdian, Ethiopian, and others. The *Fihrist* also shows that he has a decided bias toward the Greek sciences, Muʿtazilī theology, and Twelver Shiite Islam, and against Ḥanbalī law and Ashʿarī theology. He is decidedly attracted to minority groups in general, and this perspective grants his work an unusual perspective that makes it an extremely valuable complement to examinations of Islam's learned traditions penned by Sunni scholars who were more interested in producing narratives of moderation and consensus.

REFERENCES

A.J. Arberry, "New Material on the Kitāb al-Fihrist of Ibn al-Nadīm," in *Islamic Research*

Association Miscellany, vol. 1, Islamic Research Association 12 (1948), 19-45;

François De Blois, "Iranian Material in the *Fihrist*," *Encyclopedia Iranica*, s.v. "Fehrest, II";

Josef van Ess, "Die Muʿtazilitenbiographien im *Fihrist* und die muʿtazilitische biographische Tradition," in *Ibn an-Nadim und die mittelalterliche arabische Literatur: Beiträge zum 1. Johann Wilhelm Fück-Kolloquium* (Halle, 1987; repr. Wiesbaden: Harrassowitz, 1996), 1-6;

H.G. Farmer, *Tenth Century Arabic Books on Music as Contained in Kitab al-Fihrist of Abu'l-Faraj Muhammad ibn al-Nadim* (Leiden: Brill, 1959);

Manfred Fleischhammer, "Johann Fücks Materielen zum Fihrist," *Wissenschaftliche Zeitschrift der Martin-Luther-Universität Halle: Geistliche-Sozialwissenschaftiliche Reihe* 25:6 (1976): 75-84;

Gustav Flügel, "Ueber Muḥammad bin Isḥāk's Fihrist al-ʿulūm," *Zeitschrift der Deutschen Morgenländischen Gesellschaft* 13 (1859): 559-650;

Gustav Flügel, *Mani, seine Lehre und seine Schriften: ein Beiträge zur Geschichte des Manichäismus* (Leipzig: F. A. Brockhaus, 1862);

Siegmund Fraenkel, "Zum Fihrist," *Zeitschrift der Deutschen Morgenländischen Gesellschaft* 46 (1892): 741-743;

D. Frolow, "Ibn al-Nadīm on the History of *Qur'anic* Exegesis," *Wiener Zeitschrift für die Kunde des Morgenlandes* 87 (1997): 65-81;

J.W. Fück, "Neue Materialien zum Fihrist," *Zeitschrift der Deutschen Morgenländischen Gesellschaft* 90 (1936): 298-321;

J.W. Fück, "Some Hitherto Unpublished Texts on the Muʿtazilite movement from Ibn al-Nadīm's *Kitāb al-Fihrist*," in S.M. Abdullah (ed.), *Professor Muḥammad Shafīʿ Presentation Volume* (Lahore: Majlis-e-Armughān-e ʿIlmi, 1955), 51-74;

J.W. Fück, "The Arabic Literature on Alchemy According to an-Nadīm (A.D. 987): a Translation of the Tenth Discourse of The Book of the Catalogue (AL-FIHRIST) with Introduction and Commentary," *Ambix* 4 (1951): 81-144;

L.H. Gray, "Iranian Material in the *Fihrist*," *Le Muséon*, 3rd series 1 (1915): 24-39;

M.Th. Houtsma, "Zum K. al-Fihrist," *Wiener Zeitschrift für die Kunde des Morgenlandes* 4 (1890): 217-35;

Ibn an-Nadim und die mittelalterliche arabische Literatur: Beiträge zum 1. Johann Wilhelm Fück-Kolloquium (Halle, 1987; repr. Wiesbaden: Harrassowitz, 1996);

J. Lippert, "Ibn al-Kūfī, ein Vorgänger Nadīm's," *Wiener Zeitschrift für die Kunde des Morgenlandes* 11 (1897): 147-155;

August Müller, *Die Griechischen Philosophen in der Arabischen Überlieferung* (Halle: Waisenhauses, 1873);

L. Osti, "Authors, Subjects and Fame in the *Kitāb al-Fihrist* of Ibn al-Nadīm: the Case of al-Ṭabarī and al-Ṣūlī," *Annali di Ca' Foscari* (Venice) 38 (1999): 155-170;

V.V. Polosin, *"Fikhrist" Ibn an-Nadima kak istoriko-kul'turnyĭ pamiatnik X veka* (Moscow: Nauka, 1989);

Valeriĭ V. Polosin, "Izuchenie *Fikhrista* Ibn an-Nadīma posle I. Fiukka i aktual'nost' novogo nauchnogo izdaniia ego teksta," in *Ibn an-Nadim und die mittelalterliche arabische Literatur: Beiträge zum 1. Johann Wilhelm Fück-Kolloquium* (Halle, 1987; repr. Wiesbaden: Harrassowitz, 1996), 32-37;

Holger Preissler, "Ordnungsprinzipen im *Fihrist*," in *Ibn an-Nadim und die mittelalterliche arabische Literatur: Beiträge zum 1. Johann Wilhelm Fück-Kolloquium* (Halle, 1987; repr. Wiesbaden: Harrassowitz, 1996), 38-43;

H. Ritter, "Philologika I. Zur Überlieferung des *Fihrist*," in: *Der Islam* 17 (1928), 1-23;

V. Rosen, "Byl-li v 988 g. v' Konstantinopol avtor Fihrista?," *Zapiski Vostochnago Otdieleniya Imperatorskago Russkago Arkheologicheskago Obshchestva* 4 (1889): 401-404;

Rudolf Sellheim, "Das Todesdatum des Ibn an-Nadīm," *Israel Oriental Studies* 2 (1972): 428-432;

Rudolf Sellheim, "Tārīkh wafāt Ibn an-Nadīm," *Majallat Majmaʿ al-Lughah al-ʿArabiyyah* (Damascus) 50 (1975): 613-624, 933; 51 (1976): 206;

Rudolf Sellheim and M. Zakeri, "Al-Fehrest," *Encyclopedia Iranica*, s.v.;

Devin J. Stewart, "Scholarship on the *Fihrist* of Ibn al-Nadīm: the Work of Valeryĭ V. Polosin," *al-'Uṣūr al-wusṭā: the Bulletin of Middle East Medievalists* 18:1 (April 2006): 8-13;

Devin J. Stewart, "The Structure of the *Fihrist*: Ibn al-Nadīm as a Historian of Islamic Law and Theology," *International Journal of Middle East Studies* 39 (2007): 369-387;

Devin J. Stewart, "Emendations of the Legal Section in the *Fihrist* of Ibn al-Nadīm," in *Abbasid Studies: Occasional Papers of the School of Abbasid Studies*, Leuven, 28 June-1 July 2004, ed. John Nawas (Leuven: Uitgeverij Peeters en Departement Oosterse Studies, 2010), 211-244;

Devin J. Stewart, "Ibn al-Nadīm's Ismāʿīlī Contacts," *Journal of the Royal Asiatic Society*, Series 3, 19:1 (2008): 1-20;

Dieter Sturm, "Der *Fihrist* des Ibn an-Nadīm als Quelle für die kenntnis sozialer Zusammenhänge am Beispiel der dritten *Maqāla*," in *Ibn an-Nadim und die mittelalterliche arabische Literatur: Beiträge zum 1. Johann Wilhelm Fück-Kolloquium* (Halle, 1987; repr. Wiesbaden: Harrassowitz, 1996), 44-50;

Werner Sundermann, "The Representation of Manicheism in the *Fehrest*," *Encyclopedia Iranica*, s.v. "Fehrest, III,"

Hans H. Wellisch, *The First Arab Bibliography: Fihrist al-'Ulum* (Champaign-Urbana: University of Illinois, 1986);

Friedrich W. Zimmermann, "On the Supposed Shorter Version of Ibn an-Nadīm's *Fihrist* and its Date," *Der Islam* 53 (1976): 267-73.

Muḥammad Ibn Dānīyāl

(ca. 1248-1310)

AMAL EQEIQ

University of Washington

WORKS

Ṭayf al-khayāl (The Shadow Spirit);

'Ajīb wa-gharīb (The Amazing Preacher and the Stranger);

Mutayyam wa 'l-ḍāi' al-yuttim (The Love Stricken and the Lost One who Inspires Passion).

Editions

al-Mukhtār min shi'r Ibn Dānīyāl, al-Ḥākim Shams al-Dīn Muḥammad Ibn Dānīyāl al-Mawṣilī 'l-Kaḥḥāl, ed. Khalīl ibn Aybak Ṣafadī and Muḥammad Nāyif Dulaymī (Mosul: Maktabat Bassām, 1979).

Translations

Three Shadow Plays, transl. Paul Kahle, E.J.W. Gibb Memorial, New series, no. 32 (Cambridge, England: E.J.W. Gibb Memorial Trust, 1992) .

Shams al-Dīn Muḥammad Ibn Dānīyāl Yūsuf al-Khuzāʿī was a pioneer dramatist and a playwright from the Islamic middle ages. His work has been translated and studied because the three shadow plays he wrote under the title *Ṭayf al-khayāl* are by far the oldest works of Arabic drama known to us and the only dramatic pieces that have come down to us from the Islamic middle ages. A written collection of his work was put together in Egypt only in the 15th and 16th century, about a century and a half after the death of Ibn Dānīyāl. In the early 20th century, a scholar by the name of Georg Jacob (1862-1937) conducted research about shadow plays in the world, recovering the work of Ibn Dānīyāl and bringing attention to his plays. Ibn Dānīyāl's manuscripts have been scattered in many libraries in different parts of the world, and only in 1963 did a first publication of his plays come out.

Ibn Dānīyāl was born in Mosul, Iraq around 1248. At the time, Mosul was a thriving center of Arab and Islamic cultures and Ibn Dānīyāl grew up studying *Qur'ān*, *ḥadīth*, and literature. Troubled by the political unrest and economic decline that resulted from the Tatar invasion of Mosul in 1262, Ibn Dānīyāl immigrated to Cairo in 1267. In Cairo, he studied literature at the hands of Mu'īn al-Dawlah al-Fahrī (1208 or 1209-1287). Later, he became active as an ophthalmic surgeon (*kaḥḥāl*), a profession that granted him the nickname of *al-Ḥakīm* (the doctor) and had a considerable influence on his style, language and popularity. Although he ran his own clinic in the area of Bāb al-Futūḥ, Ibn Dānīyāl did not earn a lot of money. His insufficient income caused problems with his wife, and his married life become unsettled as a result. It was also possible because of his financial situation Ibn Dānīyāl took an interest in creating plays as a source of additional income.

Ibn Dānīyāl wrote poetry and prose. Although his poetry was not collected in a Dīwān, critics categorize his poetry into two types: poetry that depicts his poverty and lack of happiness that reflected the conditions of his early life, and, the poetry that came after his shadow plays became popular. After his plays became well-known among the elite, Ibn Dānīyāl's financial situation improved, and his poetry moved away from its former focus on misery and poverty. New subjects and forms appeared in his poetry, including elegant eulogy, praise of the Prophet Muḥammad (d. 632), Sufi symbolism and didactic *muwashshaḥāt*.

There is no documented evidence concerning the literary significance of Ibn Dānīyāl in his time, although literary critics often consider his work when studying the development of the *maqāmah*, another genre that was prominent among the Arabs in medieval times. Some critics would argue that Ibn Dānīyāl's plays developed from the *maqāmah*. For many modern scholars, however, Ibn Dānīyāl's work should be considered significant because of the high level of sophistication that characterizes his plays. The plays, written in poetry and versed prose, were produced by Ibn Dānīyāl himself. Not only would he write the music and choose the plot he depicted, but he would also participate in the actual shows. Moreover, he wrote specific instructions for their performance.

The three plays of Ibn Dānīyāl are: *Ṭayf al-khayāl* (The Shadow Spirit), *'Ajīb wa-gharīb* (The Amazing Preacher and the Stranger) and *Mutayyam wa 'l-ḍāi' al-yuttim* (translated literally as the Love Stricken One and the Lost One who Inspires Passion). The plays are set in Cairo in the early Mamluk period, during the rule of Sultan al-Malik al-Ẓāhir Rukn al-Dīn Baybars (1223?-1277), who forbid the consumption of alcohol in 1266 and banned the contemporary equivalent of night clubs in Cairo in 1267. All plays begin with a short introduction in which the author briefly explains his intentions. The introductions are written in rhymed prose in classical Arabic. The plays are dialogues between characters and are rich with references to the social life of Cairo. Some of these dialogues are written in colloquial Arabic, depending on the characters involved.

Ṭayf al-khayāl is the longest and most developed play in terms of plot and characters. It is about the political atmosphere and socio-cultural conditions during the reign of the Mamluk Sultan al-Ẓāhir Baybars. The play begins with the usual praise to "the Lord God Almighty, the majestic, exalted, above all the world," and goes on to "bless the Prophet and his family," and prays for "a long life for our Sultan, who alone preserves us from evil." Sultan Baybars had certainly protected his subjects, for it was he and his Mamluk armies who had dealt the Mongols a historic defeat in 1260, thus saving Cairo from the devastation that had befallen Baghdad and Damascus. Yet Ibn Dānīyāl's comment shortly after that a recent order of the sultan had "put Satan's army to flight," appears to refer not to the Mongols but to drug peddlers who had recently been expelled from the city.

The plot of *Ṭayf al-khayāl* focuses on the story of Prince Wisāl. Realizing that his life is full of meaningless entertainment and indulgent wine drinking, Prince Wisāl declares his intentions to repent and decides to get married. He calls for a marriage broker, Umm Rashīd, and asks her to find him a wife of exceptional beauty, excellent character and great wealth.

Umm Rashīd informs him immediately that she has the perfect bride for him. She enumerates for him the beauties of a divorced woman and tells him about her unfortunate experience with her previous husband. Then, she asks him to pay a huge amount of money as a dowry and other marriage expenses. Prince Wisāl, who has managed to squander all his fortune on his riotous lifestyle, accepts Umm Rashīd's offer while trying to figure out how to raise the necessary amount. In addition to demanding an expensive *mahr*, Umm Rashīd prevents Prince Wisāl from seeing the bride until the day of the wedding, as the customs dictated at the time. On the day of the wedding, when Prince Wisāl, lefts the veil from his bride's face, he is shocked to find that she is monstrously ugly. She utters a sound like the braying of a donkey, and he faints. When he later awakes, he calls for Umm Rashīd to punish her for cheating. Her husband, Shaykh ʿAflaq appears instead and tells him that she passed away a few hours earlier. Realizing that he cannot take revenge on Umm Rashīd, Prince Wisāl concludes that his misfortune is only a divine punishment for his extravagant lifestyle. Therefore, he decides to go on a pilgrimage to Mecca seeking repentance for his past sins.

'Ajīb wa-gharīb is a collection of sketches that depict numerous scenes of a market where actors enter one after another and introduce their products. The play does not include a linear plot. It begins with a Presenter who says a brief prologue. The Presenter, usually referred to as *al-Rayyis*, is the Master of Ceremonies. He is the first to appear on the stage and introduce the show. Here, the Presenter embodies the character of Gharīb (Stranger). He introduces himself as one of the Banū Sāsān, explaining how historical circumstances led his people into a life of wandering, living on their wits and resorting to trickery in order to survive.

Among the sketches in the play, there is a scene in which a snake-charmer plays with snakes in the market. As he plays with the snakes, he tells the audience that he has a remedy that heals a snake bite, and later he tries to sell it to them. Another sketch includes an astrologer who urges people to learn about their destiny, so they can plan ahead for their future. He offers them his astrological skills for a specific amount of golden coins. Other characters that appear in the sketches include a quack-doctor, a hawker of medicinal herbs, an ophthalmologist, a goat-trainer, a juggler, and a trader in amulets.

Mutayyam wa 'l-ḍāi' al-yuttim, the last play, has a story and a plot. Like the other plays it begins with a greeting from the Presenter. Here, the main character, al-Mutayyam, is the Presenter. After introducing himself to the audience, al-Mutayyam tells how he has spoiled his chances with women by falling in love with a very attractive young man, who is the object of desire of all the men around him. Al-Mutayyam describes how he fell in with the man after seeing him naked in a public bath. To describe the seductive beauty of this man, al-Mutayyam recites a love poem for the audience in the *muwashshaāḥah* form that he had composed for the man. Later on, a misshapen young man enters the stage and introduces himself as al-Mutayyam's former lover. He accuses al-Mutayyam of leaving him for the handsomer, al-Yuttim. He goes on reciting prose in favor of small things. In response, al-Mutayyam recites a poem to refute his argument, and so poetic debates begin between the two about the pros and cons of small versus big things. The play includes a scene of bull fighting and cocks and cock-fighting, sports that are seen as entertainment.

The shadow plays were performed with figures held by sticks against a back-lit canvas screen. The audience sitting in front of the screen saw only the shadows of the figures. The man behind the screen moved the figures and spoke or sang the text so that the moving figures appear to speaking or singing. The performance takes place in a theatrical space in which a screen separates the stage from the auditorium. In addition, the shadow play remained the only performing tradition in the medieval period that relied on a written script.

In terms of style, Ibn Dānīyāl's work remains significant not only in the field of oral drama, but also in the development of colloquial Arabic written literature. As scholars of his work have observed, Ibn Dānīyāl uses a remarkably flexible type of Arabic, ranging from the classical to the colloquial in a single work. In addition to that, a combination of argot, obscure jargon and even gibberish were used in places in these plays. This linguistic mixture facilitated the use of speeches, a central element to drama. It also legitimized the use of colloquial Arabic in literary forms that include comedy and irony, and in literature characteristic of a period of economic decline.

In the context of modern Islamic theatre, scholars have seen the work of Ibn Dānīyāl as an example of drama for the masses. Often, it is used to describe the collective performance of *ta'ziyyah*, which is a Shiite dramatic celebration for the memorial of Ḥusayn's murder. The *ta'ziyyah* often includes forty or fifty scenes, a Presenter who chants lamentations, a speech, and a recitation of poetry and prose.

REFERENCES

ʿAlī Ibrāhīm Abū Zayd, *Tamthīliyyāt khayāl al-ẓill* (Cairo: Dār al-Maʿārif, 1982);

Ali Zargar, "The Satiric Method of Ibn Dānīyāl: Morality and Anti-Morality in *Ṭayf al-Khayāl*," *Journal of Arabic Literature*,37:1 (Mar. 2006): 68-108;

Ibrāhīm Ḥamādah, *Khayāl al-ẓill, wa-tamthīliyyāt ibn Dānīyāl* (Cairo: al-Mu'assasah al-Miṣriyyah al-ʿĀmmah li 'l-Ta'līf wa 'l-Tarjamah wa 'l-Ṭibāʿah wa 'l-Nashr, 1963);

Li Guo, "Paradise Lost: Ibn Daniyal's Response to Baybar's Campaign against Vice in Cairo," *The Journal of the American Oriental Society*, 121:2 (2001): 219-235;

Muhammad Mandūr, *al-Masraḥ* (Cairo: Dār al-Maʿārif, 1963);

Three Shadow Plays, transl. Paul Kahle, E.J.W. Gibb Memorial, New series, no. 32 (Cambridge, England: E.J.W. Gibb Memorial Trust, 1992) .

Ibn Ḥamdīs

(ca. 1055-1132)

WILLIAM GRANARA

Harvard University

WORKS

Dīwān (Collected Poems).

Edition

Dīwān Ibn Ḥamdīs, ed. Iḥsān ʿAbbās (Beirut: Dār Ṣādir, 1960).

Translations

William Granara, "Remaking Muslim Sicily: Ibn Hamdis and the Poetics of Exile," *Edebiyat* 9:2 (1998), 167-198;

James Monroe, *Hispano-Arabic Poetry: a Student Anthology* (Berkeley: University of California Press, 1974), 202-205;

Celestino Schiapparelli, *Ibn Hamdis: Il Canzoniere* (Palermo: Sellerio, 1909).

ʿAbd al-Jabbār Ibn Ḥamdīs remains today as the best known figure from the Arabo-Muslim period of medieval Sicily. Despite the scant information in the extant Arabic bio-bibliography, the contours and trajectory of his life may be reconstructed through the pages of his relatively large anthology (*dīwān*) which contain some 370 poems, ranging from long standard *qaṣīdahs* to short two-line pieces, testifying to a long and prolific career. In addition to the momentous political events he spoke of, the patrons he praised, and the loved ones he eulogized, we have the powerful autobiographical voice that guides us through the tumultuous times he lived, from Sicily to Seville and back to North Africa, and the people and events that shared his life.

Ibn Ḥamdīs was born in the city of Syracuse in 1055 to a family of the Azdī tribe which emigrated from the Arabian peninsula to North Africa at the end of the first Islamic century, and who were among the first Muslim settlers in Sicily following the Muslim conquest in 827. His father, Abū Bakr, and his grandfather Muḥammad, were most likely the scions of military commanders who, by the time of his birth, had settled as landed gentry in the south-east corner of the island. His mother died while he was a child, leaving him and his sister. His father remarried a young Sicilian woman and the two children went to live in the house of their grandfather. He was raised by his paternal aunt, a widow whose husband, Yūsuf Ibn Abī 'l-Dār, had also recently died. The aunt had two children of her own, a boy named ʿAlī (who would be later mentioned as a physician), and a girl who would later become the young ʿAbd al-Jabbār's first wife. The four children shared one household.

There exists no mention of a formal education, teachers or schools, but his poetry strongly suggests deep grounding in Arabic language and literature. Snippets of his poetry suggest a life of comfort and ease, as well as an early falling in love with a young Sicilian girl that was foiled by the pressures of his grandfather and aunt to marry his cousin.

The political climate of his early years had an ominous impact on the young ʿAbd al-Jabbār, who was already showing a strong affinity for poetry. Since 1053, with the dissolution of the government of the Kalbid dynasty that had ruled Muslim Sicily continuously since 954, and the subsequent political fragmentation of the island by local petty warlords, Sicily had become vulnerable to the ambitions of the Norman armies from the North. The fall of Palermo in 1071 to Robert Guiscard (1031-1101) accelerated the Norman conquest and mass emigration of the island's Muslims to North Africa, Spain (al-Andalus) and Egypt. With aspirations to becoming a famous court poet, Ibn Ḥamdīs chose exile as the only course to achieve his goals. Like most of the island's Muslim population, he selected Ifrīqiyā (modern Tunisia) where most Sicilian Muslims had their roots.

Ibn Ḥamdīs's first port of exile was the city of Safāqus (modern Sfax) where his wife, children, aunt and cousins preceded him. His father chose to remain in Sicily, and there is a passing reference in one of his poems that his grandfather had died before his departure. Shortly after settling in Sfax, his wife gave birth to a [second] son, ʿUmar. Again, we know hardly anything of the short time he spent in Sfax, but given the fact that the city, located on the eastern littoral of the Tunisian coast, was not a major cultural center, and given the fact that the political climate was equally unstable due to the onslaught of the Banī Hilāl Arabian tribes (since 1050) who were wreaking havoc in both the North African urban and rural areas, we can surmise why Ibn Ḥamdīs set his sights elsewhere. In less than a year since departing his beloved Syracuse, he left his family in the "relative" safety of the family compound in Sfax, and in the company of his oldest son, Bakr, he set out on a journey to al-Andalus in search of literary fame and fortune.

The long and arduous journey across North Africa to the Iberian peninsula is amply documented through Ibn Ḥamdīs's *dīwān*, extending into a recurring *topos* for lifelong exile (*Dīwān*, #98: Leaving Sicily and Traveling to Ifrīqiyā):

5- What is it with me that I endure a long estrangement from my homeland?
Have I been born fated to live in exile?
6- Forever shall I squander my resolve in a distant land,
for a hope only to be dispersed in faraway places?
7- How many a hostile terrain will I cross on the back of a sturdy she-camel,
bleeding at the hooves and foaming at the nostrils?

In other verses, the young poet draws on his budding literary talents to express the experiences of life on the road: from sleepless and flea bitten nights, (*Dīwān*, #172, #216), to the pride and exhilaration in traveling in the company of noble Bedouins (*Dīwān*, #269: Remembering Bedouin Traveling Companions and Praising Compatriots of Syracuse):

9- Bedouins, noble and pure of stock, bred among the finest horses and camels,

they spur to battle their hard-hoofed horses and camel stallions.
10- I've had the pleasure of their company in the most hostile terrain,
a wasteland where wolves howl and gazelles bleat.

In 1079, Ibn Ḥamdīs and his son Bakr arrived at the outskirts of Seville and sent word to the royal court requesting an audience with Prince al-Muʿtamid Ibn ʿAbbād (1039-1095). In the aftermath of the fall of the Umayyad Caliphate of Cordoba in 1031, the ʿAbbādid princes had emerged as one of the most successful petty ruling dynasties, and Seville boasted a thriving court culture. Al-Muʿtamid, an accomplished poet himself, had by this time established a reputation for receiving and patronizing poets and other intellectuals. After a grueling period in which Ibn Ḥamdīs had received no royal response, he made the difficult decision to pack his bags and hit the road once again. Suddenly, on the eve of his departure from Seville, a young page appeared in the dark of night, leading a horse with one hand and holding a lantern in the other, called out the name of the dejected poet and summoned him to meet the prince. When he arrived at the palace, al-Muʿtamid offered him a seat, and then asked him to rise and look out a window. In the distance a woman was stoking the flames from an ironsmith's furnace. Al-Muʿtamid suddenly unleashed a line of poetry at Ibn Ḥamdīs describing the fire and challenged him to match it or best it. After three quick rounds of poetic sparring, al-Muʿtamid was sufficiently impressed and invited Ibn Ḥamdīs to join his royal retinue.

The dozen years he spent in Seville were professionally rewarding. In his many panegyric odes to al-Muʿtamid and his son al-Rashīd, the Sicilian exile expresses gratitude for and comfort in the protection of the ʿAbbādid court. It was especially in Seville, amidst a thriving literary production and fierce competition among hordes of poets battling for royal favors and critical reviews, where Ibn Ḥamdīs perfected his poetic talents. His literary repertoire at this time came to branch out from nostalgic verses of exile and per-forma panegyrics to include descriptive poems (*waṣf*) and meditations that displayed an extraordinary command of figurative language and metaphor. In a wine song poem, Ibn Ḥamdīs conjures a scene of the company of imbibers seated around a brook into which the server places rounds of wine; each man takes a cup as he desires and returns the empty one which sails back to the server. The poet likens the brook to a great river, the guests to cities along the river, and the cups of wine as ships sailing between them. More than a celebration of nocturnal male bonding in intoxication, the poem reads as a highly romanticized metaphor for the ʿAbbādid court where ships sailed on calm waters and men drank merrily in sumptuous, paradisiacal gardens.

The Seville years were also a period when Ibn Ḥamdīs was called upon to compose elegies (*rithāʾ*) to loved ones he left behind. News of his father's death came to him in Seville and his elegy [*Dīwān*, 330] mentions the double pain of death and exile. A later panegyric to al-Muʿtamid [*Dīwān*, 101] collapses the death of his father, exile, and refuge in his new patron:

22- You never disappointed one hopeful of your magnanimity,
you never left a thirsty man with nothing to quench his thirst.
23- I now have no distance in my distant wandering from my homeland,
after it you have made *Ḥima* a country for me.
24- As a substitute for my closest kin I was given your kin;
May God not separate me from them in all eternity.
25- How many of my people in a far away land the earth embraces,
I could not see any of them because of my distance.
26- The death of my father did not make me travel from your abode,
even though the death of a father may greatly distress the son.

In the year 1086 the ʿAbbādid court of Seville faced its greatest threat in Alfonso VI of Castile (1030-1109) and the Spanish reconquest. Having exhausted his resources combating fellow Muslim warlords in al-Andalus, al-Muʿtamid was unable to pay his tribute tax to

Alfonso and faced the threat of a military attack. In desperation al-Muʿtamid sought the intervention of Yūsuf Ibn Tāshfīn (1061-1106), Berber warlord and founder of the Almoravid dynasty in Morocco, by calling for a large-scale jihad. The Battle of Zallāqa was fought and the combined Muslim forces repelled the Castillian offense. On the occasion Ibn Ḥamdīs composed a celebratory ode to the victorious but seriously wounded al-Muʿtamid, mixing clusters of imagery ranging from the pagan swashbuckling lover/warrior to the defender of the faith and commander of the faithful [*Dīwān*, 283]. But the writing was on the wall and five years later, in 1091, Yūsuf and his Almoravid army, brandishing their fundamentalist swords, returned to claim Seville and put a decisive end to the godless ʿAbbādid principality. Ibn Ḥamdīs found himself one more time on the lonely path of exile.

As if the trauma of his friend and patron's demise was not enough, Ibn Ḥamdīs would face another hardship in the drowning of his beloved slave girl, Jawharah, as they crossed the treacherous waters of the Straits of Gibraltar back to the North African coast. He composed two poems on the occasion [*Dīwān*, 131 and 325], in one of which he likens the sea to an enraged jealous competitor for Jawharah's affections.

The return to North Africa would not be an easy one. The memory of defeat in Seville would linger, as reflected in the exchange of correspondence, in the form of poems, to and from al-Muʿtamid, who was lingering in a prison in the desert town of Aghmāt, just south of Marrakesh. From his cell, al-Muʿtamid addressed one of his poems to his former panegyrist and loyal boon companion, pondering his own fate, and expressing his painful longings for a homeland, wondering if there will ever be a return, questions, feelings, and poetic themes all too familiar to the Sicilian exile.

Political turmoil seems to have cast its shadow with a vengeance on Ibn Ḥamdīs, as he continued to encounter the familiar bickering and rivalries among Arabs on the one hand, and the dramatic success of the Christian reconquest on the other. By 1091, the Norman conquest of all of Sicily was in its final stages, and the urban centers of Ifrīqiyā were undoubtedly teeming with hordes of Arab Sicilian expatriates, crude reminders of the catastrophic events of his falling homeland, from which he was shielded during his thirteen year sojourn in Seville. In addition, the emergence of rival petty warlords along the North African littoral, although increasing the opportunities for a court poet to find employment, contributed to an atmosphere of political and economic instability. Thus we find Ibn Ḥamdīs at this time shuttling from court to court, especially the Ḥammādid court in Biyāja (modern Bougie in Algeria) and the Zīrid court of al-Mahdiyyah (Tunisia), peddling his poetic wares in search of making a living. He maintained contacts and spent periods of time with his family in Sfax, but his career called him to other places. Several poems of correspondence, particularly one composed in response to his cousin and brother-in-law, ʿAlī Ibn Abī 'l-Dār Abū 'l-Ḥasan in Sfax, expresses the pain of perpetual exile and sorrow for being unable to rejoin the family [*Dīwān*, #282]

4- How can I see myself heading in your direction,
if the hand of fate holds the reins of my life?
5- For mine is nothing more than an enduring exile,
in which I face my old age after my youth.
17- Do not think of me enjoying life without you,
taking pleasures in music and imbibing wine.
20- [But] do not think about my fear of crossing the wasteland that never ends,
with the hooves of my steeds bleeding in exhaustion.

The second forty years of Ibn Ḥamdīs's life were largely spent in the service of the Zīrid ruling family (ruled 1016-1152) which, in achieving autonomous rule of Ifrīqiyā in the aftermath of the Fatimid caliphate's move to Egypt towards the end of the 10th century, took it as their responsibility to defend and rearm Muslim Sicily against the Norman invasions. Tamīm Ibn al-Muʿizz (1061-1107) was the first Zīrid prince to be lauded by the poet, and in his only panegyric to him, Ibn Ḥamdīs used the occasion to lament the fall of Syracuse in 1092, berate his compatriots for failing to stand united, and urge a pan-Muslim front (*Dīwān*, #27: Panegyric to Tamīm and Lament on Norman Invasion of Sicily):

36- If my country were free I would go to it with a resolve
that sees separation as a constant affliction.
37- But how can my country be ransomed from captivity,
while it sits in the clutches of the usurping infidels?
38- These dogs have prevailed by devouring my lands,
and after a lull they lunged for the veins.
39- Before my eyes my compatriots succumbed to civil strife,
in which every woodsman lit a bonfire.
40- And their desires for it became such that they conducted themselves
in ways contrary to our faith.
41- Kinfolk showed no mercy to their own people,
as swords dripped with the blood of kin.

Since this composition, Ibn Ḥamdīs remained professionally engaged and prolific. In addition to elegies to friends and loved-ones, devotional poems (*zuhdiyyāt*), and occasional pieces on youthful memories and events, he composed twelve panegyrics to Tamīm's son, Yaḥyā (ruled 1107-1115), and twenty-seven to his grandson ʿAlī ibn Yaḥyā (ruled 1115-1121). These "Zīrid" panegyrics in the main documented and eulogized Muslim Sicily's decline and the rise of Norman supremacy over the central Mediterranean, addressed as much to the Zīrid patrons as to the throngs of Sicilian expatriates and their fellow Arab and Muslim sympathizers throughout Ifrīqiyā. In 1016, for example, during an attempted assassination of Prince Yaḥyā ibn Tamīm, resulting from political machinations and court intrigue, Ibn Ḥamdīs's friend and Sicilian compatriot, and the prime minister, al-Sharīf al-Fihrī 'l-Ṣiqillī, succumbed to his wounds. Once again, the poet documents the occasion with a poignant elegy [*Dīwān*, #96], giving voice to the perilous times in which he was living.

In the summer of 1123, the armies of Roger II, the King of Sicily (d. 1154) and Zīrid Prince al-Ḥasan ibn ʿAlī (1121–1152) battled at an ancient fortress (*al-Dīmās*) on a small island off the coast of the Tunisia. The "unexpected" Muslim victory sparked a glimmer of hope for the rulers of North Africa and their exile Sicilian communities, especially given that Norman Sicily had emerged by now as the uncontested dominant force in the central Mediterranean. Ibn Ḥamdīs, the seasoned seventy-year old court poet, composed a 67 line celebratory ode for the occasion, at the end of which he attached a *de rigeur* 8 line panegyric to the twelve year old Prince, al-Ḥasan, who stumbled into rulership following the premature death of his father, ʿAli. The poem documents in detail the battle's sequence of events and cites its military commanders and all the tribes who participated in it. With invective hurled at the enemy and praise and encouragement aimed at the Arab forces, Ibn Ḥamdīs delivered perhaps his last significant political poem. The *Dīmās* poem, although tired in style and hackneyed in language, nonetheless reflects a political obsession and commitment to the historical moment we see as hallmarks of his life and work. The nostalgia for a homeland and the burning desire to return would remain constant themes until the end of his long life.

The twilight of Ibn Ḥamdīs's life is recorded in a moving elegy he composed on the death of one of his daughters. In an ironic twist, the woman died shortly after hearing a false report of her father's death. The strong autobiographical voice which accompanied much of his poetry once again comes forth as the poet, referring to himself as a blind octogenarian, mixes feelings of guilt, existential angst, and that lingering loss of homeland.

9- Eighty years have I lived and I found them
destroying what they achieved, tearing down what they erected.
10- Here I am living in a world of speaking of hope which,
when I coveted it, I only found it dying in deed.
28- I see myself as a stranger crying over a stranger,
as though we were both yearning for a homeland and family.
29- She cried for me thinking that I had died before her.

But I live, and she has died and is now mourned by me.
38- May their tears water a tomb for Kifāḥ on a moist land,
with rain that has on fertility the same effect as drought.

ʿAbd al-Jabbār Ibn Ḥamdīs died in 1132, bemoaning until his last breath the loss of his beloved homeland of Sicily and holding out hope for its restoration to Arab sovereignty. Accounts vary on his burial site, some claiming it was as far away as the island of Majorca off the coast of Spain.

REFERENCES

Iḥsān ʿAbbās, *al-'Arab fī Ṣiqilliyyah: dirāsah fī 'l-tārīkh wa 'l-adab* (Cairo: Dār al-Maʿārif, 1959);

Francesco Gabrieli, *Ibn Hamdis*. (Mazara: Società editrice siciliana, 1948);

William Granara, "Remaking Muslim Sicily: Ibn Ḥamdīs and the Poetics of Exile," *Edebiyat* 9:2 (1998), 167-198;

al-Sanūsī, Zayn al-ʿĀbidīn, *'Abd al-Jabbār Ibn Ḥamdīs: hayātuh wa adabuh* (Tunis: al-Dār al-Tūnisiyyah li 'l-Nashr, 1983.

Abū Muḥammad Ibn Ḥazm

(994-1064)

TERRI DEYOUNG
University of Washington

WORKS

Ṭawq al-ḥamāmah fī 'l-ulfah wa 'l-ullāf (The Dove's Neck-Ring Concerning Love and Lovers);

al-Taqrīb li-ḥadd al-manṭiq wa-madkhūluh (Facilitating the Definition of Logic and Introduction Thereto);

Risālah fī faḍl al-Andalus wa-dhikr rijālihā (Treatise on the Excellence of al-Andalus and the Mention of Its Famous Men);

Jamharat al-ansāb al-'Arab (A Digest of the Genealogies of the Arabs);

Naqt al-'arūs fī akhbār al-khulafā' (Embroidery for the Bride Concerning Anecdotes about the Caliphs);

Jawāmi' al-sīrah (The Compilation of The Prophet Muḥammad's Biography);

Kitāb al-fiṣal (al-faṣl) fī 'l-milal wa 'l-ahwā' wa 'l-nihal (The Book of Distinctions Concerning Religions, Sects, and Denominations);

Kitāb al-iḥkām (al-aḥkām) fī uṣūl al-aḥkām (Book of the Establishment of the Roots of Legal Decisions);

Mulakhkhaṣ ibṭāl al-qiyās wa 'l-ra'y wa 'l-istiḥsān wa 'l-taqlīd wa 'l-ta'līl (Summary of the Nullification of Analogy, Opinion, Discretion, Adoption of a Legal Decision Already Approved, and Justification);

Kitāb al-muḥallā bi 'l-athār fī sharḥ al-mujallā bi-ikhtisār (Book of Ornaments Concerning Works That Explain One Revealed Succinctly);

Risālat marātib al-'ulūm (Treatise on the Categories of the Sciences);

Risālah fī 'l-radd 'alā Ibn al-Naghrīlī 'l-Yahūdī (Treatise in Reply to Ibn al-Naghrīlī the Jew);

Risālatān la-hu 'ajāb 'an risālatayn su'il fīhimā su'āl ta'nīf (His Two Treatises Replying to Two Treatises in Which a Question of Rebuke Was Asked);

Risālah fī 'l-radd 'alā 'l-hātif min bu'd (A Treatise in Reply to One Calling from Afar);

Risālat al-tawqīf 'alā shāri' al-najāt bi 'khtisār al-ṭarīq (Treatise Intended to Arrest One on the Road of Deliverance by Shortening the Way);

Risālah fī 'l-ghinā' al-mulahhī: a mubāḥ huwa am maḥẓūr (A Treatise on Pleasurable Singing: Is it Permitted or Forbidden);

Risālah fī mudāwāt al-nufūs wa-tahdhīb al-akhlāq wa 'l-zuhd fī 'l-radhā'il (Treatise on the Therapy for Souls and the Instruction of Character and Asceticism Concerning Vices);
Risālah fī alam al-mawt wa ibtālih (Treatise on the Pains of Death and How to Frustrate Them);
Risālat al-talkhīs li-wujūh al-takhlīs (Abridged Treatise on the Varieties of Purification);
Risālat al-bayān 'an ḥaqīqat al-īmān (Treatise of Clarification Concerning the Truth of Faith);
Risālah fī 'l-imāmah (Treatise on the Leadership of the Muslim Community in Prayer and Politically);
Risālah fī ḥukm man qāl inna 'l-arwāḥ ahl al-shaqā' mu'adhdhabah ilā yawm al-dīn (Treatise Concerning the Judgment of One Who Says that the Souls of the Wretched Are Punished Until the Day of Judgment);
Faṣl fī ma'rifat al-nafs bi-ghayrihā wa-jahlihā bi-dhātihā (Section on the Knowledge of the Soul about Others and Its Ignorance of Itself);
Akhlāq wa-siyar (Character and Conduct).

Editions

Ṭawq al-ḥamāmah, ed. D.K. Petrov (Leiden: E.J. Brill, 1914);
Ṭawq al-ḥamāmah fī 'l-ulfah wa 'l-ullāf, ed. al-Ṭāhir Aḥmad Makkī (Cairo: Dār al-Ma'ārif, 1977);
al-Taqrīb li-ḥadd al-manṭiq wa-madkhūluh, ed. Iḥsān 'Abbās (Cairo: Manshūrāt Dār Maktabat al-Ḥayāt, 1959);
al-Taqrīb li-ḥadd al-manṭiq wa-madkhūluh, ed. 'Abd al-Ḥaqq ibn Mulāḥiqī 'l-Turkmānī (Beirut: Dār Ibn Ḥazm li 'l-Ṭibā'ah wa 'l-Nashr wa 'l-Tawzī', 2007);
Jamharat ansāb al-'Arab, ed. Evariste Levi-Provençal (Cairo: Dār al-Ma'ārif, 1948);
Jamharat ansāb al-'Arab, ed. 'Abd al-Salām Muḥammad Hārūn (Cairo: Dār al-Ma'ārif, 1971);
Naqt al-'arūs, ed. Shawqī Ḍayf (Cairo: Maṭba'at Jāmi'at Fu'ād al-Awwal,1951);
Jawāmi' al-sīrah wa-khams rasā'il ukhrā li-Ibn Ḥazm, ed. Iḥsān 'Abbās and Nāṣir al-Dīn al-Asad (Gujrānvālah: Idārah-i Iḥyā' al-Sunnah, 1970);
Kitāb al-fiṣal (al-faṣl) fī 'l-milal wa 'l-ahwā' wa 'l-nihal, 5 vols. (Cairo: al-Maṭba'ah al-Adabiyyah, 1899-1903);
Rasā'il Ibn Ḥazm al-Andalusī, 2 vols., ed. Iḥsān 'Abbās (Cairo: Makatabat al-Khanijī, 1954);
Rasā'il Ibn Ḥazm al-Andalusī, volume 3, ed. Iḥsān 'Abbās (Beirut: al-Mu'assasah al-'Arabiyyah li 'l-Dirāsāt wa 'l-Nashr, 1981);
al-Muḥallā bi 'l-athār fī sharḥ al-mujallā bi-'khtisār, 11 vols., ed. Aḥmad Muḥammad Shākir, 'Abd al-Raḥmān al-Jazīrī and Muḥammad Munīr al-Dimashqī (Cairo and Damascus, 1929-1934);
al-Muḥallā sharḥ al-majallā, 11 vols., ed. Lajnat Iḥyā' al-Turāth al-'Arabī (Beirut: Manshūrāt Dār Āfāq al-Jadīdah, 1980);
Mulakhkhaṣ ibṭāl al-qiyās wa 'l-ra'y wa 'l-istiḥsān wa 'l-taqlīd wa 'l-ta'līl, ed. Sa'īd al-Afghānī (Damascus: University of Damascus Press, 1959-1960);
Iḥkām li-uṣūl al-aḥkām, ed. Muḥammad Aḥmad 'Abd al-'Azīz (Cairo: Maktabat 'Āṭif, 1978);
Kitāb al-akhlāq wa 'l-siyar fī mudāwāt al-nufūs, ed. Aḥmad 'Umar al-Maḥmaṣānī 'l-Azharī (Cairo: Maṭba'at al-Sa'ādah, 1908);
al-Akhlāq wa-siyar, ed. al-Ṭāhir Aḥmad Makkī (Cairo: Dār al-Ma'ārif, 1981).

Translations

A Book Containing the Risala Known as the Dove's Neck-Ring About Love and Lovers, trans. A.R. Nyckl (Paris: Librairie Orientaliste Paul Geuthner, 1931);
The Ring of the Dove by Ibn Ḥazm, trans. Arthur Arberry (London: Luzac and Company, 1953);
Hispano-Arabic Poetry: a Student Anthology, ed. and trans. James T. Monroe (Berkeley: University of California Press, 1974), 170-177;
Naqt al-'arus, ed. C.F. Seybold, trans. (into Spanish) Luis Seco de Lucena (Valencia: Textos medievales, 1974);
Abenhazam de Cordoba y su Historia Critica de las Ideas Religiosas, 5 volumes, trans. (into Spanish) Miguel Asin Palacios (Madrid: Rev. de Archivos. Bibliotecas y Museos, 1927-1932);

"The Categories of the Sciences," in Anwar Chejne, *Ibn Ḥazm* (Chicago: Kazi Publications, 1982), 189-213;
In Pursuit of Virtue: the Moral Theology and Psychology of Ibn Ḥazm al-Andalusi (384-456 AH 994-1064 AD) with a Translation of His Book al-Akhlaq wa 'l-Siyar, trans. Muhammad Abu Laylah (London: TaHa Publishers Ltd., 1990).

Abū Muḥammad ʿAlī ibn Aḥmad Ibn Ḥazm was an Andalusian literary figure who has long been seen as one of the most important representatives of Islamic thought between the death of Abū ʿAlī 'l-Ḥusayn ibn ʿAbd Allāh Ibn Sīnā (980-1037) and the maturity of Abū Ḥāmid ibn Muḥammad al-Ghazzālī (1058-1111). A report going back to his son Faḍl credits Abū Muḥammad with writing over 400 volumes in a wide range of fields, on religion, history, politics, literature, ethics and morals, language and grammar, and poetry. Even allowing for exaggeration in this enumeration, there is no doubt he was a very prolific author. Despite the fact that some of his works were proscribed, and (according to contemporary sources) burned, during his lifetime, several dozen of Ibn Ḥazm's books and treatises have been published and are available today, quite a number in translation.

Many of his religious works continue to be studied actively today, if only because it is impossible to write a history of the rise and fall of the Ẓāhirī school of law (which flourished between the ninth and fifteenth centuries) without reference to Ibn Ḥazm. Yet, somewhat surprisingly, he is probably most famous now for a work from his youth, *Ṭawq al-ḥamāmah* (*The Dove's Neck-Ring*), which survived into the nineteenth century almost by accident in a single manuscript copy. Its theme is the anatomy of love, enlivened by anecdotes taken from Ibn Ḥazm's own life and illustrated by poems of his own composition. Because of its enormous cross-disciplinary and cross-cultural appeal, this book has, since its re-discovery, been translated into several European languages, including twice into English.

Early on in his career, Abū Muḥammad also wrote an important (though controversial) work on logic, *al-Taqrīb li-ḥadd al-manṭiq*. This is a valuable work because it gives us exceptional insight into how Aristotelian logic was understood in Islamic culture at a time when Greek philosophy was becoming increasingly influential—especially in religious discourse—and can be usefully to compared to works of the scholastic movement in Europe, especially the work of his near contemporary, Peter Abelard (1079-1142). The *Taqrīb* incorporates detailed summaries of (and original contributions to) the basic curricular manuals by Aristotle on logic and argumentation, known collectively as *The Organon*.

In the middle period of his life, Ibn Ḥazm devoted himself increasingly to religious studies. During this time he composed major works on theology and (religious) history, especially in the context of supporting and expounding the orientation of the Ẓāhirī school of law, of which he was almost the only adherent in the Andalus of his day, where the Mālikī school dominated. Probably in the late 1020s, he also began a study of religious beliefs in a comparative context, *Kitāb al-fiṣal* (or *faṣl*) *fī 'l-milal wa 'l-ahwā' wa 'l-nihal* (The Book of Distinctions Concerning Religions, Sects, and Denominations), that was one of the first works to undertake such a study systematically. It is still an important source for material on how educated Muslims understood the other religious traditions (most notably Christians and Jews, but also including groups as varied as Hindus and Mazdeans) with which they interacted.

Finally, at the end of his life, he produced a volume now known as *Kitāb al-akhlāq wa 'l-siyar* (*In Pursuit of Virtue*), in which he provides, in the tradition of Aristotle's *Nichomacean Ethics*, an explanation for human behavior on the basis of reason and reflection, and suggests how human desire can be directed and molded. His conclusions represent an important and quite original contribution to the literature on moral philosophy in Islam, one that is more psychological than religious, but also not so dependent on Greek philosophy as some attempts made earlier in the century to address this subject.

He also composed many shorter works on the numerous subjects that would have been of concern to an educated person in his milieu—from history, to politics to education, to the defense of Islam from enemies both within and without, or the achievements of Andalusian Muslims in comparison with their Eastern brethren. All these works can be said to exhibit an interest in human psychology and are imbued with a lively dose of human emotion, whether to the benefit of the work (examples would include *The Dove's Neck-Ring* or *In Pursuit of Virtue*) or occasionally to its detriment, like some of the polemics (where he all too often allows his emotions to carry him away) or religious works.

We have a great deal of information on Ibn Ḥazm and his life, especially in comparison to many of his contemporaries. This is partly because he tells us much about his early life in *The Dove's Neck Ring*. The wealth of information we have from that source is supplemented by the fact that one of the earliest comprehensive biographical dictionaries from Andalus to be preserved, *Jadhwat al-muqtabas*, is by a lifelong pupil of Ibn Ḥazm, Abū ʿAbd Allāh Muḥammad ibn Abī Naṣr Fattūḥ al-Ḥumaydī, who drew upon his master for the information in many of his entries. Al-Ḥumaydī traveled eastwards after Ibn Ḥazm's death, dying in Baghdad in 1095. Thus, Abū Muḥammad's works—narrated on the authority of al-Ḥumaydī—were transmitted to the East, and he appears in the major biographical compilations from that area as well.

Thus, it is possible to reconstruct the narrative of Ibn Ḥazm's life in very great detail. Nevertheless, it is also true that establishing some facts (like the exact chronology of his works) can be quite difficult. So there remain many corners of his biography that are dark and can be illuminated only through conjecture.

This difficulty is clearly illustrated by any attempt to establish with certainty his family origins. Al-Ḥumaydī tells us that Ibn Ḥazm's family could trace their ancestry back to Persia at the time of the Prophet Muḥammad (d. 632). According to this version, their forefather, Yazīd, converted to Islam and became a client of Yazīd ibn Abī Sufyān (d. 640), the brother of Muʿawiyah ibn Abī Sufyān (the first Umayyad caliph, d. 680). The historian Abū Marwān Ḥayyān ibn Khalaf Ibn al-Ḥayyān (987 or 988-1076)—a contemporary of Ibn Ḥazm—cast doubt, however, upon this genealogy and states unequivocally that his grandfather, Saʿīd, had been a new convert to Islam from the Christian Spaniards of the area around Niebla, in the southwest of the Peninsula. This would conform well with the fact that, at the end of his life, Ibn Ḥazm retired to the family estate at Mant Lisham near Niebla in southwestern Andalus to live in provincial retirement. Yet it would also be difficult to understand why Ibn Ḥazm would feel compelled to manufacture an illustrious background if it were not true, since many of the men at court in the later Umayyad and ʿĀmirid periods did not have impeccable Islamic pedigrees, and it did no harm to their careers. Nor did those who could document such ancestry—like Abū Muḥammad's friend Abū ʿĀmir Aḥmad Ibn Shuhayd (992-1035)—particularly benefit from that kind of claim. The difficulty is further compounded by an examination of Ibn Ḥazm's work *Jamharat ansāb al-ʿArab*, where he endorses both the importance of Muslim piety (irregardless of birth) in evaluating a person's character, and yet, at the same time, emphasizes that everyone should be able to trace in minute detail his or her family tree. Given the information we have, however, the true antecedents of Ibn Ḥazm's family must remain a mystery.

Whatever the case may be, it seems that Abū Muḥammad's grandfather Saʿīd took the family to Cordoba in the mid-tenth century, where his son Aḥmad prospered (as did Aḥmad's brother ʿAbd al-Raḥman) as a government official. Aḥmad was especially respected for his writing skills, serving loyally under al-Ḥakam al-Mustanṣir (d. 976) and (especially) the Chamberlain al-Manṣūr ibn Abī ʿĀmir, (939-1002), whose close confidant he was.

Thus Ibn Ḥazm was brought up among the elite of Cordoba. According to his own description in *The Dove's Neck-Ring*, during his childhood he lived mostly in the women's quarters and seldom ventured beyond his family's palace in Balāt al-Mughīth on the western side of the city. But, most importantly, he tells us in this work that he received his first education from these women (*Ṭawq*, ed. Makkī, 79):

I have observed women and have come to know
their secrets in a way almost

> no one else has. I was raised in their care and grew up among them, not knowing anyone but them. . . .They taught me the *Qur'ān* and schooled me in the recitation of many poems. They trained me in good handwriting. I had no interest or any way to exercise my mind and excite my understanding, when I was still a young child, except to get to know their motivations, and search out and obtain stories about them

The prominence of women in general in his writings is notable. Besides the abundant material about women's lives found in *The Dove's Neck-Ring*, at a later period (when he is more preoccupied with religious issues) he devotes a long discussion in *Kitāb al-fiṣal* to the question of whether or not women can be considered prophets, ultimately deciding that such a designation was possible for women like Mary the mother of Jesus, who had direct contact with the divine, a position that was not usual among contemporary Muslim theologians.

Education was also a topic of great interest to Ibn Ḥazm throughout his life, and he more than once describes in more conventional terms than here the subjects a child should be taught—the *Qur'ān*, poetry, grammar and writing—early on. But in the passage quoted above, he shows how important the role of women could be in early childhood education (thus also demonstrating how many educational opportunities upper-class women had in the Islamic world of his time). Yet it is also interesting that, despite the intimacy and revealing nature of such a passage, we never learn anything about Ibn Ḥazm's female relatives, even the identity of his mother. Similarly, he gives few details about his siblings, only once referring to a brother who died during the plague that swept through Cordoba subsequent to the fighting that occurred in the city in mid-1009. We know equally little about his marriage or family life, except that he had three sons, all of whom survived him

He does speak incidentally in *The Dove's Neck-Ring* about some of his teachers—as well as serving as an authoritative source for their lives in al-Ḥumaydī's biographical dictionary—and these references allow us to reconstruct some of the curriculum he followed once he began to pursue a more formal education. Ibn Ḥazm's first tutor was Aḥmad ibn Muḥammad Ibn al-Jasūr (d. 1010). He is also identified as Aḥmad ibn Muḥammad ibn Aḥmad ibn Aḥmad ibn Sa'īd in *The Dove's Neck-Ring* and was a close acquaintance of Ibn Ḥazm's father. He was well-known as a *ḥadīth* scholar and transmitter of the historian Muḥammad ibn Jarīr al-Ṭabarī's (838?-923) works, having studied with one of his pupils. This would account for Ibn Ḥazm's familiarity later in life with the techniques and ideas found in the work of this famous historian and commentator on the *Qur'ān*. But it is nevertheless worth noting that, with the exception of *The Dove's Neck-Ring*, Ibn Ḥazm's historical works are quite different from al-Ṭabarī's, making little use of personal anecdote, and he is often later quite critical of this illustrious curriculum author.

Among the religious works Abū Muḥammad studied with his new teacher was the authoritative handbook of Mālikī law, the *Muwaṭṭa'*. Ibn al-Jasūr, however, also worked as a clerk (or *kātib*) for the judge Mundhir Ibn Sa'īd al-Ballūṭī, (886-966), known as "the first Ẓāhirī scholar in al-Andalus" (though he rendered legal decisions according to Mālikī views). It is thus likely that Ibn al-Jasūr imparted some Ẓāhirī ideas to his young student, and that this influenced Ibn Ḥazm's interest in that legal school. Thus the path that led to Ibn Ḥazm's Ẓāhirism can be seen to have begun very early indeed. Nor was Ibn al-Jasūr the only Ẓāhirī Abū Muḥammad studied with, he also took lessons from another prominent jurist who favored Ẓāhirī ideas, Abū 'l-Khiyār Mas'ūd ibn Sulaymān ibn Muflit al-Lughawī (d. 1034), who he mentions as a favored teacher in *The Dove's Neck Ring*. He also pursued studies in the Shafi'i texts with Abū 'l-Qāsim Salāmah ibn Sa'īd al-Anṣārī 'l-Astajī (mentioned in al-Ḥumaydī), who had studied in Mecca before returning to al-Andalus.

But Ibn Ḥazm's early exposure to *ḥadīth* and Islamic law (usual in the educational milieu of time) seems not to have kept him from also pursuing the serious study of philosophy, including an exposure to Porphyry's (ca. 234-ca. 305) *Isagogue* (in Arabic translation) and the books that make up the *Organon* of Aristotle. It is possible that his first taste of logic and dialectic (as taught through this curriculum) came at the hands of Muḥammad ibn al-Ḥasan Ibn al-Kattānī (d. 1029), the personal physician of al-Manṣūr and his son al-Muẓaffar, who was also a recognized expert in the "lore of the ancients" (a frequent circumlocution for "the Greeks" in Arabic intellectual discourse). Ibn al-Kattānī was also a noted poet, and it may have been he who introduced his pupil to Qudāmah Ibn Ja'far's (ca. 873or 874–948) *Naqd al-shi'r*, a work Ibn Ḥazm would later recommend in his book on logic as an introduction to poetry for those who sought a concise and systematic treatise that showed clearly the connection between poetry and philosophy. The warmth of Abū Muḥammad's reminiscences of Ibn al-Kattānī in the biographical literature indicates the continued cordiality of their relationship.

Ibn Ḥazm also seems to have pursued more conventional literary studies in depth. He tells us in *The Dove's Neck Ring* of reading commentaries on the famous poems from Preislamic times known as the *Mu'allaqāt* and describes how he attempted to use the poem of Ṭarafah ibn al-'Abd included in this collection as a basis for one of his own compositions. He tells us he studied these commentaries with a certain Abū Sa'īd al-Fatā 'l-Ja'farī (d. ca. 1034), a client of the famous vizier Ja'far ibn 'Uthmān al-Mushafī (who had vied for power with al-Manṣūr but lost to his rival in 978 and died several years later in prison). Al-Mushafī was a skilled writer and poet, as well as a youthful friend of Ibn Ḥazm's father, and it may have been that members of his household continued to teach those arts in Ibn Ḥazm's youth. Credit for his literary education at this time should also be given to Ibn Ḥazm's favorite teacher Abū Yazīd al-Azdī (d. 1019). He had come from Egypt in the year 1003, and would leave again for that country before a decade had passed. His main expertise was in religious matters, but while he was in Cordoba he undoubtedly imparted to his pupils the latest in Eastern intellectual fashions, which would have explained his popularity with young students like Abu Muḥammad.

All of this intellectual activity came to an abrupt end in 1009 when fighting broke out between supporters of the various Umayyad factions that attempted to seize power in the wake of the death of al-Manṣūr's younger son, 'Abd al-Raḥman (also known as Sanchuelo). Ibn Ḥazm's family had apparently been known as supporters of the Umayyad cause (even though his father had loyally served al-Manṣūr). But, following the triumph and return in 1010 to the throne of Hishām al-Mu'ayyad (d. ca. 1013)—the son of the last effective Umayyad ruler al-Ḥakam al-Mustanṣir (d. 976)—Aḥmad ibn Sa'īd Ibn Ḥazm was disgraced and fell from power, apparently because he had not supported Hishām with sufficient resolution. His son was thus transformed almost instantaneously from a carefree youth to a prisoner in his own house and—as he tells us in *The Dove's Neck Ring*—the entire family was eventually obliged to go into hiding during new fighting that broke out at the end of the year. Then, first his elder brother Abū Bakr and later his father, succumbed to rounds of the plague that broke out in the summers of 1011 and 1012.

Suddenly, at the age of eighteen, Abū Muḥammad found himself an orphan, and a year later he fled Cordoba with one of his friends, Abū Bakr Muḥammad ibn Isḥāq, for the relative calm of the Umayyad loyalist city Almeria. Ibn Ḥazm would spend three years in Almeria, continuing to study and waiting for the return of peace to Cordoba. One of the few signs that he continued to study is his report in *The Dove's Neck Ring* that he frequented the shop of the Jewish doctor Ismā'īl ibn Yūnis. It was common at the time for Muslim (and non-Muslim) scholars to supplement their income by trade. Abū Yazīd al-Azdī, for example, is also reported to have worked as a wool merchant. Thus, Ibn Ḥazm may have been learning about subjects like the Jewish scriptures or continuing his education in philosophy or medicine by frequenting Ismā'īl ibn Yūnis's shop.

It may have also been at this time he came to be acquainted with Ismā'īl Ibn al-Naghrīlah (or "al-Naghrālī"), likewise a fugitive from Cordoba, living in Almeria, who would later become chief vizier in the city of Granada. Probably late in his life, Ibn Ḥazm would compose a tart and sharply worded treatise refuting some propositions that were circulating under Ibn al-Naghrīlah's name. These propositions drew attention to certain inconsistencies in the *Qur'ān*, which Ibn Ḥazm sought vigorously to refute using largely *ad hominem* arguments, accusing Ibn al-Naghrīlah of being a freethinker and materialist, as well as not having the background (as a non-Muslim and non-Arab) to give proper readings of the sacred text. This certainly was not one of the high points of Ibn Ḥazm's religious polemic, but it illustrates a technique (*ad hominem* attack) that he resorted to—all too often—in dealing with Muslim, as a well as non-Muslim, opponents. In this, he was going against a rising tide in Islamic discourse of the time that discouraged direct attacks against those with whom one disagreed, and put Ibn Ḥazm outside the mainstream.

Yet, on the other hand, Ibn Ḥazm could be quite circumspect when the circumstances suited him, especially in his early writings. As with the details about his father's relationship with Hishām, Abū Muḥammad gives us little guidance in *The Dove's Neck Ring* about his political activities while in Almeria. He does tell us directly that he was imprisoned in 1016 by Khayrān (d. 1028), the ruler of Almeria, along with his friend Abū Bakr, and eventually banished from the city. It is reasonable to assume, as several scholars have done, that during this period he was increasingly involved in some sort of plotting to place another Umayyad, besides Hishām, on the throne. Khayrān had originally been an Umayyad legitimist, like Ibn Ḥazm, but by mid-1016 he had decided to join ʿAlī Ibn Ḥammūd (d. 1018), governor of Ceuta and a Berber leader descended directly from the Prophet, in a move to take over the city of Cordoba, which was successful. It is likely that Khayrān believed that an active Ibn Ḥazm in Almeria was an inconvenience in these changed circumstances, and therefore he had to be removed from the scene.

After leaving Almeria, Abū Muḥammad went eastwards to the small town of Ḥiṣn al-Qaṣr (not to be confused with the modern Aznalcazar), where he stayed briefly, and then sailed for the much larger eastern city of Valencia. From there, probably late in 1017, he joined a movement—spearheaded by the now disaffected Khayrān—to place a legitimate claimant from the Umayyad family on the throne. The assassination of ʿAlī in April 1018 gave heart to the rebels and the Umayyad ʿAbd al-Raḥmān (d. 1018) (who had been living in Valencia) was proclaimed Caliph, with the regnal title of al-Murtaḍā, in the same month. Supported by a large body of troops, including Christian allies of Khayrān, al-Murtaḍā marched westwards toward Granada, where the Berber governor, Zāwī ibn Zīr (d. 1019), refused to acknowledge al-Murtaḍā's legitimacy. The troops met in battle, and al-Murtaḍā, betrayed and abandoned by Khayrān, was forced to flee and was eventually killed. Ibn Ḥazm was captured and again, briefly, imprisoned.

By February 1019, Ibn Ḥazm was back in Cordoba. During the rule of Qāsim Ibn Ḥammūd (d. 1039-40), ʿAlī's brother and successor, Abū Muḥammad seems to have pursued his religious studies (most likely consolidating his knowledge of Mālikī legal doctrine as well as furthering his knowledge of Ẓāhirism), and lived a quiet, private life. For a while during this period he seems to have toyed with an allegiance to the Shafiʿi school of law (which appears to have had even fewer adherents in Andalus than Ẓāhirism). The association with Shāfiʿism seems to have followed him long after Ibn Ḥazm ceased to be interested in the school, because this is how Abū 'l-Ḥasan ibn ʿAlī Ibn al-Bassām al-Shantarinī (d. ca. 1147) would refer to him a half-century later. Similarly, the late medieval author Kâtip Çelebi (1609-1657) would mistakenly call *Iḥkām fī uṣūl al-Islām* a Shafiʿi work.

A colorful anecdote preserved only in later sources suggests that Abū Muḥammad may have felt the need during this period to further his education, particularly in Islam, which is pictured as woefully inadequate. He joins a funeral being held at a local mosque but is unable to behave according to the proper etiquette such occasions demand. His embarrassment, he tells us, causes him to seek out a teacher who will instruct him in the practices of Islam. This anecdote has sometimes been cited as evidence that Ibn Ḥazm did not begin his studies until this age, which is demonstrably false, given the extensive anecdotes we have about his early education and teachers. But it may not be entirely spurious. What it may suggest, rather, is that he returned to more formal studies during this time, after his long absence in Almeria. In a sense, then, he would have been trying to return to the routines he followed at a younger age, before his life had been so rudely turned upside down.

But some things had irrevocably changed. It is probably to this period, for example, that we owe one of the most heart-breaking and personal anecdotes of *The Dove's Neck-Ring*, where Ibn Ḥazm speaks of encountering a young woman—once owned by his family and trained by them as a singing girl, of surpassing beauty—who had been so altered by her sufferings during the chaos following his family's downfall that he barely recognized her. He reports that she had always before behaved as the perfectly aloof and unattainable beloved, never responding to his evident feelings for her, thus increasing his youthful passion for her. But now he finds that he can no longer summon the emotion he once felt for her (*Dove*, trans. Arberry, 208).

It may well have been because of this experience that he was moved to compose one of the poems he includes just before recounting this anecdote (*Ṭawq*, ed. Makkī, 144):

If anyone had said to me before
  "You will forget the one you love."
I would have sworn a thousand oaths
  that this would never, never be.
But long separation makes forgetting
  something one cannot escape.
By God, thankfully, separation sought
  over and over, laboring, to heal me.
So now, I can wonder at how easy it is to forget,
  where once I wondered at my torment.
Yet I see my passion for you like an ember
  beneath ashes not yet dead.

The emotions expressed in the final line—referring to the embers of his passion waiting to be reawakened—conform more to the Ibn Ḥazm's theory, stated at the beginning of *The Dove's Neck-Ring*, that love, as the true longing of two souls that had once been an undivided whole (which he supports by citing a passage from Plato's *Symposium* and verses from the *Qur'ān*), can never be assuaged, than it does to the evidence of his anecdote. The piquancy of the contradiction, however, adds force to both, and illustrates his awareness that human experience is subject to the power of time, and does not always conform to abstract ideals.

Yet on the surface, much continued as before. His companion in exile, Abū Bakr, may have gone back to Almeria and remained there, but he made contact again with, and enjoyed the company of, his old friend Ibn Shuhayd and his paternal cousin Abū 'l-Mughīrah (d. 1046-1047), a son of ʿAbd al-Raḥmān, who was actually more renowned as a literary figure than Ibn Ḥazm during his lifetime. He also seems, on the basis of evidence preserved in al-Ḥumaydī and elsewhere, to have renewed his acquaintance with Yūsuf ibn ʿAbd Allāh Ibn ʿAbd al-Barr (978 or 979-1071). This contemporary of Ibn Ḥazm had often shared teachers with him in his youth, and had been equally attracted to Ẓāhirism, but later embraced Mālikism, eventually becoming the chief judge in Lisbon.

The only apparent blemish on this temporarily placid picture was the ousting of Qāsim in 1021 and his replacement by ʿAlī's son, Yaḥyā Ibn Ḥammūd (d. 1035). This, however, was a harbinger of more troubled times to come. By 1023, Qāsim had again been invited back by the Cordovan elite to replace Yaḥyā and rule the city, but he was not able to bridge the interests of the various groups. In September he was once more forced to leave. Ibn Ḥazm then joined a group pushing for an election to be held between three rival Umayyad claimants for the throne. This was done in December and the choice fell upon a brother of al-Mahdī (executed in 1010), who chose the regnal title of al-Mustaẓhir (d. 1024).

Prior to his election, al-Mustaẓhir had mainly been known as a poet, and for his famous love affair with his cousin Ḥabībah (daughter of his cousin Sulaymān al-Mustaʿīn, who had ruled briefly in 1009 and again in 1013-1016). He and Ibn Ḥazm had frequented the same literary circles in their younger days. He now appointed his two friends, Ibn Ḥazm and his cousin Abū 'l-Mughīrah, as his chief ministers, with several other literary figures, like Ibn Shuhayd, also receiving official positions in his entourage. The new ruler, like his predecessors, was unable to weld together the disputing factions, and after only a few weeks in power, al-Mustaẓhir was assassinated in turn by a cousin, who assumed the caliphate as al-Mustakfī (d. 1025). Al-Mustakfī imprisoned Ibn Ḥazm and his cousin Abū 'l-Mughīrah, but he himself—like his cousin—was unable to achieve any stability, and he only remained in power until the middle of 1025, when he escaped the city disguised as a woman, dying shortly thereafter in exile. Toward the end of his book on logic, *Taqrīb li-ḥadd al-manṭiq*, Ibn Ḥazm remembers this short-term caliph with special rancor, as "a sultan who acted as a tyrant and enemy, one of little religion and much ignorance, neither trustworthy nor to be relied upon" (*Taqrīb,* 610).

This vitriol may have been because al-Mustakfī, before his final downfall, destroyed the last traces of the neighborhood where Ibn Ḥazm had grown up, ripping up the lead liners of the irrigation canals and cannibalizing even the doors and windows of the ruined buildings for their valuable metal that could be turned into ready cash. The resulting devastation is reflected in a description conveyed to him in Játiva of his family's house in Balāt al-Mughīth (*Ṭawq*, ed. Makkī, 127):

Its traces had become effaced, its boundaries erased, and the places we used to
haunt had all disappeared. Ruin had changed it and it had become a desert after having been a place filled with people.

The evocative power of this description, drawing on motifs and vocabulary familiar from Preislamic poetry, made it a set piece that was repeated in historical and literary works for several centuries after Ibn Ḥazm's death, and show that *The Dove's Neck-Ring* was in circulation and influential among medieval Andalusians even though it survived into modern times in only one complete manuscript.

Once released from al-Mustakfī's dungeon, Ibn Ḥazm fled eastwards again, this time to the city of Játiva between Denia and Valencia. It was likely here, in 1027, that he finished *The Dove's Neck-Ring* (though he may have begun it much earlier). The dispute over the dating of this work is illustrative of the difficulties encountered in reliably establishing an exact chronology of Abū Muḥammad's writings. There are a large number of anecdotes in the treatise that belong to the period of Ibn Ḥazm's return to Cordoba in 1019 and his residence in the partially ruined city until 1026. An earlier generation of scholars took the position that Ibn Ḥazm began and completed *The Dove's Neck-Ring* during this time, mostly because there is no mention of the traumatic events of al-Mustazhir's caliphate, in which Abū Muḥammad was so intimately involved.

Yet, on the other hand, Ibn Ḥazm clearly states in the preface to this work that he is writing from the city of Játiva to an unnamed friend, who has asked him "to compose a treatise about love, its root causes and the accidental qualities that result from it. . . ." Ibn Ḥazm is not recorded as having spent time in Játiva before 1026. His long stay in the city at this time, with little else to do, would have given him ample opportunity to begin and finish *The Dove's Neck-Ring.* Further, he mentions in the text a brief period of hostilities between Khayrān and Mujāhid, ruler of Denia, which took place in 1026. This would seem to argue for the later date. It is not impossible, however, that the treatise was written at an even later date than that.

Similar ambiguities in dating plague other works by Ibn Ḥazm. We can often be fairly certain they were written within a certain time span, yet not be able to pin down an exact year of composition. The problem is exacerbated by the fact that a work we know to have likely been written before another will refer to that later work somewhere in the text and so on. This would argue that Ibn Ḥazm may have made revisions during his long life to many of these works. In fact, the argument has been made that *The Dove's Neck-Ring* was revised and abridged at a later period, possibly by the author himself, so that considerable material in the original version was lost.

Whatever problems the dating of *The Dove's Neck-Ring* pose, it is clear that the work is a very personal product with many elements—principally seen in his choice to focus for illustrations on his own life, people he knew personally, and citations of his own poetry—that set it apart from the norm of medieval literature (which generally favors appeal to authority over personal experience). Yet it is also clear that Ibn Ḥazm is writing within an Arabic tradition on addressing the theoretical question of love as an emotion—well catalogued by Lois Giffen and Joseph N. Bell—that had already produced notable works and would continue to do so for several centuries. He was, furthermore, writing within a specifically literary tradition of poetry, and of stories about lovers, that had been well-established before his time.

Even in Preislamic times, a section of the polythematic *qaṣīdah* (the *nasīb*) was devoted, by convention, to a lament for a love affair that had come to an end unhappily. In early Islamic times, the first new genre of poetry (the *ghazal*) that developed took the theme of unhappy love as its focus, but transformed the character of the lover into someone who could not forget his beloved, becoming obsessed with the object of his affections, and the nature of love itself into an eternal (and ever unsatisfied) desire that could not be overcome. A typical example can be seen in the following short lyric by Jamīl ibn ʿAbd Allāh al-ʿUdhrī (d. 701) (*Dīwān Jamīl*, 105):

Had I a choice between this time just passed
And living forever, eternally,
I would say: "Give me an hour, and Buthayna,
With no hidden spies--
Then pass final judgment on me."
There is a tiny gap between her front teeth,
If the medicine of her kisses were brushed on the lips of the dead
They would rise from the grave.
If I try to compose poetry on any subject but her
By my father's life, it refuses to obey.
May she not bestow her favors on anyone after me.
May I not live after her.
May the world endure for us
Until the meeting at the Resurrection.

The religious imagery that compares the effect of Buthayna's (his beloved's) kisses to medicine that revives a dead person and brings him back to life is more than faintly blasphemous, and is certainly very different from the love poetry we find in the Greek and Latin traditions. That verse is more focused—for the most part—on celebrating the pleasures of love and describing how to seduce a beloved than it is on the effects of desire on a lover.

For Ibn Ḥazm, these Umayyad poets would have been as distant as the troubadours were from authors of the High Renaissance, and their work as ripe for reformulation and revaluation. In fact, in the century before Ibn Ḥazm's birth the poetry of these early love poets would be stitched together to form narratives (often presented as truthful, not fictional, though it was well recognized that the poets themselves might not be actual historical figures). Around the time of Abū Muḥammad's death, the Arabic narratives began to form the basis for avowedly mystical treatments of love such as we see in the Persian verse romance by Niẓāmī Ganjavī (1140 or 1141-1202 or 1203), *Laylī va Majnūn*. Yet *The Dove's Neck-Ring* shows no trace of mystical influence, and Ibn Ḥazm is uncompromising elsewhere in his writings in his hostility to mystical ideas. Thus this treatise comprises a particularly valuable instance, from the literary historian's viewpoint, of the genre of love literature in Arabic, because it can be seen as a kind of bridge between earlier forays and later works. Also, because of Ibn Ḥazm's place in Andalusian (and therefore Western) writing, it represents an especially interesting work for comparison with both troubadour poetry as it emerged in southern France during the latter part of the twelfth century, as well as with works like Andreas Capellanus's treatise *De Amore* (*The Art of Courtly Love*), composed at the court of Marie of Champagne in northern France.

This latter similarity did attract a certain interest among scholars in the years immediately before and after World War II in both Europe and the Arab world. In the wake of the demonstration, however, that there was unlikely to have been a direct influence of Arabic on the European literary tradition, the implications of this resemblance has been less enthusiastically pursued and is an area that would benefit from further comparative (rather than genetic) study.

Like the stories of lovers in Arabic, however, *The Dove's Neck-Ring* has a distinctly narrative (and teleological) structure, especially in its latter half, where its overt purpose, according to the author's preface, is to catalogue the "signs of love." In the first chapter this section Abū Muḥammad does provide a very detailed inventory of the ways—from movements of the eyes, involuntary sighs, secret whispers, unexplained anxiety, sleeplessness—by which the secret sufferings of the lover are made public. The following chapters, however, chronicle what Ibn Ḥazm sees as important temporal milestones in the narrative of a love affair from beginning to end. He starts by devoting chapters to the ways that people fall in love and concludes by describing the end of a love affair in separation, forgetting, and ultimately death. Each chapter in this section follows an, in some ways, a rather rigidly formal pattern. Typically, the general principles of each stage are described first. Prose anecdotes are then given illustrating the kind of love that has been outlined. Following that, the section concludes with one or more poems of Ibn Ḥazm's own composition on the aspect of love under discussion.

Then—very similar to the way his French counterpart Andreas Capellanus concludes his treatise on love a century and half later—Ibn Ḥazm suddenly shifts tone and concludes *The Dove's Neck-Ring* with chapters that condemn the very sort of love relationship he has just been describing—if it should stray into consummation of the desire—as being unacceptable from a religious (in his case Islamic) moral point of view. Neither the theoretical treatises in the Arabic tradition nor the stories of lovers that preceded Ibn Ḥazm had ever presented the experience of love in quite this way.

Despite its engaging content, and straightforward style that make it immediately accessible even in translation for readers who have little familiarity with the cultural background of the text, there is much about *The Dove's Neck-Ring* that is inexplicable upon immediate encounter and should provoke deeper thought in the reader's mind. The first issue is why and for what purpose Abū Muḥammad chose to compose the treatise. He himself tells us at the beginning that the composition is in response to a request made by an anonymous friend (both Abū Bakr Muḥammad ibn Isḥāq and Ibn Shuhayd have been proposed as candidates for the friend), to "present in categories . . . a description of love and its various significations, how it is caused and the accidental characteristics associated with it; what occurs in it, and on account of it, realistically and with no [fanciful] additions or branching off into side issues" (*Ṭawq*, ed. Makkī, 16). Such an opening, however, is conventional in Arabic letters, and cannot therefore be taken as a sufficient explanation. Treatises—from their earliest appearance in Arabic—have been framed as letters to friends or patrons, replying to requests. There is, of course, nothing to prevent such a scenario from being true. But we should never forget that these are first and foremost formal compositions designed for public consumption and not principally private communications. So we should at least make an attempt to place a work like this in a broader context, even if it resists easy pigeonholing, as *The Dove's Neck-Ring* apparently does. Characterizations by scholars have emphasized a variety of aspects in this text, from its personal, psychological element, to its moralization, to its philosophical content, to the valuable historical information it imparts, but none has captured the essence of the text's difference from earlier (and later) Arabic works that take love as a theme.

One element to keep in mind in seeking to characterize it is that *The Dove's Neck-Ring* is not an isolated work. If in an earlier period, Ibn Ḥazm seemed to have composed very little, in the latter half of the 1020s this seems to have shifted markedly. For example, at about this same time, Abū Muḥammad was also engaged in writing his first formal, pedagogical work, *al-Taqrīb li-ḥadd al-manṭiq* (Facilitating the Definition of Logic). This is a tract devoted to presenting an introduction to the study of logic and argumentation, focusing on defining terms and the problematic nature of using language (in this case Arabic) in doing so. Both Porphyry's *Isagogue* and Aristotle's introductory work, the *Organon* are mentioned by Ibn Ḥazm in the introduction, the first specifically by name: "This is where we begin, God Almighty willing, with His power and might, as we have intended. We will commence by clarifying the introduction to the aforementioned books. In Greek this is called "the *isagogue*." "*Isagogue*" means in the Greek language "introduction," and it is special among the compositions of Porphyry the Syrian. The books that follow are among the compositions of Aristotle, the teacher of Alexander and the organizer of his realm. In God Almighty there is success, so to Him we adhere and seek support. There is no God but Him" (*Taqrīb*, ed. al-Turkmānī, 325).

The didactic tone of the work gives rise to the impression that Ibn Ḥazm intended the *Taqrīb* to be an introductory manual for students interested in the study of logic. Once the principles of this field were assimilated by the student, he could then proceed to the exposition on dialectic (based on a summary chapter incorporating Aristotle's *De Interpretatione, Prior and Posterior Analytics*, and *Sophistical Refutations*). This was followed by brief treatments of rhetoric and poetry, little more that notes giving an outline for further study, but invaluable for the literary scholar in their sketch of the curricular materials Ibn Ḥazm alludes to.

Unfortunately, the *Taqrīb* was viewed by Ibn Ḥazm's immediate successors—including his own student, Sa'īd of Toledo—as too idiosyncratic for an introductory manual, and it was roundly criticized by them as not conveying accurately enough Aristotle's original observations. Thus it did not have an important impact on subsequent scholarship in Andalus or elsewhere. In fact, it would be fairer to say that the work is clearly intended by Ibn Ḥazm as his own interpretation of the issues in logic and dialectic raised by Aristotle (and to a lesser degree Porphyry), and thus should have been recognized as an original contribution to the Arabic understanding of Greek logic during this period. This is especially clear in his initial interest in issues such as definitions (not covered in Porphyry's *Isagogue*) and in how he consistently uses examples from Islamic discourse to illustrate his points. Though aspects of the work have been studied with some thoroughness (as in Arnaldez, Rosenthal or Yafūt), its place in the medieval Islamic revaluation of the heritage of Antiquity has yet to be properly carried out.

Despite the individualism of its arguments and conclusions, Ibn Ḥazm maintains an impersonal tone throughout the *Taqrīb*, very unlike his method in *The Dove's Neck Ring*, where every heading is illustrated by the author's personal experience. The one place where he violates this decorum comes at the end of the main section, where he speaks about his imprisonment at the hands of al-Mustakfī and how he found his enforced idleness an opportunity to think about the kind of difficult logical issues discussed in the *Taqrīb* (ed. al-Turkmānī, 610):

> I thought for a long time about these issues [in prison], day and night, until the clear explanation became apparent to me and the truth was revealed and was shown to be right to me in judgment. It was as if the sun suddenly appeared over the horizon, though I was in the situation I described—by God, than whom there is no other God, the First Creator, He who orders the world, Who will not permit Himself to be divided, I swear. My happiness that day, though I was in such a situation, in finding victory over the truth, when I had been so preoccupied with this problem, and the solution shed its rays on me, was greater than the day I was eventually set free. Nor is it likely I would have composed this book of mine, and many others that I have written, without being in exile far from my homeland my family and my children, fearing in my soul tyranny and enmity. I don't conceal this, but say it openly. There is no seeker who can deny our words in this. To God we complain, from Him we seek judgment—and no other—there is no God but He.

Clearly, in this passage Ibn Ḥazm is recording how, for him, the sheer intellectual pleasure of the search for truth is what allows one to overcome the pain of exile. This is why he compares his feelings in exile to the time he spent in prison. In both cases, the fear and anxiety lead him to concentrate with greater intensity on intellectual pursuits.

This revelation also suggest that *The Dove's Neck-Ring*—composed most likely at virtually the same time—may have had some of the same intellectual genesis as the *Taqrīb*. Such a presupposition would help account for its systematic formal structure juxtaposed with the choice of emotionally charged subject matter (love and the destruction of his happy past life). He uses the patterned formality of Aristotelian logical principles about evidence and dialectic to control the emotional chaos that might result from too free an indulgence in the consideration of the pathos of his own history.

The fact that the rules of evidence and proof that he drew from Aristotle's work and presented in the *Taqrīb* requires exhaustive consideration of all sides of an argument might also be helpful in understanding the two most notable features of *The Dove's Neck-Ring*: its extensive teleological depiction of the different elements of a love affair, and its abrupt shift at the end to chapters that condemn love from a strictly moral point of view. To fulfill the requirement of a complete presentation of the phenomenon under consideration, he would need to pursue such a plan. Similar operative principles have been convincingly examined by Don Monson and others, with reference to Andreas Capellanus's *De Amore*, which may have been produced under a similar interest in Aristotelian logical principles during the height of European Scholasticism (Monson, 80-85).

Ibn Ḥazm's newfound interest in rigorous intellectual study does not, however, seem to have prevented him from involvement in one last attempt to restore the Umayyad caliphate. The ill-fated al-Murtaḍā's older brother, Hishām (d. 1031), had taken refuge after his brother's death in the city of Alpuente, living under the protection of its ruler Muḥammad ibn Qāsim al-Fihrī (d. ca. 1030). Alpuente is not far from Játiva, where Ibn Ḥazm was living in exile, and when in 1027 the Cordovans decided to make one more attempt to restore the caliphate and sent representatives to pledge their allegiance to Hishām, who now called himself Muʿtadd (in some sources his title is given as al-Muʿtamid), Ibn Ḥazm may have joined him there. At any rate, he composed a panegyric poem, included in *The Dove's Neck-Ring*, in Muʿtadd's honor. According to some accounts of these events, Hishām made Abū Muḥammad one his viziers. If this was the case, then Ibn Ḥazm would very likely been part of the entourage who accompanied the new sovereign back to Cordoba. Hishām's progress across the country took over two years, plagued by money troubles and the opposition of local rulers. When he finally entered the city, according to the historian Abū Marwān Ḥayyān ibn Khalaf Ibn Ḥayyān (987 or 988-1076), the people of Cordoba were taken aback by al-Muʿtadd's shabbiness and the underwhelming nature of his presence and stature. Matters then quickly deteriorated as Muʿtadd and his ministers engaged in a frenzied search for ready cash to recruit and support new troops. In the end, by the end of 1031, Hishām had alienated enough of the locals to be exiled from Cordoba and sent packing to a refuge in Lerida. Following this debacle, a council of notables in Cordoba, lead by Ibn Jahwar (d. 1043), formally declared the office of caliph defunct.

After 1031, the nature of Ibn Ḥazm's activities turns somewhat murky for a number of years, until he surfaces in the eastern province of Denia and the Balearics in 1038, where he was invited to live at the court of Mujāhid (d. ca. 1044), a former general of al-Manṣūr, and a man of great appreciation for the heritage of Arabic and Islamic culture, who proved a generous patron to his former companions in Cordoba's literary salons. Abū Muḥammad seems to have fled there to escape the hostility of the Mālikī jurists in his hometown. Later, he took up residence on the island of Majorca, at the invitation of Abū 'l-ʿAbbās Aḥmad Ibn Rashīq (d. ca. 1048), a *ḥadīth* scholar, who was Mujāhid's governor there. It was on Majorca that Abū Muḥammad set up a sort of "school" for legal studies, called the Ḥazmiyyah, and it was there that al-Ḥumaydī became his pupil. He would remain on Majorca until 1048.

Prior to 1038, Ibn Ḥazm certainly spent some time in Cordoba in 1035, where he supervised the funeral services for his old friend Ibn Shuhayd, who died in April of that year. He also must have spent some time in the eastern town of Alpuente in the early 1030s, because it is from there that he addresses a treatise in the form of a letter to his old friend Abū Bakr Muḥammad ibn Isḥāq, entitled *Risālah fī faḍl al-Andalus* (Treatise on the Merit of al-Andalus). This work provides a valuable overview of the state of scholarship in Islamic Spain during Ibn Ḥazm's lifetime, in the guise of a reply to an insulting letter written to Abū Bakr by an unnamed "inhabitant of Tunisia," suggesting that the scholars of Andalus are ignorant barbarians. Besides its obvious utility in highlighting the achievements of Spanish intellectuals, the work illustrates Ibn Ḥazm's continuing interest in educational topics, especially the divisions of knowledge and the construction of an ideal curriculum, issues he had already touched upon in the *Taqrīb*. He would return to the subject again in a much more exhaustive fashion in his work *Marātib al-'ulūm* (*The Categories of the Sciences*), which has been translated into English in Anwar Chejne's book on *Ibn Ḥazm*.

Certainly during this period Abū Muḥammad was also engaged in compiling the first of his monumental works on religious topics, *Kitāb al-fiṣal fī milal wa 'l-ahwā' wa 'l-nihal* (The Book of Distinctions Concerning Religions, Sects, and Denominations). This book was published in five volumes—based on a manuscript preserved in Cairo—early in the twentieth century, and this text has been reprinted several times by printers in various countries. There are, however, several other manuscripts of the work preserved in various libraries and no proper edition of the text has yet been prepared. The problems this engenders can be seen in the discussions that have taken place over the very title of the work. The original Cairo edition indicated that the first word of the title should be vocalized as *fiṣal*, which would be the plural of *faṣlah*. This plural, however, is unattested, not even in Ibn Ḥazm's day, so more recently scholars have proposed it should be vocalized as the singular *faṣl*. The book is referred to in scholarly works and library catalogues under both headings, but it is exactly the same work. I have chosen to use the older title, because it is still referred to more frequently in that form.

Adding to the textual difficulties associated with the *Fiṣal*, it is clearly a composite work. A first draft was probably completed in the time of al-Mu'tadd (who is mentioned early in the text as the reigning caliph), but it was almost certainly begun even earlier, since it is mentioned briefly toward the end of the *Taqrīb* as an already existing text, although this may not be anything resembling the *Fiṣal* we now possess. There are also references to much later dates in the text, which suggest that it underwent at least two extensive revisions during the time Ibn Ḥazm was living in Denia and Majorca.

The initial inspiration for the work is clearly the kind of Islamic heresiographical treatise called *maqālāt*, which were already being produced in the preceding century, and would continue to be so long after Ibn Ḥazm's death. The most famous of these was by the theologian Abū 'l-Ḥasan ʿAlī ibn Ismāʿīl al-Ashʿarī (873 or 874-935 or 936). He was much disliked by Ibn Ḥazm for his use of analogy (*qiyās*), which Abū Muḥammad associates in the *Taqrīb* with inductive reasoning (*istiqrā'*), a type of reasoning that he considers productive of unclear thinking whose conclusions cannot be relied on. Thus it is no surprise that he criticizes these works in his own introduction to the *Fiṣal*, and intimates that he can do better, principally by relying on the methodology of examining dialectical claims of truth developed in the *Taqrīb*. This certainly suggests that by the time the *Fiṣal* was actively in the process of composition, the *Taqrīb* was substantially complete.

Following the introduction, Ibn Ḥazm then turns to the specific beliefs of certain sects of Islam and religious groups (as well as non-religious claims of truth made by intellectuals like philosophers), and enumerates those he wants to examine. These include ideas like the eternity or createdness of the world, whether the world—once created—has a Creator who intervenes in its development, whether there are many creators or only one, and the nature of prophecy and the number of prophets. It is in these last two categories where he ends up most prominently highlighting the beliefs of various Christian and Jewish sects he has either read about or encountered in during his research in Andalus itself. His willingness to pursue analysis of the exact words of the Bible (though he shows no familiarity with either Hebrew or Latin) is perhaps the most original element of the *Fiṣal*, and should be very attractive to modern scholars interested in understanding the nature of Biblical studies in this time period. Ibn Ḥazm also indicates an interest into inquiring about the doctrines of transmigration of souls, and whether "every kind of animal has its own prophets" (*Fiṣal*, 1:62). He does follow up on all these plans, and it is in the last two categories that he begins to examine the beliefs of Hindus, Mazdeans, and various smaller and more exotic religious groups.

Abū Muḥammad, in the context of exploring these categories, turns as well to an examination of the claims of philosophers, especially the then fashionable claims, based on some interpretations of Neoplatonic ideas, that the world was eternal and that Islamic (as well as Jewish and Christian) notions of a Creator God were untenable. In the end, he makes a spirited defense of the pursuit of philosophy (at least in its logical aspect) in ways that will anticipate his future analysis of morals in his book *Character and Conduct* (*Fiṣal*, 1:75):

> [Philosophy] is nothing but the reform of the soul, since you can use it in this world for its virtues and as good path to follow, leading safely to the hereafter . . . . This itself is nothing other than the goal of the religious law (*sharī'ah*), which is no different than that found among the scholars of philosophy.

The idea that philosophy and religious studies can be reconciled and have the same goal is a constant theme of Ibn Ḥazm's work. In this way he illustrates a particular phase of Islam during the period of its consolidation, which would not last long. By the time of al-Ghazzālī (d. 1111), philosophy would be accorded a much narrower place in the curriculum, considered useful mainly for its teachings about logic. By the time of Aḥmad ibn ʿAbd al-Ḥalīm Ibn Taymiyyah (1263-1328) even that field would be denied usefulness, as is exemplified in Ibn Taymiyyah's famous formulation "he who studies logic, has become an unbeliever" (*man tamantaq, tazandaq*).

It is also during the period of his residence in Majorca that Ibn Ḥazm produced his other two monumental religious works, both summations of his ideas as influenced by Ẓāhirī precepts of religious law. The *Kitāb al-iḥkām fī uṣūl al-aḥkām* (Book of the Establishment of the Roots of Legal Decisions) is Abū Muḥammad's attempt to formulate the principles of understanding how religious law can be derived according to Ẓāhirī presuppositions. Again, like the *Taqrīb* and *Fiṣal*, it relies on the logical precedent of Aristotle for the formulation of its arguments. It was first published in eight parts, later reduced to two volumes. The *Kitāb al-muhallā bi 'l-athār fī sharḥ al-mujallā bi-'khtisar* (Book of Ornaments Concerning Works That Explain One Revealed Succinctly), consisting of eleven volumes in its original format, is a more conventional presentation of the formal precepts and daily rituals of Islam according to Ẓāhirī rules, very similar to the *Iḥyā' 'ulūm al-dīn* (Revival of the Religious Sciences) produced by al-Ghazzālī at the close of the eleventh century. Each of them required considerable time and effort to produce, and argue strongly for Ibn Ḥazm's almost exclusive dedication to religious studies during this period.

By the end of 1048, Ibn Rashīq had died, and Ibn Ḥazm had had a confrontation with a well-known Mālikī scholar, Sulaymān ibn Khalaf al-Bājī (1012 or 1013-1081?), in which he came off second best. We don't known if either, or both, of these factors were dominant in Abū Muḥammad's decision, but he left Majorca, and seems to have taken up residence in Seville. There, he quickly ran afoul of the local Mālikī jurists, and al-Muʿtadid (d. 1068)—the ruler of Seville—ordered him to leave and had some of his works publicly committed to the flames. Ibn Ḥazm wrote a poem about this incident that was preserved in Ibn al-Bassām al-Shantarinī (1/1:171):

If you wish to burn these sheets of paper, you cannot burn
What those sheets contain, for that is in my heart.
It goes with me, wherever my riding camels alight
They dismount with me, and they will be buried in my grave.
Spare me the burning of parchment and paper,
Speak rather of knowledge so the people will see what they know.
If not, then go back to the times when writing was done as it was in the beginning
For how often without your interference God has placed veils.

The poem is obviously an occasional piece, addressed to Muʿtadid to point out the futility of seeking to burn books as long as their author is able to retain their contents within his being, and presumably eventually communicate them to others. But then the speaker shifts his approach and points out that the real harm comes, not from the action against himself as an individual, but its wider implication, as an attack against the people's right to know rather than remain in ignorance. After all, the speaker points out, only God has the right to control knowledge (and the search for it), not the individual human being. In this Ibn Ḥazm anticipates the cry of the intellectual throughout the Middle Ages and into modern times, against the state's desire to control knowledge and how it is disseminated. Such frankness is unusual in medieval Arabic poetry, though not unique.

Ibn Ḥazm, as was the case with his attitude toward the tools afforded by philosophy for seeking knowledge—especially those of formal logic—never gave up his interest in poetry and continued (as can be seen in the above example) to compose it all his life, even in the face of the fact that it was disapproved in the *Qur'ān*, as long as it lacked a moral basis. He was apparently very proud of his abilities in producing it, from the time of *The Dove's Neck-Ring* (which contains so much of it), but often the stated reasons for his pride—his ability to craft elaborate metaphors, for example—have been somewhat puzzling to modern scholars. Even his contemporaries were not as receptive to it as they were to the verse of other Andalusian authors, like Ibn Zaydūn (c. 1003-May 1071) or Ibn Shuhayd, which were much more to medieval Arab taste. Thus, although he is recorded in Ibn Bassām as having left a *dīwān* arranged "according to the letters of the alphabet," this work has not come down to us. And, even though in the *Taqrīb* he endorses the commonly held view that "the best poetry is that which lies the most," it is in its bold power of conceptual statement that his work shines. While this kind of poetry often translates well, it may not be so compelling in the original. This may be why Abū Muḥammad became known to subsequent generations mainly as a religious scholar and not as a poet.

After Ibn Ḥazm was forced to leave Seville, he took up residence in his family's ancestral home village of Mant Lishām near Neibla, in the interior of south western Spain. It was probably there that he composed what is now considered to be the last work he produced, the ethical treatise *al-Akhlāq wa 'l-siyar* (*In Pursuit of Virtue*). It is not mentioned in the earliest lists of his works, so the common assumption is that it is a late product, although, of course, it may have been initially drafted much earlier and subsequently revised, as so many of Ibn Ḥazm's works appear to have been. In a general sense, however, it should be noted that the speaker presents himself as someone who has thought for a long time about the issues he is discussing, which would argue for the posteriority of the work. Even so, scholars are undoubtedly correct in their belief that *In Pursuit of Virtue* has stylistic links to *The Dove's Neck-Ring*. It follows the same structure as that early work in presenting definitions first, then specific illustrations (*aḥwāl*) of ethical behavior in certain situations. It even has a section on love. Furthermore, the last two sections—on the importance of knowledge and the etiquette to be observed when attending a class—at first appear on tangentially concerned with the main topic. It is only through reading the sections and assimilating the evidence they contain about ethical behavior that they can be related to the other sections.

Because of its likely lateness in Ibn Ḥazm's body of writings, however, it would not be incorrect to see *In Pursuit of Virtue* as a work profoundly influenced by Islamic morality and ethical principles. In fact, before he moves to specific cases in moral behavior, Abū Muḥammad tells us that: "I have found that action [in this world] with the afterlife in mind, is [the way] safe from every sort of fault, unmixed with any sort of stain" (*Akhlāq*, ed. Makkī, 87) This active insistence to keep the Judgment Day in mind is appended, however, to a broader principle that has a great deal more to do with Greek ethical thought: that human beings—whatever their background, seek as their ultimate goal in life "to repel anxiety." This is not exactly a definition of good that can be taken from any precise Greek ethical writing that we now have access to, not even that of Aristotle (whose *Nicomachean Ethics* probably had the greatest impact on Arab authors in the tenth and eleventh centuries). It would thus be tempting to see in this formulation—as several scholars have done—a certain response to the political upheavals of Ibn Ḥazm's own time, in which as we have seen, he was so intimately involved. But Ibn Ḥazm—true to form—does not admit to this possibility so easily in the text itself. He says, instead, that he arrived at this definition because the concept of pleasure or happiness (a staple of Greek ethical theories, including that of Aristotle) was too varied an idea to allow its use as a basis for definition. Thus, his reliance on what is basically a negative formulation to express his judgment of what the goal of human beings is. That here, as earlier, he couples this idea with a religious stricture, that anxiety can only be reliably repelled by following the precepts laid down by God, illustrates his continued commitment to the belief that the basics of philosophical inquiry are compatible with Islam.

Like his guide to Aristotelian logic, the *Taqrīb*, *In Pursuit of Virtue* seems to have had little immediate impact on the direction of Islamic thought, only reaching a wide audience when it was published several times in Egypt (coinciding with a general resurgence in interest in Islamic ethics) early in the twentieth century. Ibn Ḥazm's religious treatises seem to have had a better fortune. Late in the twelfth century, the second Almohad ruler, Abū Yaʿqūb Yūsuf (d. 1184), sponsored the Ẓāhirī school—and with it the works of Ibn Ḥazm—as the officially sanctioned school of law in Andalus. Thus we find even the great Sufi Muḥyī 'l-Dīn Ibn al-ʿArabī (1165-1240)—who was born in Murcia, Spain—expressing great admiration for Ibn Ḥazm. It is probable that Ibn Ḥazm's writings did not fall completely out of favor until the Ẓāhirī school was finally suppressed in the East in the wake of an unsuccessful political rebellion (which had adopted the ideology of the school) in the mid-fourteenth century. After that period all of Ibn Ḥazm's works were little known until they were rediscovered, by Western and Arab scholars alike, in the nineteenth and twentieth centuries.

REFERENCES

Iḥsān ʿAbbās, *Tārīkh al-adab al-Andalusī*, rev. ed., vol. 1 (Beirut: Dār al-Thaqāfah, 1969), 303-322;

Andreas Capellanus, *De Amore: the Art of Courtly Love*, trans. John Jay Parry, ed. Frederick W. Locke (New York: Frederick Ungar Publishing, 1957);

Roger Arnaldez, *Grammaire et théologie chez Ibn Ḥazm de cordoue: essai sur la structure et les conditions de la pensée musulmane* (Paris: Librairie Philosophique J. Vrin, 1956);

Joseph Norment Bell, *Love Theory in Later Hanbalite Islam* (Albany: State University of New York Press, 1979);

Anwar Chejne, *Ibn Ḥazm* (Chicago: Kazi Publications, 1982);

Peter Dronke, *Medieval Latin and the Rise of the European Love Lyric*, vol. I: Problems and Interpretations (Oxford: Clarendon Press, 1965);

Israel Friedlaender, "The Heterodoxies of the Shiites in the Presentation of Ibn Ḥazm," *Journal of the American Oriental Society* 28 (1907), 1-80;

Niẓāmī Ganjavī, *Layla and Majnun*, trans. Rudolf Gelpke in collaboration with E. Mattin and G. Hill (Boulder, Colo.: Shambala Publications, 1966);

Lois Anita Giffen, *Theory of Profane Love Among the Arabs: the Development of the Genre* (New York: New York University Press, 1971);

Lois Anita Giffen, "Ibn Ḥazm and the *Ṭawq al-Ḥamāma*," in *The Legacy of Muslim Spain*, 2 volumes, ed. Salma Khadra Jayyusi (Leiden: E.J. Brill, 1994), 420-442;

Ignaz Goldziher, *The Ẓāhirīs: Their Doctrine and Their History*, ed. and trans. Wolfgang Behn (Leiden: E.J. Brill, 1971), first published as Die Ẓâhiriten, Leipzig, 1884;

Muḥammad ibn Fattūḥ al-Ḥumaydī, *Jadhwat al-muqtabas fī dhikr wullāt al-Andalus* (Cairo: al-Dār al-Miṣriyyah li 'l-Ta'līf wa 'l-Tarjamah, 1966);

Abū 'l-Ḥasan ʿAlī Ibn Bassām al-Shantarinī, *al-Dhakīrah fī maḥāsin ahl al-Jazīrah*, ed. Iḥsān ʿAbbās, vol. 1, pt. 1 (Beirut: Dār al-Thaqāfah, 1975);

Abdelilah Ljamai, *Ibn Ḥazm et la polémique islamo-chrétienne dans l'historie de l'islam* (Leiden: E.J. Brill, 2003);

Jamīl ibn ʿAbd Allāh al-ʿUdhrī, *Dīwān Jamīl*, ed. Ḥusayn Naṣṣār (Cairo: Dār Miṣr li 'l-Ṭibāʿah, 1967);

Don A. Monson, *Andreas Capellanus, Scholasticism and the Courtly Tradition* (Washington, D.C.: The Catholic University Press, 2005);

A.R. Nykl, *Hispano-Arabic Poetry and its Relations with the Old Provençal Troubadors*

(Baltimore: Hispanic Society of America, 1946);
Eric Ormsby, "Ibn Ḥazm," in *The Literature of al-Andalus*, ed. Maria Rosa Menocal, Raymond P. Scheindlin, and Michael Sells (Cambridge: Cambridge University Press, 2000), 237-251;
Abdel-Magid Turki, "L'engagement politique et la théorie du califat d'Ibn Ḥazm de Cordoue," *Théologiens et juristes de l'Espagne musulmans: aspects polémiques* (Paris: Masionneuve et Larose, 1982);
Jean-Claude Vadet, *L-Ésprit courtois en Orient dans les cinq premiers siècles de l'Hégire* (Paris: G.-P Maisonneuve et Larose, 1968);
Sālim Yafūt, *Ibn Ḥazm wa 'l-fikr al-falsafī bi 'l-Maghrib wa 'l-Andalus* (Casablanca: al-Markaz al-Thaqāfī al-ʿArabī, 1986).

Muḥammad ibn Aḥmad Ibn Jubayr

(1145-1217)

NATHANIEL GREENBERG
University of Washington

WORKS

Riḥlat Ibn Jubayr (The Travels of Ibn Jubayr);
Shi'r Ibn Jubayr (The Poems of Ibn Jubayr).

Editions

Riḥlat Ibn Jubayr (Baghdād: al-Maktabah al-ʿArabiyyah, 1937);
Riḥlat Ibn Jubayr (Bayrūt: Dār Ṣādir li 'l-Ṭibāʿah wa 'l-Nashr: Dār Bayrūt, 1959);
Riḥlat Ibn Jubayr: fī Miṣr wa-bilād al-'Arab wa 'l-'Irāq wa 'l-Shām wa-Ṣiqilliyyah 'aṣr al-Ḥurūb al-Ṣalībiyyah, ed. Ḥusayn Naṣṣār (Cairo: Yutlabu min Maktabat Miṣr, 1992);
Dīwān al-raḥḥālah Ibn Jubayr al-Andalusī wa mā waṣal ilaynā min nathruh Shi'r Ibn Jubayr, collected and ed. Fawzī 'l-Khuṭabā.ʿ (Amman: Dār al-Yanābīʿ li 'l-Nashr wa 'l-Tawzīʿ, 1991).

Translations

Voyages, trans. Maurice Gaudefroy-Demombynes (Paris: Libraire Orientaliste Paul Geuthner, 1949);
Travels of Ibn Jubayr, ed. by William Wright (Leyden: E.J. Brill; London: Luzac, 1907);
The travels of Ibn Jubayr, being the chronicle of a mediaeval Spanish Moor concerning his journey to the Egypt of Saladin, the holy cities of Arabia, Baghdad the city of the caliphs, the Latin kingdom of Jerusalem, and the Norman kingdom of Sicily, trans. Ronald J.C. Broadhurst (London, J. Cape, 1952);
Viaggio in Ispagna, Sicilia, Siria e Palestina, Mesopotamia, Arabia, Egitto, trans. Celestino Schiaparelli (Roma: Casa Editrice Italiana, 1906).

Abu 'l-Ḥusayn Muḥammad ibn Aḥmad ibn Jubayr was born in 1145 in Valencia, Spain, then part of the territory of al-Andalus, which stretched from Toledo to Cadiz. Muslims held power in al-Andalus from the time of the Umayyad caliphate (711-1031) to the fall of the Alhambra and subsequently the kingdom of Granada in 1492. The same year Ibn Jubayr was born, the second European crusade began. The Reconquista had already established its principle doctrines; and the kingdom of Granada was in disarray with two dynasties, the Almohades and the Almoravides, bidding for power. It was against a background of social and political turmoil, in the last decade of the twelfth century, that Ibn Jubayr composed one of the great historical chronicles of the medieval period.

The ingenuity of his work is manifest in the content and succinctness of his observations. But, as J.C. Broadhurst notes when quoting the Andalusian writer, Lisān al-Dīn Ibn al-Khaṭīb (d. 1375), it was also the poetry that he derived from his journey, much of which is incorporated into his *Riḥlah*, that distinguished him "above all others" (*Travels*, Broadhurst, 20). The list of successors who reproduced his descriptions in their own chronicles of pilgrimage is substantial. Perhaps most notably, the renowned explorer Ibn Batuta (1304-1377), or, more specifically, as Maurice Guadefroy-Demombynes notes in his introduction to the French translation, his secretary Muḥammad ibn Aḥmad Ibn Juzayy 'l-Kalbī (1294-1340) may have imported passages from Ibn Jubayr's work, including descriptions of Mecca and Medina, the great convoys of Iraqi pilgrims, and numerous descriptions of Iraq, Mesopotamia and Syria, into Ibn Batuta's *Riḥlah* (*Voyages*, 26).

Ibn Jubayar's life preceded that of the famous Andalusian thinker Ibn Khaldūn (1332-1406) by half a century. Among his contemporaries were the first great philosophers of medieval al-Andalus, including Muḥammad ibn ʿAbd al-Malik Ibn Ṭufayl (d. 1185) and Ibn Rushd, i.e. Averroës (1126-1198). His languages were Arabic, Greek, Hebrew, Latin and Spanish. He was raised and educated in Játiva by his father, who was the city's public notary and chancellor secretary under the Almoravid dynasty. By 1183, rule over the kingdom had changed hands. Ibn Jubayar, then a geographer and writer living in Játiva, was chosen to be secretary to Abū Saʿid ʿUthmān, an Almohad prince and the governor of Granada. Abū Saʿid was the brother of Abū Yaqūb, who ruled the Almohad dynasty, the North African capital of Ceuta. While dictating a letter one day, the prince, who was already drunk, ordered his pious secretary to drink seven glasses of wine. Ibn Jubayr reluctantly did so and was immediately overcome with guilt. He explained to the prince his need to perform the pilgrimage that very year, the man agreed, also perhaps out of guilt, and filled the same cup seven times with gold currency, thus enabling the journey (*Travels*, Broadhurst, 15; *Voyages*, 4). It is unlikely, however, that guilt alone propelled his will to reach not just Mecca, but most of the great cities of the Arab-Muslim world. As a geographer, a poet and an Arab whose origins traced back to the tribe of Kinānah near Mecca, Ibn Jubayr's journey across the Muslim world seems to have been as much an exploration of an imagined ancestral land as it was an expedition or pilgrimage.

Ibn Jubayr's voyage to Mecca began on February 3, 1183, most likely in the month of Ṣafar, the month of the Muslim calendar named for the spiritual event of travel, and it lasted just over two years. With his friend Aḥmad ibn Ḥassan, he first traveled from Granada to Ceuta in the Maghreb and then on to Alexandria by way of Sardinia, Sicily, and Crete. From Alexandria he went to Cairo and from there to the Nubian coast of the Red Sea before crossing to the Arabian Peninsula. From Mecca and Medina he traveled to Baghdad, Mosul and then Damascus where he spent two months. He traveled through Acre, Aleppo and Sicily where because of bad tides he stayed three and half months before returning to Granada on May 3, 1185. Ibn Jubayr would repeat the pilgrimage two more times in 1189 and 1217 before his death in 1219 in Alexandria.

On his first voyage he began taking notes immediately. He considered his work a chronicle and intended to provide cartographic and geographic information of the lands he visited. He recorded dates with great precision using both the Muslim and Gregorian calendars. It appears that he attempted to record the names of not only the towns he passed, but every monument, mosque, college, hospital, bridge, and waterway. His attention to detail seems compulsive at times, but provides the reader with extensive, often vivid imagery. Here is one such passage concerning a flashpoint of conflict, "where the fires of discord burned bright," on the border of the Frankish kingdom of Jerusalem. Ibn Jubayr and his group of pilgrims were southwest of Damascus, near the town of Banyas or Belinas on the "frontier of the Muslim territories."

> Halfway on the road, we came upon an oak-tree of great proportions and with wide-spreading branches. We learnt that it is called 'The Tree of Measure,' and when we enquired concerning it, we were told that it was the boundary on this road between security and danger, by reason of some Frankish brigands who prowl and rob thereon. He whom

> they seize on the Muslim side, be it by the length of the arms or a span, they capture; but he whom they seize on the Frankish side at a like distance, they release. This is a pact they faithfully observe and is one of the most pleasing and singular conventions of the Franks (*Travels, Broadhurst,* 314).

Restrictions on free-speech under the historically rigid Almohad dynasty, in addition to Ibn Jubayr's own religious beliefs, ironically freed his writing from many of the idiosyncrasies that tend to characterize European medieval prose. As with the description of "The Tree of Measure," his writing was guided by a voracious inclination for truth and the veracity of his descriptions are preserved by full disclosure. He seldom discussed a political movement or social phenomenon without attributing it to a specific source. His writing was neither journalistic nor autobiographical, yet his vigorous commitment to knowledge as derived from perception seemed to echo the Aristotelian tradition of Abū ʿAlī ʾl-Ḥusayn ibn ʿAbd Allāh Ibn Sīnā (980-1037), i.e. Avicenna, and to foreshadow, by nearly six hundred years, a certain Cartesian sensibility.

Ibn Jubayr's chronicles intersect with the great northern advance of the army of Saladin into the crusader controlled lands of greater Syria. In August of 1184, after having traveled through eastern Iraq and northern Syria (including the crusader fortress of Aleppo where he took note of the need to alter the route because of the nearby Assassin fortress), Ibn Jubayr arrived in Damascus in 1184, soon after the emperor Saladin and his army had left to march on the crusader fortress of Kerak. On his return passsage, two months later, he stopped in Damascus for a second time. According to Ibn Jubayr, the Sultan's army at that time had left its position outside Kerak to block the crusaders' path to a nearbye watering hole, forcing them to retreat from their hold on the fortress by a circuitious route across the desert. The Sultan took advantage of this opening and "schemed an incursion" onto Frankish territory, attacking the town of Nablas (314). According to Ibn Jubayr, the result was a "raid the like of which had not been heard of in the land" (314).

For the most part, Ibn Jubayr's chronicle tends less towards descriptions of historical events than of material conditions (*Travels*, Broadhurst, 314). However, the specificity of his observations created a view of the world that was both local and timeless. On his first voyage he spent over seven months in Mecca. Here is a typical passage from the month of Ramadan in the holy city. It is from the months of December and January, 1183-1184 (*Travels*, Broadhurst, 144):

> During this blessed month there was much ceremony in the sacred Mosque, making necessary the renewal of the mats, and the increasing of the candles and firebrands and other appointments until the Ḥaram blazed with light and shone with brightness. The imams formed separate groups in order to recite the *tarwīḥ*. The Shafiites, who had precedence over the others, had set up an imam on one side of the Mosque, and the Hanbalites, the Hanafites, and the Zaydis had done the same. As for the Malikites, they had gathered round three reciters who recited in turn. In this year, the attendance of this sect was greater than usual and it possessed more candles, because a party of Malikite merchants had vied with each other, bringing to the imam of the Kaʿbah a vast quantity. Two of the largest, weighing each a qinṭār, were placed in front of the miḥrāb, and round them were the lesser candles, some big, some small. Thus the Malikite part of the Mosque excited wonder for its beauty and overpowered the eyes with its radiance.

Ibn Jubayr's ability to illuminate his world is exemplary. His religious images were reserved to the likes of the Mosque glowing in the blackness of the desert, or the Lead Dome of the Cathedral Mosque in Damascus where, "as we had previously been assured," he writes (*Travels*, Broadhurst, 307), "in the venerated mosque no spider spun its web." He included countless blessings to God and described fulfilling the duties of Islam with great pleasure. But he did not turn from the complexities of the Muslim world. The modern day reader will be surprised by the familiarity of the social problems he observed. Of Baghdad, "the city of peace;" then shackled by the decline of the Abbasid Caliph, he wrote (*Travels*, Broadhurst, 226): "in comparison with its former state, before misfortune struck it and the eyes of adversity turned towards it, it is like an effaced ruin, a remain washed out, or the statue of a ghost."

Throughout the *Travels* Ibn Jubayr paid great attention to sectarianism and religious strife. North of Damascus he observes (*Travels*, Broadhurst, 291): "The Shiʿites are more numerous than the Sunnis, and have filled the land with their doctrines." He does not reserve judgment in this matter and is quick to identify blasphemy. He decried the Christian Agnes of Courtenay, mother of Baldwin IV, as (*Travels*, Broadhurst, 316) "the sow known as Queen who is the mother of the pig who is the Lord of Acre— may God destroy it." And he lamented the condition of Muslims in Sicily (*Travels*, Broadhurst, 346). Yet, he reconciled differences with an obedient focus on the unconditional truths of his journey.

In addition to his sentiment for truth, the student of Cartesian enlightenment will be quick to take note of familiar stylistic motifs. The subject of time and water compels some of the traveler's finest descriptions. Including this wonderful description of a remarkable time piece in the Cathedral Mosque of Damascus (*Travels*, Broadhurst, 281):

> To the right of him who leaves by the Bab Jayrun, in the wall of the portico in front of him, is a gallery in the form of a large archway set with yellow arches in each of which opens a small door to the number of the hours of the day. An engineering contrivance has been arranged whereby at the end of each hour of the day two brass balls falls each from the mouths of two brazen falcons set above two brass cups, one below each bird. One falcon is beneath the first door, and the other beneath the last (and twelfth). The cups are perforated so that when the balls fall into them, they return through the inside of the wall to the gallery. You may see the two falcons stretching forth their necks with the balls (in their mouths) towards the cups, a noise is heard from them, and the yellow door corresponding to that hour closes upon the instant.

From the context of simple, yet solid truths, Ibn Jubayr's world, a time now entrenched in our collective imaginations as one of great importance, emerges with haunting clarity. Like the workings of the clock in the mosque, or the black bitumen he finds gathering on the desert fields of southern Iraq, the revelations of his journey, although peripatetic, are free from sophistry. His words remain whole and in a sense real.

REFERENCES

Ibrāhīm D. ʿAwaḍ, *Riḥlat Ibn Jubayr al-Andalusī: dirāsah fī 'l-uslub* (Cairo: Maṭbaʿah al-Ūfsit al-Ḥadīth, 1992);

Munjid Muṣṭafā Bahjat, *Dīwān al-raḥḥālah Ibn Jubayr al-Andalusī wa-mā waṣala ilaynā min nathruh* (al-Riyāḍ: Dār al-Rifāʿī, 1999);

Dale F. Eickelman, and James Piscatori, *Muslim Travellers: Pilgrimage, Migration, and the Religious Imagination* (London: Routledge, 1990);

Albert Gateau, *Quelques observations sur l'intérêt du voyage d'Ibn Jubayr pour l'histoire de la navigation en Méditerranée au XII-e siècle* (1949);

Muḥammad ibn Aḥmad Ibn Jubayr, *The Travels of Ibn Jubayr, Being the Chronicle of a Mediaeval Spanish Moor Concerning his Journey to the Egypt of Saladin, the Holy Cities of Arabia, Baghdad the City of the Caliphs, the Latin Kingdom of Jerusalem, and the Norman Kingdom of Sicily*, trans. Ronald J.C. Broadhurst, (London: J. Cape, 1952), introduction;

Muḥammad ibn Aḥmad Ibn Jubayr, *Voyages*, trans. Maurice Gaudefroy-Demonbynes (Paris: Librairie orientaliste P. Geuthner, 1949), introduction;

Muḥammad ibn Aḥmad Ibn Jubayr and ʿAlī Kanʿān, *Umarā' wa-asrā wa-khawātīn: ḥikāyāt Ibn Jubayr mustakhlaṣah min riḥlatih* (Abū Ẓaby: Dār al-Suwaydī li 'l-Nashr wa 'l-Tawzīʿ; Beirut: al-Mu'assasah al-ʿArabīyah li 'l-Dirāsāt wa 'l-Nashr, 2009);

Ian R Netton, *Golden Roads: Migration, Pilgrimage, and Travel in Mediaeval and Modern Islam*, (Richmond, Surrey, U.K: Curzon Press, 1993);

Yaacov Kahanov, and Iskandar Jabour, "The Westbound Passage of Ibn Jubayr from Acre to Cartagena in 1184-1185," *al-Masaq* 22, 1 (2010): 79-101.

ʿAlī ibn al-Husayn Hāshimī 'l-Najafī, *Sa'īd ibn Jubayr aw Shahīd Wāsiṭ* (Beirut: Mu'assasat al-Tārīkh al-ʿArabī, 2004);

Studies on Ibn Ğubair (d. 1217), collected and reprinted by Fuat Sezgin in collaboration with Mazen Amawi, Carl Ehrig-Eggert, and Eckhard Neubauer, Islamic geography v. 173 (Frankfurt am Main: Institute for the History of Arabic-Islamic Science at the Johann Wolfgang Goethe University, 1994)

Abū Isḥāq Ibrāhīm ibn Abī Fatḥ Ibn al-Khafājah

(1058 or 1059-1138 or 1139)

MATTHEW ERICKSON

University of Washington

WORKS

Dīwān (Complete poems).

Editions

Dīwān, ed. Muṣṭafā 'l-Najjārī (Cairo: al-Maṭbaʿah al-Khāṣṣah bi-Jamʿīyat al-Maʿārif, 1869);

Dīwān, ed. Karam al-Bustānī (Beirut: Dār Ṣādir, 1961);

Dīwān, ed. Sayyid Muṣṭafā Ghāzī (Alexandria: Munsha'at al-Maʿārif, 1960).

Admired since his death as one of the most prolific and versatile literary figures of the late Almoravid and early Almohad periods in Spain, Ibn al-Khafājah has gained recognition over the centuries as the unequaled master of nature poetry in al-Andalus. Well-read in the classical descriptive poetry of Arabia and the Mashriq, Ibn al-Khafājah applied his pastoral inspiration to the genre, adding to it natural settings evocative of the particular landscape around him. This, as well as frequent resort to personification, introduced a new sensibility into Arabic poetry with his work. His poetic talent, combined with his prodigious output and a long life, established a corpus that is considered to include some of the best nature poetry ever produced, having a lasting influence on subsequent Arab poets, both peninsular and beyond.

Ibn al-Khafājah was highly regarded by his contemporaries, especially those who wrote biographical works on Andalusian writers. His contemporaries, al-Fatḥ ibn Muḥḥammad Ibn Khāqān (d. 1134) and Abū 'l-Ḥasan ibn ʿAlī Ibn al-Bassām al-Shantarinī (d. 1147). Abū 'l-Ḥasan ʿAlī Ibn Bassām (d. 1147) included lengthy entries on Ibn al-Khafājah in their respective biographical works, *Qalā'id al-'iqyān* and *al-Dhakhīrah*. Both of these authors saw Ibn al-Khafājah as primarily a descriptive (*wasfī*) poet and secondarily as a skilled writer of *sajʿ* prose. It was not until the treatise *Risālah fī Faḍl al-Andalus* by Abū 'l-Wālid Ismāʿīl al-Shaqundī (d. 1231 or 32) that the special genius of Ibn al-Khafājah's nature poetry is recognized, and it is al-Shaqundī who first calls Ibn al-Khafājah "the gardener," the nickname by which he was later widely known (Shaqundī, trans. Garcia Gomez, 72 and Maqqarī, 2:338). The great Andalusian historian, Aḥmad ibn Muḥammad al-Maqqarī (1578 or 79-1632), and the author of the most authoritative eastern biographical dictionary, Ibn

Khallikān (1211-1282), both enthusiastically agreed with this characterization, and al-Maqqarī makes many admiring references to Ibn al-Khafājah and quotes samples of his poetry (where nature is often conjoined to the themes of love and wine drinking) in his own work. Although Ibn al-Khafājah has perhaps not been as celebrated as some other Andalusian poets and authors in different epochs of Arabic literary history, his modest, yet consistent, reputation and fame have continued into modern times and even been enhanced by several studies devoted to his work in recent years.

Born into the landed gentry outside of Valencia, Ibn al-Khafājah is recognized as the Andalusian master of nature poetry. Ibn al-Khafājah transmitted the classical nature poetry of Arabia and the Mashriq to al-Andalus, applied the genre to his pastoral inspiration as well as the natural settings evocative of the east, and mastered both with skill and depth. His poetic talent, combined with his prodigious work and a long life, established a corpus that is considered to be the best of Andalusian nature poetry ever produced, and lasting to influence subsequent Arab poets, both peninsular and beyond.

Born in 1058 in Alcira (in Arabic *Jazīrat Shuqr*), just outside of Valencia, Ibn al-Khafājah was raised on his family's estate and this region was to be his principal physical point of reference. From his own introduction as penned in his *Dīwān*, we know that he was educated in the study of *fiqh* (Islamic jurisprudence) to a level where he could be considered a master of it. He probably obtained most of his expertise in this field from being a pupil of Ibn Abī Talīd (b. 1052 or 53), the chief muftī (and highly respected legal scholar) of Játiva (in Arabic *Shātibah*) a town to the south east of Valencia. Since Ibn Abī Talīd never left Játiva, Ibn al-Khafājah must have traveled there to study with him. Other than this individual, Ibn al-Khafājah's teachers are no more than names without any background. Nevertheless, it was probably during this time that Ibn al-Khafājah was introduced to the work of two eastern poets, Mihyār al-Daylamī and al-Sharīf al-Raḍī (970-1016), who had a significant influence on his work. After participating in the Meccan pilgrimage on a number of occasions, al-Sharīf al-Raḍī had developed an interest in poetry describing the desert of the Arabian peninsula, and produced a number of verses dealing with this topic, called collectively *al-ḥijāziyāt*, after the strip of desert that bordered Mecca and Medina. Mihyār, al-Sharīf's protégé, had followed in the footsteps of his master with his own compositions. Ibn al-Khafājah seems to have been inspired to substitute descriptions of the Andalusian landscape for the desert world described by al-Sharīf and Mihyār.

His wealth and landed status, however, meant Ibn al-Khafājah in his youth had no need for employment and could devote himself to the cultivation of a persona solely focused on the occupations of poet and nature lover. Included by Ibn Bassām (618) in a selection of the poetry from this early period of his life is this short lyric where he describes what he calls a *khayriyyah* "gillyflower" (a plant frequently found in its wild state in the Arabian Peninsula and often mentioned by Preislamic Arab poets). Given the profile of the flower as described in the poem, however, it is more likely to be the evening scented stock or even the carnation (national flower of modern Spain) to which Ibn al-Khafājah refers:

I remember a gillyflower that was joined with the breeze in conversation:
when the darkness fell, it began to smell so sweet,
Possessing an aroma that traveled with the night full of perfume,
like one there with a secret who startles you and makes you doubtful.
It steals in with the evening, as though it has a beloved,
[hidden] behind the curtain of darkness.
And it hides when morning's light appears, as if morning
were a spy sent to find it.

In contrast to the ambitions or preoccupations that often give rise to great poets, Ibn al-Khafājah acknowledges in the preface to his *Dīwān* that this is the kind of composition he prefers and that he was neither drawn to asceticism nor to the life of a court poet producing panegyrics in praise of others.

Nonetheless, Ibn al-Khafājah lived during an intensely political period for the Arabs of the Iberian Peninsula. In his lifetime, the small *Ṭā'ifah* city states that had emerged after the reversals suffered by the Almoravid dynasty came under increasing assault from the Spaniards in the north. In 1094 Ibn al-Khafājah's own home town of Valencia fell to Díaz de Vivar, Rodrigo, called El Cid (d. 1099?), the famed soldier who was the subject of what is generally regarded as the first epic poem in Spanish. El-Cid's successors were not able to hold Valencia for long after his death in 1099, however, and the Spanish were soon expelled from the city, to be replaced again by Arab rulers in 1102, though the city changed hands several times in the ensuing decade.

Fortunately, his pastoral life on his estate outside Valencia kept Ibn al-Khafājah fairly insulated from many of the effects of military campaigns and incursions of the day, save a few years he spent in northern Africa during the siege of Valencia. This interlude produced, however, a poem where Ibn al-Khafājah mourned the loss of his home in heartrending terms:

The vicissitudes of time have despoiled your courtyards, [my] dwelling,
fire and slow disintegration have erased your beauties.
And when an onlooker caresses with his eyes your august self,
long does he see much to consider and to weep over.
A land whose inhabitants have been kicked back and forth [like pebbles],
and the fates have been racked with labor pains in bringing forth its ruins.
The hand of events has written among its precincts:
"You are not you and the dwellings are not dwellings."

The poem makes telling use of Ibn al-Khafājah's trademark technique of personification in the striking image of fate "giving birth" to the ruined houses, reversing the usual association of labor pains with the production of new life. The vividness of personification is again used to give a kind of malevolent humanity to fate, in the form of the reference to "the hand of events" in the last line. The verses also resort to constant evocation of earlier poems by the targeted use of a specifically poetic lexicon, as with the "precincts" (*'arasāt*) mentioned in the last line, which is a word made famous by the earliest of the Preislamic poets, Imru' al-Qays (497-545), at the beginning of his *mu'allaqah*. Similarly, the image of the people who once lived on the deserted site as "having been kicked back and forth" evokes an image similar to one found in a famous Preislamic elegy by Abū Dhu'ayb al-Hudhalī (7th century), where he describes himself as " a white pebble . . . , daily trodden and knocked about" (Ibn 'Abd Rabbih, vol. 3, 253) after the loss of all seven of his sons. But perhaps the most notable use of quotation in the poem is Ibn al-Khafājah's direct borrowing of a line that begins a poem by the famed Abbasid panegyrist Abū Tammām ((796 or 804-842/843 or 845/846) for the conclusion of his own verses, "you are not you, and the dwellings are not dwellings." These instances of quotation, if nothing else, have the effect of giving some semblance of structure and control to what would otherwise be inchoate and inexpressible grief. It should not be surprising that this poem has always been considered to be one of the most effective examples (if not the earliest) of a genre of poetry, *rithā' al-mudun* (elegies for cities) that came to be associated with the Andalusians and the long, slow process of exile from their former lands that they endured.

Once he was able to go back to his estates after the fall of El-Cid, Ibn al-Khafājah returned to his poetry of nature (often mixed with the themes of love and wine drinking) and proceeded to live out his genteel life in undisturbed peace, eventually earning the nickname of *al-Jannān*, "the gardener." There was, however, an extended period in his mid-life during which he did not compose any works At the age of 64, he organized his *Dīwān* according to his own aesthetic criteria rather than thematically or alphabetically. In the preface to the collection, he defends his earlier poems to his critics as products of his youth. Outliving many of his peers, Ibn al-Khafājah died in 1139 C.E. after reaching his eighties.

In relation to other personas that often give rise to great poets, Ibn al-Khafājah acknowledges that he was neither drawn to asceticism nor the life of a court poet producing panegyrics. Moreover, he lived during an intensely political period for the Arabs of the Iberian Peninsula. In his lifetime, *Ṭā'ifah* kingdoms were under assault from the Spaniards in the north, and his home of Valencia had fallen to El-Cid. However, his pastoral life kept Ibn al-Khafājah fairly removed from much of the military campaigns and incursions of the day save a few years in northern Africa during the siege of Valencia. As his poetry and love of nature became more widely known, he earned the nickname of *al-Jannān*, "the gardener," and continued to write and live out his genteel life. At the age of 64, he organized his dīwān according to his own aesthetic rather than thematically or alphabetically. He defends his earlier works to his critics as products of his youth, and had an extended period in hid mid-life during which he did not compose any works. Outliving many of his peers, Ibn al-Khafājah died in 1139 C.E. after reaching into his eighties.

While the bucolic settings of Ibn al-Khafājah's Iberian home gave rise to many of his odes to nature, it is his "Mountain Poem" (*Dīwān*, ed. Sayyid Muṣṭafā Ghāzī, 215-217) that is cited as the exemplar of his poetic prowess and skill. Interestingly, the setting is not the verdant pastoral of al-Andalus, but rather the barren and harsh desert that recalls the Arabian east. Ibn al-Khafājah begins "The Mountain Poem" with a solitary traveler in the expanse of a land and journey that pass through day and night without encountering another. The elements of nature—the wind, the stars—do little in terms of providing companionship to the traveler. Drawing on a familiarity of the traditional *qaṣīdah*, one might assume that it will be the memories of the traveler will be the source of contemplative thought. At this point, Ibn al-Khafājah asserts his true source of inspiration, and the night begins the anthropomorphizing elements that then turn to the mountain. As the traveler (and all of us) center life's experiences around one's self, it is the "life" of the mountain he truly experiences--a solitary and unending existence. The mountain speaks of its past, the violence of nature paling in comparison to the cruelty of seeing all those who have encountered the mountain pass before it. Sorrow for those long past do not escape the mountain, but the infinite cycle of seeing those you know pass before you has left the geologic entity at a point beyond expressing grief or the ability to lament. The traveler sees the tragedy of a long-lived life and acknowledges, in his solitary journey, the value of the best of traveling companions: the lone mountain. The ultimate injustice is then commited again by the traveler, leaving the mountain behind yet again to wait for its next encounter with the living, and perpetuating the cruel cycle we are all vulnerable to. The power of the poem is undeniable, and we are fortunate that the late Magda al-Nowaihi concluded her volume *The Poetry of Ibn Khafājah: A Literary Analysis* with an excellent close reading of "The Mountain Poem."

REFERENCES

Iḥsān ʿAbbās, *Tārīkh al-adab al-Andalusī: 'asr al-tawā'if wa 'l-murābitūn*, Studies in Arabic literature, v. 16 (Beirut: Dār al-Thaqāfah, 1962);

J. C. Bürgel, Man, Nature and Cosmos as Intertwining Elements in the Poetry of Ibn Khafāja, *Journal of Arabic Literature,* 14 (1983): 31-45;

Ḥamdān Ḥajjājī, *Ḥāyah wa-āthār al-shā'ir al-Andalusī Ibn Khafājah* (Algiers: al-Sharikah al-Waṭaniyyah, 1974);

Aḥmad ibn Muḥammad Ibn ʿAbd Rabbih, *Kitāb al-'iqd al-farīd*, ed. Aḥmad Amīn, Aḥmad al-Zayn and Ibrāhīm al-Abyārī (Beirut: Dār al-Kitāb al-ʿArabī, 1982);

ʿAlī Ibn Bassām al-Shantarīnī, *al-Dhakhīrah fī maḥāsin ahl al-Jazīrah*, ed. Iḥsān ʿAbbās, vol. 3, pt. 2 (Beirut: Dār al-Thaqāfah, 1975);

al-Fatḥ ibn Muḥammad Ibn Khaqān, *Qalā'id al-'iqyān*, ed. Muḥammad al-ʿInābī (Tunis, al-Maktabah al-ʿAtiqah [1966?];

Salma Khadra Jayyusi, "Nature Poetry in al-Andalus and the Rise of Ibn Khafaja," in *The Legacy of Muslim Spain*, ed. S.K. Jayyusi (Leiden: E.J. Brill, 1992 rev), 367-397;

ʿAbd al-Raḥmān Jubayr, *Ibn Khafājah al-Andalusī* (Beirut: Dār al-Āfāq al-Jadīdah, 1980);

ʿAbd al-Raḥmān Jubayr, "al-Ṭabīʿah fī shiʿr Ibn Khafājah," *al-Risālah* 1:23, 24, 25 (11 December 1933, 18 December 1933, and 25 December 1933), 22-23, 22-23, 23-24.

Sam Liebhaber "al-Shanfara and 'The Mountain Poem' of Ibn Khafaja: Some Observations on Patterns of Intertextuality," *Journal of Arabic Literature*, 34, no. 1-2 (2003): 106-121;

James Monroe, *Hispano-Arabic Poetry: a Student Anthology* (Berkeley; Los Angeles: University of California Press, 1974);

Magda M. al-Nowaihi; *The Poetry of Ibn Khafajah: a Literary Analysis* (Leiden: E.J. Brill, 1993);

Raymond P. Scheindlin, "*Is There a Khafajian Style: Recent Studies on Ibn Khafaja*," Edebiyat: the Journal of Middle Eastern Literatures, 6, no. 1 (1995): 123-130;

Arie Schippers and John Mattock "Love and War: a Poem of Ibn Khafājah," *Journal of Arabic Literature* 17 (1986): 50-68;

Nadia Yaqub "Some of Us Must Depart: an Intertextual Reading of the Mountain Poem by Ibn Khafajah," *Journal of Arabic Literature*, 30, no. 3 (1999 Oct): 240-256.

Abū Bakr ibn ʿAbd al-Malik Ibn Quzmān

(1078 or 1080-1160)

JAMES T. MONROE

University of California at Berkeley

WORKS

Dīwān.

Editions

Le divan d'Ibn Guzman, texts with trans. and commentary by David Günzburg (Berlin, S. Calvary & Co., 1896);

El cancionero del šeih, nobilísimo visir: maravilla del tiempo, ed. A. R. Nykl (Madrid: Impr. de E. Maestre, 1933);

Todo Ben Quzmān, ed. Emilio García Gómez, 3 vols. (Madrid: Gredos, 1972);

Dīwān Ibn Quzmān al-Qurṭubī: naṣṣan wa-lughatan wa-ʿurūḍan, ed. Federico Corriente (Madrid: al-Maʿhad al-Asbānī al-ʿArabī li 'l-Thaqāfah, 1980);

Dīwān Ibn Quzmān al-Qurṭubī (555 H./1160 M.): iṣābah al-aghrāḍ fī dhikr al-aʿrāḍ, ed. Federico Corriente (Cairo: al-Majlis al-Aʿlā li 'l-Thaqāfah, al-Maktabah al-ʿArabiyyah, 1995).

Translations

Le divan d'Ibn Guzman, texts with trans. and commentary by David Günzburg (Berlin, S. Calvary & Co., 1896);

El cancionero del šeih, nobilísimo visir: maravilla del tiempo, ed. and trans. A. R. Nykl (Madrid: Impr. de E. Maestre, 1933);

Ibn Quzmān, poète hispano-arabe bilingue: Chansons X, XIX, XX, LXXIX, LXXXIV, LXXXVII, XC, edition critique O.J. Tuulio., Studia orientalia, v.9 (Helsinki, Societas Orientalis Fennica, 1941);

Todo Ben Quzmān, ed. Emilio García Gómez, 3 vols. (Madrid: Gredos, 1972);

Dīwān Ibn Quzmān al-Qurṭubī: naṣṣan wa-lughatan wa-ʿurūḍan, ed. and Spanish trans. Federico Corriente (Madrīd: al-Maʿhad al-Asbānī al-ʿArabī li 'l-Thaqāfah, 1980);

Gramática, métrica y texto del cancionero hispanoárabe de Aban Quzmān: reflejo la situacion linguistica de al-Andalus tras concluir el periodo de las Taifas, ed. Federico Corriente (Madrid: Institute Hispano-Arabe de Cultura, 1980);

El cancionero hispanoarabe, ed. and trans. Federico Corriente (Madrid: Editora Nacional, c1984);

Cancionero andalusí, ed. Federico Corriente (Madrid: Hiperión, 1989).

The extraordinary complexity and sophistication of Ibn Quzmān's poetry clearly indicate that he is not only a great Arab poet, but also one of great international standing. Despite this, and until very recently, his superlative value has hardly been recognized in the Arabic-speaking world, since he has been discovered, edited, translated, and studied largely, though not entirely, by foreigners. Why is this so? It has been pointed out by Everett K. Rowson in his article "Two Homoerotic Narratives from Mamlūk Literature" in *Homoeroticism in Classical Arabic Literature* (151-191), the canon of classical Arabic literature was closed with Abū 'l-ʿAlā' al-Maʿarrī (973-1058) in poetry, and Abū Muḥammad al-Ḥarīrī (1054-1122) in prose. From then on, and until the Napoleonic invasion of Egypt in 1798, some scholars speak of a seven-century long 'Age of Decadence' (*ʿaṣr al-inḥiṭāṭ*) that they view as in no way rivaling in excellence with what came before it. Part of the problem that arises from excluding Ibn Quzmān's work from the Arabic literary canon is that the so-called 'decadent' period saw the rise of new genres that partially or totally abandoned classical Arabic diction and/or the courtly environment, in favor of a more or less colloquial medium of expression and/or popular, non-courtly themes, as is the case with the *maqāmah*, the shadow play, and the *zajal* itself. The dim view of Postclassical literature taken by traditional linguistic purists is, however, tantamount to defending the argument that Cervantes, Dante, Goethe, Molière, and Shakespeare, to name but a few writers, were 'decadent' authors because they abandoned Classical Latin in favor of the vernacular languages of Europe. A fairer and more balanced assessment would be reached by conceding that those Arab authors who abandoned Classical diction as their vehicle of expression, contributed significantly to creating, in the Arabic language (to be understood in a broad sense that includes the non-classical), one of the richest and most varied literatures the world has ever seen. If this heterodox view were to be adopted, the extraordinary poetry of Ibn Quzmān would most certainly be awarded the place of honor it rightfully deserves in a greatly expanded and enriched canon of Arabic literature.

Not much is known about the life of Abū Bakr ibn ʿAbd al-Malik ibn Quzmān. One of the few reliable points of reference is that he flourished during the Almoravid period (483/1091-535/1145), which he outlived, having been born somewhere between the years 470/1078 and 472/1080, in Cordoba, where he died in 555/1160. Such meager biographical data stand in stark contrast to the extraordinary value of his poetry, which provides a unique perspective on the colloquial Andalusian *zajal*, as it was cultivated by an author already recognized in medieval times as the supreme master of the genre. The manuscript of his *Dīwān*, which is missing a few pages, contains 149 extant poems that have fared somewhat better. A single copy of the manuscript has survived, and is located in the Asiatic Museum of Saint Petersburg. In 1896, Baron David de Günzburg published a photographic reproduction of the text. The poetry of Ibn Quzmān was then introduced to Western readers by Julián Ribera y Tarragó, who composed a lengthy study in Spanish, describing its contents. Subsequently, in 1933, A. R. Nykl produced a paleographic edition, in Romanized transliteration, accompanied by Spanish translations of the *zajal*s, in those places where he was able to understand the dead Andalusī dialect in which they were couched, and of general summaries, where he was unable to translate with greater precision. In 1941, O. J. Tuulio, a Finnish scholar who, according to the custom of his time, also went by a Swedish name (Tallgren), published a detailed philological analysis and highly imaginative French translation of seven *zajal*s. In 1972, Emilio García Gómez brought forth a critical edition of the entire text, to which he added fragments of 43 extra poems, culled from disparate sources other than the Saint Petersburg manuscript. This edition, also in romanized transliteration, was accompanied by a complete translation into Spanish verse that attempted to approximate the rhythms, line-lengths, and strophic patterns (though not the rhyme-schemes) that he perceived to exist in the original Arabic poems. According to García Gómez, the *zajal* poetry of Ibn Quzmān, like that of the *zajal*'s putative Romance congeners, namely the medieval French *virelai*, the Provençal *dansa*, the Italian *ballata*, the Galician *cantiga*, and the Castilian *villancico*, is based on the Romance, stress-syllabic system of versification, and not on the quantitative, Khalilian system used in Classical Arabic poetry. The editor was, therefore, suggesting a hypothesis with far-ranging implications, namely that the *zajal* poetry of Andalus had been influenced by, and was ultimately derived from, a native Romance genre, at least insofar as its form was concerned. In 1980, Federico Corriente, who was trained as a linguist with expertise in Arabic dialectology, published a second critical edition of the Quzmānī manuscript, couched in the Arabic script, and accompanied by romanized transliterations, which often, and significantly, improved upon his predecessor's attempts. This was followed, in 1984, by Corriente's prose translation into Spanish, of which a revision appeared in 1989, plus a further, revised edition of the Arabic text, published in 1995. In contrast to García Gómez's Romance-inspired metrical theory, Corriente proposed a prosodic system derived from the Arabic, and which he described as a modification of the Khalılian system, in which long, stressed syllables are replaced by stress alone. Unfortunately, the actual stresses he proposes in his edition are so irregular as to indicate that stress, by itself, cannot be the basis of this system. A third, conciliatory possibility, also exists, to wit: that the metrical system of the *zajal* is, simultaneously, both Romance and Arabic; i. e., that it derives from the Romance *syllabic*, if not *accentual* system of scansion (on the regularity of stress in Romance popular poetry, García Gómez was entirely wrong), to which it has accommodated the principles of Arabic scansion (after Corriente), thereby producing meters not always recognizable according to strict Khalilian principles. According to this view, the system would be a hybrid one. According to Corriente, the Andalusian Arabic dialect did not know quantity, and substituted stress alone for the long, stressed syllables of the Khalilian system. Therefore, any quantitative patterns found in the dialect poetry are orthographic rather than acoustic. Furthermore it should be noted that, from a Romance perspective, the strophic patterns, rhyme-schemes, line-lengths, and combinations thereof, exhibited by the *zajal* genre, all coincide with patterns well known to Hispano-Romance popular poetry. For more information on this possibility, see James T. Monroe, "Elements of Romance Prosody in the Poetry of Ibn Quzmān," *Perspectives on Arabic Linguistics*, vol. 6, ed. Mushira Eid, *et al.*, Current Issues in Linguistic Theory, vol. 115 (Amsterdam: John Benjamins Publishing Co, 1994), 63-87.

While many obscurities in the manuscript are still in need of clarification, there exists, then, no dearth of editions and metrical theories for Ibn Quzmān's poetry, each of which has succeeded in producing progressive improvements in our understanding of the corpus. In contrast, little headway has been made in the literary analysis and exploration of the Quzmānī *zajal*. In the hope that such an endeavor will lead us to new horizons, I have, over the years, studied the *Dīwān* from the latter perspective. While I am painfully aware that literary analysis, when based upon non-definitive editions (and there is, after all, no such thing as a definitive edition), is a risky undertaking at best, I would like to think that literary analysis, insofar as it seeks to uncover deeper layers of meaning in a poem, can contribute to the establishment of a more reliable text, from which, in turn, more reliable editions may eventually follow, while these, in turn, may supply the basis for further, less unreliable literary interpretations (there likewise being no such thing as a definitive literary interpretation), and so on, with no amen. More recently, a most welcome addition to Quzmānī literary criticism has appeared in *A poesia Árabe-Andaluza: Ibn Quzman de Córdova* by Michel Sleiman.

Concerning the much debated question of whether the *zajal* and its classical cognate, the *muwashshaḥah* were of native Iberian or of Eastern origin, attempts have been made to derive both these Andalus strophic forms from the Classical Arabic strophic *musammaṭ*, but here we are faced with two problems: (1) The individual lines of the strophic *musammaṭ* never contain internal caesuras, while its *matla'* or initial refrain, if without any supporting evidence, what in fact is the first strophe of the poem may be called a refrain, normally contains four times (aaaa, bbba, ccca, etc) rather than twice the number of lines normally found in the *simṭ*/*vuelta* of the *zajal* (AA, bbb*a*, ccc*a*, etc. [the structure of the *muwashshaḥah* is AA, bbb*aa*, ccc*aa*, etc.]). (2) The *musammaṭ* is a very rare form both in the East and in the West, of which hardly a dozen examples are known. It is, therefore, highly unlikely that a rare form composed in classical Arabic, such as the strophic *musammaṭ*, could have given rise to an extremely popular genre of poetry. (3) The oldest *musammaṭ* in Arabic (and it is not strophic) is from the early ninth century, and is attributed to the Eastern poet Abū Nuwās (d. 200/815) whereas at least one strophic, *zajalesque* poem, the *Táin Bó Cúalnge*, that is certainly of the same age, and very possibly older, has survived in the Western tradition.

Concerning a second much debated question, namely which came first, the *zajal* or the *muwashshaḥah*, medieval sources inform us that the *zajal* was already in existence in al-Andalus as early as ca. 319/931, although no individual is singled out as being the inventor of the genre. Since the *zajal* is couched in colloquial rather than classical Arabic, this circumstance would tend to suggest that the genre was originally popular and oral, and that it flourished among minstrels. In contrast, we are informed that the *muwashshaḥah* (which, with the exception of its colloquial *farja* is entirely in classical Arabic), was invented by a poet at the court of the Cordovan Amir ʿAbdullāh (ruled 275/888-300/912) around the end of the ninth or the beginning of the tenth centuries. That same source informs us that, in those cases where the poems had internal, blank or unrhymed caesuras either in the *simṭs*/*vueltas* or *ghuṣns*/*mudanzas*, a series of later poets introduced the innovation of adding internal rhymes, first in the *simṭ*s/*vueltas* and then in the *ghuṣn*s/*mudanzas*. The earliest poems to have survived, however, are from the late tenth century, after these innovations had already been incorporated into the genre. Therefore, we have no examples of *muwashshaḥah*s with internal blank caesuras. Such forms have, however, survived in the *zajal*, which did not experience the process of assimilating internal rhymes to such an extent as did the *muwashshaḥah*. This alone, would tend to suggest that the *muwashshaḥah* is a learned, more complex derivative of the more humble *zajal*, and not the reverse.

As far as the sticky question of the metrical nature of these strophic poems is concerned, the *muwashshaḥah*, being in classical Arabic, exhibits regular quantitative patterns. These patterns, however, do not always coincide with those of the classical Arabic Khalilian system, and sometimes depart from them entirely. Indeed, they seem to have been superimposed on, and made to harmonize with, an Ibero-Romance syllabic system. According to recent research by Teresa Garulo, not only were classical Arabic monorhymed poems composed in al-Andalus with non-Khalilian meters, but also without any discernably regular quatitative patterns whatsoever. In the *muwashshaḥah*, as in medieval Spanish popular poetry, there are no lines longer than twelve syllables, and the only regular stress in each line falls on the accented syllable of its rhyme-word. In this sense, it would seem to be a hybrid system. In the case of the *zajal*, matters are even more complicated. Since the *zajal* is in colloquial Andalusian Arabic, which dialect, according to Leonard Patrick Harvey, lacked quantity, we might expect its metrical system to be purely syllabic. Nevertheless, the *zajals* are written in Arabic script, whose nature inherently differentiates between long and short vowels and syllables. In these cases, the metrical system manipulates orthography to provide the illusion of long and short syllables and thus, of a regular quantitative meter when, in fact, all the syllables are linguistically and phonetically of equal duration. In the *zajal*, as in the *muwashshaḥah*, not to speak of popular Ibero-Romance poetry, the only regular stress falls on the accented syllable of the rhyme-word. Hence, the merely orthographic quantitative system superimposed on a non-quantitative language seems to be an Arabic way of dignifying what is, in essence, a non-Arabic metrical system for, as in the case of the *muwashshaḥah*, and of medieval Spanish popular poetry, in the *zajal* too, there are no lines longer than twelve syllables. Here again, we seem to have a case of hybridization on the metrical level.

It is also necessary to consider the question of whether the Andalusian strophic texts were primarily songs, rather than poems intended only for recitation. Here, we have abundant evidence from the medieval as well as the modern period, that both *muwashshaḥah* and *zajal* were normally composed for singing to previously existing melodies. In fact, in a tradition such as that of the medieval Arabs, in which musicians lacked a system of notation, melodies were transmitted orally, from teacher to student. Another way in which melodies could be transmitted, was by quoting, in the body of the poem, an easily remembered line, or group of lines (usually the refrain), of an earlier song whose melody was well known. This is the technique used in the *muwashshaḥah*, in which the *farja*, quoted from another poem, normally its initial refrain, and often that of a previously known *zajal*, had the function of alerting the singers to the melody to which the poem was intended to be sung. The *farja*s themselves, when in Romance, betray evidence of remarkable archaism in their usage of formulaic diction. The *muwashshaḥah* is, therefore, primarily a case of musical *contrafactura*. This method of proceeding stands in sharp contrast to classical Arabic poetry, in which poems were composed mainly for recitation, although there is no reason why they could not be set to music later. In sum, in the case of the *muwashshaḥah* and the *zajal*, the melody came first, and the words were written for it, whereas in classical Arabic poems, the words were composed first, for the purpose of recitation, and could either be set to music or not, at the discretion of musicians. Moreover, the very fact that *muwashshaḥah*s often quoted refrains from earlier *zajal*s as their *farja*s, clearly indicates that the *muwashshaḥah* was based upon the *zajal*, that the *zajal* antedated the *muwashshaḥah* and that, insofar as the *zajal* was the source of the *muwashshaḥah*'s melody, it had to be a song.

Thematically, the *zajal* contains elements that hint at potential relationships with earlier genres of Arabic literature. Arabic literature provides us with an unbroken, multi-secular tradition of invective poetry known as *hijā'*. This tradition begins with the earliest poetry that has come down to us from Preislamic times, all of it both oral and formulaic, and it continues into the Umayyad period, at which time the poets al-Farazdaq (ca. 641-728) and Jarīr ibn ʿAṭīyah (d. 728) engaged in an extended poetic slanging-match the details of which were compiled into a famous collection known as *al-Naqā'iḍ* ('poems that contradict one another'). In this tradition, everything pertaining to the opponent was fair game. In particular, his womenfolk were often the target of ridicule. Thus, on many occasions Jarīr made disparaging sexual remarks about Jiʿthin, the sister of al-Farazdaq, accusing her (without foundation, according to the commentators) of having been the victim of a gang rape. This tradition of invective poetry was introduced by the Arabs to al-Andalus, and references to it survive from the early period. It was largely composed in classical Arabic, and followed the classical system of prosody. For example, the chronicler of the Andalusian Umayyads, Abū Marwān Ḥayyān ibn Khalaf Ibn Ḥayyān (376/987-467/1076), informs us that, in the year 312/925, the Caliph of Cordoba ʿAbd al-Raḥmān III (ruled 299/912-350/961) defeated and captured the rebel lord of Lorca, named ʿAbd al-Raḥmān ibn Waḍḍāḥ, whom the Caliph brought back with him as a hostage to Cordoba. The rebel was famous for the length of his beard, and for a large dog he brought with him on a chain, by which it was rumored that he used to have his enemies devoured. A Cordovan satirist said about him:

> Ibn Waḍḍāḥ came to Cordoba by daylight with his dog in front of him, but his dog can do us no harm;
> He came with his beard dragging along the ground, so that at times you could see him, and at times he was hidden within its midst.
> Seventy beards a day could emerge from what his alone produces, nor would they be short ones.
> In it, there is a load of wool and hair so abundant that, if it were to be woven, it would clothe the poor.

Very interestingly, after these four lines of invective, the chronicler ceases to quote any further from the poem, and merely states: "what follows is too indecent to mention (Ibn Ḥayyān,

196-197)." As in the case of Jarīr and al-Farazdaq, we are told by Abū 'l-Ḥasan ibn ʿAlī Ibn al-Bassām al-Shantarinī (d. 541/1147) that the Andalusian poet ʿAbd Allāh ibn Muḥammad Ibn Ṣāra 'l-Shantarinī (d. 517/1123) specialized in satirizing the notables of his time by writing love poems to their wives (Ibn Bassām al-Shantarīnī, 2:834-835).

If we turn from the classical to the Andalusian colloquial tradition, we once more find Ibn Ḥayyān reporting that, in the year 299/912, ʿAbd al-Raḥmān III conquered the fortresses of the Alpujarras in Granada, which were supporting the insurrection of the famous rebel ʿUmar ibn Ḥafṣūn (ca. 854-917). The chronicler proceeds to narrate the following incident that took place during the campaign:

> All the fortresses of the Alpujarras were also conquered, since they had joined forces with Ibn Ḥafṣūn, but [ʿAbd al-Raḥmān III] al-Nāṣir li-Dīn Allāh reduced them to submission during that campaign of his, for the signs of [divine] approval were clear, so that both his warlike and peaceful activities toward them were goodly and successful. One of the insolent fools in those haughty fortresses showered down blame and scorn upon him, saying: "*Ruddū ruddū aban ummuh fī fummuḥ*" ["Cast down, cast down, the son of his mother, onto his mouth"], but a muleteer in charge of the baggage who was in the ranks near [the Caliph], refuted [the fool, answering]: "*Wa-'llāh lā naruddu-hā 'illā bi-rās aban* Ḥafṣūn *fī ḥukmuh*" ["By God, we will not cast it (i.e., 'his mouth') down, save when the head of Ibn Ḥafṣūn is in his power"] (Ibn Ḥayyān, 64).

This passage contains the earliest known poetic text in colloquial Andalusian Arabic, and that text constitutes a satirical exchange. Whether or not it is also a proto-*zajal*, as Corriente claimed in his *Cancionero andalusí* (22), is a matter about which serious reservations may be entertained. But this does lead us to the question of whether the colloquial *zajal*, known to us largely from the clearly literate poetry of Ibn Quzmān, could have (1) had an earlier oral, and largely undocumented stage, and (2) whether that stage might have served as a vehicle for invective, as it often did later on.

As far as the first question is concerned, Ibn Quzmān himself provides an answer in the prologue to his *Dīwān*, in which he expresses unusual scorn for the literary achievements of his immediate predecessors, despite the fact that these very same predecessors were held in great esteem by the public of his time. Among the various defects of the poets Ibn Quzmān inveighs against, was one with which he was deeply concerned: they committed what the poet considered to be the unpardonable indiscretion of using occasional classical inflexions (*i'rāb*) in their colloquial poems, a practice that he proudly claims to have banned from his own production (Corriente, *El cancionero hispanoarabe*, 17): "I stripped [the *zajal*] of the classical inflexions [used by my predecessors] for [classical inflexions] are the ugliest feature to appear in a *zajal*, and more unpleasant than the arrival of death." To this he adds: "The usage of colloquial wording within the classically inflected diction of *qaṣīdah*s and *muwashshaḥah*s is no uglier than the usage of classical inflexions in the *zajal*." As has been pointed out elsewhere, insofar as the use of *i'rāb* is viewed as a lapse from perfection, it is a clear indication that such poets were literate; that their lapses were literate ones and, therefore, that their poetry was not the product of oral composition. In contrast, truly illiterate poets could not have known the subtleties of literate, classical inflexions and, thus, could hardly have used them. Moreover, since Ibn Quzmān insists that the true, pure, and original *zajal* did not make use of *i'rāb*, we may conclude that that true, pure, and original *zajal* (today lost to us), must have been the product of an illiterate and oral milieu. As we now know, the colloquial *zajal* was a very ancient Andalusi genre; it was popular in origin and, at the outset, it flourished within a purely oral environment. At some point in time, it began to attract the attention of learned poets who began to imitate it with greater or lesser success. One of these poets was Ibn Quzmān, whose poetry is practically all that is left to us of the Andalusian tradition.

As to whether the early *zajal* served as a vehicle for invective, we can only state that, before the appearance of Ibn Quzmān, who has left us a *dīwān* containing poems of which the vast majority are covertly satirical, we have little by which to go. Nonetheless, there are some early references to the *zajal* that suggest its obscene and scurrilous nature. For example, we have a copy, finished by a Mozarabic monk named Binjant ('Vicente'), on Tuesday, October 17, 1046, of a manuscript entitled *Kitāb 'Abd al-Malik al-Usquf* ('The Book of Bishop ʿAbd al-Malik'). A passage in this work states (Monroe, Ibn Quzmān on *I'rāb* 45-46):

> It is not permitted for clergymen to attend performances or *zajal*s in weddings and drinking parties; but rather, they must leave before the appearance of such musical performances and dancers, and withdraw from them.

What was valid for Christians was equally valid for Muslims for, in his treatise on the regulation of markets (*ḥisba*), the inspector Ibn ʿAbd al-Ra'ūf (fl. ca. 319/931) states ((Monroe, Ibn Quzmān on *I'rāb* 46-47):

> Those who go about the markets singing *zajal*s, *azyād* [?], and other types [of song] are forbidden to do so when [people] are being summoned to Holy War, or when they are being exhorted to go to the Ḥijāz [in pilgrimage]. But [if] they exhort people to participate [in the above enterprises] in a seemly manner, there is no harm in it.

If the singing of scurrilous songs in colloquial Arabic offended Muslims as well as Christians, it was also a matter of great concern to Hispano-Jewish scholars for, in a passage on the subject, Moses Maimonides (529/1135-600/1204) comments on the scurrilous nature of strophic songs in Arabic, Hebrew, and Romance (Monroe, *Maimonides*, 19):

> Know that poems composed in any language whatsoever, are only valued for their content, and that they follow the classifications of speech that we have established. I have explained this, even though it is self-evident, only because I have observed that, when certain religious scholars and learned men of our nation attend a wine party, a wedding, or the like, and someone begins to sing in Arabic, even though the subject of the poem is praise of courage or generosity, which belongs to the category of what is commendable, or praise of wine, they disapprove of it from every possible angle, nor do they consider listening to it to be permissible, whereas if the singer sings a *muwashshaḥah* in Hebrew, it meets with neither disapproval nor disdain, even though such speech may contain what is forbidden or reprehensible. This is downright ignorance, for speech is not forbidden, permitted, recommended, or reproved, nor is its utterance commanded, on the basis of its language, but on the basis of its content instead. Thus, if the poem's subject is a virtue, its utterance is required, regardless of its language, whereas if its subject is a vice, it must be shunned, regardless of its language. Indeed, there is more to the matter, in my opinion, for if there are two *muwashshaḥah*s on the same subject, namely one that arouses and praises the instinct of lust, and encourages the soul to [practice] it (despite the fact that [lust] is a vice, so that [the poem] will belong to the category of defect in character, as is explained by our words in Chapter Four), and if one of these two *muwashshaḥah*s is in Hebrew, and the other is either in Arabic or is in Romance, why then, listening to, and uttering the one in Hebrew is the most reprehensible thing one can do in the eyes of the Holy Law, because of the excellence of the [Hebrew] language, for it is inappropriate to employ [Hebrew] in what is not excellent, especially if to this is added the use of a verse of the *Torah* or of the *Song of Songs* on the same subject, for then [the poem] departs from the category of the reprehensible, only to enter that of the forbidden and the prohibited, since the Holy Law itself forbids prophetic discourse from being applied

to types of songs about vices and unworthy acts.

From this passage we may infer that Maimonides too, attests to the existence of an obscene genre of poetry composed in colloquial Andalusian Arabic, in Hebrew, and in Hispano-Romance. The recitation of such poetry in Hebrew was particularly offensive to Jews because, in comparison to Arabic, which has both a classical and colloquial form, Hebrew was until very recently, a largely liturgical and literary language, rather than a spoken one. In Arabic, the *muwashshaḥah* was a classical, literary form, whereas the *zajal* was colloquial. In contrast, Hebrew writers made no distinction between the two literary forms under consideration, and referred to either, be they *muwashshaḥah*s or *zajal*s, with the same term, namely *muwashshaḥah*. The above passage is, thus, fully applicable to the *zajal*, the strophic form of which does exist in Hebrew.

Be that as it may, when we come to a period of greater documentation, as exemplified by the poetry of Ibn Quzmān, a curious feature stands out: The vast majority of Ibn Quzmān's *zajal*s are, ostensibly, panegyric in nature, while, at the same time, the poet ridicules his patrons by placing his praise in the mouth of a literary *persona* who is presented as a ritual clown or buffoon. By so doing, the poet manages to be devastating in criticizing his patrons, while at the same time not offending their sensibility. One may therefore suspect that, in this respect, Ibn Quzmān represents a literate, as opposed to an oral, approach to satire. Whereas earlier, oral invective had been entirely direct in its approach, this new kind of invective, belonging to a written tradition, was more subtle and circumspect. We have thus gone full circle, from a direct, to an indirect, and even ironic form of satire. Consider the following three examples of the above.

(1) In *Zajal 90,* Ibn Quzmān begins by boasting of his innate penchant for debauchery. First of all, he is an inveterate winebibber, and hopes that, upon his death, his companions will hold a drinking session over his grave, in which Satan himself will participate. Then he goes on to describe, in vivid detail, an adventure he had in a brothel. In it, a Berber prostitute catches his fancy, and the two go to bed. Next morning, however, when the time comes to pay the woman for her services, it turns out that he has no money, whereupon he is soundly beaten by the brothel's managers. In the process, such a scandal is caused, that the poet is shamed in public, and loses his reputation. With such a background to recommend him, he then proceeds to praise a certain unidentified vizier named Abū Isḥāq. The title of vizier, incidentally, had, in the Andalus of this time, become debased, and meant no than "Mister," hence the recipient of the panegyric is hardly a man of high social rank.

(2) In *Zajal 87*, Ibn Quzmān first describes the days of his youth, in which he was a dandy and, consequently, extremely careful about getting fashionable hair cuts, and wearing fine clothes. He had a charming *garçonnière* in a neighborhood lacking in men of religion, but full of "pretty widows without husbands" (87:7,2), who streamed by his house to ask for favors, the nature of which the poet professes to avoid mentioning out of modesty. One day, as he is loitering at the door of his house, a beautiful Berber woman walks by. He immediately declares his eternal love to her, whereupon she replies that she loves him even more, and invites him to visit her house at night, and in disguise, when her husband is away, attending lessons at a *Qur'ānic* school. When the poet does so, all the neighborhood comes out to jeer at him, from which it may be inferred that the Berber woman had previously alerted her neighbors to the poet's arrival, thus playing a trick on him, so that he is, once again, publicly disgraced. With such dubious qualifications to recommend him, he delivers a panegyric to another unidentified patron.

(3) In *Zajal 20*, the poet begins by portraying himself as an accomplished seducer: he is very much attracted to his neighbor's wife, but fears for his safety and reputation, should that lady inform her husband of the poet's advances. Either the irate husband will grab a door-bar and chase the poet down the street in order to thrash him or, if he is the intellectual type, he will upbraid the poet publicly, where all may hear, whereupon his reputation will be ruined. The poet

adds that he is an expert at handling women, in proof of which he cites the cleverness with which he controls his own cunning wife. Then he declares that, one evening, his neighbor's wife slipped into his house for a night of love-making. Eventually, when she was thoroughly bored with what must have been the endless chatter of a vain and inept lover, she hints broadly to him that it is time to go to bed. But alas, there is no blanket on the bed! The poet then takes pen and paper, and writes (there is no oral composition here!) a panegyric to another unidentified patron, this time a grammarian and *ḥadīth* expert named Abū 'l-Qāsim, to whom he then takes his petition for money to buy a blanket with which to cover the lady with whom he intends to commit an act of fornication. In the process, he leaves the lady abandoned in his home. The jurist, who should have known better than to aid and abet an act of fornication (since the latter is a *ḥadd* crime, that is, a crime against God and religion, rather than against fellow mortals, and which merits the death penalty), generously grants the poet his request, by interpreting that Law both narrowly and literally. At the same time that the poet is granted the money to buy a blanket, the jurist turns a blind eye to the illicit usage to which that blanket will be put, thereby revealing that he ignores and perverts the spirit of the Law. The jurist is, therefore, a fool if not a corrupt individual. Not only is the panegyric subverted, and the patron indirectly mocked, but the reader/listener is left wondering where the poet's wife was that night while he was sneaking strange women into their home. Was she too, out for the night, in the arms of another man and, if so, did the poet know that this was the case and, consequently, that the coast would be clear for him to bring another woman into his home? If so, the poet is no less than a wittol!

The three examples summarized above, along with many others, indicate that, by adopting the literary *persona* of a clown, the poet was able to get away with criticizing certain corrupt members of the Almoravid society in which he lived. Why did he do so?

In a recent and important article, Raymond K. Farrin stresses the enormous influence wielded by the Andalusian Mālikī jurists on the Almoravid rulers of their day and, specifically, relates this fact to the poetry of Ibn Quzmān, thereby opening up a significant new dimension in our understanding of that poet's corpus. These jurists were primarily interested, not in interpreting the Holy Law in a sense broad enough to accommodate its spirit, but rather, in applying it in a most narrow and literal way. Needless to say, accounts of their practices, all of which were written in later times, during the age of the Almohads (539/1145-627/1230), who overthrew the Almoravids and were their mortal enemies must, for this reason, be used with extreme caution. Nonetheless, these accounts paint the portrait of a narrow-minded, legalistic, and thoroughly corrupt school of jurists, who exercised enormous influence at a court from which poets were completely excluded. There was, then, no love lost between poets and jurists.

The Almoravids were Berbers with little understanding either of the Arabic language or of the subtleties of its poetry. During their rule, the two greatest Andalusian poets were Ibrāhīm ibn Abī 'l-Fatḥ Ibn al-Khafājah (1058 or 1059-1138 or 1139), who abandoned the panegyric *qaṣīdah*, adapting the genre instead, to praise the beauties and mysteries of nature, and Ibn Quzmān, who abandoned the classical Arabic language altogether, to write mock panegyrics, not of sublime rulers, but of his everyday fellow citizens, in colloquial Andalusian Arabic, and in a native, Ibero-Romance form, the *zajal*. This is one indication, among others, that the panegyric *qaṣīdah* had ceased to be viable in al-Andalus, for lack of a courtly environment to sustain it. The major center of literary patronage for poets under the *mulūk al-ṭawā'if* was the Seville of the ʿAbbādids, particularly during the reign of al-Muʿtamid (ruled 461/1069-484/1091), who was himself a poet. However, as García Gómez pointed out, after that monarch had been deposed by the Almoravids, and literary patronage had disappeared, the *topos* of "hatred of Seville" became a commonplace among disgruntled poets, whose productions were no longer appreciated in that city.

It has also been suggested elsewhere, that the *maqāmah* arose within similar circumstances. It does not deal primarily with rulers in their courts (when it does so, it is ironic, and not sincerely encomiastic); instead, it deals with society at large, which it views with a suspicious eye, providing us with a negative portrait of its pretensions, activities, and aspirations. If the *qaṣīdah* is a genre for the consumption of insiders, privy to royal courts, the *maqāmah* may be viewed as the literature of rejected and disgruntled outsiders no longer welcome at those courts, and who turn a critical eye on society at large. Finally, to take this argument one step farther, one suspects that, in the poetry of Ibn Quzmān, the praise-poem has either come to be influenced by the *maqāmah*, from which it has acquired a clownish, ironic, and picaresque approach to society in general, along with a deceptive surface that, nonetheless, masks a very serious underlying purpose, or else, the very same social conditions that led to the rise of the *maqāmah*, and its adoption and cultivation in al-Andalus, also brought about the radical changes introduced into the panegyric *qaṣīdah* by Ibn Quzmān and his predecessors. There is, nevertheless, an important difference in perspective between the *maqāmah* and the Quzmānī *zajal*. In the *maqāmah*, a narrator, who is often (but not always) a victim, normally informs the reader, in the first person, either about how he was successfully deceived by a trickster, or about how he observed that trickster successfully deceiving others. In the *zajal*, in contrast, a would-be trickster normally narrates, also in the first person, how he attempted to deceive a potential victim. The attempted deceit is, however, more often than not, a dismal failure. In this respect, the *zajal* and the *maqāmah* constitute literary inversions of one another: The classical *maqāmah* records the triumph of deceit, whereas the colloquial *zajal* records its failure. Both genres are, nonetheless, didactic, insofar as both teach by negative example.

REFERENCES

Discursos leídos ante la Real Academia Española en la recepción pública del Sr. D. Julián Ribera y Tarragó el día 20 de mayo de 1912 (Madrid: Maestre, 1912), reprinted in Julián Ribera y Tarragó, "El cancionero de Abencuzmán," *Disertaciones y opúsculos* (Madrid: Maestre, 1928), 1:3-92;

Alan Dundes, *Fables of the Ancients? Folklore in the Qur'ān* (Lanham, Maryland: Rowman & Littlefield, 2003);

The Naqā'iḍ of Jarīr and al-Farazdaq, ed. Anthony Ashley Bevan, 3. vols. (Leiden: E.J. Brill, 1905) 1:211-231, 2:25-29;

Raymond K. Farrin, "Season's Greetings: Two *'Īd* Poems by Ibn Quzmān," *Journal of Arabic Literature*, 35, 3 (2004): 247-269 (On *Zajal*s *8* and *48*);

Francisco Fernández y González, *Discursos leídos ante la Real Academia Española: Influencia de las lenguas y letras orientales en la cultura de los pueblos de la península ibérica* (Madrid: Maestre, 1894);

E. García Gómez, "Nuevos testimonios del 'odio a Sevilla' de los poetas musulmanes," *al-Andalus*, 14, 1 (1949): 143-148;

E. García Gómez, "Un eclipse de la poesía en Sevilla: la época almorávide," *al-Andalus*, 10 (1945): 285-343;

Teresa Garulo, "En torno a Granada: reflexiones sobre la poesía en la época almorávide," *Qurṭuba*, 4 (1999): 73-96;

Teresa Garulo, "Wa-huwa wazn lam yarid ʿan al-ʿarab: métrica no jaliliana en al-Andalus," *al-Qanṭara*, 26, 1 (2005): 263-267;

Leonard Patrick Harvey, "The Arabic Dialect of Valencia in 1595," *al-Andalus*, 36 (1971): 81-115;

Henk Heijkoop and Otto Zwartjes, *Muwaššaḥ, Zajal, Kharja: Bibliography of Strophic Poetry and Music from al-Andalus and their Influence in East and West* (Leiden and Boston: E. J. Brill, 2004);

Guillermo E. Hernández, "El arte satírico de Ibn Quzmān: Zéjel núm. 20," *Actas del Congreso Romancero-Cancionero*, ed. Enrique Rodríguez Cepeda (Madrid: Gredos, 1991), 2:383-408;

Guillermo E. Hernández, "Jarcha Antecedents in Latin Inscriptions," *Hispanic Review*, 57, 2 (1989): 189-202;

ʿAlī Ibn Bassām al-Shantarīnī, *al-Dhakhīrah fī maḥāsin ahl al-Jazīrah*, ed. Iḥsān ʿAbbās, 8 vols. (Beirut: Dār al-Thaqāfah, 1978);

Abū 'l-Ṭāhir Muḥammad ibn Yūsuf al-Tamīmī 'l-Saraqusṭı Ibn al-Aštarkūwī, *al-Maqāmāt al-Luzūmīyah*, trans. James T. Monroe, Studies in Arabic Literature, vol. 22 (Leiden: E. J. Brill, 2002);

Abū Marwān Ḥayyān ibn Khalaf Ibn Ḥayyān, *al-Muqtabas V*, ed. Pedro Chalmeta Gendrón and Federico Corriente (Madrid: al-Maʿhad al-Isbānī 'l-ʿArabī li 'l-Thaqāfah; Rabat: Kulliyyat al-Ādāb, 1979), 196-197;

María Rosa Lida de Malkiel, *Two Spanish Masterpieces: The "Book of Good Love" and "The Celestina,"* Illinois Studies in Language and Literature, vol. 49 (Urbana: The University of Illinois Press, 1961);

Samuel Liebhaber, "Al-Shanfarā and the 'Mountain Poem' of Ibn Khafāja: Some Observations on Patterns of Intertextuality," *Journal of Arabic Literature,* vol. 34, 1-2 (2003): 107-121;

James T. Monroe and Mark F. Pettigrew, "The Decline of Courtly Patronage and the Appearance of New Genres in Arabic Literature: the Case of the *Zajal*, the *Maqāma*, and the Shadow Play," *Journal of Arabic Literature,* 34, 1-2 (2003): 138-177;

James T. Monroe, "Elements of Romance Prosody in the Poetry of Ibn Quzmān," in *Perspectives on Arabic linguistics VI: annual symposium on Arabic linguistics*, ed. Mushira Eid, V. Cantarino and K. Walters (Amsterdam: Benjamins, 1994), 63-87;

James T. Monroe, "Formulaic Diction and the Common Origins of Romance Lyric Traditions," *Hispanic Review*, 43, 4 (1975): 341-350;

James T. Monroe, "Hispano-Arabic Poetry During the Almoravid Period: Theory and Practice," *Viator: Medieval and Renaissance Studies*, 4 (1973): 65-98;

James T. Monroe, "Ibn Quzmān on Iʿrāb: a zéjel de juglaría in Arab Spain?," in *Hispanic Studies in Honor of Joseph H. Silverman*, ed. Joseph V. Ricapito (Newark, Delaware: Juan de la Cuesta, 1988), 45-56;

James T. Monroe, "Ibn Quzmān's *'Zajal* 118': an Andalusian 'Ode to the Onion'," in *Los quilates de su Oriente: Homenaje a Francisco Márquez Villanueva,* ed. Mary Gaylord, Luis Girón Negrón, and Ángel Sáenz-Badillos (Newark: Juan de la Cuesta, 2006), (Forthcoming);

James T. Monroe, "Improvised Invective in Hispano-Arabic Poetry and Ibn Quzmān's *'Zajal 87'* (When Blond Meets Blonde)," in *Voicing the Moment: Improvised Oral Poetry and Basque Tradition*, ed. Samuel G. Armistead and Joseba Zulaika (Reno: University of Nevada, Center for Basque Studies, 2005), 135-160;

James T. Monroe, "Literary Hybridization in Ibn Quzmān's *'Zajal 147'* (The Poet's Repentance)," in *Handbook of Oral Literature*, ed. Karl Reichl, Weisbaden, (forthcoming);

James T. Monroe, "Literary Hybridization in the *Zajal*: Ibn Quzmān's '*Zajal 88*' (The Visit of Sir Gold)," *Journal of Arabic Literature*, 38:3 (2007): 324-351;

James T. Monroe, "Maimonides on the Mozarabic Lyric (A Note on the *Muwaššaḥa*)," *La Corónica*, 17 (1988-1989): 18-32;

James T. Monroe, "The Mystery of the Missing Mantle: the Poet as Wittol? (Ibn Quzmān's *Zajal 20*)," *Journal of Arabic Literature*, 37:1 (2006): 1-45;

James T. Monroe, "On Re-reading Ibn Bassám: 'Lírica Rómanica' After the Arab Conquest," *Actas del Congreso Romancero-Cancionero, UCLA (1984),* ed. Enrique Rodríguez Cepeda and Samuel G. Armistead, 2 vols. (Madrid: Porrúa, 1990), 2:409-446;

James T. Monroe, "Oral Composition in Pre-Islamic Poetry," *Journal of Arabic Literature*, 3 (1972): 1-53;

James T. Monroe, "Poetic Quotation in the *Muwaššaḥa* and its Implications," *La Corónica*, 12 (1984): 230-250;

James T. Monroe, "Prolegomena to the Study of Ibn Quzmān: the Poet As Jongleur," in *El Romancero hoy: historia, comparatismo, bibliografía crítica*, Samuel G. Armistead, Diego Catalán, and Antonio Sánchez Romeralo, eds. (Madrid: Gredos, 1979), 78-128 (On *Zajal 12*);

James T. Monroe, "Prolegómenos al estudio de Ibn Quzmān: el poeta como bufón," *Nueva Revista de Filología Hispánica*, 34 (1985-1986): 769-799 (On *Zajal 137*);

James T. Monroe, "Salmà, el toro abigarrado, la doncella medrosa, Kaʿb al-Aḥbār y el conocimiento del árabe de don Juan Manuel: prolegómenos al *Zéjel Núm. 148* de Ibn

Quzmān," *Nueva Revista de Filología Hispánica*, 36 (1988): 853-878;
James T. Monroe, "The Striptease That Was Blamed on Abū Bakr's Naughty Son: Was Father Being Shamed, or Was the Poet Having Fun? (Ibn Quzmān's *Zajal No. 133*)," in *Homoeroticism in Classical Arabic Literature*, J.W. Wright Jr. and Everett K. Rowson, eds., 94-139;
James T. Monroe, "The Tune or the Words? (Singing Hispano-Arabic Poetry)," *al-Qanṭara*, 8, 1-2 (1982): 265-317;
James T. Monroe, "The Underside of Arabic Panegyric: Ibn Quzmān's (Unfinished?) *Zajal* No. 84," *al-Qanṭara*, 17 (1996): 79-115;
James T. Monroe, "Wanton Poets and Would-be Paleographers (Prolegomena to Ibn Quzmān's *Zajal No. 10*)," *La Corónica*, 16 (1987): 1-42;
James T. Monroe, "Which Came First, the *Zajal* or the *Muwaššaḥa*? Some Evidence for the Oral Origins of Hispano-Arabic Strophic Poetry," *Oral Tradition*, 4, 1-2 (1989): 38-64;
Magda M. al-Nowaihi, *The Poetry of Ibn Khafājah: a Literary Analysis*, Studies in Arabic Literature, vol. 16 (Leiden: E. J. Brill: 1993);
Ismail El-Outmani, "La *maqāma* en al-Andalus," in *La sociedad andalusí y sus tradiciones literarias*, ed. Otto Zwartjes, Foro hispánico, vol. 7 (Amsterdam and Atlanta, Georgia: Rodopi, 1994), 105-125;
Everett K. Rowson, "Two Homoerotic Narratives from Mamlūk Literature: al-Ṣafadī's *Law'at al-shākī* and Ibn Dānīyāl's *al-Mutayyam*," in *Homoeroticism in Classical Arabic Literature*, ed J. W. Wright Jr. and Everett K. Rowson (New York: Columbia University Press, 1997), 158-191;
Gregor Schoeler, "Musammaṭ," *Encyclopedia of Islam*, 2nd ed., ed. P. Bearman, Th. Bianquis, C.E. Bosworth, E. van Donzel and W.P. Heinrichs (Brill, 2008, Brill Online) http://www.brillonline.nl./entry?entry=islam_COM-0807;
Michel Sleiman, *A poesia Árabe-Andaluza: Ibn Quzman de Córdova* (São Paulo: Perspectiva, 2000);
Táin Bó Cúalnge: From the Book of Leinster, ed. and trans. Cecile O'Rahilly, Irish Texts Society, vol. 49 (Dublin: Dublin University Press, 1967), 99-100, 234-235;
David A. Wacks, "Framing Iberia: the Medieval Iberian Frametale Tradition" (Ph.D. diss., University of California, 2003);
Nadia Yaqub, "Some of Us Must Depart: an Intertextual Reading of the Mountain Poem by Ibn Khafājah," *Journal of Arabic Literature*, vol. 30, 3 (1999): 240-255;
Michael Zwettler, *The Oral Tradition of Classical Arabic Poetry: Its Character and Implications* (Columbus: Ohio State University Press, 1978).

Ibn Sanā' al Mulk

(ca. 1155-1211)

GABRIEL SKOOG
University of Washington

WORKS

Dār al-ṭirāz fī ' 'amal al-muwashshaḥāt;
Dīwān.

Editions

Dār al-ṭirāz fī 'amal al-muwashshaḥāt, ed. Jawdat al-Rikābī (Damascus, 1949);
Dīwān, ed. Muḥammad ʿAbd al-Ḥaqq (Hayderabad: Dā'irat al-Maʿārif al-ʿUtmāniyya, 1958);
Dār al-ṭirāz fī 'amal al-muwashshaḥāt, ed. Jawdat al-Rikābī (Damascus: Dār al-Fikr, 1977);

Dīwān, ed. Muḥammad ʿAbd al-Ḥaqq (Hayderabad: Dā'irat al-Maʿārif al-ʿUtmāniyya, 1958) . Reprinted. (Beirut: Dār al-Jīl, 1975).

Abū 'l-Qāsim Hibat Allāh ibn Abī' Faḍl Jaʿfar ibn al-Muʿtamid Ibn Sanā' al-Mulk was born in Cairo circa 550/1155 and died there in 608/1211. An Arabic poet of the Ayyubid period, his most famous contribution to the literary field is his work *Dār al-ṭirāz fī 'amal al-muwashshaḥāt*, which first introduced the Andalusian *muwashshāḥ* poetic form into the eastern part of the Islamic empire. The blossoming of the *muwashshāḥ* poetry in the eastern part of the Arabic-speaking world can be directly traced to Ibn Sanā' al-Mulk's work, and while his *Muwashshaḥāt* are not the most profound examples of the genre, he has the singular privilege of being the first to compose them in the East. In addition to compiling and composing *muwashshaḥāt*, Ibn Sanā' al-Mulk also included a long introductory essay outlining his own theory of the compositional elements of *muwashshaḥāt*, and this essay has been a useful resource for scholars from when it was written until the present. In addition to his *Dār al-ṭirāz*, his *Dīwān*, or collection of poetry, has also been published. As many of the poems in the posthumous collection were composed for Ibn Sanā' al-Mulk's patrons and friends, it gives some insight into the author's biography and character.

Ibn Sanā' al-Mulk came from an esteemed and pious family of religious judges (*qāḍī*). His father Abū 'l-Faḍl Jaʿfar al-Qāḍī 'l-Rashīd was the son of al-Muʿtamid Sanā' al Mulk, from whom Ibn Sanā' al-Mulk takes his name. His father al-Qāḍī 'l-Rashīd was more than likely an important judge in his lifetime.

As the son of a respected member of the community, Ibn Sanā' al-Mulk received a well rounded education, studying the *Qur'ān* with al-Sharīf Abū 'l-Futūḥ, and grammar with the famous grammarian and scholar ʿAbd Allāh Ibn Barrī (1106-1187), also know as Ibn Barrī. Ibn Sanā' al-Mulk is reported to have traveled to Alexandria some time between the years 570/1174 and 576/1180 to learn at the feet of the well known Imam Ḥāfiẓ Abū Ṭāhir Aḥmad ibn Muḥammad al-Silafī (1078 or 1079-1180), also known as al-Ḥāfiẓ al-Silafī. Students from all over the Muslim world came to learn *ḥadīth* from al-Ḥāfiẓ al-Silafī, but Ibn Sanā' al-Mulk's learning with al-Ḥāfiẓ al-Silafī was cut short when the latter died in 576/1180.

While Ibn Sanā' al-Mulk had many important figures in his life, by far the most important part was played by ʿAbd al-Raḥīm ibn ʿAlī 'l-Qāḍī 'l-Fāḍil (1135-1200), also known as al-Qāḍī 'l-Fāḍil. Al-Qāḍī 'l-Fāḍil was a famous writer and stylist of the age, and, as a close friend of the family, came into frequent contact with Ibn Sanā' al-Mulk, and encouraged the latter in his compositions, going so far as to correct some of his informal pupil's poetry and prose. In addition to being Ibn Sanā' al-Mulk's mentor, al-Qāḍī 'l-Fāḍil also served as vizier to Ṣalāḥ al-Dīn al-Ayyūbī (1137-1193), known as Ṣalāḥ al-Dīn al-Ayyūbī in Europe, and was forced to accompany his master to Damascus in 570/1174. In 571/1175 Ibn Sanā' al-Mulk traveled to Damascus to be with his patron and teacher. He established a reputation for himself there as a fine poet and witty conversationalist. From Damascus the poet and the vizier went on to visit Ḥamāh and Buṣrā. Ibn Sanā' al-Mulk's poems from that period show a young man very much consumed with homesickness. In the first part of 572/1176 Ibn Sanā' al-Mulk was able to return to his native Cairo.

Shortly after his return to Cairo, it appears that Ibn Sanā' al-Mulk was appointed to the position of clerk (*kātib*). While it is clear that both his father and grandfather served as Qāḍī's, it is unclear as to the extent that Ibn Sanā' al-Mulk followed in their footsteps. His title "al-Qāḍī 'l-Saʿīd" could possibly be due to an important political position, but is more likely adopted due to his father's position. Nevertheless, he was not without his own documented success. In addition to receiving the continual patronage of al-Qāḍī 'l-Fāḍil until his death in 596/1199, he also appears to have included as his patrons Ṣalāḥ al-Dīn al-Ayyūbī and his brothers, composing multiple praise poems concerning the Sultan up until his death in 589. Starting at around 580/1194 we begin to see reference in Ibn Sanā'al-Mulk's writings to al-Qāḍī 'l-Fāḍil of his desire to receive a robe of honor (*khil'at*) from the Sultan. It is unclear when exactly his request was granted, but there is an undated poem from the poet thanking his patron for interceding on his behalf.

In 583/1187 Ibn Sanā' al-Mulk traveled first to Jerusalem and then to Damascus to visit his patron. Al-Qāḍī 'l-Fāḍil was seriously ill at the time, and Ibn Sanā' al-Mulk stayed only a few days before traveling on to Ṣūr (Tyrus). At that time, when a powerful vizier or sultan died, it was common for those in his family and entourage to suffer greatly in the transition from the old to the new power, and it is probably because of this that Ibn Sanā' al-Mulk was reticent to stay at his patron's side. Upon hearing of his master's recovery, Ibn Sanā' al-Mulk was filled with remorse and composed a poem in which he apologized for his ignoble action. It appears that al-Qāḍī 'l-Fāḍil excused his friend and eventually the slight was forgiven.

As vizier to Ṣalāḥ al-Dīn al-Ayyūbī, al-Qāḍī 'l-Fāḍil was forced to travel extensively, accompanying his masters' armies on excursions of conquest and protection. Consequently, the latter was forced to appoint a trusted agent to look after his holdings in Egypt. The position was widely coveted. At some point Ibn Sanā' al-Mulk was appointed the agent of his patron and more than likely held the position until al-Qāḍī 'l-Fāḍil's death in 596/1199. In addition, Ibn Sanā' al-Mulk was also asked to tutor the vizier's son al-Qāḍī al-Ashraf Aḥmad al-Qāḍī 'l-Fāḍil (1177-1245). All of this combined to make Ibn Sanā' al-Mulk an important and powerful figure in the learned and aristocratic aspects of Cairene society.

After Ṣalāḥ al-Dīn al-Ayyūbī's death in 588/1193 al-Qāḍī 'l-Fāḍil, unable or unwilling to continue working in the new political climate, decided to retire from the world to his personal estate. Ibn Sana' al-Mulk, still relatively young and full of vigor, decided to seek patronage among the new elite of Cairo, while simultaneously continuing to compose poems for his longtime patron and friend al-Qāḍī 'l-Fāḍil. Ibn Sanā' al-Mulk composed at least eight odes to Ṣalāḥ al-Dīn al-Ayyūbī's son al-Malik al-ʿAzīz. After al-ʿAzīz's death in 594/1197, Ibn Sanā' al-Mulk turned his attention to al-Malik al-Afḍal, the regent of the young son of al-Malik al-ʿAzīz, composing as many as eleven odes in his honor. Shortly thereafter, in 596/1199, al-Afḍal was ousted by al-Malik al-ʿĀdil, and Ibn Sanā' al-Mulk was yet again forced to switch allegiance under a new power. A somewhat sticky situation arose when Ibn Sanā' al-Mulk found himself torn between loyalty to his patron al-Qāḍī 'l-Fāḍil and the wrath of al-Malik al-ʿĀdil's new vizier Ṣafī 'l-Dīn 'Abd Allāh ibn 'Alī Ibn Shukr (1153-1225). It is well known that Ibn Shukr harbored much ill will towards the old vizier, and if it were not for his patron's timely death in 596/1199, Ibn Sanā' al-Mulk might have found himself at a political impasse that not even his impressive skills would have been able to solve. Ibn Sanā' al-Mulk consistently adapted to changes in the political climate in Egypt, and it is this adaptation that granted him his long and successful career.

Dār al-ṭirāz, Ibn Sanā' al-Mulk's most well known and respected work, was probably completed shortly before the death of al-Qāḍī 'l-Fāḍil in 596/1199. The work is a collection of *muwashshaḥāt*, a strophic poetic form developed in al-Andalus and northern Africa. The text includes 34 Andalusian and north African pieces collected by the author, 35 pieces composed by Ibn Sanā' al-Mulk himself, and a long introduction which outlines the author's theory on the structure and prosody of the *muwashshaḥāt* genre. The longer theoretical introduction facilitated the spread of the *muwashshaḥāt* form at that time and is also an important resource for contemporary scholars interested in both the eastern and western *muwashshaḥāt* literary lineages.

Between natural poetic wit and the patronage of al-Qāḍī 'l-Fāḍil, Ibn Sanā' al-Mulk was able to leverage himself into a strong financial position, a status that was often coveted by his fellow poets. His enemies nicknamed him "Frog" due to the prominence of his eyeballs. Additionally, some biographies state that his grandfather had once been a rich Jewish money lender in Cairo and that his father was not learned at all but instead a businessman. Finally, some baseless claims have been made that Ibn Sanā' al-Mulk was a Shiite Muslim, when in all likelihood he was a follower of the Shafiʿi doctrines of the Sunni sect. All of these statements have been shown to be incorrect, and it is generally believed that they are all more than likely the consequence of Ibn Sanā' al-Mulk's jealous fellow poets trying to sully his name.

In 606/1209 al-ʿĀdil's son, the prince al-Malik al-Kāmil, Sultan of Egypt and Syria (ruled 1218-1238), offered the aging poet complete control over the Military Office (*Dīwān al-Jaysh*). Feeling himself too old and therefore unsuited for the position, Ibn Sanā' al-Mulk composed a short poem politely declining the prince's request. That three verse poem was the last he composed before his death on the 4th of Ramadan, 608/1211.

REFERENCES

Muḥammad ʿAbd al-Ḥaqq, "Introduction," *Dīwān*, ed. Muḥammad ʿAbd al-Ḥaqq (Hayderabad: Dā'irat al-Maʿārif al-ʿUtmāniyya, 1958) . Reprinted. (Beirut: Dār al-Jīl, 1975);

Jawdat Rikābī, *La poésie profane sous les Ayyûbides, et ses principaux représentants* (Paris: G.P. Maisonneuve, 1949), 69-86.

Abū ʿĀmir Aḥmad Ibn Shuhayd

(992-1035)

TERRI DEYOUNG
University of Washington

WORKS

Dīwān (Collected Poems);

Risālat al-tawābiʿ wa 'l-zawābiʿ (The Treatise of Familiar Spirits and Demons).

Editions

Dīwān Ibn Shuhayd al-Andalusī, ed. with intro. Charles Pellat (Beirut: Dār al-Makshūf, 1963);

Dīwān Ibn Shuhayd al-Andalusī, ed. Yaʿqūb Zākī (James Dickie) (Cairo: Dār al-Kātib al-Miṣrī, 1969);

Dīwān Ibn Shuhayd al-Andalusī wa-rasā'ilih, ed. with intro. Muḥyī 'l-Dīn Dīb (Beirut: al-Maktabah al-ʿAṣriyyah, 1997);

Risālat al-tawābiʿ wa 'l-zawābiʿ, ed. with intro. Buṭrus al-Bustānī (Beirut: Maktabat Ṣādir, 1951; repr. Beirut: Dār Ṣādir, 1967).

Translations

James T. Monroe, *Risālat al-tawābiʿ wa 'l-zawābiʿ: the Treatise of Familiar Spirits and Demons* (Berkeley: University of California Press, 1971), 106-111;

James T. Monroe, *Hispano-Arabic Poetry: a Student Anthology* (Berkeley: University of California Press, 1974), 160-169.

Abū ʿĀmir Aḥmad Ibn Shuhayd was an Andalusian literary figure whose body of work, though not as extensive as that of many of his contemporaries, is quite varied and defies easy categorization. Trained in the art of government chancellery writing and a notable prose stylist, he was also a prolific poet in a variety of genres, including panegyric and elegy as well as love and wine poetry. When his family fortunes were reduced following the violent break-up of Cordovan society in the early eleventh century, he seems to have made his living largely as a highly influential and respected teacher of rhetoric and boon companion to the notables remaining in the city. One strand of Arabic biographical studies, represented by early works such as the *Maṭmaḥ al-anfus* of al-Fatḥ ibn Muḥammad Ibn Khāqān (d. 1134), highlights this aspect of Ibn Shuhayd's literary output. These authors characterize him as a *bon vivant* and rebel against convention, though they do not necessarily neglect the panegyrics he composed celebrating the varied factional political leaders of his times. Another strand, less influential until modern times, gives a more rounded and complete view of his literary activity. Most of these works rely on the extensive entry found in Abū 'l-Ḥasan ibn ʿAlī Ibn al-Bassām al-Shantarinī (d. 1147)'s *al-Dhakhīrah fī maḥāsin ahl al-Jazīrah* (Treasury of the Merits of the Inhabitants of the Peninsula), composed in the century after Ibn Shuhayd's death. Today Ibn Shuhayd is best known for his highly original and unusual treatise on the literary arts, *Risālat al-tawābiʿ wa 'l-zawābiʿ* (*The Treatise of Familiar Spirits and Demons*), a work that seems to have been well-known in al-Andalus and elsewhere until the thirteenth century, but then disappeared from critical ken until it was reconstructed from quotations found in Ibn Bassām and other medieval sources by Buṭrus al-Bustānī in the twentieth century. This work provides us with an almost unparalleled insight into the new critical ideas that were circulating in Ibn Shuhayd's lifetime among the class of practicing poets and prose writers (rather than simply educators and rhetoricians, who were the more usual authors of literary critical works).

Unfortunately for him, Ibn Shuhayd's life span neatly coincided with the period when the Umayyad caliphate in Spain imploded with stunning swiftness. This meant that his life became a succession of upheavals and misfortunes. In the generation before his birth, a talented chamberlain for the Umayyad rulers by the name of al-Manṣūr ibn Abī ʿĀmir (d. 1002) became the actual ruler of al-Andalus, when the Umayyad caliph al-Ḥakam suddenly died in 976, leaving only a fourteen-year-old son, Hishām (d. ca. 1013), as heir. After their ascension to virtual rule of al-Andalus, al-Manṣūr's family became widely known collectively as the Amirid dynasty for the tribal name, the Banū ʿĀmir, of their ancestors. Since he had no son by this name, Ibn Shuhayd probably received his *kunya* (Abū ʿĀmir), in recognition of his close association with the family of Abū Manṣūr.

Abū ʿĀmir's own ancestors, the Banū Shuhayd, had originally entered the Peninsula at the time of ʿAbd al-Raḥmān I (731-787 or 788) and were for a long time mainstays of the Umayyad dynasty there, serving them loyally as viziers and courtiers. But after 981, once al-Manṣūr had consolidated his power, Ibn Shuhayd's father, Abū Marwān ʿAbd al-Malik (d. 1003), transferred his allegiance to the new chamberlain and his family. Abū Marwān served as an official at court, joining al-Manṣūr on festive occasions where he would recite poetry and entertain his patron with stories, and he also accompanied al-Manṣūr on his regular military campaigns throughout the Peninsula. Particularly notable among these campaigns was al-Manṣūr's expedition northwards and his sack of the shrine of St. James at Compostela in 997, but a decade earlier, in 985, he had marched eastwards to Barcelona, where he defeated its ruler, Count Borrel, and sacked the city. Following this foray, al-Manṣūr appointed the elder Ibn Shuhayd governor of the provinces of Valencia and Tudmir, south along the eastern coast of Spain, where the latter remained for nine years, amassing a considerable fortune in the process.

Soon after Abū Marwān's return to Cordoba, when he was 59, his son Abū ʿĀmir Aḥmad, was born. It is unclear whether he was the oldest child. Abū ʿĀmir mentions having brothers, but they are shadowy figures, and no details are known about their lives, including whether they lived to maturity. They certainly did not outlive Ibn Shuhayd himself, since his friend and executor, Abū Muḥammad ʿAlī ibn Aḥmad Ibn Ḥazm (994-1064), tells us he was the last survivor of his family. Equally, we know virtually nothing about his mother, not even her name.

We are fortunate that the premier literary biographer of this period, Ibn Bassām, preserved a great deal of Ibn Shuhayd's voluminous correspondence in his anthology *al-Dhakhīrah*. This includes not only the major surviving sections of *The Treatise of Familiar Spirits and Demons*, but also sections from letters he wrote to al-Mu'taman (d. 1060), the grandson of al-Manṣūr, and himself ruler of Valencia from 1021-1060. In one of these letters to the heir of al-Manṣūr, Abū ʿĀmir recounts one of his earliest memories, of being taken at the age of five to visit the great chamberlain in his palace. Lying on the table before al-Manṣūr was a ripe, tempting apple that drew the boy's eyes like a magnet. Seeing the child's longing, al-Manṣūr offered him the apple, but Ibn Shuhayd's tiny hands could not hold it and his mouth was too small to bite into it. So al-Manṣūr, using his own teeth, cut the apple into bite-sized pieces that he proceeded to feed to his young guest. Then he called to his own teenage son, ʿAbd al-Raḥmān, and commanded him and a companion to carry Ibn Shuhayd to the women's quarters where they were to play with him to keep him amused during the long rainy afternoon. These vignettes give us an unguarded insight into the life of a man more often portrayed as a ruthless warrior and a pious ruler in the grand tradition. Even more valuable is the brief glimpse they give us of ʿAbd al-Raḥman's mother ʿAbdah, the favorite wife of al-Manṣūr and daughter of Count Sancho Garcia of Navarre. She is described as wearing a sort of crown and beautifully worked embroidered robes as she greets Abū ʿĀmir in her elaborately decorated chambers in the women's section of the palace. That she had access to considerable personal wealth is revealed by the portrayal of her calming the young Ibn Shuhayd with a gift of money that his father later confiscates.

As can be seen from the above, the letters also reveal that Ibn Shuhayd's relationship with his father was volatile. Late in the latter's life, Abū Manṣūr withdrew from the world and became an ascetic, compelling his son, at the age of only eight, to share his lifestyle, shaving his head and abandoning the fine clothes and other comforts of life the child loved. It was only through the intervention of al-Muẓaffar (d. 1008), al-Manṣūr's older son, that Abū ʿĀmir Ibn Shuhayd was restored to his accustomed, privileged way of life. Given their relationship, it was unlikely to have been a great disappointment to Abū ʿĀmir, at only eleven, when his father suddenly died.

On the other hand, the Abū Marwān most likely had an important role in his son's early education. He himself was a scholar of some repute, with an extensive knowledge of *ḥadīth* and historical lore, as well as poetry and other works from the literary tradition. He is reported to have left behind at his death a detailed history of the Umayyad dynasty, *al-Tārīkh al-kabīr fī 'l-akhbār 'alā 'l-sinīn* (The Great History Containing the Annals of the Years) in more than one hundred volumes. Abū Marwān has also been reported as teaching other young men about *ḥadīth* and legal scholarship. It is unlikely that a man with such intellectual interests would have been indifferent to his son's education.

Yet, it is also the case that we have almost no knowledge of who Abū ʿĀmir studied with, or the subjects he pursued. This lack of information may have inspired the historian Abū Marwān Ḥayyān ibn Khalaf Ibn Ḥayyān (987 or 988-1076)—frequently quoted as a source by Ibn Bassām—to assert that Ibn Shuhayd was self-taught and had had no share in the conventional upper-class education of his time. This is at least partially contradicted, however, by Abū ʿĀmir's own statement at the beginning of *The Treatise of Familiar Spirits and Demons* that he, in the days of his early studies, used to desire the company of men of learning and to long to compose written works similar to theirs. He then began, he tells us, to read many *dīwāns* of poetry while sitting at the feet of various professors. This would give credence to the idea that Ibn Shuhayd was a learned poet and trained rhetorician, not a natural talent, despite his championship of innate genius in his critical writings.

As is the case with his education, we know relatively little about Ibn Shuhayd's life for several years after his father's death. We do know that he composed his first poem before mid-1004 as a contrafaction (in the same rhyme and meter) of a poem sent to him by the vizier Abū Marwān ʿAbd al-Malik ibn Idrīs al-Jazīrī (d. 1003 or 1004), who was strangled in prison in August of that year on al-Manṣūr's order. The poem is a slight product, politely replying to al-Jazīrī's query about whether the last or first roses plucked in summer are the most fragrant by noting that—like the vizier's fame—the fragrance of the final roses should remind those around him of the aroma of the first. But it shows that Ibn Shuhayd was early on trained in the practice of *mu'āradah*, or contrafaction, a method of writing that undergirds *The Treatise of Familiar Spirits and Demons*, and about which he will have some important critical precepts to impart in his other writings about poetry.

In 1009-1010, when Ibn Shuhayd was in his late teens, Cordoba was sacked as Umayyad pretenders and their supporters fought to take control of the caliphate, and the recently constructed suburb of al-Ẓahirah, where the Shuhayd family residence was located, was destroyed. We know that Abū ʿĀmir remained in the city, but we know little else of his activities during this uncertain time.

One of the major claimants during this period was a scion of the Umayyad family known as Sulaymān al-Mustaʿīn (d. 1016). Sulaymān, allied with the Berber elements of the Army that had fled from Cordoba when his cousin al-Mahdī (d. 1010) took the caliphate, was able to take control of the city briefly in 1009 and for a longer period between 1013 and 1016. The new Caliph had been better known as a talented poet and an eloquent prose writer before he became embroiled in the dynastic conflicts of the Umayyad family. He now surrounded himself with an extensive entourage of poets and scholars of literature—which seems to have included Ibn Shuhayd as one of its core members. Several of the latter's poems that are preserved in early sources like Ibn Bassām (including several in *The Treatise of Familiar Spirits and Demons*) and Ibn Khāqān have been characterized as having originally been addressed to Sulaymān.

This group includes a poem (later incorporated in *The Treatise of Familiar Spirits and Demons*) in which the poet seems to celebrate a return to Umayyad allegiance (*Dīwān*, ed. Dīb, 111):

Is it a lightning bolt that has appeared, or the flash of a white, sharp [sword]
And is that the echo of singing, or the echo of a whinnying roan steed?
Truly, it is a war I have reaped in a moment this day
With a group of Arabs, the choicest, on the Day of the Sandhill.
A passion belonging to the Taghlibī tribe has overcome my heart,
And enfolded an inner grief [as a token] of a pang there.
Bring, O Skilled One, the horses, O offspring of the Wā'il tribe,
Your steeds have not made any nearer the distance to Thārthār valley.
We repaid the day of Marj [Rāhit] with another like it
Satisfying the thirst of a branch like a tooth, dark, pliant, made into a spear.
The lightning came again and again there, until I thought it
Was fingers pointing to the stars on hills.

The remainder of the poem is quoted in the section of *The Treatise of Familiar Spirits and Demons* where Ibn Shuhayd seeks to impress the familiar spirit of the famous Eastern poet Abū 'l-Ṭayyib al-Mutanabbī (915-965). But in these verses, the invocation of the battle of Marj Rāhit in Syria, where the poet's ancestor first became involved with the Umayyads, coupled with his reference to "another like it"—an occasion where his backing is represented as having been essential—clearly seems to indicate a change in the author's allegiance, or perhaps more properly a remembrance that his loyalty should be focused on the Umayyads, rather than on the Amirids. In addition, this poem, in its allusion to topoi like the "Tharthar valley" and the "Taghlib tribe," recalling the Preislamic period, already shows fully realized Ibn Shuhayd's mature poetic style, which is decidedly antiquarian in its tone.

The most notable of this group, however, is a poem that gives us a plausible reason for the composition of *The Treatise of Familiar Spirits and Demons (Dīwān*, ed. Dīb, 78):

I have been told of people whose hearts
Simmer against me, though I have nothing against them.
They listened closely to my words and I made them hear a miracle [they could not duplicate].
They dove deep [looking] for my secret, but they tired before [reaching] what was in my mind.
One party said: "This poetry is not his."
Another party said: "We swear by God, we do not know!"
Don't they know that I have always kept my eyes raised to learning?
And that I am the one who runs before all others to its root?
Not every one who leads racehorses can manage them,
Nor can every one who starts a race complete it.

So let him who wishes speak. For I am here and present.
Nothing will dispel doubts more thoroughly than [disclosing] information.

This poem was apparently first recited to Sulaymān al-Mustaʿīn after three members of his entourage accused Ibn Shuhayd of plagiarism. One of them has been securely identified as Abū 'l-Qāsim Ibrāhīm ibn Muḥammad Ibn al-Iflīlī (963-1049), an Umayyad supporter and government bureaucrat, best known for his extensive linguistic knowledge, showcased for his contemporaries in one of the earliest commentaries designed to explain the difficult vocabulary found in the poetry of the Eastern author al-Mutanabbī. Ibn Shuhayd seems to have had a longstanding love-hate relationship with him, that included much jesting and lampooning of each other, as well as a perhaps more serious rivalry over preferment at court. This rivalry came to a head later, in the short reign of the caliph Mustakfī (d. 1025), when Ibn al-Iflīlī became head of the caliphal chancery and Ibn Shuhayd found himself a fugitive.

This poem was later incorporated in the second section of the *The Treatise of Familiar Spirits and Demons*, where the narrator recites it when the *jinn* bring up the subject of how unfairly Ibn Shuhayd has been slandered by the very individuals, well-versed in literature, who should appreciate his talent. The fact that Ibn Shuhayd resuscitates such an old poem at this juncture and recites it suggests that a longstanding desire to prove his accusers wrong was at least one of the reasons he chose to present a collection of his poems in a framework like *The Treatise of Familiar Spirits and Demons*, where the *jinn* (those who inspire both poets and prose writers in Ibn Shuhayd's universe) give their unqualified endorsement to his writings as legitimate emulations of his predecessors.

By 1016 Sulaymān had alienated enough elements of the Andalusian polity that one of his governors, ʿAlī ibn Ḥammūd (d. 1016), was able to mount an effective challenge to his rule. ʿAlī, along with his elder brother Qāsim (d. 1039-1040), belonged to an old Arab family—descended from the Prophet's cousin and son-in-law ʿAlī ibn Abī Ṭālib (ca. 600-660)—who had in the course of their residence in the west become Berberized and perhaps adopted Shiite ideas as well (though evidence for this is less clear). But, certainly based on their lineage, they were able to claim sufficient legitimate authority to challenge Sulaymān and the Umayyads, backing this up by the support of Berber troops from North Africa (as well as an inherent appeal to Sulaymān's own Berber forces). When he went out to lead the troops in battle, then, Sulaymān was promptly betrayed to ʿAlī's forces, taken back to the city and executed there.

What happened to Ibn Shuhayd when ʿAlī became ruler of Cordoba is not entirely clear. His biographers suggest, however, that he was eventually put in prison, either during ʿAlī's reign, or during the two years that Qāsim ruled the city after his brother's assassination in 1018. When Qāsim, in turn, was driven out of Cordoba in August 1021, Ibn Shuhayd's fortunes improved when ʿAlī's son Yaḥyā (d. 1035) took power that same year. Yaḥyā was apparently more receptive to Ibn Shuhayd's poetic productions than his predecessors had been, though he as well seems to have briefly jailed the poet. Nevertheless, Abū ʿĀmir composed many panegyrics for Yaḥyā, some of which also made their way into *The Treatise of Familiar Spirits and Demons*, most notably his contrafaction of a poem by the iconic pre-Islamic poet Imrū' al-Qays (497-545). Ibn Shuhayd describes himself at the beginning of his tour of the land of the *jinn* as meeting Imrū' al-Qays' familiar spirit there and impressing him by the recitation of this poem that he had originally composed for Yaḥyā.

But it would appear Ibn Shuhayd was also playing something of a double game because it was most probably at this time that he began writing to al-Mu'taman, al-Manṣūr's grandson, who had received the allegiance of all the Amirid supporters, and been set up in Valencia as ruler in 1021 by al-Mujāhid (d. 1044), one of al-Manṣūr's generals and now king of Denia and the Balearics. Al-Mu'taman at the time was only fourteen years old, so it is unlikely that Ibn Shuhayd's letters to him began much before that year, but once initiated, the letters contain several panegyrics that seem intended to encourage al-Manṣūr's heir to reclaim his lands in the East (*Dīwān*, ed. Dīb 126-127):

Time passed judgment that [those usurpers] should be oppressed
By fate, and the behavior of fate is oppressive.
So the attack of a fierce lion
Will return once again the splendor of [Amirid] rule,
And resolute fighters will marshal themselves, straightening
Their belts, those whose belts are worn high, for all to see.
One strong male springs upon another
And one sword leaps upon another.
Yes! Here is ʿAbd al-ʿAzīz [al-Mu'taman]!
And he is the one who casts stones in the places where they should be thrown.
[He is] a moon by which affairs cast light
Upon the coal-black, moonless nights at the end of the month.
The winds spread his glory far and wide,
And their breezes fill the corners of the Ghūr valley [with its scent].
He has not finished quenching his thirst from the water of youth,
Yet every graybeard finds a tent near him, [seeking]
To be a shepherd for al-Mu'taman, who has been the guardian
Among us for unprecedented events, as well as traditions from the past
Whose beginnings have been well established, and he has returned
To uncover their final tyrannies.
So do not leave to the severity of time
The blades of those upright ones.
But cast upon affairs the like of them
In determination, for you should be a contributor to them.
And this is sent to you from a man endowed with speech
Who calls to you when dumb beasts are silent.

Unlike the prose passages in these letters, which are nostalgic, full of reminiscence (like the description of the five-year-old Ibn Shuhayd's visit to al-Manṣūr's palace), these lines appear to be more than just complimentary salutations. They seem rather intended to encourage al-Mu'taman to return and reclaim his birthright by defeating those who, according to the poet, have usurped power. Here, memory is not retrospective or meditative—as it is in so many *qaṣīdahs*—but a spur to action in the present or future. It would, therefore, not be easy to reconcile the sentiments expressed in these panegyrics with his commendations of Yaḥyā ibn Ḥammūd or the various Umayyad claimants that appear in poems of roughly the same period. Perhaps they can all most usefully be viewed as exercises in composition, as the poetic expression of views on how rulers should behave and act, rather than the consistent endorsement of one political faction or another. This would justify Abū ʿĀmir's later inclusion of such a wide variety of these praise poems in his *Treatise*. Nevertheless, Ibn Shuhayd seems to have been more satisfied with the panegyrics produced for the Ḥammūdids and the Umayyads than for al-Mu'taman, since it is these that appear most frequently in the *Familiar Spirits and Demons*.

Ultimately, however, it would be ill-advised to portray Ibn Shuhayd as ever completely severing his connections to the Amirids and their supporters for at least one panegyric originally addressed to al-Muʿtaman is quoted *The Treatise of Familiar Spirits and Demons*. Furthermore, his most penetrating and extensive literary critical observations are contained in a series of letters he addressed to Abū Bakr Muḥammad ibn Qāsim al-Ishkimiyāt, who fled Cordoba after the turbulent period of the Ḥammūdid and Umayyad struggle for power, and found refuge in the 1020s with al-Mujāhid (al-Mu'taman's early protector) in Denia, which would seem to indicate that there was considerable correspondence passing back and forth between Ibn Shuhayd and his compatriots in the Eastern part of al-Andalus.

The final (and most active) stage of Ibn Shuhayd's political career begins in 1023, sparked by the Cordovans' last flirtation with a series of Umayyad candidates for caliph, a process that continued until a leader of the Cordovan notables, Abū 'l-Ḥazm Ibn Jahwar, finally abolished the caliphate in 1031, shortly before Ibn Shuhayd's own death in 1035. A number of poems that can be dated to this period are cited in *The Treatise of Familiar Spirits and Demons*, including an elegy for an otherwise obscure political figure, Ḥassān ibn Mālik ibn Abī ʿAbdah, who died in 1026 (or possibly even as late as 1029), thus giving us a point before which the work was unlikely to have been composed. We also find a poem praising Ibn Shuhayd's childhood friend Ibn Ḥazm, characterizing him as a Shafiʿi, which would have been inappropriate after 1027, when Ibn Ḥazm adopted the Ẓāhirī orientation. However, it is likely that Ibn Ḥazm was not in Cordoba during at least part of this period, so Ibn Shuhayd may not have known immediately about his friend's conversion to a different legal school. Ibn Ḥazm, however, was back in Cordoba after 1029, and by that time it is unlikely that Ibn Shuhayd would have been ignorant of the change in his friend's attitudes.

This period (between 1026 and 1029) coincides with a period when Ibn Shuhayd would have been at loose ends, since he had been part of the government (along with Ibn Ḥazm) put together by one Umayyad claimant, al-Mustaẓhir, who had been brutally assassinated at the beginning of 1024 after only slightly more than one month in power. With the change in administration, Ibn Shuhayd fell from favor. Abū ʿĀmir would not then return to government until 1029, when he would be appointed minister by yet another Umayyad, al-Muʿtadd. In between these two dates, Ibn Shuhayd may have spent time with Yaḥyā ibn Ḥammūd in Malaga, where the latter had established a power base. Yaḥyā toyed with a return to Cordoba in 1025-1026 but ultimately remained in Malaga. It is to this time period that a famous poem by Ibn Shuhayd (not included in *The Treatise of Familiar Spirits and Demons*) is conventionally ascribed. This poem begins with an almost frantic characterization of the dangers that threaten the speaker on every side (*Dīwān*, ed. Dīb, 117-118):

I see eyes staring at me as though
Speckled snakes among them assault my sides.
I turn but I do not encounter any but a combatant,
I strive, but meet no man who would make peace with me.
My understanding brings me only different varieties of suffering
And the most miserable man in a land of ignorance is a man with knowledge.

The poem ends with a comparison of the speaker's tears to pearls collecting around his closed eyes:

We commanded our eyelids to hold back the tears
So that any blamer or critic would not be quick to reveal what is concealed.
But the tears of the eye continued confused,
As though on the corners of our eyes pearls were harmoniously arranged.
Our tears refused to flow [further than that], fearing one who gloats
Or a master pearl stringer arranging them on the cheek bones.
And [other] noble eyes have overwhelmed this passion of ours
Smiling until smiles clearly appear.

Ibn Bassām extensively analyzes this simile, noting with approval how it relies on use of pearls as a vehicle—which could be applied equally to the tears clustered around the speaker's eyelids and teeth in a smiling mouth—to effect an emotional transfer from a state of sorrow to one of happiness and joyful smiles (Ibn Bassām, 1, 1:322).

A timeframe encompassing the period from 1026 to 1029 is thus the most likely for the composition of *The Treatise of Familiar Spirits and Demons*. Establishing such a precise chronology is more important than it might otherwise be, because of the uncertainty among critics over whether *The Treatise of Familiar Spirits and Demons* or another important literary work with a similar structure, Abū 'l-ʿAlā' al-Maʿarrī's (973-1058) *Risālat al-ghufrān* (Epistle of Forgiveness)—conventionally dated on the basis of internal references in the text to 1032—was composed first, and whether or not the two could have influenced one another. Many have assumed that *Risālat al-ghufrān* (perhaps because of al-Maʿarrī's greater fame) preceded *The Treatise of Familiar Spirits and Demons*. But Buṭrus al-Bustānī, in his pioneering work reconstructing *The Treatise of Familiar Spirits and Demons*, provided compelling evidence that the latter work had priority. Subsequent research by James Dickie and James Monroe has corroborated that point of view, and has further shown that the most likely date for the composition of

The Treatise of Familiar Spirits and Demons is the last half of the 1020s. This conclusion is particularly pertinent since it helps us date more accurately a likely intermediate source for the transmission to al-Maʿarrī of *The Treatise of Familiar Spirits and Demons*, the anthology *Yatīmat al-dahr* (The Unique Pearl of Time) by ʿAbd al-Malik ibn Muḥammad Thaʿālibī (961-1038), and documents that such a transmission could have occurred.

Yatīmat al-dahr is perhaps the most important anthology produced in Iraq during the late tenth and early eleventh centuries. Its author, al-Thaʿālibī, tells us in his introduction that he first began work on his anthology in 994 and finished a second and final revision of his work in 1016. Yet its second volume contains an extensive section on Andalusian authors that includes a selection of writings by Ibn Shuhayd. Al-Thaʿālibī says that these were related to him by a certain al-Ḥākim Abū Saʿīd ʿAbd al-Raḥmān ibn Muḥammad Ibn Dūst (d. 1040) on the authority of the Andalusian legal scholar al-Walīd ibn Bakr. Interestingly, most of these poems and prose pieces also occur in *The Treatise of Familiar Spirits and Demons* (although rarely in absolutely identical form). Indeed, the first eight poems in *Yatīmat al-dahr* occur in precisely the same order as they are found in *The Treatise of Familiar Spirits and Demons*, which is quite surprising since there they are neither chronologically presented there nor in rhyme order, as would be expected if they had been transmitted through a *dīwān* or another independent source. Since these poems do include Ibn Shuhayd's elegy for Ḥassān ibn Mālik ibn Abī ʿAbdah, who died at the earliest in 1026, it is virtually impossible that they could have been incorporated into the *Yatīmah* before that date, despite al-Thaʿālibī's own contention that he had completed the anthology by 1016. Further, the arrangement of the section on Ibn Shuhayd's poetry in the *Yatīmah* suggests that, however al-Thaʿālibī's informant Ibn Dūst may have precisely learned of the poet's work, it is very likely that he would also have learned in the process something about *The Treatise of Familiar Spirits and Demons* and at least a summary of its contents. This makes it very likely that al-Maʿarrī, who—though he lived in a small village in Syria—visited Baghdad at least once and kept in touch with correspondents in the capital, could easily have heard about Ibn Shuhayd's work before composing *Risālat al-ghufrān*. This preponderance of evidence, circumstantial though it may be, means that it is more likely that *The Treatise of Familiar Spirits and Demons* influenced *Risālat al-ghufrān* rather than the other way around. This, of course, does not entirely preclude the possibility that the two were produced independently.

It is less easy to establish what sources Ibn Shuhayd may have had for his work. The central conceit of *The Treatise of Familiar Spirits and Demons*—that a poet is inspired in composition by a supernatural being, either a devil (*shaytān*) or a demon (*jinnī*)—was a very ancient belief among the Bedouin Arabs, traces of which appear at the end of Sūrah 26 (The Poets) of the *Qur'ān*. It is not, however, a belief that receives much attention in Arabic literary critical works prior to the time of Ibn Shuhayd. Thus it would seem that the decision to highlight this theory of poetic composition was very much his own, and may indeed have been—as James Monroe has suggested—an attempt to construct something similar to the Greek doctrine (popularized by Plato) of inspiration by the Muse in an Islamic context. It is entirely plausible that Ibn Shuhayd, living in al-Andalus at a time when Greek philosophy was making heavy inroads from Islamic lands to the East, was exposed to general references to this idea, but there are no particular references (in the sources Ibn Shuhayd indicates familiarity with) to the similarities between Greek and Preislamic beliefs in the supernatural inspiration of the poet (or its connection with madness). Thus, the choice to explore this idea may have been his own.

Similarly, it is difficult to pinpoint an actual source contemporary with Ibn Shuhayd that would have suggested to him a trip to the "land of the jinn" as a framework for a specifically literary journey. To be sure, stories giving details of Muḥammad's heavenly journey to meet with God and the prophets (and to witness the punishment of the damned) had already been long current, but there is no trace of religions eschatology in *The Treatise of Familiar Spirits and Demons* as there is in al-Maʿarrī's *Risālat al-ghufrān* or, even less arguably, in Dante's *Divine Comedy* (a work that has been connected to the Islamic tradition of the *mi'raj*, heavenly journey, by several authors, including the Spanish Orientalist Miguel Asin Palacios). The closest element in the *The Treatise of Familiar Spirits and Demons* to a reference to the *mi'raj* would be that his jinnī, Zuhayr, transports Ibn Shuhayd on "the back of a steed" to the other world (specifically designated "the land of the jinn," not Paradise), similar to the way the angel Gabriel mounts Muḥammad (d. 632) on the magical steed Burāq, but Zuhayr's horse has none of the supernatural characteristics of Burāq. So, again, the choice of the journey framework could certainly have been entirely Ibn Shuhayd's, and not inspired by any religious motive.

Modern reconstructions of the work divide *The Treatise of Familiar Spirits and Demons* into four sections plus an introduction. In the Introduction, Ibn Shuhayd recounts how he first met his own *jinnī*, Zuhayr, who appears, mounted on a black horse, to help the young poet on an occasion when he finds it difficult to finish a poem about his beloved, who has just died prematurely. The *jinnī* helps Ibn Shuhayd to finish his work, and, at the end of their encounter, Zuhayr teaches his new charge some verses he can use to summon him whenever he has need of him and rides away.

Later, one day, when Zuhayr and Ibn Shuhayd are discussing the merits of earlier poets, and the identities of the *jinn* who inspired them, Abū ʿĀmir asks whether it might be possible to visit some of these familiar spirits and demons in their homeland. Zuhayr mounts him on his horse, and the three fly up into the sky, crossing over vast tracts of land until they reach the place where the *jinn* dwell. There, Ibn Shuhayd asks to meet the *jinn* of the poets he admires most, and Zuhayr proceeds to introduce him to them in roughly chronological order, beginning with that of the Preislamic poet Imrū' al-Qays and ending with the tenth-century poet al-Mutanabbī, whose work was widely admired in al-Andalus. As we have seen, Ibn al-Iflīlī, one of the poets in Sulaymān's entourage who accused Ibn Shuhayd of plagiarism, was the author of a commentary on the poetry of al-Mutanabbī.

At each encounter, Ibn Shuhayd is asked by the *jinnī* to recite one of his own poems. All of these poems are either true contrafactions or in the style of the earlier poet. After listening, the *jinnī* declares that Abū ʿĀmir is "well qualified"—a phrase familiar by this time as part of formal graduation in the Islamic educational system—and tells him he can leave. These confrontations seem to carry the implication, not only that Ibn Shuhayd is recognized each time as a competent poet, but also that his poems, though they may resemble those of his predecessors, are not seen by the *jinn* that originally inspired those poets as simple copies. They also suggest some of the complexities in Ibn Shuhayd's attitudes toward recognition of the importance of natural talent versus a need for training and education in the poetic art. Elsewhere (in the letters to Ishkimīyāt), he gives priority to natural talent and accords training and study at best a supporting role. But here, he focuses more on education as process that allows the development of poetic talent, which would give it a necessary, rather than simply additive, role in the development of a new poetic talent.

The importance of training, for example, can be seen in the episode where Ibn Shuhayd is introduced to the *jinnī* of Imrū' al-Qays, and he recites a poem that contrafacts a famous poem (now considered spurious) in which Imrū' al-Qays describes his journey to Constantinople to seek help from the emperor Justinian (d. 565) in pursuing blood vengeance for his father. Justinian promises to help, as the legend goes, but then reneges when he finds out that Imrū' al-Qays has seduced his daughter, and he has the poet murdered on his return to Arabia. The lesson seems to be that reliance on outsiders for help, particularly those from a different background and religious community, is an undertaking fraught with danger.

The poem Ibn Shuhayd recites was originally a panegyric dedicated to Yaḥyā Ibn Ḥammūd, most likely in the first flush of his arrival in Cordoba, when he seemed to be the rescuer of the city from the factional fighting that threatened to engulf it, leaving it prey to depredations by outside allies (Berber and Christian) of the contenders for the throne. The work, with its archaic diction and imagery, appears to celebrate

Yaḥyā as a truly Arab ruler, from an ancient lineage, who can appreciate Ibn Shuhayd's mastery of the old style of poetry. The echoes of Imrū' al-Qays, then, serve to reinforce subtly the elaborate message the poem is constructing (as far as we can be sure, since we do not possess the entire text). The poems recited at the other encounters in the text, if their contexts are explored, seem to convey similar messages.

One of the more overt elements—or messages—in this section of *The Treatise of Familiar Spirits and Demons*, tied up not so much with any individual encounter in itself, but with the choice of authors and the order in which they are introduced, would seem to be the registration of Ibn Shuhayd's position vis-à-vis the question of which style of poetry—natural or artificial—should be preferred in composition. In his day, the natural style, eschewing rhetorical ornament and vocabulary drawn from scientific disciplines or philosophy, was conventionally represented by the work of the ninth-century poet al-Walīd ibn ʿUbayd al-Buḥturī (821-897 or 898). The artificial, or mannered, style was epitomized by al-Buḥturī's contemporary Abū Tammām (796 or 804-842/843 or 845/846). Elsewhere, Ibn Shuhayd championed the cause of naturalness and expressed the belief that poets were born, not made. So it is not surprising to find him first being interviewed by Abū Tammām's familiar spirit, and then encountering the *jinnī* of al-Buḥturī. Yet his meeting with the familiar spirit of al-Buḥturī has surprisingly ambivalent aspects. He and Zuhayr are actually on the way to meet the familiar spirit of the eighth-century Bacchic poet Abū Nuwās (ca. 756-ca. 810), whose love and wine poetry Ibn Shuhayd especially admired. On the way, Zuhayr offers to introduce his companion to al-Buḥturī's *jinnī*, who is staying at a palace on their way. Abū ʿĀmir replies that this would be a wonderful opportunity, for he has considered al-Buḥturī as one of his masters, a fact he has unaccountably forgotten. But, once the poet and the *jinnī* are introduced to one another, Ibn Shuhayd recites a poem in which he vaunts his own ancestry and poetic talent, thus not paying due deference to the influence of al-Buḥturī on his work. Though at the end of the episode, al-Buḥturī's familiar spirit acknowledges Ibn Shuhayd's poetic talent, he parts from Ibn Shuhayd and Zuhayr with a curse, and expressing a desire not to meet them again, thus signaling his displeasure with the poet.

Thus Ibn Shuhayd does not present himself in this encounter as a complete, wholehearted champion of natural—as opposed to artificial, learned—poetry. This supposition is reinforced by the final episode of the section, where he and Zuhayr meet the familiar spirit of al-Mutanabbī. Critical opinion of Mutanabbī by Ibn Shuhayd's time saw this brilliant poet as the one who had, to an extent, synthesized the natural idiom of al-Buḥturī with the rhetorical flourishes of Abū Tammām. By presenting their encounter as a much more amicable one (and the final one of the piece), Ibn Shuhayd seems to indicate that he also aspires to wield this same synthesizing power in his own work. The affinity between the two poets is reinforced by the fact that Mutanabbī was frequently accused of plagiarism in his work, just as Ibn Shuhayd had been.

The second section of *The Treatise of Familiar Spirits and Demons* continues the framework of the first, but this time Ibn Shuhayd is introduced to a series of familiar spirits who have inspired the prose writers who have achieved fame and recognition prior to Abū ʿĀmir's own time but also within his own circle of acquaintances. Again, the selection of prose writers and the order in which they appear would seem to be significant. Chronological order does not play as much of a role as it did in the earlier section, however. Zuhayr introduces his companion to the familiar spirits of both the earliest important prose stylist, ʿAbd al-Ḥamīd ibn Yaḥyā 'l-Kātib (d. 750) and the much later Abū ʿUthmān ʿAmr ibn Baḥr al-Jāḥiẓ (d. 868 or 869), who are sitting together conversing, even though they belonged to very different generations of prose writers. And, in fact, al-Jāḥiẓ's familiar is introduced first and speaks to Ibn Shuhayd first, thus indicating his greater importance. He accuses Ibn Shuhayd of being too fond of using the most elaborate form of rhymed prose (*sajʿ*) in contradistinction to his own style, which used parallelism but rarely rhymed. Ibn Shuhayd skillfully defends himself against this charge, actually using a style in this section closer to al-Jāḥiẓ's own style than is typical of his writing, which does resort—more frequently than not—to rhyme. The familiar spirit of ʿAbd al-Ḥamīd then points this out, suggesting that Ibn Shuhayd is trying—unfairly—to associate himself with al-Jāḥiẓ (who was very popular in al-Andalus at the time). Following this, Ibn Shuhayd does not reply directly, but changes the direction of the conversation by pointing out ʿAbd al-Ḥamīd's own infelicities of language, and suggests that it is their lack of control over the finer points of Arabic grammar that has caused the plainer prose style of ʿAbd al-Ḥamīd's generation to lose popularity. All of the repartee in this section is very consistent with the kinds of debates about prose stylistics that were current in the Arab world generally—and al-Andalus in particular—during the tenth and eleventh centuries.

This section also shows an important development in the character of Ibn Shuhayd as portrayed in *The Treatise of Familiar Spirits and Demons*. In the first section, he was much more deferential to the familiar spirits of the poets, especially at the beginning. Although he slowly becomes more forthright—as in his encounter with al-Buḥturī's familiar spirit—any effort at confrontation he makes seems to be expressed through the customary (and indirect) medium of contrafaction. Here, in the prose section, he expresses his point of view with much greater confidence and is not at all reluctant to critique earlier masters.

This new attitude is even more on display in the second half of the section on prose writers where Ibn Shuhayd compares himself with (first) his contemporary and rival Ibn al-Iflīlī and (second) a near contemporary from the East, Badīʿ al-Zamān Aḥmad ibn al-Ḥusayn al-Hamadhānī (ca. 969-1008), whose writings (including the first fictional prose, in the form of the *maqāmāt*) had made him a force to be reckoned with in Arabic literary circles. Ibn Shuhayd bests them both in competitions based on description, and further asserts that he is superior to Ibn al-Iflīlī because of his God-given natural talent, even though Ibn al-Iflīlī's familiar spirit lays claim to greater formal study under the most highly respected teachers of the literary arts in al-Andalus.

Fresh from his humbling of Ibn al-Iflīlī and Badīʿ al-Zamān al-Hamadhānī, the third section of *The Treatise of Familiar Spirits and Demons* depicts Ibn Shuhayd fully accepted as a literary expert in a gathering of *jinn* who are discussing the merits of various human poets of the past. They compare poets who have treated similar themes, thus returning to the questions involved in contrafaction (as had been treated in the first section of *The Treatise of Familiar Spirits and Demons*), albeit on a wider scale. Here, Ibn Shuhayd puts into the mouth of one of the *jinn*, Fātiq ibn al-Saqʿab (not affiliated to any poet), an anecdote where he describes a teacher of poetry giving his young son a lesson in composition:

> If you [should consider] relying on a theme (*ma'nā*) that someone else has treated before you, and composed it well, filling in with refinements all its various interstices, then avoid it entirely. But if there is no way to evade it, then [treat it] in another meter (*fī ghayr al-'urūd*) than the one used before by the one who excelled in it, so that you will give fresh stimulus to your nature (*ṭabī'ah*), and strengthen your weakness (Ibn Bassām, 1, 1:287).

Here, although the boy is encouraged not to imitate a predecessor directly—if that precursor has already excelled at treating the theme—he is encouraged to treat such a theme by less direct methods of imitation, if necessary. Fātiq, the *jinnī*, endorses this view and offers an example of why he agrees with this advice. The early Islamic poet ʿUmar ibn Abī Rabīʿah (643 or 644-712) had, in a famous incident, sought to emulate a line from Imrū' al-Qays' iconic *mu'allaqah* poem where Imrū' al-Qays describes how he approaches his beloved as she sleeps, in order to seduce her:

I rose (*samawtu*) toward her after her family had fallen asleep
as water bubbles (*ḥabāb al-mā'*) rise time after time.

ʿUmar was recognized as having failed badly when he composed a line in the same meter (though not the same rhyme) where he compared himself to a snake (*ḥubāb*). The similarity of sound in the Arabic words "bubbles" and "snake" used by these two poets underscores

ʿUmar's lack of decorum in comparing himself to a dangerous animal, where Imrū' al-Qays had compared himself to the much more attractive bubbles of water. Fātiq then accounts himself much more successful than the unfortunate ʿUmar in composing a set of lines (actually by Ibn Shuhayd himself) that describe a similar seduction scene, albeit in a different meter (as well as rhyme) from the Imrū' al-Qays original:

I creep upon him as slumber creeps
and I rise (*asmū*) to him as breath (*al-nafas*) does.

A breath is even more refined and ethereal than Imrū' al-Qays' "bubbles of water," so in the sense of fulfilling the rules of decorum, Fātiq (Ibn Shuhayd's mouthpiece) has succeeded. And, in an interesting reversal of the first section, the character Ibn Shuhayd (once the suppliant and student), is depicted as congratulating the *jinnī* on the success of his composition.

Fātiq then asks Abū ʿĀmir to give some of his own successful evocations (rather than true contrafactions) of his predecessors. Interestingly, Ibn Shuhayd quotes the same contrafaction of Imrū' al-Qays with which he began Section 1 of *The Treatise of Familiar Spirits and Demons*, this time claiming that it outstrips a line of al-Mutanabbī in which he alludes to his sword as a metonym for military glory and the hard life of a warrior. Ibn Shuhayd counters this by invoking a line in his poem (quoted earlier) where he makes similar references to his sword and his spear (Ibn Bassām, 1, 1:288):

The first is a thing flowing in its sheath, from which the thirst of desires
are quenched,
The other is a branch [held] in an outstretched hand, that is
stripped bare, yet then bears fruit.

Fātiq then congratulates Ibn Shuhayd for having added to, and refined, al-Mutanabbī's original line.

Ibn Shuhayd then proceeds to give several other examples where he has gone beyond al-Mutanabbī's original lines and, in his opinion, improved on them. He concludes the section citing several poems in which his father, brothers and ancestors have performed similar rhetorical prodigies. Thus he suggests that talent may have—contrary to his earlier emphasis on his own prowess—an innately genealogical element, and be inherited. Such a notion of literary ability coming from a dynamic interchange of innate ability with training (largely through *mimesis*, in the sense of "imitation of models") is reminiscent of those found in the work of Hellenistic rhetoricians like Dionysius of Halicarnassus and pseudo-Longinus, who were influenced by the rhetorical more than the Aristotelian tradition of literary criticism, and certainly had their own impact on late Antique ideas of what literature could and should be (see Russell, 108-110). While it would probably not be possible to trace direct relations between these authors and someone like Ibn Shuhayd, it would nevertheless be of interest to trace their similarities and differences, a task that has yet to be taken seriously in hand.

The last section of *The Treatise of Familiar Spirits and Demons* poses the greatest challenges for modern interpretation. This is because the main protagonists—with the exception of Ibn Shuhayd and Zuhayr—are all animals. Obviously, the animals' species and characteristics all embodied a richly humorous set of references to Ibn Shuhayd's contemporaries, but the allusions pose a difficult task for reconstruction at this distance in time.

Two points worth noting do emerge out of this section, however. First, Ibn Shuhayd presents himself as having completed the journey from student to authority (while simultaneously poking fun at the cultural seriousness of this role) when he is asked, at the beginning of the section, to judge the poetic competition between a mule and an ass. Thus, this can only be the last section of the original treatise, and the order in which these sections appear in *The Treatise of Familiar Spirits and Demons* (though they may at first appear independent) have a fixed chronological, or teleological, logic that would not allow them to be presented in any other order.

Second, more seriously, Ibn Shuhayd makes an effort at the end of this section to codify some of his ideas about the importance of natural ability over instruction in the advice he gives to a goose he encounters, who has the temerity to try to engage him in dialectic (Ibn Bassām 1, 1:301):

> I said: "Which is better? Training (*al-adab*) or native intellect (*al-ʿaql*)?" It said: "Native intellect." I said: "Do you know any creature among God's creatures stupider than a goose, saving the bustard?" It said: "No." I said: "Then seek over and over again the intelligence of empirical experience (*ʿaql al-tajribah*), since you [a goose] have no path to natural intelligence (*ʿaql al-ṭabīʿah*). Then, if you succeed in obtaining a share of that [intelligence] and bring back a portion of it, then engage in argument (*nāẓirī*) as part of your training (*al-adab*)." It departed and so did we.

At the conclusion of *The Treatise*, then, Ibn Shuhayd gives us a clearer sense of his hierarchy of ability: 1) the highest level of ability comes from innate talent (*al-ṭabʿ* or *al-ṭabīʿah*); next 2) actual experience can either enhance or—more atypically—substitute for natural talent. Finally, 3) the use of more formalized pedagogical practices, like dialectic or formal disputation (*munāẓarah*) brings up the rear, because they can at best give support to natural ability already present in the intellect.

The doctrines we find in *The Treatise of Familiar Spirits and Demons* receive more nuanced support in the series of letters (probably more or less contemporary to *The Treatise*) that Ibn Shuhayd addressed to his friend (and sometime rival) Abū Bakr al-Ishkimiyāt, once he had taken refuge from the troubles in Cordoba with al-Mujāhid in eastern al-Andalus. First, Ibn Shuhayd uses some of the ideas of later Neoplatonism (probably made accessible to him through the *Theology of Aristotle* or the treatise known as *The Sayings of the Greek Sage*, both of which were circulating in al-Andalus during his lifetime) to suggest that natural talent can only manifest itself in individuals where the soul controls the body (Ibn Bassām 1, 1: 231):

> The extent of an individual's natural ability (*ṭabʿ*) is based on the extent to which his soul (*nafs*) is mixed together with his body. Anyone whose soul, in the essence of his constitution, dominates his body will be naturally disposed to a spiritual nature (*maṭbūʿ rūḥānī*), with the instantiations of words and themes appearing in their best possible configuration and purest costume. Anyone whose body dominates his soul, in the essence of his constitution, and controls his sensations, the instantiations [of words] will appear in him as deficient in the first degree of perfection and completeness.

Here, the soul (intermediate between the Intellect and the material body in classical Neoplatonian thought) would seem to be occupying the same position as "the intelligence of empirical experience" did for the goose at the end of *The Treatise of Familiar Spirits and Demons*. The difference would seem to be that here, Ibn Shuhayd is talking about a person, a being who does possess a soul, while in *The Treatise of Familiar Spirits and Demons* he was advising an animal which can never possess such a faculty capable of guiding it toward the higher Intellect.

Probably more representative of Ibn Shuhayd's thinking about the relationship between experiential knowledge and innate talent is his well-known anecdote about "the eloquent Jew," where a young Jewish man sitting in on Abū ʿĀmir's lessons is represented as being instinctively able to grasp principles of literature that are beyond the discernment of his official student from the Cordovan elite:

> One day Yūsuf ibn Isḥāq Ibn Baklārish al-Isrāʾīlī, who was the student with the most understanding who has ever passed by me, sat down with me during a time when I had agreed to tutor a man dear to me among the inhabitants of Cordoba, and I was saying to him: "Indeed consonants have relations of kinship and closeness, which become apparent in words. If a kinsman is placed in a neighborly relation to another relative, or a family member mingles with a family member, the intimacy is pleasant and the companionship [between them] is a fine thing. . . . do you understand?" He said: "Yes, by God!" . . . . All the time, that

> Jew was sitting silently, paying attention to what I was saying. Then the Cordoban came the next morning and he recited to me:

I swear by the Lord of Mecca and the camels
That my sorrows are truly comparable to mountains.

and other lines of poetry resembling this. Then the Jew came forward and recited to me (Ibn Bassam, 1, 1: 234-35):

Did their riders turn toward a fertile land
having enclosed your heart in the camel litter?

> And he continued to the end of the poem, bringing in every beauty. Then that Cordoban said to me: "The poetry of the Jew is better than my poetry." I said: "There is nothing bad about your understanding if you have come to realize that."

This anecdote certainly gives us unusual insight into the teaching process, and into the relationship of different religious groups in the Cordoba of Ibn Shuhayd's time—and this is often why it is quoted. But it also represents, in action, the principles elucidated at the end of *The Treatise of Familiar Spirits and Demons*. Although the young Jewish man has no connection, or particular allegiance to, Arab Islamic culture, his innate talent allows him to grasp the literary ideas Ibn Shuhayd is illustrating, while the young man from the Cordovan elite—who has every motive to profit from his studies, but no innate talent—completely misses the point. Certainly the message of Ibn Shuhayd's lesson can help someone who already talent to compose a better poem, but without that grounding the instruction is worthless. Nor is talent necessarily a trait that must be handed down, for someone who is a complete outsider (thus the emphasis on the young man's Jewish background) is equally likely to possess the talent that will enable him to take better advantage of experiential learning.

Finally, in the letters to al-Ishkimiyat, Ibn Shuhayd elucidates a principle of relativism that is important in the understanding of literary history (Ibn Bassām 1, 1: 236):

> Just as it is said, "For every place of standing, there is an appropriate form of speaking," so too there is for every age, [an appropriate form of] rhetoric, for every age there are [appropriate] words, and for every group among the nations . . . there is a kind of oratory and a sort of rhetoric that will not be congruent with any other or give cheer to anyone else.

As several modern critics have noted, this relativism is a highly original critical notion of Ibn Shuhayd. For him, there are no absolute standards of excellence. Everything can change with time and with the cultural presuppositions that are being examined.

It is difficult to tell if Ibn Shuhayd might have used these critical ideas—as expressed in *The Treatise of Familiar Spirits and Demons* and his letters to al-Ishkimiyāt—to produce more systematic examinations of Arabic literature and its heritage. In 1029, he became involved in Cordovan political life once again. About one and one-half years before this, a group of Umayyad supporters (including Ibn Shuhayd's friend Ibn Ḥazm) had prevailed upon one of the last active members of the Umayyad royal family, Hishām ibn Muḥammad al-Muʿtadd to accept the caliphate. Al-Muʿtadd had been living in the eastern Andalusian town of Alpuente ever since Qāsim ibn Ḥammūd had become ruler of Cordoba in mid-1018.

It took al-Muʿtadd more than a year to reach his new capital, after allegiance had been officially paid to him. When he finally entered Cordoba, his most pressing aim was to fill the virtually empty caliphal coffers. He appointed one of his followers, Ḥakam ibn Saʿīd al-Qazzāz (formerly a silk weaver, who had distinguished himself militarily), his chief minister. Al-Qazzāz's task was to find his master as much ready money as possible. Ḥakam sought out the help of Ibn Shuhayd, who became a minister and confidant of al-Qazzāz. When the leaders of the dominant Mālikī community of Muslims, outraged by the new caliph's financial exactions, turned against the authorities in 1030, Ḥakam ordered Ibn Shuhayd to denounce them, which he did with much energy, in both prose and poetry. Eventually, al-Muʿtadd's depredations led to his overthrow, and in the last years of his life Ibn Shuhayd avoided political entanglements, no doubt soured by this recent experience.

Ibn Shuhayd's mind seems to have stayed sharp to the end of his life, and he composed many occasional poems during this period that have been preserved. One of his most haunting works, which uses the conventions of the traditional *naṣīb* to lament the final destruction of Cordoba as it had been under al-Manṣūr, has sometimes been attributed to this time. Certainly, it would have gained added poignancy after the destruction of the last remnants of the royal suburb of Madīnat al-Zahrā' (mentioned in the poem) during the brief caliphate of al-Mustakfī in 1024-1025, when Ibn Shuhayd was out of favor and perhaps in exile. Equally, however, the poem may have become attached to Ibn Shuhayd's name only after his death, since it was not mentioned in such a context until some three centuries later, in a history (*A'māl al-a'lām*) by the Granadan and Moroccan government official Lisān al-Dīn Ibn al-Khaṭīb (d. 1375). Thus it may not be Ibn Shuhayd's poem at all, but if it is, it provides a fitting requiem for the end of the Umayyad caliphate, which was declared at the end of 1031.

Ibn Shuhayd's last poems are preoccupied with the immanence of death. While his mind was still lucid, his physical health began to fail well in advance of his final demise. He had long been deaf, though that condition may have worsened and become more noticeable at the end of the 1020s. Sometime in his last years he began to suffer from increasing paralysis, and, finally, about three weeks before he died, he suffered a stroke that "turned his body to stone." At this point he considered suicide, but in the end resigned himself to the will of God. He commemorated these internal struggles, and his sorrow at parting from his friends in a number of poems that have been singled out for their moving and personal qualities.

One of his last works was a poem addressed to his childhood friend Ibn Ḥazm, asking him to take care of the arrangements for his funeral. Ibn Ḥazm dutifully carried out his friend's request, and Ibn Shuhayd was buried just outside the city where had be born on 12 April 1035.

REFERENCES

Iḥsān ʿAbbās, *Tārīkh al-adab al-Andalusī*, rev. ed., vol. 1 (Beirut: Dār al-Thaqāfah, 1969), 270-302;

James Dickie, "Ibn Shuhayd: a Biographical and Critical Introduction," *al-Andalus* 29 (1964): 243-310;

Jaakko Hameen-Anttila, *Maqama: a History of A Genre* (Wiesbaden: Harrassowitz Verlag, 2002), 219-229;

Abū 'l-Ḥasan ʿAlī Ibn Bassām al-Shantarinī, *al-Dhakhīrah fī maḥāsin ahl al-Jazīrah*, ed. Iḥsān ʿAbbās, 4 vols. (Beirut: Dār al-Thaqāfah, 1975);

Abū Naṣr al-Fatḥ Ibn Khāqān, *Maṭmaḥ al-anfus wa-masraḥ al-ta'annus fī mulaḥ ahl al-Andalus* (Beirut: Dār ʿAmmār, Mu'assasat al-Risālah, 1983);

Abd Allāh al-Maʿattānī, *Ibn Shuhayd al-andalusī wa-juhūduhu fī 'l-naqd al-adabī* (Alexandria: Mansha'at al-Maʿārif, 1994);

A.R. Nykl, *Hispano-Arabic Poetry and its Relations with the Old Provencal Troubadors* (Baltimore, 1946), 103-105;

Donald A. Russell, *Criticism in Antiquity* (London: Duckworth, 1981).

Aḥmad ibn ʿAbd Allāh Ibn Zaydūn

(ca. 1003-May 1071)

TERRI DEYOUNG
University of Washington

WORKS

Dīwān (Collected Poems);
Rasā'il (Letters).

Editions

Dīwān Ibn Zaydūn wa-rasā'iluh, ed. Kāmil Kilānī and ʿAbd al-Raḥmān Khalīfah (Cairo: Maṭbaʿat Muṣṭafā 'l-Bābī 'l-Ḥalabī, 1932);
Dīwān Ibn Zaydūn, ed. Karam al-Bustānī (Beirut: Dār Ṣādir, 1975);
Dīwān Ibn Zaydūn wa-rasā'iluh, ed. ʿAlī ʿAbd al-ʿAẓīm (Cairo: Dār Nahḍat Miṣr, 1980);
Sharḥ al-'uyūn fī sharḥ risālat Ibn Zaydūn [*al-hazliyyah*], ed. Jamāl al-Dīn Ibn Nubātah al-Miṣrī, rev. Muḥammad al-Faḍl Ibrāhīm (Cairo: Dār al-Fikr al-ʿArabī, 1964);
Tamām al-mutūn fī sharḥ risālat Ibn Zaydūn [*al-jiddiyyah*], ed. Khalīl ibn Aybak al-Ṣafadī, rev. Muḥammad al-Faḍl Ibrāhīm (Cairo: Dār al-Fikr al-ʿArabī, 1969).

Translations

A.J. Arberry, *Arabic Poetry: a Primer for Students* (Cambridge: Cambridge University Press, 1965), 114-117;
James Monroe, *Hispano-Arabic Poetry: a Student Anthology* (Berkeley: University of California Press, 1974), 178-187.

Ibn Zaydūn is considered the greatest love poet to have emerged in the Iberian peninsula (al-Andalus) during Islamic rule there. He also produced works in most of the other genres of Arabic poetry fashionable at the time, and was a noted prose stylist. He made a career as a *kātib*, or chancellery clerk, and then as a roving ambassador for the rulers of Cordoba and subsequently the ʿAbbādid family that ruled Seville in the eleventh century. He was also a mentor and teacher for al-Muʿtamid Ibn ʿAbbād (1039-1095), the last ruler of that dynasty, who himself became a noted poet. In the centuries immediately following Ibn Zaydūn's death, the case can be made that he was more famous for his prose than his poetry (with the exception of his best known poem, the "*Nūniyyah*" (Poem Rhyming the Consonant "N"), which remained widely popular), since his *al-Risālah al-hazliyyah* (Jesting Letter) and *al-Risālah al-jiddiyyah* (Serious Letter) attracted the attention of (and lengthy commentary by) two important Egyptian scholars in the fourteenth century.

Following this, his reputation gradually faded, so that by the nineteenth century, his work seems to have been little known and he was certainly not considered a major literary figure. In the early twentieth century, however, Ibn Zaydūn's reputation as a great love poet received an important boost when his most famous love lyric, the *"Nūniyyah,"* was contrafacted by the famous Egyptian Neoclassical poet Aḥmad Shawqī (1868-1932) during the time he was exiled to Spain by the British government in World War I. The pubic interest sparked by this episode led to the publication of Ibn Zaydūn's full *dīwān* (collected poems) in 1932. Since the end of World War II, his poems have received further attention from Western literary scholars eager to establish the possible connections between Arabic poetry in al-Andalus and the rise of the courtly love lyric in Provence and Italy. Today his poetry is a staple of secondary and college curricula on Arabic literature and several translations (and analyses) of his more famous works have been made in Western languages.

Aḥmad ibn ʿAbd Allāh Ibn Zaydūn was born in 394/late 1003 or early 1004, probably in Rusāfah, a suburb of Cordoba, to a family of

Islamic legal scholars (*faqīhs*) with roots in the city of Elvira, near Granada. Cordoba was at that time one of the largest cities in Europe, with a population in the hundreds of thousands, drawn from all parts of the Islamic world and a variety of religious traditions, including substantial numbers of Christians and Jews as well as Muslims. Ibn Zaydūn's family, however, prided themselves on their pure Arab ancestry, tracing their forebears back to the clan of the Banī Makhzūm, a branch of the Quraysh tribe to which the Prophet Muḥammad (d. 632) belonged.

We know very little about Ibn Zaydūn's early life. His father, ʿAbd Allāh, was a teacher as well as an authority on the Mālikī school of Islamic law, so it is entirely possible that he personally taught his son in his early years. This background would account for Ibn Zaydūn's familiarity with material from the *Qurʾān* and the Muslim religious tradition, which is obvious in his work. Given that he had close ties to the family of the chief judge in Cordoba at the time, Abū ʾl-ʿAbbās Aḥmad ibn ʿAbd Allāh Ibn Dhakwān (d. 1022), ʿAbd Allāh may have sent his son to study Islamic subjects in that household as well. At any rate, Ibn Zaydūn became a close friend to Ibn Dhakwān's son Abū Bakr, a year younger than himself, and would write one of his most moving elegies for his childhood comrade upon the latter's premature death in 1043.

We do know of one outside teacher, the grammarian, author and transmitter of poetry Abū Bakr Musallim ibn Aḥmad Ibn Aflaḥ (d. 1041 or 1042), with whom Ibn Zaydūn seems to have maintained cordial relations until the former's death. When Ibn Zaydūn was seeking release from prison in 1041, he addressed a letter and a poem to Abū Bakr that recalls in some detail their relationship. This would suggest that Ibn Zaydūn received a thorough, yet conventional, education in Islam and Arabic letters for the time, with the emphasis on literature and composition, which would accord well with the fact that he was eventually employed as a chancery clerk (*kātib*), ambassador and general factotum by more than one ruling family in al-Andalus. He does not appear to have composed much poetry in his early life that he considered worth preserving; at least, it has not come down to us. The earliest poems we have would probably date from the period when he was in his late twenties, after his experience of the precipitous fall of the unified caliphal state in al-Andalus.

Ibn Zaydūn was born a year after the death of the last truly strong and effective leader al-Andalus was to know for a generation, al-Manṣūr ibn Abī ʿĀmir (939-1002). Al-Manṣūr had not been a member of the Umayyad family, the dynasty that had historically ruled in al-Andalus, but had seized power as regent for Hishām II al-Muʾayyad (d. ca. 1013), whose father had died when he was only ten or eleven. Al-Manṣūr had ruled effectively in Hishām's name for over a quarter of century, the result of sound fiscal policy and an aggressive stance toward the Spanish Christian kingdoms situated to the north of al-Andalus. In 997, he even penetrated as far as the northern edge of the Iberian Peninsula, sacking the shrine of St. James of Compostela, one of the holiest Christian pilgrimage sites in Europe.

Al-Manṣūr's elder son, ʿAbd al-Mālik al-Muẓaffar (d. 1008), continued his father's policies when he succeeded him in 1002. Although not as forceful as his father had been, al-Muẓaffar was effective as a ruler, and surmounted several challenges, including plots against his life. But he died suddenly, most likely from diphtheria, while on his annual campaign against the Christians of the north in October 1008, when Ibn Zaydūn would have been around five years old.

Al-Manṣūr's younger son ʿAbd al-Raḥmān, who next succeeded to the throne, was a far less effective ruler. His mother, ʿAbdah, was the daughter of the King of Navarre and she nicknamed her son Sanchuelo (Arabic Shanjūl), a constant reminder of his status as the child of a foreign woman. But more important than this, ʿAbd al-Raḥmān was cowardly, indolent and vain, quickly alienating—after his accession to power—all the important elements of the bureaucracy and the army. Taking advantage of ʿAbd al-Raḥmān's absence from the capital, in March of 1009, the populace rose against him, deposed the figurehead caliph Hishām II, and put a new member of the Umayyad family in his place, with the regnal title of al-Mahdī (the

Rightly Guided One). For good measure they pillaged and utterly destroyed al-Manṣūr's palace complex of al-Zahīra' to the south-east of the city center.

Al-Mahdī (d. 1010), even though a member of the traditional ruling family, did not turn out to be any wiser a ruler than his predecessor. He quickly alienated the Berber troops in the army, who had been the mainstay of al-Manṣūr's and al-Muẓaffar's rule. This included on several occasions allowing mobs to attack houses in the Rusāfah area, where many Berbers lived (as well as Ibn Zaydūn's family). The Berbers reacted to the provocation by promptly naming their own, rival, caliph, al-Mahdī's cousin Sulaymān al-Mustaʿīn (d. 1016). Then they left Cordoba, heading north, where eventually they were successful in obtaining aid from Sancho Garcia, Count of Castile. They were able to re-take Cordoba, but al-Mahdī escaped and made his own deal with the Catalans, who provided him with 10,000 mercenaries. At the end of May 1010, Sulaymān and the Berbers left the city to meet Muḥammad al-Mahdī and his new allies. Muḥammad al-Mahdī was killed in the battle that followed on July 23, but fighting continued sporadically with much destruction inside the city. In one battle late in 1012, for example, both Rusāfah and the Umayyad palace complex al-Zahrā' to the north-west of the city center were attacked and partially destroyed.

Adding to the turmoil in Ibn Zaydūn's life at this time was the death of his father in 1014. Although it does not seem to have been connected to any political event, the eleven-year-old Ibn Zaydūn suddenly found himself the ward of his maternal grandfather, Abū Bakr Muḥammad Ibn Hadāhīd (d. 1040 or 1041), who was the administrator of market regulations (*muḥtasib*) in Cordoba and a legal scholar of some note. Undoubtedly he ensured that his grandson continued his studies, despite the turmoil in the city.

In 1015, ʿAlī Ibn Ḥammūd (d. 1018), governor of the port of Ceuta on the North African coast opposite Gibraltar, accused Sulaymān of having murdered the old caliph Hishām II and rose against him. The troops of Ibn Ḥammūd defeated Sulaymān's forces and in July 1016 entered Cordoba. Eventually ʿAlī was assassinated and neither of his successors, his brother Qāsim (d. 1039-40) or his son Yaḥyā (d. 1035) were able to control the contending factions within the city and impose order. By the middle of the 1020s they had withdrawn to their stronghold in Malaga and the Cordovans were left to their own devices to pacify the city. Various members of the Umayyad family sought to claim the caliphate in dizzying succession. By this time, of course, Ibn Zaydūn was an adult, in his twenties himself and beginning to be involved in these events.

The period of Umayyad restoration was even more tumultuous than the Ḥammūdid interlude. But one of the myriad of contending claimants, al-Mustakfī (d. 1025), stands out from the rest because of the brutality of his brief tenure in the caliphate and because he was the father of the woman who was to become famous as the beloved to whom Ibn Zaydūn is considered to have directed the preponderance of his love poems: Wallādah.

Al-Mustakfī's reign lasted for less than a year and he died in ignominious flight from the city in June 1025. But his daughter Wallādah bint al-Mustakfī, d. 1091 or 1092 (at that time in her teens) remained in Cordoba and, according to the historians, took advantage of the absence of a father or guardian to establish her residence as a place where poets, literary figures, intellectuals and even government ministers gathered. This, together with the disordered conditions of those years, seems to have given her a freedom in behavior and ability to surmount criticism rarely accorded upper-class women in the Islamic world. On the one hand, a scandalous anecdote circulated that she had embroidered in gold on the left side of her cloak a verse of her own composition:

By God, I am most deserving of noble things,
  as I walk my walk and proceed with pride.

This was matched by another verse on the right side of her garment:

I present my lover with the dish of my cheek
  and give my kiss to the one who desires it.

For this and other outrages to convention, literary historians of al-Andalus like Ibn al-Bassām al-Shantarinī (d. 1147) criticized her for her "outspokenness and concern with satisfying her own pleasures" (1, 1:429). Yet they also praised her beauty and wit. The fourteenth-century scholar Khalīl ibn Aybak al-Ṣafadī (ca. 1297-1363) even went so far as to say that he had found her famous for her "respectability and chastity" (*Dīwān,* ed. ʿAbd al-ʿAzīm, 634). Certainly she paid no serious price for her behavior, dying unmarried but secure and well regarded in her hometown in 1091.

Other women of her age seem to have exercised considerable power behind the scenes, and some in earlier centuries had been able to carve out the kind of public role she enjoyed but no contemporary seems to have been able to equal the achievement of Wallādah. She remained, as the historian Aḥmad ibn Muḥammad al-Maqqarī (d. 1631 or 1632) put it, "unique in her time" (5:336). Certainly we see in Ibn Zaydūn's early poetic descriptions of her traces of this dual attitude of familiarity and adulation. Although it is not easy to date his love poetry for her—except in the most general way—the following verses probably represent an early expression of his feelings for her (*Dīwān*, ed. ʿAbd al-ʿAzīm,169):

Although in years you may be kin to the crescent moon
in beauty you exceed the moon at full.
As for there being one who might never be reached
because it is so far away,
My motives will allow me to engage your passion, so that
I will no longer have a care.
So say to passion "Run free!"
the arena of my heart is wide open.

Though he begins the poem by comparing her to the cold and distant moon in the sky, by the end their passion has become one, sporting together in the playing field of his heart.

But if this period was a heady time for Wallādah, it was even more so for her lover Ibn Zaydūn, who now emerged from obscurity into prominence among the men of position in Cordoba. There would be one last attempt to install a caliph from the Umayyad family, the unfortunately ill-qualified Hishām al-Muʿtadd. Although the Cordovan officials gave him their allegiance in June 1027, he was living far to the East, in exile in Alpuente, and he did not appear to claim his patrimony until late in 1029. Once installed, he proceeded to appoint a vizier, Ḥakam Ibn Saʿīd, whose arrogance and high-handedness alienated all the urban notables, including most especially Ibn Zaydūn's grandfather and guardian. Once al-Muʿtadd and his vizier were, inevitably, deposed (in 1031), Ibn Zaydūn joined a coalition of officials, led by the former vizier Ibn Jahwār (d. 1043), in declaring the caliphate to be at an end and Cordoba to an independent city governed by its own inhabitants. Eventually Ibn Jahwār would become the de facto ruler, but he always maintained the formality of governing in the name of a *shūrā*, or council. Ibn Zaydūn became his right-hand man, his chief minister. He briefly also served Cordoba as supervisor of the Christian and Jewish minorities in the city, but his main occupation eventually involved serving as Ibn Jahwār's ambassador to the other emerging city-states on the Peninsula, including Granada and Valencia, as well as Seville and Badajoz closer to home.

During this period, subsequent to 1031, Ibn Zaydūn's relationship with Wallādah became more complex. There are a number of different versions of what happened between them, but whatever the initial cause, at some point Wallādah became infatuated with Abū ʿĀmir Ibn ʿAbdūs, a rival minister in the employ of Ibn Jahwār. Either before or after this, the two former lovers exchanged insulting verses and Ibn Zaydūn ended up by composing a famous invective he sent to Ibn ʿAbdūs that also manages to disparage Wallādah (*Dīwān*, ed. ʿAbd al-ʿAzīm,196):

Be deferential to Wallādah, such a prize for the collector!
If only she knew the difference between a veterinarian (*baytār*) and a perfumier (*ʿattār*).
They say: "Abū ʿĀmir now dances attendance on her."
I say: "The moth has drawn near to the fire."
They seek to insult me by saying: "He has become your successor
with the one you love," but that's no insult.
She was a tasty mouthful that we took the sweetest parts of,
and we left the rest for the mouse.

Ibn ʿAbdūs was well known by the pet name "Mouse," and here Ibn Zaydūn uses it to cruel effect. About this same time, Ibn Zaydūn intensified his attack on the lovers by composing an elegant letter he also sent to Ibn ʿAbdūs as though from Wallādah in order to stir up trouble between them. He says, in her name, that she has just been visited by a lady who praised Ibn ʿAbdūs to the skies—in order to excite her affection for him—but that she realizes the go-between would not have been so generous in her praise were she not an old lover of his, anxious to foist her discarded sweetheart off on Wallādah. But she, Wallādah, knows him for what he is, including, among other insults, a hideous deformed fool with a stutter and bad breath. The first part of the letter, containing the go-between's praise, is a veritable catalogue of learned allusions to famous Arab poets and heroes from Islamic history and classical antiquity, while the second half is a treasure trove of rare terms, unusual proverbs and poetic quotations. It is no wonder that the great fourteenth-century scholar Ibn Nubātah (d. 984 or 985) decided to devote an entire lengthy commentary to unraveling the network of references. The letter, of course, may have functioned in its context as an indirect compliment to Wallādah's learning (as well as heightening the impact of the enumeration of Ibn ʿAbdūs's defects), but to later generations it became a tool for teaching students the knowledge necessary for someone aspiring to obtain an advanced education.

We do not know the immediate impact of the poetic exchanges or the letter, but Ibn Zaydūn by the beginning of the 1040s found himself out of favor with Ibn Jahwār and, sometime after October 1040 he was imprisoned for almost a year and a half by a corrupt judge on a charge of helping defraud the heir of a man who, it has been suggested, was one of Ibn ʿAbdūs's freedmen. After Ibn Zaydūn escaped from his confinement, he addressed a letter to his old teacher Ibn Aflaḥ that gives details of the episode and describes at length the harsh conditions of his incarceration. He tells his old friend that the cause of his troubles was passion (*hawā*), and this may be an indirect allusion to some personal vendetta involving Ibn ʿAbdūs and Wallādah. But he also says that the immediate reason for his decision to escape was the reception of a letter from someone he thought was a friend, condemning him for what he had done and blaming him for causing his own troubles. It may not be too much of a leap to connect this answer to the other letter he sent that survives from this episode. This is the so-called *al-Risālah al-jiddiyyah* (The Serious Letter) that he sent to Ibn Jahwār begging for his forgiveness. This letter, like *al-Risālah al-hazliyyah*, was considered a masterpiece of the epistolary art and was, like the latter, the subject of a lengthy commentary in the fourteenth century, this time by Ibn Nubātah's colleague Khalīl ibn Aybak al-Ṣafadī (ca. 1297-1363). *Al-Risālah al-jiddiyyah* is, similar to its counterpart, a massive display of learned erudition, but in this case all the allusions are to either *Qur'ānic* material or great Arab poets in the traditional mold, mostly from the Preislamic period, so the tone of the work (entirely aside from its subject matter) is quite different from *al-Risālah al-hazliyyah*, implying an attitude of sober self-analysis and restraint. But it is hardly a work solely about apology and supplication. It also implies, frequently, that Ibn Zaydūn feels he was acting during this period as a faithful executor of Ibn Jahwār's wishes—he was merely following orders. This justification does not conform well with the actual details of the charge that landed him in jail, which suggests that he was reminding Ibn Jahwār that what had happened was a cover for something else, perhaps retaliation for something he had done while carrying out a commission for Ibn Jahwār.

Ibn Zaydūn probably escaped from prison in early 1043. He may have remained for some time in hiding in the environs of Cordoba, before eventually proceeding to Seville, where he was warmly welcomed by the newly installed ruler of the city, al-Muʿtadid (d. 1068). It is certainly to this period that another of his letters, *al-Risālah al-bakriyyah*, may be dated. It is probably also the time (or shortly before this) when his three most famous love poems—"*al-Lāmiyyah*" (The Poem Rhyming in the consonant "L"), "*al-Qāfiyyah*" (The Poem Rhyming in the consonant "Q"), and "*al-Nūniyyah*" (*The Poem Rhyming in the consonant "N"*)—were composed. Though it is impossible to date these poems with precision, they all share a powerful sense of nostalgia for the past, and are concerned in one way or another with leave-taking and farewell, which suggests a connection with the poet's departure from his birthplace for the city of Seville.

None of the poems mention Wallādah by name, but commentators have traditionally associated all of them with her. Of the three, "*al-Lāmiyyah*" contains material that may be most closely identified with the precise circumstances of Ibn Zaydūn's personal life. It begins with lines using very legalistic terminology, which suggests an affiliation with the charges against Ibn Zaydūn and his quick and irregular trial (*Dīwān*, ed. ʿAbd al-ʿAẓīm, 187):

Truly despair of you has cut all hope short
 and your unjust accusation blocks any defense.
That envious man has whispered untruths concerning me,
 and then you gave him—in a very public way—what he asked.
You find the slanderous pretenses of my enemies pleasing
 and you are deceived by their fabricated falsehoods.
You have turned toward them—concerning me—the face of acceptance
 and your gladdened joy repays them.
I will never cease to keep the claims of passion alive, preserved,
 just as I have always done.

Here, the beloved is defined by her inconstancy to her lover and the change from a state of desire to indifference or even active hostility to her former sweetheart, which is brought on by the untrue insinuations of another man. This parallels very closely the reports of the love triangle between Ibn Zaydūn, Wallādah, and Ibn ʿAbdūs, and—if it does refer to the trial—conforms to events surrounding his imprisonment as well (an unjust accusation based on an untrue representation of the case). But more importantly for the development of the lover's persona in Ibn Zaydūn's other poems, the lover himself is depicted (in line 5) as unrelentingly steadfast, unwavering in his loyalty and faithfulness (as opposed to the celebration of his passion, which in earlier Arabic love poetry would have taken pride of place, over and above the value of fidelity).

This value of loyalty is emphasized in the subsequent lines as well. Then, suddenly it turns to depict the situation when the poet, as lover, ventures to express a criticism of the beloved to her face:

Whatever blame I brandish at you
 you attire yourself with different kinds of excuses.
As though you were seeking to contend with the scholasticians
 or had been given an understanding of the art of disputation.
If you wished, you could revert to freedom of action,
 and return to that initial nature.

Here, there is of course (perhaps a somewhat grudging) a recognition of the intellectual capacity of the beloved, consistent with the character of Wallādah as she is constructed in *al-Risālah al-hazliyyah*, with its many learned allusions. But the poet's language wavers uncertainly between language appropriate to warfare and language appropriate to theological disputation, especially Muʿtazilism (a religious orientation that strongly endorses free will). In the end this inability to control his framing of the conflict (Is his criticism a hostile attack on the beloved or a rule-bound and therefore ultimately unthreatening debate?) seems to lead the poet to the conclusion that the only solution to his unhappiness is to break off his relations with his lady and leave:

My salutations to you, the salutations of farewell,
 farewell to a passion that has died before its time.
And it is not by choice that I would forget you
 but I am one subject to others' dictates, not a hero.

These lines, in their masterful rhetorical parallelism and balance, are frequently quoted in Arabic literary histories and stand on their own. But if they were actually written in the aftermath of Ibn Zaydūn's desperate escape from jail, his flight from Cordoba, and his realization that his passion for Wallādah was hopeless, this would add to their poignance. Certainly, they dramatize the poet's failure, under the pressure of circumstance, to maintain his declaration of unswerving devotion to his love.

The impact of the *qāfiyyah* may also be better appreciated by placing it in the context of Ibn Zaydūn's spectacular fall from power and his forced departure from his natal city. Despite its brevity (15 lines), it has become a far more famous poem than the *lāmiyyah* and it was the Ibn Zaydūn poem chosen by Arthur Arberry in his anthology containing the most significant poems in Arabic literature.

The poem begins where "*al-Lāmiyyah*" left off, with the poet nostalgically recalling an idyllic past, to which he has already bidden farewell (*Dīwān*, ed. ʿAbd al-ʿAẓīm, 139):

Full of longing, I remember you as you were in al-Zahrā'
the horizon unfettered and the earth before our eyes clear and unmuddied.

The reference to al-Zahrā' is particularly evocative. The feminine form of a word in Arabic that means "most shining, resplendent," it was the name bestowed upon the palace complex built in Cordoba at the height of Umayyad rule (in the tenth century) by its most powerful caliph, ʿAbd al-Raḥmān III al-Naṣr. It was reported to have taken more than ten years to complete and to have cost something in the neighborhood of 400,000 *dīnārs* {the Umayyad's gold coin). It was sacked and at least partially destroyed in the Berber attacks on the city in 1010 and 1012, but its final destruction was carried out under the orders of Wallādah's father, al-Mustakfī. By the time Ibn Zaydūn reached adulthood, it was largely uninhabited, and historical works are replete with stories of famous individuals roaming the ruined buildings and deserted gardens, and using them as a fitting setting for mourning the vanished glories of the past and marveling at the ravages of time and fate.

Since Wallādah's father was the final architect of Zahrā''s destruction it might be natural (and full of irony) to associate her with the place, but it is important to remember that she is never explicitly named here. The beloved—whoever she may be—also begins to be absorbed, as the lines proceed, into the physical features of the garden and she loses her human identity:

The meadow smiles, revealing its silver water
just as you used to loosen the collar fastenings from the hollow of your throat.
This is a day like our days of pleasure that have fled, we lingered in them as
thieves while destiny slept.
We amused ourselves, watching the flowers that so attract the eye
where the dew wells up, until the necks bend over.
As though their eye-like pistils, when they see how I cannot sleep
weep for my affliction, until the tears well up, overflowing.

The poet here begins by personifying the meadow, describing it as "smiling" in a human way, as the rippling winds pull back the overhanging grasses in half circles, like smiles, to reveal the hidden pools of water shining in its center. But not content with this, he directly links this image to his own beloved by comparing this action of the wind on the meadow to her as she undid the buttons fastening her bodice tight around the base of her throat, no doubt smiling at him as she did it. In a related figurative maneuver, the poet in the next section of the poem singles out the flowers, telling how the lovers spent their time staring at them with eyes that resembled the centers of the flowers (in Arabic, the pistil of the flower is called its "eye"). This creates a sort of mirroring effect, eyes gazing into eyes, which makes to easier to accept the personification technique then used to turn the dewdrops dotting the flower petals and collecting in the center into tears the flowers are weeping at the sight of the lover's unhappiness. The blending of human and nature in these lines is reinforced by the consistent resort to a grammatical license common in Arabic that allows a writer to use the generic definite article ("the") instead of the specific possessive pronouns. Thus it is "the" necks that bend over in line 5, overwhelmed by the weight of the dew/tears, not "our" necks or "their" necks. This leaves the reader free to interpret it either way, the necks of the human lovers, or the stems of the flowers, or both. Similarly, in the next line it is "the" tears, rather than "their" tears or "my" tears, which rise up. The use of the definite article allows the poet to delicately suggest a unity of action among all the figures involved in the scene, crossing the boundary between the human and the inanimate. This sustained use of pathetic fallacy (a rhetorical strategy where the writer attributes human feeling to the natural world surrounding him) to enliven the poem is seldom encountered—with the exception of the work of Ibn Zaydūn's fellow Andalusian, the nature poet Ibn al-Khafājah—in the Arabic literary tradition before the nineteenth century and the rise of poets (mainly in Egypt and Lebanon) influenced by Romanticism. It takes the implicit parallelisms drawn between the natural and the human world in much earlier Arabic poetry a significant step further.

Here, use of the technique allows the poet to distance the trauma of his separation, to fill the past with life, as it were. But in the end his innate intellectual honesty causes him to acknowledge in the last line of the poem (as he had done as well in "*al-Lāmiyyah*") that the faithfulness he has so scrupulously observed in preserving his love can be instantly brought to nothing, if the beloved does not honor the compact with equal commitment, which she does not.

The theme of separation, farewell and loss—as opposed to faithfulness and loyalty—also forms a central concern of the poem that has been considered for many centuries to be Ibn Zaydūn's masterpiece, the *nūniyyah*. Yet the *nūniyyah* is also very different in its impact from its predecessors.

The poem is quite long for an Arabic love poem, fifty lines, and its length gives the opportunity for complex effects to be developed, which in turn has evoked complex responses articulated in the many interpretations that have been given to the poem, both by Arab and Western critics. It would be difficult to summarize all these insights and do justice to every one. Adding to the web of complexity, Ibn Zaydūn himself was probably inspired by a much earlier poem in the same rhyme and meter, composed in the ninth century by the Syro-Iraqi poet al-Walīd ibn ʿUbayd al-Buḥturī (821-897 or 898). This would make the *nūniyyah*—whatever else it may be—a kind of commentary, or response, to the earlier poet's work.

Al-Buḥturī has always been highly admired by devotees of traditional Arabic poetry, and he was regarded in his time and for subsequent generations as the supreme representative of the school of poetry that avoided too much reliance on ornate and showy rhetorical devices in their poems. Ibn Zaydūn has been frequently characterized as "the Buḥturī of al-Andalus," emphasizing the natural and straightforward style he chose to use. So it is probably not without significance that a connection was made between these two poems. Certainly, whether Ibn Zaydūn's choice of rhyme was consciously modeled on al-Buḥturī or not (and there have been some who have been unpersuaded that Ibn Zaydūn is contrafacting his predecessor), he used it very effectively in dramatizing the relationship between him and the beloved (who is, again, not named as Wallādah, but conventionally assumed to be so). Many different categories of words in Arabic end in the consonant "n," and al-Buḥturī ranges freely among them in choosing his rhyme words. Ibn Zaydūn, on the other hand, limits himself in his poem to three categories of n-rhyme words: verbs in the "we" form, and the possessive pronoun "our," and the object pronoun "us." Thus the end of the line, the rhyme word, emphasizes over and over again the now-lost unity of the lovers, as their actions in the past are reported in the we form, and things are shown as being done to them as a pair, and any things they once possessed are possessed by them both. This grammatical usage is particularly effective in underscoring the overt theme of much of the poem, which is—as in the *lāmiyyah* and the *qāfiyyah*"—the separation of the lovers in the present, contrasted with their intense togetherness in the past. The emphasis on "we" and "us" may help to explain why, when the *nūniyyah* was later contrafacted by other poets, it was frequently the inspiration for elegies, poems that mourn the loss of someone close to the poet.

Along with this morphological dimension of the poem, the *nūniyyah* also exhibits structural features and repetitions that tie the lines of the poem together and heighten its impact as a finished work of art and an homage to the most idealized formalism of the Arabic literary tradition. They also create a sense of balance and order, as though the emotional experience described in the poem is being recalled after a considerable period of time has passed. There is, for instance, its use of antitheses, like black and white, far and near, high and low, without necessarily resolving them into a synthesis. The individual lines are also strongly broken in most cases by the caesura required in traditional Arabic poetry, without allowing any enjambment. Even more noticeable is that the poem observes in general a kind of chiastic structure, or ring composition, which is especially marked by the placement of the homage to the beloved at the very center of the poem. Such placement is found not infrequently in earlier panegyric poems, where the patron is described (or the first mention of his name occurs) in the central line of the poem. By this time in Arabic poetic tradition, an expectation had developed that there might be a connection implicitly drawn by the poet between his relationship to the beloved mentioned in the *nasīb* of the formal panegyric *qaṣīdah*, and his actual emotional relationship to the patron who was the focus of the rest of the poem. Ibn Zaydūn, however, innovated in the *nūniyyah* by treating his beloved like a patron, and placing her description at the middle of the poem. This extreme idealization of the beloved, it should be remarked, differs significantly from the actual course of his love affair with Wallādah, where the two engaged in mutual invective and Wallādah was hardly the shy, retiring beloved, so easily idealized, that we find in Dante's Beatrice or Petrarch's Laura. Certainly, Arabic literary tradition also abounded in examples of quite different treatments of love affairs. It has never been adequately determined—or seriously explored—why Ibn Zaydūn chose to depict his love relationship in the way he did, so different from the real relationship with Wallādah. Nor has there been any consistent attempt to compare Ibn Zaydūn's depiction of the love relationship with that of his slightly older Cordovan contemporary Abū Muḥammad ʿAlī ibn Aḥmad Ibn Ḥazm (994-1064), who attempted an ambitious theoretical examination of love in his *Ṭawq al-ḥamāmah* (*The Dove's Neck Ring*) that draws extensively on the Greek philosophical heritage—an element that does not appear to be present in the formulation of love implicit in Ibn Zaydūn's poetry.

There are several alternative chronologies for the composition of Ibn Zaydūn's love poems (though all agree that the three discussed above were written around this date). With his arrival in Seville, however, we enter more secure ground. Al-Muʿtadid welcomed him warmly, and Ibn Zaydūn showed his gratitude by composing several panegyrics for his host, including one that celebrated his marriage to the daughter of the ruler of Denia, which took place between al-Muʿtadid's accession in late 1041 and the death of the bride's father in 1044—most likely in 1042, when Ibn Zaydūn was newly arrived at court. The poem itself has a light-hearted tone that does not prevent it from being conventional in the extreme and forms a sharp contrast to the intensity and sobriety of his love poetry from this period. Ibn Zaydūn first congratulates his host on the good fortune he has brought to Seville by this auspicious marriage to a lady with illustrious kin, who herself resembles a star falling from the sky. He then goes on to say that this should be no surprise, since time and fortune respond generously to al-Muʿtadid's requests. He needs only say "I would like this," and fortune responds by saying: "Here it is!" If fate is always ready to help al-Muʿtadid, however, his new status as a husband will perhaps not allow him to reciprocate by being attentive to his old friends. The poet gently warns him (*Dīwān*, ed. ʿAbd al-ʿAzīm, 438):

This will be a week of intimacy that will introduce me to loneliness
knowing that during it I will not see you.
I will be tormented although I may know that
you are in bliss, but there it is.
But shouldn't I give thanks as long as you live, after
your hands have filled mine with the things of this world?

This poetry of graceful compliment, urbane friendship and conviviality will become very much a hallmark Ibn Zaydūn's work during the next decade as it fulfills more and more the role of valuable adjunct to his diplomatic missions and his cultivation of relationships at the courts where he serves.

One instance that may be seen as running counter to this pattern is his elegy for his childhood friend Abū Bakr Ibn Dhakwān who died young in 1043. This poem does at times cross the boundary of conventionality to express deeper emotion. At some point either before or shortly after this event, Ibn Zaydūn was able to effectuate a reconciliation with Ibn Jahwār and he had been allowed to return to Cordoba. The aged ruler was already close to death, however, and 1043 he died, to be succeeded by his son, Abū 'l-Walīd Ibn Jahwār, who was Ibn Zaydūn's good friend. The elegy for Ibn Dhakwān mentions all three events, gracefully combining the sorrow the poet (and those around him) feel at the loss of Ibn Dhakwān with their grief for Ibn Jahwār the elder. The poem concludes by declaring that what will rescue the mourners from the burden of their sorrow is the knowledge that Abū 'l-Walīd stands ready to take over his father's position, and to follow Ibn Dhakwān in his example of kindness and generosity. The poet begins by turning to address the absent Ibn Dhakwān, emphasizing his separation from the other mourners, and his unique ability to recognize how the presence of his friend can compensate for their loss (*Dīwān*, ed. ʿAbd al-ʿAẓīm, 530):

So, if a fate must overtake you—after having been so long safe from it—to
everything once safe comes a time when it is lost.
A perceptive person will guard those whom you have left behind
in preserving what you sought to preserve, not falling short.
The minister (*wazīr*) Abū 'l-Walīd has undertaken to comfort them
indeed the minister is well known to act in things like this.
A ruler (*malik*) whose nature is loyalty, who has never,
in friendship, breached a trust.

The sentiments expressed in this poem would seem to represent Ibn Zaydūn's optimistic hope at this time for a rosy future, and, indeed, this does seem to have been the case for many years.

Ibn Zaydūn became Abū 'l-Walīd's chief diplomatic emissary, even more than he had been for his father, well rewarded for his efforts, and he continued, throughout the rest of 1040s, to travel throughout the entire breadth and width of al-Andalus in the service of Cordoba. But in 1048, when Ibn Zaydūn would have been in his mid-forties (and thus by the standards of the time well advanced in years), the family of the Banū Dhakwān rose in rebellion against Abū 'l-Walīd. The rebellion was put down, and the head of the clan at that time, Abū ʿAlī, was imprisoned for the rest of his life (until 1058). Although Ibn Zaydūn disclaimed any involvement in the rebellion—and even wrote a poem to that effect—suspicion dogged him. So, after exploring and abandoning plans to stay in Valencia during one of his diplomatic missions, he opened negotiations with al-Muʿtadid through an old friend, Abū ʿĀmir Ibn Maslamah, now working for al-Muʿtadid in Seville. He followed this up with correspondence he exchanged with al-Muʿtadid himself. This move was conducted in a much more leisurely fashion, with extensive negotiations involved, and suggests that Ibn Zaydūn had learned much from his unfortunate experience in the early 1040s.

In mid-1049, Ibn Zaydūn moved for good to Seville, and shortly after his arrival there presented his host with a carefully crafted panegyric glorifying his house, his ancestry and his exploits. It is one of Ibn Zaydūn's longest poems at over eighty verses, and begins with a lengthy traditional *naṣīb*. The praise for the ʿAbbādid family and al-Muʿtadid himself, is introduced—as is customary—at approximately the mid-point of the poem:

At the house of ʿAbbād I alight, where my aspirations
are fastened, where the mountains rise high.
Descendents of the Preislamic Lakhmid kings, they tower
above their fellows like hills overtop the valleys.
A people whose heirs can be numbered, in comparison
to the sons of Mundhir Māʾ al-Samāʾ, as even greater.

A house whose support beams the shooting stars in their
orbits would love to be.

Then a few lines later, he turns to describe al-Muʿtadid himself:

He is a king whose majestic characteristics will seduce everyone
whose number cannot be counted.

The way Ibn Zaydūn structures this more traditional panegyric can be usefully compared with his longer love poems like the *nūniyyah.*

When Ibn Zaydūn arrived in Seville this time, he also met and formed an attachment to al-Muʿtadid's second son, al-Muʿtamid Ibn ʿAbbād (1039-1095), who was nine or ten years old by this time. At this time, al-Muʿtamid was not slated to inherit his father's position, but he had already shown himself a precocious poet, and Ibn Zaydūn became his instructor in the art. Numerous poems they exchanged survive from this time, and they are testimony to the affectionate relationship between the two, which lasted until Ibn Zaydūn's death. Notable in particular are the riddle poems describing different species of birds that the boy and his teacher exchanged with Abū Ṭālib Muḥammad ibn ʿAlī 'l-Makkī (d. 996) that are found at the end of Ibn Zaydūn's *Dīwān*.

Relations with al-Muʿtadid were less smooth than they would be with his son. Despite his generosity and his cultivated appreciation of literature and learning, al-Muʿtadid was also known for his irascible temper and frequent rages. In one of these he killed al-Muʿtamid's older brother Ismāʿīl, and so the second son was suddenly elevated to the position of heir apparent. But he always lived thereafter in fear of his father. Ibn Zaydūn, too, was said to have expressed relief at al-Muʿtadid's death, saying that the experience of living with him was like clinging to the ears of a lion—one knew that whether one held on or let go, one's life would be in danger. This mistrust was exacerbated by the fact that, on occasion al-Muʿtadid seemed to encourage rival ministers and literary figures at the court to challenge Ibn Zaydūn and involve themselves in quarrels with him. But matters were always smoothed over, and Ibn Zaydūn continued until the end of his life to help al-Muʿtadid achieve what appeared to be his ultimate goal: the consolidation of rule in the Peninsula in ʿAbbādid hands.

Back in Cordoba, in 1064 Abū 'l-Walīd decided to turn over most of his royal duties to his two sons, which turned out to be a disastrous move. A rivalry grew between the young men and al-Muʿtadid was able to encourage the younger, ʿAbd al-Mālik, to assassinate his father's able chief minister, Ibn al-Saqqā'. In the ensuring disorder, the ruler of Toledo, al-Ma'mūn Ibn Dhī 'l-Nūn (d. ca. 1074), decided to take Cordoba, and besieged the city. Al-Muʿtadid, by this time approaching death, entered into secret negotiations with al-Ma'mūn and promised him a free hand with Cordoba in exchange for other territory. But then, in reply to an appeal from ʿAbd al-Mālik and the people of Cordoba in 1069, al-Muʿtamid (who had by this time succeeded his father) rode to attack the Toledan troops. As soon as al-Ma'mūn's army was defeated, however, al-Muʿtamid doubled crossed ʿAbd al-Mālik, deposing him and taking the throne for himself. Both sons, and their ailing father Abū 'l-Walīd Ibn Jahwār, were exiled from the city.

It has been said that Ibn Zaydūn participated in the planning for this plot against his old friend's family. At any rate, he accompanied al-Muʿtamid into Cordoba and in his last days was able to return to his childhood haunts and see once again his old friends in the city. While the poet and his protégé were enjoying their triumph in Cordoba, news arrived that disorders had broken out in Seville. Although by this time Ibn Zaydūn was an old man nearing seventy, and ill as well, his rivals in al-Muʿtamid's entourage encouraged the prince to send him back to quell the rioting. Ibn Zaydūn was successful in his mission but the strain and exertion took its toll, and he died in Seville at the beginning of May 1071. His son, Abū Bakr (d. 1091), had remained with al-Muʿtamid in Cordoba, and would assume many of his father's duties in the ʿAbbādid state.

REFERENCES

ʿAlī ʿAbd al-ʿAẓīm, *Ibn Zaydūn* (Cairo: Dār al-Kitāb al-ʿArabī, 1967);

Shawqī Ḍayf, *Ibn Zaydūn* (Cairo: Dār al-Maʿārif, 1967);

Raymond Ferrin, "The *Nūniyya* of Ibn Zaydūn: a Structural and Thematic Analysis," *Journal of Arabic Literature* 34, 1-2 (2003): 82-106;

Th. Emil Homerin, "In the Gardens of al-Zahrā': Love Echoes in a Poem by Ibn Zaydūn," in *The Shaping of an American Islamic Discourse: a Memorial to Fazlur Rahman*, ed. Earle H. Waugh and Frederick M. Denny (Atlanta: Scholars Press, 1998), 215-231;

Abū 'l-Ḥasan ʿAlī Ibn Bassām al-Shantarinī, *al-Dhakīrah fī maḥāsin ahl al-Jazīrah*, ed. Iḥsān ʿAbbās, 1, 1 (Beirut: Dār al-Thaqāfah, 1975);

Salma Khadra Jayyusi, "Andalusi Poetry in the Golden Period," in *The Legacy of Muslim Spain*, ed. by Salma Khadra Jayyusi, (Leiden: E.J. Brill, 1990), 1:317-366;

Sieglinde Lug, *Poetic Technique and Conceptual Elements in Ibn Zaydun's Love Poetry*, (Washington, D.C.: University Press of America, 1982);

Aḥmad ibn Muḥammad al-Maqqarī, *Nafḥ al-ṭīb min ghuṣn al-Andalus al-raṭīb*, 10 vols. (Cairo: Maṭbaʿat al-Saʿādah, 1949);

Devin Stewart, "Ibn Zaydūn," in *The Literature of al-Andalus*, ed. Maria Rosa Menocal, et al. (Cambridge: Cambridge University Press, 1990), 306-318.

ʿAbd al-Qāhir al-Jurjānī

(d. ca. 1081)

JOCELYN SHARLET

University of California at Davis

WORKS

Asrār al-balāghah;

al-'Awāmil al-mi'ah al-naḥwiyyah fī usūl 'ilm al-'Arabiyyah;

Bayān al-'arūḍ;

Dalā'il al-i'jāz;

Durj al-durar fī tafsīr al-Qur'ān al-'Aẓīm;

Kitāb al-jumal fī 'l-naḥw;

Kitāb al-miftāḥ fī 'l-ṣarf;

Kitāb al-muqtaṣad fī sharḥ al-īḍaḥ;

al-Risalah al-shāfiyyah fī 'l-i'jaz;

al-'Umdah.

Editions

Asrār al-balāgha, ed. Maḥmūd Muḥammad Shākir (Jiddah: Dār al-Madanī; Cairo: Maktabat al-Khānjī, 1991);

al-'Awāmil al-mi'ah al-naḥwiyyah fī usūl 'ilm al-'Arabiyyah [also called *Mi'at 'Amil*], ed. al-Badrāwī Zahrān (Cairo: Dār al-Maʿārif, 1983);

Bayān al-'arūḍ, ed. Qays ʿAṭṭār (Qum: Intishārāt Saʿīd ibn Jubayr, 1996);

Dalā'il al-i'jāz, ed. Maḥmūd Muḥammad Shākir (Jiddah: Dār al-Madanī; Cairo: Maktabat al-Khānjī, 1992);

Durj al-durar fī tafsīr al-Qur'ān al-'Aẓīm, ed. Talʿat Ṣalaḥ and Muḥammad Adīb Shakkūr (Amman: Dār al-Fikr, 2008);

Kitāb al-jumal fī 'l-naḥw, ed. Yusrī ʿAbd al-Ghanī ʿAbd Allāh (Beirut: Dār al-Kutub al-ʿIlmiyyah, 1990);

Kitāb al-miftāḥ fī 'l-ṣarf, ed. ʿAlī Tawfīq Ḥamad (Beirut: Mu'assassat al-Risālah, 1987);

al-Mukhtar min dawāwīn al-Mutanabbī wa 'l-Buḥturī wa-Abī Tammām in *Tarā'if adabiyyah*, ed. ʿAbd al-ʿAzīz al-Maymūnī (Cairo: Lajnat al-Ta'līf wa 'l-Tarjamah wa 'l-Nashr 1937), 195-305;

Kitāb al-muqtaṣad fī sharḥ al-īḍaḥ [by Abū ʿAlī ibn Aḥmad ibn ʿAbd al-Ghaffār], ed. Kāẓim Baḥr al-Murjān (Baghdad: Dār al-Rashīd li 'l-Nashr, 1982);

al-Risālah al-shāfiyyah fī 'l-i'jaz, ed. ʿAbd al-Qādir Ḥusayn (Cairo: Dār al-Fikr al-ʿArabī, 1998);
al-'Umdah: kitāb fī 'l-taṣrīf, ed. al-Badrawī Zahrān (Cairo: Dār al-Maʿārif, 1988).

Translations

Die Geheimnisse der Wortkunst (Asrār al-balāga) des 'Abdalqāhir al-Curcānī, tr. Hellmut Ritter. Bibliotheca Islamica, Band 19 (Wiesbaden: In Kommission bei F. Steiner, 1959).

ʿAbd al-Qāhir ibn ʿAbd al-Raḥmān Abū Bakr al-Jurjānī was born in Jurjān in northeastern Iran. He remained there and studied with Abū 'l-Ḥusayn Muḥammad ibn al-Ḥusayn ibn ʿAbd al-Wārith al-Fārisī. At this time, the Ziyarid dynasty ruled Jurjān, mostly under the sway of the Seljuks to the West or the Ghaznavids to the East. Al-Jurjānī was affiliated with the Shafiʿi school of law and Ashʿarī theology and was known as a scholar of the Arabic language. Unlike many scholars of his time, al-Jurjānī is not known to have traveled extensively in his professional life, or to have made extensive use of court patronage to support his work. As a scholar living and working in Iran in Arabic, al-Jurjānī was by no means unusual at this time. Scholars from this region, many of whom may have been ethnically Persian, played an important role in the development of Arabic scholarly production in a range of fields. He died in 471 or 474 Islamic Era/1078 or 1081 C.E.

Al-Jurjānī is best known for his book on rhetoric, *Asrār al-balāghah* (The Secrets of Rhetoric) and his book on the miraculous nature of the *Qur'ān* as verbal expression that cannot be imitated by mankind, *Dalā'il al-i'jāz* (The Indications of the Inimitability [of the *Qur'ān*]), although a number of other works by him have survived. Although these two works have ensured al-Jurjānī an important place in the history of Arabic theology and literary criticism, it is worth noting that Brockelmann's bibliography shows that his work on more technical aspects of language, the *al-'Awāmil al-mi'ah* or *Mi'at 'Amil*, was far more popular, probably due to its usefulness for more general instruction, judging by the numerous manuscripts, commentaries, and versifications of this work. Al-Jurjānī is particularly well-known for his original and insightful treatment of the intersection between these two scholarly projects. Al-Jurjānī stands out among the dozen or so major authors of works on medieval Arabic poetics as a unique figure who offered original and systematic approaches to issues that were dealt with in only vague terms in the work of earlier scholars.

For al-Jurjānī, Muslims not only have the option to use reason to analyze the inimitable quality of the *Qur'ān* as discourse, they are obliged to do so. For it is this inimitable quality that defines the excellence of the discourse in the *Qur'ān*, and the excellence of *Qur'ānic* discourse is the main proof that Muḥammad was a prophet. Al-Jurjānī's conclusions about the inimitability of the *Qur'ān* are intertwined with his conclusions about the use of fine discourse in the human sphere, so it is necessary to explore his theological views in order to investigate his literary criticism. His approach to discourse was a reaction to the work of scholars who emphasized the distinction between meaning and verbal expression.

The dualism between meaning and verbal expression took shape in the work of ʿAbd Allāh ibn Muslim Ibn Qutaybah (828-889), an earlier scholar of religion and literature. It appears in the famous statement by the scholar Abū ʿUthman ʿAmr ibn Baḥr al-Jāḥiẓ (d. 868 or 869) that meanings are to be found cast in the road. In this statement, al-Jāḥiẓ is saying that meaning is not relevant to the quality of discourse, which is instead defined exclusively by verbal expression. For al-Jāḥiẓ, meaning is like the gold used by a goldsmith, whose skill is evaluated by his work on the gold, not by the gold itself. Al-Jāḥiẓ was affiliated with Muʿtazilī theology, a movement that is known for using reason as a method in the study of theology. For Muʿtazilī theologians such as Qāḍī (Judge) ʿAbd al-Jabbār, to suggest that the *Qur'ān* is uncreated and eternal like God would imply that God's speech disrupts His essential unity. For such theologians, God's speech is viewed as an external attribute of God, not an aspect of His essential unity. As a result, these theologians asserted that the *Qur'ān* is the created, temporal speech of God, an attribute that is separate from His essential unity. ʿAbd al-

Jabbār expands on this idea of God's speech as an attribute that is separate from His essential unity. He views human discourse as verbal expression that is separate from thought and meaning. As a result, for ʿAbd al-Jabbār, verbal expression is divorced from the inner life of the speaker. According to his view, human discourse is related to the actual presence of that which is described in the world more than it is to the inner life of the speaker.

In contrast with these views, al-Jurjānī advocates a different perspective that is related to his affiliation with Ashʿarī theology. The Ashʿarī movement is related to the Muʿtazilī movement. Both movements involve using reason in theology, and the Ashʿarī movement was founded by a former Muʿtazilī. However, there is an important difference between the two movements that is central to understanding al-Jurjānī's approach to discourse in the *Qur'ān* and in the human sphere. Muʿtazilī theology emphasizes the unified essence of God as opposed to His attributes, including the *Qur'ān*. The Muʿtazilah therefore define the *Qur'ān* as God's created speech. As a result, the Muʿtazilī movement defines divine and human speech as separate from the thought and meaning that are used to produce it. For this movement, divine and human discourse relates more closely to that which they signify in the world than they do to the speaker's intended meaning. In contrast, Ashʿarī theology emphasizes that the *Qur'ān* is the uncreated, eternal speech of God. For Ashʿarī theologians like al-Jurjānī, God's speech is primarily the meaning that is part of His essence, and the verbal expression of the *Qur'ān* is a series of signs connecting mankind with this inner meaning. As a result, this movement, including al-Jurjānī, considers meaning and thought to be integrated with verbal expression, both in the *Qur'ān* and in human discourse. The modern scholar Margaret Larkin explains that for al-Jurjānī, "We may even go so far as to say that thought and expression are two sides of the same coin." (*Theology of Meaning*, 60) For al-Jurjānī, the miracle of God's speech as inimitable discourse cannot inhere in verbal expression to the exclusion of meaning, since the verbal expressions in the *Qur'ān* were present in the language before the revelation. Likewise, the miracle cannot inhere in the meaning of the *Qur'ān* alone, since if that were the case, it would be enough to simply state that Muḥammad (d. 632) is a prophet. Instead, al-Jurjānī views the miracle of God's speech and the more limited excellence of fine human discourse to be the result of the configuration of meaning and verbal expression, or *naẓm*. Since al-Jurjānī links verbal expression to thought and meaning in the speaker's mind, he views verbal expression not as signs of that which is described in the real world, but as expressions of the speaker's meanings, which are images of that which is in the real world. This theory of the configuration of discourse is a rejection of the distinction between meaning and verbal expression in the work of scholars such as Ibn Qutaybah, al-Jāḥiẓ, and Qāḍī ʿAbd al-Jabbār.

Al-Jurjānī's Ashʿarī theory of configuration of discourse in which meaning and verbal expression are linked has important implications for the relationship between a speaker and his audience, including the relationship between God and mankind as well as the relationship between a human speaker and his audience. If meaning and verbal expression are linked, the capacity of discourse to allow an audience to perceive a speaker's thought is foregrounded. This access to the speaker's meaning through verbal expression is crucial in the case of the *Qur'ān*, since it means that mankind has access to God's intended meaning about the ethical parameters of social order as they are elaborated in His speech. If intellectual and verbal activity are linked in discourse, then discourse is a way for a speaker to share his inner life, and a way for an audience to connect with the intellect of the speaker. As a result, al-Jurjānī's view of discourse suggests an interest in the subjectivity of a speaker and the possibility for an audience to connect with this subjectivity. In the contexts of divine and human speech, this possibility of connecting with the speaker's subjectivity through discourse is at least as important as the articulation of that subjectivity. That is, the importance of subjectivity in this cultural context is its role in relationships more than its role in individuality. This phenomenon shows how the articulation of individual identity is bound up with relationships.

The theologically-grounded fascination with the conjunction between the intellectual and verbal dimensions of communication is the defining feature of al-Jurjānī's work on rhetoric. While ordinary discourse combines meaning and verbal expression to connect an audience to a speaker, artistic discourse also includes the dimension of form or *sūrah*. In addition to meaning and thought, form foregrounds the intention of the speaker. As a result, form further emphasizes the articulation of individual subjectivity in and through discourse and the access of an audience to that subjectivity through discourse. In other words, form enhances the elaboration of individual subjectivity and especially the potential for individual subjectivity to contribute to relationships. The elaborate rhetoric that characterizes fine, aesthetic discourse in this period is not just about the intellectual prowess needed to produce it, but also the intellectual activity of deciphering it. Elaborate rhetoric is often identified with *badī'*, a term that varies from a type of metaphor to a range of figures of speech. The modern scholar Suzanne Stetkevych has suggested that the elaborate rhetoric of *badī'* is actually the obverse of interpretation or *ta'wīl*. (Abū Tammām, 8) This relationship between encoding meaning in elaborate rhetoric and decoding it in interpretation implies the social interaction of intellectual life. By emphasizing the intellectual dimension of discourse and fine discourse in particular, al-Jurjānī emphasizes the intellectual exchange that takes place in the encoding and decoding of meaning in elaborate rhetoric.

Al-Jurjānī's interest in the conjunction of thought and verbal expression in discourse shapes his approach to rhetorical devices. The use of elaborate rhetoric was a central issue in medieval Arabic cultural production for two reasons. First, the use of elaborate rhetoric and especially figurative language in the *Qur'ān* meant that analytic approaches were needed to articulate the meaning of scripture as an indication of the ethical parameters of social order. Persuasive explanations of figurative language could clarify these *Qur'ānic* passages and avoid the implication of multiple meanings in elaborate rhetoric. In particular, persuasive explanations of figurative language in the *Qur'ān* could avoid any confusion between God and man in anthropomorphic images. Analysis of elaborate rhetoric in the *Qur'ān* could point the way toward certainty about the meaning of the revelation. Second, mannerist development in medieval Arabic poetry led to conflicts about the validity of this mannerist expression. The analysis of elaborate rhetoric could better enable its consumers among the cultural elite to understand and enjoy this type of discourse. For al-Jurjānī, reason is not simply used to analyze figurative language as verbal expression. Instead, it is used to explore the intellectual activity that takes place in the use of elaborate rhetoric. This intellectual work is not a dry or technical activity for al-Jurjānī, but a source of pleasure. He explains that pleasant companionship for souls occurs when you move them from that which is concealed to that which is revealed, and bring them from that which is implicit to that which is explicit. (*Asrār* 121) In other words, listeners do not do this work just because they have to in order to make sense of elaborate expression. They do it because it is pleasing and engaging for them. The analytic approach to elaborate rhetoric had implications for the role of mannerist expression in social life. The opposition to mannerist change implied the priority of ancient Arabic poetry and, by extension, contemporary Arab identity in cultural production. Approval of mannerist change, which did not suggest opposition to ancient Arabic poetry, implied the shared and dynamic heritage of ancient Arabic poetry and mannerist poetry and, by extension, the shared and dynamic interaction of Arab and non-Arab, especially Persian identity in cultural production. Al-Jurjānī's insightful approaches to mannerist change contributed indirectly to the cultural integration of Arab and non-Arab, especially Persian heritage in Arabic poetry.

Al-Jurjānī's theory of configuration or *naẓm* should not be confused with ideas about organic unity of the text. Like other rhetoricians, al-Jurjānī focused his attention on the individual verse or short sequence of verses. The conjunction of meaning and verbal expression has important implications for the formal feature of segmentation in discourse. Segmented composition is not merely a superficial feature of verbal expression. Instead, segmented composition offers a multifaceted and comparative perspective on that which is described. For example, in the case of the short segments of poetry that are offered as examples in the rhetorical analysis of al-Jurjānī and other scholars, the segments of poetry may describe relationships of patronage or love. In poetry about patronage or love, segmented composition offers a multifaceted perspective on such relationships. Other segments may deal with the process of observation in the description of objects. In descriptive poetry, the segmented composition offers a multifaceted perspective on the process of observation. Al-Jurjānī's theory of configuration means that what may at first appear to be superficial, formal features are actually the configuration of the speaker's thought and meaning in verbal expression. Al-Jurjānī observes in his description of a figure that involves the enumeration of details, "I mean that you have two or more descriptions and you look at them one at a time and consider them one at a time... or that you look at one thing from more than one perspective." (*Asrār*, 166) In discussing a range of figures that segment meaning, he points out that "...they say the first look is foolish because you see the description as a whole, and then you see the details when you look again...." (*Asrār*, 160) While this theory is important for the study of fine discourse in general, it is particularly important in the context of medieval Arabic poetry, in which elaborate rhetoric was valorized. The theory of configuration therefore has an important implication for the use of fine discourse in social life. In medieval Arabic culture, the ability to produce, appreciate, and comment upon elaborate rhetoric in fine discourse was a measure of social status and a criterion for social mobility. If such elaborate rhetoric were merely external verbal expression related to that which is in the world, social status would be more about verbal art as a material craft rather than an intellectual pursuit. However, if such elaborate rhetoric is instead the product of the configuration of meaning, as images of the outside world in the mind of the speaker, as a process of thinking in language, then this measure of social worth is identified with intellectual acumen. Al-Jurjānī seems to be aware of the social implications of his approach to refined rhetoric. He explains, "Do you not see that none but those whose intellect and perspicacity raise them above the common class can truly understand this?" (*Asrār*, 94) He also asserts that not all those who seek knowledge of refined rhetoric can attain it, just as not all who seek entry into a ruler's presence are allowed in. (*Asrār*, 141) It is by understanding the role of configuration in God's discourse as a way of determining what makes it the finest discourse of all that al-Jurjānī suggests the role of configuration in human discourse and its use as a measure of social value.

The role of segmented discourse in al-Jurjānī's work is implicit, in the way he, like other critics, uses examples. In contrast, the role of approaches to figurative language in his work is explicit. In the context of divine discourse, understanding figurative language was important for several reasons. First, figurative language appears in divine discourse and so analyzing it is part of analyzing the inimitability of the *Qur'ān*. This inimitable quality of the *Qur'ān* is the main proof of Muḥammad's prophethood. The *Qur'ān* contains legal guidance for social order, so it is necessary to understand its exact meaning to determine this legal guidance. It includes figurative language, so it is necessary to interpret this language in a precise way to avoid multiple meanings of the law. The *Qur'ān* contains anthropomorphic descriptions of God. An analysis of figurative language is necessary to avoid any confusion between God and man. In the earliest discussions of figurative language in the *Qur'ān*, the term *majāz* seems to refer to something like the interpretation of any language that is not straightforward in one way or another. In the work of the scholar Ibn Qutaybah this term begins to refer to a range of non-straightforward uses of language rather than the interpretation of those uses of language. Later, the term was further emphasized as non-straightforward language in the opposition between *majāz* and *ḥaqīqah*, in which *ḥaqīqah*, which literally means reality itself, is used to refer to straightforward uses of language rather than reality itself. Early Arabic literary criticism deals with different categories of figurative language, but does not make extensive use of this concept of non-straightforward language in general. In contrast, al-Jurjānī organizes the appropriation of this concept from theology for the purpose of literary criticism. Al-Jurjānī recognizes the value of the concept of non-straightforward language in general as an overarching concept that includes the different types of figurative language in poetry, and that excludes types of expression that, though not straightforward, are not figurative either. Al-Jurjānī transforms the vague concept of non-straightforward language in theology into a very precise and carefully categorized concept of figurative language in poetry. The modern scholar Wolfhart Heinrichs notes that "...the *majāz* treatment in the *Asrār*, which is after all a book mainly devoted to poetry, has a strong *Qur'ānic* and theological flavor, whereas the passages in the *Dalā'il*, whose main theme is the inimitability of the Koran, seem much more geared to poetry." ("Contacts," 277)

Al-Jurjānī is known for his articulation of the categories of figurative language and for the application of the concept of imagination or *takhyīl* (this translation is too loose but convenient) to the study of figurative language. Al-Jurjānī was the first to use this term and to identify the figurative language to which it refers. This work was particularly important because in it al-Jurjānī offers literary critical approaches that cope with the problems presented by mannerism in medieval Arabic poetry. The proliferation of complex figurative language in medieval Arabic poetry led many critics to complain about the impossibility of images. Al-Jurjānī emphasizes that in images, the speaker affirms or negates in discourse, and does not affirm or negate the existence of things in reality. Instead of being put off by complexity in images, he views it as a challenge. He observes that the nice thing about images is that they give you a lot of different meanings in a small number of words, like a number of pearls from a single shell or varieties of fruits from a single branch, or like a number of branches from the trunk of a tree with fruit upon each branch. (*Asrār*, 43, 136) Al-Jurjānī sorts out the differences between images based on a single point of comparison and images based on a sentence-length analogy. The fact that analogy-based metaphors require more work on the part of the listener is considered a good thing by al-Jurjānī. He cites the scholar al-Jāḥiẓ's emphasis on the aesthetic and intellectual value of long perception, in which he contrasts an animal's immediate pleasure in killing with the very different pleasure that comes from perseverance, as in the horse race or the competition between archers. (*Asrār*, 145) Another feature of elaborate rhetoric that is sometimes opposed by other medieval Arabic critics but is embraced by al-Jurjānī is the combination of figurative expressions in series. In addition to this valorization of intellectual work in figurative language, al-Jurjānī demonstrates and valorizes the role of imagination in this type of discourse. Imagination may involve an imaginary ascription of one thing to another or the use of imaginary logic that serves as an alternative to the logic that governs knowledge of the real world, such as mock etiologies or mock analogies. Al-Jurjānī's interest in analogy-based metaphors, combinations of figurative language, and the alternative worlds of imagination in figurative language all share an emphasis on the extended duration and/or depth of thought in the production and consumption of fine discourse. This type of fine discourse allows speakers and listeners to explore topics in more detailed and in-depth ways. Al-Jurjānī clears the way for more extensive roles for both the intellect and the imagination in the analysis of fine discourse. His emphasis on the relationship of discourse to the meaning in the speaker's mind as opposed to the external reality of the world allows him to make sense of figurative expressions that other critics found problematic.

The division of knowledge into distinct disciplines was an important feature of scholarly progress in medieval Arabic culture. Disciplines allowed scholars to systematize knowledge in the context of particular disciplines, and to develop ways of evaluating each others work. At the same time, the interaction of distinct disciplines also led to scholarly progress. Al-Jurjānī's work is a significant example of the successful interaction between the fields of theology and literary criticism. Since the unsurpassed excellence of the *Qur'ān* is the main proof of Muḥammad's prophethood, and since the *Qur'ān* contains indications of God's guidance for mankind, it is imperative for theologians to clarify the nature of this unsurpassed excellence as well as the meaning of the indications that the *Qur'ān* contained. At the same time, elaborate rhetoric in poetry becomes a central feature of social life for the cultural elite, and mannerist changes in the use of fine discourse transforms the use of language in literature. Al-Jurjānī's work on theology and literary criticism tackles these very different problems together. By shifting attention away from the relationship of discourse to external reality, and downplaying the dichotomy between meaning and verbal expression, al-Jurjānī opens the way for a more central role of thought, including intellectual and imaginative activity, in discourse.

REFERENCES

Iḥsān ʿAbbās, *Tārīkh al-naqd al-adabī 'inda 'l-'Arab: naqd al-shi'r min al-qarn al-thānī ḥattā 'l-qarn al-thāmin al-Hijrī.* (Beirut: Dār al-Thaqāfah, 1971), especially 419-438;

Kamāl Abū Dīb, "al-DJurDJānī, Abū Bakr ʿAbd al-Ḳāhir b. ʿAbd al-Raḥmān (d. 471/1078)" in *Encyclopedia of Islam, Second Edition*, ed. P. Bearman, Th. Bianquis, C.E. Bosworth, E. van Donzel and W.P. Heinrichs (Brill, 2008, Brill Online) http://www.brillonline.nl./entry?entry=islam_SIM-8516;

Kamāl Abū Dīb, *Al-Jurjānī's Theory of Poetic Imagery* (Warminster, England: Aris and Phillips Ltd., 1979);

Mansour Ajami, *The Alchemy of Glory: the Dialectic of Truthfulness and Untruthfulness in Medieval Arabic Literary Criticism* (Washington, DC: Three Continents Press, 1988);

Jābir Aḥmad ʿAṣfūr, *al-Ṣūrah al-fanniyyah fī 'l-turāth al-naqdī wa 'l-balāghī* (Cairo: Dār al-Thaqāfah, 1974);

Carl Brockelmann, *Geschichte der arabischen Literatur*, 2nd ed., 4 vols. (Leiden: 1943-1949), 1: 287-288 and Supplement, 3 vols. (Leiden: 1937-1942), 1: 503-505;

Carl Brockelmann, *Tārīkh al-adab al-'Arabī*, 10 vols., tr. Maḥmūd Fahmī Ḥijāzī (Cairo: al-Hay'ah al-Miṣriyyah al-ʿĀmmah li 'l-Kitāb, 1993), 3:203-210;

Wolfhart Heinrichs, "Contacts Between Scriptural Hermeneutics and Literary Theory in Islam: the Case of Majāz," *Zeitschrift für Geschichte der Arabisch-Islamischen Wissenschaften* 7 (1991/1992): 253-284;

Wolfhart Heinrichs, "Istiʿārah and Badīʿ and Their Terminological Relationship in Early Arabic Literary Criticism," *Zeitschrift für Geschichte der Arabisch-Islamischen Wissenschaften* 1(1984): 180-211;

Wolfhart Heinrichs, "Paired Metaphors in Muḥdath Poetry" *Occasional Papers of the School of Abbasid Studies* 10 (1986), 1-22;

Wolfhart Heinrichs, "Takhyil" *Encyclopedia of Islam, 2nd ed.*, ed. P. Bearman, Th. Bianquis, C.E. Bosworth, E. van Donzel and W.P. Heinrichs (Brill, 2008, Brill Online) http://www.brillonline.nl.lib.washington.edu/.entry=islam_COM-1156;

Margaret Larkin, "The Inimitability of the *Qur'ān*: Two Perspectives," *Religion and Literature* 20:1 (1988): 31-47;

Margaret Larkin, *The Theology of Meaning: 'Abd al-Qāhir al-Jurjānī's Theory of Discourse* (New Haven, Connecticut: American Oriental Society, 1995);

Muḥammad Mandūr, *al-Naqd al-minhajī 'inda' l-'Arab* (Cairo: Dār Nahḍah Miṣr li 'l-Ṭabʿ wa 'l-Nashr, 1972);

Suzanne Stetkevych, *Abū Tammām and the Poetics of the 'Abbasid Age* (Leiden: E.J. Brill, 1991);

Tāj al-Dīn Abī Naṣr ʿAbd al-Wahhāb ibn ʿAlī ibn ʿAbd al-Kāfī 'l-Subkī, *Ṭabaqāt al-Shāfi'iyyah al-kubrā*, 10 vols. (Cairo: ʿĪsā 'l-Bābī 'l-Ḥalabī, 1964-1967), 5:149-50;

Jalāl al-Dīn al-Suyūṭī, *Bughyat al-wū'āh fī ṭabaqāt al-lughawiyyīn wa 'l-nuḥah*, 2 vols., ed. Muḥammad Abū 'l-Faḍl Ibrāhīm (Beirut: al-Maktabat al-ʿAṣriyyah, n.d.), 2:106.

Takhyīl: the Imaginary in Classical Arabic Poetics, ed. Marle Hammond and Geert Jan van Gelder (Cambridge: E. J. Gibb Memorial Trust, 2008);

al-Badrawī Zahrān, *'Alim al-lughah 'Abd al-Qāhir al-Jurjānī* (Cairo: Dār al-Maʿārif, 1979).

ʿAlī ibn ʿAbd al-ʿAzīz al-Qāḍī ’l-Jurjānī

(ca. 902 or 928–976 or 1002)

ALI HUSSEIN
University of Haifa

WORKS

al-Wasāṭah bayna ’l-Mutanabbī wa-khuṣūmih; *Dīwān*.

Editions

al-Wasāṭah bayna ’l-Mutanabbī wa-khuṣūmih: kitāb adab wa-naqd wa-lughah (The Mediation between al-Mutanabbī and his Adversaries: a Book of Literature, Criticism, and Language) (Sidon: Maṭbaʿat al-ʿIrfān, 1913);

al-Wasāṭah bayna ’l-Mutanabbī wa-khuṣūmih (The Mediation between al-Mutanabbī and his Adversaries), ed. and explained by Muḥammad Abū ’l-Faḍl Ibrāhīm and ʿAlī Muḥammad al-Bijāwī (Cairo: ʿĪsā ’l-Bābī ’l-Ḥalabī, 1961); ed. and explained by Muḥammad Abū ’l-Faḍl Ibrāhīm and ʿAlī Muḥammad al-Bijāwī (Beirut: Dār al-Qalam, 1966);

al-Wasāṭah bayna ’l-Mutanabbī wa-khuṣūmih, ed. by Hāshim al-Shādhilī (n. p.: Dār Iḥyā’ al-Kutub al-ʿArabiyyah, 1985);

al-Wasāṭah bayna ’l-Mutanabbī wa-khuṣūmih, ed. by Aḥmad ʿĀrif al-Zayn (Sūsa, Tunis: Dār al-Maʿārif li ’l-Ṭibāʿah wa ’l-Nashr, 1992);

Dīwān al-Qāḍī ’l-Jurjānī, ʿAlī ibn ʿAbd al-ʿAzīz, ed. Samīḥ Ibrāhīm Ṣāliḥ (Damascus: Dār al-Bashā’ir li ’l-Ṭibāʿah wa ’l-Nashr wa ’l-Tawzīʿ, 2003).

Al-Qāḍī ’l-Jurjānī (The Judge of Jurjān) was a title given to many judges of the Persian region or city of Jurjān (also Gurgān), which was situated, according to Richard Hartmann and John A. Boyle, at the south-east corner of the Caspian Sea. One of these judges, the subject of this entry, was Abū ’l-Ḥasan ʿAlī ibn ʿAbd al-ʿAzīz. This judge, poet and scholar was born and lived for some part of his life in Jurjān. No date of birth is given in contemporary sources, but ʿAbd al-Laṭīf Muḥammad al-Sayyid al-Hadīdī has suggested 902 or 903 as a possible year. As indicated later, the year 928 is also a possibility. Yāqūt ibn ʿAbd Allāh al-Ḥamawī, 1179?-1229 and other classical scholars claim that he visited Naysābūr (Nīshāpūr), one of the great towns of Persia in medieval times, in the year 948, together with his older brother Abū Bakr Muḥammad. There they spent some time in study. Aḥmad Badawī assumes that the reason that Abū ’l-Ḥasan left Jurjān, despite his young age, might have been due to the death of his father, meaning that his older brother had to take care of him and take him along as a companion in his travels.

Scholars such as ʿAbd al-Malik ibn Muḥammad al-Thaʿālibī (961 or 962-1037 or 1038) in his literary anthology *Yatīmat al-dahr fī maḥāsin ahl al-ʿaṣr* (The Ages’ Rare Pearl on the Admirable Attributes of the People of this Time) mention that Abū ’l-Ḥasan visited many places in Iraq and Syria seeking knowledge. This probably occurred at a later stage of his life, after he had traveled to Nīshāpūr, and his poetry confirms this assumption. Yāqūt al-Ḥamawī cites certain excerpts of Abū ’l-Ḥasan's poetry, some of which were composed after he left Baghdad, for in them he recalls his life in this capital. If this poetry truly expresses his life, then we may conclude that he enjoyed a pleasant life there. In one *mīmiyyah* (a poem rhyming with the letter *m*), he alludes to having traveled to some distant place north of Baghdad. He suffers intense longings for past days in that city and reminisces about lost relationships with his former friends (or perhaps his former beloved?). In other excerpts, he weeps because of his longing for Baghdad and his friends (perhaps beloved?) and wishes he could visit it once again.

There is a very interesting *rā'iyyah* (a poem rhyming with the letter *r*) in which he recalls a gloomy love affair in Baghdad. He states there that he is still very sad over that affair. If these poetic statements really reflect Abū 'l-Ḥasan's life, then this pleasant interlude in Baghdad most probably occurred during his youth since It would be more difficult to assume that he had such love affairs in his old age after having become a judge. For some unknown reason, perhaps because of his search for knowledge or work, he had to leave the city for another place where he was not so happy.

His poetry includes other love lyrics. Maḥmūd al-Samrah assumes that these lyrics express the poet's life in Baghdad, an assumption which appears to be reasonable but cannot be proved. In addition, he assumes that they do not always refer to female beloveds, but also to men who were adored by Abū 'l-Ḥasan. Such a conclusion seems quite probable. ʿAbd al-Malik ibn Muḥammad al-Thaʿālibī in his *Yatīmat al-dahr* mentions a six-verse poem, rhyming with the letter *j*, in which Abū 'l-Ḥasan expresses his love and desire for a man called Abū 'l-Qāsim. ʿAbd al-Malik ibn Muḥammad al-Thaʿālibī also includes another excerpt in which the poet describes a certain romantic night which he spent with his male lover. As al-Samrah claims, finding such love motifs in the poetry of Abū 'l-Ḥasan is not strange, since male lovers were a frequent phenomenon in the communal society of the tenth century. Neither the common people nor the elite condemned homosexuality because they were only too familiar with it. In addition, al-Samrah mentions that Abū 'l-Ḥasan, while he was in Baghdad, used to drink a lot of wine and became intoxicated, but this was not reflected in any of the verses consulted for this entry.

His extant poetry shows that besides living in Baghdad, Abū 'l-Ḥasan lived in Syria as well. ʿAbd al-Malik ibn Muḥammad al-Thaʿālibī in his *al-Muntaḥal* (The Plagiarized/The Borrowed) cites an eight-verse extract in which Abū 'l-Ḥasan expresses his great longing for his life in this country. In the poem, he alludes to having lived there during his youth, preferring it to Jurjān, the place of his birth and childhood. However, it is not known exactly when or during which period, Abū 'l-Ḥasan visited Syria. Was it before his visit to Iraq or after?

Abū 'l-Ḥasan lived not only in Nīshāpūr, Iraq and Syria, but seems to have spent some period of time in Rāmhurmuz (Ramhormuz), situated to the east of al-Aḥwāz in the south-western area of Persia. It seems that his life in Rāmhurmuz was also very pleasant. ʿAbd al-Malik ibn Muḥammad al-Thaʿālibī in his *Yatīmat al-dahr* quotes a poem rhyming with the letter *'ayn*, in which he recalls his beautiful life in Baghdad and alludes to his joy in an unnamed place. The author of this book mentions that Abū 'l-Ḥasan wrote this poem during his stay in Rāmhurmuz.

The knowledge that Abū 'l-Ḥasan acquired was manifold as can be perceived in the works that he composed. Classical scholars mention the following books by him: a commentary on the *Qur'ān*, a book on history, a book on genealogy, a book on jurisprudence, some prose letters, and a *dīwān* (collection) of poetry. However, none of these books are extant. ʿAbd al-Malik ibn Muḥammad al-Thaʿālibī in his *Yatīmat al-dahr* cites two extracts from his book on history. In the first, Abū 'l-Ḥasan deals with the need to know history, and in the second he describes his aim in composing his book. It appears that the major part of this book dealt with the history of the Prophet and his invasions. As for his *dīwān*, only a few excerpts are extant and they are mainly found in the books written by ʿAbd al-Malik ibn Muḥammad al-Thaʿālibī, in his *Yatīmat al-dahr* and Yāqūt al-Ḥamawī. Regarding the prose books, it is not known when or at what stage they were composed, whether before Abū 'l-Ḥasan became a judge or during that period.

The extant poetry of Abū 'l-Ḥasan reveals that, after having finished his studies, he suffered from poverty and had bad relationships with people. It is not known for certain in which country this occurred. Aḥmad Badawī assumes that this might have occurred in Jurjān, while Maḥmūd al-Samrah assumes on the contrary that it was in Baghdad. As mentioned above, his poetry shows that his life in Baghdad was not an unhappy one at all. The first assumption is therefore the more likely one, and it seems that Abū

ʾl-Ḥasan returned to his homeland after his travels to other places.

In his *mīmiyyah* poem mentioned by Yāqūt al-Ḥamawī, Abū ʾl-Ḥasan presents himself as an educated person who kept his distance from people for fear of being humiliated by them. He mentions that he did not study in order to serve people, but to be served by them. This might indicate that he was not given the respect due to him, and it is not unlikely that he considered himself more important than other people in his country. Taqī ʾl-Dīn Abū Bakr ibn ʻAlī Ibn Ḥijjah al-Ḥamawī (d.1434) mentions a longer version of the poem (11 verses), introducing it with a short account of the poet in which he is described as someone who does not salute the people he encounters. A friend of his blames him for this, and in response Abū ʾl-Ḥasan composes this poem.

In a *nūniyyah* (a poem rhyming with the letter *n*) of two verses, he speaks about his poverty and being advised by some people to travel and seek money (a job), but he refuses to do so. These verses show that Abū ʾl-Ḥasan, perhaps after his return to Jurjān, was jobless. In a *rāʾiyyah* of three verses, he alludes to the fact that he refused to ask for financial help from other people, and that it was better to suffer poverty than to beg for money. In another *rāʾiyyah* of eight verses, he rejects advice from some other persons to humiliate himself in order to gain money. All these verses show the suffering of Abū ʾl-Ḥasan after having acquired knowledge and before becoming a judge. In a *sīniyyah* (a poem rhyming with the letter *s*) of three verses, he decides to leave society and spend all his time at home together with his books. It is not unlikely that some of his prose works might have been composed during this period.

From a reading of his poetry it also appears that Abū ʾl-Ḥasan, at some stage of his life, was acquainted with certain noble persons. Classical scholars, mainly ʿAbd al-Malik ibn Muḥammad al-Thaʿālibī in his *Yatīmat al-dahr* and Yāqūt al-Ḥamawī, mention some panegyrics of his in praise of certain persons, including noble figures such as rulers, viziers, and even highly educated persons. One of the two main patrons whom he praised were the *Amīr* Shams al-Maʿālī Qābūs ibn Wushmakīr (or Wushmagīr) who reigned, according to C.E. Bosworth, between 977 and 981 and again from 998 to 1012 or 1013 in Tabaristan and Jurjān. However, it is not known in which of these two periods Abū ʾl-Ḥasan was in contact with him. The second patron was al-Ṣāḥib ibn ʿAbbād (938-995) who, according to Claude Cahen and Charles Pellat, was a vizier of the Buwayhids from 976 onwards in Rayy which is located in central Persia, to the south of the present-day capital, Tehran.

If Abū ʾl-Ḥasan praised the *Amīr* during his first reign, then it would be possible to conclude that, in order to overcome his poverty and lack of social position, he attempted to create a relationship with the elite of Jurjān. However, the later relation between him and al-Ṣāḥib ibn ʿAbbād was of greater benefit, since he was appointed by the vizier as a judge in Jurjān, and then filled the position of chief judge (*qāḍī ʾl-quḍāt*) in Rayy. From that time onwards he was known as al-Qāḍī ʾl-Jurjānī (The Judge of Jurjān). Not much is known about his work as a judge, except for his characterization by some classical critics such as Ibn Khallikān (1211-1282), Khalīl ibn Aybak al-Ṣafadī (ca. 1297-1363) and Ibn Sulaymān al-Yāfiʿī (d.1366 or 1367) as being a righteous and highly renowned person.

During the lifetime of al-Qāḍī ʾl-Jurjānī there was a wide-ranging literary controversy over the poetry of one of most famous poets in the Arab world, Abū ʾl-Ṭayyib al-Mutanabbī (915-965). Several books and treatises were composed either in support of his poetry or in condemnation of it. Wen-Chin Ouyang mentions these works and argues that most of the condemners attacked al-Mutanabbī because of his arrogance. One of them was the aforementioned sponsor of al-Qāḍī ʾl-Jurjānī, al-Ṣāḥib ibn ʿAbbād, who composed the *Risālah fī ʾl-kashf ʿan masāwī ʾl-Mutanabbī wa-ʿuyūbih* (Treatise on the Disclosure of the Shortcomings of al-Mutanabbī and his Defects). Modern scholars, such as Wen-Chin Ouyang, believe that al-Qāḍī ʾl-Jurjānī, in a response to this treatise and all those who professed an opinion of that poet, composed his only extant work called *al-Wasāṭah bayna ʾl-Mutanabbī wa-khuṣūmih* (The Mediation between al-Mutanabbī and his Adversaries). Aḥmad Badawī assumes that this book was composed after the death of al-Ṣāḥib ibn ʿAbbād, or at least that he composed it after having become a judge. Maḥmūd al-Samrah also argues that the book was composed after the author became a judge.

Al-Qāḍī ʾl-Jurjānī did not originally divide his book into chapters or sub-sections. This division was later made by the editors. But he did begin by presenting his aim in composing this book. While scholars have been divided in their opinions on al-Mutanabbī, with one group exaggerating in defense of him and the other exaggerating their blame of him, al-Qāḍī expresses the belief that both groups are unjust in their views of al-Mutanabbī and literature in general. He sets himself up a judge or a mediator between the two groups with the intention of admitting the faults of al-Mutanabbī, but also of indicating those places in which al-Mutanabbī composed good poetry.

Before doing so, al-Qāḍī argues that even Preislamic and early Islamic poets made mistakes such as in grammar or meanings (motifs). Yet there are many who are not ready to admit this fact and often attempt to defend them because they believe that old Arabic poetry is the best kind of poetry and has no faults. The author does not mention clearly why he begins his book with such an opinion, but he seems to have a double aim. The first is to convince the condemners that, although al-Mutanabbī has some faults in his poetry, this should not make them condemn all his poetry as several scholars do, because even the great poets had their faults. The second is to respond to those who might have condemned the poetry of al-Mutanabbī simply because, for the period of al-Qāḍī, he was seen as a modern poet and not a classical one.

Al-Qāḍī states that the value of poetry has no connection with the period in which it is composed. Aḥmad Badawī believes that al-Qāḍī is influenced here by ʿAbd Allāh ibn Muslim Ibn Qutaybah (828-889). Poetry, al-Qāḍī argues, is one of the Arab sciences and includes four elements: a talent for not composing poetry artificially (*ṭabʿ*); knowing poems, and even knowing them by heart (*al-riwāyah wa ʾl-ḥifẓ*); intelligence (*dhakā*); and training (*durbah*). A good poet, whether ancient or modern, should be recognizable according to the inclusion or absence of these elements. Here too, al-Qāḍī does not state clearly the reason for providing this analysis. Perhaps he is trying to convince his audience, especially al-Mutanabbī's adversaries, to judge the poet according to these elements and not according to personal hatred or according to the period in which he lived. This critical opinion on how to evaluate poetry influenced later scholars such as Abū ʾl-ʿAbbās Aḥmad Ibn Rāshiq (d. ca. 1048).

In addition, al-Qāḍī gives some rules for distinguishing between good and bad poetry. The first rule is the one mentioned above, *tabʿ* (naturalness). He emphasizes the fact that poetry should not be composed artificially, since this makes the audience dislike it. Al-Qāḍī explains clearly what he means by *tabʿ*:

1. Not to imitate Preislamic or early Islamic poetry by using its Bedouin expressions and words which are no longer familiar to civilized Abbasid society.
2. Not to exaggerate by including what is called the *badīʿ* (literally: the new style) which is the rhetorical branch for commendatory poetry.

He defines certain types of *badīʿ* and he promises that he will compose another book on some of them. Later critics such as Ibn Rashīq refused to accept some of the examples of this type of poetry as presented by al-Qāḍī.

Another rule is clarity. Al-Qāḍī highlights the fact that poetry should be clear to its audience and easily understood. There should be clarity in both meanings and expressions. Meaning should not be complicated. It should not, for example, include complex metaphors that make it difficult for the audience to understand or imagine them. Words and expressions should not be obscure and obsolete, and vulgar expressions should not be used.

A third rule he puts forth concerns making a comparison between two verses from two different poems. One should give the expressions (*alfāẓ*) used in them more importance than the meanings (*maʿānī*). That is because expressions are the first thing that the audience appreciates when hearing or reading a poem. For this reason, if one of the two verses includes a certain theme (*maʿnā*) that is not original, this should not make one reject the verse as unsuccessful.

The fourth rule that al-Qāḍī gives for evaluating a poem is to see whether the poet pays attention to the opening part of the poem, to its closure and to the transition verses connecting its different parts. His opinions in this regard are quoted extensively by Ibn Rashīq.

After this introduction, al-Qāḍī begins dealing with the poetry of al-Mutanabbī. He argues that although it includes some shortcomings, this should not make scholars consider al-Mutanabbī a bad poet and reject all of his poetry. Al-Qāḍī devotes several pages to examples taken from other famous poets with many shortcomings far more serious than those of al-Mutanabbī, such as Abū Nuwās (ca. 756-ca. 810) and Abū Tammām (796 or 804-842/843 or 845/846). One should not consider them bad poets, although they wrote both good and bad poetry, and this applies to al-Mutanabbī as well.

Then al-Qāḍī presents the major shortcomings that al-Mutanabbī's adversaries noticed in his poetry. Unfortunately, in many instances, he only mentions certain examples of poetry without defining and discussing the shortcoming found in each. An examination of these examples would reveal that the main shortcomings are related to the above-mentioned rules of good poetry:

1. Complex and intricate meanings in al-Mutanabbī's poetry. This has two main causes: his exaggerated use in some of his verses of one of the *badīʿ* elements, *tajnīs* (paronomasia), and his use of difficult and obsolete words.
2. Superficial meanings such as "not every gray-haired man is considered an old man."
3. The use of obscene and vulgar meanings.
4. Unsuccessful transitions between the different parts of the poem and also unsuccessful beginnings.

Al-Qāḍī admits these shortcomings, but he asserts that they appear only in a very few instances in the poetry of al-Mutanabbī. On the other hand, he advances what he considers many other beautiful and successful examples of this poet's work. In addition, he mentions his successful transitions, arguing that the number of unsuccessful transitions is very small in comparison with the successful ones. He then provides other examples of successful beginnings. Here too, in most cases he only provides examples without indicating why these verses are considered good beginnings of al-Mutanabbī's poems. But, when these examples are studied, they reveal three main reasons for considering them as good beginnings:

1. The expressions are clear and precise.
2. The meanings are clear.
3. The meanings are not frequently used (the author does not know any other poet that used them before).

Al-Qāḍī concludes that the poetry of al-Mutanabbī does include some shortcomings, but that it includes many other attributes which make it impossible to consider it bad poetry and to regard him as an unsuccessful poet.

The main shortcoming for which al-Mutanabbī is attacked is his plagiarism or borrowing of meanings and expressions from other poets. Many scholars accused the poet of this defect. Al-Qāḍī admits this fact, but he argues that not all influences should be considered plagiarism. For this reason he defines what plagiarism is and speaks of praiseworthy and blameworthy plagiarism. Plagiarism, according to ʿAbduh ʿAbd al-ʿAzīz Qalqīlah, and other scholars such as Gustave von Grunebaum and Wolfhart Heinrichs, had already been discussed before by scholars such as al-Ḥasan ibn Bishr al-Āmidī (d. 980), and it was discussed by later scholars such as ʿAbd al-Qāhir ibn ʿAbd al-Raḥmān Abū Bakr al-Jurjānī (d. ca. 1081). Al-Qāḍī, in his work, collects all the examples that he can find in the poetry of al-Mutanabbī which seem to be influenced by other verses composed by earlier poets. He does not analyze many of these examples of plagiarism, except to say whether they are considered praiseworthy or blameworthy. Al-Qāḍī occasionally implies that these examples should not lead scholars to consider al-Mutanabbī as an unsuccessful poet, since being influenced by the verses of other poets is permissible.

At the end of the book al-Qāḍī deals with other shortcomings that are found in the poetry of al-Mutanabbī such as errors in language and grammar, using hyperbole in presenting his meanings, and using unsuccessful metaphors.

Here too, he admits some of these shortcomings but he defends al-Mutanabbī in two ways. Firstly, he asserts that if the poet were given the chance to recompose these defective verses, he would have been able to write successful ones. Secondly, earlier poets have also committed such errors. Since scholars did not attack them, they should not attack al-Mutanabbī. As previously shown, his good poetry is greater in quantity than his defective poetry.

It is very interesting to see in this book how the characteristics of the judge are clearly portrayed. He presents himself as a judge in a law court in which he first announces the charges against his "accused-poet" and then presents the points in his favor. However, he does not make his judgment a conclusive one; he only presents the material and asks his audience to judge. Despite this, one can confidently declare that al-Qāḍī makes an implicit judgment in more than one instance in his book. As mentioned above, he tries to persuade his audience not to consider al-Mutanabbī an unsuccessful and unskillful poet, but on the contrary, to decide that al-Mutanabbī's many attributes in his literary work cancel out his defects and shortcomings and, consequently, to consider him a great modern poet.

Al-Qāḍī held his position as *Qāḍī ʾl-quḍāt* until his death. Most scholars mention the year 1001/1002 as the year of his death, while some scholars such as Ibn Khallikān and Ibn Sulaymān al-Yāfiʿī, mention the year 976. Ibn Khallikān says that he was probably 76 years old when he died. If this is true, then he was born either in the year 928 or in 902 or 903. It is not clear whether or not his death was in Nīshāpūr as the same critic mentions, but all the scholars mentioned in this entry agree that his body was sent to Jurjān where he was buried.

REFERENCES

Aḥmad Badawī, *al-Qāḍī ʾl-Jurjānī* (Egypt: Dār al-Maʿārif, 1964);

C.E. Bosworth, "Ḳābūs b. Wushmagīr b. Ziyār, Shams al-Maʿālī Abu ʾl-Ḥasan," *Encyclopedia of Islam,* 2nd ed., ed. P. Bearman, Th. Bianquis, C.E. Bosworth, E. van Donzel and W.P. Heinrichs (Brill, 2008, Brill Online) http://www.brillonline.nl./entry?entry=islam_SIM-3749;

Claude Cahen, "Ibn al-ʿAmīd: Abu ʾl-Fatḥ ʿAlī b. Muḥammad," *Encyclopedia of Islam,* 2nd ed., ed. P. Bearman, Th. Bianquis, C.E. Bosworth, E. van Donzel and W.P. Heinrichs (Brill, 2008, Brill Online) *http://www.brillonline.nl./entry?entry=islam_COM-0315*

Claude Cahen and Charles Pellat, "Ibn ʿAbbād, Abu ʾl-Ḳāsim Ismāʿīl b. ʿAbbād b. al-ʿAbbās b. ʿAbbād b. Aḥmad b. Idrīs," *Encyclopedia of Islam,* 2nd ed., ed. P. Bearman, Th. Bianquis, C.E. Bosworth, E. van Donzel and W.P. Heinrichs (Brill, 2008, Brill Online) http://www.brillonline.nl./entry?entry=islam_SIM-3024;

ʿAbd al-Laṭīf Muḥammad al-Sayyid al-Ḥadīdī, *Naẓarāt fī Wasāṭat al-Qāḍī ʾl-Jurjānī* (Contemplations on the Book *al-Wasāṭah* by al-Qāḍī ʾl-Jurjānī) (Cairo: Jāmiʿat al-Azhar, Kulliyyat al-Lughah al-ʿArabiyyah, 1995);

Richard Hartmann and John A. Boyle, "Gurgān," *Encyclopedia of Islam,* 2nd ed., ed. P. Bearman, Th. Bianquis, C.E. Bosworth, E. van Donzel and W.P. Heinrichs (Brill, 2008, Brill Online) http://www.brillonline.nl./entry?entry=islam_SIM-2565;

Wolfhart Heinrichs, "An Evaluation of Sariqa," *Quaderni Di Studi Arabi,* 5-6 (1987-1988):357-368;

Taqī al-Dīn Ibn Ḥijjah, *Ṭīb al-madhāq min thamarāt al-awrāq* (The Good Taste of the Fruits of Papers), ed. Abū ʿImād al-Sakhāwī (Sharja: Dār al-Fatḥ, 1997), 364-365;

Abū ʾl-ʿAbbās Aḥmad ibn Muḥammad Ibn Khallikān, *Wafayāt al-aʿyān wa-anbā Ibn al-Zamān* (Dead Important Persons and News on the Sons of the Time), ed. by Yūsuf ʿAlī Ṭawīl and Maryam Qāsim Ṭawīl (Beirut: Dār al-Kutub al-ʿIlmiyyah, 1998), 3:243-246;

Wen-Chin Ouyang, *Literary Criticism in Medieval Arabic-Islamic Culture: the Making of a Tradition* (Edinburgh: Edinburgh University Press, 1997), 146-154;

ʿAbduh ʿAbd al-ʿAzīz Qalqīlah, *al-Naqd al-adabī ʿinda ʾl-Qāḍī ʾl-Jurjānī* (Literary Criticism according to al-Qāḍī ʾl-Jurjānī) (Cairo: Maktabat al-Anjlū ʾl-Miṣriyyah, 1976);

al-Ḥasan ibn Rashīq al-Qayrawānī, *al-'Umda fī maḥāsin al-shi'r wa-ādābih* (The Pillar on the Attributes of Poetry and its Rules), ed. Muhammad Qarqazān (Beirut: Dār al-Maʻrifa, 1988), 1:249, 407-408, 462, 561-562; 2:724-725, 993-994;

Ṣalāḥ al-Dīn ibn Aybak al-Ṣafadī, *Kitāb al-wāfī bi 'l-wafayāt* (The Complete [data] on Dead Persons), ed. Aḥmad al-Arnā'ūt and Turkī Muṣṭafā (Beirut: Dār Iḥyā' al-Turāth al-ʿArabī, 2000), 21:157-159;

Maḥmūd al-Samrah, *al-Qāḍī 'l-Jurjānī: al-adīb 'an-nāqid* (al-Qāḍī 'l-Jurjānī: the Writer and Critic) (Beirut: al-Maktab al-Tijārī, 1979);

ʿAbd al-Malik ibn Muḥammad al-Thaʿālibī, *al-Muntaḥal* (The Plagiarized/The Borrowed), ed. Aḥmad Abū ʿAlī (Cairo: Maktabat al-Thaqāfah al-Dīniyyah, 1997), 14, 50-51, 83, 250, 252-253, 277-278;

ʿAbd al-Malik ibn Muḥammad al-Thaʿālibī, *Yatīmat al-dahr fī maḥāsin ahl al-'aṣr* (The Ages' Rare Pearl on the Admirable Attributes of the People of this Time) (Beirut: Dār al-Kutub al-ʿIlmiyyah, 1983), 4:3-29;

Gustave E. Von Grunebaum, "The Concept of Plagiarism in Arabic Theory," *Journal of Near Eastern Studies*, 3 (1944): 234-253;

Abū Muḥammad ibn Sulaymān al-Yāfiʿī, *Mir'āt al-janān wa-'ibrat al-yaqzān fī ma'rifat mā yu'tabar min ḥawādith al-zamān* (The Mirror of Heart and the Exhortation of the Awake on Knowing what can be Considered of the Incidents of Time), ed. Khalīl Manṣūr (Beirut: Dār al-Kutub al-ʿIlmiyyah, 1997), 2:290-291;

Yāqūt al-Ḥamawī, *Mu'jam al-udabā'* (The Dictionary of Writers), ed. Iḥsān ʿAbbās (Beirut: Dār al-Gharb al-Islāmī, 1993), 4:1796-1805.

Abū 'l-ʿAlā' al-Maʿarrī

(973-1058)

SINAN ANTOON

New York University

WORKS

al-Fuṣūl wa 'l-ghāyāt (Chapters and Endings);
Rasā'il (Letters);
Risālat al-ghufrān (The Epistle of Forgiveness);
Risālat al-ṣāhil wa 'l-shāḥij (The Epistle of the Neigher and the Brayer);
Risālat al-malā'ikah (Epistle of Angel);
Saqt al-zand (Dīwān);
Luzūm mā lā yalzam (Dīwān);
Zajr al-nabiḥ (Driving Away the Barker).

Editions

'Abath al-Walīd fī 'l-kalām 'alā shi'r Abī 'Abādah al-Walīd ibn 'Ubayd al-Buḥturī, ed. Nādiyā ʿAlī 'l-Dawlah (Damascus: al-Sharikah al-Muttaḥidah li 'l-Tawzīʿ,1987);

al-Fuṣūl wa 'l-ghāyāt fī tamjīd Allāh wa 'l-mawā'iẓ, ed. Maḥmūd Ḥasan Zanātī (Cairo: Maṭbaʿat Ḥijāzī;, 1938);

Luzūmiyyāt, aw, Luzūm mā lā yalzam, 2 vols., ed. ʿAzīz Zand (Cairo: Maṭbaʿat al-Maḥrūsah, 1891-1895);

Dīwān Luzūm mā lā yalzam: mimmā yasbiqu ḥarf al-rawī, first ed., ed. Kamāl al-Yāzijī, 2 vols. (Beirut: Dār al-Jīl, 1992);

Rasā'il Abī 'l-'Alā' 'l-Ma'arrī, ed. D. S. Margoliouth (Oxford: The Clarendon Press, 1898); ed. Iḥsān ʿAbbās (Cairo: Dār al-Shurūq, 1982);

Risālat al-ghufrān, fourth ed., ed. ʿĀ'ishah ʿAbd al-Raḥmān "Bint al-Shāṭi'" (Cairo: Dār al-Maʿārif, 1965);

Risālat al-ṣāhil wa 'l-shāḥij, ed. ʿĀ'ishah ʿAbd al-Raḥmān "Bint al-Shāṭi'" (Cairo: Dār al-Maʿārif, 1975);

Saqt al-zand wa-ḍaw'uhu li-Abī 'l-'Alā' 'l-Ma'arrī, 363-449 H: bi-ākhir riwāyatihimā 'anh, riwāyat al-Aṣfahānī, ed. al-Saʿīd al-

Sayyid ʿIbādah (Cairo: Maʿhad al-Makhṭūṭāt al-ʿArabiyyah, 2003);

Sharḥ Dīwān Abī 'l-Ṭayyib al-Mutanabbī: Mu'jiz Aḥmad, ed. ʿAbd al-Majīd Diyāb (Cairo: Dār al-Maʿārif, 1986);

Zajr al-nabiḥ "muqtaṭafāt," ed. Amjad al-Ṭarābulusī (Damascus: Majmaʿ 'l-Lughah al-ʿArabiyyah bi-Dimashq, 1965).

Translations

The Letters of Abu l-'Alā of Ma'arrat al-Nu'mān, ed. D. S. Margoliouth. (Oxford: The Clarendon Press, 1898);

R. A. Nicholson, *Studies in Islamic Poetry* (Cambridge: Cambridge University Press, 1921), 43-298;

"From Abu 'l-ʿAla' al-Maʿarri, Risalat al-Ghufran" in Salma Khadra Jayyusi, *Classical Arabic Stories: an Anthology* (New York: Columbia University Press, 2010), 375-381.

Aḥmad ibn ʿAbd Allāh ibn Sulaymān Abū 'l-ʿAlā' al-Maʿarrī, was one of the most important poets of the late Abbasid age and certainly one of the great figures of the Arabic literary tradition. His virtuosity, complex works, and various contributions in poetry, prose, epistles, letters, and commentaries on the poetry of some of his predecessors, secured his permanent place in the Arabic literary canon. He was highly regarded by his contemporaries for his vast knowledge. However, his skepticism, heterodox lifestyle and views, particularly his relentless criticism of organized religion and derision of popular beliefs made him a controversial figure and drove many to accuse him of heresy. Much of his work, especially those from later in his life, engaged philosophical themes and concerns, earning him the sobriquet of "the philosopher poet."

Al-Maʿarrī was born in Maʿarrat al-Nuʿmān, near Aleppo in Syria, to a family of notables and learned men. His grandfather was a judge. Al-Maʿarrī was afflicted with smallpox at the age of four, lost sight in his left eye, and soon thereafter lost sight in both eyes. He studied in Maʿarrat al-Nuʿmān at first, but then went to Aleppo to continue his studies. He was very precocious and had an astounding memory. He began to compose poetry when he was eleven and wrote a poem elegizing his father's death when he was fourteen. He also traveled to Antioch and Tripoli in search of their libraries and passed through Latakia, where he might have been exposed to the Hellenistic philosophy and ideas that were to influence his skepticism. He returned to his hometown when he was twenty and remained in Maʿarrat al-Nuʿmān for fifteen years, a period about which very little is known. He lived on the income from an endowment belonging to his family.

Al-Maʿarrī's early poetry is collected in *Saqt al-zand* (The Spark of the Fire-Stick) and it encompasses all the poems he composed in his early years, up until shortly after his return from Baghdad. The poems are relatively conventional in structure and themes when compared to his later work. In addition to *al-Dir'iyyāt*, a group of poems describing armor, *Saqt al-zand* contains some poems about the ongoing battles between Muslims and Byzantines taking place close to his home, and some panegyrics. Nevertheless, al-Maʿarrī's mastery of the poetic tradition and his virtuosity and descriptive powers, especially for a blind man, are fully displayed. Here is a famous line describing a night (*Saqt*, 178):

This night of mine is a Negro bride
adorned with pearl necklaces

Saqt al-zand includes seven *rithā'* poems (elegies), one of which, written for a relative, Abū Ḥamzah al-Faqīh, is one of al-Maʿarrī's most famous poems and is considered one of the best elegies in classical Arabic literature. Its opening lines are preserved in the collective memory of literate Arabs (*Saqt*, 389-392):

It is of no use in my creed and belief
for the wailer to wail, or the singer to sing
Lamenting death is akin, if compared,
to good tidings in every circle
Was that dove crying, or singing,
on the edge of its swaying branch?
My friend, our graves fill the vast earth
Where are the graves from the times of Ād?
Tread gently for I think the earth's
skin is made of these bodies

Beyond the elegiac tone predetermined by the occasion and the demands of the genre itself, one can discern the pessimism and fatalism that would later figure very prominently in al-Maʿarrī's poetry. Later in the same poem, al-Maʿarrī expresses his despair (*Saqt*, 393):

"Life is all toil and I wonder
at those who ask for more of it"

But despite his pessimism, al-Maʿarrī was well aware of his talents and potential and did not shy away from expressing his desire to leave his mark on the tradition. The young al-Maʿarrī was highly influenced by Abū al-Ṭayyib al-Mutanabbī (915-965) and held him in very high esteem. It is not surprising, then, that when al-Maʿarrī expressed his grand ambitions for literary glory, he sounded like the great poet he so admired (*Saqt*, 199-200):

Although I am the last to come
I shall bring forth what predecessors could not
I set out even though the morning is sharp swords
At night I venture out against legions of darkness

The Mecca of poetry and culture at that time was Baghdad, and if al-Maʿarrī was to make his mark, he had to go there. Thus, in 1007, when he was about thirty years old, he made the trip east. He arrived in Baghdad the day the father of the two poets, al-Sharīf al-Raḍī (970-1016) and ʿAlam al-Hudā ʿAlī ibn al-Ḥusayn al-Sharīf al-Murtaḍā (966-1044) died. Al-Maʿarrī attended the crowded funeral and tripped on the foot of one of those attending who said "Where are you going you dog?" Al-Maʿarrī responded by saying "A dog is one who does not know seventy names for a dog." (Yāqūt: 3,123) Irrespective of the veracity of this incident, it underscores the perception of al-Maʿarrī's incredible knowledge. Al-Maʿarrī's reputation had already preceded him to Baghdad and afforded him the respect of its literati. However, for several reasons, he was not able to stay there. Poets depended on patronage for their income and al-Maʿarrī was not the kind of poet who would sell his poetry by composing panegyrics. The pride of the free-spirited poet unwilling to subjugate his name and poetry to any political power, was itself a theme in his later poetry. Despite the generosity of many in Baghdad, he was not able to settle there permanently. Moreover, news of his mother's illness had also reached him in Baghdad, compelling him to return home after a year and a half from his arrival. In one of his letters to the people of Maʿarrat al-Nuʿmān, al-Maʿarrī wrote of his trip, assuring them that it was not made for financial gain, and that did he have anything more to learn in Baghdad (*Rasā'il*, 40-43):

> "I left Baghdad, with my honor still in a vessel that did not leak; not one drop of it had I | spilt in quest of either wealth or learning. Indeed, since I passed my twentieth year, it | never occurred to me to seek knowledge from any inhabitant of Iraq or Syria. . . And I | swear that I did not travel to increase my means, nor to gain by interviewing my | fellows. What I wanted was to stay in a place of learning; and I found out the most | precious of spots, only fate did not allow me to stay there, and only a fool will quarrel | with destiny"

Al-Maʿarrī's mother died before his return and this only added to his profound sorrow and alienation. Two of the elegies in *Saqt al-zand* were for his mother. The impact of her death is viscerally felt in lines such as these two (*Saqt*, 605-609):

She went away when I had aged
Yet I felt I was still an unweaned infant

. . .

I asked when we would meet and was told:
when the sleeping awake from the unknown

Upon his return to Maʿarrat al-Nuʿmān, al-Maʿarrī decided to renounce the world and seclude himself in his home. While his failure to settle in Baghdad might have been an important factor in this decision, he claimed that this drastic decision was the culmination of many years of reflection. He himself said in a letter to the people of Maʿarrat al-Nuʿmān when on his way to Baghdad, explaining his reasons (*Rasā'il*, 43-44):

> "I have found that the best course for me to pursue in the days of my life is to go

into | retreat, such as shall make me stand towards mankind in the relation that the chamois in | the plain stands to the ostriches that are there. . . It is no offspring of an hour, no nursling | of a month or year; it is the child of past years and the product of reflection. I have | hastened to inform you of this for fear that one of you out of courtesy might be fain to go | to the house it is my custom to inhabit in order to meet me."

Al-Maʿarrī called himself "*rahınu al-miḥbasayn*," i.e the twice confined, in reference to the two prisons he inhabited,his blindness and his house. In one of his poems he added his body as a third prison. Al-Maʿarrī extended his self-imposed confinement into the poetic realm as well, by composing a collection of poems with two rhyme consonants instead of the usual mono-rhyme. He composed poems on every rhyme letter and in four different forms for the three vowel endings and the unvowelled ending. Hence the collection's title *Luzūm mā lā yalzam,* also known as *Luzūmiyyāt,* or, restricting oneself to what is not obligatory. This collection was not as popular as *Saqt al-zand*, probably due to its departure from conventions. In lieu of the traditional *qaṣīdah*, it features short pieces with philosophical and ascetic themes. His philosophy cannot be neatly categorized or labelled. Although, since he affirms his belief in God, he cannot be characterized as an atheist. However, al-Maʿarrī was skeptical of prophecy and doubtful of resurrection and he expressed that repeatedly. The *Luzūmiyyāt* includes many poems deriding commonly held beliefs. For al-Maʿarrī, reason was only true guide in this world (*Luzūm*, 2:206):

The people of the earth are two: one with reason
and no religion, another with religion and no reason

The style of the *Luzūmiyyāt* is generally highly ornate with unusual diction and a certain level of opacity, perhaps to ward off reductive readings. Al-Maʿarrī alludes to the fact that he might be still keeping a few thoughts to himself (*Luzūm*: 1:382):

I have secret that cannot be mentioned
Hidden from those who can see when it is as clear as day

Al-Maʿarrī's unorthodox views earned him many an enemy. One of his arch enemies was Abū 'l-Faraj ʿAbd al-Raḥmān ibn ʿAlī Ibn al-Jawzī (ca. 1116-1201). There were, however, defenders as well. Kamāl al-Dīn ʿUmar ibn Aḥmad Ibn al-ʿAdīm (1192-1262), a scholar from Aleppo, took it upon himself to write a book in defense of al-Maʿarrī, *al-Inṣāf wa 'l-taḥarrī fī dafʿ al-ẓulm wa 'l-tajarrī 'an Abī 'l-'Alā'' al-Ma'arrī* (Fairness and Investigation in Warding off Injustice and Offense against Abū 'l-ʿAlā' al-Maʿarrī). It includes important biographical information as well as the names of al-Maʿarrī's students and those with whom he was in contact.

At the behest and insistence of his students, al-Maʿarrī composed *Zajr al-nābih* (Driving Away the Barker) to clarify and explain controversial verses in his *Luzūmiyyāt* and almost explain away the various accusations leveled at him as being weak in his belief or even a heretic. In his rebuttal, al-Ma'arrī marshals his mastery of rhetoric and of the tradition. His responses are not addressed to specific persons, but to the abstract category of the detractor. His tone ranges from the quiet and collected to angry and sarcastic.

Despite his self-imposed seclusion and intense desire to keep to himself, which he reiterated in his poetry,

Ultimate comfort is in being alone
It is cumbersome to be in the world among people

he could not refuse those who came to learn from him. His home became a pilgrimage site for those seeking his knowledge and mentorship. Still, al-Maʿarrī refused any compensation from his students, who were numerous and included Yaḥyā ibn ʿAlī al-Tibrīzī (d. 1109).

In the forty nine years since his return from Baghdad, al-Maʿarrī left his home only once, when he was compelled to do so by the people of Maʿarra to intercede on their behalf with Ṣāliḥ b. Mirdās (d. 1029), the ruler of Aleppo, who had come to quell a rebellion. Ṣāliḥ was persuaded by al-Maʿarrī and asked him to recite poetry. Al-Maʿarrī said (*Luzūm*, 1:329):

I was absent in my home for a period
  envied by none, my defects covered
When life was all but gone
  and my soul was destined to depart my body
I was sent to Ṣāliḥ as an intercessor
  The people's defective opinion it was
He heard the cooing of doves from me
  While I heard the roaring of a lion from him

Al-Maʿarrī's most famous prose work is *Risālat al-ghufrān* (The Epistle of Forgiveness). It was composed in 1033, when al-Maʿarrī was about sixty years old, in response to a letter he received from ʿAlī ibn Manṣūr Ibn al-Qāriḥ (d. 962), a poet who was in many ways al-Maʿarrī's antithesis. He was more than willing, like most poets, to put his poetry at the services of various patrons, and he led a bohemian life. Ibn al-Qāriḥ had been patronized by one of the powerful families in Cairo and had written panegyrics for them. However, when the political tide turned, he composed invectives against them. He decided to retire to Aleppo, at which point he wrote to al-Maʿarrī, showing off his own knowledge and alluding to heretics. In *Risālat al-ghufrān*, al-Maʿarrī sends Ibn al-Qāriḥ on an imaginary journey to heaven and hell, where he meets various poets, scholars, and heretics from previous eras. The first part describes Ibn al-Qāriḥ's sojourn. The second is a detailed response to the contents of Ibn al-Qāriḥ's epistle. The obvious model for this work is the *Mi'rāj* of the Prophet Muḥammad. There are speculations that *Risālat al-ghufrān* might have influenced Dante's *Divine Comedy*, but there is no consensus.

Before his departure to Baghdad al-Maʿarrī had started *al-Fusūl wa* 'l-*ghāyāt fī tamjīd Allāh wa 'l-mawā'iz* (Paragraphs and Periods in Glorifying God and the Sermons). He completed it after his return to Maʿarrat al-Nuʿmān. It is a series of chapters written in rhymed-prose and arranged alphabetically. Its thematic focus is God's omnipotence, justice, and eternity, but it also illustrates al-Maʿarrī's pessimism and despair for this world and its wayward inhabitants. His style in this work, which echoes *Qur'ānic* discourse and oaths, led many, unjustly, to accuse him of attempting to rival, whether implicitly or explicitly, the inimitable Qur'āān.

One of al-Maʿarrī's other prose works is *Risālat al-ṣāhil wa 'l-sāhij* (The Epistle of the Neigher and the Brayer). A number of animals address some of the political events of al-Maʿarrī's time. Not unlike most of his works, it also features philological digressions, ornate language, and a display of his immense knowledge.

Al-Maʿarrī also produced a number of commentaries on the poetry of other poets. *Mu'jiz Aḥmad* (The Immaculate [or the "*Qur'ān*"] of Aḥmad) is a commentary on the *dīwān* of al-Mutanabbī (915-965), hence "Aḥmad." It is unremarkable and it seems that al-Maʿarrī wrote it early on in his life. Another commentary, *al-Lāmi' al-'azīzī*, on selections from al-Mutanabbī's poems was commissioned much later in al-Maʿarrī's life, but no edited edition exists. *'Abath al-Walīd fī 'l-kalām 'alā shi'r Abī 'Abādah al-Walīd ibn 'Ubayd al-Buḥturī*, was a commentary on selections from the latter's (820-897) poems that were sent to al-Ma'arrī to correct. Although it did not survive, al-Ma'arrī's commentary on selections from Abū Tammām (796 or 804-842/843 or 845/846), *Dhikrā Ḥabib*, is incorporated into Tibrīzī's commentary on Abū Tammām's *Dīwān*.

Late in his life, al-Maʿarrī exchanged correspondence with the Ismāʿīlī *dā'ī* al-Mu'ayyad fī 'l-Dīn Hibat Allāh ibn Mūsā (d. 1078), who had been dispatched to Syria to mobilize local rulers against the Saljūqs. The letters include a debate about al-Maʿarrī's views and his veganism. He refused to eat meat, yogurt, or eggs.

Al-Maʿarrī never married and died of natural causes. In addition to his cousins, Ibn Buṭlān (d. ca. 1068), the famous physician, was at his side. Al-Maʿarrī wished to dictate one last work, but when he did so, it was full of errors, upon which Ibn Buṭlān said "Abū al-ʿAlā' has already died. Al-Maʿarrī asked that the following be inscribed on his grave: This, my father, committed against/And I have not committed against anyone." In 1098, the Crusaders invaded Maʿarrat al-Nuʿmān and many of al-Maʿarrī's other works were destroyed and lost.

Al-Maʿarrī's philosophical and controversial views continued to attract attention and debate throughout the following centuries. In the modern period, attention has focused more on the literary aspects of his work as opposed to his heterodox philosophical ideas, but modern admirers of the Arab poet have also given their due to the originality of al-Maʿarrī's thinking.

Impressed by the early printed edition *Dīwān Luzūm mā lā yalzam* published in two volumes in Cairo during the early 1890's, the pioneering Lebanese American poet Ameen Fares Rihani (al-Rīḥānī) (1876-1940) translated a number of Abū al-ʿAlā''s poems into four line English lyrics reminiscent of the form used to great acclaim by Edward Fitzgerald in the Victorian period to translate the quatrains of the eleventh-century Persian poet ʿUmar al-Khayyām. Al-Khayyām had been deeply influenced by the lyric meditations of al-Maʿarrī and al-Rīḥānī felt that a judicious selection of the Arab poet's best short works would be an appropriate way of introducing the genius of Arabic poetry to English-speaking readers. Al-Rīḥānī was not reticent about his admiration for Abū al-ʿAlā', calling him "besides being a poet of the first rank, was also the foremost and profoundest thinker of his age, not excepting his learned contemporary Ibn Sīnā, known to European scholars as Avicenna" (Rihani, "Introduction," 1903, xv). His volume would not entirely succeed in its goals, but al-Rīḥānī's effort was to herald a resurgence of interest in al-Maʿarrī in the Arab world that would persist beyond the end of World War II.

In 1916, the soon-to-be-influential Egyptian Romantic literary critic, ʿAbbās Maḥmūd al-ʿAqqād, began his career with a series of articles for the Nationalist newspaper *al-Dustūr*, where he subjected a group of famous figures from the Arab literary heritage to searching psychological analyses, based in part on the new theories of the European psychiatric researcher Sigmund Freud. His first subject was al-Maʿarrī, and this shed a new and entirely more personal light on the work of the famous poet.

Shortly before the publication of al-ʿAqqād's work, the doyen of Arabic literature, Ṭāhā Ḥusayn (1889-1973), like al-Maʿarrī, himself blind from childhood, had written his first doctoral thesis "Dhikr Abī 'l-ʿAlā'" (The Memory of Abū al-ʿAlā') on al-Maʿarrī in 914 for the Egyptian University. He would publishe this work as a monograph in 1922 under the title *Tajdīd Dhikra Abī 'l-'Alā'*. He would eventually write and publish three other books, *Ta'rīf al-Qudamā' bi- Abī 'l-'Alā'*, *Ṣawt Abī 'l-'Alā'* (The Voice of Abū al-'Alā', volume 23 of the popular Iqra' series, published in Cairo) and *Ma'a Abī 'l-'Alā' fī sijnih* (With Abū al-ʿAlā' in His Prison). It was undoubtedly due to Ṭāhā Ḥusayn's and al-ʿAqqād's influence that a special edition of the Egyptian magazine *al-Hilāl* (The Crescent) was devoted to al-Maʿarrī and his times in 1938. The editing of the issue was supervised by Emile Zaydān, the publisher of *al-Hilāl*. The contributors to included a roll call of the most eminent men of letters in Egypt at the time, led by the Minister of Education (and author of the foremost Egyptian Romantic novel, *Zaynab*) Muḥammad Ḥusayn Haykal, Ṭāhā Ḥusayn himself, Aḥmad Amīn, and Zakī Mubārak, among many others. Zaydān also solicited studies from his fellow Lebanese among the emigré community, including the great Lebanese poet residing in Egypt, Khalīl Mutrān, and Ameen al-Rihani's colleagues in North America, the poets Kahlil Gibran and Mikhā'il Nu'aymah. Though some of the contributions are simply short appreciations, many are substantial studies detailing the vastly varied aspects of al-Maʿarrī's work and subsequent literary influence.

Despite the war during the next decade, a Millennial event in honor of al-Ma'arrī was held in a number of Syrian cities in 1944. Egypt's gift on that occasion was the aforementioned work edited under the guidance of Ḥusayn, *Ta'rīf al-Qudamā' bi Abī 'l-'Alā'* (The Ancient Scholars' Introduction to Abū 'l-ʿAlā'). It is a comprehensive compilation on al-Ma'arrī culled from pre-modern biographical compendia. It was also during this decade that the well-known traditional Iraqi poet, Maʿrūf al-Ruṣāfī, composed a sprited defense of al-Ma'arrī against accusations of atheism entitled ʿAlā bāb sijn Abī 'l-ʿAlā' (At the Prison Door of Abū al-ʿAlā'). In the course of his presentation, al-Ruṣāfī—like al-Rīḥānī—underscores the value of al-Maʿarrī's unequaled contributions to Arabic literature. Because of al-Ruṣāfī's somewhat troubled reputation as a freethinker himself, however, the book was not published in its entirety until 2002.

In addition to being one of the great poets of Arabic literature, for contemporary Arab secular and atheist intellectuals and readers, al-Maʿarrī stands out as the freethinker, par excellence, and one of the towering figures of rational thought in the Arabo-Islamic tradition.

REFERENCES

ʿAbd al-Karīm al-Khaṭīb, *Rahīn al-maḥbasayn: Abū 'l-'Alā' al-Ma'arrī* (Riyad: Dār al-Liwā' li 'l-Nashr wa 'l-Tawzī', 1980);

"Adad Khāss: Abū 'l-ʿAlā' al-Ma'arrī," *al-Hilāl* 46:8 (June 1938): 842-968;

Bint al-Shāti', *Ma'a Abı 'l-'Alā'* (With Abū 'l-ʿAlā') (Beirut: Dār al-Kitāb al-ʿArabī, 1972);

Bint al-Shāti', *al-Ghufrān li Abī 'l-'Alā' al-Ma'arrī: dirāsah naqdiyyah* (Cairo: Dār al-Maʿārif, 1968);

Ṭāhā Ḥusayn, *Ma'a Abī 'l-'Alā' fī sijnih* (Cairo: Dār al-Maʿārif, 1962);

Ṭāhā Ḥusayn, *Ṣawt Abī 'l-'Alā'* (Cairo: Maṭbaʿat al-Maʿārif, 1954);

Ṭāhā Ḥusayn, *Tajdīd Dhikrā Abī 'l-'Alā'* (Cairo: Maṭbaʿat al-Maʿārif, 1922);

Ṭāha Ḥusayn, ed., et al, *Ta'rıf al-Qudamā' bi-Abī 'l-'Alā'*, (Cairo: Dār al-Kutub, 1944);

Abdelfattah Kilito, *Abū al-'Alā' al-Ma'arrī aw Matāhāt al-qawl* (Abū al-ʿAlā' al-Maʿarrī or The Labyrinths of Speech) (Casablanca: Dār Tūbqāl li 'l-Nashr, 2000);

Ameen F. Rihani, *The Quatrains of Abū 'l-'Alā'* (New York: Doubleday, Page & Company, 1903);

Ma'ruf al-Ruṣāfī, *'Alā bāb sijn Abī 'l-'Alā'* (Baghdad: Dār al-Ḥikmah li 'l-Nashr wa 'l-Tawzīʿ, 1946); special edition, 2002.

Abū 'l-Ḥasan ʿAlī 'l-Masʿūdī

(ca. 890 – 956)

MICHAEL COOPERSON
University of California, Los Angeles

WORKS

Akhbār al-khawārij (History of the Khawarij)=*al-Intisār*;

al-Akhbār al-Mas'ūdiyyat (al-Masʿūdī's Historical Reports);

Akhbār al-zamān wa-man abādahu l'īdthān min al-umam al-māḍiyyah wa 'l-ajyāl al-khāliyyah wa-al-mamālik al-dāthirah (Accounts of World History, Bygone Times, Ancient Nations, Past Generations, and Vanished Kingdoms);

al-Awsaṭ (The Intermediate);

al-Bayān fī asmā' al-a'immah al-qaḍ'iyyah (An Explanation of the Names of the Twelver *Imāms*);

al-Da'āwā 'l-shanī'ah (On Abominable Claims);

Dhakhā'ir al-'ulūm wa-mā kān fī sālif [*or: sā'ir*] *al-duhūr* (The Treasuries of Knowledge and an Account of the Events of Past [or: All] Time);

Fī aḥwāl al-imāmah (Modes of the Imāmate);

Funūn al-ma'ārif wa mā jarā fī 'l-duhūr al-sawālif (The Branches of Knowledge and an Account of History);

Ḥadā'iq al-adhhān fī akhbār Āl Muḥammad [*or al-Nabī*] *wa-tafarruqihim fī 'l-buldān* (Gardens of the Mind, on the Descendants of the Prophet Muḥammad and Their Dispersion Across the World);

al-Ibānah fī [*or: 'an*] *usūl al-diyānah* (A Clarification of the Premises of Religion);

al-Istibsār fī 'l-imāmah wa-wasf aqāwīl al-nas fīhā (An Examination of the Imāmate and a

Description of the Various Opinions Regarding It);

al-Istidhkār bi-mā marra [*or: limā jarā*] *fī sālif al-a'ṣār* [*or: al-a'mār*] (A Review of the Events of History);

al-Istirjā' fī 'l-kalām (A Demand for Restoration, on Theology);

al-Intiṣār al-mufrad li-firaq al-Khawārij (The Triumph, a Work Devoted to the Khārijī Sects);

(attr.) *Ithbāt al-waṣiyyah li 'l-Imām 'Alī* (A Confirmation of the Designation of ʿAli as *Imām*);

Khāwass al-ashyā' (Special Properties of Objects);

Khazā'in al-dīn wa-sirr al-'ālamīn (The Treasuries of Religion and the Secret of the Universe);

al-Mabādi' wa 'l-tarākīb (The Primary and the Composite);

al-Maqālāt fī usūl al-diyānāt (Discourses on the Premises of Religions);

Maqātil fursān al-'ajam (The Death-tales of Persian Knights);

al-Masā'il wa 'l-'ilal fī 'l-madhāhib wa 'l-milal (Questions and Arguments Regarding Creeds and Sects);

(attr.) *al-Masālik wa 'l-mamālik* (Routes and Kingdoms);

Maẓāhir al-akhbār wa sarā'if al-āthār fī Āl Abī Ṭālib [*or: Āl al-Nabī*] [*al-akhyār*] (Luminous accounts and Precious Reports Concerning the [Good] Family of Abū Tālib [or: the Prophet]);

Murūj al-dhahab wa-ma'ādin al-jawhar (Meadows of Gold and Mines of Gems);

Naẓm al-adillah fī usūl al-millah (Arrangement of Evidence for the Premises of Islam);

Naẓm al-a'lām fī usūl al-aḥkām (Arrangement of Indicants [or: Authorities] on the Premises of Legal Rulings);

Naẓm al-jawāhir fī tadbīr al-mamālik wa 'l-'asākir (Arrangement of Gems, on Managing Kingdoms and Armies);

al-Nuhā wa 'l-kamāl (Reason and Perfection);

al-Qaḍāyā wa 'l-tajārib (Inquiries and Experiences);

Rāḥat al-arwāḥ (Repose of Souls);

al-Rasā'il (Epistles)=al-Rasā'il wa 'l-istidhkār?;

al-Rasā'il wa 'l-istidhkār bi-mā marra fī sālif al-a'ṣār (Epistles and a Review of the Events of History)=*al-Istidhkār bi-mā marra* [*or: limā jarā*] *fī sālif al-a'ṣār* [*or: al-a'mār*] (A Review of the Events of History);

Risālat al-Bayān: see *al-Bayān*;

al-Ru'ūs al-sab'ah [*sab'iyyah?*] *fī 'l-siyāsah al-madaniyyah* (The Seven Heads [or: The Septenary Principles] on Politics);

al-Ru'yā wa 'l-kamāl (Vision and Perfection [probably an error for *al-Nuhā wa 'l-kamāl*]);

al-Ṣafwah fī 'l-imāmah (The Quintessence, on the Imāmate);

Sirr al-ḥayāh (The Secret of Life);

al-Tanbīh wa 'l-ishrāf (Reference Guide and Overview);

Taqallub al-duwal wa taghayyur al-arā' wa 'l-milal (The Alternation of Dynasties and the Alteration of Opinions and Creeds);

al-Ta'rīkh fī akhbār al-umam min al-'arab wa 'l-'ajam (The History of the Arab and Non-Arab Nations);

Ṭibb al-nufūs (Treatment of the Soul);

al-Wajib fī 'l-furūd wa 'l-lawāzim [or: *lawāzib*] (The Essential Book on Religious Obligations and Duties);

Waṣl al-majālis bi-jawāmi' al-akhbār wa-mukhtalit [*or mukhallat*] *al-athār* [*or: al-ādāb*] (Miscellaneous Historical Anecdotes to Be Recounted at Literary Gatherings);

al-Zāhī (The Shining Book);

al-Zulaf (Stages) or *al-Zulfā* (Closeness).

Editions

(Attr.) *Akhbār al-zamān* (Cairo: ʿAbd al-Ḥamīd Aḥmad Ḥanafī, 1938; repr. Beirut: Dār al-Andalus, 1966, 1980);

(attr.) *Ithbāt al-waṣiyyah li 'l-Imām 'Alī* (Tehran: Dār al-Ṭibāʿah, 1902 or 1903; repr. Najaf: al-Ḥaydariyyah, 1955);

Murūj al-dhahab wa-ma'ādin al-jawhar (Būlāq: Idārat al-Ṭibāʿah al-Mūnīriyyah, 1867); ed. Muḥammad Muhyī 'l-Dīn ʿAbd al-Ḥamīd, 5th ed., 4 vols. (Beirut: Dār al-Fikr, 1973); ed. Yūsuf Asʿad Dāghir, 4 vols. (Beirut: Dār al-Andalus, 1965-1966); ed. Charles Pellat, 7 vols. (Beirut: al-Jāmiʿah al-Lubnāniyyah, 1965-1979);

Murūj al-dhahab wa-ma'ādin al-jawhar, on the margins of al-Maqqarī, *Nafḥ al-Ṭīb* (Cairo: al-Azhariyyah, 1884-1885);
Murūj al-dhahab wa-ma'ādin al-jawhar, on the margins of Ibn al-Athīr, *al-Kāmil fī 'l-ta'rīkh* (Būlāq: Idārat al-Ṭibāʿah al-Mūnīriyyah, 1885-1886);
Murūj al-dhahab wa-ma'ādin al-jawhar, ed. with a French translation, by Barbier de Menard et Pavet de Courteille, 9 vols. (Paris, Imprimerie impériale, 1861-1877);
al-Tanbīh wa 'l-ishrāf, ed. M.J. de Goeje (Leiden, 1893-1894; repr. Beirut: Maktabat Khayyāt, 1965; repr. Leiden: Brill, 1967); ed. ʿAbd Allāh Ismāʿīl al-Ṣāwī (Cairo: Dār al-Ṣāwī, 1938; repr. Baghdad, al-Muthannā, 1967); (Beirut: Dār al-Turāth, 1968); ed. Qāsim Wahb (Damascus: Wizārat al-Thaqāfah, 2000).

Translations

(attr.) *l'Abrégé des merveilles*, trans. into French by Bernard Carra de Vaux (Paris: C. Klincksieck, 1898; repr. Paris, Sindbad, 1984; reprinted Frankfurt am Main: Institut für Geschichte der arabisch-islamischen Wissenschaften an der Johann Wolfgang Goethe-Universität, 1994);
Les Prairies d'or, trans. into French by Barbier de Menard et Pavet de Courteille, 9 vols. (Paris, Imprimerie impériale, 1861-1877); rev. by Charles Pellat (Paris: Société asiatique, 1962-1971);
El-Masūdī's Historical Encyclopedia, entitled Meadows of Gold and Mines of Gems, selections trans. by Aloys Sprenger (London: Oriental Translation Fund., 1841), vol. 1;
Bis zu den Grenzen der Erde. Ausz. aus d. Buch der Goldwäschen, selections trans. into German by Gernot Rotter (Tübingen: Erdmann, 1978);
Le Livre de l'avertissement et de la revision, trans, into French by Carra de Vaux (Paris: Imprimerie nationale, 1896; repr. Frankfurt am Main: Institut für Geschichte der arabisch-islamischen Wissenschaften an der Johann Wolfgang Goethe-Universität, 1986);
Hyeong Gi Kwon, *Le Kitāb al-tanbīh wa 'l-ishrāf d'al-Mas'ūdī: étude comparative avec traduction partielle annotée* (Lille: A.N.R.T. Université de Lille III, 1989);
The Meadows of Gold by Mas'udi. Vol. 1: The Abbasids, selections trans. by Paul Lunde and Caroline Stone (London: Kegan Paul, 1989);
Religion & society in the India of the 10th century as described by the Arab scholar al-Mas'udi, selections trans. by Mahmudul Ḥasan (Patna: Khuda Bakhsh, 1994);
The book of golden meadows (Islamabad: Alhamra, 2001);
From the Meadows of gold (London: Penguin, 2007).

Abū 'l-Ḥasan ʿAlī ibn al-Ḥasan ibn ʿAlī ibn ʿAbd Allāh al-Hudhalī 'l-Masʿūdī was a widely traveled geographer, historian, and student of religion. In his two surviving works, *Murūj al-dhahab* (*Meadows of Gold*) and *al-Tanbīh wa 'l-ishrāf* (Reference Guide and Overview), he surveys the regions and peoples of the world and describes his experiences in Iraq, Persia, India, Arabia, the Levant, Central Asia, the Caucasus, and Egypt. In both works, he presents the history of the Muslim community from its origins to the mid-tenth century. He also devotes chapters or digressions to various subjects, including astronomy, oceanography, zoology, Egyptian antiquities, Persian literature, Greek philosophy, Preislamic religious beliefs, Muslim creeds and sects, foreign languages and Arabic dialects, trade and commerce, clothing and fashion, and cuisine and diet. Because of his curiosity about matters usually ignored by other chroniclers, he remains an indispensable source for the cultural history of medieval Islam.

As the name al-Masʿūdī indicates, his family claimed descent from a prominent companion of the Prophet Muḥammad (d. 632), ʿAbd Allāh ibn Masʿūd (d. ca. 652). Al-Masʿūdī himself was born in the Abbasid capital of Baghdad, probably around 890. In his discussion of the seven climes (regions) into which ancient Greek geographers had divided the earth, he says that "the middlemost [clime] is that of Babylon," meaning central Iraq, "where I was born." Within Babylon, he says, the most favored of all places is Baghdad, his hometown. He adds that he was later forced to leave it, a circumstance he regrets; but he offers no account of when or why this event occurred.

Al-Masʿūdī's surviving works prove his familiarity with the so-called "ancient sciences," which included geography, astronomy, medicine, music, and philosophy, as well as the so-called "Arabic sciences" of grammar, poetry, *Qur'ān*, *ḥadīth*, history, jurisprudence, and theology. Some of his learning was doubtless memorized in his youth or acquired in the traditional study circles that formed around prominent scholars. In his books, he frequently attributes material to teachers whom he heard in person. The authorities whose death dates indicate that he must have encountered them early in his career are the *ḥadīth*-scholar Ibrāhīm ibn ʿAbd Allāh al-Kajjī (d. 904); the theologian ʿAbd Allāh ibn Muḥammad Ibn Shirshīr al-Nāshi' (d. 905 or 906); the grammarian al-Qāsim ibn Muḥammad al-Anbārī (d. 916); the chronicler and genealogist Abū Khalīfah al-Jumaḥī (d. 917); the philologist Wakī' al-Dabbī (d. 918); the famous jurist, *Qur'ān*-exegete, and historian Muḥammad ibn Jarīr al-Ṭabarī (838?-923), whom he describes as "the most discerning and abstemious scholar of the age"; the grammarian Abū Isḥāq Ibrāhīm ibn al-Sarī 'l-Zajjāj (d. 923); and the *ḥadīth*-scholar Ibn 'Ammār (d. 926).

As much as he learned from teachers, al-Masʿūdī derived as much if not more from books. By his time, the ready availability of paper had given rise to a learned culture that relied increasingly on literacy. In the introduction of *Meadows of Gold*, he discusses his predecessors in the field of history (*ta'rīkh wa-akhbār*, literally "chronology and reports") and lists over eighty works in the field. Among the authors he mentions are ʿAbd Allāh Ibn al-Muqaffaʿ (d. ca. 760), translator of Middle Persian fables and wisdom literature; Muḥammad ibn Isḥāq (d. ca. 767), biographer of the Prophet; Ḥammād ibn Ṣābūr al-Rāwiyah (713 or 714-772 or 773), compiler of classical Arabic poetry; Isḥāq al-Mawṣilī (767-850), composer and musician; Abū ʿUthman ʿAmr ibn Baḥr al-Jāḥiẓ (d. 868), essayist, whose writings "will clean the rust from your brain"; ʿAbd Allāh ibn Muslim Ibn Qutaybah (828-889), exegete, *ḥadīth*-scholar, and literary anthologist; Aḥmad ibn Abī Ṭāhir Ṭayfūr (819 or 820-893), poet, critic, and historian of the caliphate; and ʿUbayd Allāh ibn ʿAbd Allāh Ibn Khurradādhbih (ca. 820-ca. 911), geographer.

In addition to the "Arab sciences," al-Masʿūdī also mastered the "ancient sciences" of the Greeks, which he considered the basis for all subsequent human knowledge. He writes that the "divine philosophy" of Socrates—that is, metaphysics—was taught by Plato, Aristotle, and their successors, until the philosophers were driven from Athens. The Academy, he says, moved to Alexandria and from there to Antioch and Harran (both in what is today south-central Turkey) and finally to Baghdad, where it was represented by Yaʿqūb Ibn Isḥāq al-Kindī (d. ca. 873), Aḥmad Ibn al-Ṭayyib al-Sarakhsī (d. 899), and Abū Naṣr al-Fārābī (d. 950). Al-Masʿūdī mentions his acquaintance with the latter's student, Yaḥyā Ibn ʿAdī (ca. 893-974), whom he calls the only living authority on philosophical matters. In a passage based on al-Fārābī's *Opinions of the People of the Virtuous City*, a work itself inspired by Plato's *Republic*, al-Masʿūdī lists the topics of philosophical enquiry. These include the cause and degrees of being, the soul, the intellect, sleep, human association, kingship, the different kinds of government, and the neo-Platonic doctrine of emanation, according to which the earth is not governed directly by the Creator but rather by a hierarchy of "intellects" corresponding to the celestial spheres. He claims to have discussed all these topics in works now lost. His extant works often cite philosophers, especially Aristotle, as well as the physician Galen and the geographers Marinus of Tyre (d. 130) and Ptolemy (d. 168).

In addition to learning from Greek thinkers and their Muslim heirs, al-Masʿūdī was influenced by the teachings of the Muʿtazilah (literally, "the separatists"), a group of theological and scientific thinkers originally associated with the southern Iraqi town of Basra. He appears to have met several contemporary representatives of the Muʿtazilah, although--as with most of his teachers--one can only guess when or where such meetings would have taken place. In any case, he was clearly sympathetic to many of the opinions they professed. Like them, he believed that the world was an orderly place, governed by laws that God had established and was unlikely to violate. Like them, too, he had little patience for scholars who explained phenomena by referring to older authorities rather than to reason and the evidence of their own eyes. In his *Meadows of Gold*, he states that unless an assertion is backed by universal assent or corroborating evidence, "it remains neither excluded nor necessary, and thus only in the realm of the possible."

Al-Masʿūdī's extant works contain no explicit profession of sectarian allegiance. They do, however, narrate early Islamic history in a manner that reveals his belief that certain descendants of the Prophet were the best qualified to rule as caliphs. In particular, his treatment of the Prophet's cousin ʿAlī ibn Abī Ṭālib (ca. 600-660) indicates that al-Masʿūdī was a Shiite, probably of the Twelver branch. The Shiites held that God had designated a specific member of the Prophet's family in each generation to serve as the *imām*: that is, the person assigned to guide the community to salvation. In this respect, the Shiites disagreed with the Muʿtazilah, who believed that the Muslim community was free to choose its own *imām*. A Twelver Shiite was one who recognized a particular set of twelve *imāms* beginning with ʿAlī and ending with his descendant Muḥammad al-Mahdī, who had gone into hiding in 873 or 874 and was expected to return and usher in a millennial reign of justice.

Because al-Masʿūdī's specifically sectarian works have not survived, it is difficult to accept or reject the suggestion that his apparent Twelver affiliation served merely as a cover for his membership in another, smaller Shiite sect, that of the Ismailis. The Ismailis recognized seven *imāms*, not twelve, and espoused cosmological doctrines that diverged from those of mainstream Shiism. André Miquel's argument for al-Masʿūdī's Ismailism is based on circumstantial evidence, including al-Masʿūdī's interest in cosmology; his voyages to places such as Oman, where there were communities of Ismailis; and his unexplained departure from Baghdad shortly before the coming of the Twelver Buwayhid dynasty, which would presumably have regarded him as a heretic. Other modern scholars, including Charles Pellat, Ahmed Shboul, and Tarif Khalidi, have found Miquel's arguments for al-Masʿūdī's Ismailism unconvincing.

In 915 or 916, al-Masʿūdī embarked on the first of his many voyages. Because he left no complete itinerary or travelogue, his journeys must be reconstructed from the incidental remarks in his two extant works. According to two modern scholars, S. Maqbul Ahmad and Ahmad Shboul, al-Masʿūdī's first trip took him to parts of what are today Iran, Afghanistan, Pakistan, and India. He appears to have begun the journey by traveling from Baghdad to Basra on the Persian Gulf. Although Basra itself was doubtless too familiar to readers to merit description, he does mention that one can fish there at night using lamps: attracted by the light, the fish leap out of the water into the fishermen's boats. This phenomenon, he says, supplies Zoroastrians with an argument for the extraordinary attractiveness of fire, which they consider an intermediary between God and His creation. In this as in many other cases, al-Masʿūdī presents the beliefs of non-Muslims as faithfully as he can. He often makes an effort to demonstrate why those beliefs might seem reasonable, and only occasionally expresses disapproval of them.

While in Basra, al-Masʿūdī met Abū Zayd Ḥasan ibn Yazīd al-Sīrāfī, author of a book about India and China, and a copious source of Eastern lore. Among the stories Abū Zayd passed on to al-Masʿūdī is the one told by an Arab traveler who claimed to have met the emperor of China. After asking about the Arabs and their religion, the emperor shows the traveler a scroll containing pictures of the prophets, including Noah, Jesus, and Muḥammad. As transmitted by Abū Zayd and al-Masʿūdī, this report contains what seems to be a description of a Christian devotional text. What remains unknown is the narrator's reason for putting such images into the hands of the Chinese emperor, a figure who in this period is unlikely to have taken an interest in the religious beliefs of Christians and Muslims. Whatever the case, it is easy to guess why the story appealed to al-Masʿūdī. Fascinated as he was with the beliefs of others, he may have been unable to resist a story about the impression his own faith had made on them.

From Basra, al-Masʿūdī appears to have followed the Persian Gulf coast eastward through Khuzistan as far as Sīrāf. From there he turned north to cross the province of Fārs, the heartland of the ancient empires of Persia. The first of these empires, that of the Achaemenids, had ruled Southwest Asia from the seventh to the fourth centuries B.C.E. Al-Mas'ūdī reports that Achaemenid history, though not forgotten, was difficult to reconstruct because it was preserved only in divergent oral traditions. Thus it was that he visited Persepolis, the dynasty's most spectacular monument, without knowing exactly what he was looking at. In the *Meadows*, he refers to the site as a Zoroastrian fire temple. (In reality, it had been a ceremonial complex where representatives of subject nations had come to pay tribute to the Achaemenid king.) His description emphasizes the same features that may be seen today: the "vast courtyard" and "the marvelous stone pillars, which are topped with impressive carvings of horses and other animals." He adds that the inhabitants of the region regard the reliefs (which depict Persian and Median soldiers and representatives of the tributary nations) as images of the prophets. They also believe that King Solomon imprisoned the wind there, a conclusion that al-Masʿūdī finds reasonable given that "the temple is located at the foot of a mountain, and the wind roars through it night and day" (*Murūj*, 2:399-400=§ 1403).

In the nearby town of Istakhr, al-Masʿūdī added to his knowledge of another Persian dynasty, that of the Sassanians, who had ruled Persia and Iraq before the Arab conquest. Unlike the Achaemenids, the Sassanians were relatively well known thanks to the translation of Middle Persian books into Arabic during the eighth and ninth centuries. In Istakhr, al-Masʿūdī discovered a new book of the same kind. Compiled in 731 on the basis of Sassanian archival material and translated into Arabic for the caliph Hishām (reigned 724-743), it contained information about "the kings, the monuments, and the policies" of the Sassanians. It also contained vivid color portraits of the dynasty's twenty-five emperors and two empresses. The last ruler, Yazdegerd (d. 651 or 652), for example, was depicted "in a figured green mantle, figured sky-blue trousers, and a crimson crown, holding a lance and leaning on a sword" (*Tanbīh*, 106-107).

From Fārs al-Masʿūdī seems to have traveled east through Kirman and Sijistan before turning north to Khurāsān, a vast region that includes what is today northeastern Iran as well as parts of Turkmenistan and Afghanistan. He mentions Balkh, Bukhara, and other cities of the Oxus River delta on the Aral Sea, and lists the distances between them. In January, he reports, the Oxus floods, leaving nearby towns stranded on their hilltops like fortresses, with no passage between them possible except by boat. At its eastern extremity, the river disappears into forests and swamps. Some authorities claim that it runs underground, resurfaces in Kirman, and empties into the Persian Gulf; but al-Masʿūdī, who took a special interest in rivers and their courses, was unpersuaded. "I have gone through every part, chilly and torrid alike, of Fārs, Kirman, and Sijistan," he declares firmly, "and found no sign that such is the case" (*Tanbīh*, 66). Here as elsewhere, he shows does not hesitate to reject the testimony of others when it conflicts with the evidence of his own eyes.

Al-Masʿūdī's next destination was Hind, a term that covers the territory of the modern state of Pakistan as well as that of India. From his north-to-south description of the territories of the Indus, it appears that he reached the Punjab and Sind (today, the northeastern and southern provinces of Pakistan) by taking the caravan route from Khurāsān through the Indus Valley. At the time of his visit, which lasted from 915 to 916 or 917, parts of the valley had been under Muslim control for two centuries, but the local population appears to have been predominantly Buddhist. The kings of the region "are often at odds, and fight one another" and "the people speak different languages and hold clashing opinions, with most of them believing in reincarnation and the transmigration of souls" (*Murūj*, 1: 91=§169). His description of the city of Multan, in what is today Pakistan, indicates that some communities had nevertheless achieved a relatively peaceful form of coexistence. He reports that Multan is ruled by a Muslim king but serves as a pilgrimage center for non-Muslims, who flock to the city to venerate a statue. Rather than destroy the statue, the Muslim king keeps his treasury full by taxing the pilgrims' offerings of money, gems, aloes, and perfumes.

South of Multan was al-Manṣūrah, where al-Masʿūdī was particularly taken with the two enormous elephants owned by the king. One of the elephants was famous for having mourned the death of one of his keepers by weeping, moaning, and refusing to eat or drink. The same elephant had also once blocked a street to prevent passerby from looking at a woman who had fallen to the ground in an indecorous posture. In another kingdom, that of Dahram, al-Masʿūdī learned of the rhinoceros, which he describes in some detail. He takes the opportunity to correct a claim made in the writings of the eminent essayist al-Jāḥiẓ. Al-Jāḥiẓ had written that the rhinoceros has a gestation period of seven years and that the fetus feeds by poking its head outside the womb. Finding this report unlikely, al-Masʿūdī consulted a number of informants, all of whom were astounded to hear it. The gestation period of the rhinoceros, they informed him, is the same as for water buffalo and cattle. The alleged behavior of the fetus seems to have been too absurd for comment. This incident illustrates another of al-Masʿūdī's habits: his practice of consulting local experts, whose testimony he preferred to that of armchair scholars.

After following the Indus down to the sea, al-Masʿūdī appears to have traveled south along the coast as far as present-day Bombay. Unlike the regions he had visited so far, these were ruled not by Muslims but by Brahmins. Among the places he mentions visiting is Cambay, a region of coconut groves populated by peacocks, parrots, and other birds, where the ruler made a practice of debating with visitors of other faiths. Uncharacteristically, al-Masʿūdī does not appear to have debated him. He does, however, have more to say about Cambay in the course of a discussion of the tides. The city, he reports, is located on a bay some two days' journey from the sea. At low tide, the water recedes to the point that the sandy bottom of the bay is exposed. At high tide, the water comes rushing back, moving so quickly that dogs cannot outrun it and are drowned. The same phenomenon, he says, may be witnessed on the Persian Gulf coast between Basra and Aḥwāz, where the tide rushes in with "a great roaring and boiling" (*Murūj*, 1:136=§ 270). Elsewhere he says that he thinks it likely that tides are caused by the action of the moon.

Further south along the Indian coast was Saymur, where al-Masʿūdī witnessed a young man's ritual suicide. After being paraded through the streets by a crowd playing drums and cymbals, the young man cut open his own belly with a dagger to indicate his contempt for death. Throughout his ordeal, he chewed on betel leaves, presumably because of their narcotic effect. Al-Masʿūdī comments that the leaves, which also freshen the breath and strengthen the teeth and gums, have become a popular commodity in western Arabia and Yemen. At the end of the ceremony, the young man flung himself into a bonfire. In a rare expression of disgust, al-Masʿūdī comments that such rituals "are horrifying and make the skin crawl" (*Murūj*, 1:248-249=§ 515-516). Nevertheless, he admits having described more of them in his (now lost) second book on universal history, *al-Awsaṭ* (The Intermediate).

Although al-Masʿūdī's works describe places beyond the western coast of India, there is no evidence that he visited those places himself. In one passage, he describes a royal funeral in Sarandib, now Sri Lanka. Yet, as Shboul points out in *al-Masʿūdī and his World*, the passage is borrowed from the work of another traveler. Moreover, the phrase "I saw" that occurs in some editions does not appear in all the manuscripts and may be a copyist's error. In another passage, al-Masʿūdī claims to have crossed the China Sea, and in yet another, China itself. From other parts of the book, nevertheless, it is clear that he considered the "China Sea" to be part of the Indian Ocean, meaning that the reference "may be considered the result of imprecision." As for China, "there is no evidence in his surviving works to indicate personal acquaintance" with it. Shboul therefore suggests that al-Masʿūdī's claim to have gone there "be viewed in the context of his especial pride over his wide journeys" (*Masʿūdī*, 7). From India, al-Masʿūdī apparently sailed westward across the Indian Ocean to the port of Ṣuḥār in Oman. There he joined Omani seafarers who took him south along the Arabian and East African coasts to an island he calls Qanbalū. Of all the seas he had ever crossed, this one, he says, was the most terrifying. He quotes a song the sailors sang to keep up their courage as their ship rose and fell in high seas, and describes how they would strike wooden clappers to frighten off whales. He adds that all of the men he sailed with were later lost at sea. As for Qanbalū, which has been variously identified as Madagascar, Zanzibar, or one of the Comoros Islands, he says that its inhabitants are Africans ruled by Muslim invaders who now speak a local language. On his way to or from Qanbalū, he may also have stopped at Socotra, an island off the coast of Yemen. Its inhabitants, he says, are the descendants of Greeks sent there by Alexander the Great on the advice of Aristotle.

Although he does not appear to have landed on the coast, al-Masʿūdī has much to say about the East African mainland. He discusses the commodities exported from the region, including leopard skins, tortoiseshell, and emeralds; and describes the elephant, the water buffalo, and the giraffe. He also made an effort to learn what he could about the *zanj* or native East Africans. His comments reflect his interest, which is evident also from his reading of Plato and al-Fārābī (d. 950), in the ways in which human beings use their religious beliefs to organize themselves into communities. The *zanj*, he says, have no divinely revealed law, but rather follow customs established by their kings. They call their king the son of God unless he oppresses them, in which case they withdraw his title, kill him, and forbid his descendants to ascend the throne.

On the way back to Ṣuḥār, or after returning there, al-Masʿūdī may have traveled southwest along the Arabian coast to Yemen and then possibly also north to the Ḥijāz (western Arabia). It is clear from various references in his works that he did visit these places, although none of the references are dated. Speaking of the Arabian coast, he notes the poverty of the inhabitants as well as their distinctive dialect. In Oman and Yemen, he asked local informants about the genealogy of their tribes, which was a matter of interest for historians of early Islam. In Ṣanʿāʾ, today the capital of Yemen, he visited the ruins of the once-famous palace of Ghumdān, built, he says, by a Preislamic king in honor of Venus. He reports being impressed by the abilities of Yemeni trackers, who could identify people by their footprints. In Mecca and Medina, he doubtless performed the pilgrimage, a ritual incumbent upon all capable Muslims; and in Medina copied the inscription on the tomb of Fāṭimah (d. 632 or 633), the Prophet's daughter, from whom the Shiite *imāms* were descended.

By 918, al-Masʿūdī was back in Baghdad. There, according to a report preserved in a later biographical source, he was among those who attended the legal scholar Aḥmad ibn ʿUmar Ibn Surayj (863-918) during his final illness. He also copied Ibn Surayj's summary treatise on the principles of jurisprudence according to the Shafiʿi school, one of the Sunni schools of legal interpretation. This report is one of the few references to al-Masʿūdī's study of law. In his day, the Shiite minority and Sunni majority disagreed not only on the definition of the imamate but also on certain points of ritual and law. Shiites, for example, permitted temporary marriage, while Sunnis did not. Al-Masʿūdī was interested in such matters, and wrote three books dealing with them. Unfortunately, all three are lost. Therefore, his opinions can be reconstructed only on the basis of references to legal matters in his surviving works.

In a study of one such passage, Devin Stewart argues that al-Masʿūdī supported literal (that is, not figurative) readings of the *Qur'ān* and the *ḥadīth*. Consequently, he rejected the use of analogy (*qiyās* or *ijtihād*), personal opinion (*ra'y*), and juridical preference (*istiḥsān*). In other words, he upheld the idea that legal and ritual matters should be decided on the basis of revelation rather than reason. This position was characteristic of Shiite jurists, who considered the text of the *Qur'ān* and the practice of the Prophet and the imams to be the only valid sources of law. Among Sunnis, a similar position was characteristic of the Ẓāhirī (literally, "exoteric") school of jurisprudence. The Ẓāhirīs argued that legal verdicts must be based on a precise understanding of the actual words of the *Qur'ān* and the *ḥadīth* rather than extrapolation from the presumed intention behind the text. Because Shiite and Ẓāhirī views overlapped, Shiite scholars who wished to study with Sunni teachers could call themselves Ẓāhirīs without betraying their own beliefs. According to Stewart, al-Masʿūdī may have been one of the scholars who did so, possibly in order to participate more fully in the interpretation of Islamic law.

Al-Masʿūdī's next journey or journeys took him from Baghdad to the Mediterranean coast, Syria, and northern Iraq. In 921 or 922 he visited the northern Syrian town of Aleppo. During the same journey, along the coast of what is today Lebanon, he spoke with naval commanders and sailors who were engaged in fighting against the Byzantines on the Mediterranean Sea. Among those he met was the Greek convert Leo of Tripoli, who died at sea shortly thereafter; as well as the commander of the Muslim garrison at Adana, in what is today south-central Turkey. From these sources, it seems, al-Masʿūdī acquired his information about Constantinople, the capital of the Byzantine Empire. He mentions its sea walls, towers, and churches, and describes the Golden Gate, one of its most famous landmarks. As for the Byzantines themselves, he remarks that their ancient Greek ancestors attained great knowledge of the sciences, including the quadrivium of arithmetic, geometry, astronomy, and music; but that all these sciences have been forgotten by the Greeks since their conversion to Christianity.

Despite his criticism of the Byzantines, al-Masʿūdī was eager to consult Christian sources on world history and church doctrine. During his travels in Syria and Iraq, he visited churches and monasteries in search of scholars and books. In 925 or 926, in the Iraqi town of Tikrīt, he met the Jacobite Christian Abū Zakariyyā Dankhā and debated with him on the nature of the Trinity. Al-Masʿūdī offers no detail about the debate, although his description of Dankhā as "contentious" suggests that the Christian may have bested him. Whatever the case, it is clear that al-Masʿūdī was familiar with church history and doctrines. In the *Reference Guide*, he provides an account of the ecumenical councils, and mentions a now lost work of his that explains the disagreements among the Melkites, Maronites, Jacobites, and Nestorians regarding the nature of Christ.

After visiting the northern Iraqi town of Mosul, al-Masʿūdī appears to have headed westward again, this time to the region now occupied by the modern states of Israel and Jordan. In 926 or 927 he was in Tiberias. There he met a diehard partisan of the Umayyad dynasty—which had been overthrown in the east in 750 but subsequently revived in far-off Spain—who showed him a book full of arguments to the effect that the Umayyads had been true imams and would return to usher in the millennium. Such a doctrine would have been particularly obnoxious to a Shiite like al-Masʿūdī, but even here he confines himself to an objective description of the other point of view. At an unknown date, but possibly during this period, he also visited Petra, in what is today Jordan. He identifies this ancient Nabatean city as the dwelling of the Arabian tribe of Thamūd, whose extinction is described in the *Qur'ān* (7:73-79; 11:61-68). Noticing that the entranceways of Petra are low and the chambers small, he dismisses the claim of "storytellers" that the tribesmen of Thamūd were giants.

In Tiberias, as well as Ramlah, Nablus, and Jerusalem, al-Masʿūdī investigated the beliefs and practices of the local Jews and Christians. He reports on the existence of the Samaritan sect, whose members consider Moses to be the last of the prophets and the city of Nablus to be the site of the Temple. He notes that Lake Tiberias is where Jesus recruited followers by inviting them to become "fishers of men" (Matthew 4:19; Mark 1:17). In Nazareth, he visited a church where the tombs of those buried there exude a thick oil with supposedly miraculous properties. In Jerusalem, he saw Solomon's temple, which he identifies with al-Aqsā mosque; the Church of the Resurrection, "the greatest church the Christians have in Jerusalem," and the churches of Zion and Gethsemane. He also visited the Dead Sea (which he calls the "Stinking Lake") and the cavern (in present-day Jordan) reported to house the grave of Moses. Finally, he reports having debated many times in Palestine and Jordan with Abū Kathīr Yaḥyā ibn Zakariyā 'l-Ṭabarānī, a Jewish scholar who helped translate the Torah from Hebrew into Arabic. Among the topics they debated was the abrogation of the scriptures: the question of how (or whether) later revelations from God, such as the *Qur'ān*, override older ones, such as the Torah.

At some point before 927, al-Masʻūdī visited Damascus. He cites a report that the city had been founded by Jayrūn, a Preislamic Arab king, and is identical with the "many-columned Iram" mentioned in the *Qur'ān* (89:7). The gate of Jayrūn's palace, he says, was now part of the city market. He toured the Umayyad Mosque, which even today is the city's major monument, and he copied an inscription by its founder, the caliph al-Walīd I (reigned 705-715). He also visited the tomb alleged to be that of Muʻāwiyah ibn Abī Sufyān (d. 680), the first caliph of the Umayyad dynasty (661-750), and reports that it was open to the public two days a week.

It was probably before his return to Baghdad in 926 or 927 that al-Masʻūdī visited Baʻlabakk, in what is today Lebanon's Bekaa Valley; Palmyra, in the Syrian desert; and al-Raqqah, near the border of the present-day state of Iraq. Baalbek he describes as two large and impressively decorated temples built by the Greeks to house their idols. These ruins, which are in fact Roman, still exist today. Palmyra, an Arab city-state that flourished in the third century A.D., he describes as a marvelous construction made of stone, with an amphitheater. These ruins, too, remain in existence. Regarding al-Raqqah, once a major Abbasid settlement, he mentions only that he debated there with two Jewish scholars.

The northernmost point that al-Masʻūdī mentions in Syria is Harran, then the cultic center of the Sabean sect. He explains that the members of this sect once built temples to the First Cause, the Active Intellect, and other entities described by Greek philosophers, as well as to the planets. In his time, however, there remained only one temple, associated with the father of the Biblical and *Qur'ānic* Abraham. In its cellars are idols that frighten children by speaking to them; but the speech, al-Masʻūdī says, is that of priests hidden in an adjoining chamber and speaking through tubes. The Sabeans, he concludes, have preserved some of the wisdom of ancient Greece but they are not true philosophers because they have no wisdom of their own.

In 928, al-Masʻūdī left Syria, apparently by sailing downstream on the Euphrates. Shortly before reaching Baghdad, he was forced to stop in the town of Hīt, which was being attacked by members of the dissident Qarmatī sect. In the *Tanbīh*, he provides an eyewitness account of the siege. After the garrison succeeded in driving the attackers back from the walls, the citizens of Hīt were alarmed by a great glow in the sky. They were relieved to learn that the source of the glow an enormous fire outside the city: the Qarmatīs had decided to burn their own equipment and abandon the siege. At some point in the course of these events, al-Masʻūdī managed to speak with Qarmatī missionaries who explained to him the teachings of their sect. Although he has nothing good to say about their religious and political doctrines, he admits to being impressed with their learning and piety.

Al-Masʻūdī's travels over the next several years cannot be dated precisely. After a return trip to the Iranian provinces of Aḥwāz and Fārs in 930 or shortly thereafter, he traveled to the Caspian Sea region, probably in the period between 932 and 941. Hoping to learn whether there was a passage from the Caspian to the Black Sea, he sailed from Abaskun on the coast of Jurjān (now Gorgan, in present-day Iran) to a number of Caspian ports, making inquiries of ship captains and tradesmen. He also inquired about a series of shipborne raids carried out shortly before his visit by the Russians against the Caspian shores. If the two seas were connected, he says, the Russians would have gone on to attack Constantinople. Since they did not, he concludes (correctly) that the two bodies of water are separate. While traveling on the Caspian, he also visited Baku (in what is today Azerbaijan), where a continuous roaring flame issued from the ground, filling the sky with light and smoke for miles around. He compares the phenomenon with Mount Aetna in Sicily and the oil geysers he had seen in South Arabia. The latter comparison is the more apt, since, as he notes, the flame was fueled by oil rising to the surface of the ground.

On the northern shore of the Caspian, al-Masʻūdī visited ʻĀṭil (near present-day Astrakhan), the capital of the Khazars, where he was struck by the diversity of peoples and religions. The ruling family, he reports, were converts to Judaism, while the vizier and many of the soldiers were Muslims. The city was also home to Christians as well pagan Russians and "Slavs," a term of vague application in this period. The pagans, he says, burn their dead. When a man dies, his widow is cremated; but when a woman dies, her husband is not. Al-Masʿūdī points out that Indians have a similar custom, although (he claims) they will not cremate a woman without her permission. Among the other peoples of the Caspian region, he mentions the Burtas, a Turkic tribe that trades in furs and pelts; and the Bulgars, who in his time were ruled by a Muslim king who had carried out raids on Constantinople.

Al-Masʿūdī appears to have traveled extensively in the Caucasus, which he describes as a mountainous region populated by seventy-two nations, each with its own language. Although he perpetuates this and other legends, his account of the region is (according to Shboul in *al-Mas'ūdī and his World*) "the most original and complete description in classical Muslim sources of the geography, ethnography, and politics of this area" at the time (*Mas'ūdī*, 171-172). He concludes by thanking God for the mountainous terrain and fortified passes that separate the various Caucasian peoples from the heartland of Islam. The Muslim community, he says, is now divided, in much the same way Alexander the Great's kingdom was divided after his death; if not for God's disposition of the terrain, the Muslims would be easy prey for their warlike neighbors.

In the period after 941, al-Masʿūdī continued to travel, making what he describes as frequent visits to Damascus, Antioch, and the Byzantine frontier. He does not appear to have returned to his native region of Iraq. His seeming unwillingness to travel there has been linked to political and also with religious circumstances. In 941, Baghdad was seized by the Barīdī family of Basra. Soon afterwards, the caliph al-Muṭīʿ placed himself and his capital under the protection of the Buwayhid dynasty. The accompanying disorder in Iraq may have dissuaded al-Masʿūdī from going there. If, furthermore, he was indeed an Ismaili, as Miquel has suggested, he may have avoided Iraq for fear of persecution by the Twelver Shiite Buwayhids. There is, however, no direct evidence for these proposals.

On January 6, 942, al-Masʿūdī was in Fusṭāṭ, the major site of Muslim settlement in Egypt. There he attended the celebration of the Christian festival of Epiphany. He reports that the sultan, Muḥammad ibn Tughj al-Ikhshīdī, set up torches on the banks of the Nile. Muslims as well as Christians gathered on the shore, carrying food, drink, games, and musical instruments, and "the Muslims and the Christians displayed no hostility to each other." Many of the revelers leapt into the Nile, whose waters were supposed to cure illness and prevent disease. He reports that Epiphany "is the most enjoyable festival in Egypt" (*Murūj*, 2:69-70=§780).

From 942 until his death, al-Masʿūdī appears to have been based in Fusṭāṭ and to have traveled extensively within Egypt. He visited Alexandria on the Mediterranean coast and Aswan, Akhmim, Qifṭ, and Qus in the south, asking local informants about the pyramids, temples, languages, and writing systems of ancient times. As it appears in the *Meadows*, some of this material is legendary: for example, the story of Alexander the Great and the sea monsters. Other reports are speculative but reasonable, such as the claim that the pyramids were built up in stages and then smoothed from the top down. Others again are entirely matter-of-fact, such as the detailed description of the contents of a Pharaonic tomb.

Al-Masʿūdī's two surviving works, *Murūj al-dhahab* (*The Meadows of Gold*) and *al-Tanbīh wa 'l-ishrāf*, were composed in Egypt. Of his other works, twenty-three are mentioned in *Meadows*, and must therefore have been written before 947, but they are lost and cannot be dated more precisely. The two surviving works belong to the series of books he wrote on universal history: that is, the description of the earth, its regions, and its peoples, and the history of the great nations, with particular attention to the history of the Muslims. The first and largest work in this series was the *Akhbār al-zamān* (Accounts of World History), to which the reader of his extant books is constantly referred for more detail. (A volume purporting to represent the first part of this book has been published, but it appears to be an apocryphon, possibly with some borrowings from the genuine *Akhbār al-zamān*.) The second work in the series was called *al-Awsaṭ* (The Intermediate), evidently because it was smaller than its predecessor. The title suggests that al-Masʿūdī already planned to write a third, shorter universal history, as indeed he did. This third work is the *Meadows of Gold*, of which he had completed the first 33 chapters by January 944 and the entirety (consisting of 132 chapters of unequal length) at some time in 947 or 948. Several years later, he produced a revised and expanded version, which is now lost.

The *Meadows* begins with an account of the creation of the world, or more exactly with several accounts: in this as in other disputed matters, al-Masʿūdī provides several reports. In this case, the one he appears to favor reports that God placed a portion of light into a form corresponding to the Prophet Muḥammad. God then created the heavens and the earth and unfurled time. Adam, the first man, and certain of his descendants contained in themselves the light that would one day appear as the Prophet Muḥammad. After Muḥammad's death, the light continued to be manifest in his descendants, the imams, who provide guidance and salvation to those who acknowledge them.

In the next sections of the *Meadows*, al-Masʿūdī summarizes the story of the ancient patriarchs, prophets, and kings according to the Hebrew Bible and the *Qur'ān*. He retells the life of Jesus based on the Gospels and sketches out the progress of religious ideas in Arabia in the period before Muḥammad. He then turns to India, which some scholars regard as the original source of philosophical and religious ideas. He reports on the foundation of the first kingdom in India and reproduces a Brahmanic discussion of the meaning of life. Here, as Tarif Khalidi has argued, al-Masʿūdī's choice of themes reflects his interest in the problem of whether human societies can have attained a proper understanding of the nature of the universe and of their place in it without the help of divine revelation (*Islamic Historiography*, 60-70, 81-113).

Before resuming his account of ancient history, al-Masʿūdī devotes several chapters to geography. The earth, he knew, was round. He gives various figures for its circumference, of which Ptolemy's figure of 25,000 miles comes closest (assuming that the miles in question are the same length) to the modern figure of 24,901.55. Al-Masʿūdī describes the inhabited world, which for him extended from the Canary Islands in the west to "farthest China" in the east, and from "an island called Thule, in Britain" in the north to "an island between Ethiopia and India" in the south. He gives figures for the distances and diameters of the sun, moon, and planets. He describes the major rivers of the world, including the Nile, the Ganges, and the Tigris; as well as the seas of the world, including the "Sea of Ethiopia" (that is, that part of the Indian Ocean that adjoins Africa), the Mediterranean Sea, the Black Sea, and the Caspian. After a discussion of the early history of the Turks and the Chinese, he returns to the subject of oceans and of geographical regions in general. Here he describes some of the places he had visited in Persia, Arabia, India, and the Caucasus, as well as places such as Tibet that were known to him only through hearsay.

Returning to ancient history, the *Meadows* takes up the "Syrians," the Assyrians, the Babylonians or Chaldeans, the Persians, the ancient Greeks, Alexander and his successors, the Romans, the Byzantines, and the Egyptians. These sections, based on a combination of Jewish, Greek, and Persian sources, are not surprisingly full of errors, especially in regard to the most ancient periods; but they are nevertheless impressive for their attempt to construct dynastic lists for the major empires and to relate them to each other.

According to Tarif Khalidi, al-Masʿūdī's treatment of the ancient nations reflects a philosophy of history according to which "wise men are able to deduce the principles of social organization without the benefit of a revealed law" (*Islamic Historiography*, 63). When rulers govern justly, as was most famously the case in ancient Iran, societies approximate the highest ideals of virtue. Nevertheless, al-Masʿūdī suggests, the ancient civilizations eventually failed and collapsed when their leaders rejected the promptings of the intellect and choose instead "to follow a course of unquestioning obedience to tradition or to the subtleties of charlatans" (*Islamic Historiography*, 53). Fortunately, the accumulated wisdom of the ancient nations, including their arts and sciences, has survived, and remains available to those few who choose to avail themselves of it.

In addition to illustrating a philosophy of history, al-Masʿūdī's account of the ancient nations reveals an unusual breadth of interest in what today would be called social, cultural, and material history. He comments, for example, on the Babylonians' invention of new techniques in irrigation, agriculture, and military engineering; on the qualifications for serving as a jester at the court of the Persian emperor; and on the Byzantines' practice of writing in Ancient Greek because of the inadequacy of their own (spoken) language for scholarly purposes.

In the section on the Byzantines, as well as in the following sections on the peoples of Africa and Europe, the *Meadows* moves from ancient (that is, Preislamic) history to a description of the non-Muslim societies of later periods up to al-Masʿūdī's own time. The chapter on Africa deals largely with geography, although there is some discussion of Arab settlement, slavery, and land tenure. The chapters on the European peoples describe the Slavs, whom al-Masʿūdī had encountered in his travels, as well as the Franks, the Galicians, the Lombards, and the Spaniards. For the chronology of the Frankish kings, he drew on a work by Godmar, a Catalan bishop, who in 939 or 940 had presented a history of the Franks to al-Ḥakam II al-Mustanṣir (d. 976), the heir apparent to the caliphate of Cordoba. According to Bernard Lewis, there are only three pre-modern Muslim descriptions of Western Europe, of which al-Masʿūdī's is the earliest (Lewis, "al-Masʿūdī on the Kings of the Franks," 10).

Having thus covered the entirety of the inhabited world as he knew it, al-Masʿūdī establishes the background for the rise of Islam by devoting several chapters to Arabia. He reports traditions regarding ʿĀd and Thamūd, two extinct tribes mentioned in the *Qur'ān*. He surveys the history of Mecca, whose shrine, according to Muslim tradition, had been founded by Abraham as a temple to the one God, although Arabian pagans later took over the shrine and worshipped idols there. The next chapter, which along with several others seems out of order (at least in this first draft of the *Meadows*), deals with the climate of the various parts of the Muslim world, with homesickness, and with the importance of studying history and writing books.

The historical narrative resumes with an account of Yemen. In Preislamic times, the region had supported powerful kingdoms, and a Yemeni queen had been mentioned in the *Qur'ān* (27:20-44). Yet, much of Yemeni history was legendary, and al-Masʿūdī expresses his discomfort with it. After mentioning a report that the queen, identified as Bilqīs, was the daughter of a demon, he comments that certain reports may appear incredible but have support in the *Qur'ān* or the testimony of reliable transmitters. Evidently, he felt obliged to explain that, if not for religious tradition, he would find such claims difficult if not impossible to believe.

The next sections of the *Meadows* deal with the Preislamic Arab kingdoms of Mesopotamia and Syria, the Bedouin Arabs, and the nomadic Berbers and Kurds. Al-Masʿūdī depicts the religious beliefs of the Arabs as having degenerated from Abrahamic monotheism into the veneration of idols and angels. He devotes attention to the Arab belief in the existence of ghouls and other demons. Such beliefs, he says, are neither imposed nor excluded by revealed religion, although they are dismissed by "those who practice theoretical inquiry and apply rational investigation" (*Murūj*, 2:293=§1205). He offers a rational explanation of his own, namely that demonic apparitions result from the fear of traveling through deserted places at night.

The next chapters deal with divination and soothsaying, and include digressions on such matters as Zoroastrian and Christian beliefs about the nature of God. The discussion then turns to the systems of timekeeping used by the Persians, the Nabateans, the Syrian Christians, and the ancient Arabs, including the folklore associated with the names of the months and the days of the week. The following chapters, ostensibly devoted to fire and other natural forces, address such matters as fetal development, the connection between lunar phases and fevers, the earth's gravity, the four humors, the doctrine of the cyclical cosmos, and the effect of climate on the body. Al-Masʿūdī eagerly pursues evidence of connections between different natural phenomena, but continues to express skepticism regarding reports of monsters and other wonders.

Returning to the history of religion, al-Masʿūdī devotes several chapters to ritual practices and cultic buildings. He again raises the question of religion before revelation, reporting that the Indians worshipped idols representing God and the angels but later began worshipping the stars, a practice encouraged (he says) by the Buddha. The Persians, meanwhile, worshipped fire; although they, like the Indians, believed themselves to be worshipping God. He then describes the great temples of the world, including one in China reputed to contain a treasury of all the wisdom of the ages. In connection with such legends, he remarks that similar stories may be found in translated works of fiction such as the *Thousand and One Nights*. This remark is one of the earliest references to the *Nights*. Next follows a long list of marvels and wonders, including the attempts by the Romans to dig a canal between the Red Sea and the Mediterranean. The last Preislamic topic discussed is world chronology. Al-Masʿūdī surveys various positions on when (and indeed if) the earth was created, and reports the belief that it is some 6000 years old.

The remainder of the *Meadows* is devoted to the history of the Muslim community beginning with the life of the Prophet Muḥammad. Doubtless because detailed accounts were readily available in other books, the biography is telegraphic, containing only brief notes, chronologically arranged, on the major events in the Prophet's career, supplemented by a collection of his memorable pronouncements. The remainder of the Islamic history section is divided into chapters corresponding to the reigns of the caliphs--or more exactly, the reigns of those who succeeded in seizing power, since al-Masʿūdī did not recognize the legitimacy of all the claimants. Each chapter opens with an account of the ruler's date of accession and of death and an estimate of the length of his rule. The remainder of each chapter is devoted to the subject's reign, but without offering comprehensive or even chronologically ordered coverage. As al-Masʿūdī himself explains, the *Meadows* contains only those items not mentioned in his earlier works. Throughout the *Meadows*, the reader is advised to consult the now-lost *Akhbār al-zamān* or *al-Awsaṭ* for a fuller account.

In al-Masʿūdī's retelling of early Islamic history, the first two caliphs, Abū Bakr (d. 634) and ʿUmar ibn al-Khaṭṭāb (d. 644), were virtuous, pious, and ascetic; and the third, 'Uthmān ibn ʿAffān (d. 656), was generous. In this respect, al-Masʿūdī is not representative of Shiite historians, who usually have nothing good to say about these figures they deem to have been usurpers. Al-Masʿūdī's Shiite sympathies do, however, become apparent in his treatment of the fourth caliph, ʿAlī ibn Abī Ṭālib, whom Shiites consider to be the only legitimate successor of the Prophet. In al-Masʿūdī's account, ʿAlī is an invincible warrior and an incorruptible ruler who can foretell the future (the idea being that Muḥammad confided to him, and only to him, knowledge of what was to come). Some of the most gripping passages in the *Meadows*, and indeed in classical Arabic historiography generally, are those al-Masʿūdī devotes to the Battle of Siffīn, at which ʿAlī and his rival Muʿāwiyah fought to a standstill; the arbitration intended to resolve the conflict; and the deception practiced by Muʿāwiyah's representative to gain the upper hand in the negotiations.

The chapters devoted to the caliphs of the Umayyad dynasty (661-750) reflect al-Masʿūdī's belief that all of them, with the possible exception of the righteous ʿUmar ibn ʿAbd al-ʿAzīz, were illegitimate rulers. As polemical as it is, this section nevertheless contains many points of interest, again thanks to al-Masʿūdī's curiosity about social, cultural, and intellectual matters. The chapter on Muʿāwiyah, for example, contains a series of anecdotes about the character of the common people, who are depicted as staggeringly ignorant of the basic tenets of Islam. The chapter on al-Walīd ibn Yazīd reports that he was the first to hire singers from the provinces, and was also famous for his devotion to horse racing, whose special terminology al-Masʿūdī pauses to explain. Most unexpectedly, the chapter on Yazīd ibn al-Walīd contains an extended discussion of the characteristic positions of the Muʿtazilah, the Shiites, and the Khārijīs (the "dissenters" who opposed both Sunnis and Shiites) on free will, divine justice, and the definition of a legitimate *imām*.

Al-Masʿūdī's account of the Abbasid dynasty (750-1258, nominally to 1517 in Egypt) is more sympathetic, doubtless because the Abbasid claim to legitimacy was similar to that of the ʿAlīds: that is, it was based on kinship to the Prophet (the Abbasids were descended from

Muḥammad's uncle.) Again, however, the interest of this section derives less from what al-Masʿūdī reports about the caliphs themselves--who in some cases hardly appear in the chapters nominally dedicated to them--than in the digressions and asides. These include, in the chapter on the Barmakid family of viziers, a report on what the representatives of various sects had to say when asked to define love; in the chapter on the caliph al-Ma'mūn (786-833), a comical story about party-crashers and the misadventures that befall them; in the chapter on al-Muʿtamid Ibn ʿAbbād (1039-1095), a list of requirements for being a good dancer; and in the chapter on al-Mustakfī (d. 1025), versified descriptions of various foods, including asparagus, pickles, and rice pudding. The last caliph mentioned is al-Mutīʿ, of whom al-Masʿūdī reports that he exercises no power, but rather serves as a figurehead, the real rulers being the princes of the Buwayhid dynasty. The *Meadows* concludes with an exhortation to the reader to treat the work indulgently, along with a stern warning not to alter or misrepresent its contents.

Like many Arabic works of the classical period, the *Meadows* consists of loosely joined prose passages, many of which contain citations of verse. Al-Masʿūdī's prose style is famously clear and unaffected. It also serves as a remarkable demonstration of the extent to which the Arabic language of the tenth century had acquired the vocabulary necessary to describe everything from the cosmological doctrines of India to the sauces best eaten with fish. As for the poetry, none of it is al-Masʿūdī's own, but his selections reveal a thorough knowledge of the tradition. The *Meadows* contains love poems, including one spoken by a donkey; invective poems, such as the savage denunciations of the caliph al-Amīn; elegies, such as those composed in honor of ʿAlī ibn Abī Ṭālib and the viziers of the Barmakid family; and poems and songs one might characterize as ethnographic, such as sea-shanties, diviners' chants, and prayers for rain. In some cases, al-Masʿūdī cites poems as historical evidence, even for events from ancient history, evidently working from the assumption that other peoples, like the Arabs, commemorated notable occurrences in verse. He also cites poems, as well as sermons and orations, because he thinks they are noteworthy in themselves, often because of their apt expression of a particular theme, and often, too, because they are witty. In a few cases, finally, he cites verses to convey his own state of mind, as when he discusses the hardships of travel and the poignancy of homesickness.

After finishing the first draft of the *Meadows* in 947 or 948, al-Masʿūdī wrote at least four more books: *Funūn al-ma'ārif* (The Branches of Knowledge), *Dhakhā'ir al-'ulūm* (The Treasuries of Knowledge), *al-Istidhkār li-mā jarā fī sālif al-a'ṣār* (A review of the events of history), and the *Tanbīh*, which was completed in Fusṭāṭ in 956 and is the only one on this list to have survived.

Al-Masʿūdī's work was briefly interrupted on January 5, 956, when an earthquake struck Fusṭāṭ. In the *Tanbīh*, he describes the event as follows: "It felt as if there were some enormous object passing under the earth and pressing against it, causing it to move and shake, as if it were bigger than the earth, and the earth were glancing off it; accompanied by a great thundering in the air; but we all survived, thank God, and there was only minor damage to buildings" (*Tanbīh*, 48). With his lifelong interest in tides, earthquakes, and other forms of terrestrial motion, al-Masʿūdī appears eager to learn as much as he can about this phenomenon by describing its effect as closely as possible.

The *Tanbīh*, which appears to be al-Masʿūdī's last work, is intended to serve as an outline of universal history, a supplement to his previous works on the same subject, and a guide to the places in his other works where he treats particular topics more fully. Broadly speaking, its categories of subject matter and order of arrangement are largely the same as that of the *Meadows*: the cosmos, the regions and peoples of earth, ancient civilizations, and the reigns of the caliphs. Even so, it is neither an abridgement of the *Meadows* nor apparently of any other work. Certain subjects discussed in the *Meadows* are passed over, while others--notably philosophy, astronomy, and Byzantine history--are given fuller treatment. The chapter on each caliph begins with a preface that includes the name of the ruler's mother (if known), a description of his appearance, and the text of his signet ring, information that does not appear in the *Meadows*. Though a much smaller work than its predecessor, the *Tanbīh* is equally prone to digression: the chapter on the caliph al-Muʿtaṣim (794?-842), for example, contains a long excursus on the seven new cities founded by Muslims. Finally, the *Tanbīh* contains several important expressions of authorial opinion.

Among the most famous of these expressions is the discussion of scientific progress. It is true, al-Masʿūdī admits, that the precise dimensions of the continents remain unknown. Nevertheless, Muslim geographers know more about the earth than did their Greek predecessors (*Tanbīh*, 76):

> Even though we are living centuries after these ancient authors, we hope not to fall short of them in our writings and in our aspirations... On occasion, a later thinker may surpass an earlier one, because the later one enjoys greater experience, fears becoming a mere imitator, and has the benefit of seeing the errors of his predecessors. As one thinker after another discovers what his predecessors did not, scientific knowledge grows and expands. This process appears to be infinite and to have no predetermined end.

In another important passage, al-Masʿūdī evaluates the Islamic polity of his day by the standards he used to assess the ancient nations. Comparing the state of Islam to that of Alexander's empire after the death of its founder, he explains: "Every [leader] has a patch of territory he calls his own, which he defends and seeks to enlarge, while all around, people have stopped building, roads are no longer passable, entire regions have become uninhabitable, provinces fall away, and Byzantines and slave soldiers hold sway over the frontiers of Islam and many of its cities" (*Tanbīh*, 400). Despite having received the favor of divine revelation, the Muslim community is now repeating the errors of the ancient nations, whose neglect of religion and of justice precipitated their downfall.

At the end of the *Tanbīh*, al-Masʿūdī gives the date on which he completed the work according to the Islamic calendar: 345 after the Hijrah, corresponding to 956 of the Gregorian calendar. In a gesture characteristic for its universalism as well as its exotic erudition, he mentions the years elapsed since the accession of four ancient monarchs: Nebuchadnezzar; Alexander the Great; Ardashir, the founder of the Sassanian dynasty, and Yazdegerd, its last emperor.

Al-Masʿūdī died in September 956. He was reportedly buried in the so-called cemetery of al-Shāfiʿī (a Muslim jurist, d. 820, near whose tomb other notables were buried), although his gravesite is unidentified. The cemetery, as well as the site of Fusṭāṭ, is now surrounded by the massive and rapidly expanding city of Cairo, which was founded by the Shiite Fātimid dynasty shortly after al-Masʿūdī's death.

Perhaps because al-Masʿūdī spent the most productive period of his life in a region that in his time was still on the margins of the literary world, the few biographies devoted to him contain little information. His fellow Baghdadī Ibn al-Nadīm (d. 990) imagines him to have been a North African. A later biographer, Yāqūt ibn ʿAbd Allāh al-Ḥamawī (1179?-1229), corrects the error by citing al-Masʿūdī's account of his birth in the *Meadows*, but has little else to say. His other biographers are no more forthcoming.

Of the forty-two works attributed to al-Masʿūdī, only two survive. Even if five or six works of doubtful attribution are dropped from the count, the survival rate seems poor. It may be that Sunnis avoided his works because of their Shiite orientation, while Shiites avoided him because he nowhere (in his extant works, at any rate) makes an explicit declaration of allegiance to their cause. It may also be the case that, as both Sunnism and Shiism became increasingly self-contained and dogmatic orthodoxies, scholars of all stripes came to find his interest in non-Muslim peoples and creeds irrelevant or even dangerous. In later periods, he is often cited--usually inaccurately--as a source of Egyptological legend. He was appreciated fully only by Ibn Khaldūn (1332-1382), the historian and philosopher of history, who, despite finding him too credulous in certain respects, cites him "hundreds of times" (Fischel, 54). Particularly grateful for his predecessor's coverage of non-Muslim societies, Ibn Khaldūn called on the historians of his own day to "set down the situation of the world among all regions and races, as well as the customs and sectarian beliefs that have changed for their adherents, doing for this age what al-Masʿūdī did for his" (*Muqaddimah*, cited in Fischel, 58).

The qualities that appealed to Ibn Khaldūn appealed also to European scholars, who rediscovered al-Masʿūdī in the nineteenth century. In 1839, the French Orientalist Etienne Quatremère published a brief study of his life and works. By 1877, Barbier de Menard and Pavet de Courteille had completed a nine-volume edition and French translation of the *Meadows*. In 1894, the Dutch Orientalist M. J. de Goeje published an edition of the*Tanbīh*, which three years later was translated in its entirety into French. By the mid-twentieth century, al-Masʿūdī had become an object of interest among Slavicists, notably Tadeus Lewicki, who used the *Meadows* as a source for the history of the central and eastern European peoples. In 1974, Charles Pellat completed a revision of the 1877 Arabic edition and French translation of the *Meadows*, producing what is now the standard edition of that work.

Commenting on the appearance of the first French translation of the *Meadows*, the French Orientalist Ernest Renan spoke in glowing terms of al-Masʿūdī's "simplicity of style, breadth of knowledge, and lively curiosity, not to mention his taste and delicacy" ("Les Prairies d'or," in *Mélanges*, 255). Pellat, editor and translator of the *Meadows*, went so far as to argue that al-Masʿūdī was neither a historian nor a geographer but rather an *adīb*, that is, a collector of literary anecdotes on a variety of subjects. This claim is exaggerated: al-Masʿūdī, as he himself points out in the *Meadows*, went to see things for himself rather than relying on what others said about them. A more recent and more judicious assessment of his style is that of Tarif Khalidi, who argues that his prose represents a conscious attempt to enact the ideals of clarity and concision expounded by writers such as al-Jāḥiẓ and critics such as Qudāmah ibn Jaʿfar (ca. 873or 874–948) (Khalidi, *Islamic Historiography*, 14-23).

In 1958, the millenary of al-Masʿūdī's death was marked by a conference held at Aligarh Muslim University in India and attended by scholars from India, Iran, Europe, and the United States. (The Arab countries were represented only by a single scholar, though congratulatory telegrams were dispatched by King Faisal II of Iraq and President Nasser of Egypt.) The conference proceedings convey a sense of the qualities that make al-Masʿūdī an appealing object of study. He "traveled about with open eyes, open ears, an open heart, and an open mind" (Nicola A. Ziadeh, "Speech," 142); he "suppresses nothing; he neither blackens nor whitewashes, but seeks out the truth and tells it as he sees it" (Lewis, "Masʿūdī and the Muslim Renaissance," 136); he left "to the world two works whose clarity of outline and unaffected style have secured them transcultural effectiveness after a thousand years" (von Grunebaum, "Statement," 139). More recently, al-Masʿūdī has been the subject of two major studies, one by Tarif Khalidi (*Islamic Historiography*) on the practical and theoretical dimensions of his work as a historian, and one by Ahmad Shboul (*al-Mas'ūdi and his World*) on his interest in non-Muslims.

REFERENCES

Note: Al-Mas‘ūdī and his works are mentioned in numerous general surveys of Arabic literature and in studies devoted to particular historical and geographical topics. A bibliography that includes such references up to 1979 may be found in Shboul, *al-Mas'ūdī and his World*, which may also be consulted for items in Polish and Russian.

Camila Adang, *Muslim Writers on Judaism and the Hebrew Bible From Ibn Rabban to Ibn Ḥazm* (Leiden: Brill, 1996), 44-48;

K.J. Ahmad, "Masudi. (One of the greatest encyclopedists and travelers in Islam.)," in *Proceedings of the Pakistan Historical Conference 6* (1956):133-138;

S. Maqbul Ahmad., "Geographical materials in the writings of al-Masʿūdī," (Ph.D. diss., University of Oxford, 1947);

S. Maqbul Ahmad, "Arabic Source Materials on Indo-Arab Relations," *Medieval India Quarterly* (Aligarh) 3:1-2, 100-108;

S. Maqbul Ahmad and A. Rahman, editors, *al-Mas'ūdī Millenary Commemoration Volume* (Calcutta: The Indian Society for the History

of Science and The Institute for Islamic Studies, Aligarh Muslim University, 1960);
S. Maqbul Ahmad, "al-Masʿūdī on the kings of India," in *al-Masʿūdī Millenary Commemoration Volume*, edited by S. Maqbul Ahmad and A. Rahman (Calcutta: The Indian Society for the History of Science and The Institute for Islamic Studies, Aligarh Muslim University, 1960), 97-112;
S. Maqbul Ahmad, "al-Masʿūdī's Contributions to Medieval Arab Geography," *Islamic Culture* 27 (1953): 61-27; 28:275-86;
S. Maqbul Ahmad, "The travels of Abu 'l Ḥasan ʿAli b. al-Husayn al-Masʿūdī," *Islamic Culture* 28 (1954): 509-24;
S. Maqbul Ahmad, "Two Early Arab Geographers Describe India," *The Aligarh Magazine* 1952: 22-31;
Sawsan Al Abtah, *Sentiments religieux et valeurs dans les Murūj al-dhahab d'al-Masʿūdī* (Lille: A.N.R.T, Université de Lille III, 1992);
Ziauddin Alavi, "al-Masʿūdī's conception of the relationship between man and environment," in *al-Masʿūdī Millenary Commemoration Volume*, ed. S. Maqbul Ahmad and A. Rahman (Calcutta: The Indian Society for the History of Science and The Institute for Islamic Studies, Aligarh Muslim University, 1960), 93-96;
Jawwād ʿAlī, "Mawārid Ta'rīkh al-Masʿūdī," *Sumer* 20 (1964):1-8;
S.M. Ali, "Some geographical ideas of al-Masʿūdī," in *al-Masʿūdī Millenary Commemoration Volume*, ed. S. Maqbul Ahmad and A. Rahman (Calcutta: The Indian Society for the History of Science and The Institute for Islamic Studies, Aligarh Muslim University, 1960), 84-92;
Muḥsin al-Ḥusaynī 'l-ʿĀmilī, *Aʿyān al-Shīʿah*, 56 vols. (Dimashq: Maṭbaʿat Ibn Zaydūn, 1935-1949): 41:198-213; ed. Ḥasan al-Amīn 10 vols., (Beirut: Dār al-Taʿāruf li 'l-Maṭbūʿāt, 1984), 8:220-226.
Ibrāhīm ibn Yūsuf Aqṣam, *al-Dawlah al-Umawiyyah fī kitābāt al-Masʿūdī, 41-132 H/661-750 M: dirāsah taḥlīliyyah muqāranah* (Jiddah: Dār al-Mujtamaʿ li 'l-Nashr wa 'l-Tawzīʿ, 2003);
Ḥusayn ʿĀsī, *Abū 'l-Ḥasan al-Masʿūdī al-muʾarrikh wa 'l-jughrāfī* (Beirut: Dār al-Kutub al-ʿIlmiyyah, 1993);
ʿAzīz al-ʿAzmah, *al-Masʿūdī. al-muntakhab min mudawwanāt al-turāth* (Beirut: Riyāḍ al-Rayyis li 'l-Kutub wa 'l-Nashr, 2001);
Ibn Ḥajar al-ʿAsqalānī, *Lisān al-mīzān*, 6 vols. (Hayderabad: Dā'irat al-Maʿārif al-ʿUthmāniyyah, 1911-1913), 4:224-225;
ʿAbd al-Raḥmān Ḥusayn ʿAzzāwī, *al-Masʿūdī muʾarrikhan* (Baghdad: Ittiḥād al-Mu'arrikhīn al-ʿArab, 1982);
A. Bausani, "Le maree nei Murūğ adh-Dhahab di al-Masʿūdī (m.956)," *Oriente Moderno* 60 (1980): 63-67;
S. Bochartum, *Historia imperii vetustissimi Joctanidarum in Arabia felice ex Abulfeda, Hamza Ispahanensi, Nuweirio, Taberita, Mesoudio; accesserunt denuo hac editione Monumenta vetustiora Arabiae, sive Specimina quaedam illustria antiquae memoriae et linguae, ex manuscriptis codicibus Nuweirii, Mesoudii, Abulfedae, Hamasa* [*etc. etc. etc.*], excerpta ab Alberto Schultens; et Colonia Joctanidarum, deducta per S. Bochartum, Geogr. sacr. libro II (Harderovici Gelrorum [Harderwijk (Gelderland)]: Ioannem van Kasteel, 1786);
Carl Brockelmann, *Geschichte der arabischen Litteratur* (Leiden: Brill, 1937-1949) 1:150-152; *Supplementband* 1: 20-21;
Carl Brockelmann, "al-Masʿūdī," in *Encyclopaedia of Islam*, 1st ed. (Leiden: Brill, 1919-1938), 3: 403-404;
Joseph Brunet y Bellet, *Un autor mahometà del sigle X, el Maçoudí; apuntacions preses de l'obra d'aquest autor Les praderes d'or* (Barcelona: l'Avenç 1897);
Bernard Carra de Vaux, "Note sur un ouvrage attribué à Maçoudi," *Journal Asiatique* n.s. 7 (1896):133-144;
A. Czapkiewicz, "al-Masʿūdī on Balneology and Balneoltherapeutics," *Folia Orientalia* 3 (1961): 271-275.
Shams al-Dīn al-Dhahabī, *al-ʿIbar fī khabar man ghabar*, 4 vols., ed. Abū Hājar Muḥammad al-Saʿīd ibn Basyūnī Zaghlūl (Beirut: Dār al-Kutub al-ʿIlmiyyah, 1985), 2:71;

Shams al-Dīn al-Dhahabī, *Siyar aʿlām al-nubalā*, 23 vols., ed. Shuʿayb al-Arnā'ūt and Ḥusayn al-Asad (Beirut: Mu'assasat al-Risālah, 1981-1985), 15:569;

D.M. Dunlop, *Arab Civilization to AD 1500* (London: Longman; Beirut: Librarie du Liban, 1960), 99-114 and index;

D.M. Dunlop, "A Source of al-Masʿūdī: the Madīnat al-Fāḍilah of al-Fārābī," in *al-Mas'ūdī Millenary Commemoration Volume*, ed. S. Maqbul Ahmad and A. Rahman (Calcutta: The Indian Society for the History of Science and The Institute for Islamic Studies, Aligarh Muslim University, 1960), 69-71;

Nadia Maria El Cheikh, *Byzantium viewed by the Arabs* (Cambridge: Harvard University, 2004), index;

Walter J. Fischel, "Ibn Khaldūn and al-Masʿūdī," in *al-Mas'ūdī Millenary Commemoration Volume*, edited by S. Maqbul Ahmad and A. Rahman (Calcutta: The Indian Society for the History of Science and The Institute for Islamic Studies, Aligarh Muslim University, 1960), 51-59;

Charles Genequand, "Alexandre et les sages de l'Inde," *Arabic and Middle Eastern Literatures* 4:2 (2001): 137-144;

H. Ghulam Mustafa, "Use of Poetry by al-Masʿūdī in his works," in *al-Mas'ūdī Millenary Commemoration Volume*, edited by S. Maqbul Ahmad and A. Rahman (Calcutta: The Indian Society for the History of Science and The Institute for Islamic Studies, Aligarh Muslim University, 1960), 77-83;

Jūrj Ghurayyib, *Adab al-riḥlah: tārīkhuhu wa-'ālamuhu, al-Mas'ūdī, Ibn Baṭūṭah, al-Rayḥānī* (Beirut: Dār al-Thaqāfah, 1966);

J. Gildemeister, "Über den Titel des Masudischen Werkes Muruj al-Dhahab," *Wiener Zeitschrift für die Kunde des Morgenlandes* 5 (1844): 202-204;

G. E. von Grunebaum, "Statement," in *al-Mas'ūdī Millenary Commemoration Volume*, ed. S. Maqbul Ahmad and A. Rahman (Calcutta: The Indian Society for the History of Science and The Institute for Islamic Studies, Aligarh Muslim University, 1960), 137-139;

Yāqūt al-Ḥamāwī, *Mu'jam al-udabā'*, 20 vols. (Beirut: Dār Ihyā' al-Turāth al-'Arabī, 1988), 13:90-94;

Ḥādī Ḥusayn Ḥammūd, *Manhaj al-Mas'ūdī fī baḥth al-'aqā'id wa 'l-firaq al-dīniyyah* (Baghdad: Dār al-Qāḍsiyyah li 'l-Ṭibāʿah, 1984);

Mohibbul Hasan, "al-Masʿūdī on Kashmir," in *al-Mas'ūdī Millenary Commemoration Volume*, edited by S. Maqbul Ahmad and A. Rahman (Calcutta: The Indian Society for the History of Science and The Institute for Islamic Studies, Aligarh Muslim University, 1960), 25-27;

al-Ḥasan ibn ʿAlī Ibn Dāwūd al-Ḥillī (d. 7th/13th c.), *Kitāb al-rijāl*, ed. Muḥammad Ṣādiq Āl Baḥr al-ʿUlūm (Najaf: al-Maṭbaʿah al-Ḥaydariyyah, 1972), 137;

al-Ḥasan ibn Yūsuf Ibn al-Muṭahhar al-Ḥillī, *Rijāl al-'Allāmah* [=*Khulāsat al-aqwāl fī 'ilm al-rijāl*] (Najaf: al-Maṭbaʿah al-Ḥaydariyyah, 1961), 100;

E. Honigmann, "Notes sur trois passages d'al-Masʿoudi," *Annuaire de l'Institut de philologie et d'histoire orientales et slaves* 12 (1952): 177-184;

J.F.P. Hopkins and Nehemia Levtzion, *Corpus of early Arabic sources for West African history* (Princeton, N.J.: Markus Wiener, 2000);

Mahmoud Hossein and Philippe Calderon, *A la rencontre de l'autre 2, Les arpenteurs du monde=Encountering others; they surveyed the world* (videorecording), with the cooperation of FIT Production, La Cinquième, Canal Sur Televisión. When the world spoke Arabic: the golden age of Arab civilization (Princeton, N.J.: Films for the Humanities & Sciences, 2001);

al-Ḥurr al-ʿĀmilī, *Amal al-Āmil fī 'ulamā' Jabal 'Āmil*, 2 vols. (Baghdad: Maktabat al-Andalus, 1965-1966), 2:180-81;

Ibn al-ʿImād, *Shadharāt al-dhahab fī akhbār man dhahab*, 5 vols. ed. Maḥmūd al-Arnā'ūt (Beirut: Dār Ibn Kathīr, 1986), 4:242;

Ibn al-Nadīm, *al-Fihrist*, ed. Riḍā Tajaddud (Tehran: Dār al-Masīrah, 1988), 171;

Ibn Taghrībirdī, *al-Nujūm al-zāhirah*, 16 vol. (Cairo: al-Muʿassassah al-Miṣriyyah al-ʿĀmmah li'-Taʾlīf wa 'l-Ṭibāʿah wa 'l-Nashr, 1963-1971), 3:315-316;

Rajab ʿAbd al-Jawwād Ibrāhīm, *Alfāẓ al-ḥaḍārah fī 'l-qarn al-rābi' al-hijrī: dirāsah fī ḍaw' Murūj al-dhahab li 'l-Mas'ūdī* (Cairo: Dār al-Āfāq al-ʿArabiyyah, 2003);

M. Idel, "Magic Temples and Cities in the Middle Ages and the Renaissance: a Passage of Masʿūdī as a Possible Source for Yohanan Alemanno," *Jerusalem Studies in Arabic and Islam* 3 (1982): 185-189;

Mīrzā ʿAbd Allāh Afandī 'l-Iṣfahānī, *Riyāḍ al-'ulamā' wa-ḥiyāḍ al-fuḍalā'*, 6 vols., ed. Aḥmad al-Ḥusaynī (Qum: Maṭbaʿat al-Khayyām, 1401), 3:428-432;

Muhammad Reza Kazimi, "Masʿūdī and Cultural Geography," *Journal of the Pakistan Historical Society* 46, 3(1998): 75-79;

Tarif Khalidi, *Arabic Historical Thought in the Classical Period* (Cambridge: Cambridge University Press, 1994), 131-136 and index;

Tarif Khalidi, *Islamic Historiography: the Histories of Mas'ūdī* (Albany: State University of New York Press, 1975);

Tarif Khalidi, "Masʿūdī's lost works: a reconstruction of their content," *Journal of the American Oriental Society* 94 (1974): 35-41;

M.S. Khan, "al-Masʿūdī and the Geography of India," *Zeitschrift der Deutschen Morgenländischen Gesellschaft* 131 (1981): 119-136;

ʿAlī Ḥusnī 'l-Kharbutlī, *al-Mas'ūdī* (Cairo: Dār al-Maʿārif, 1982);

Muḥammad Bāqir ibn Zayn al-ʿĀbidīn al-Khuwānsārī, *Rawḍāt al-jannāt fī aḥwāl al-'ulamā' wa 'l-sādāt*, 8 vols. (Beirut: al-Dār al-Islāmiyyah, 1991), 4:272-280;

M. Kowalska, "al-Masʿūdī's Stellung in Geschichte der arabischen Literatur," *Folia Orientalia* 32 (1996): 115-121;

J.H. Kramers, "La littérature géographique classique des musulmans," *Analecta Orientalia*, 1 (1954): 172-204

Ibn Shākir al-Kutubī, *Fawāt al-wafayāt*, 2 vols., ed. ʿAlī Muḥammad Muʿawwad and ʿĀdil Ahmad ʿAbd al-Mawjūd (Beirut: Dār al-Kutub al-ʿIlmiyyah, 2000), 2:81;

Hyeong Gi Kwon, *Le Kitāb al-tanbīh wa 'l-ishrāf d'al-Mas'ūdī: étude comparative avec traduction partielle annotée* (Lille: A. N. R. T. Université de Lille III, 1989);

U. Lewicka-Rajewska, "Falconry in Muslim Countries During the Tenth Century in Light of *Murūj adh-Dhahab* by al-Masʿūdī," *Rocznik Orientalistyczny* 50, 2 (1997): 133-143;

Tadeusz Lewicki, "al-Masʿūdī on the Slavs," in *al-Mas'ūdī Millenary Commemoration Volume*, ed. S. Maqbul Ahmad and A. Rahman (Calcutta: The Indian Society for the History of Science and The Institute for Islamic Studies, Aligarh Muslim University, 1960), 11-13;

Bernard Lewis, "Masʿūdī and the Muslim Renaissance" in *al-Mas'ūdī Millenary Commemoration Volume*, ed. S. Maqbul Ahmad and A. Rahman (Calcutta: The Indian Society for the History of Science and The Institute for Islamic Studies, Aligarh Muslim University, 1960), 134-135;

Bernard Lewis, "Masʿūdī on the Kings of the Franks," in *al-Mas'ūdī Millenary Commemoration Volume*, ed. S. Maqbul Ahmad and A. Rahman (Calcutta: The Indian Society for the History of Science and The Institute for Islamic Studies, Aligarh Muslim University, 1960), 7-10;

Bernard Lewis, *The Muslim Discovery of Europe* (New York: Norton, 1982);

J. S. Meisami, "Masʿūdī on Love and the Fall of the Barmakids," *Journal of the Royal Asiatic Society* 1989, 2: 252-277;

A. Miquel, *La Géographie humaine du monde musulman jusqu'au milieu du 11e siècle*, 2 vols. (Paris, La Haye: Mouton & Co., 1967-1975), 1:202-212;

J.J. Modi, "Maçoudi on Volcanoes," *Journal of the Bombay Branch of the Royal Asiatic Society* 22 (1905-1908): 135-142;

J.J. Modi, "Masʿūdī's Account of the Pesdadian Kings," *Journal of the K. R. Cama Oriental Institute* 27 (1933): 6-35;

J.J. Modi, "Zarathustra and Zoroastrianism in Macoudi's Kitab-i Muruj al-Zahab va Ma'adan al-Jauhar," *Journal of the K. R. Cama Oriental Institute*, 25 (1931): 148-158;

M. Moʿin, "Masʿūdī on Zaraouštra," in *al-Mas'ūdī Millenary Commemoration Volume*, ed. Ahmad S. Maqbul and A. Rahman (Calcutta: The Indian Society for the History of Science and The Institute for Islamic Studies, Aligarh Muslim University, 1960), 60-68;

G. Morrison, "The Sassanian Genealogy in Masʿūdī," in *al-Mas'ūdī Millenary Comme-*

moration Volume, ed. Ahmad S. Maqbul and A. Rahman (Calcutta: The Indian Society for the History of Science and The Institute for Islamic Studies, Aligarh Muslim University, 1960), 42-44;

E.M. Murzaev, "The Significance of al-Masʿūdī for the Works of Russian and Soviet Geographers," in *al-Mas'ūdī Millenary Commemoration Volume*, ed. Ahmad S. Maqbul and A. Rahman (Calcutta: The Indian Society for the History of Science and The Institute for Islamic Studies, Aligarh Muslim University, 1960), 14-19 (with further bibliography of studies in Russian).

Aḥmad ibn ʿAlī 'l-Najāshī, *Kitāb al-rijāl* (Qum: Markaz-i Nashr-i Kitāb, n.d.), 192;

Ahmad Nazmi, "The King of al-Dār in al-Masʿūdī's Murūj adh-Dhahab," *Studia Arabistyczne i Islamistyczne* 2 (1994): 5-11;

Charles Pellat, "La España musulmana en las obras de al-Masʿūdī," *1. Congreso de estudios árabes e islámicos, Cordoba, 1962, Actas*, 257-264;

Charles Pellat, "al-Masʿūdī, Abu 'l-Ḥasan ʿAlī b. al-Ḥusayn," *Encyclopedia of Islam*, 2nd ed., ed. P. Bearman, Th. Bianquis, C.E. Bosworth, E. van Donzel and W.P. Heinrichs (Leiden: Brill, 2008*)*; VI: 784-789; (Brill Online) http://www.brillonline.nl./entry?entry=islam_COM-0704

Charles Pellat, "Masʿūdī et l'imamisme," *Le Shî'isme imâmite. Colloque de Strasbourg (6-9 mai 1968),* ed. R. Brunschvig and T. Fahd (Paris: Presses universitaires de France, 1970), 69-80;

Charles Pellat, "A Project for a New Edition of al-Masʿūdī's Murūj al-Dhahab Based on That of Barbier de Menard and Pavet de Courteille," in *al-Mas'ūdī Millenary Commemoration Volume*, ed. Ahmad S. Maqbul and A. Rahman (Calcutta: The Indian Society for the History of Science and The Institute for Islamic Studies, Aligarh Muslim University, 1960), 3-4;

Charles Pellat, "Was al-Masʿūdī a Historian or an Adib?" *Journal of the Pakistan Historical Society* 9 (1961): 231-234;

Giancarlo Pizzi, *al-Mas'ūdī e i prati d'oro e le miniere de gemme: la enciclopedia di un umanista arabo del decimo secolo* (Milan: Jaca, 2001);

Etienne Quatremère, "Notice sur la vie et les ouvrages de Masoudi," *Journal Asiatique*, 3 (1839): 7, 1-31;

A. Rahman, "al-Masʿūdī and Contemporary Science," in *al-Mas'ūdī Millenary Commemoration Volume*, ed. Ahmad S. Maqbul and A. Rahman (Calcutta: The Indian Society for the History of Science and The Institute for Islamic Studies, Aligarh Muslim University, 1960), 45-50;

M. Reinaud, *Géographie d'Aboulféda*, 2 vols. (Paris: Imprimerie nationale, 1848-1883; repr. Frankfurt am Main: Institute for the History of Arabic-Islamic Science at the Johann Wolfgang Goethe University, 1998), 1:64-72;

Ernest Renan, "Les Prairies d'or de Maçoudi," in *Journal des débats*, 1 and 2 October 1873; repr. in *Mélanges d'histoire et de voyages* (Paris: Lévy, 1878), 253-275; and in *Oeuvres complètes de Ernest Renan*, ed. Henriette Psichari, 10 vols. (Paris: Editions Calmann-Lévy, 1947), 2:502-519;

Peggy Saari, Daniel B. Baker, and Nancy Pear, *Explorers & Discoverers: from Alexander the Great to Sally Ride* (New York: UXL, 1995);

George Sarton, *Introduction to the History of Science*, 3 vols. in 5 (Baltimore: Williams and Wilkins, 1948), 1:637;

Ulrich Schädler, "Sphären-Schach," zum sogenannten "astronomischen Schach" bei al-Masʿūdī, al-Āmolī und Alfons X," *Zeitschrift für Geschichte der Arabisch-Islamischen Wissenschaften /Majallat Tārīkh al-'Ulūm al-'Arabiyyah wa"l-Islāmiyya*, 13 (1999): 205-242;

C.F. Seybold, "Līnškh-Lbnškh in Masʿūdī's Tenbīh 68, 15 Verderbnis aus Basta Bazar," *Le monde orientale* 13 (1919), 126-128;

Fuat Sezgin, *Geschichte der arabischen Schrifttums*, 12 volumes to date (Leiden: Brill, 1968-present), 1:332-336;

Studies on Qudama b. Ga'far (d. after 932) and al-Mas'udi (d. 956) collected and reprinted, Fuat Sezgin ed., in collaboration with Mazen Amawi, Carl Ehrig-Eggert, and Eckhard Neubauer, (Frankfurt am Main: Institute for the

History of Arabic-Islamic Science at the Johann Wolfgang Goethe University, 1992);

Ursula Sezgin, "al-Masʿūdī, Ibrāhīm b.Watīfšāh und das Kitāb al-ʿAǧāʾib: Aigyptiaka in arabischen Texten des 10. Jahrhunderts n.Chr," *Zeitschrift für Geschichte der Arabisch-Islamischen Wissenschaften /Majallat Tārīkh al-'Ulūm al-'Arabiyyah wa 'l-Islāmiyyah* 8 (1993): 1-70;

Ursula Sezgin, "Pharaonische Wunderwerke bei Ibn Wāṣif aṣ-Ṣābi' und al-Masʿūdī. Einige Reminiszenzen an Ägyptens vergangene Grösse und an Meisterwerke der alexandrinischen Gelehrten in arabischen Texten des 10. Jahrhunderts n. Chr," *Zeitschrift für Geschichte der Arabisch-Islamischen Wissenschaften /Majallat Tārīkh al-'Ulūm al-'Arabiyyah wa 'l-Islāmiyyah* 9 (1994): 229-291; 11 (1997): 189-249; 14 (2001): 217-256; 15 (2003): 281-312;

Mohammad Shafi, "al-Masʿūdī as Geographer," in *al-Mas'ūdī Millenary Commemoration Volume*, ed. Ahmad S. Maqbul and A. Rahman (Calcutta: The Indian Society for the History of Science and The Institute for Islamic Studies, Aligarh Muslim University, 1960), 72-76;

Ahmad M. H. Shboul, *al-Mas'ūdī and his World: a Muslim Humanist and his Interest in non-Muslims* (London: Ithaca, 1979);

S.M. Stern, "al-Masʿūdī and the Philosopher al-Fārābī," in *al-Mas'ūdī Millenary Commemoration Volume*, ed. S. Maqbul Ahmad and A. Rahman (Calcutta: The Indian Society for the History of Science and The Institute for Islamic Studies, Aligarh Muslim University, 1960), 28-41;

Devin Stewart, "The Formation of the Twelver Madhhab," paper delivered at the 3rd International Schacht Conference on Islamic Law, Boston, May 2000;

Devin Stewart, "al-Masʿudī's Lost Manual of Legal Theory," paper delivered at Text and Context: Recent Research in Middle Eastern and South Asian Studies conference, Emory University, February 15-16, 2004;

Caroline Stone, "Masudi: Imam of the Historians," *Ur*, 1984, 2: 6-9;

Caroline Stone, "The Model of the Historians," *Saudi Aramco World* 56: 2 (2005): 18-23;

Tāj al-Dīn al-Subkī, *Ṭabaqāt al-shāfi'iyyah al-kubrā*, 10 vols., ed. ʿAbd al-Fattāḥ al-Ḥilw and Maḥmūd Muḥammad al-Ṭanāḥī (Cairo: Hajr, 1992), 3:456-57;

Sulaymān ibn ʿAbd Allāh al-Mudayd Suwaykit, *Manhaj al-Mas'ūdī fī kitābat al-tārīkh* (Riyāḍ: al-Suwaykit, 1986);

P. Voorhoeve, "Note on the Leiden MSS of the Murūj al-Dhahab," in *al-Mas'ūdī Millenary Commemoration Volume*, ed. S. Maqbul Ahmad and A. Rahman (Calcutta: The Indian Society for the History of Science and The Institute for Islamic Studies, Aligarh Muslim University, 1960), 4-6 + 3 plates;

ʿAbd al-Fattāḥ Muḥammad Wuhaybah, *Jughrāfiyyat al-Mas'ūdī bayna 'l-naẓariyyah wa 'l-wāqi' min al-adab al-jughrāfī fī 'l-turāth al-'Arabī* (al-Iskandariyyah: Munsha'at al-Maʿārif, 1995);

Nicola A. Ziadeh, "Diyār al-Shām according to al-Masʿūdī," in *al-Mas'ūdī Millenary Commemoration Volume*, ed. S. Maqbul Ahmad and A. Rahman (Calcutta: The Indian Society for the History of Science and The Institute for Islamic Studies, Aligarh Muslim University, 1960), 20-24.

Nicola A. Ziadeh, "Speech," in *al-Mas'ūdī Millenary Commemoration Volume*, ed. S. Maqbul Ahmad and A. Rahman (Calcutta: The Indian Society for the History of Science and The Institute for Islamic Studies, Aligarh Muslim University, 1960), 142-143.

al-Mu'tamid Ibn 'Abbād

(1039-1095)

KATHLEEN ALCALÁ
University of Washington

WORKS

Dīwān.

Editions

Abū 'l-Qāsim Muḥammad Ibn 'Abbād al-Mu'tamid 'Alā Allāh, *Dīwān al-Mu'tamid Ibn 'Abbād,* ed. Aḥmad Aḥmad Badawī and Ḥāmid 'Abd al-Majīd (Cairo: al-Maṭba'ah al-Amīriyyah, 1951).

Translations

al-Mu'tamid Ibn 'Abbād, *Poesias de 'l-Mu'tamid Ibn 'Abbād*, a biographical introduction and anthology in Spanish translated by María Jesús Rubiera Mata, Clásicos Hispano-Arabes Bilingues no. 3 (Madrid: Instituto Hispano-Arabe de Cultura, 1987).

Al-Mu'tamid is now considered the most outstanding Andalusian poet of the second half of the eleventh century. His mentor was Aḥmad ibn 'Abd Allāh Ibn Zaydūn (*ca. 1003-May 1071*), and al-Mu'tamid grew up surrounded by poets in the court of his father, al-Mu'tadid (1014-1069). Most of al-Mu'tamid's 190 known poems are in the style of the Andalusian *qaṣīdah*. Lacking the tripartite form of the early *qaṣīdah* as defined by 'Abd Allāh ibn Muslim Ibn Qutaybah (828-889), the poems nevertheless maintain formality of language, the monorhyme, and a regular meter. In addition, like his mentor Ibn Zaydūn, al-Mu'tamid's poetry uses simple, straightforward language in its descriptions of love and emotion, and concentrates on the contrasts between black and white. His mastery of the form enabled him to heighten the sense of anticipation and resolution between the first and second stanzas of a verse, and was manifest in his ability to stretch and even subvert the form in a way that maximized its emotional impact.

It is not known what al-Mu'tamid's contemporaries thought of his poetry. The anthologists and biographers offer only vague hyperboles, rarely making favorable or adverse comments. The question that arises is whether al-Mu'tamid's poetry was popular because of its excellence, or because of his fame, the splendor of his court, and the romantic tragedy of his fate. Because of his position, say some sources, al-Mu'tamid could make poetry his servant, rather than being at its service, as most court poets were of necessity. "If the Andalusians had celebrated style, their indisputable hero would have been the king al-Mu'tamid of Seville," according to one of his biographers, María Jesús Rubiera Mata.

Al-Mu'tamid's full name was Abū 'l-Qāsim Muḥammad Ibn Abī 'Amr 'Abbād Ibn Muḥammad Ibn Ismā'īl al-Lakhmī 'l-Ẓāfir bi-Ḥawl Allāh al-Mu'ayyad bi Allāh al-Mu'tamid 'Ala Allāh. He was born towards the end of Rabī' al-Awwal, 431 (December, 1039 or January 1040) in Beja, and became ruler of Seville on the death of his father, al-Mu'tadid, on 3 Jumādā 'l-Ulā, 461 (28 February, 1069). He was deposed in 1092, and died in prison in Aghmat, Morocco, in Rabī' al-Awwal or Dhū 'l-Ḥijjah, 488 (March-April or December, 1095). As one of the most eminent men of eleventh-century Andalus, a good deal is known about his life. He was the third and last member of the 'Abbādid dynasty of Seville and the epitome of the cultivated Muslim Spaniard of the Middle Ages—liberal, tolerant, and a patron of the arts.

Al-Mu'tamid was the second son of 'Abbād ibn Abī 'l-Qāsim, King al-Mu'tadid. If Abū Marwān Ḥayyān ibn Khalaf Ibn Ḥayyān (987 or

988-1076) did not exaggerate, al-Muʿtadid had a harem of seven hundred wives, carefully chosen for their beauty. Al-Muʿtamid, then known as Prince Muḥammad, was born to an anonymous concubine in Beja, but grew up in Seville. Shortly after his birth, al-Muʿtamid's older brother died in Carmona, after leading a rebellion against his father, and al-Muʿtamid became the principal heir in 1042. Al-Muʿtadid made his son governor of Silves (in present-day Portugal) when he was twelve years old. Prince Muḥammad Ibn ʿAbbād, as he was known before he became a monarch, found his two loves in Silves: Ibn ʿAmmār (d. 926) and Rumaykiyyah.

Al-Muʿtadid surrounded himself with *literati* who served as ministers and secretaries, and were preceptors to his children. His minister Ibn Zaydūn, the great Cordovian poet, taught the art of poetry to the prince Muḥammad, and some of the poems that passed between them were classical exercises of rhetoric between teacher and disciple. Little else is known about al-Muʿtamid's education. Although he was highly regarded as a poet, one source states explicitly that he was not knowledgeable about any branch of learning except *adab* (poetry).

But it was his father, al-Muʿtadid who cultivated the love of poetry in his second son. One day, the future al-Muʿtamid wanted a shield of gold, and described it in one of his first poems (Ibn al-Abbār, 2:56):

It is a shield, with artifice made like the sky
  To show that it will exhaust the longest lances;
They have forged on it the Pleiades,
  Stars that auger victory;
Its circles revolve like stars, the same as
  The horizon one sees clothed in the dawn.

Al-Muʿtamid's early poems tell us of the life of a prince. He recited them to his daunting father, in a tone both respectful and affectionate, calling himself "your little slave," asking for gifts such as horses, shields of gold, saddles, etc., always objects appropriate for war, with the promise that he would use them against his father's enemies. Besides cultivating a love of poetry in his son, al-Muʿtadid wanted to make him a soldier, as accomplished in arms as in letters.

In 458 (1065-1066) al-Muʿtamid was sent by his father to Malaga at the head of Sevillian troops to support an insurrection against the ruler Bādīs ibn Ḥabbūs of Granada. After easily capturing the city, the young prince was duped by his Berber officers into allowing his soldiers to relax and drink wine, rather than pursuing the siege of the citadel. He was assured that the citadel would surrender of its own accord, and he might as well divert himself with feasting and drinking. While he and his troops were so occupied, the garrison in the citadel managed to inform Bādīs of the attack. Bādīs sent fresh troops, who were able to enter Malaga unopposed and retake the city.

Al-Muʿtadid was enraged over the foolish loss, and ordered his son imprisoned. Under these circumstances, al-Muʿtamid was moved to write one of his most famous poems. He must have recalled, under the circumstances, that in 449 (1057-1058) his elder brother, Ismāʿīl, had been caught by their father in open rebellion and killed by his own hand. Al-Muʿtamid must have realized that this petition of forgiveness to his father might mean the difference between life and death. The poem, addressed not to his father, but to himself, strikes a careful tone between humility, praise for his father, and optimism .

Entrust to God the matter which you fear
  And rely on He-Who-Seeks-the-Help-of-God to forgive.

...goes one couplet. It suggests a new-found maturity and caution that would serve the future king well. Al-Muʿtadid spared his son, and it has been posited that he was more lenient with the younger al-Muʿtamid, perhaps recognizing his more artistic nature, and feeling that he had been too harsh with Ismāʿīl.

At age twenty four al-Muʿtamid commanded a military expedition that had been sent against the city of Silves. The venture was successful, and he was appointed governor of this and another district. In 1069 his father died, and al-Muʿtamid acceded to the throne of Seville. He was destined to rule in difficult times: neighboring princes were resuming the inexorable advance that in time would bring all of Spain once again under Christian rule. Yet his first efforts were successful. In 1071 he conquered and annexed the principality of Cordoba, although his rule was not effectively secured until 1078. During that time he also brought the kingdom of Murcia under his rule.

Al-Muʿtamid lived his life in an atmosphere in which poetry was an important form of personal expression. One was judged by the facility with which one could spontaneously compose a poem, and the cleverness and insight exemplified by that poem. An apocryphal story is that he and his companion since childhood, Ibn ʿAmmār, went in disguise to walk along the river to a place called the Meadow of Gold. The breeze ruffled the water, and al-Muʿtamid improvised a verse:

The breeze has made of the water a coat of mail.

It was their practice that Ibn ʿAmmār would continue the poem, in the same meter and an identical rhyme, but at that moment inspiration did not arrive, but a feminine voice recited:

What a boon for combat if it became solid!

Surprised, al-Muʿtamid turned to the woman, who in some versions was bathing in the river, and found a beautiful face with which he was enamored; he asked who she was and if she was married. The girl answered that she was Rumaykiyyah, and her job was to take care of the pack animals of her master, Rumayk ibn al-Ḥajjāj and she was unmarried. Al-Muʿtamid took her to his palace and possessed her.

The story is a literary creation: the verses pertain to Abū Muḥammad ʿAbd al-Jalīl ibn Wahbūn of Murcia (1039 to 1049-ca. 1092) and ʿAbd al-Jabbār Ibn Ḥamdīs (ca. 1055-1132) of Syracuse, who spoke them together at Guadalquivir, but the episode recreates a historical fact: the infatuation of the Prince al-Muʿtamid with a slave named Rumaykiyyah on the edge of the River Silves, immortalized in his own verses, and in which, perhaps, we can identify the girl with the curvaceous bracelet, who is remembered as standing out from the rest.

Rumaykiyyah became the only legitimate wife in his populous harem, and was given the title of al-Sayyidah al-Kubrā, or great lady, and the name Umm Rabīʿ Iʿtimād. Queen Iʿtimād became the great love of al-Muʿtamid's life, and the subject of many of his poems. Below is an example (Ibn al-Abbār, 2:61):

Iʿtimād

Invisible are you to my eyes,
    You are present in my heart
Tis the force of my passion that sends you my love
    With tears of suffering, with insomnia;
Indomitable am I, and you dominate me,
    And find the task easy;
My desire is to be with you always,
    If only you can concede me that desire!
Assure me that the oath that unites us,
    Will not break with distance;
Designed into the verses of this poem,
    Lies your sweet name, Iʿtimād.

The poem is an acrostic, incorporating Iʿtimād's name in the first letter of each couplet. (more on the techniques he favored).

The love between the two lasted all of their lives. Al-Muʿtamid forgot his dominant personality and became submissive before her feminine love, like perfect courtly love. He says this to Iʿtimād:

You dominate me, a difficult thing to achieve
    You have discovered that my love is easy to take.

And Rumaykiyyah tried to win the heart of her love, sometimes elusive, sometimes available, in a game that allowed the persistence of her youthful name to burn in Seville. That is how al-Muʿtamid laments her avoidance of him in this lovely poem:

The heart persists and does not cease;
    The passion is great and does not dim;
The tears run like drops of rain
    The body ages to a yellow color;
And this happens when the one I love and I are united;
    What would happen if she left me?

At no other time in the history of al-Andalus did such a brilliant and genial poetry flourish as during the reign of the third and last ʿAbbādid king of Seville, al-Muʿtamid Ibn ʿAbbād.

The personality and reign of al-Muʿtamid contributed much to the definitive framework of certain traits that are now identified with "the Andalusian." For example, what we can call the "joyful fatalism" in the following story:

> After a long time of terrorizing the roads near Seville, the authorities succeeded in capturing the famous bandit nicknamed "the Grey Falcon," and they crucified him on the outskirts of the city. While he waited for death, with his wife and children at the foot of the cross in great lamentation, a merchant of clothing passed by on the road. The Grey Falcon implored the man to draw near. He explained to him how he came to be in this sorry situation, and that he wanted to end his life with a work that would benefit those who were about to become a widow and orphans. A little while ago, he said, he had stolen a large quantity of money and, before his arrest, he flung it in a well he had found not two steps from where they were. He indicated the road, begging the merchant to recover the money and give it to his wife. Quickly the avaricious merchant went into the well by using a rope, and the thief sent his wife to cut it. Following his instructions, she took the merchant's burro and all of its goods to the market of Seville and sold all of it for a large sum of money. When the sharp cries from the dry bottom of the well were finally heard, and the man rescued from it, the news of the event ran through Seville. Al-Muʿtamid, marveling, ordered that the thief be lowered from the cross and brought into his presence. He asked how it was possible that, suspended between heaven and hell, it occurred to him to commit one more crime. The Grey Falcon answered that, if the king knew how delicious it was to deceive people, he would leave his throne and dedicate his life to banditry. Al-Muʿtamid granted him his life and gave him a place in the royal guard.

This story demonstrates not only the generosity of al-Muʿtamid, and the cunning of the thief, but also, and this is more important, the appreciation the Sevillians had for these two qualities.

The last anecdote, in addition to its strong romantic flavor, demonstrates the many social levels affected by the poetic sensibility among the Sevillians during this stage of Andalusian culture. It now practically constitutes a commonplace to talk about the life of al-Muʿtamid as "pure poetry in action," as Emilio García Gómez said. From a later vantage point, that affirmation is certain, but it is no less true that the King of Seville and her inhabitants provided the fundamental ambiance in which poetry flourished in such a general way, from the humblest slave to the self-same king.

The theme of generosity in the poetry of al-Muʿtamid is a constant throughout his poetic development. He liked the public to see him as such. This included the funding of an academy of poets of sorts, founded by his father, in which the best poems were splendidly rewarded. Other monarchs of these times, also dedicated to poetry, brought together poets in their courts of lesser quality since, as was observed, "he (al-Muʿtamid) was one of the masters of the art (of poetry), and many times the poets avoided him because of it, unless they knew their superiority and had confidence in it." There is an endless series of stories about the prodigious generosity of the last ʿAbbādid king, some true, others, not so.

On one occasion Ibn Wahbūn expressed in verse his doubt concerning a fabulous king who awarded a thousand pesos (*mizqál*) to a poet whose verses were to his taste. On hearing this, al-Muʿtamid ordered that this exact amount immediately be given to him. Besides these gifts, he had to pay "protection" money, as we would say today, to Alfonso VI, King of Castile and Leon, 1030-1109, as he had to his father Fernando I, King of Castile and León, 1016?-1065.

Not all of the poets were satisfied with life in the court of al-Muʿtamid. Abū 'l-Muzarrif ibn al-Dabbāgh, for example, was accused of painting his fingers, something only permitted of women. So he composed these verses:

Seville disdains the noble, accusing them of reproachable acts,
While praising imbeciles, it insults the valorous.

To this Ibn ʿAmmār responded:

Your poem is ridiculous, and your actions frivolous.
When did Seville not honor the noble, or
Scorn other than vile criminals?

But the poet with whom he had the most contact, and who changed his life and the history of his reign, was the poet-adventurer Ibn ʿAmmār. One day while they were walking together, they heard the distant call of the muezzin. Al-Muʿtamid improvised:

The muezzin began his call.

To this Ibn ʿAmmār responded:

Begging forgiveness from Allah.

Al-Muʿtamid:

Blessed is he who testifies to the truth.

Ibn ʿAmmār:

Only if his intent is as true as his tongue.

Not even in the adverse military times that clearly announced the impending fall, could they refrain from seeking the perfect metaphor or the most elegant and refined expression. To the contrary, it was as though the Sevillians sought grounding in art when the circumstances seemed desperate.

Nevertheless, when he survived the disaster of 1091, the magic continued of the commingling of the king and his kingdom. Al-Muʿtamid, after his penurious exile in North Africa, composed the best poems of his dīwān, using to great effect one of the sentimental elements in Arabic poetry: nostalgia for the abandoned campsite as used in the *naṣīb* section of the *qaṣīdah*.

It was a felicitous and lively mix of poetry and townspeople, townspeople and poetry, that permitted the realization of both so commingled that they can hardly be distinguished. The Sevillian world carried all of this in a dream state and the feeling, not entirely false, of well-being.

When Iʿtimād al-Rumaykiyyah had been al-Muʿtamid's favorite for a number of years, who not only loved her, but allowed his unbridled love for her to "trump" him, she looked out of a window of the royal palace one day and saw some women trampling clay to prepare bricks. This reminded her of her days of servitude, when she used to go out and do the same, and she broke out in nostalgic sobs. She asked her husband, with a great display of vexation, if he would allow her to do the same. Al-Muʿtamid, according to D. Juán Manuel, had mud filled with "sugar, cinnamon, ginseng, amber and algalia with other spices and perfumes." Then he ordered that they all be mixed together with rosewater. In this clay he allowed Iʿtimād to happily tread in the company of her friends and young daughters.

Later sources, influenced by the literary historiography that surrounded al-Muʿtamid and Iʿtimād, accuse the latter of being the cause of the moral decadence of the king of Seville. The "statement of the religious leaders" (*faqīhs*) say that she was the cause of the weakness of Islamic practice among the population. It is difficult to blame this important paper on the corruption of the Sevillians on Iʿtimād, who, according to sources of the time, was not distinguished from the other concubines accompanying al-Muʿtamid into exile as the mothers of his children. It is interesting to note, on the contrary, that the only archaeological artifact attesting to the existence of Iʿtimād is an inscribed stone commemorating the construction of the minaret of a mosque in Seville, and that she paid for it, a fact far distant from the anachronistic image of the corruptor of the people. The truth is that Iʿtimād always followed her husband, as much in his successes as his failures. She went with him into exile, and her presence, as the grieving mother, appears in the poems of exile.

Al-Muʿtamid's relationship with Ibn ʿAmmār is more complex. His court poet from Silves, Ibn ʿAmmār was not allowed to accompany al-Muʿtamid to Seville when he became the heir apparent, and was considered a bad influence on him by his father's advisors, including Ibn Zaydūn. As al-Muʿtamid's power grew, he was constantly petitioned by Ibn ʿAmmār to appoint him to an important post. When al-Muʿtamid met and married Iʿtimād, the differences between them, always complicated, deepened.

When Prince Muḥammad (al-Muʿtamid) was named the governor of Silves, he added Abu Bakr Muḥammad Ibn ʿAmmār, a professional court poet from Lusitania, to his retinue. Nine years older than the prince, he was handsome and intelligent, and soon won the heart of the sovereign. In his company, al-Muʿtamid learned about the pleasures of wine and beautiful women. Given the difference in their ages, Ibn ʿAmmār became al-Muʿtamid's teacher in the ways of love and poetry. Ibn ʿAmmār was cerebral and ambitious, and preoccupied with ideas of power, although his greatest poems were love poems, often to eunuchs. Al-Muʿtamid, by contrast, was emotional and sensual.

It was easy for Ibn ʿAmmār to adulate al-Muʿtamid, who had opened the doors to power for him, but Ibn ʿAmmār did not count on the fact that to an ʿAbbādid ruler, to love meant to possess, in every sense of the word. Much later, Ibn ʿAmmār accused al-Muʿtamid of sodomizing him against his will. The sexual humiliation was a symbol of social humiliation, since the two were not equals, al-Muʿtamid the prince, and Ibn ʿAmmār his subject. A sexual relationship between them would have reduced Ibn ʿAmmār to an object of pleasure, like a eunuch or a woman. There are several anecdotes about this relationship, which eventually led to tragedy. One is that al-Muʿtamid, drunk, struck Ibn ʿAmmār in the head by throwing tableware at him, and refused to apologize to the hosts of the party. Ibn ʿAmmār also had dark premonitions, dreaming that al-Muʿtamid would murder him. But the greatest rift between the two was caused by al-Muʿtamid's devotion to Rumaykiyyah, whom he elevated from a slave to Queen Iʿtimād. In one story, Ibn ʿAmmār became jealous because al-Muʿtamid made a separate, curtained room for himself and his wife during one of the celebrations of daybreak that were so popular among the Andalusians. Ibn ʿAmmār continued to bide his time, however, driven by ambition.

When al-Muʿtamid returned to Seville as the principal heir, Ibn ʿAmmār accompanied him, but King al-Muʿtadid considered the poet a bad influence on his son. Ibn ʿAmmār was forced to leave, afraid of the wrath of the king of Seville, and took refuge in Zaragoza. From there he sent al-Muʿtadid a magnificent poem, considered by many one of the best Andalusian compositions. The king, however, was not moved by his blandishments, and Ibn ʿAmmār was only able to return to Seville after his death. Ibn ʿAmmār had scarcely returned to al-Muʿtamid's side when he asked for the governorship of Silves, perhaps because he was aware of the hostility of the prime minister, the famous Ibn Zaydūn. Upon Ibn Zaydūn's death in 463/1070, al-Muʿtamid appointed Ibn ʿAmmār as prime minister for external affairs, at which post he remained for ten years. Here he encountered, as both ally and adversary, a personality of equal measure to his own, Alfonso VI of Castile. One story that captures the frontier flavor of the times tells of Ibn ʿAmmār and the king of Castile playing chess over the fate of Seville.

Al-Muʿtamid allowed himself to succumb to his natural indolence, allowing his prime minister to negotiate in his stead with the surrounding Christian monarchs. This went well until Ibn ʿAmmār conspired with the count of Barcelona, Ramón Berenguer II (1053?-1082), to conquer Murcia in exchange for a large sum of money and the delivery of al-Muʿtamid's son al-Rashīd, the principal heir, as a hostage.

When the money did not arrive immediately, Berenguer kept the prince in chains while the Sevillian army, under Ibn ʿAmmār, left Murcia, only to encounter al-Muʿtamid on his way with the money and other gifts to redeem his son. The hapless al-Rashīd was involuntarily the first, and later, part of the final rift between al-Muʿtamid and Ibn ʿAmmār. The prime minister's rash ambition had endangered the life of the prince, who, according to the emir ʿAbd Allah, Ibn ʿAmmār treated with disrespect.

Al-Muʿtamid's politics had one aim: the expansion of his kingdom. He conquered Cordoba, intended to conquer Granada, annexed Murcia, and finally Lorca. All of this was accomplished with the help of Alfonso VI, king of Castillo, except in the case of Murcia. In that case, Alfonso VI did nothing to stop al-Muʿtamid, and al-Muʿtamid did the same when Alfonso VI conquered Toledo. Only when the king of Castile became a bothersome ally, such as when he pretended that his wife Constanza needed to stay in Madīnat al-Zahrā, near Cordoba, during her pregnancy, did it occur to al-Muʿtamid to ask the Almoravids to come to al-Andalus, thinking that he could divide the Almoravid tribes and get them fighting against each other.

The arrival of the Almoravids meant the loss of Algeciras, but the outcome of the campaign was positive: the North Africans defeated Alfonso VI in Sagrajas/Zallaqa in 479/1086. So al-Muʿtamid called on them again when Alfonso VI made a move for Murcia, which al-Muʿtamid hoped to regain for his son al-Rāḍī.

The Andalusians understood their precarious position. With the advance of the Reconquest and two invasions from North Africa, they realized that they would either become swineherds in Spain or camel drivers in North Africa. The king of Granada, Muḥammad II, according to Ibn Khaldūn (1332-1406), hesitated to ask for help from North African mercenaries, fearing to be placed in the same position as al-Muʿtamid. The Granadian author of *al-Ḥulal al-Mawshiyyah fī dhikr al-akhbār al-Marrākishiyyah*, attributed to Ibn Simmāk, or Ibn al-Khaṭīb (d. 1374) dramatized the dilemma of the Andalusians, putting in al-Muʿtamid's mouth the famous phrase (I would rather be a slave in North Africa than a swineherd in Castile) in a dialogue with his son, al-Rashīd.

In reality, al-Muʿtamid did not understand the danger posed by the Almoravids until the last minute. When Yūsuf ibn Tāshfīn (1061-1106) destroyed ʿAbd Allāh of Granada, al-Muʿtamid went to congratulate him and ask if he would give al-Muʿtamid Granada as compensation for Algeciras. The response from the Almoravid emir was so chilling that al-Muʿtamid finally understood the reality of the situation, and said to Ibn al-Aftas, the king of Badajoz, who accompanied him: "Save yourself, because what happened to the lord of Granada yesterday will happen to me tomorrow."

It was also the first time that he realized that the other *Ṭā'ifah* kings were in the same boat as he. Until then, the king of Seville had viewed his colleagues only as prey for his own territorial ambitions. He announced his first conquest, Cordoba, in a poem that is interesting from a literary point of view, because the city is represented as a bride, courted by the kings, a figure remembered in later Spanish literature in the romance of Abenámar (al-Maqqarī, 1:297):

Who has arrived among the kings, at last this valiant king?
Generous! The king of *Mahdi* has arrived among us;
He asked in marriage for Cordoba the beautiful, when she
Had rejected those who pretended with swords and lances;
How much time she was naked! Until I presented
Myself, and covered her in beautiful tunics and jewels.
A royal wedding! We were married in her palace,
While the other kings were in the courtyard of timidity;
Look, sons of bitches, the attack of a lion draws near
Wrapped in a mantle (loriga) of valor.
"They can take my kingdom…
but they cannot take my noble character."

When Yūsuf ibn Tāshfīn began the conquest of the kingdom of Seville, al-Muʿtamid vainly asked for help from Alfonso VI. Instead, the king of Castile gave his enemies moral reasons for defeating the ʿAbbādids.

Al-Muʿtamid's sensuous lifestyle was transformed into a burden, and the end of his dynasty was proclaimed from the pulpits by the clergy. His son al-Ma'mūn died in Cordoba, and his son al-Rāḍī heroically resisted in Ronda until ordered to surrender by his father. Al-Muʿtamid only wanted to die in battle rather than suffer the humiliation of defeat. He did not obtain his desire. After a fierce battle, Seville fell on the 7th of September, 22 Rajab 484/1091.

Al-Muʿtamid was taken prisoner, and his harem became the booty of General Sīr ibn Abī Bakr, allowing only the concubines who had born him children to accompany al-Muʿtamid into exile. Yūsuf ibn Tāshfīn ordered that the king of Seville be taken to Maruecos. The moment of parting was described by Muḥammad ibn ʿĪsā Ibn al-Labbānah (d. 1113) at the end of a long poem about the fall of the ʿAbbādids:

I will never forget the dawn

Beside the Guadalquivir, when they boarded the ships
Like the dead to their graves.
The people clustered on the banks
Looking at them as they floated
Upon white beds of foam.
The virgins cast off their veils
Uncovered their faces that, cruelly,
Were more obscured by pain
Than by their cloaks.
When the moment arrived, What a tumult
Of goodbyes! What a clamor was launched
By the ladies and gentlemen!
The vessels departed, accompanied by sobs,
Like the wandering caravan
Urged on by the cry of the camel driver.
Oh, how many tears the water carried!
Oh, how many hearts were broken in those insensible galleys!

Al-Muʿtamid saw the death of his most beloved sons, those born to Rumaykiyyah, and he mourned them in his poems of exile. The king of Seville had many children–some sources say one hundred seventy, but only the names of a few have been preserved, especially Rumaykiyyah's sons who received political appointments: ʿAbbād Sirāj al-Dawlah, the eldest, born in Silves and made governor of Cordoba when it came under the crown of Seville in 462/1070, who died fighting against Ibn ʿUkāsha when he conquered the city on behalf of the king of Toledo in 467/1075. Al-Muʿtamid did not rest until he had reconquered the city and avenged his son by crucifying Ibn ʿUkāsha beside a dog.

Next in line was ʿUbayd Allāh al-Rashīd, who became principal heir upon the death of his brother. He was refined, loved poetry, song and music, and was a fan of lute-playing. He was taken prisoner at the fall of Seville and ended his days in exile with his father.

The third son of Rumaykiyyah was named ʿAbd Allāh al-Mu'tadd. He was the governor of Mértola, which he bravely defended from the Almoravids, only surrendering when ordered by his father. Next was al-Fatḥ Abū Naṣr al-Ma'mūn, governor of Cordoba after it was reconquered from the Toledans. He was killed by the Almoravids upon its fall in 484/1091. It is possible that his widow was Zaydah, a mis-spelling of the title al-Sayyidah al-Kubrā, who became the wife of Alfonso VI.

The fifth son was named Yazīd Abū Khalīd al-Rāḍī, the best poet of al-Muʿtamid's children, and perhaps his favorite. He was the governor of Algeciras, the outpost that the ʿAbbādids ceded to the Amoravids during their first expedition to al-Andalus. It was he who took Ibn ʿAmmār as a prisoner from Segura to Cordoba. He was very studious, and received a reprimand from his father when he neglected to participate in the assault on Lorca. With his terrible irony, al-Muʿtamid told his son that he should dedicate himself to his books, where he would find power and glory, and not to war, which was his official duty as a prince. In this poem, he suggests that al-Rāḍī circles his study the way a devout Muslim would circle the Kaʿbah.

Al-Muʿtamid lamented al-Ma'mūn and al-Rāḍī in one of his poems of exile (al-Maqqarī, 5:381):

The turtledove cries to see two lovers together in their nest,
Having recently lost her love
She cries without tears, while mine
Are more abundant than drops of rain;
She discovers her pain, and prefers to keep her
Secret, without emitting a moan;
Besides that, why should I not cry? Is my heart made
Of stone? Sometimes rocks break loose from the rivers.
She cries for a single loved one she has lost,
I cry for many of mine!
For my little son, for my loyal friend,
For that one torn by misery, for this one drowned in the sea;
And for those two stars, ornaments of the world,
Who lie in their tombs, one in Cordoba, one in
Ronda. I would be culpable if my eyelids kept me from crying
But one only cures the soul with resignation;
Tell the brilliant stars to cry with me
For those two, who were like stars, stars shine.

We know the names of two more of Iʿtimād's sons, Abū Sulaymān Tāj al-Dawlah, and Abū 'l-Hāshim al-Muʿālla Zayn al-Dawlah. The last was a small child when they went into exile, and the subject of the following poem, remembered during the last battle of Zallaqa (al-Maqqarī, 6:10):

Abū Hāshim, the swords destroy me
How I resisted in that battle!
I remember your little person and my love for you
My impulse was to flee;

His sadness and fear upon seeing his father in chains exacerbated al-Muʿtamid's grief (al-Maqqarī, 3:389):

My chains, don't you know that I am a Muslim?
And without a doubt you refuse me compassion or mercy
My blood is your drink, you eat my flesh,
Although you have not broken my bones;
Abū Hāshim sees me like this and cringes,
With his heart broken;
Have compassion for a child who is shaken,
But does not dare come to you to ask for clemency.
Have compassion for his little sisters who, like him
Must drink venom and bitterness;
Some understand some things and I fear
That the flood of tears will blind them;
Others understand nothing, and only
Open their mouths to nurse.

Al-Muʿtamid's daughters are only recorded in exile as ravenous and tearful ghosts who oppress the spirit of the prisoner (al-Maqqarī, 6:9-10):

Look at your daughters in rags and starving,
Spinning for others, because they possess nothing;
They come to you, to greet you, with downcast eyes,
Low-spirited;
They step barefoot on the mud, as though they had not
Stepped on musk and camphor;
There are on their cheeks only the tracks of hunger
And they do not refresh themselves except with tears of pain.

Only one name emerges from this anonymous chorus, Buthaynah, who was taken prisoner at the fall of Seville and sold as a slave. She later wrote to her father in Agmat, asking permission to marry for love, to which al-Muʿtamid agreed.

Other of al-Muʿtamid's children found their destinies far from Agmat. Yaḥyā and al-Ḥakam, sons of an anonymous concubine, became scribes in Fez and Marakesh. Another son, ʿAbd al-Jabbār, rebelled against the Almoravids in Montemayor and Arcos, but was defeated and killed the same year as the death of his father, 1095. After that, no other ʿAbbādids attempted to regain power.

His wife's illness increased al-Muʿtamid's desperation. He who so loved life, said to the doctor who cared for Iʿtimād:

Since death is not preferable to life,
Why the shame of a long lie?
If each of us desires to find his love,
I do not desire it, unless I find death.

With both hope and Iʿtimād dead, the prisoner rapidly declined. Sensing his impending death, al-Muʿtamid composed his epitaph in which he describes, if it did not happen, what he would have liked:

Build up the clouds with perennial tears
Your gentle land, oh tomb of exile
That the king Ibn ʿAbbād covers the balances
Guard with the three illustrious virtues
Science, grace, and clemency gathered;
The fertile abundance that the appetites
Came to exterminate, and the water to dry out.
Quell him who leads the endless quarrel
With the sword, the lance, and the bow,
He whom to the lion's fury was a hard death;
Rival to destiny in vengeance
Of the ocean in dispensing favors
Of the moon in shining in the darkness;
Leader of the salon. It is certain:
Not without justice, with rigorous exactitude,
A celestial design came to wound me.
But, before I became a cadaver, I never knew
That a tall mountain could
End in a trembling bed.
What more do you want, oh tomb? Be merciful
With such honor as will be entrusted to your custody.
The crashing lightning closes in,
When it quickly crosses these environs,

For me, its brother–I ask an eternal rain
Of compassionate refrains of your praise –
Cry without consolation. And the white frost
Of your gentle tears, drop by drop
Will distill from your eyes the stars,
Giving me no greater fortune.
The blessings of Allah descend,
Without number, incessant,
Upon he who still has a warm breast!

After the passing of Iʿtimād, al-Muʿtamid lingered only a few months before following her (488/1095). His best epitaph was undoubtedly the words of Muḥammad ibn ʿAbd Allāh Ibn al-Abbār (1199-1260), faithfully written down by Ibn al-Labbānah:

"He won the love and compassion of the people: even now they cry for him."

In the third/ninth to fifth/eleventh century, three major changes produced the Abbasid panegyric *qaṣīdah*–in which form it would reach al-Andalus. First, the *qaṣīdah* now celebrated and commemorated the religious and political ideals of the Muslim community. It extolled the ideal Islamic ruler and offered a vision of the Arabo-Islamic past and future. Its themes were reimagined to fit this new function. In general, urban themes supplanted nomadic elements. Descriptions of spring, gardens and wine, blame of fate, and lament for lost youth often replaced the traditional *naṣīb*. The *raḥīl* was frequently dropped, and in the panegyric, battles with unbelievers superseded tribal skirmishes. Descriptions of palaces, parades, and religious festivals supplied new themes of praise. The *qaṣīdah*'s central figure became the perfect ruler, God's instrument and recipient of his grace, guarantor of right guidance, and mediator between God and his subjects. A skilled poet was still allowed to resurrect and adapt any older theme, even one temporarily eclipsed.

Second, through its quasi-official function, the *qaṣīdah* became a court genre and its author a court poet, dependent on the caliph or another patron. But the poet might still exert a limited moral hold over a patron through modes of address, ranging from praise and felicitation (*tahni'ah*), to admonition (*wa'ẓ*) and reprimand (*'itāb*) to implied threat of slander. Thus the eloquent poet might balance his weaker position by publicly placing a *qaṣīdah*'s recipient under moral pressure–a strategy perfected by ʿAlī ibn al-ʿAbbās Ibn al-Rūmī (836-896) who developed a specific dramatic style for this purpose.

Finally, the relationship of poetry to reality was redefined in the "new" (*muḥdath*) style. The Abbasid poet could combine existing images to create various effects by transferring them between themes or overlaying them with rhetorical figures, such as paronomasia (*jinās*) and antithesis (*ṭibāq*). The binary character of the last two figures allowed expansion into a larger dialectic structure, one in which the just government of a divinely instated caliph could be contrasted with the chaotic injustice of fate. The intellectual, and sometimes surreal, nature of this new style first drew the poetic critics' protest, but gradually, with the acclaim of its illustrious representatives, Abū Tammām (796 or 804-842/843 or 845/846) and al-Walīd ibn ʿUbayd al-Buḥturī (821-897 or 898), it became the panegyric standard. The gradual Islamization of the *qaṣīdah*'s world view, its role as a nexus between poet and patron, and its new mannerist style allowed the genre to adapt to the caliphal court and its literary circles.

The Andalusian *qaṣīdah* was joined by two other genres in dispensing *madīḥ*. In the late fourth/tenth century, the *nawriyyah* came into fashion. This short panegyric consisted of few verses of varying complexity, describing a flower, and ending with a reference to the addressee attached by an image or figure. Yūsuf ibn Hārūn al-Ramādī (d. 1012), while in prison, changed the genre to a short bird description, concluding with a plea for forgiveness. The *qaṣīdah*'s second rival, the *muwashshaḥ*, was first reclaimed for classical Arabic *madīḥ* in the mid-twelfth century by Ibn al-Labbānah in praise of al-Muʿtamid ibn ʿAbbād. It either contained praise alone or connected with another theme, such as a festive occasion or the description of wine, love, or gardens.

The poetry of al-Muʿtamid of Seville is, for the most part, free of the stilted language which is often employed in medieval Arabic poetry and which is difficult for the uninitiated to read. The key to his clarity may lie in an extra-literary fact:

his royal station in life, that permitted him to use poetry rather than to serve it.

His poetry is not entirely free of rhetoric, but uses various wordplays typical of the Arabic poem: parallel structure and interplacement, including acrostics, but always with a refined balance. His lexicon, is simple, without archaisms or obscure words. The usual vehicle for his poetry is the cadence and meter of classical Arabic.

Al-Muʿtamid's poetic language seems to focus on the antithesis, especially in the counterpoint of light/darkness, which his poetry converts, in its first epoch, into nocturnal and astral: the night illuminated by the stars is the only description of nature one finds in his poems. The other elements of nature (the garden, flowers, animals, water) only appear as human comparisons. In the poems of exile, the lion will become warfare; the gazelle, woman; the water a metaphor for generosity, like dew or like clouds. What will be crying, is hyperbolically transformed into rain and ocean; birds become, also in Aguat, metaphors for freedom. Woman will become a perfumed garden, a branch for her belt, and a rose for her cheeks, but above all remain the stars.

The *qaṣīdah* was designed to be practiced before highly educated hearers. With increasing familiarity, however, the modern reader may approach an impression of the fulfilled or flouted expectations that thrilled earlier audiences. Recent *qaṣīdah* scholarship has advanced in three general directions: 1) the various themes, motifs, figures and styles of the *qaṣīdah*–as opposed to the monothematic *qiṭ'ah*–have led to studies of its textual unity with special regard for the way in which these elements contribute to the *qaṣīdah*'s overall coherence. 2) the diachronic position of the *qaṣīdah* within the literary tradition has been examined in intertextual studies. These pursue the development of single themes or motifs across poems, so as to delimit a poet's share in a reused motif as well as the audience's pleasure occurring *between* works and not *within* one monolithic work. 3) The *qaṣīdah* has given rise to broadly synchronic studies that complement a close reading of the poetry with the search for an underlying (ritual, ethical, or ideological) rationale, thus motivating a *qaṣīdah*'s play on the tradition by its function. Many of these approaches identify a situational meaning at the intersection of historical context and poetic text.

The textual norms for the *qaṣīdah* include a courtly, ornate, and formal register of speech, the Arabic lexicon and motifs, and a prosody employing one of sixteen meters with a single rhyme. The structure is flexible but generally linear and transformational (e.g., ascending from the physical to metaphysical world), containing several themes arranged into two or three parts. Over time, the recurring themes and motifs have themselves become polysemic or symbolic, conveying secondary, situational meanings. The cultural norms include performance in a public setting with a ceremonial or celebratory purpose, the moral code of Islamic statehood and Arabo-Islamic morality, and the social function of praising those who wield God-given power, chastising their adversaries and admonishing their subjects to respect it.

The Abbasid panegyric *qaṣīdah* was at the center of, and conditioned by, a social and literary exchange. Its material value, iconographies, and *modus vivendi* place this *qaṣīdah* type in a class of its own–in the same way *qaṣīdahs* serving devotional, didactic, or ideological functions warrant consideration in light of their context.

The true sophisticate, according to the fourteenth century literary critic Khalīl ibn Aybak al-Ṣafadī (ca. 1297-1363), was one who "wears robes of white and rings of carnelian, recites the *Qu'rān* according to the readings of Abū ʿAmr Zabbān ibn al-ʿAlā' (d. 770), knows the sacred law according to the tradition of Muḥammad ibn Idrīs al-Shāfiʿī (767 or 768-820), and relates the poetry of Ibn Zaydūn. Described as a master of passion and longing, Ibn Zaydūn is generally held to be the outstanding Arab poet of al-Andalus and ranks among the most illustrious love poets in all Arabic literature. His stormy love affair with Wallādah bint al-Mustakfī (d. 1091 or 1092), the daughter of the Umayyad caliph al-Mustakfī (d. 1025) and a leading figure in Cordovan society, inspired much of his poetry. Ibn Zaydūn's work captures the essence of Andalusian poetry, especially in two areas characteristic of Andalusian literature: the description of gardens, and the relatively unstylized presentation of emotion and experience.

A native of Cordoba, Ibn Zaydūn left due to political intrigues and served al-Mu'tadid and then his son al-Mu'tamid for the next two decades, as vizier and ambassador. It was he who advised King al-Mu'tadid that Ibn 'Ammār was a bad influence on the principal heir, al-Mu'tamid, and kept Ibn 'Ammār from the court of Seville until al-Mu'tadid's death. His own rather public and outrageous affair with Wallādah may have equally influenced the young prince, who showed a proclivity for wine and beautiful women. When the 'Abbādids captured Cordoba and made it their new capital, Ibn Zaydūn was able to return to his native city. After his death in 463/1091, his son Abū Bakr continued to serve al-Mu'tamid. It is assumed that al-Mu'tamid obtained his education from Ibn Zaydūn.

Besides love poetry, Ibn Zaydūn was also a master of satire. He and Wallādah exchanged biting, even obscene, epistles after the end of their affair, but Ibn Zaydūn also wrote his most heartfelt and immortal verse, the *Nuniyyah*, a fifty-two verse *qaṣīdah* rhyming in *–inah* that expresses longing for the lost days of bliss with Wallādah. It is one of the most famous love poems in all of Arabic literature, and it was said that he who memorized it was doomed to die far from home. Many poets composed *mu'āraḍahs* (imitations in the same rhyme and meter) of the *Nuniyyah*, both during the author's life and afterward. Ibn Zaydūn also wrote a famous letter pleading his case when imprisoned by the Jahwarid ruler of Cordoba, *al-Risalah al-jiddiyyah* (The Serious Epistle), panegyrics for the various royals he served, and exchanged a series of riddle poems playing on the names of birds with al-Mu'tamid and the jurist Abū Ṭālib Muḥammad ibn 'Alī 'l-Makkī (d. 996).

The descriptions of a 'tamed' or urban view of nature–the moon as viewed from an enclosed garden, likening women to various natural elements–are evident in al-Mu'tamid's work, but his panegyrics to himself are certainly the product of his royal position. His satiric exchanges with Ibn 'Ammār were in the spirit of Ibn Zaydūn's satires sent to Wallādah and her new lover, except that Ibn 'Ammār forgot his place in relationship to the king and subsequently lost his life. It is possible that Ibn Zaydūn's *al-Risalah al-jiddiyyah* served as inspiration, if not a model for al-Mu'tamid's own poem sent to his father after the botched siege of Malaga.

Ibn Zaydūn's poetry can be characterized as neoclassical. Through the union of Neoplatonic doctrines with the tradition of Arabic verse, Ibn Zaydūn was able to produce a more humane Neoclassical verse that cultivated true human emotion. He especially admired al-Buḥturī, among the earlier Arabic poets, and al-Ṣafadī suggests that the *Nuniyyah* was intended as a *mu'āraḍah* of a poem by al-Buḥturī. Ibn Zaydūn also aspired to compose excellent prose and often expresses this dual concept of ideal literary talent in his own writings, holding up as paragons not only the poets al-Buḥturī and Abū Tammām, but also the prose writers Abū 'Uthman 'Amr ibn Baḥr al-Jāḥiẓ (d. 868 or 869) and the famous secretaries al-Faḍl ibn Sahl (d. 818) and Ja'far al-Barmakī. Like al-Jāḥiẓ, Ibn Zaydūn preferred the use of structurally parallel cola without rhyme and avoided the constant use of *saj'*, rhymed and rhythmic prose, which had become popular among court secretaries during the tenth century.

Ibn Zaydūn's prose is also classicizing in its constant references to obscure proverbs and aphorisms, Preislamic lore, *Qur'ānic* narratives, and earlier poetry. The lack of these allusions in the work of al-Mu'tamid may account for the assertion that he lacked any classical education, but he was clearly exposed to them by Ibn Zaydūn.

As ambassador to the courts of the party kingdoms, Ibn Zaydūn lived a life where eloquence translated directly into noble charges and political prominence. His poetry, linguistically perfect, is at the same time restrained. It has attained full maturity and independence from Eastern tutelage. The brilliant colors and glittering decoration of his predecessors are toned down and reduced to sober and masterly contrasts between black and white which distract less from the depth and sincerity of meaning. Likewise, his language, is simple and natural, yet embellished enough to reach an elevated poetic tone. Ibn Zaydūn died on a negotiation mission on behalf of al-Mu'tamid, having been sent from Cordoba to use his powers to quell a revolt in Seville.

In spite of their descriptions by other scholars, Raymond Scheindlin says that, of the 190 poems attributed to al-Muʿtamid, not one could properly be called a *qaṣīdah* as defined by the Ibn Qutaybah. The anthologists and historians who preserved al-Muʿtamid's work usually introduce his poems with *qāla* (he said), *anshada* (he sang), *wa-min shiʿrihi* (the following is one of his poems) as opposed to 'following is a *qaṣīdah* by al-Muʿtamid.' That is because these terms apply to a different literary milieu, and bear no direct meaning to the kind of poetry al-Muʿtamid wrote.

The most characteristic genre of the *qaṣīdah*, the *madīḥ,* has its counterpart in *Dīwān al-Muʿtamid* in a number of poems which al-Muʿtamid addressed to his father, while the *marthiyyah* has as its counterpart a number of elegies composed on the death of al-Muʿtamid's sons. But none of these poems shows the sequence of themes characteristic of the traditional *qaṣīdah*. Most notably, the traditional opening *naṣīb* is completely lacking. In fact, a single general subject is addressed by all of his poems. Thematically, al-Muʿtamid's poems, both short and long, are unified entities.

Al-Muʿtamid was not a professional poet, but King al-Muʿtadid had raised him to be a poet and warrior. He had probably saved his own life by writing an exceptional *madīḥ* to his father, and his position as a patron to poets demanded that he be able to maintain a certain standard of excellence. He became the Western protector of poets par excellence after the Normans invaded Sicily and Qayrawan was overrun by Bedouin tribes, and he himself led a life full of poetry and romance. His reputation as a poet was formidable enough to daunt professional court poets who aspired to join his academy.

To enter his intimate circle of confidantes, one had to demonstrate not only a great talent for versifying, but also of improvisation. After the conquest of Sicily by the Normans in 1078, a poet of Syracuse named Ibn Ḥamdīs went to al-Andalus after a short stay in Tunis. He was intent on garnering the favor of al-Muʿtamid, but for a long time went unnoticed. At last, one night the ʿAbbādid monarch called him to the palace to put his poetic abilities to the test. Through a window, he could see at a distance a glass factory in which one could observe two lights coming, one from each furnace. Al-Muʿtamid improvised:

Look at them, like two stars in the darkness.

Ibn Ḥamdīs responded:

Like the orbs in the darkness of the lion.

When the doors of the furnaces closed, al-Muʿtamid said:

He opens his eyes, then he shuts them.

Ibn Ḥamdīs:

Like the lids of inflamed eyes.

Said al-Muʿtamid when he saw that the doors opened again and then only one closed:

But Destiny overcomes the one fire.

Ibn Ḥamdīs ended thus:

Who is saved from his claws?

Al-Muʿtamid loved his brilliant salons (*majlis*), surrounded by his poet friends, slender cupbearers and flirtatious slave singers. Al-Muʿtamid's liberal court, that held excellence in poetry above all else, included at least one Mozarab, Ibn al-Mir'issī al-Naẓrānī, and one Jew, Abu 'l-ʿAlā ibn Zuhr, the court physician.

In addition, diplomatic communication was in the form of poetry, from asking for favors to expressing insults, and as earlier illustrated, this was a sport in which all of the populace participated. Most of his love and wine poetry was extemporaneously composed in the context of the poetic games so frequently engaged in by Andalusian aristocrats, during their parties and pleasure-outings. Similarly, the poems addressed to friends and political associates generally take as their starting point a particular message which al-Muʿtamid wished to convey. Even his longer and more serious poems, the *marthiyyah* and the laments on his exile and imprisonment in Aghmat, deal with a single idea, and display no great leaps that would invoke the tradition of the ancient *qaṣīdahs*.

There is one bit of information about his literary interests. When Ibn al-Labbānah visited him in Aghmat, al-Muʿtamid discovered that he had salvaged from Seville a copy of the commentary by Abū 'l-Hajjāj Yūsuf ibn Sulaymān al-Aʿlam al-Shantamarī (1019 or 1020-1083 or 1084) on the *dīwāns* of the poets of the *Muʿallaqāt*. Al-Muʿtamid borrowed the book so that his children could copy it for him. But it is not known if he would have sought out such a book if it had not been available to him, and he had not had so little to occupy himself during his last, lonely years in captivity.

Al-Muʿtamid's verse is occasionally compared to the verses of earlier poets, but it is not known if he was consciously alluding to these poets. One anecdote recounts that a visitor from Baghdad criticized a verse by Ibn ʿAmmār, and al-Muʿtamid defended the latter by pointing out that Ibn ʿAmmār's verse contains an allusion to a verse by a Huhaylite poet, which he then quoted. Only one direct quotation from an earlier poet has been noted in al-Muʿtamid's own poetry so far, and the verse quoted is so famous that it does not warrant any conclusions about al-Muʿtamid's education.

In view of the occasional nature of al-Muʿtamid's poetry, we would not expect to find patterns such as those in the *qaṣīdah*. But many of them have definable structures that attest to a conscious technique of organization present in the mind of the poet. Often, just as there exists parallelism between the first and second hemstitches of a verse, there may be parallels between whole verses, and even between groups of verses. In other instances, balanced wordplay may offset random wordplay, emphasizing the bipartite structure of certain verses and calling attention to their positions of resolution and closure.

Unlike Ibn Zaydūn, al-Muʿtamid was not averse to using the vernacular for some of his poetry. There are instances of combining Arabic with the Romance vernacular of the time, and it is possible that Rumaykiyyah, with her humble origins, spoke this language as well.

In an early *qaṣīdah* to his father requesting forgiveness for having allowed himself to fall into a trap set for him by the Berbers of Granada, the personal tone he was to adopt in his later poetry is already present. The poem is composed in a simple, natural language containing relatively few rhetorical devices. This allows him to speak straight from the heart to his notoriously violent father. Al-Muʿtamid casts aside all excessive rhetoric and in the initial soliloquy, tries to calm his own fears. He employs the poetic convention of addressing himself in the second person singular *ka*, "your." This has the effect of suggesting a dialogue because it seems to include the father in the poet's musings. By saying, "Rest your heart, let not your cares overcome you. What good will grief and apprehension do you?" the poet is on one level calming his own fears, as though his reason were speaking to his emotion. The device thus makes possible a lyrical dimension whereby the poet's psychology is revealed. On another level, it seems to suggest that it is the father speaking to the son. It assumes sadness rather than anger on the father's part, a disposition in favor of clemency rather than punishment. By attempting to arouse the father's compassion and his nobler instincts, the poet hopes to mitigate his wrath. On a third level, the use of *ka* might even be taken to suggest that it is the father who is sad, and must be comforted by the son. Thus the *ka* has an expressive function that goes far beyond its mere grammatical and logical function. It encircles and emphasizes the main theme of the poem, a request for forgiveness.

After his defeat at the hands of the Almoravids, al-Muʿtamid spent his final years in poverty and exile, writing poems filled with deep emotion in which he mourned his fall from power. His production from this period is in some ways comparable with that of the Ḥamdānid Abū Firās ibn Saʿīd ibn Aḥmad ibn Ḥamdān al-Ḥamdānī (932-968), which the latter wrote during his captivity in Constantinople. Both poets make of their personal sorrow the main subject of their poetry, and by this means they rise above the commonplaces found in occasional verse. Every aspect of al-Muʿtamid's life was reflected in his poetry, from the escapades of his early youth to the captivity of his later years.

It is unclear when al-Muʿtamid's poetry was first collected into a *dīwān*. We know that such a *dīwān* existed in the Middle Ages from Ibn al-Abbār. The earliest works known to have included a large number of his poems were written by Ibn al-Labbānah, who joined the court of Seville shortly before al-Muʿtamid was deposed, and who visited him in exile in Aghmat. These works were entitled *Saqīṭ al-durar wa-laqīṭ al-zahīr* and *Naẓm al-sulūk fī mawā'iz al-mulūk.* There is, unfortunately, no evidence that these books still exist, although later anthologies quote from them. Another contemporaneous work which may have recorded some of his poems was the collection of anecdotes compiled by Abū Bakr Muḥammad Ibn Yūsuf Ibn Qāsim al-Shiblī, one of al-Muʿtamid's secretaries. This work is quoted several times by Ibn al-Abbār, who regarded its author as more reliable than Ibn Bassām.

The two manuscripts of the *Dīwān* of Ibn Zaydūn preserved in the Egyptian National Library have an appendix with a large number of poems by al-Muʿtadid and al-Muʿtamid. It is not known when this *dīwān* was compiled, and it may be fairly recent. However, the poems by al-Muʿtamid collected in this *dīwān* include only love poems, wine poems, and poems addressed to his father, his own courtiers, and to ambassadors from other courts. None of the famous exile poems are included. The appendix ends with a poem addressed to Ibn ʿAmmār dated 1078, after the death of Ibn Zaydūn in 1071. This implies that the collector intended to include not only the works of al-Muʿtamid written during the life of his mentor Ibn Zaydūn, but all of al-Muʿtamid's important works known to the editor. The lack of al-Muʿtamid's poems of exile, his last and most popular work, implies that the appendix was compiled before they were written, or that the exile poems had not yet had time to reach Spain.

Among the poets who remained faithful to al-Muʿtamid after his fall was the Sicilian, Ibn Ḥamdīs, who had escaped to Seville after the Normans invaded his homeland, and Ibn al-Labbānah, famous for his *qaṣīdah* in which he mourns his former protector's departure into exile.

Al-Muʿtamid, the Lion of Seville and last of the ʿAbbādid monarchs, asks in his epitaph to be remembered not only as a warrior, but also as the generous leader of the literary salon, surrounded by the three muses of science, grace and mercy. His life as a king and a poet exemplified the values of al-Andalus during the reign of the party kings.

REFERENCES

Reinhard Dozy, *Scriptorum Arabum Loci de Abbadidis* 3 vols. (Leiden, 1846-1863);

Ramón, A. Guerrero, "Enemistad de Al-Muʿtaṣim Ibn Ṣumādih hacia al-Muʿtamid Ibn ʿAbbād," *Miscelánea de Estudios Árabes y Hebraicos* vol. 32-33, no. i (1984): 181-187;

ʿAlī ibn Mūsā Ibn Saʿīd, *Moorish Poetry: a Translation of the Pennants, an Anthology compiled in 1243 by the Andalusian Ibn Sa'id*, trans. A.J. Arberry (Cambridge: University Press, 1953);

Abū ʿĀmir Aḥmad ibn Shuhayd, *Risālat at-Tawābi' wa z-Zawābi': The Treatise of Familiar Spirits and Demons*, James T. Monroe. University of California Publications, Near Eastern Studies 15 (Berkeley: University of California Press, 1971);

Muḥammad ibn ʿAbd Allāh Ibn al-Abbār, *Kitāb al-Ḥullah al-siy*arā, ed. Ḥusayn Mu'nis. 2 vols. (Cairo: al-Sharikah al-ʿArabiyyah, 1963);

Ibn Zaydūn, *Dīwān* (Cairo: Dār Nahḍat Miṣr, 1980);

The Literature of al-Andalus, ed. Maria Rosa Menocal, Raymond P. Scheindlin, and Michael Sells. Cambridge History of Arabic Literature,(Cambridge: Cambridge University Press, 2000), 212-216;

Aḥmad ibn Muḥammad al-Maqqarī, *Nafḥ al-ṭīb ghuṣn al-Andalus al-raṭīb wa-dhikr wazīrihā Lisān al-Dīn ibn al-Khaṭīb*, ed. Muḥammad Muḥyī al-Dīn ʿAbd al-Ḥamīd. 10 vols. (Cairo: al-Maktabah al-Tijāriyyah al-Kubrā, 1949);

J.S. Meisami, "Unsquaring the circle: rereading a poem by al-Muʿtamid Ibn ʿAbbād," *Arabica* no. 35 (1988): 293-310;

James T. Monroe, *Hispano-Arabic Poetry: a Student Anthology* (Piscataway: Gorgias Press LLC, 2004);

"Muʿtamid, al-," in Encyclopædia Britannica. 2005. Encyclopædia Britannica Premium Service. 29 Dec. 2005 http://www.britannica.com/eb/article-9054487;

A.R. Nykl, *Hispano-Arabic Poetry and Its Relations with the Old Provençal Troubadours* (Baltimore, 1946);
Raymond P. Scheindlin, *Form and structure in the poetry of al-Mu'tamid Ibn 'Abbād* (Leiden, Brill, 1974);
Raymond P. Scheindlin, "Poetic structure in Arabic: three poems by al-Muʿtamid Ibn ʿAbbād," *Humaniora Islamica* no. 1 (1973): 173-186;
Salah Serour, "Poesía Arabe de Al-Andalus (Siglos X-XII) y Su Paralelo en el Oriente," http://web-linux.unisi.it/tdtc/ricerca/burgos/lezioni/1.%20Historia%20literaria/2.%20Salah%20Serour.doc.

al-Mutanabbī

(915-965)

Andras Hamori
Princeton University

WORKS

Dīwān (Collected poems).

Editio princeps

Dīwān Abī 'l-Ṭayyib al-Mutanabbī, ed. by Aḥmad al-Yamanī 'l-Shirwānī (Calcutta, 1230/1814) Said to be unfindable.

Selected editions with commentary

Mutanabbii carmina cum commentario Wahidii, 2 vols., ed. by Friedrich Dieterici (Berlin: E.S. Mittler, 1861); Repr: *Dīwān, wa fī athnā' matnih sharḥ al-imām al-'allāma 'l-Wāḥidī wa-arba'at fahāris* (Baghdad: Maktabat al-Muthannā, 1964?);

Dīwān Abī 'l-Ṭayyib al-Mutanabbī bi-sharḥ Abī 'l-Baqā' al-'Ukbarī 'l-musammā bi 'l-Tibyān fī sharḥ al-dīwān (commentary ascribed to Abū 'l-Baqā' al-ʿUkbarī), 4 vols., ed. Muṣṭafā 'l-Saqqā, Ibrāhīm al-Ibyārī, and ʿAbd al-Ḥāfīẓ Shalabī (Cairo: Muṣṭafā 'l-Bābī 'l-Ḥalabī, 1936);

Nāsīf al-Yāzijī, *al-'Arf al-ṭayyib fī sharḥ dīwān Abī 'l-Ṭayyib,* 2 vols. (Beirut: Dār Ṣādir, 1964).

Translations

Johann Jacob Reiske, *Proben der arabischen Dichtkunst in verliebten und traurigen Gedichten, aus dem Motanabbi*; Arabisch und Deutsch, nebst Anmerkungen (Leipzig: s.n., 1765);

Joseph v. Hammer-Purgstall, *Motenebbi, der grösste arabische Dichter* (Vienna, 1824);

A. J. Arberry, *Poems of al-Mutanabbi*; a selection with introduction, translations and notes (London: Cambridge University Press, 1967).

Of the medieval Arab poets who made a living from panegyrics, few can match the best of al-Mutanabbī's, and there is more of his best than of anyone else's. Powerful language, brilliant conceits, lapidary verses about daring, hope, and disillusionment, and a haughty stare in the face of fate and human sleaziness have brought his work passionate admirers from his own age to ours. It does not translate particularly well. Much depends on rhetorical techniques. The conceits are mannered according to the fashion of the time. The modern reader also tends to look with distaste on the adulatory extravagances of the genre, sniffing hypocrisy. This was not the medieval view. The panegyrist created objects of pomp and ceremony that doubled as enduring monuments. For conveying truth other vehicles existed. When late in life al-Mutanabbī said "The Sun and the Moon will not outlast what I have bestowed on these princes," it was with a touch of poetic license but not out of keeping with the attitudes of his world.

Abū 'l-Ṭayyib Aḥmad ibn al-Ḥusayn al-Juʿfī, later known as al-Mutanabbī, was born into a poor family in the Mesopotamian city of Kufa in 303/915. The Kinda quarter, which the family inhabited, is described in one report as having consisted of three thousand households, mostly of weavers and water-carriers. His father was one of the latter. The name al-Juʿfī indicates that he traced his lineage to a Yemenite tribe, a matter of immense importance to al-Mutanabbī who was, in an age of Turkic and Iranian ascendancy, fiercely proud of his Arab blood. According to the same source, as a child al-Mutanabbī attended school with the children of the notables of Kufa, and had there his first lessons in poetry, lexicon, and grammar. His memory was superb. A much repeated anecdote tells of his learning by heart a poetry book of thirty sheets while browsing in a bookseller's stall. We are told that his knowledge of poetry came mainly from such booksellers' notebooks, although one at least partially confused report also records some distinguished teachers. He was born into an age of turmoil. In early youth, as one source puts it, al-Mutanabbī "lived among the Arabs of the desert and after some years came back a pure Bedouin." The relative safety of the desert steppe stretching from Kufa to Syria may have been sought by the family on one or more occasions, because in 312/924-925, and again in 315/927-928, Kufa was sacked by the Qarmatīs. (The Qarmatīs were a revolutionary sect of Ismaili origin, whose propaganda met with considerable success and whose violence contributed to the decline of central authority in the fourth Islamic century. They looked forward to the appearance of a divinely guided religious leader, the Hidden Imam, who would establish justice in the world and usher in the last age. They had broken with the main Ismaili movement, which supported ʿUbayd Allāh al-Mahdī, Caliph (872 or 873-934), later the founder of the Fatimid state in Egypt. Their first wave of pillage and murder in Syria ended with a defeat in 294/907, but by then they had established a mini-state in Bahrain, from where they harried the Abbasid caliphate. In 317/930 they seized and sacked Mecca, and perpetrated a massacre of pilgrims. From the Kaʿbah they carried off the black stone itself, and held on to it for some three decades.) At a certain point, possibly after a poverty-stricken trip to Baghdad, al-Mutanabbī traveled to Syria, where he meant to launch his career as a panegyrist. Régis Blachère estimates he must have been there by 318/930.

His choice of a profession made literary sense. In the latter half of the second Islamic century (corresponding to the quarter centuries before and after the year 800) the most interesting and innovative Arabic poetry was characterized by accessible vocabulary and syntax. Love poems and wine songs sparkled with the witty or gallantly sentimental, and moderately rhetorical, expression of I-oriented, if conventionally apprehended, experience. Shortly afterward, panegyrics, which had existed in the Preislamic age and never stopped being written, re-emerged as the genre where the most exciting innovations could be made. In the verse of Abū Tammām (796 or 804-842/843 or 845/846) and al-Walīd ibn ʿUbayd al-Buḥturī (821-897 or 898), a new style of linguistic grandeur and rhetorical intricacy dazzled the public. Mostly, the vehicle for their panegyrics was the *qaṣīdah*, a traditional poetic form in which preliminary themes, usually the evocation of past love in a desert setting (the *naṣīb*) and a desert journey, precede the main topic. Al-Mutanabbī made a careful study of these poets, and is said to have carried their *dīwān*s (collected poems) on all his travels. After his death, the man who came into possession of his copy of al-Buḥturī's *dīwān* reported seeing al-Mutanabbī's corrections on the margins.

In the course of his career, al-Mutanabbī would write touching and delicate *naṣībs*; his *qaṣīdahs* would at times display his talent for descriptions of nature; there would be fine pieces of occasional verse or even hunting poems when his patrons called for them; but he had no interest in writing love poems, wine poems, or working in the other lyric genres developed by the "modern poets" of the early Abbasid period. According to one account, he claimed that he didn't know the work of the "moderns" at all. He specialized in, and was to excel at, the grand style.

The beginnings in Syria were not promising. The panegyrics he composed in the first few years celebrated men of no particular renown, and earned him little fame or recompense. In several cases all that is known about a patron is the town he adorned, as the panegyrist tells us, by living there. Al-Mutanabbī's ambition, and perhaps idealism, sought a different outlet. By 322/933 the great adventure of his youth was over and he was in prison at Homs (Arabic Ḥims, the ancient Emesa), but the precise nature of the adventure is obscure. He seems to have been involved in, or led, an abortive Bedouin rebellion. Perhaps it did not get far beyond planning. In a poem addressed from prison to the local governor (Isḥāq ibn Kayghulugh, the successor of Lu'lu' al-Ghūrī who had made the arrest) al-Mutanabbī begs him to distinguish between "you did" and "you intended." Several sources report that he set himself up as a prophet. According to one, al-Mutanabbī first declared himself to be a descendant of the Prophet Muḥammad's (d. 632) son-in-law ʿAlī ibn Abī Ṭālib (ca. 600-660)and grandson al-Ḥusayn (d. 680), then claimed prophethood, and at last downshifted to his first claim again. This version of the story may reflect the young man's confusion, or everybody else's confusion about what he actually did. A famous narrative attributed to a certain Muʿādh ibn Ismāʿīl al-Lādhiqī goes as follows (al-Badīʿī, *al-Subh*, 50-55):

> Abū 'l-Ṭayyib al-Mutanabbī came to Latakia (Arabic Lādhiqiyyah, the ancient Laodicea) some time after the year 320, when the down on his cheeks was just beginning to show and his locks were down to his earlobes. I showed him honor because of his eloquence and beauty. Once, when we were already on easy terms and I found occasion to be alone with him, wishing to look at him and to profit from his literary knowledge, I said: "By God, you're a noble young man, fit to be a great king's table companion." He said: "Do you know what you're saying? I am a prophet sent by God." I thought he was joking, but then recalled that in all our acquaintance, I had never heard as much as a single jesting word from him. So I said: "What are you saying?" He said: "I am a prophet sent by God." I said to him: "Sent to whom?" He said: "To this community that has gone astray, and leads men astray." I said: "To do what?" He said: "To fill the world with righteousness, as it is now filled with injustice." I said: "How?" He said: "By offering ample sustenance and quick reward to those who submit and join me, and cutting off the heads of those who disobey and refuse."

Abū Muʿādh shows some alarm at this idea, whereupon the young man recites the following extempore verses:

Abū ʿAbdallāh Muʿādh, you do not know how I stand my ground in battle.
You say what I seek is prodigious, and that I am risking my dear life-blood for it.
Does misfortune diminish one like me? Does such a man worry about dying?
If Fate itself took human shape and challenged me, my sword would redden the hair of his head.

The anecdote goes on to describe a miracle worked by al-Mutanabbī (later seen to be sleight of hand) that causes the narrator to accept his prophethood. Passages are cited from al-Mutanabbī's "*Qur'ān*." It all smacks of fabulation. The poem appears in the *dīwān*, and Muʿādh al-Lādhiqī is named in yet another one of al-Mutanabbī's poems, but he is not otherwise known. Nothing in the poetry speaks of filling the earth with justice.

It is likely enough that if al-Mutanabbī was involved in a Bedouin rebellion, it had a religious coloring. The reports claiming that before being released he was required to make public confession of his errors and "return to Islam" are historically plausible. The religious coloring would have been Shiite. Shiism, based on the view that the Prophet's descendants had been deprived of their right to the caliphate, could be quietist, resigned to the state of political affairs. But the belief that the existing government was illegitimate and the world full of injustice, and that at length the Hidden Imam, the last in a line of Muḥammad's divinely guided descendants (the Imams), now deathless in preternatural concealment, would manifest himself and set things right could also be embraced by millenarian revolutionary movements, each with its own preferred line of Imams and its candidate for the Messianic job. Some scholars have seen a kind of Qarmatī revolutionary in the young al-Mutanabbī. It has been proposed that far from being the son of a humble water-carrier, he was born to the cast-off wife of an ʿAlid of high station, and that he was asserting that family's claims to the caliphate. Wolfhart Heinrichs, in a prudent and comprehensive study of the meaning of the nickname al-Mutanabbī–"the would-be prophet"-points out that the Qarmatīs sent out propagandists on behalf of a Hidden Imam, but their belief had no room for prophets after Muḥammad. There were however the *ghulāt*–the 'extravagant ones'-men given to all kinds of gnostic speculations, including, on their fringe, the notion that divinity is infused in the Imams, the men who—according to Shiite belief—were to lead the Muslim community. Such people, who considered the Imams to be God, were ready to call the advocates of their cause prophets. It follows that if al-Mutanabbī did put forward a claim to prophecy, his religious claims belonged to the world of the *ghulāt*. This would not be far-fetched, since the city of his birth was a stronghold of all kinds of Shiite sympathies. On the other hand, perhaps the religious tincture of the rebellion was indeed Qarmaṭī. This too would be possible, because Qarmaṭī operatives had been thoroughly active among the Bedouins of the Iraqi-Syrian desert. In that case the claim to prophecy–not attested in the earliest biographical notices-was a later invention. The poetry suggests that al-Mutanabbī was familiar with some *ghulāt*, and was quite aware of Qarmatī violence. In a poem written in his early youth, in Kufa, a certain Abū 'l-Faḍl is addressed in the following terms (*Mutanabbī*, 19-20):

O prince whose pure substance derives from God, the Possessor of Kingship! O loftiest of those who rise aloft!
A divine light is manifested in you so that you all but know what will remain hidden.

There is no telling whether such extravagant language reflects al-Mutanabbī's own beliefs at the time, or his knowledge of what the recipient of the poem wanted to hear. In another poem, his own dreams of violent advancement are cast in terms that seem to make explicit reference to Qarmatī atrocities. He speaks of going into battle (*Dīwān*, vol. 1, ed. al-Yāzijī, 138):

With resolute men who have waited for me to give them power over the empire of slaves,
Each one a shaykh who regards the five prayers as supererogatory and permits shedding the blood of pilgrims in the sacred enclosure.

It is probably pointless to try to extract a consistent structure of religious thought from poetic imagery. Al-Mutanabbī himself was not fond of his nickname. To one inquiry about its origin he is said to have replied "That's just on account of something that happened in my youth." There are explanations of the nickname that have nothing to do with prophecy. One attaches to a verse in which al-Mutanabbī speaks his mind about the men of his time by comparing himself to a personage named in the *Qur'ān* as a prophet rejected by his own kin: "I am a stranger among a people–may God set them right!–as Ṣāliḥ was among the Thamūd."

The dating, and even the relative chronology, of al-Mutanabbī's activities and compositions in the period before his imprisonment and for several years after his release depend largely on the identification of certain events mentioned in the poems. The received *dīwān* (which al-Mutanabbī helped edit not long before his death) begins to attach dates to poems only in 336/948. It does offer a rudimentary relative chronology by placing, with one trivial exception, all the poems headed "he recited in his youth" before the poem in which al-Mutanabbī beseeches the governor of Homs to set him free, but it is not clear that the poems placed after that entreaty were all composed after his release. Régis Blachère, to whose outstanding biography of al-Mutanabbī we owe the most scholarly attempt at dating the early work, thinks the poem from prison was written in 324/936, because it refers to a certain al-Kharshanī routed by the local governor's cavalry. This would be Badr al-Kharshanī, later for a short while a patron of al-Mutanabbī's, whom the caliph's weak central government in Baghdad had sent to assume authority in Aleppo. He is known to have been ejected from there with the help of forces sent from Homs and loyal to Muḥammad ibn Tughj (d.334/946), a Central Asian Turk whom the caliph had made governor of Syria in 319/931. Homs was controlled by Ibn Kayghulugh on Ibn Tughj's behalf. (Ibn Tughj, later known by the honorific title al-Ikhshīd, was competent, with an independent streak. In 323/935 he was appointed to bring order to a turmoil-ridden and externally threatened Egypt, and did so to such purpose that he gradually made himself the de facto ruler of that country, Palestine and much of Syria.) Blachère also thinks, very plausibly, that some of the poems placed in the *dīwān* after the entreaty from prison were also written before al-Mutanabbī's arrest. For example, one of several poems written to members of the Tanūkhī family in Latakia mentions a military expedition by ʿAlī ibn Ibrāhīm al-Tanūkhī, which Blachère identifies with the campaign in which the Banū 'l-Qaṣīṣ, a rebellious sub-clan of Tanūkh, were subdued in 319/931. The violent tone of the poem adds force to dating it to before the trouble that led to the period of imprisonment. In the report already cited, the mysterious Muʿādh ibn Ismāʿīl says that the meeting in which the poet claimed prophethood took place in Latakia "a bit after the year 320." The approximate date seems a likely one for the mischief that got al-Mutanabbī into trouble. The sources suggest that the poet spent two years in prison. This would have lasted from 322/933 to 324/936. In the prison poem al-Mutanabbī describes himself as not yet having reached the age at which prayer becomes a legal requirement. This would make him impossibly young, and has to be hyperbole.

The most striking thing about al-Mutanabbī's early poems, whether they are panegyrics, poems of quasi-heroic self-praise, or short pieces, is the repeated expression of boundless pride and a manic self-exhortation to violence in search of glory and rank. For example (*Dīwān*, vol. 1, ed. al-Yāzijī, 114-16):

My bed-roll is the saddle on my horse, but my shirt is woven of iron,
Ample, it shines like a pool of water, supple, as if King David himself had woven it.
Where is my excellence if I am contented with a life all whose vexations have already set upon me?
....

Live in high honor, or die nobly amidst the thrusting spears and the beating banners
The spear points are better at dispelling rage, and at curing the spite of the malicious–
Not as you have been living, unpraised, unmissed if you died.
Seek glory then in the fire of Hell itself, and forsake humiliation, were it in the very garden of Eden!
.....

If I speak haughtily, it is the pride of one to be marveled at, who has found nothing greater than himself.
I am the bosom-friend of generosity, the lord of rhymes, poison to my foes and the rage of the envious!
I am a stranger among these people–may God set them right-as Ṣāliḥ was among the Thamūd.

This was an age of political fragmentation. The power that had been the caliphs' was now in the hands of Turkish generals, history re-enacting the praetorians' rise to power over the Roman emperors. The central government was ineffectual, the finances of the empire were in disastrous shape, and in many places local princelings fought over the spoils. Such was the background to al-Mutanabbī's expressions of disdain for the foreigners ruling what had once been an Arab empire, and to his dreams of power (*Dīwān*, vol. 1, ed. al-Yāzijī, 137-38):

In me the sword will have a companion like its own edge, and I will be famed as the bravest of the brave.
I forbore until there was no further forbearance, and now I will plunge into battle reckless of peril.
I will make the horses' cheeks gaunt, as war is more firmly set than a leg on a foot,
As spear thrusts inflame them, as shouted urgings trouble them to madness,

When the lances have wounded them, and they bare their teeth, as if a bitter plant were fastened to the bits.
[I will do this] With resolute men who have waited for me to give them power over the empire of slaves,
Each a shaykh who regards the five prayers as supererogatory, and permits shedding the blood of pilgrims in the sacred enclosure.
....

The swords are thirsty and the birds are starved: will men who are no more than meat on a butcher's block continue to rule?...

The idea is put with sharp concision in a short poem (*Dīwān*, vol. 1, ed. al-Yāzijī, 140):

Abu Saʿīd, do not blame me–opinion can miss the mark.
Princes have throngs of chamberlains and porters to bar their gates.
Sharp-edged swords, yellowish-brown lances, and Arab horses
Will clear the way to them!

At times one gets the impression that true self-knowledge appears in the poems that speak of an unappeasable drive (*Mutanabbī*, 50):

The ignorant does not know that if I possessed all of the Earth I would still feel impoverished; that I tread on the backs of the stars.
My great soul finds every ambition paltry; the farthest goals fall short in my eyes...

or (*Mutanabbī*, 60):

What station shall I not attain? What mighty ones would I fear?
All that God has created and all that he has not
Is paltry measured by the greatness of my soul, a mere hair of my head.

On being released from prison, al-Mutanabbī embarked on fresh travels in Western Iraq and Syria in search of a patron. It was an itinerant, hand to mouth existence. One poem per addressee, or two at the most, is the rule. One patron offered ten *dirhams* for a poem and then doubled it–a ludicrous sum. In 328/939, Badr ibn ʿAmmār al-Kharshanī (the very man whose expulsion from Aleppo al-Mutanabbī had celebrated in his prison poem) was made governor of Tiberias. Al-Mutanabbī sought and received this man's patronage, and wrote five panegyrics to him, one of which includes an unusual, colorful passage about the killing of a lion. Court intrigues, for which al-Mutanabbī evidently had no talent, turned Badr against the poet, who had to flee once again. In the first poem the *dīwān* places after the pieces for Badr, he writes in the grim gnomic style that he is by now a master of: "To bear injury and continue to look upon the one who gave it is a food that emaciates a man's body." But the old resolve is there too (*Mutanabbī*, 245-246):

A contemptible man finds it easy to bear slights: the wound causes no pain to the dead.
My fate could not deal me blows I could not deal with; men of noble mind saw my nobility.

In the next placed poem he addresses the chief intriguer (*Mutanabbī*, 251-252):

I travel alone through the dark night, as if I were its shining moon!
You may speak of desires, very dear to me, of which nothing was attained
But speak also of a soul that does not submit to the base...

In the next poem, written to a judge in Antioch, the introductory part of the *qaṣīdah* is devoted to the ignoble character of the men of the time, including its princes who "more than the idols of the heathen, deserve to have their heads knocked off." A bitter combativeness asserts itself in a backward glance at his poetic career: "I have praised such people that if I live, I will compose for them *qaṣīdah*s of mares and stallions / Their rhymes lean horses under the dust of battle, their recital not meant for the ear..." The old dream combines with contempt for the people of the age, and indeed for the world itself in a poem that begins with imagining leading battle-hardened men into war "to seek what is due to me," but continues like this (*Mutanabbī*, 297-298):

If I wish it, I will be surrounded by men on horses that seem to swim as they gallop, each man [rushing forward] as if death were honey in his mouth.

I chide this world and its tiny people, the wisest of them dullards, and the most resolute, base wretches.
The noblest among them are dogs, the most insightful blind, the most alert sleepy as lynxes and the bravest but apes.
It is one of the trials of the world for the noble to see an enemy to whom he must show friendship.
In my heart there is a weariness of the world, although I have not had my fill of it...

The poem debouches into panegyric. The passage above probably expresses al-Mutanabbī's true feelings about the world, but it is also an original compositional strategy. He had, on an earlier occasion, introduced a panegyric with a meditation on the fugitive nature of human existence, prompting a later commentator to remark that such verses were appropriate to funerary elegies but not poems celebrating the living. Here, finding a more personal voice that he was to use many times in his career, he certainly knew that the gritty introduction would set off the praise of the patron that was to follow. That introduction is a latecomer's reinvention of the heroic voice of the Preislamic warrior poet. Where in Preislamic poetry the ultimate victory of Time–the certainty of death, without hope of a pleasing afterlife–is the background to a grim readiness to venture all for honor and glory, in al-Mutanabbī, the poet's grandeur of spirit is set against the depravity of human nature and the ignoble cast of a society in which the great-souled man has no place. No pious solace is offered.

Unusually for al-Mutanabbī, this period also produces a poem of private mourning: an elegy written on his grandmother's death. We do not know how al-Mutanabbī felt about his mother or his wife, but his love for this woman who brought him up shines through the conventional ideas (*Dīwān*, vol. 1, ed. al-Yāzijī, 344-345):

I wept, fearing for her when she was alive. Each of us tasted in advance the loss of the other.
My letter reached her after she had despaired of me, and grieved, and she died of joy on my account, just as I died of sorrow.
....
She marveled at my words, at my handwriting, as if the letters ranged in a line were rare as ravens with white feathers in their wings.
She kissed the letter until the ink dyed black the circuits of her eyes, and her teeth.
The tears have ceased to run; her eyes are dry. Love for me has quit her heart, the heart it had caused to bleed.
Death alone consoled her, but harder than the disease was the cure.
I sought for her a share of the good things of the world, and she, and it, eluded me. She would have been contented with me as her share. How I wish I had been contented with her!

A funerary elegy for a powerful personage would end with praise of his tribe or clan. Oddly for a private poem, but not so oddly for al-Mutanabbī, this poem ends with self praise. After the transitional verse "Had you not been the daughter of the noblest of fathers, your being my [grand]mother would have been a father grand enough" the poet is on the way to familiar territory.

In 330/942, Ibn Rā'iq, the general who at this time held real power in what was left of the Abbasid empire, was murdered, and the forces of the Ikhshīd, ready to take advantage, pushed deeper into Syria. In 334/946, al-Mutanabbī, whose reputation was by now secure although his circumstances were not, was asked for a poem by the Ikhshīd himself, but luck trifled with him once again, for the Ikhshīd died shortly afterward. After a brief interval al-Mutanabbī is found in Ramleh, at the provincial court of the Ikhshīd's nephew, Abū Muḥammad al-Ḥasan ibn ʿUbayd Allāh. Later he was to say "this was when my fortunes first brightened." Nevertheless, he was not to stay long. In and around Aleppo an Arab prince was rising to power: Sayf al-Dawlah (915 or 916-967), the younger brother of Nāṣir al-Dawlah, the prince of Mosul. (The family, known as Ḥamdānids, had advanced through their service in the army. Nāṣir al-Dawlah was finally acknowledged by the central government as tributary ruler of Mosul in 323/935.) Sayf al-Dawlah's conflicts with the Ikhshidids ended in 336/947 with a treaty that gave him the province of Aleppo, including territories as far south as

Homs. This prince was a patron of literature, science, and scholarship, and attracted men of extraordinary talent to his courts in Aleppo and Mayyāfāriqīn. ʿAbd al-Malik ibn Muḥammad al-Thaʿālibī (961 or 962-1037 or 1038) writes that except for the caliphs, no ruler ever assembled such brilliant company. Among those patronized by Sayf al-Dawlah were the philosopher al-Fārābī (d. 950), the celebrated preacher Ibn Nubātah (d. 984 or 985), and such poets as ʿAbd al-Wāḥid ibn Naṣr al-Babbaghā' (d. 1007 or 1008) and Abū 'l-Ḥasan ibn Aḥmad al-Sarī 'l-Raffā'. He was also a dashing, magnificent warrior and unlike the Ikhshidids, he was an Arab. For al-Mutanabbī who had once written (*Mutanabbī*, 148-149):

Men may be judged by their princes. Arabs whose princes are non-Arabs will never prosper.
They have no culture, no nobility, no compacts and no loyalty.
In every land whose earth I have trodden the people are herded by slaves like so many sheep

the attraction was irresistible. Many years earlier (in 321/ 933), he seems to have attempted to approach a very young Sayf al-Dawlah, and composed for him a panegyric that remained unheard. Now he went about his goal by indirection. In 336/948, after a roundabout journey that included an escape from Tripoli where Isḥāq ibn Kayghulugh, the very man who had once held him in prison, was moved to fresh malice by al-Mutanabbī's refusal to praise him, the poet arrived in Antioch (Arabic Antāqiya) and offered his panegyrics to Abū 'l-ʿAshā'ir, a relative of Sayf al-Dawlah's. The following year the prince himself visited Antioch, and al-Mutanabbī seized the opportunity. His first panegyric was designed to surprise: it describes Sayf al-Dawlah as he is shown, receiving homage, on a tapestry-woven tent or sunshade, and only then speaks of him directly. It was evidently a success, and al-Mutanabbī was to remain at Sayf al-Dawlah's side for a period of about nine years. There was mutual esteem. Al-Mutanabbī stipulated that he would come to Sayf al-Dawlah's court only if he would not have to kiss the ground before the emir, and would not have to recite standing: conditions that members of Sayf al-Dawlah's entourage thought were those of a lunatic. Sayf al-Dawlah accepted.

The panegyrist must rejoice when spectacular action relieves the routine ascription of virtues. The fact that Sayf al-Dawlah was an indefatigable campaigner was a true blessing to al-Mutanabbī's talent. His descriptions of battle amazed the critics. Comparing al-Mutanabbī with his two great predecessors among neo-classical panegyrists, al-Sharīf al-Raḍī (970-1016) called Abū Tammām an orator, al-Buḥturī a subtle painter in words, and al-Mutanabbī a leader of armies. Al-Mutanabbī was also lucky in that, by and large, fortune favored the prince during the period al-Mutanabbī spent with him. Between 338/950 and 343/954 Sayf al-Dawlah managed to subdue rebellious tribes that were encroaching on the cultivated areas, and put down a major revolt in 344/955. His principal opponent was more dangerous. The Byzantine Empire, now in a period of resurgence, was incomparably more powerful than the shining but small emirate of Aleppo. It threatened the Muslim-occupied lands of Cilicia (which were indeed to fall to Nicephorus II Phocas in 354/965), and Sayf al-Dawlah spent most of his enormous energies in defending the frontier and from time to time raiding the lands beyond it. Booty and self-assertion appear to have been the goals of these raids; there can hardly have been any serious thought of conquering Byzantine territory. Still, in the first decade after his definitive establishment in Aleppo, Sayf al-Dawlah was on the whole successful in the frontier war (notwithstanding a raid in 339/950 that, after some initial ravaging of Byzantine towns, turned out so badly that it is known as the "raid of annihilation" in the chronicles). A series of crushing defeats was to come after 350/961, and the last years of Sayf al-Dawlah's life were attended with the miseries of military defeat, family tragedy, and sickness. He died in 356/967. It is certain that al-Mutanabbī truly admired, indeed loved, this prince for his impulsive and generous spirit. The chronicles report that he accompanied Sayf al-Dawlah on most of his campaigns. Sayf al-Dawlah's cousin, the poet Abū Firās ibn Saʿīd ibn Aḥmad ibn Ḥamdān al-Ḥamdānī (932-968), hated al-Mutanabbī and claimed that he barely knew how to mount a horse, but al-Mutanabbī is said to have ridden with Sayf al-Dawlah when at the unfortunate end of the "raid of annihilation" the prince and a handful of his closest companions fought off the enemy and escaped with their lives.

One of al-Mutanabbī's most famous poems is a fine example of his style in this period. It celebrates the battle for al-Ḥadath, an important fortification in Cilicia, in 343/954. Some years earlier, Sayf al-Dawlah had to surrender al-Ḥadath to the Byzantines, who burned it. He now re-entered it and began to make repairs. A huge Byzantine army led by the Domesticus Bardas Phocas, and recruited from many parts of the empire, marched against the Muslims. It is reported that the Muslims were about to break when Sayf al-Dawlah slashed his way to the Domesticus himself, putting the Byzantines to rout (*Dīwān*, vol. 2, ed. al-Yāzijī, 202-208):

Resolutions are as great as the men who make them; actions are as noble as their actors.

.... (Hamori, *Composition*, 10-11, 109)

Sayf al-Dawlah demands from men valor like his own, to which even lions cannot pretend.
The longest lived birds pledge their lives to his weapons, the desert vultures, from their fledglings to their ancient ones.
It cannot harm them that they were created without hard talons, for his hilts and blades have been created.
Can al-Ḥadath, the red fort, distinguish its own color? Does it know which of the two rains was shed by the clouds?
Before his arrival, the white clouds had rained on it, but after he had come it was watered by men's skulls.
He built it, and then raised it high as spear struck on spear, as the waves of death clashed about it.
Something like a demonic possession had held it in its grip, and then it was strung with amulets made of the bodies of the slain.
Changeable Time had driven it off as plunder, but you with your spear brought it back to the Faith in spite of Time.
You force the passing nights to renounce what you have seized, while they, when they seize something of yours, remain your debtors.

....

The Byzantines came against you heavy with iron; in the long chain mail their horses seemed without legs.
When the sunlight flashed from them, their swords could not be distinguished because their armor and helmets sparkled just like the blades.
Theirs was a fivefold army whose march filled east and west, and whose thunder reached the ears of Gemini.
All tongues and nations mingled in it, so that only interpreters could make the speakers understand each other.
God, what a time it was! Its fire melted the ignoble alloy, and there remained only the sharp sword and the bold champion.
What could not cut through armor and spear was cut to pieces; the knights who could not bear the brunt of the clash had to flee.
You took your stand where none could doubt that death awaited him, as if you stood enclosed by the very eyelid of destruction while destruction slept.
Wounded warriors moved past you in defeat, but your face was radiant and your mouth wore a smile.
You exceeded the limits of valor and intelligence until it was said that you knew the things hidden from man.
You folded the two wings of that army back against its heart (and their plumes died in that folding)
With a blow that fell upon their heads when victory was remote and reached their collarbones as victory arrived.
You despised the Rudaynī spears and cast them aside, so that the swords seemed to rebuke the spears.
Whoever seeks a glorious victory–the keys to it are the quick, sharp, white blades.
You scattered their dead all over Uhaydib hill, as silver dirhams are scattered over a bride;
In pursuit of the fleeing, your horses trampled the nests of vultures on the mountain

peaks, although all around them you left ample food.

Their fledglings think you brought their mothers to them, but you came with strong, noble horses.

When their feet slipped, you made them crawl on their bellies, as dappled snakes crawl on the face of the earth.

Will that Domesticus advance day after day, although the back of his neck reproaches his face for advancing?

Does he not know the lion's smell before he meets him? The very beasts recognize the smell of a lion......

The poem goes on to enumerate the relatives of the Domesticus who were killed in (or after) this battle, and praises Sayf al-Dawlah as a champion of Islam, the ornament of all Arabs, and wishes him a long and happy career in war.

When things went badly, it was al-Mutanabbī's job to put the appropriate eloquent spin on them. In his poem about the disastrous campaign of 339/950, which began with the cheerful sack of town after town but ended with the slaughter of the invaders as they passed through a narrow defile on their way home, Sayf al-Dawlah is the true "knight of the cavalry, steadying it when it grew unsteady in the defile where spurts of blood flecked the walls" and as for the men captured by the Byzantines, the Domesticus is to be told that "those delivered over to you had betrayed the prince and he repaid them for what they had done." "Can you be disgraced," al-Mutanabbī addresses Sayf al-Dawlah, "by a time whose champion you were, while others were incapable and weak?" All this is a little hard on the men who died because Sayf al-Dawlah had overreached and chosen a bad route for his return, but pitying the victims of war is no part of the medieval Arab panegyric. The emphasis in the poem is on the part that went well. The devastation inflicted in the early stages of the expedition is rendered with particular relish relish (*Dīwān*, vol. 2, ed. al-Yāzijī, 91):

Never letting up, he led his armies with such speed that the horses were given to drink but once, with the bits still in their mouths.

No town kept him from marching on to another (he was like death itself, which is never contented, never sated)

Until he stood at the outskirts of Kharshana, to the grief of the Byzantines, their crosses and churches,

With the women they would marry fated to be slaves, their children to be slaughtered, the wealth they amassed devoted to plunder, and their sown fields to be burned....

A particularly fine example of the panegyrist as manager of the news is provided by a poem celebrating a campaign that was broken off because of icy weather. Only a throwaway reference to a frozen river, tucked into a single line, records the abortive character of the affair (*Dīwān*, vol. 2, ed. al-Yāzijī, 102-03):

The people, although not at prayer, are prostrate on the ground and around them the land, daubed with the saffron dye of blood, is like so many painted mosques.

You unhorse them though they take to the mountains–those are now their fast horses–and you thrust at them the lances of your stratagems;

You hew them to pieces though they hide beneath rocks as snakes hide in the belly of the earth

And the lofty strongholds on the mountaintops are encircled with your horsemen, a necklace around their necks.

They annihilated them [=the Byzantines] in the battle of the Luqān river, and drove them at Hinzīt, till Āmid was white with captives;

They made Safsāf join in the fate of Ṣābūr and it fell; their people, their very stones, tasted destruction.

In the wadi there rode with your cavalry ......

A man of many raids whose swords are never absent from their necks unless the Sayhān freezes,

So that not one of them has been left except those whom their dark lips and high breasts protect from the sword.

The patricians weep over them in the gloom, while among us they are unwanted goods cast aside on the market...

At Sayf al-Dawlah's court al-Mutanabbī enjoyed high prestige and dizzying financial rewards. In one anecdote, Sayf al-Dawlah asks his office of gifts for a report on the moneys bestowed on al-Mutanabbī. The total is found to have been thirty five thousand *dīnārs* disbursed over a period of four years–a colossal sum. (It is probable that a Ḥamdānid gold *dīnār* weighed about 4.25 grams and that its gold content was around 98%. Al-Mutanabbī's emoluments for the four years would have come to a hair under 150 kilograms of gold, which today would be worth over two million dollars.) But the poet's years with Sayf al-Dawlah were not free of friction. Literary jealousies and the poet's difficult personality created numerous enemies, some of them within the Ḥamdānid family, and Sayf al-Dawlah was affected. A major clash, probably in 341/952, is described in one of the sources. Abū Firās reportedly said to Sayf al-Dawlah: "You give him three thousand *dīnārs* per year, for three *qaṣīdah*s. For just two hundred you could have twenty poets who would bring you better verses." The first sentence was true enough: al-Mutanabbī was a careful worker, and not one for tossing off one poem after another. A chill in Sayf al-Dawlah's attitude toward the poet soon became apparent. Al-Mutanabbī decided to carry the war home to his enemies, and recited a poem of extreme boldness. It begins (*Dīwān*, vol. 2, ed. al-Yāzijī, 118-119):

Oh for the heart burning with pain for one whose heart is cold, who thinks ill of me, body and soul!
Why do I hide a love that has worn me thin when every folk declaims its love for Sayf al-Dawlah?
If love for his radiant face unites us, I wish we shared [in his love] each according to the degree of his.
I came to him when the Indian blades were sheathed, and I looked upon him when they seemed to be so much blood.

Blachère is surely right in saying that the second line is a challenge flung at the intriguers, no doubt present in the audience, and that the fourth refers to the disastrous campaign of 339/950 when al-Mutanabbī was among the few who stayed at the prince's side. Calls went up for killing the poet on the spot. Abū Firās contented himself with accusing al-Mutanabbī of plagiarism, line after line. The poem moves on to proud verses. "I am known to horses, night and desert, to war and striking swords, to the parchment and the pen." Soon a lover's language returns: the poet speaks of the sorrow he would feel at parting. Sayf al-Dawlah, it is said, was brought around by the line "If it is your pleasure to treat me harshly, if the slanderers' talk gives you joy, I will not complain or show distress"–a line out of the repertoire of the sentimental love lyric. In this way there came reconciliation with the prince, although not with al-Mutanabbī's enemies who are said to have had more than one try at assassination. Once more, splendid panegyrics followed, gifts and honors were received, but the first intimacy could not be restored. In 346/957, a ludicrous incident occurred. In Sayf al-Dawlah's presence, in the course of a philological debate al-Mutanabbī insulted Abū 'Abd Allāh al-Ḥusayn Ibn Khālawayh (d. 980 or 981), a grammarian of Iranian origin. "You're a Persian from Khuzistan," he said, "what business can you have with the language of the Arabs?" Ibn Khālawayh pulled a key from his sleeve and with it struck al-Mutanabbī in the face. Sayf al-Dawlah sat immobile. After this al-Mutanabbī had no choice. He asked Sayf al-Dawlah's permission to visit a landed property he had been given, south of Aleppo. His destination lay elsewhere. With all his movable possessions, which by now included great wealth and slaves, he traveled on towards Damascus, and crossed into Ikhshidid territory. In Ramleh he was warmly welcomed by al-Ḥasan ibn ʿUbayd Allāh, the Ikhshīd's nephew, whom he had praised a dozen years earlier, but when Abū 'l-Misk Kāfūr (d. 357/968), now the effective ruler of the Ikhshidid realm, wrote to al-Ḥasan requesting that he send al-Mutanabbī to him, the poet traveled to Fusṭāṭ, the Egyptian capital on the Nile, just south of modern Cairo. It is hard to know his frame of mind. Kāfūr was a man of great military and administrative talents, the master of a rich province, and known as a generous patron. He was also a black eunuch who had started his career as a slave. For al-Mutanabbī, the contrast with Sayf al-Dawlah could not have been more pronounced.

Kāfūr was brought to Fusṭāṭ as a child. Years later, he became the property of the Ikhshīd who saw his abilities, freed and educated him, and promoted him to important political and military roles. After the Ikhshīd's death Kāfūr became regent to the Ikhshīd's small sons Anujūr and ʿAlī. He was in fact for the rest of his life the sole ruler of Egypt, Syria as far north as Damascus, and the Ḥijāz. He received al-Mutanabbī with great respect: the poet was permitted to recite with his boots on and a sword at his side. Since al-Mutanabbī was a precious and prickly commodity, Kāfūr may also have used extravagant temptation. Several sources report that he dangled before his guest the possibility of a governorship in Sidon or somewhere else in Syria. Slowly, the panegyrics were forthcoming, but their author was disappointed with the sluggish returns. In the same year, he already reproaches Kāfūr: "Is there anything left for me in your cup? For a long while now, I've been singing but only you got to drink." It was not long before al-Mutanabbī began to write, for his own satisfaction, poems ridiculing Kāfūr's race and character. In poems recited in public, he allowed himself considerable ambiguities. In a panegyric celebrating the putting down of a rebellion, all the emphasis is on the valor shown by the rebel. The relationship with the regent deteriorated, and there was less and less to hold al-Mutanabbī in Fusṭāṭ. The one man al-Mutanabbī admired, and was admired by, in Egypt, Abū Shujāʿ al-Fātik, a young military hero of vast wealth, fitting generosity, and insensate courage, met the poet in 348/959, received a panegyric, and, less than two years later, died. Kāfūr forbade al-Mutanabbī to leave Fusṭāṭ, and set spies on him, but the poet packed his bags–and a lot of them there were by now–and toward the end of 350 (beginning of 962), as Kāfūr busied himself with the distribution of gifts to his troops on the occasion of the Feast of Sacrifices (the *ʿĪd*), he stole away. As Kāfūr expected, vicious satires were to follow. Al-Mutanabbī eluded pursuit and, after an adventurous journey the stages of which were to last several months, during which some Bedouin chiefs robbed and others protected him, arrived in Kufa. He received a present from Sayf al-Dawlah there, and thanked him in a poem forwarded in 351/962. If this was a mutual attempt at patching things up, it was interrupted by the crushing defeat (including the sack of Aleppo by the Byzantines) that Sayf al-Dawlah suffered at the hands of Nicephorus Phocas the following year.

From Kufa, al-Mutanabbī proceeded to Baghdad. Predominant power in Iraq and Iran was now in the hands of the Buwayhid family. The three brothers who had established the family's fortunes had started their career as military adventurers leading mercenaries from Daylam, a mountainous area southwest of the Caspian, whose recently converted population was at this time a reservoir of soldiers for Muslim armies. Much of Iraq was the province of Muʿizz al-Dawlah (915 or 916-967), who entered Baghdad in 334/945 and was duly appointed "commander of all commanders" by the enfeebled caliph. Muʿizz al-Dawlah had no use for culture, but his vizier Abū Muḥammad al-Ḥasan ibn Muḥammad al-Muhallabī (903-963) had gathered a very impressive constellation of scholars and literati around him, including Abū 'l-Faraj al-Iṣbahānī, (897 or 898-967), author of the monumental *Book of Songs*, the famous secretary and historian Hilāl ibn al-Muḥassin al-Ṣābī (970-1056), and the literary expert Abū ʿAlī Muḥammad ibn al-Ḥasan al-Ḥātimī (d. 998). Al-Mutanabbī remained true to himself. On his first visit to Muhallabī's court, he impressed the gathering with a display of his vast knowledge of Arabic poetry. The next day, he was expected to deliver a panegyric to the vizier but refused to do so, disgusted, it is said, with the frivolity of the man and his coterie. His enemies now included al-Muhallabī and his friends. They got Abū ʿAbd Allāh al-Ḥusayn ibn Aḥmad Ibn al-Hajjāj (ca. 931-24 May 1001), an extraordinarily foulmouthed poet, to accost him in the street with scurrilous verses. Al-Mutanabbī heard him out in contemptuous silence. The professional failure was of benefit to posterity, because al-Mutanabbī was at leisure to sit with a company of his admirers, go over his collected poems, establish the text and explain difficult passages. These sessions in Baghdad are at the origin of the redaction of his work that has come down to us, and of the commentaries on it.

Shortly, a new prospect turned up. Ibn ʿAbbād, now a rising bureaucrat, later a statesman and great litterateur, invited the poet to join him in Rayy, in Iran. Al-Mutanabbī ignored him, refusing to praise a mere bureaucrat. Al-Ṣāḥib ibn ʻAbbād (938-995) was to return the favor by writing an acid attack on al-Mutanabbī's poetry (which, it was thought, did not keep him from recycling al-Mutanabbī's conceits in his own eloquent conversation and writings). In 352/963 al-Mutanabbī returned to Kufa. Possibly, he wanted to wait and see whether Sayf al-Dawlah, who was by now seriously ill, would recover sufficiently to call him back to Aleppo. A poem dated in the *dīwān* to that year, and as having been written after his departure from Baghdad, is particularly bitter. His travels are unceasing, but his very camel would laugh at the people he needs to seek out, who are no better than idols but not as innocuous. Loyalty and sincerity are not to be found. Life has been a vain expense of time.

While the poet was still in Kufa, another invitation came from Iran, and it was too good to resist. Abū 'l-Faḍl Ibn al-ʿAmīd (d. 360/970), a most cultivated poet and epistolarian, powerful and generous vizier to Rukn al-Dawlah, the Buwayhid ruler of Northern Iran, asked al-Mutanabbī to meet him in the town of Arrajān, just north-east of the Persian Gulf, where he traveled on official business. With his son, his secretary, and some of his closest literary friends, in 354/965, al-Mutanabbī set out. Perhaps he intended his stay in Iran to be temporary. Some verses in poems written there seem to indicate that he left his wife (or wives) in Kufa. Arrajān did not impress al-Mutanabbī, but Ibn al-ʿAmīd received him as an honored guest. Three panegyrics had been presented to Ibn al-ʿAmīd when he was outbid by ʿAḍud al-Dawlah, the most powerful of the Buwayhid princes, who invited al-Mutanabbī to his court in Shiraz. ʿAḍud al-Dawlah was a man of wide cultural attainments, a generous patron, and an admirer of al-Mutanabbī's. According to an anecdote, on one feast day as the prince sat in a garden, surrounded by his closest associates, a courtier said: "The only thing missing from our master's party is an Abū Tammām or al-Buḥturī." ʿAḍud al-Dawlah replied: "If al-Mutanabbī came, he would be worth the two of them." In the event, al-Mutanabbī was hesitant at first, but when ʿAḍud al-Dawlah gave assurances that he would be free to stay as long as he liked, and to go whenever he wished, he accepted the offer. At a distance of four parasangs from Shiraz, he was met by an escort led by the prince's special emissary. It was a foretaste of the reception and rewards he was to have. After one of his panegyrics, ʿAḍud al-Dawlah is said to have presented to al-Mutanabbī a quantity of camphor, ambergris, musk and aloe, a horse of his that had been acquired in exchange for fifty thousand sheep, a purse of silver coins, a splendid robe lined with Byzantine silk brocade, a turban valued at five hundred *dīnārs*, and an Indian sword with a sword-belt set with precious stones and a scabbard of gold. The first two poems al-Mutanabbī recited in Shiraz contain expressions of nostalgia for the Arab lands–especially Syria, the country of his youth-but it is hard to know whether these verses, conforming to a conventional theme, express personal emotion or were thought by him appropriate to arrival in a foreign land. In any case, before the year was out, al-Mutanabbī asked for a leave of absence, promising in a poem to return. In Wāsiṭ, in Iraq, he was cautioned of marauding Bedouins, but shrugged off the danger. Between Wāsiṭ and Baghdad his party was attacked. According to one account, the Bedouins were led by a chief intent on avenging a satire al-Mutanabbī had directed at his brother. According to other, more fantastical ones, al-Muhallabī, or Kāfūr, or even ʿAḍud al-Dawlah, had hired assassins. Perhaps robbery was the sole motive. Some versions of the end carry details that may have sprung from spirited story-telling. Al-Mutanabbī, it is said, was about to flee when one of his slaves quoted the line from the poem in which he had first reproached Sayf al-Dawlah. "Aren't you the one who said," the slave called out, "I am known to horses, night and desert, to war and striking swords, to the parchment and the pen?" The poet turned to face his enemies and was cut down. One report asserts that his son al-Muḥassad escaped, turned back to gather up his father's manuscripts, and paid with his life. It was the end of Ramadan 354/September 965.

The poetry illuminates essential aspects of al-Mutanabbī's character. The anecdotes whose point is to throw light on his virtues and faults are to be read with caution. On his haughtiness there is general agreement. In one report, he recalls the extreme poverty of his youth to justify his love of money, another frequently mentioned trait. He abhorred intoxication. Despite the suspicious symmetry, there is the ring of truth to the statement that he had "three good and three bad qualities: He never lied, fornicated, or engaged in pederasty; he never fasted, prayed, or read the *Qur'ān*."

Passionate admirers and detractors fought over al-Mutanabbī's poetry during his lifetime and for a generation after. Hostile critics thought him too much given to bizarre expressions and conceits that call for mental acrobatics. They also accused him of having derived many of his conceits from other poets. Books and pamphlets were published by both sides. The first objective and thoughtful treatise was written by ʿAlī ibn ʿAbd al-ʿAzīz al-Qāḍī 'l-Jurjānī (ca. 902 or 928–976 or 1002) under the title *The Mediation Between al-Mutanabbī and His Adversaries.* Al-Mutanabbī's reader, the Qāḍī 'l-Jurjānī thought, will come across ten beautiful passages for every flawed one. This, by and large, was the judgment of posterity. He is certainly the most quotable of the medieval Arab poets. Al-Thaʿālibī tells us that al-Mutanabbī's poetry flourishes in scholarly assemblies and friendly conversations, and is quoted by orators and writers of letters in art prose. The biographer Ibn Khallikān (1211-1282) knew of more then 40 commentaries on al-Mutanabbī's poetry, which he regarded as an unequalled mark of popularity. The highest praise came from Abū 'l-ʿAlā 'l-Maʿarrī (973-1057), himself a great poet. When he quoted the verses of others, he would attribute them in the usual way, but when the verse came from al-Mutanabbī, he would just say "The Poet says."

REFERENCES

Julia Ashtiany, "al-Mutanabbi's elegy on Sayf al-Dawla's son," in *Festschrift Ewald Wagner zum 65. Geburtstag*, vol 2, ed. by Wolfhart Heinrichs and Gregor Schoeler (Beirut; Stuttgart: F. Steiner, 1994), 362-372;

Kūrkīs and Mīkhā'īl ʿAwwād, *Rā'id al-dirāsah 'an al-Mutanabbī* (Baghdad: Dār al-Rashīd li 'l-Nashr, 1979);

ʿAbd al-Wahhāb ʿAzzām, *Dhikrā Abī 'l-Ṭayyib ba'd alf 'ām* (Cairo: Dār al-Maʿārif, 1968);

Peter Bachmann, "Oryx-Antilopen in arabischen Gewändern: zu einigen Versen al-Mutanabbis," in *Gelehrte Dichter, dichtende Gelehrte, Göttinger Symposium über arabische Dichtung zu Ehren von Peter Bachmann, anlässlich seines 65. Geburtstages*, ed. by Lale Behzadi (Hildesheim: Olms, 2003), 144-154;

Yūsuf al-Badīʿī, *al-Subh al-munbi' 'an haythiyyat al-Mutanabbī*, ed. by Muṣṭafā 'l-Saqqā, Muḥammad Shattā and ʿAbduh Ziyāda ʿAbduh (Cairo: Dār al-Maʿārif, 1963);

Régis Blachère, *Un poète arabe du IVe siècle de l'Hégire (Xe siècle de J.-C.): Abou t-Tayyib al-Motanabbî* (Paris: Adrien-Maisonneuve, 1935);

Seeger A. Bonebakker, *Hātimī and his encounter with Mutanabbī: a biographical sketch* (Amsterdam: North-Holland, 1984);

Seeger A. Bonebakker, "Some commentaries on the poet al-Mutanabbi," in *Verse and the fair sex: studies in Arabic poetry and in the representation of women in Arabic literature* (Utrecht: Houtsma Stichting, 1993);

Francesco Gabrieli, *Studi su al-Mutanabbī* (Rome: Istituto per l'Oriente, 1972);

Geert Jan van Gelder, "Al-Mutanabbī's encumbering trifles," *Arabic and Middle Eastern Literatures* 2 (1999): 5-19;

Andras Hamori, *The Composition of Mutanabbī's panegyrics to Sayf al-Dawla* (Leiden: Brill, 1992);

Andras Hamori, "Reading Mutanabbi's ode on the siege of al-Hadath," in *Studia arabica et islamica: Festschrift for Iḥsān Abbās on his sixtieth birthday* (Beirut: Imprimerie catholique, 1981);

Wolfhart Heinrichs, "The meaning of *al-Mutanabbī*," in *Poetry and Prophecy*, ed. James L. Kugel (Ithaca: Cornell University Press, 1990), 120-139;

Ṭāhā Ḥusayn, *Ma'a 'l-Mutanabbī* (Cairo: Dār al-Maʿārif, 1949);

ʿAbd Allāh al-Jabbūrī, *Abū 'l-Ṭayyib al-Mutanabbī fī āthār al-dārisīn* (Baghdād: Manshūrāt Wizārat al-Thaqāfah wa 'l-Funūn, 1977) A collection of references to al-Mutanabbī in pre-modern sources;

Margaret Larkin, "Two examples of rithā': a comparison between Aḥmad Shawqī and al-Mutanabbī" *Journal of Arabic Literature*, 16 (1985): 18-39;
J.D. Latham, "The elegy on the death of Abū Shujā' Fātik by al-Mutanabbī," in *Arabicus felix: luminosus Britannicus, essays in honour of A.F.L. Beeston on his eightieth birthday*, ed. by Alan Jones (Reading: Ithaca Press for the Faculty of Oriental Studies, Oxford University, 1991), 90-107;
J.D. Latham, "al-Mutanabbī: some reflections and notes on his Egyptian valedictory," in *Studies in honour of Clifford Edmund Bosworth*, vol. 1, ed. by I.R. Netton (Leiden: Brill, 2000), 15-31;
J.D. Latham, "Towards a better understanding of al-Mutanabbī's poem on the battle of al-Hadath," *Journal of Arabic Literature* 10 (1979): 1-22;
M.C. Lyons, *Identification and Identity in Classical Arabic Poetry* (Warminster, Wiltshire: E.J.W. Gibb Memorial Trust, 1999), 192-225;
Julie Scott Meisami, "Al-Mutanabbī and the critics," *Arabic and Middle Eastern Literatures* 2 (1999): 21-41;
James E. Montgomery, "Al-Mutanabbī and the psychology of grief," *Journal of the American Oriental Society* 115 (1995): 285-292;
al Mutanabbi: recueil publié à l'occasion de son millénaire (Beirut: L'Institut français de Damas, 1936). Studies by L. Massignon, J. Sauvaget, M. Canard and others;
Fuat Sezgin, *Geschichte des arabischen Schrifttums*, vol. 2 (*Poesie bis ca. 430 H.*) (Leiden: E.J. Brill, 1975), 484-497;
Maḥmūd Muḥammad Shākir, *al-Mutanabbī*, 2 vols. (S.l.: s.n. 1976-1977);
Suzanne Pinckney Stetkevych, "Abbasid panegyric: the politics and poetics of ceremony," in *Tradition and modernity in Arabic language and literature*, ed. by J.R. Smart (Richmond, Surrey: Curzon Press, 1996), 119-143;
Suzanne Pinckney Stetkevych, *The Poetics of Islamic Legitimacy* (Bloomington: Indiana University Press, 2002), 180-240.

Qudāmah ibn Ja'far

(ca. 873 or 874 – 948)

ALI HUSSEIN
University of Haifa

WORKS

Jawāhir al-alfāẓ (Jewels of the Expressions);
Kitāb al-kharāj wa-ṣinā'at al-kitābah (The Book of the Land Tax and the Craft of Writing, or of the State-Secretary);
Naqd al-shi'r (The Criticism of Poetry).

Editions

Jawāhir al-alfāẓ, ed. by Muḥammad Muḥyī' al-Dīn 'Abd al-Ḥamīd (Cairo: Maktabat al-Khānjī, 1932);
al-Kharāj wa-ṣinā'at al-kitābah, ed. by Muḥammad Ḥusayn al-Zubaydī (Baghdad: Dār al-Ḥurriyyah li 'l-Ṭibā'ah, 1981);
Kitāb al-kharāj wa-ṣinā'at al-kitābah, facsimile ed. by Fuat Sezgin (Frankfurt am Main: Institute for the History of Arabic-Islamic Sciences, 1986);
Kitāb naqd al-shi'r (Constantinople: Maṭba'at al-Jawā'ib, 1885);
The Kitāb naqd al-ši'r of Qudāma b. Ǧa'far al-Kātib al-Baġdādī, ed. by S.A. Bonebakker (Leiden: E.J. Brill, 1956);

Translations

A. Ben Shemesh, *Taxation in Islām*, Vol. II: Qudāma b. Ja'far's Kitāb al-Kharāj, Part Seven and Excerpts from Abū Yūsuf's Kitāb

al-Kharāj (Leiden: E.J. Brill; London: Luzac & Co. Ltd., 1965);
Vicente Cantarino, "Texts: Qudāma from *Naqd ash-shi'r*" in *Arabic Poetics in the Golden Age* (Leiden: E.J. Brill, 1975), 118-124.

Qudāmah ibn Jaʿfar was one of the most influential classical Arab critics and scholars. He was given the *kunyah* of Abū 'l-Faraj, and also became known as *al-Kātib al-Baghdādī*, i.e., "the state-secretary of Baghdad." Seeger A. Bonebakker in his article about Qudāmah for *The Encyclopedia of Islam*, assumes that the earliest possible date of his birth may be around the year 873 or 874, and mentions another scholar who says it was 878. A third scholar, Muḥammad ʿAbd al-Munʿim Khafājī, in his introduction to Qudāmah's book suggests the years 873 or 874 or 889.

Not much is known about Qudāmah's life, and only a small amount of information concerning his religion, education, work and parentage. Regarding his religion, he is mentioned as being of a Christian family and of converting to Islam when he was about thirty years old, at the suggestion of the Muslim Abbasid Caliph al-Muktafī (who reigned during 902-908). As for his education, some scholars list as his teachers three scholars, all of whom lived for some period of their lives in Baghdad. Some consider him to have been a pupil of the grammarian Aḥmad ibn Yaḥyā 'l-Thaʿlab (ca. 816-904) who was born and died in the capital while some others consider him to have been a pupil of Muḥammad ibn Yazīd al-Mubarrad (ca. 826-899), the Basran scholar who lived in the capital during the last period of his life, or of ʿAbd Allāh ibn Muslim Ibn Qutaybah (ca. 828-889), the famous scholar who lived in Baghdad and Kufa in Iraq. These assumptions have no definite confirmation according to Bonebakker, and in his encyclopedia entry he mentions another assumption that Qudāmah was the pupil of a scholar of Basra in Iraq named Abū Saʿīd al-Ḥasan ibn al-Ḥusayn al-Sukkarī (827 or 828-888 or 889).

Yāqūt ibn ʿAbd Allāh al-Ḥamawī (1179?-1229) (5:2235-2236) says that Qudāmah worked in several *dīwāns* (i.e., state-offices or state-registers) in Baghdad. Bonebakker concludes from Yāqūt's statement that Qudāmah held unimportant positions in these *dīwāns*. Yāqūt adds that it was only in the year 910 that Qudāmah was appointed as the head of a certain *majlis* (section, department) in the *dīwān al-mashriq* (Office of the Eastern Provinces), called *majlis al-zimām* (Section of Control). ʿAbd al-ʿAzīz Dūrī shows that this *dīwān* was in the capital Baghdad and was in charge of the *kharāj* (land taxes) of the eastern provinces. The section headed by Qudāmah controlled the work in this *dīwān*, and was responsible for keeping copies of the documents concerning lands that were in that *dīwān*, for checking assessments and orders for payments and receipts. But Badawī Ṭabānah was mistaken in thinking that Qudāmah was the head of the Department of Control in the *dīwān al-khātam* (Office of the Seal).

All the information about Qudāmah's life indicates that, if he was not born in Baghdad, he at least lived there for a long time. If the assumption that he was also a student of al-Sukkarī is correct, then this might be an indication to that he spent some of his time in Basra. However, it would be impossible to consider him one of the Basran scholars, or "a son of al-Basra" as Khafājī assumes, and Bonebakker denies categorically the assumption that Qudāmah is of a Basran family.

Classical sources are divided about his father Jaʿfar ibn Qudāmah, some considering him as being uneducated, while others consider him as learned. Bonebakker suggests that there were two learned persons with the same name of Jaʿfar ibn Qudāmah. The first was Qudāmah's father, a Christian and a professional secretary who occupied a minor position in the central administration, and the second was a Muslim scholarly official of some reputation in that period not related to our Qudāmah.

Qudāmah died in Baghdad and the year of his death is also a matter of controversy. More than one date is given, such as the year 922 which seems to be quite untenable because Yāqūt states that Qudāmah attended the scholarly *munāẓarah* (controversy) that took place in the year 932 between the grammarian Abū Saʿīd al-Sīrāfī (d. ca. 979) and the logician Mattā ibn Yūnus al-Qunnā'ī (d. 940) on the merits of logic and grammar. Other years have been given, such as

932, and 939-940. The latest year presented here is 948, which is mentioned in most of the sources.

According to classical critics such as Abū 'l-Faraj Muḥammad Ibn al-Nadīm (d. 990) (144) and Yāqūt, Qudāmah was identified as a scholar who possessed a high degree of eloquence, and was also a philosopher and a logician. Bonebakker adds that Qudāmah was also a good historian, a philologist and an expert on administration. Many works ascribed to Qudāmah are mentioned in classical texts, but only three books are extant, and it is not known which of these works was composed first.

Qudāmah's books are: *al-Kharāj wa-sinā'at al-kitābah* (Land Tax and the Craft of Writing or "of the State Secretary"); *Kitāb naqd al-shi'r* (The Book of the Criticism of Poetry); and *Jawāhir al-alfāẓ* (Jewels of the Expressions). A fourth book, which is wrongly ascribed to Qudāmah, is *Kitāb naqd al-nathr* (The Book of the Criticism of Prose). This is the same book as the one called *Kitāb al-burhān fī wujūh al-bayān* (The Proof Concerning Aspects of Eloquence) which was written by a contemporary of Qudāmah, a scholar called Isḥāq ibn Ibrāhīm ibn Sulaymān ibn Wahb al-Kātib (no date of death is given). The wrong ascription of this book to Qudāmah is discussed by Bonebakker in his entry "Kudāma b. Dja'far" in The *Encyclopaedia of Islam*. According to the extant material in the three books listed above, Qudāmah could be classified mainly as an expert of administration, a critic of old Arabic poetry, or an expert and teacher of Arabic literary prose.

Though a complete edition of *Kitāb al-kharaj wa sinā'at al-kitābah* was only recently edited, parts of the book were edited and included with other works much earlier. Chapter 11 of Section 5 and chapters 2-7 of Section 6 are printed at the end of the book of 'Ubayd Allāh ibn 'Abd Allāh Ibn Khurradādhbih (ca. 820-ca. 911). *Al-Masālik wa 'l-mamālik* (The Ways and Regions), edited by M.J. De Goeje (Leiden: E.J. Brill, 1899), 184-266. The same chapters are printed in Qudāmah ibn Ja'far, *Nubadh min kitāb al-kharāj wa-san'at al-kitābah* (Chosen Pieces of the Book of Land Tax and the Craft of Writing), edited by Muḥammad Makhzūm (Beirut: Dār Ihyā' at-Turāth al-'Arabī, 1988). Section 7 has been translated into English: A. Ben Shemesh, *Taxation in Islām*, Vol. II: *Qudāma b. Ja'far's Kitāb al-Kharāj, Part Seven, and Excerpts from Abū Yūsuf's Kitāb al-Kharāj*.

There is no clear date for the composition of this book. Some modern researchers, such as Bonebakker, assume that it was written between the years 928 and 932. Only half of the book, Sections 5-8, is extant, the rest of the material is lost, and we only know about the missing parts from the remaining sections of this book and through other classical works. The original book included, according to some reports, seven, eight or nine sections. The four extant sections each begin with the title *manzilah*, which literally means a "rank."

The book reveals the wide knowledge that Qudāmah had gained in the field of administration or *kitābah*. The term *kitābah* means both "writing" and "the craft of the state-secretary." Paul L. Heck has extensively described the relation between writing and the job of the state-secretary. During the first four Islamic centuries, the state-secretary had to be highly expert in the art of writing and in the use of the Arabic language because it was assumed that without such expertise administration and governance would cease to function or at least to function properly.

It was mainly in the Abbasid era that the failure of state representatives such as the state-secretaries, to make a correct use of the Arabic language, the language of the *Qur'ān*, could cast doubts upon the relation between the state and its Islamic identity. Qudāmah felt that it was important to explain to the state-secretaries of his period everything relating to the writing process, especially how to use the language correctly, and only then provide them with the knowledge they needed in order to fulfill their administrative work properly and successfully. Therefore the first kind of knowledge, the correct usage of language and writing, was the subject presented in the earlier but missing sections of Qudāmah's book.

Heck asserts that at least Sections 2 and 3 dealt with this aspect of knowledge. In Section 2, Qudāmah dealt with the tools involved in the writing process, the handling and using the writing instruments such as pen, quill, penknife, inkwell, and also with orthography. Section 3 dealt with the language itself especially rhetoric, and includes examples of good and bad usage of language. It seems that the book as a whole was a guidebook for the state-secretaries, both for the older and the newly appointed ones.

Qudāmah deals in the extant sections with four main branches of knowledge: the state-offices, geography, taxation, and politics. Section 5 on the state offices includes 11 chapters concerning the different state-offices (*dīwāns*) and the most important departments (*majlis*es) included in them. According to Heck, this branch is also treated in the lost Section 4. It is not known whether Qudāmah implied that all the state-secretaries should have some knowledge of all these offices, or whether each needed to know only his own office.

The *dīwān al-jaysh* (Office of the Army) included two main departments, one being responsible for payments and for the salaries of the soldiers and the other for recording the names of the soldiers and registering all the required information about them. Each department in this *dīwān* was divided into sub-departments called *'asākir* (plural of *'askar*), such as the *'askar* of the elite soldiers (*al-khāssah*) and that of the soldiers who have lower ranks (*al-'āmmah*). Soldiers were registered as well as the mounts used in fighting, especially horses. Qudāmah lists the terms that the state-secretary should use when registering a soldier or an animal. Although some of these terms do not fit the rules of the Arabic language, he mentions them because they were often used by state-secretaries.

The *dīwān al-nafaqāt* (Office of Expenditures), according to Dūrī, was connected with all the other offices, examined their expense accounts and drew up their reports. Later it dealt mainly with the needs of the *dār al-khalīfah* (House or Palace of the Caliph). It is not clear from Qudāmah's book whether the expenditures were connected with the *dār al-khalīfah* or with the state in general. It dealt with the payments of the monthly salaries (a work-month was 45 days), and it is not known whether the salaries were for those who worked in the Caliph's palace or the salaries paid to all the state employees in general. Another payment was for the merchants who provided the *wazā'if*, i.e. daily provision of food and other supplies for the employees. The Caliph apparently ordered certain merchants to provide the employees with the *wazā'if* and this office paid them for it as well as for the feeding and treatment of the animals belonging to the state or the Caliph. Payments were also made for the construction of new buildings or for the renovation of old ones.

The *dīwān bayt al-māl* (Office of the Treasury) mainly controlled the work of the Head of the Treasury and checked income and expenditures. Any errors that were made were brought to the attention of the Vizier who ordered the Head of the Treasury to explain their occurrence.

In the *dīwān al-rasā'il* (Office of Correspondence), the chief secretary had to deal with all kinds of correspondence, normally at the request of the vizier or the caliph. Qudāmah brings examples of letters for the secretaries to use whenever they wanted to write on similar subjects. From these letters Vassilios Christides deduced certain naval information about Qudāmah's period.

Two other *dīwāns*, the *tawqī'* (Writing a Response) and the *dār* (Palace/House, perhaps "the Ministerial House or Residence") were connected with each another. It seems that the *dīwān al-dār* was not the same office established by al-Muʿtadid (ruled 892-902) and that dealt with land taxes, as Dūrī explains, but was associated with the vizier himself. Through this office he received queries or demands from different sources. He then made a *mu'āmarah* (lit., "a consultation"), a list of the queries sent to that office, and also noted what was done regarding each query. He then presented this *mu'āmarah* to the caliph who wrote down the decision he made regarding each query. These decisions were then taken to the office of the *dīwān al-tawqī'* where a letter was written and addressed to the chief secretary of the *dīwān al-dār* asking him to send letters to the relevant *dīwāns* requesting them to carry out the decisions of the caliph.

The *dīwān al-khātam* (Office of the Seal) dealt with all letters that had to be signed with the seal of the caliph, and a note regarding the content of the sealed letter was written and saved there. Dūrī mentions that a copy of each letter, not a summary of its content, was kept in this *dīwān*.

The *dīwān al-fadd* (Office of Letter-Opening or Seal-Breaking) dealt with all the letters sent to the caliph. These were opened and classified, and notes were written summarizing each letter. The caliph read the summaries and wrote his decision on the letter itself. Later it was the vizier who personally read the letters or petitions and wrote his decisions regarding them.

The *dīwān dār al-darb* (Office of the Minting House) and the *dīwān al-jahbadhah* (free translation: Office of Treasury Control) are not clearly described by Qudāmah. It seems that the first office controlled the amount of money made in *dār al-darb* (Minting House). Regarding the second office, Walter J. Fischel suggests that its director was required to prepare a monthly or yearly statement accounting for all income and expenditure of the Treasury.

In the *dīwān al-mazālim* (Office of Complaints), the chief secretary collected all the complaints sent during the week and sometimes wrote a summary of them before submitting them to the caliph for his decision. Letters were then sent to the relevant *dīwāns* or persons asking them to carry out the caliph's orders. Qudāmah's description contradicts that of Dūrī who states that a judge sat in this office. According to Qudāmah, the judge was the caliph himself.

Qudāmah then deals with the rules and punishments for those who committed crimes and refers to an office called the *dīwān al-shurṭah* (Office of the Police). In his view the chief secretary of this office should be aware of each crime committed.

The *dīwān al-barīd* (Office of the Post) was probably located in the capital Baghdad, since the main task of its chief secretary was to present the caliph with all the reports arriving from the chiefs of the *barīd*s (the Posts) located in different regions of the Islamic state. The director of each *barīd* wrote reports concerning his city or region and sent them by messengers to the capital. The chief secretary of the *dīwān al-barīd* sometimes wrote summaries of these reports and also controlled the work of the messengers. He appointed the employees in the *dīwān al-barīd*, and was responsible for paying them. Most of this chapter concerns the postal routes and locations that the chief of this office should know.

Section 6 presents another branch of knowledge especially intended for those *kuttāb* who wished to reach high positions (*rashshaha nafsahū li 'l-ri'āsah al-'āliyyah*; i.e., "one who runs for the elite or high chairmanship"). This branch of knowledge consists of geography, in which Qudāmah presents himself as an expert. Qudāmah does not explain what he means by the term *ri'āsah 'āliyyah*, but it may indicate a chief of an important office and not of a minor one such as the short term offices established for temporary needs only, as Dūrī suggests. Some *dīwāns* were occasionally put under one secretary, and the term *ri'āsah 'āliyyah* may indicate the position of a secretary who is the chief of more than one office. Paul Heck, however, translates the term as "the ruling elite" and as "those holding the highest administrative posts of state," and refers to the secretary of a minister as one of the ruling elite.

This section is divided into seven chapters beginning with world geography and then dealing more specifically with the geography of the Islamic state. Chapter 1 deals generally with the relationship between astronomy and knowledge about the earth. Qudāmah shows how astronomy can calculate the size of the earth, and indicates which parts of the earth are inhabited or are desolate. Qudāmah was influenced by Ptolemy (d. ca. 170) in his geographical classifications and quotes him directly.

In Chapter 2 he mentions the different divisions of the inhabited parts of the earth, first making a theological division of the earth among the three sons of Noah: Sām, Hām, and Yāfith. The holy lands (Mecca, Jerusalem and Mount Sinai) were allotted to the first son. Qudāmah then describes the way Persian kings divided the earth into four parts, while the Greeks divided it into three regions. The last part of this chapter deals with the division of the inhabited regions of the earth into seven parts, and according to Heck, this division is also of Greek origin.

In Chapter 3 Qudāmah names the seas and indicates their measurements and their islands. In chapter 4 he names the famous mountains of the earth and their height, mentioning about 207 mountains. In Chapter 5 he mentions the numbers of rivers, their divisions, their descriptions, their measurements, and the names of the most famous ones.

Heck divides geographical writings by the Arabs into two schools: the 'Irāqī (Iraqi) school which describes the whole world with an emphasis on the regions connected with the Islamic world, and the Balkhī school (named after a certain scholar called Aḥmad ibn Sahl al-Balkhī (849 or 850-934), which deals only with the Islamic regions and rarely mentions non-Muslim lands. Qudāmah's approach in Chapters 1-5 is ascribed to the first school. Heck argues that this school was influenced by Indian, Persian and Greek geographical writings, and he calls Qudāmah's approach in these chapters "the Ptolemaic approach," i.e., the mathematical and physical approach to geography, on which Qudāmah depends.

After dealing with the earth in general in the first five chapters, Qudāmah reviews the different administrative regions of the Islamic Empire in Chapter 6. According to him, the center of Islamic lands is Iraq, and he locates the regions of the Islamic State according to their distance from this country. He mentions each region, the names of its districts, townships and villages, and states the amount of tax revenue collected from each. At the end of the chapter he lists these major regions of the Islamic states and the tax revenue collected from them. This list reflects, as Heck believes, "Qudāmah's habit of organizing the various elements of his survey in an orderly fashion," and he calls this "the administrative approach."

Finally, in Chapter 7, Qudāmah mentions the frontiers (*thughūr*) of the Islamic lands that border the non-Islamic countries. Many pages are dedicated to describing the frontiers that border the Byzantine lands. He also mentions the amount of tax revenue collected at each frontier. Qudāmah describes the Byzantine forces, the number of soldiers in certain locations, and certain Islamic invasions across the Byzantine borders. The chapter also deals with other frontiers, such as those with Persia. His approach is called by Heck "the descriptive approach," since it describes certain locations and the habits of people living along the frontiers. Heck believes that Qudāmah's present chapter is a product of the state's interests in its enemies. However, Qudāmah's approach in Chapters 6 and 7 can be ascribed to the aforementioned Balkhī approach.

Qudāmah does not mention why the two approaches of geography are so important and necessary for the secretaries who wish to attain high administrative positions. On the one hand, it is difficult to guess the reason for the necessity of the first approach by Qudāmah, the "Ptolemaic" one. But there is reason for the necessity of the second approach. This may be important since it provides the secretary with considerable knowledge about two important issues for the Islamic state: all the regions that fall under it and the revenues that should be collected from them. It also gives the elite secretaries vital information about the geographic sources from which the Islamic treasury should be filled.

As previously mentioned, Qudāmah held the position of chief of the Department of Control in one of the largest offices of the land tax, i.e. the *dīwān al-mashriq*. It is not unlikely that Qudāmah's work in taxation led him to devote the greater share of the extant sections to the subject of taxes gathered from the Islamic lands and from the people who lived in the Islamic state. Qudāmah's career was probably the reason for entitling his book not only as "The Craft of Writing (or of the State-Secretary)" but including the term "land tax" at the head of the title to indicate the main domain in which state-secretaries should be expert.

Section 7 of his book is devoted to the subject of taxation. This section consists of more than 200 pages (equal to the sum of pages of the other three extant sections), and has nineteen chapters, in which many sources of tax revenue of the Islamic state are mentioned. In the first chapter, Qudāmah summarizes the sources of tax revenue that appear in the following chapters of this section.

Qudāmah deals here with several kinds of taxes, firstly with land taxes, and he describes many sources of land taxes. One is taken from land conquered by the Muslims (*'ard al-'anwa*), and several opinions are given about what kind of tax should be taken from this type of land. One of the opinions is that the caliph has the right to make *takhmīs*, i.e., to divide the land into five parts, taking one part for himself and dividing the others among the persons who conquered the land. In this case, the conquerors should pay one tenth of their land's production to the state as a tax. If the original owners of the land do not convert to Islam, they become the slaves of the conquerors.

Alternatively, the caliph has the right to consider the conquered land as a *fay* (lit. "a grant"). In this case, he does not take a fifth part, and the whole land is considered as the property of the Muslim community. However, there is no clear indication here whether these lands are considered a possession of the state, and they remain in the hands of their original people, perhaps as rented land that they cultivate and for which they pay a land tax. This assumption is justified to some degree by Sayyid Sābiq in his *Fiqh al-sunnah* (Traditional Islamic Jurisprudence). The original owners are freed but they pay a *jizyah* (poll tax).

The second source of land taxes is the tax taken from the people who do not submit to Muslims by force, but by reconciliation (*'ard al-ṣulḥ*). Here too Qudāmah's treatment of the subject is not clear. It seems that the lands remain in the hands of their original owners, and perhaps they still possess them, but their land taxation is similar to that of the *fay*, i.e., they pay *kharāj* (i.e., a land tax). The difference between this land and that of the *fay* seems to be that for the *fay*, the original owner of the land cannot sell it, while in case of his reconciliation, he may do so.

A third source of land taxes is for wasteland brought under cultivation. Another source is the land tax taken for land granted by the Caliph to other Muslims in order to cultivate it. Qudāmah raises the question as to which lands can be granted by the Caliph to the Muslims.

In addition to land taxes, Qudāmah presents himself as an expert on another type of taxation, the poll tax (*jizyah*). At first, Qudāmah says that only Jews and Christians (*ahl al-kitāb*; lit., the Owners of the Book) and the *majūs* (Zoroastrians) must pay the poll tax. Pagan Arabs were not required to pay such a tax but were given two choices: either to convert to Islam or to die. In addition, poll tax is taken from every adult man or woman and every person who is protected from being killed, such as children, priests, monks, and blind persons. Qudāmah discusses the amount of poll tax and divides people into three financial groups: the elite (the rich), the middle class, and the lower classes (the poor), and the tax is assessed according to these ranks.

Another type of taxation is the *ṣadaqah* (alms). However, according to Thomas H. Weir and Aron Zysow, the term has more than one meaning and indicates different kinds of alms. For Qudāmah it seems to mean the obligatory alms taken for the cattle (camels, cows, and sheep). This is an annual alms that is paid according to the amount of cattle that a person owns.

Taxation is also taken for whatever is found buried under the earth such as money, mines, and the *rikāz*, which, according to Ismā'īl ibn Ḥammād al-Jawharī (d. ca.1003) (3:880), is the property that pre-Islamic people buried under the earth. There is no doubt that one who finds a *rikāz* should pay a fifth of its value to the state. The problem is with mines, which some scholars consider to be like the *rikāz* while others say that it should be paid as alms (without defining how much it should be). Taxes are also paid for what is taken from the sea, such as pearls. Here also, scholars are divided. Some say that one should pay a fifth of the value while others say that no tax should be paid.

Qudāmah devotes a chapter to tax payments taken from Muslim and non-Muslim merchants for the money that they possess. Regarding Muslims, a Muslim should pay a certain sum (about one fortieth) of the money that he gains. The state does not ask him to do so, but he should do this by his own volition. A Muslim that does not pay will not be punished; God alone will punish him. Regarding the *ahl al-dhimmah* (the free non-Muslims (Jews and Christians) who are under the Muslim rule), they should pay one twentieth of their money in addition to the poll tax for each person. But it is not known whether or not the state obliges them to pay this amount. In addition, non-Muslim merchants who are not under Muslim rule (*ahl al-ḥarb*, lit., "persons of war"), whenever they trade in or pass through Muslim lands, they should pay one tenth of their merchandise as tax.

Even lost money or property that is found, as well as whatever is recovered from thieves and robbers, is dealt with by Qudāmah. Regarding lost money or property, it should be deposited in the treasury for a year pending claims by the owner, and then it becomes the property of the state. If its owner is found after a year, he is paid some compensation.

An additional source of taxes is the inheritance of a man who has no legal relatives to inherit from him. His property is given to the chief of his tribe, but if his tribe is unknown the caliph is allowed to do whatever he wants with it.

The last branch of knowledge is presented in Section 8. This Section deals with the science of politics. Unlike Sections 5-7, in which it is stated clearly that Qudāmah is addressing the state-secretaries and that the aim of the sections is mainly to guide them in their work, this section does not seem to be connected with the state secretaries at all but with another branch of administrative affairs: the administration of states by kings and caliphs. Bonebakker's assumption that this section does not originally belong to Qudāmah's present book but to another lost book called *Kitāb al-Siyāsah* (Book of Politics), is not unlikely. However, if his assumption is correct, it is not known why this chapter is attached to this book. Was it the fault of the transmitters of the book, or was it done by Qudāmah himself for some unknown purpose?

Qudāmah devotes more than half of the section (eight chapters out of twelve) to explain gradually, in a philosophical manner, why human beings need politics. He then devotes four chapters to certain principles or aspects of politics. Here Qudāmah might be considered a philosopher and an expert in politics. On the subject of philosophy, Qudāmah explains that human beings need to protect and preserve themselves by food, clothing and propagation. Since their needs are many, and since one person alone is unable to accomplish them, humans must help each other. They must live in groups in certain places (cities), and they need certain people in each place to guide them, to help them achieve what they need, and to live in the right way without oppressing each another. God gave human beings certain rules to guide them and needs to have someone who will oblige them to respect these rules. Such a person is the king himself, or the *imām* (leader, ruler or caliph).

Qudāmah believes that religion and kingship cannot exist without each other. He quotes the opinions of a Persian king and a Greek philosopher (Aristotle) to support his assumption, and says it would be wrong to have two kings in one place, since they may differ in their opinions. Since ruling means to follow the rules of God, different opinions undoubtedly means that one of the two kings does not obey the rules of God and causes much damage to the community. In order to rule the people, the king or the *imām* needs politics. Politics, according to Qudāmah, is the science that every king should study so that his opinions and actions are righteous and trustworthy (*istaqāmat ārā'uhum*) and be of advantage to the community. A nation suffers misfortunes because of the bad opinions and actions of its king.

Regarding the principles or aspects of politics, Qudāmah is presented here as a guide or teacher for kings, giving them the principles of politics and helping them to manage their states more successfully. These principles are dealt with in a few pages of chapter 8 and in chapters 9-12. The first principle here is the concept of *rahbah* (dread). The king should know how to keep the people in dread of him in order to make them do whatever he commands and to obey the rules of God. He also keeps his enemies in dread of attacking him. Love for the king must be combined with fear of him, and hating the king may be a sign of his success in obliging his people to do what is right, even though they dislike doing so. In presenting these opinions, Qudāmah depends on Persian, Greek and Arabic sources.

The second principle of the science of politics is the attributes of the king. Kings should learn certain attributes and develop others. One of these attributes is "reason" (*'aql*), which Qudāmah divides into two kinds: "natural reason," i.e. that which is innate, and "acquired reason," which this is the reasoning power that one gains through studying sciences, personal experiences, and communicating with wise people. If the king does so, he brings himself and his nation great happiness. The king should prevent whatever may damage his reason such as inordinate desire. Another attribute is the *'iffah*, which can be translated as "chastity" or "virtue," and includes virtuous habits such generosity. Other attributes are: courage, forbearance and clemency (*ḥilm*), justice and modesty.

Kings should read the biographies of other kings in order to learn the good attributes they possessed. An important attribute of the king is thinking deeply before making any decision, and consulting wise and trustworthy people. Qudāmah lists the required attributes of the consultants and advisors of the king. He tells the story of Alexander the Great who became one of the greatest kings in the world thanks to having Aristotle, the great wise philosopher, as a consultant. Another principle of politics is the choice of good and appropriate viziers. Qudāmah lists the attributes the viziers should possess and even the way that the king should treat *viziers. He also mentions the attributes that employees* and persons close to the king should possess and lists more than twenty such attributes.

Looking at the section as a whole, Heck argues that in the first eight chapters that stress the need for politics, Qudāmah is influenced by an Arabic translation of the letter of Themistius (d. ca. 388) to the Byzantine Emperor Julian, and that Qudāmah's chapters can be recognized as an expanded version of that letter. The last four chapters (9-12 and some part of chapter 8 too) derive from Greco-Hellenistic and Persian sources. In them, Qudāmah mixes foreign elements with Arab Islamic material by quoting some verses of Arabic poetry, some *Qur'ānic* verses, and extracts from *ḥadīth* literature (the Prophet's Tradition) connected with politics. Heck argues that Qudāmah was the first to amalgamate foreign and Arab Islamic materials dealing with politics.

One of the outstanding qualities of Qudāmah is his great knowledge in several areas of Arabic learning. In *Kitāb naqd al-shi'r* (The Book of the Criticism of Poetry) he is a totally different scholar from the one presented in *al-Kharāj wa-sinā'at al-kitābah*. Here he acts as a critic of old Arabic poetry. It is not known when he composed this book. Qudāmah's main aim here seems to be to present the readers with rules by which they can decide whether a verse or verses of poetry should be considered good or bad.

The book includes a short introduction and three chapters. In the introduction Qudāmah explains the aim of this book. In the first chapter he deals with the definition of poetry and gives some rules regarding good and bad meanings in poetry. In the second chapter he deals with good poetry, and in the third chapter he deals with bad poetry. Since the material of this book has been profoundly studied by several scholars, especially by Ṭabānah and Bonebakker, we will not discuss all the chapters of this book. It will be sufficient to deal with three of its main issues: Qudāmah's aim in composing the book, his definition of the poetry, and some rules he gives for distinguishing good poetry.

In his introduction, Qudāmah states that the knowledge or science of poetry (*al-'ilm bi 'l-shi'r*) includes: meter; rhyme; difficult words (*gharīb*) and language (*lughah*, including grammar); meanings and what the poet intends to achieve through them (known to Arab critics as *aghrāḍ al-shi'r*, lit., "aims of poetry"); and distinguishing between good poetry and bad poetry. Qudāmah explains that many books have been undertaken about the first four, but no book has been composed about the fifth branch of poetic knowledge, and that his present book is the first attempt to write about this subject. It seems that Bonebakker in his entry "Kudāma b. D̲jaʿfar," and Iḥsān ʿAbbās (177-202) are not totally confident about this statement and allude to other works that had appeared before Qudāmah in which there was some material on this fifth branch. But Qudāmah was to some degree right in his assertion, for the other works were not entirely devoted to this issue. Wen-Chin Ouyang (115-117) also gives some credit to Qudāmah and believes his assertion to be true in some degree.

In order to convince his readers that the fifth branch of poetic knowledge deserves to have an entire book written about it, Qudāmah argues that this branch is the one most related to poetry, while the third and fourth branches are related to the writing of prose and not only of poetry. As for the first two branches, although they are related only to poetry, Arabs of that time were able to know them without studying them. On the other hand, knowing how to differentiate between bad poetry and good poetry is a branch of knowledge that many people know nothing about it. Qudāmah's aim here is similar to the one presented in *al-Kharāj wa-sinā'at al-kitābah*, although different readers are addressed in each book.

In the first chapter he defines the basis on which he can establish the rules for good poetry discussed in the second chapter and bad poetry in the third chapter. He first explains that *shi'r* (poetry) is rhymed speech expressing a certain meaning and has a *wazn*. The term *wazn* is problematic. This term is translated by Anṭwān Daḥdāḥ as "measure." Bonebakker translates the term as "meter" and translates Qudāmah's definition of poetry as "metrical, rhymed speech expressing a certain meaning." There is no doubt that for Qudāmah the term means "meter," but it seems he is not alluding to meter alone.

Although Qudāmah devotes Chapters 2 and 3 to providing rules for readers or critics of poetry in order to decide whether a certain verse is good or bad, he mentions three of these rules in Chapter 1. The first rule is that it is wrong to think that repetition of a certain meaning by different poets is bad. Qudāmah argues that meanings are an essential element of poetry to be used by all poets, and they are not the monopoly of one poet. Poetic meanings can thus be compared with wood commonly used by all carpenters. The second rule is that the use of revolting and uncouth meanings (*fuḥsh al-ma'nā*) in poetry does not indicate that the poem is bad. The third rule is that contradictory meanings in different poems by the same poet does not have a bad effect on his poetry, but may even be a proof of his poetic skill.

Qudāmah indicates that there are four main elements in poetry: *lafẓ* (expression); *wazn* (meter and measure); *qāfiyyah* (rhyme); and *ma'nā* (*meaning*). From these elements he derives four combinations between a) expression and meaning; b) expression and *wazn*; c) meaning and *wazn*; d) meaning and rhyme. In order to define whether a certain verse is good or not, Qudāmah provides certain rules to be applied to each element. Their full application makes the poem a good one, and their absence makes it a bad one. If the rules are only applied partially, the poem is either partially good or partially bad.

Qudāmah states, in his rules of expression, that expressions in a poem should be *samḥ*, a term which Bonebakker says means "fluent" or easily pronounced and eloquent rather than "ugly" or unattractive (*khālī mina 'l-bashā'ah*).

Qudāmah gives two rules for *wazn*, by which he means both meter and measure. The first rule is that the *wazn* should be easy. Here the term means meter, which should not include too many variations so that the reader can easily recognize the meter of the verse. Ṭabānah's assumption that easy meter means, for Qudāmah, those Arabic meters with short feet (*tafā'īl*), seems to be unacceptable, and Ṭabānah himself admits that this assumption is problematic. The same might be said regarding the assumption of Dāwūd Sallūm (191), who assumes that an easy *wazn* is that which has less than four feet in every hemistich. Upon reflection, this assumption does not seem to be reasonable, and Sallūm himself says that he is not sure of his idea.

The second rule for *wazn* is that some of the poem's verses should include some *tarṣī'* (translated as "isocolon," by Magdi Wahba and Kamel al-Muhandes (55)). According to Qudāmah, the *tarṣī'* is at least two words or phrases in the verse that are either rhymed, semi-rhymed, or are at least similar in their measure. According to this rule, *wazn* does not indicate the meter but the measure of the words or phrases inside the verse as well as the rhyming or semi-rhyming words or phrases. Qudāmah states that if a poet makes a lot of *ṭarsī'* in his poem, it will make the poem bad, since the *tarṣī'* will not be composed naturally but artificially.

As for rhyme, two rules are mentioned. A good rhyme should be *'adhbat al-ḥarf salisat al-makhraj*. Bonebakker translates this rule as "sweet-sounding, and of simple pronunciation." The second rule is to include *taṣrī'*, which means making the *maqta'* (lit. the "end," or perhaps the "rhyme") of the first hemistich in a certain verse similar to the rhyme of the second hemistich. However, the letters in the two rhymes should not be identical except for the rhyming letter, which should be the same for both. Qudāmah deals here with three cases of *taṣrī'*: that which is found only in the first verse of the poem; that which is found in other verses of the poem; and that which found in both the first and in few other verses of the poem. Qudāmah does not say clearly which of the three cases is the best, but he implies that poems that have verses with more *taṣrī'* should be considered as better poems.

The largest number of rules are connected with meaning. Qudāmah devotes about sixty pages to this subject. In addition to three general rules mentioned in the first chapter, Qudāmah precedes these with another two general rules. The first is that meanings must suit the aims that the poet intends to achieve (*an yakūna 'l-ma'nā muwājihan li 'l-gharadi 'l-maqsūd ghayra 'ādilin 'ani 'l-amri 'l-matlūb*). This rule is the basis for all the other rules mentioned in his book. The second rule is to express meanings with *mubālaghah* (hyperbole), and cites Greek philosophers in saying that the best poetry lies the most.

Qudāmah deals only with rules for those meanings related to "well-known poetic aims and intentions" (*al-a'lām min aghrād al-shu'arā'*). Bonebakker's translation of this sentence as "the principal genres of the poets" seems to be problematic, and the term *gharaḍ* is discussed more usefully by ʿAlī Ḥusayn). The poetic aims Qudāmah lists are: praise, lampoon or invective, elegy, simile, description, and amorous affairs (*naṣīb*).

Praise is discussed by Qudāmah only in relation to the praise of men. The best praise includes the four virtues: *'aql* (reason), *shajā'ah* (courage), *'adl* (justice or honesty), and *'iffah* (chastity or virtue), that distinguish human beings from animals, and the more virtues included in a poem the better it is. Bonebakker states that Qudāmah is influenced by the doctrine of the four virtues derived from Greek sources.

Praise should be considered good if it suits the social position of the person praised. A poet should praise a king with royal attributes, and viziers and state secretaries should be praised by what characterizes their position. Qudāmah also refers to the proper praise of those of the lower classes of society such as laborers, and even thieves and robbers. People should be praised according to their social and professional rank. This opinion on adapting the praise to the professional or social rank is adopted by later scholars such as ʿAlī ibn ʿAbd al-ʿAzīz al-Qāḍī 'l-Jurjānī (ca. 902 or 928–976 or 1002) (75), who discusses a verse in which a certain poet mentions that he is in bad physical condition and turns to his patron to heal him. But he criticizes this kind of praise as being unworthy since only physicians can heal the poet, not the patron.

Lampoon or invective is treated by Qudāmah as contrary to praise. A good lampoon or invective should show the lack of the four virtues. The poet may admit that the person or tribe has some good characteristics but that they lack others. This will prove his objectivity and reliability in his characterizations in the poem, and at the same time will convince the audience that the person or tribe he is lampooning truly lacks certain admirable characteristics. Qudāmah gives an example of a certain poet who admits that a certain tribe is very large in number and their men are able bodied, but says that the tribe is not faithful and does not help those who seek its aid.

Elegy for Qudāmah is the same as praise, since it is praise for a dead person. The only difference is that it is related to the past and not to the present. All the rules for praise should therefore apply to elegy. Another two rules are, firstly, that a poet may say that the death of a person was a loss to the society of all his attributes, such as generosity. Secondly, a poet may express not only his own feelings of loss, but of those who were related to him. Here Qudāmah deals with two kinds of feelings: the sadness of things or persons benefited by the eulogized person in the past, and the happiness of those who were burdened by him.

Simile refers to what is common between the two things that are compared with each another. The greater the degree of comparison, the better the simile. Common aspects should be more than the differences between them. It will be to his credit if the poet can introduce many similes into one verse using only a few words. Another rule is that the poet mentions two similes that have the same subject, but describes each subject in reference to a different situation. For example, a poet describes his head before and after cutting off his hair. The head is first likened to a great rock with an eagle sitting on its peak, and then likened to a rock after the eagle has flown away.

Another rule is that to make an untraditional simile. In this case, it is noted that battle helmets had been usually likened by poets to ostrich eggs, but a certain poet broke this tradition and likened them to stars.

Description is not dealt with in detail by Qudāmah but he says that a good description is that which includes many features of the thing described. In other words, it entails whatever makes the audience see the described thing more clearly.

Amorous affairs (*naṣīb*) are dealt with in greater detail. Qudāmah first explains the meaning of this term and the difference between it and another term (*ghazal*) which is normally used by Arab critics to indicate amorous affairs. He does so, he says, because many people do not know the difference between them. His explanation is not very clear, but it seems that *ghazal* is whatever happens between a lover and his beloved, the feelings of a lover regarding love and his beloved, and the physical and internal attributes of a certain woman that attracts the lover to her. The term *ghazal* does not seem to be a poetic term at all, but a psychological and social one.

Expressing all these amorous feelings in poetry is the *naṣīb*. The rule for a good *naṣīb* is to present the lover as a passionate person who is very malleable and humble. The more he is presented so, the better a *naṣīb* it is. The lover should be weak and humble rather than arrogant and powerful. The poet should speak about the love situations familiar to his audience, either by having experienced them or by anticipating their experience. The poet need not be truthful about his personal feelings and wishes, and the poet need not be the lover presented in the poem. Qudāmah differentiates between the literary persona of the lover in a certain poem and the poet. This point, traditional in Arabic literary criticism, parallels the twentieth-century call by Ronald Barthes (49-55) to separate the author from the hero of a literary work.

Qudāmah also deals with the rules relating to poetic meanings in general, such as rhetorical elements that can be used for expressing any meaning, regardless of whether they are used for a lampoon, for praise or for anything else. The presence of rhetorical elements makes the verse fall under the definition of good poetry. He then deals with the rules that are related to the four combined elements, and devotes about forty pages to presenting certain aspects that, if they are found in poetry, will cause it to be considered as bad poetry.

Three important notes by Bonebakker should be mentioned to close the discussion of this critical work. The first is that Qudāmah does not show great interest in the modern poetry of his time (the poetry of the Abbasids), and his references are taken from Preislamic and early Islamic poetry. The second is that Qudāmah derives some of his material from his predecessors such as 'Abd Allāh ibn Muslim Ibn Qutaybah (828-889) and Ibn al-Mu'tazz (246 or 247-296/862-908). Despite this, he is unique in his theory of poetry. The third is that this theory was rarely adopted by later critics with the exclusion of his definition of some of the rhetorical elements. Bonebakker mentions that this theory was the subject of several refutations, none of which has survived.

Jawāhir al-alfāẓ was the third and last extant book by the state secretary of Baghdad. Here too, the date of composition is unknown. The editor of the book mentions another title, *Kitāb al-alfāẓ* (Book of Expressions), and is not sure which of the two titles is the original one.

Unlike the two previous books by Qudāmah, this book has unfortunately not yet been thoroughly studied. The reason for this may be that, unlike the two preceding books, it does not include any theory or any theoretical material. It contains 452 pages and resembles nothing more than a dictionary of expressions.

Despite this, it seems that the book is of great importance, especially for those who want to study the eloquence of the Arabic language or those who wish to learn how to write eloquent and beautiful sentences. Here too, Qudāmah adopts the same role of teacher or guide as is found in the previous two books, but he is now a teacher of Arabic literary prose. His book includes a huge number of eloquent and literary expressions in many fields.

Qudāmah divides his book into several *abwāb* (chapters), each one dealing with one topic, and under each topic the author brings many expressions that one can use in order to express this topic in a literary manner in his writings. To give a few examples, one of the chapters deals with groups of horsemen, another with recovery from illness, a third with love, and a fourth with weeping. If one is writing about something in which these topics are mentioned, he can refer to these chapters and chose some of the expressions for his use.

By composing such a book, Qudāmah expresses his belief that literary language can be learned not only by studying literary works, but also by using books or dictionaries that conveniently present readers with ready made expressions. However, it is not known which readers were the audience addressed by the book. Are they the persons who wish to write in a more literary fashion or are they only the state secretaries whom Qudāmah addressed in his book *al-Kharāj wa-sinā'at al-kitābah*? In his introduction to this third book, Qudāmah mentions that the material of this book will improve the eloquence of *al-kuttāb*. Are these the state secretaries or writers in general?

Qudāmah also mentions certain rhetorical elements that will help to express meanings more eloquently and in better language. At the end of his treatment of these elements, Qudāmah states that these elements are very necessary for the rhetoric of speech, and every poet or orator needs to know them. This statement might imply that the readers addressed in Qudāmah's are not only the state secretaries but any writer.

The material in this book is not arranged arbitrarily. In each chapter, Qudāmah arranges the expressions according to rhymed expressions and also according to expressions that have identical or similar measures (*wazns*). This might prove what was previously mentioned regarding the Qudāmah's habit of organizing the various elements of his survey in an orderly fashion.

To sum up, the three books mentioned above show that Qudāmah was one of the classical authors who had a great knowledge in many branches of Arab civilization. Although almost the material in each one of the three books is different, and the readers addressed by them are different, Qudāmah is presented in all of them as a teacher and guide, who always tries to convey certain branches of knowledge to his readers.

REFERENCES

'Abd al-'Azīz Dūrī, "Dīwān," *The Encyclopaedia of Islam*, 2nd ed., ed. P. Bearman, Th. Bianquis, C.E. Bosworth, E. van Donzel and W.P. Heinrichs (Brill, 2008, Brill Online) http://www.brillonline.nl./entry?entry=islam_COM-0170;

'Alī Ḥussein, "Hawla dalālat al-mustalah 'gharaḍ shi'rī'" [On the indication of the term *gharaḍ shi'rī*], *al-Karmil: abhāth fī 'l-lughah wa 'l-adab* 23-24 (2002-2003): 93-110;

'Ali Ḥussein, "Classical and Modern Approaches in Dividing the Old Arabic Poem," *Journal of Arabic Literature* 35, 3 (2004): 297-328;

Anṭwān Daḥdaḥ, *A Dictionary of Arabic Grammatical Nomenclature: Arabic-English*, reviewed by Martin J. McDermott (Beirut: Librairie du Liban Publishers, 1993);

Badawī Ṭabānah, *Qudāmah ibn Ja'far wa 'l-naqd al-adabī* (Cairo: Maktabat al-Anjlū 'l-Miṣriyyah, 1954);

Dāwūd Sallūm, *Maqālāt fī ta'rīkh al-naqd al-'arabī* (Beirut: Dār al-Ṭalī'ah li 'l-Ṭibā'ah wa 'l-Nashr, 1981);

Abū 'l-Faraj Muḥammad Ibn al-Nadīm, *Kitāb al-fihrist*, ed. Riḍā Tajaddud (Tehran: Maktabat al-Asadī, 1971);

Abū 'l-Ḥasan 'Alī ibn 'Abd al-'Azīz al-Qāḍī 'l-Jurjānī, *al-Wasāṭah bayna 'l-Mutanabbī wa-khuṣūmih,* ed. and annotated by Muḥammad Abū 'l-Faḍl Ibrāhīm and 'Alī Muḥammad al-Bijāwī (Cairo: 'Īsā 'l-Bābī 'l-Ḥalabī, 1961);

Iḥsān 'Abbās, *Tārīkh al-naqd al-adabī 'inda 'l-'arab: naqd al-shi'r min al-qarn al-thānī hattā 'l-qarn al-thāmin al-hijrī* (Amman: Dār al-Shurūq li 'l-Nashr wa 'l-Tawzī', 1993);

Isḥāq ibn Ibrāhīm ibn Sulaymān ibn Wahb al-Kātib, *Kitāb al-Burhān fī wujūh al-bayān*, ed. Aḥmad Maṭlūb and Khadījah al-Hadīthī (Baghdad: Maṭba'at al-'Ānī, 1967);

Ismā'īl ibn Ḥammād al-Jawharī, *al-Ṣiḥāḥ: tāj al-lughah wa-ṣiḥāḥ al-'arabiyyah*, ed. Aḥmad 'Abd al-Ghafūr 'Attār, (Beirut: Dār al-'Ilm li 'l-Malāyīn, 1984);

Magdi Wahba and Kamel al-Muhandes, *A Dictionary of Arabic Literary & Linguistic Terms* (Beirut: Librairie du Liban, 1979);

Paul L. Heck, *The Construction of Knowledge in Islamic Civilization: Qudāma b. Ja'far and his Kitāb al-Kharāj wa-sinā'at al-kitābah* (Leiden, Boston, and Köln, 2002);

Abū 'l-Qāsim ibn Khurradādhbih, *al-Masālik wa 'l-mamālik*, ed. M.J. De Goeje (Leiden: E.J. Brill, 1899);

Qudāmah ibn Jaʿfar (wrongly ascribed to him), *Kitāb naqd al-nathr* (Beirut: Dār al-Kutub al-ʿIlmiyyah, 1980);

Roland Barthes, *The Rustle of Language*, transl. Richard Howard (New-York: Hill and Wang, 1986), 49-55;

Seeger A. Bonebakker, "Ḳudāma b. Dja'far al-Kātib al-Baghdādī, Abu 'l-Faradj," *The Encyclopaedia of Islam*, 2nd ed., ed. P. Bearman, Th. Bianquis, C.E. Bosworth, E. van Donzel and W.P. Heinrichs (Brill, 2008, Brill Online) http://www.brillonline.nl./entry?entry=islam_SIM-4478;

Sayyid Sābiq, *Fiqh al-sunnah* (Cairo: Dār al-Turāth, n.d.);

Thomas H. Weir and Aron Zysow, "Ṣadaḳa," *The Encyclopaedia of Islam,* 2nd ed., ed. P. Bearman, Th. Bianquis, C.E. Bosworth, E. van Donzel and W.P. Heinrichs (Brill, 2008, Brill Online) http://www.brillonline.nl./entry?entry=islam_COM-0956;

Vassilios Christides, "Two Parallel Naval Guides of the Tenth Century: Qudāma's Document and Leo VI's Naumachica: a Study on Byzantine and Moslem Naval Preparedness," *Graeco-Arabica* 1 (1982): 52-100;

Walter J. Fischel, "Djahbadh," *The Encyclopaedia of Islam,* 2nd ed., ed. P. Bearman, Th. Bianquis, C.E. Bosworth, E. van Donzel and W.P. Heinrichs (Brill, 2008, Brill Online) http://www.brillonline.nl./entry?entry=islam_SIM-1932;

Wen-Chin Ouyang, *Literary Criticism in Medieval Arabic-Islamic Culture: the Making of a Tradition* (Edinburgh: Edinburgh University Press, 1997);

Yāqūt al-Ḥamawī, *Mu'jam al-udabā'*, ed. Iḥsān ʿAbbās (Beirut: Dār al-Gharb al-Islāmī, 1993).

al-Rāghib al-Iṣfahānī

(fl. before1018)

ALEXANDER KEY
Harvard University

WORKS

Durrat al-ta'wīl wa ghurrat al-tanzīl fī 'l-ayāt al-mutashābihah wa 'l-muta'akhkhirah (Interpretative Pearls and Highlights of Revelation: Verses that Resemble and Repeat Each Other);

al-I'tiqādāt (On Creeds);

Kitāb al-dharī'ah ilā makārim al-sharī'ah (The Path to Nobility in the Revelation);

Kitāb min kalām al-Rāghib fī 'l-badī' (al-Rāghib on Innovative Figures of Speech);

Majma' al-balāghah (The Confluence of Eloquence);

Mufradāt alfāẓ al-Qur'ān (*Qur'ānic* Glossary);

Muḥādarāt al-udabā' wa muhāwarāt al-shu'arā' wa 'l-bulaghā' (The Replies of the Litterateurs and The Answers of the Poets and the Eloquent);

Mukhtasar iṣlāḥ al-manṭiq li-Ibn al-Sikkīt (Abridgement of ʿThe Reform of Speech' by Ibn al-Sikkīt);

Risālah fī adab al-ikhtilāt bi 'l-nās (On the Correct Way to Mix With People);

Risālah fī anna faḍīlat al-insān bi 'l-'ulūm (On Human Virtue Arising from the Disciplines of Knowledge);

Risālah fī dhikr al-wāḥid wa 'l-aḥad (On the Difference Between the Words ʿOne' and ʿAbsolute One');
Risālah fī marātib al-'ulūm wa 'l-a'māl al-dunyawiyyah (On the Ordering of Intellectual Disciplines and of Worldly Actions);
Tafṣīl al-nash'atayn wa-taḥṣīl al-sa'ādatayn (Analysis of the Two Creations and Attainment of the Two Happinesses);
Tafsīr (Exegesis of the *Qur'ān*).

Editions

Durrat al-tanzīl wa-ghurrat al-ta'wīl fī bayān al-āyāt al-mutashābihāt fī Kitāb Allāh al-'Azīz, ascribed to Muḥammad ibn ʿAbd Allāh al-Khatīb al-Iskāfī, ed, Ibn Abī al-Faraj al-Ardistānī (Beirut: Dār al-Āfāq al-Jadīdah, 1973); 4th ed. 1981; (Beirut: Dār al-Kutub al-ʿIlmiyyah, 1995); ed. with introduction Muḥammad Muṣṭafā Āydīn (Mecca: Jāmiʿat Umm al-Qurā, 2001);
Kitāb Durrat al-tanzīl wa-ghurrat al-ta'wīl fī bayān al-āyāt al-mutashābihāt fī Kitāb Allāh al-'Azīz, ascribed to Muḥammad ibn ʿAbd Allāh al-Khatīb al-Iskāfī, eds. Aḥmad Nājī al-Jamālī and Muḥammad Amīn al-Khānjī (Cairo: Maṭbaʿat Muḥammad Muḥammad Maṭar, 1909);
Ṣiddīqī, Ḥāfiẓ Muḥammad Khālid, "A critical edition of Imām Rāghib al-Iṣfahānī's manuscript Durrat al-ta'wīl wa ghurrat al-tanzīl fī 'l-ayāt al-mutashābihah wa 'l-muta'akhkhirah" (Ph.D. diss., University of London, School of Oriental and African Studies, 1977);
Luqmān, Akhtar Muḥammad "al-Iʿtiqādāt" (MA thesis, Jāmiʿat Umm al-Qurā, Mecca, 1981-1982);
al-I'tiqādāt, ed. Shamrān al-ʿAjalī (Beirut: Mu'assasat al-Ashrāf, 1988);
al-Dharī'ah ilā makārim al-sharī'ah, ed. ʿAlī Mīr Lawḥī Falāvarjānī (Isfahan: Jāmiʿat Iṣfahān, Muʿāwanīyat al-Baḥth al-ʿIlmī, 1996;
Kitāb al-Dharī'ah ilā makārim al-sharī'ah, ed. Muḥammad Najjār (Cairo: Maṭbaʿat al-Watan, 1882); ed. Ibrāhīm ibn Shaykh Ḥasan Qayūmī (Cairo: al-Maṭbaʿah al-Sharqiyyah, 1906); ed. ʿAbd al-Zahrā ʿĀtī (Najaf: al-Maṭbaʿah al-Ḥaydariyyah, 1967); ed. Ṭāhā ʿAbd al-Ra'ūf Saʿd (Cairo: al-Kulliyyah al-Azhariyyah, 1973); ed. Maḥmūd Bījū (Damascus: Dār al-Iqrā', 2001); ed. with indexes Abū Yazīd al-ʿAjamī (Cairo: Dār al-Ṣaḥwah, 1985);
Majma' al-balāghah: mukhtārāt fī 'l-lughah wa 'l-adab wa 'l-akhbār wa 'l-nawādir, ed. ʿUmar ʿAbd al-Raḥmān al-Sārīsī (Amman: Maktabat al-Aqṣā, 1986);
Mufradāt alfāẓ al-Qur'ān, in *al-Nihāyah fī gharīb al-ḥadīth wa 'l-athar wa-ma'ahā fī 'l-ṣalb al-durr al-nathīr talkhīṣ nihāyat Ibn al-Athīr li-Jalāl al-Dīn al-Sayyūṭī wa-bi 'l-hāmish kitābān aḥaduhumā Mufradāt al-Rāghib al-Aṣfahānī fī gharīb al-Qur'ān wa-thānīhumā taṣḥīfāt al-muḥaddithīn li 'l-Ḥāfiẓ Abī Aḥmad al-Ḥasan ibn 'Abd Allāh al-'Askarī* (Cairo: al-Maṭbaʿah al-Khayriyyah, 1904); ed. with introduction and indexes Ṣafwān ʿAdnān Dāwūdī (Beirut: Dār al-Qalam; Damascus: Dār al-Shāmiyyah, 1992); Reprint: Qum: Talīʿat al-Nūr, 2006);
al-Mufradāt fī gharīb al-Qur'ān, ed. Muḥammad Sayyid Kīlānī (Beirut: Dār al-Maʿrifah, 1961); ed. Muḥammad Aḥmad Khalaf Allāh (Cairo: Maktabat al-Anjlū al-Miṣriyyah, 1970);
Mu'jam mufradāt alfāẓ al-Qur'ān, ed. Nadīm Marʿashlī (Beirut: Dār al-Kātib al-ʿArabī, 1972;
Zubdat al-mufradāt li 'l-ṭullāb wa 'l-Ṭālibāt: mukhtasar al-mufradāt fī gharīb al-Qur'ān li 'l-Isfahānī, ed. ʿAbd al-Laṭīf Yūsuf (Beirut: Dār al-Maʿrifah, 1998);
al-Juz' 'al-awwal[*-al-thānī*] *min Muḥāḍarāt al-udabā' 'wa-muḥāwarāt al-shu'arā' wa 'l-bulaghaā'* (Cairo: al-Maktabah al-Āmirah al-Sharafiyyah, 1908);
Muḥādarāt al-udabā' wa muḥāwarāt al-shu'arā' wa 'l-bulaghā' (Cairo: Jāmiʿat al-Maʿārif al-Miṣriyyah, 1870); 4 vols. (Beirut, Maktabat al-Ḥayāt, 1961; Repr: 1980); ed. ʿUmar al-Ṭabbāʿ 2 vols. (Beirut: Dār al-Arqām, 1999); ed. with introduction and indexes ʿAbd al-Ḥamīd Murād, 5 vols. (Beirut: Dār Ṣādir, 2006);
Muḥādarāt al-udabā' wa muḥāwarāt al-shu'arā' wa 'l-bulaghā, abridged Ibrāhīm Zaydān (Cairo: Maktabat al-Hilāl, 1902; Reprint: 1980);

Fawzī, Mas'ūd "Mukhtasar Iṣlāḥ al-Manṭiq li-Ibn al-Sikkīt" (thesis, Jāmi'at al-Mālik Sa'ūd, Riyad, 1993);

Rasā'il al-Rāghib al-Aṣfahānī, ed. with introductions 'Umar 'Abd al-Raḥmān al-Sārīsī (Irbid: 'Ālam al-Kutub al-Ḥadīth, 2005) Includes Risālah fī dhikr al-wāḥid wa 'l-aḥad; Risālah fī adab al-ikhtilāt bi 'l-nās, Risālah fī anna faḍīlat al-insān bi 'l-'ulūm, and Risālah fī marātib al-'ulūm wa 'l-a'māl al-dunyawiyyah;

Kitāb Tafṣīl al-nash'atayn wa-taḥsīl al-sa'ādatayn, ed. Ṭāhir Jazā'irī (Beirut: al-Maktabah al-Ahliyyah, 1901); ed. Aḥmad Dakār (Oran, Algeria: Dār al-Gharb li 'l-Nashr wa 'l-Tawzī', 2006);

Tafṣīl al-nash'atayn wa-taḥṣīl al-sa'ādatayn, ed. 'Abd al-Majīd Najjār (Beirut: Dār al-Gharb al-Islāmī, 1988); ed. As'ad al-Sahmarānī (Beirut: Dār al-Nafā'is, 1988);

Muqaddimat Jāmi' al-Tafāsīr ma' Tafsīr al-Fātihah wa Matāli' al-Baqarah, ed. with introduction Aḥmad Ḥasan Farhāt (Kuwait: Dār al-Da'wah, 1984), includes Introduction and Q.1:1 (al-Fātihah) through Q.2:5 (al-Baqarah);

"Muqaddimah of *Tafsīr al-Rāghib al-Isfahānī*," appendix in al-Qāḍī 'Abd al-Jabbār ibn Aḥmad al-Asadābādī, *Tanzīh al-Qur'ān 'an al-Maṭā'in*, ed. Muḥammad Sa'īd al-Rāfi'ī (Cairo: al-Maṭba'ah al-Jamāliyyah, 1911);

"Muqaddimah of *Tafsīr al-Rāghib al-Isfahānī*," appendix in Ṣalāḥ al-Dīn 'Abd al-Laṭīf al-Nāhī, *al-Khawālid min ārā' al-Rāghib al-Isfahānī fī falsafat al-akhlāq wa 'l-tashrī' wa 'l-taṣawwuf* (Amman: Dār 'Ammār; Beirut: Dār al-Jīl, 1987), 75-134;

Tafsīr al-Rāghib al-Isfahānī: dirāsah wa-tahqīq min Sūrat al-Nisā' ayāh 114 ḥattā nihāyat Sūrat al-Mā'idah, ed. with introduction and indexes Hind bint Muḥammad ibn Zāhid Sardār, 2 vols. (MA thesis, Jāmi'at Umm al-Qurā, Mecca, 2003);

Tafsīr al-Rāghib al-Asfahānī: min awwal Sūrat Āl Imrān wa-ḥattā nihāyat al-āyah (113) min Sūrat al-Nisā', ed. with introduction and indexes 'Ādil ibn 'Alī 'l-Shidī, 2 vols. (Riyad: Madār al-Waṭan li 'l-Nashr, 2003).

Translations

Rāh-i buzurgvārī dar Islām: tarjumah-yi al-Dharī'ah ilā makārim al-sharī'ah, trans. Ḥasan ibn Muḥammad Mahdī Farīd Gulpāygānī (Tabriz: Surūsh, 1958);

The path to virtue: the ethical philosophy of al-Rāghib al-Isfahānī: an annotated trans., with critical introduction, of Kitāb al-Dharīah ilā makārim al-sharīah, trans. Yasien Mohamed (Kuala Lumpur, Malaysia: International Institute of Islamic Thought and Civilization (ISTAC), International Islamic University Malaysia (IIUM), 2006);

Karānah-i sa'ādat: baḥshī mabsūṭ dar arkān-i akhlāq-i Islāmī, ed. and trans. Mahdī Shams al-Dīn (Qum: M. Shams al-Dīn, 1997);

Yasien Mohamed, "Knowledge and Purification of the Soul: an Annotated Translation of al-Iṣfahānī's Kitāb al-Dharī'ah, (58-76; 89-92)," *Journal of Islamic Studies* 9, no., 1 (1998): 1-34;

al-Mufradāt fī gharīb al-Qur'ān, ed. Mir Muhammad Jī, trans. Muḥammad 'Abduh Fallah (Lahore, 1963);

Navādir, trans. Muḥammad Ṣāliḥ ibn Muḥammad Bāqir Qazvīnī (Tehran: Surūsh, 1993);

Der vertraute Gefährte des Einsamen, ed. Gustav Flüb (Wien: Anton Edlem von Schmid, 1829);

Tarjumah va taḥqīq-i mufradāt-i alfāẓ-i Qur'ān-i "Rāghib Iṣfahānī": bā tafsīr-i lughavī va adabī-yi Qur'ān, trans. Ghulām Riẓā Khusravī Ḥusaynī (Tehran: Murtaẓāvī, 1995);

Falsafah-i afarīnish-i insān va sa'ādat-i vāqi'ī-yi aw, trans. Zayn al-'Ābidīn Qurbānī (Tehran: Markaz-i Maṭbū'āt-i Dār al-Tablīgh-i Islāmī, 1975).

Abū al-Qāsim al-Ḥusayn ibn Muḥammad ibn al-Mufaḍḍal, known as al-Rāghib al-Isfahānī, was an influential scholar of literature, ethics, creed and scripture at the end of the tenth and beginning of the eleventh century. Al-Rāghib's biography is entirely obscured by the passage of time. This is a curious phenomenon for an author whose work would come to be used so enthusiastically, both in the *madrasah* system that would start soon after his death, and by better-known scholars such as Abū Ḥāmid ibn Muḥammad al-Ghazzālī (1058-1111). The only biographical evidence we have from the years around al-Rāghib's lifetime is a manuscript of his *Mufradāt alfāẓ al-Qur'ān*, the colophon of which is dated 1018 (409 H.) (Library of Muḥammad Luṭfī al-Khatīb, Private Collection, London). A purchase note on the manuscript's cover provides evidence that his works quickly became valuable; the scribe ʿAlī ibn ʿUbaydallāh al-Shirāzī writes that he bought the codex in Isfahan in 1029 for the library of the Abū 'l-Muẓaffar Ibrāhīm ibn Aḥmad al-Layth. In the introduction to the *Mufradāt*, al-Rāghib mentions another of his works, *al-Dharī'ah ilā makārim al-sharī'ah*, so we know that two of his major works were composed before 1018.

However, it is only in the 1090s that al-Rāghib first appears in an extant biographical work, al-Mufaḍḍal ibn Sa'd al-Māfarrūkhī's (d. ca. 1082) history of Isfahan, and in subsequent centuries biographers would display an understandable confusion about the dates of his life and death. Recent scholarship (such as that of al-Sārīsī) has nevertheless brought together a number of references to events and people in his works, and biographical notes in manuscript marginalia, all of which show that al-Rāghib lived at the end of the tenth and beginning of the eleventh century.

With al-Rāghib's works we are on much firmer ground. As can be seen from the lists at the head of this entry, the majority are extant. His books cover the fields of ethics, creed, exegesis and literature (both poetic criticism and *adab* compendia). I will now deal with each of these genres in turn.

Al-Rāghib's ethics are a catholic synthesis of Aristotelian, Islamic and pre-Islamic Iranian ideas that proved attractive to generations of scholars. The number of manuscript copies of his work that still exist around the world, and the regularity with which they have been published throughout the twentieth and twenty-first centuries, are evidence of their popularity.

An ambitious goal for humanity is at the centre of all of al-Rāghib's ethical work. His longer ethical treatise, *al-Dharī'ah ilā makārim al-sharī'ah*, is an account of the ways in which a human being can fulfill his divine potential and come to deserve to be described as God's vicegerent *(khalīfah)* on the earth. The shorter *Tafsīl al-nash'atayn wa-taḥsīl al-sa'ādatayn* is an exhortation that we should try and become as good as, or even better than, the angels.

This tremendous opportunity and potential for humanity goes hand in hand with a very high standard for what "human" means. Al-Rāghib writes that those who fail to live up to God's revelation are no longer fit to be called human, they are worse than beasts, and in the words of ʿAlī ibn Abī Ṭālib (ca. 600-660) mere "shapes of men" (*Tafsīl*, Introduction:28). Humans can achieve a quasi-divine status if their actions and their ideas *('ilm wa-'amal)* follow the prescriptions of the revelation, and if God chooses to assist them. The knowledge that they attain on this journey can be achieved through learning and is built on the foundation of human reason *('aql)*, with which God has distinguished humanity. This reason is not so much the rational calculation implied by the word in English, but rather an inborn ability *(fitrah)* to understand principles. However, and here the Sufi current in al-Rāghib's work is perhaps clearest, humans also have the potential to attain the highest level of knowledge of the divine and the realities of things *(ḥaqā'iq al-ashyā')* without any education at all, purely through divine assistance. This is the path prophetic knowledge takes, but the possibility exists that other humans, non-prophetic but still saintly, can follow it too.

Al-Dharī'ah ilā makārim al-sharī'ah has seven chapters: (1) the human being and the soul; (2) knowledge and reason; (3) the human being's concupiscent *(shahwiyyah)* faculties; (4) the human being's irascible *(ghadabiyyah)* faculties; (5) justice; (6) crafts and the process of making a living; (7) the human being's actions. The Hellenistic tradition of ethics is the source of a number of ontological structures, most notably the account of sense perception as attainment of the images of a thing in the soul, the subsequent predication of those images, the discussion of the concupiscent and irascible faculties, and the exhortation to "know thyself." Al-Rāghib also uses the *Organon* epistemology of the five universals. This synthesis of Greek ideas with Islamic scripture and a mystic commitment to self-improvement proved so attractive to al-

Ghazzālī that, as Wilfred Madelung has shown, over half of the later author's *Mīzān al-'amal* is unattributed copying from al-Rāghib's *al-Dharī'ah*.

Al-Rāghib's shorter ethical treatise is clearly aimed at a different audience from the educated readership of the *al-Dharī'ah. Tafsīl al-nash'atayn wa-taḥsīl al-sa'ādatayn* has much more *Qur'ānic* quotation, and is shorn of many of the complex epistemologies of reason and knowledge in the *al-Dharī'ah* in favor of rhetorical phrases and repetition. It may have been intended for use in teaching, or indeed as a text from which to preach. The most important slogan of the *Tafsīl* is that human reason *('aql)* and divine revelation *(shar')* are mutually dependent and jointly productive (chapter 18). The overwhelming force of its argument is the need for human beings to believe and act well in order to benefit in the afterlife, even if their actions bring them no immediate tangible reward. However, there remain tantalizing glimpses of al-Rāghib's varied influences. Most notable among these is his use of the phrase "that whose existence is necessary" *(wājib al-wujūd)* to describe God, which, as Robert Wisnovsky has shown, is an important piece of evidence that al-Rāghib's more famous contemporary Avicenna was not operating in a vacuum when he made that idea central to his metaphysics.

These ethical ideas would seem to place al-Rāghib in the company of scholars such as Aḥmad ibn Muḥammad Ibn Miskawayh (d. 1030) and Abū al-Ḥasan Muḥammad ibn Yūsuf al-ʿĀmirī (d. 992), who sought to integrate Hellenistic thought into their Islamicate culture and, especially in the latter's case, assuage the concerns of Islamic scholars that it was foreign. However, al-Rāghib is not just the author of these ethical syntheses. In his *al-I'tiqādāt* we have direct evidence of how he saw himself fitting into the sectarian landscape of his day.

Al-I'tiqādāt is a review of the standard topics of theological disagreement, discussions that had been taking place in Islamic scholarship for several hundred years by al-Rāghib's time. He does not always use the labels to which we are accustomed from better-known heresiographies, but we can identify his main targets. At the start of the work he talks about the two primary types of error into which the Islamic community has fallen (1:13-16). The first is excessive fetishization of the family of the Prophet, and of ʿAlī in particular. Although al-Rāghib uses ʿAlī as a source of ethical teaching more than he uses any other of the first four caliphs, this opening criticism in *al-I'tiqādāt* gives the lie to characterizations of al-Rāghib as Shiite in the later biographical tradition. The second major type of error into which the community has fallen is a tendency to downplay God's overwhelming *sui generis* nature and to allow God to be incapacitated by rules of justice or physics. This goes together with a tendency to befuddle the masses with esoteric proofs they cannot understand and then incite them against other Muslims with the accusation that any disagreement is evidence of unbelief. This is an example of al-Rāghib's condemnation of the Muʿtazilah as denigrators of God's power, his distaste for heated theological dispute, and his acceptance of gradations of correctness within belief. The lack of comfort with esotericism is also consistent with the pedagogical purpose of his ethical works.

It is clear from *al-I'tiqādāt* that al-Rāghib is a member of the developing Sunni consensus, and he says as much. However, he also goes further in delineating his exact sectarian position within the broad Sunni community (1:27-31). When dealing with the principles of religion he says that any religious position not based on a text or principle found in the *Qur'ān*, the Sunna or the consensus of the community is heresy *(bid'ah* and *ḍalālah)*. This is a Ḥanbalī or Mālikī position. He criticizes Ḥanafī independent opinion *(ra'y)*. Although at several points in his *Tafsīr*, when discussing a legal point and the different schools of thought regarding it, al-Rāghib tends to prefer the Shafiʿi position (*Tafsīr*, ed. al-Shidī, 287-292), he nevertheless disagrees with the idea that reasoning by analogy *(al-qiyās al-shar'ī)* should be seen as a third source of law (*Tafsīr*, ed. al-Shidī, 1289-1290). The clearest evidence for his personal allegiance comes in his *al-I'tiqādāt* review of sectarian positions on evil in the world (7:250-253). After dealing with non-Islamic dualism, he criticizes the Muʿtazilah for the confidence with which they decide what is necessary for God and then damn those who disagree with them. He then lays out and names the Ashʿarī position, and although he does not criticize it, he leaves the final correct word to another grouping: traditionalists, advanced Sufi mystics, and the wise *(ahl al-athar wa-muḥaṣṣilī 'l-ṣūfiyyah wa 'l-ḥukamā')*.

This is the group in which al-Rāghib places himself, and which he regards as the most correct. The combination of the Ḥanbalī creed and Sufism was popular in the Isfahan of his time, where a number of wealthy merchants such as the Ibn Mandah family (see the Encyclopaedia of Islam II) collected both *ḥadīth* and power. Al-Rāghib, however, distinguishes his *ahl al-athar* from the *ahl al-ḥadīth*, writing that *ḥadīth* specialists believe prophecy to be the only source of truth, and fail to understand the lesson of history that some communities have lived without a prophet. There must therefore be a second source of true knowledge, and the *ahl al-athar* recognize this to be human reason *('aql)*. In an echo of the slogans of the *Tafṣīl*, prophecy and human reason are mutually dependent (2:115-116). This criticism of *ḥadīth* specialists could well have been a factor that led the biographers of the time to exclude him from their pages.

That biographical exclusion did not, however, have an impact on the popularity of his work. The best example of this is his *Mufradāt alfāẓ al-Qur'ān*, which became a fixture of the vast majority of libraries across the Islamic world, as attested by the distribution of its manuscripts today. A work of philological exegesis firmly in the mainstream Sunni tradition, it would make al-Rāghib's name familiar to generations of *madrasah* students. In its introduction, the author writes that the alphabetical organization is designed to facilitate consultation, and that the unit of analysis is the single *Qur'ānic* word. In each entry he provides lexicographical data and a representative analysis of the occurrences of the word under consideration.

In addition to the *Mufradāt* glossary of the *Qur'ān*, al-Rāghib wrote an exegesis that is only partially extant. Its methodological introduction was highly valued by, *inter alia*, Jalāl al-Dīn al-Suyūṭī (1445-1505), who approvingly copied its judgments on the difference between exegesis *(tafsīr)* and interpretation *(ta'wīl)*, and on the meaning of *Qur'ānic* inimitability *(i'jāz)*, into his great manual for exegetes (*Itqān*, 4/77:168 and 4/64:10-12, 14).

Al-Rāghib starts this methodological introduction with the problem of language: the relationship between an expression *(lafẓ)* and the idea, or ideas, behind it *(ma'nā)* (ed. Farḥāt, 28-30, ed. al-Nāhī, 80-81). The relationship cannot be one of simple correspondence because there are an infinite number of ideas but, even with all the different combinations, the number of expressions is finite. The two planes of expression and idea interact in five different ways: (1) agreement between expression and idea, for example "human" applied to Zayd and to ʿAmr *(mutawāṭī')*; (2) disagreement between expression and idea, for example "man" and "horse" *(mutabāyin)*; (3) same idea but different expression, for example the two synonymous words for "sword" *ḥusām* and *ṣamṣām (mutarādif)*; (4) same expression but different idea, for example the homonym *'ayn*, which means "eye," "spring [water]," and "lookout" or "vanguard" *(mushtarik)*; (5) partial agreement between expression and idea, for example the derived forms "hitter" and "hit" *(mushtaqq)*. Al-Rāghib writes that problems usually arise in (1) and (4) with regard to whether the expression is intended to have a general or specific *('āmm* or *khāṣṣ)* meaning, and in (5) with regard to etymology.

Later on in the book, the fifth chapter "on what generally causes disagreements and increases doubts" is a good example of the way al-Rāghib approaches problems. It reads (ed. Farḥāt, 40-41, ed. al-Nāhī, 87-88):

> There are three problematic areas that the scholar should take care to check and where he should stop up the cracks from which disagreements and doubts spring.
>
> The first area is the doubts that occur with homonymous expressions, as discussed above.
>
> The second area is a difference of perspective *(naẓar)* on the part of those contemplating [the issue at hand]. For example, the difference between the two sects who adhere to the doctrines of compulsion and free will. When they

> consider the first cause, the adherents of the doctrine of compulsion say that all actions come from the creator and that if it were not for him nothing would exist. When the adherents of the doctrine of free will consider the final cause, which, rather than the first cause is the immediate cause of action, they say that possibilities [of action] come from us [humans].
>
> The third area is [also] a difference of perspective: whether to establish ideas on the basis of expressions, or expressions on the basis of ideas. An example of the former approach is [Ḥamd ibn Muḥammad] al-Khaṭṭābī [931-996 or 998], who looked to the expression in order to establish the essences of things. On the other hand, the wise *(al-ḥukamāʾ)* start with the essences of things and move to the expressions. An example of this difference is the discussion of the attributes of the creator. Those who start with the expression are confronted with a grave doubt by, for example, *Qurʾān* 5:64 (al-Māʾidah) "rather his two hands are outstretched," *Qurʾān* 54:14 (al-Qamar) "proceeding under our eye" and other verses like them.
>
> [However,] when specialists in the realities of things *(ahl al-ḥaqāʾiq)* demonstrate that God is one and unblemished by multiplicity (and consequently cannot have limbs or organs), they establish the expression based on that [principle]. They [therefore] see these verses as non-literal language and idiom, and by doing so are protected from the doubt that confronted the group discussed above.

In the second area, al-Rāghib characterizes the opposing sides in the common debate on God's involvement in human acts as talking past each other. While one side focuses on the first cause, the second focuses on the final cause. This analysis matches his general distaste for the to and fro of theological dialectic, and is also in accordance with his own creedal position that humans do act, but God created our abilities and therefore our actions (*al-Iʿtiqādāt*, 7:277).

The third area showcases al-Rāghib's eclectic creed. As discussed above, many of his positions are Ḥanbalī, but others are Sufi. The exegetical position he takes here, that God's hands in *Qurʾān* 5:64 should be understood metaphorically, is closer to the Muʿtazilah than the Ḥanābilah. He attributes the position to *al-ḥukamāʾ* and the *ahl al-ḥaqāʾiq*, groups that we can understand as analogous to the "advanced Sufi mystics and the wise" whom he recorded himself as agreeing with in *al-Iʿtiqādāt* (7:252). Indeed, later in the *Tafsīr*, he repeats the position in his own voice: the hands in *Qurʾān* 5:64 "mean 'continuous good favor'" (al-Shidī, 926).

After its methodological introduction, al-Rāghib's *Tafsīr* starts, of course, with the *basmalah* at the beginning of the first verse of the *Qurʾān* (ed. Farḥāt, 110-112). Here, he discusses whether the name (or noun) *(ism)* is the same as the thing named *(musammā)*. His neat analysis is that "name" *(ism)* is itself a homonymic expression *(lafẓ mushtarik)*. When "name" is used in a sentence about the act of naming, for example "my son's name is Zayd," then it does not refer to the thing named. When it is predicated in a sentence, for example "I saw Zayd," then it does refer to the thing named. The name does, of course, only refer to the thing. It cannot be that the name is the named, because they are ontologically distinct; the letters f-i-r-e do not, after all, burn people's mouths when spoken. As for the use of the *basmalah* ("in the name of God..."), the expression "name" therein is acting as a verbal noun and should be understood as "[I begin] with the act of naming God...."

This analytical technique, in which problematic words are separated into their expressions and the ideas they convey, is found in al-Rāghib's exegesis, his creedal work, his ethics, and his poetics. His manual of poetic criticism remains unpublished in a single manuscript in the Beinecke Library at Yale University (Landberg, 165, details in Key, 2010). It represents a unique take on the structure of poetics. The standard for good communication, *balāghah* (usually translated as "eloquence"), is met when an author breaks down the correspondence between the amount of idea communicated and the amount of expression used to communicate it. This correspondence is usually one-to-one, for example the single expression "horse" communicates the single idea "horse." However, the correspondence breaks down in brevity *(ījāz)*, when a large amount of idea is conveyed by a small amount of expression, and conversely when many expressions convey a single idea *(basṭ)*. The poetic techniques of repetition for emphasis *(takmīl, tablīgh, tadhyīl, ta'kīd, takrīr)* are examples of this latter category of *basṭ*. The central techniques of metaphor and metonymy (including *isti'ārah* and *tashbīh)* are understood as types of brevity.

Al-Rāghib is therefore a theorist of language and poetics, but he is also a consumer and collector of literature. His *adab* compendium *Muḥādarāt al-'udabā'* is a tightly structured, comprehensive and quality-controlled selection of the most apt quotations and the best poetry for any one of the hundreds of situations and subjects that make up the chapters, sub-chapters, and sub-sub-chapters of the work. After the *Mufradāt*, it is his best-known work. His second *adab* compendium *Majma' al-balāghah* deals with smaller units of language usage. It provides its reader with strings of related words, short phrases and linguistically significant snatches of poetry, rather than the somewhat longer stories and quotations of the *Muḥādarāt*, which themselves still rarely run beyond a short paragraph. As with the *Mufradāt*, al-Rāghib's avowed intent in both *adab* compendia is ease of use, and to this end he provides layers of sectional and sub-sectional topic organization.

Al-Rāghib is, as we have seen, an ethicist. For him therefore, *adab* is a virtue and a pattern for action more than it is a vehicle for professional advancement or a means of personal pleasure. Just as not every human can become better than the angels, so *adab* is the virtuous road less traveled (*ṭuruqu 'l-'ulā'i qalīlatu 'l-īnās*). Too many people who know their *adab* refuse to bring it out in acts of speech, they sit back and refrain from spontaneity (*tataqā'adu badāhata 'l-maqāl*) (*Muḥādarāt*, 1, Introduction 3-4, compare Thomas, 164). The introduction to the *Majma'* makes the pious action of *adab* clearer. Knowledge goes with asceticism (*zuhd*) and God gave us the goal of seeking knowledge in order that we tend to others with it, rather than repeating it for ourselves (*ri'āyatan* not *riwāyatan*) (*Majma'* 1, Introduction: 36).It is fitting that a scholar with ideas like this should see his work preserved by students, readers and book-buyers, rather than by the biographical dictionaries and courtly reports.

A number of works by al-Rāghib have not survived, but his references to them remain. In the introduction to his *Durrat al-ta'wīl*, al-Rāghib mentions his *Kitāb al-ma'ānī 'l-akbar* (The Larger Book of Literary Ideas) and his *Iḥtijāj al-qirā'āt al-mukhtaṣṣah* (Vindication of Specified Readings of the *Qur'ān*). His *Kitāb sharaf al-taṣawwuf* (On the Nobility of Sufism) and *al-Risālah al-munabbihah 'alā fawā'id al-Qur'ān* (On Calling Attention to the Lessons of the *Qur'ān*) are mentioned in the introduction to his *Mufradāt alfāz al-Qur'ān.* The *Taḥqīq al-bayān fī ta'wīl al-Qur'ān* (Determination of Clarity Concerning the Interpretation of the *Qur'ān*) is mentioned by al-Rāghib in the introduction to his *al-Dharī'ah ilā makārim al-sharī'ah*. A work entitled *Adab al-shatranj* (The Correct Way in Chess) is referred to by Theodore Menzel in *Der Islam* (17 (1928):94).

REFERENCES

Abū 'l-Ḥasan ʿAlī ibn Zayd al-Bayhaqī, *Tārīkh ḥukamā' al-Islām*, ed. Muḥammad Kurd ʿAlī (Damascus: Maṭbūʿāt al-Majmaʿ al-ʿIlmī 'l-ʿArabī, 1946), 112-113;

Carl Brockelmann, "Al-Rāghib al-Isfahānī," in *E.J. Brill's first encyclopaedia of Islam, 1913-1936*, ed. M.Th. Houtsma, Thomas Walker Arnold, René Basset, Richard Hartmann and A. J. Wensinck (Leiden: Brill, 1960-), 6:1097-1098;

Hans Daiber, *Bibliography of Islamic Philosophy*, 3 vols., Handbuch der Orientalistik Abt. 1: Der Nahe und Mittlere Osten (Leiden: Brill, 1999) 2:457, 3:206;

Hans Daiber, "Griechische Ethik in islamischem Gewande: das Beispiel von Rāghib al-Isfahānī (11. Jh.)," in *Historia Philosophiae Medii Aevi* 1 (1991): 181-192;

Geert Jan van Gelder, "Rāgeb Esfahāni," in *Encyclopaedia Iranica*, ed. Ehsan Yarshater

(New York, 2010, Iranicaonline) http://www.iranica.com/articles/rageb-esfahani
Ömer Kara and Anar Gafarov, "Râgib el-İsfahānī," in *Türkiye Diyanet Vakfı İslâm Ansiklopedisi*, ed. Kemal Güran (Istanbul: Türkiye Diyanet Vakfı, 2007), 34:398-403;
Ali Reza Karabulut, *Mu'jam al-makhṭūṭāt al-mawjūdah fī maktabāt Istānbūl wa Ānāṭūlī*, 3 vols. (Qaysarī: Dār al-ʿAqabah, 2005);
Alexander Key, "Language and Literature in al-Rāghib al-Isfahānī," in *Reflections on Knowledge and Language in Middle Eastern Societies*, ed. Bruno De Nicola, Yonatan Mendel and Husain Qutbuddin (Cambridge: Cambridge Scholars Publishing, 2011), 32-62;
Muḥammad Kurd ʿAlī, *Kunūz al-ajdād* (Damascus: Maṭbaʿat al-Taraqqī, 1950), 268-271.
Wilferd Madelung, "Ar-Rāghib al-Isfahānī und die Ethik al-Ghazālīs," in *Islamwissenschaftliche Abhandlungen Fritz Meier zum 60sten Geburtstag*, ed. R. Gramlich (Wiesbaden: Franz Steiner, 1974), 152-163; Repr, in *Religious Schools and Sects in Medieval Islam* (London: Variorum Reprints, 1985);
al-Mufaḍḍal ibn Saʿd al-Māfarrūkhī, *Kitāb mahāsin-i Iṣfahān*, ed. Jalāl-al-Dīn al-Ḥusaynī al-Ṭihrānī (Tehran: Maṭbaʿat Majlis al-Millī, 1933), 32;
al-Mufaḍḍal ibn Saʿd al-Māfarrūkhī, *Mahāsin-i Iṣfahān*, transl. Ḥusayn ibn Muḥammad Āvī (Tehran: Sāzmān-i Farhangī-i Tafrīḥī-i Shahrdārī-i Iṣfahān, 2006), 159.
Sayyid ʿAlī Mīr Lawhī, *Rāghib Iṣfahānī: zindagī va āṣār-i ū* (Isfahan: Sāzmān-i Farhangī Tafrīḥī-i Shahrdārī-i Iṣfahān, 2008);
Dagmar A. Riedel, "Searching for the Islamic episteme: the status of historical information in medieval Middle-Eastern anthological writing" (Ph.D. diss., Indiana University, 2004);
Everett Rowson, "al-Rāghib al-Isfahānī, Abū 'l-Kāsim al-Husayn ibn Muḥammad ibn al-Mufaddal," in *Encyclopaedia of Islam*, Second Edition, ed. P. Bearman, Th. Bianquis, C.E. Bosworth, E. van Donzel and W.P. Heinrichs (Brill, 2008, Brill Online) http://www.brillonline.nl/entry?entry=islam_SIM-6188
ʿUmar ʿAbd al-Rahmān al-Sārīsī, *al-Rāghib al-Isfahānī wa-juhūdahu fī 'l-lughah wa 'l-adab* (Amman: Maktabat al-Aqsā, 1987);
Jalāl al-Dīn al-Suyūtī, *al-Itqān fī 'ulūm al-Qur'ān*, ed. Muḥammad Abū 'l-Faḍl Ibrāhīm, 4 vols. (Beirut: al-Maktabah al-ʿAsriyyah, 1997);
Stephanie Bowie Thomas, "The Concept of Muḥāḍara in the Adab Anthology with special reference to al-Rāghib al-Iṣfahānī's Muḥāḍarāt al-Udabā'" (Ph.D. diss., Harvard University, 2000);
Robert Wisnovsky, "One Aspect of the Avicennian Turn in Sunni Theology," *Arabic Science and Philosophy* 14 (2004): 65-100.

al-Ṣāḥib Ibn ʿAbbād

(14 September 938–30 March 996)

MARY ST. GERMAIN
University of Washington

WORKS

al-Amthāl al-sā'irah min shi'r al-Mutanabbī (Proverbial Passages in Mutanabbī's Poetry);
Dīwān (Poetic Works);
al-Farq bayna 'l-dād wa 'l-zā' (The Difference between [the Letters] Dād and Zā');
al-Ibānah 'an madhhab ahl al-'adl bi-ḥujaj al-Qur'ān wa 'l-'aql (An Exposition of the Beliefs of Those who Hold that God is Just on the Basis of the *Qur'ān* and Reason);

al-Iqnāʿ fī 'l-ʿarūḍ wa-takhrīj al-qawāfī (Satisfaction in Poetic Meter, Exegesis and Word Play);
al-Kashf ʿan masāwī shiʿr al-Mutanabbī (An Exposition of the Faults in Mutanabbī's Poetry);
al-Muḥīṭ bi 'l-lughāh (The Scope of Language);
Nuṣrat madhāhib al-Zaydiyyah (The Zaydīs);
al-Rasāʾil (Epistles);
Risālah fī 'l-hidāyah wa 'l-ḍalālah (Epistle on Guidance and Error);
Risālah fī aḥwāl ʿAbd al-ʿAẓīm al-Ḥasanī (Epistle on ʿAbd al-ʿAẓīm al-Ḥasanī);
al-Rūznāmajah (Journal);
al-Safīnah (The Boat);
al-Tadhkirah fī 'l-uṣūl khamsah (Exposition of the Five Principles [of Muʿtazilism]);
ʿUnwān al-maʿārif wa dhikr al-khalāʾif (An Epitome of Knowledge and an Account of the Caliphs).

Editions

al-Amthāl al-Mutanabbī, ed. Zuhdī Yakan (Ṣayda, Lebanon: al-Maṭbaʿah al-ʿĀriyyah, 1950?);
al-Amthāl al-sāʾirah min shiʿr al-Mutanabbī, wa 'l-rūznāmah, ed. Muḥammad Ḥasan Āl Yāsīn (Baghdad: Maktabat al-Nahḍah, 1965);
Dīwān, ed. Muḥammad Ḥasan Āl Yāsīn (Baghdad: Maktabat al-Nahḍah, 1965);
Dīwān, ed. Ibrāhīm Shams al-Dīn (Beirut: Muʿassasat al-Aʿlamī, 2001);
al-Farq bayna 'l-ḍād wa 'l-ẓāʾ, ed. Muḥammad Ḥasan Āl Yāsīn (Beirut: Mu'assasat al-Balāgh, 1990);
al-Ibānah ʿan madhhab ahl al-ʿadl bi-ḥujaj al-Qurʾān wa 'l-ʿaql, in Nafāʾis al-makhṭūṭāt: al-majmūʿah al-ūlā, ed. Muḥammad Ḥasan Āl Yāsīn (Najaf: al-Maṭbaʿah al-Ḥaydariyyah wa-Maktabatuhā, 1952);
al-Iqnāʿ fī 'l-ʿarūḍ wa-takhrīj al-qawāfī, ed. Muḥammad Ḥasan Āl Yāsīn (Baghdad: al-Maktabah al-ʿIlmiyyah, 1960);
al-Kashf ʿan masāwī shiʿr al-Mutanabbī, wa-yalīhi dhamm al-khaṭāʾ fī 'l-shiʿr li-Aḥmad Ibn Fāris al-Qazwīnī (Cairo: Maktabat al-Qudsī, 1930-1931);
al-Kashf ʿan masāwī shiʿr al-Mutanabbī, ed. Muḥammad Ḥasan Āl Yāsīn (Baghdad: Maktabat al-Nahḍah, 1965);
al-Muḥīṭ bi 'l-lughāh, ed. Muḥammad Ḥasan Āl Yāsīn (Baghdad: Wizārat al-Thaqāfah wa 'l-Funūn, 1975-);
al-Muḥīṭ bi 'l-lughāh, ed. Muḥammad Ḥasan Āl Yāsīn, 11 vols. (Beirut: ʿĀlam al-Kutub, 1994);
Nuṣrat madhāhib al-Zaydiyyah, ed. Nājī Ḥasan (Baghdad: Maṭbaʿat al-Jāmiʿah, 1977);
Nuṣrat madhāhib al-Zaydiyyah, ed. Nājī Ḥasan (Beirut: al-Dār al-Muttaḥidah, 1981);
Rasāʾil, ed. ʿAbd al-Wahhāb ʿAzzām and Shawqī Ḍayf (Cairo: Dar al-Fikr al-ʿArabī, 1946);
Risālah fī aḥwāl ʿAbd al-ʿAẓīm al-Ḥasanī, in *Nafāʾis al-makhṭūṭāt: al-majmūʿah al-rābiyyah*, ed. Muḥammad Ḥasan Āl Yāsīn (Najaf: al-Maṭbaʿah al-Ḥaydariyyah wa-Maktabatuhā, 1955);
Risālah fī 'l-hidāyah wa 'l-ḍalālah in *Nafāʾis al-makhṭūṭāt: al-majmūʿah al-thāniyyah*, ed. Muḥammad Ḥasan Āl Yāsīn (Baghdad: Maṭbaʿat al-Maʿārif, 1954);
Risālah fī 'l-hidāyah wa 'l-ḍalālah, ed. Ḥusayn ʿAlī Maḥfūẓ (Tehran: Maṭbuʿat al-Ḥaydarī, 1955);
al-Rūznāmajah, ed. Muḥammad Ḥasan Āl Yāsīn (Baghdad: Dār al-Maʿārif li 'l-Taʾlīf wa 'l-Tarjamah wa 'l-Nashr, 1958);
al-Tadhkirah fī 'l-uṣūl khamsah in *Nafāʾis al-makhṭūṭāt: al-majmūʿah al-thāniyyah*, ed. Muḥammad Ḥasan Āl Yāsīn (Najaf: al-Maṭbaʿah al-Ḥaydariyyah wa-Maktabatuhā, 1953);
ʿUnwān al-maʿārif wa dhikr al-khalāʾif in *Nafāʾis al-makhṭūṭāt: al-majmūʿah al-ūlā*, ed. Muḥammad Ḥasan Āl Yāsīn (Najaf: al-Maṭbaʿah al-Ḥaydariyyah wa-Maktabatuhā, 1952);
al-Zaydiyyah, ed. Nājī Ḥasan (Beirut: al-Dār al-ʿArabiyyah li 'l-Mawsūʿāt, 1986).

Al-Ṣāḥib Ibn ʿAbbād was an extremely competent and influential vizier for eighteen years under the second generation of Buwayhid rulers, specifically Muʿayyad al-Dawlah (d. 984), and Fakhr al-Dawlah, (ca. 952–997). The period of his service corresponded to the height of the dynasty's power. He was also one of the foremost writers of the Buwayhid period (932-062) and a great patron of many branches of scholarship. Among his works, his epistles were the most important, because they were influential as models of ideal style and form for correspondence. He had an exceptional command of the Arabic language and was accomplished both as a writer of prose and poetry. In addition, he was proficient in most of the fields of scholarship popular in his times, such as theology, history, and grammar, lexicography, and literary criticism. He led a very active literary circle that included many of the most influential figures of the times, such as al-Sharīf al-Raḍī, (970–1016), a poet and leader of the Shiite community, and Abū Isḥāq Ibrāhīm al-Ṣābī (925–994), a historian.

Al-Ṣāḥib's full name is Abū 'l-Qāsim Ismāʿīl ibn ʿAbbād ibn al-ʿAbbās ibn Aḥmad ibn Idrīs Ibn ʿAbbād. Since he did not have a son, he apparently received his *kunyah* (patronymic consisting of Abū or "father" and a name), Abū 'l-Qāsim, when he was a child. Al-Ṭālaqānī was added to his name based on his familial association with the village of Ṭālaqān. Al-Iṣfahānī derived either from Ṭālaqān's location near Isfahan, or from the later development of his career in Isfahan. Two explanations exist that explain his *laqab*, or honorific title, al-Ṣāḥib. One presents the full form of the title as Ṣāḥib Ibn al-ʿAmīd ("the companion of Ibn al-ʿAmīd"), which refers to the vizier who trained him as a *kātib*, or secretary. The other explanation gives the full form of the title as Ṣāḥib Muʿayyad al-Dawlah ("companion of Muʿayyad al-Dawlah"), which refers to one of the Buwayhid caliphs al-Ṣāḥib served. Al-Ṣāḥib's diligence and skill earned him the additional title of Kāfī 'l-Kufāh ("the most competent of the competent").

Al-Ṣāḥib was born on September 14th in Istakhr, a city a little north of Persepolis, the capital of the Preislamic Achaemenid Empire, and somewhat further north of Shiraz. The year of his birth is not recorded. Of the years 934, 936 and 938 which have been proposed, the year 938 is the most likely. He spent his childhood in a village called Ṭālaqān. There are two villages with that name that could have been his home: one near Isfahan known as Ṭālaqān al-Qazwīn and another in eastern Khurāsān. Biographers, including Yāqūt ibn ʿAbd Allāh al-Ḥamawī (1179?-1229), who was famous for writing about his travels and for extensive biographical dictionaries, and Ibn Khallikān (1211–1282), a biographer, discussed the identity of this village in detail. The deciding factor was al-Ṣāḥib's ethnic background. Al-Ṣāḥib's lineage was recorded for five generations and all his ancestors had exclusively Arabic names. The consensus was that although both villages were located in regions with primarily Persian populations, only Ṭālaqān al-Qazwīn had a significant Arab population. The same biographers related that this population was linked either to the Banū ʿAbbās from Yamāmah in Najd, or with Daylamites of Arab stock.

Al-Ṣāḥib was born into the top echelons of power. Two previous generations of al-Ṣāḥib's family had served in high positions under the Buwayhids. His grandfather was originally a schoolteacher, but later became a vizier under Rukn al-Dawlah (d. 977), one of the three brothers who founded the Buwayhid dynasty. His father collected *ḥadīth* and was a pious Shiite and a Muʿtazilite. He too served Rukn al-Dawlah, first as a secretary and then as a vizier. The date al-Ṣāḥib's father died is not known, but it is likely he died in 946 or 947, leaving his son a relatively young orphan. Al-Ṣāḥib attended mosque schools in Isfahan for a time. His family's situation was sufficiently comfortable that his mother was able to give him some coins to give to a needy person on his way to school. Little else is know about his life during this early period.

The influence of his father in terms of Shiism, *ḥadīth*, and the training in the logical arguments typical of his Muʿtazilism had an impact throughout al-Ṣāḥib's life. He began his religious studies with his father. Although it is unlikely his father lived long enough to provide any substantial training in evaluating *ḥadīth*, al-Ṣāḥib became a *rāwī* for the *ḥadīth* he had collected. Although the work has not survived, al-Ṣāḥib wrote *al-Imāmah*, a Shiite work on faith and early Muslim religious leaders that clearly demonstrated the superiority of ʿAlī ibn Abī Ṭālib (ca. 600-660), Muḥammad's cousin, without disparaging the imamates of the first three caliphs. This is important because it suggests that al-Ṣāḥib's Shiism was, initially at least, moderate and accommodationist. Finally, al-

Ṣāḥib's *al-Tadhkirah fī 'l-usūl khamsah* explained Muʿtazilism in terms of five basic principles. He clearly had a talent for theological studies that was overshadowed by his other accomplishments.

One of his first teachers for advanced studies was Aḥmad Ibn Fāris (d.1004), a philologist, whose greatest interest was lexicography. Although he worked in a variety of subjects, Ibn Fāris showed a preference for lexicography. As his student, al-Ṣāḥib was exposed to lexicography and continued to be interested in it. Over many years, he compiled a dictionary, the *Muḥīṭ bi 'l-lughah*, in 10 volumes.

Al-Ṣāḥib left Ibn Fāris when the vizier Abū 'l-Faḍl Ibn al-ʿAmīd (d. 970)—who from 950 on was an increasingly important vizier of Rukn al-Dawlah—took charge of his training as a *kātib*, or secretary. The most important skills the latter needed for this position were a good knowledge of Arabic, proficiency in writing letters, and expertise in the use of rhetorical devices and versification. While he served the senior Ibn al-ʿAmīd, al-Ṣāḥib must have associated with his son Abū 'l-Fatḥ ʿAlī ibn Muḥammad Ibn al-ʿAmīd (948 or 949–ca. 977), a fact which would have ramifications later in his life. Ibn al-ʿAmīd was one of the finest stylists throughout the history of Arabic literature. His skill is indicated by the proverb: "Writing began with ʿAbd al-Ḥamīd and ended with Ibn al-ʿAmīd." Although they have not survived, the historian Aḥmad ibn Muḥammad Ibn Miskawayh (ca. 932–1030) stated that his collected epistles were the epitome of style and were used by all secretaries as models. Thus, he was an ideal mentor for al-Ṣāḥib at this stage of his development. In addition to gaining the skills and experience necessary for his developing political career, al-Ṣāḥib further expanded his literary development during this period by attending Abū 'l-Faḍl Ibn al-ʿAmīd's *majlis*, or salon.

Although al-Ṣāḥib became proficient in nearly all the categories of knowledge recognized in his times, his comprehensive knowledge of philology and of epistolary composition and style was due primarily to these two men. Just as Ibn al-ʿAmīd was most famous for his epistles, al-Ṣāḥib's greatest work was his *al-Rasā'il*, or the compilation of his official and private correspondence. Reports of its original length vary from ten to thirty volumes, but now only short selections survive. Ibn al-ʿAmīd's influence is clear in al-Ṣāḥib's style. Like that of Ibn al-ʿAmīd, al-Ṣāḥib's collection of letters served as a model for other writers.

Skill in writing epistles was far more important than it might seem now. It was a major factor in determining which of the great writers of the period were the very foremost. Al-Ṣāḥib was sure of his own skill and was not shy about declaring it. ʿAbd al-Malik ibn Muḥammad al-Thaʿālibī (961 or 962-1037 or 1038), a literary critic and author of anthologies summarizing cultural information, reported that al-Ṣāḥib often said,

> The writers of the world and the eloquent ones of the age are four: the Master Ibn al-ʿAmīd, and Abū 'l-Qāsim ʿAbd al-ʿAzīz ibn Yūsuf and Abū Isḥāq al-Ṣābī and if I wanted, I would mention the fourth, that is, me.

All of these men were high officials under the Buwayhids and were all known for their collected correspondence. The excellence of the correspondence of Ibn al-ʿAmīd and al-Ṣāḥib has already been discussed. Abū Isḥāq al-Ṣābī (925–994) was the chief secretary of Muʿizz al-Dawlah, (915–967), one of the three brothers in the first generation of the Buwayhid dynasty. He was famous for his collected correspondence. Abū 'l-Qāsim ʿAbd al-ʿAzīz ibn Yūsuf was the private secretary and personal advisor of ʿAḍūd al-Dawlah (936–983), Rukn al-Dawlah's oldest son. His correspondence was famous, but since it was limited to the period of ʿAḍūd al-Dawlah's reign, it was not as broadly consulted as the correspondence of Ibn al-ʿAmīd and al-Ṣāḥib.

It must be noted that works written about al-Ṣāḥib and his literary skills and influence were written after it was already clear that he was a major political figure. Thus, such works were not entirely unbiased. One work about him, the *Yatīmat al-dahr fi maḥāsin ahl al-ʿaṣr*, by al-Thaʿālibī, was intended to depict al-Ṣāḥib and the poets at his court. By virtue of its intent, this work had a positive view of him. Other writers, like Abū Ḥayyān al-Tawḥīdī (ca. 922-ca. 1014), who wrote extensively about al-Ṣāḥib in his

Akhlāq al-wazīrayn, were either jealous of his abilities and success, disappointed at failing to receive sufficient reward from him, or even offended by his demeanor. Some individuals praised him sincerely for his writings, but, due to his power, others surely flattered him in hopes of political favors or patronage for their own writings. However, even the latter group acknowledged his abilities.

Although his observers' opinions of him exhibited various types and amounts of biases, there were plenty of contradictions in al-Ṣāḥib's behavior and nature for them to exploit. Those contradictions were already apparent during the time he was learning his trade. Al-Thaʿālibī, who generally depicted the glories of al-Ṣāḥib's court, related a story depicting al-Ṣāḥib's complete willingness to dispense with earlier, less important connections as his position advanced. When al-Ṣāḥib entered Ibn al-ʿAmīd's service, he completely severed relations with his former teacher, Ibn Fāris. In time, Ibn Fāris sent al-Ṣāḥib a book entitled *Kitāb al-ḥajar* (Book of the Stone). Having looked only at its title page to determine who it was from, al-Ṣāḥib handed it back to the messenger who delivered it, with the comment, "Return the stone to the place from which you brought it."

In contrast, al-Ṣāḥib clearly recognized how much he owed Ibn al-ʿAmīd. He stated, as is recorded in al-Thaʿālibī's *Yatīmat al-dahr fī maḥāsin ahl al-ʿaṣr* (3:230):

> For twenty years I have been keeping company with poets and vying with men of culture and letters, and deliberating with the erudite; and for another twenty, I have been receiving related [*ḥadīth*] from Muḥammad ibn Yazīd and recording [information] from the followers of Aḥmad ibn Yaḥyā Thaʿlab--but never have I seen one who knows poetry with [such] precise knowledge, or criticizes it with [such] a brilliant mind, except for the master Abū 'l-Faḍl Ibn al-ʿAmīd, a man of God, may [God's] days and beauty be with him, delighting him. He goes beyond the criticism of lines of poetry to the criticism of letters and words and he is not content with the revision of meaning until he establishes the best rhyme and meter and from his *majlis* (salon), may God enhance [his state], I gained what I practice of this art.

After serving Ibn al-ʿAmīd as a *kātib* for some time, in 958 al-Ṣāḥib was assigned to the service of Rukn al-Dawlah's son Abū Manṣūr, who would take the name Muʿayyad al-Dawlah when he came to rule. Muʿayyad al-Dawlah was sent to Baghdad to seek a marriage with the daughter of Muʿizz al-Dawlah, then senior ruler of the Buwayhid dynasty. During the visit to Baghdad, al-Ṣāḥib took advantage of the opportunity to meet Baghdādī intellectual figures and to attend their *majlis*es. In particular, he studied jurisprudence, *ḥadīth* (traditions of the Prophet Muḥammad), grammar, and poetry with the judge Abū Bakr ibn Kāmil, who was a pupil of the historian Muḥammad ibn Jarīr al-Ṭabarī (838?-923). He also studied *kalām*, or the use of discursive argument to explain and defend the content of theology, with Yaḥyā ibn ʿAdī (893–974), a Christian theologian and one of the great Aristotelian philosophers of the period. Following his marriage, Muʿayyad al-Dawlah took his bride to Isfahan. Al-Ṣāḥib accompanied him and remained in his service.

During the same visit, al-Ṣāḥib met Muʿizz al-Dawlah's celebrated vizier Abū Muḥammad al-Ḥasan ibn Muḥammad al-Muhallabī (903-963), who served from 950 through 963. Like many of the figures who influenced al-Ṣāḥib's development, he was famous for his literary style and for his brilliant literary circle, which was attended, among others, by Abū 'l-Faraj al-Iṣfahānī (897–967), the compiler of the *Kitāb al-Aghānī*, by Abū Isḥāq Ibrāhīm al-Ṣābī, and by the chief judge Ibn Maʿrūf. Al-Ṣāḥib claims at this time to have met two other particularly famous men, Abū Saʿīd al-Sīrāfī (d. 979), a judge and grammarian, and Abū 'l-Fatḥ al-Marāghī (d. 986), another grammarian.

In the years following the visit to Baghdad, al-Ṣāḥib was rarely mentioned until 968, when he was recorded as being present in Rayy with Muʿayyad al-Dawlah. Up through 968, al-Ṣāḥib was developing his career and literary skills but had not yet become truly prominent. However, the gauche aspects of his behavior toward Ibn

Fāris continued. Al-Tawḥīdī indicates that, at this time, al-Ṣāḥib wrote poems in praise of himself, then had another poet read them as though they were his own work.

In 970, al-Ṣāḥib's former patron, Abū 'l-Faḍl Ibn al-ʿAmīd died. His son Abū 'l-Fatḥ Ibn al-ʿAmīd succeeded him as Rukn al-Dawlah's vizier. In 973-974, he soon committed a political error that would later cost him dearly. Bakhtiyār (d. 967 or 968) was the Buwayhid ruler in Baghdad from 967-978. He was a cousin of ʿAḍūd al-Dawlah who had great political and administrative talent. In contrast, Bakhtiyār had little ability for rule and, as a result, his troops rebelled against him in 973. Rukn al-Dawlah sent ʿAḍūd al-Dawlah to help him. In opposition to his father's wishes, ʿAḍūd al-Dawlah convinced Bakhtiyār to abdicate in his favor. When Abū 'l-Fatḥ Ibn al-ʿAmīd informed Rukn al-Dawlah of the situation, he made his son restore Bakhtiyār to power. By thwarting his efforts, Abū 'l-Fatḥ made an enemy of ʿAḍūd al-Dawlah.

Upon Rukn al-Dawlah's death in 976, his son ʿAḍūd al-Dawlah succeeded him in Shiraz as the senior Buwayhid ruler and soon took control of Baghdad as well. Muʿayyad al-Dawlah, Rukn al-Dawlah's second son, received the regions around Rayy and Isfahan. Rukn al-Dawlah's third son, Fakhr al-Dawlah (952–997), was allotted rule over Hamadhan and Dīnawar. Muʿayyad al-Dawlah also inherited Abū 'l-Fatḥ Ibn al-ʿAmīd as his vizier. Al-Ṣāḥib was by now Muʿayyad al-Dawlah's personal secretary. Although Muʿayyad al-Dawlah knew Abū 'l-Fatḥ disliked al-Ṣāḥib, he did not dismiss the former. Even when Abū 'l-Fatḥ convinced the army to rebel with the intent of killing al-Ṣāḥib, Muʿayyad al-Dawlah still took no action against the former, but instead sent al-Ṣāḥib secretly to Isfahan, where he would be safe. However, relatively soon after his succession, ʿAḍūd al-Dawlah ordered Abū 'l-Fatḥ arrested and put to death. At that point, Muʿayyad al-Dawlah made al-Ṣāḥib his vizier.

In 977, Fakhr al-Dawlah attempted to take Muʿayyad al-Dawlah's lands. His two older brothers joined together to drive him beyond the Buwayhid lands to the Sāmānids, a Persian dynasty whose rule was based in what is now Central Asia. Al-Ṣāḥib's status increased as a result of the redistribution of power and land between ʿAḍūd al-Dawlah and Muʿayyad al-Dawlah. The latter received the districts of Hamadhān and Nihawand out of his younger brother's patrimony. ʿAḍūd al-Dawlah met with al-Ṣāḥib to discuss the administration of these territories.

It is difficult to construct a timeline for al-Ṣāḥib's intellectual activities during the initial phase of his climb to power because the sources depict only its fully developed stage. However, by the time he became vizier, he had already collected an extensive library. Nūh ibn Manṣūr, who became the Sāmānid ruler in 977, invited al-Ṣāḥib to become his vizier at one point. His offer was refused ostensibly because of the difficulty of moving al-Ṣāḥib's extensive library, a task that supposedly would have required four hundred camels.

In 979, al-Ṣāḥib was sent to Hamadhan to ʿAḍūd al-Dawlah's court. He was treated with great honor and stayed there a long time, encouraging good relations between the two brothers and their courts. Eventually, Muʿayyad al-Dawlah complained of his absence and recalled him.

ʿAḍūd al-Dawlah died in 983 and Muʿayyad al-Dawlah the year after. His son Ṣamṣām al-Dawlah (964–998) succeeded ʿAḍūd al-Dawlah in Baghdad. Fakhr al-Dawlah, the oldest member of the Buwayhid family by this point, was still living in exile. Nevertheless, al-Ṣāḥib chose to approach him to succeed Muʿayyad al-Dawlah in his dominions instead of either of ʿAḍūd al-Dawlah's other sons, Ṣamṣām al-Dawlah or Sharaf al-Dawlah (961–989). Al-Ṣāḥib paid the army to ensure their support. Although he offered to resign, Fakhr al-Dawlah kept him on as vizier. Al-Ṣāḥib's action preserved the Buwayhid tradition of the oldest member of the family becoming the chief ruler. At the same time, it preserved his vizierate. His negotiations were of general benefit in that they maintained peace. He served Fakhr al-Dawlah as vizier for over eighteen years.

Throughout his employment as vizier, al-Ṣāḥib's administration was highly beneficial to the Buwayhid lands and their populace. He put the state finances on a sound footing and maintained a stable government. He successfully led the army on foreign campaigns. He built palaces, thereby contributing to the glory of the state, but also built mosques, a charitable contribution to the public good. With the economic prosperity, he was able to support culture and intellectual pursuits.

Although al-Ṣāḥib had formed his own *majlis* well before he became vizier, this position—and the peace, wealth and respect that came with it—greatly increased his ability to support writers and other intellectuals. Generally the participants in his *majlis* all wrote poetry, although as indicated within the list, some were at least as well known or even better known for other intellectual pursuits, as is indicated below. Although the participants varied over the years, the following individuals are known to have attended: Abū 'l-Ḥusayn al-Salāmī (d. 1021), a Sufi; Abū Bakr al-Khwārizmī (d. 993), a grammarian, poet and letter writer; ʿAbd al-Salām ibn al-Ḥusayn al-Ma'mūnī (d. 993), a poet; Abū 'l-Ḥasan al-Badīhī (d. 990), a poet associated with the school of Yaḥyā ibn ʿAdī the philosopher; Abū Saʿīd al-Rustamī, a poet; Abū 'l-Qāsim al-Zaʿfaranī a poet who served al-Ṣāḥib, ʿAḍūd al-Dawlah, and Fakhr al-Dawlah; Abū 'l-ʿAbbās ibn Ibrāhīm al-Dabbī (al-Kāfī 'l-Awḥad), a ministerial colleague of al-Ṣāḥib; ʿAlī ibn ʿAbd al-ʿAzīz al-Qāḍī 'l-Jurjānī (ca. 902 or 928–976 or 1002); Abū 'l-Qāsim ibn Abī 'l-ʿAlā'; Abū Muḥammad al-Khāzin (d. ca. 970), an astronomer and mathematician; Abū Hāshim al-ʿAlawī; Abū 'l-Ḥasan al-Jawharī; the Banū 'l-Munajjim; Ibn Bābak; Ibn al-Qāshānī; Badīʿ al-Zamān Aḥmad ibn al-Ḥusayn al-Hamadhānī (circa 358/969–398/1008) the first great author of *maqāmāt*, or short, amusing, fictional prose vignettes; Ismāʿīl al-Shāshī; Abū 'l-ʿAlā' al-Asdī; Abū 'l-Ḥasan al-Ghuwayrī; Misʿar ibn Muhalhil Abū Dulaf al-Yanbūʿī (d. ca. 1000), who wrote mendicant literature; Abū Hafs al-Shahrazūrī, a copyist in Isfahan who compiled a collection of aphorisms; Abū Muʿammar al-Ismāʿīlī; Abū 'l-Fayād al-Ṭabarī; al-Sharīf al-Raḍī (970–1016), a leader of the Shiites and a writer known for his poetry; Abū Isḥāq Ibrāhīm al-Ṣābī, a historian; Abū ʿAbd Allāh al-Ḥusayn ibn Aḥmad Ibn al-Ḥajjāj (ca. 931–24 May 1001), a poet more famous for his *sukhf*, or poetry espousing the opposite of social values including obscenity than for his traditional poetry; Ḥusayn ibn Muḥammad Ibn Sukkarah (d. 1120 or 1121), a poet; and Ibn Nubātah (d. 984 or 985), who wrote sermons in rhyming prose. In addition to members of his *majlis*, al-Ṣāḥib also supported individual intellectuals in Baghdad.

Despite his own personal literary talents, because of the importance of many of the participants in this *majlis* and his support for them, al-Ṣāḥib is now better known as a patron than as a writer. He gave away around 100,000 *dīnārs* per year, usually in amounts ranging from one hundred to five hundred *dirhams*. Another of the contradictory aspects of al-Ṣāḥib's nature appears in his distribution of patronage. He was credited with being both a liberal patron and simultaneously with being miserly in fulfilling his obligations to the intellectuals at his court. There were certainly writers at his court, such as al-Tawḥīdī, who did not receive patronage despite having excellent skills. At the same time, Abū Isḥāq Ibrāhīm (925–994), who was chief secretary under Muʿizz al-Dawlah and Bakhtiyār, but was imprisoned under ʿAḍūd al-Dawlah, received 1000 *dīnārs* annually from al-Ṣāḥib. Part of the issue may be the gap between the rewards economically possible in the Buwayhid period and the reports of much higher rewards in earlier periods. For example, in contrast to al-Ṣāḥib's five hundred *dirhams*, Hārūn al-Rashīd (763 or 766-809) was able to award 50,000 *dīnārs* for a single poem.

In directing his *majlis*, al-Ṣāḥib consistently avoided taking sides with any single ethnic group. As far as can be ascertained, his ethnic background was Arab. He definitely defended Arabs against insults from *ʿajamīs*, or non-Arabs. For example, when he heard an *ʿajamī* disparage Arabs for eating snakes, he would refute the person by suggesting that he was ignorant of Arab eating habits. Al-Ṣāḥib would bring up the incestuous sexual relations of the Persians and thereby demonstrate the lack of validity of ethnic stereotypes (*Dīwān*, ed. Āl Yāsīn, 286).

O you who when ignorant of their food
  Accuses the Arabs of eating snakes,
[Remember] the *ʿajamīs* whose snakes cohabit
  With their mothers and sisters throughout the night.

Although al-Ṣāḥib countered such insults, he did not go on to raise the Arabs above the *ʿajamīs*. Instead, he praised the good qualities of both groups (*Dīwān*, ed. Āl Yāsīn, 403-404).

The progeny of al-Munajjim have dazzling intellect
And the excellent qualities of Arabs and *ʿajamīs*
I ceaselessly praised them and publicized their pre-eminence
Until I was tinted by the strength of [my] advocacy.

Although al-Ṣāḥib is now more famous as a patron, in his own time, in his lifetime he was seen as a great scholar in multiple fields of knowledge. He left a *Dīwān*, or collection of his poetry, which has survived only partially. As was typical during his time, some of his *qaṣīdas* employ a neo-classical form. In others, there is a continuity of thought and connections between verses that resemble those found in Persian *masnavī*, or poems primarily identified by their rhyming couplets in the pattern aa, bb, cc, etc. Some of his poems are relatively simple, as is this example (*Dīwān*, ed. Āl Yāsīn, 229).

The snow approached then blanketed [everything] for pleasure
And for drinking by the great and by the small
And its midst approached in a gown of light
And presented gifts of scattered pearls
As if the sky had wed the earth
So that camphor was scattered.

Other poems are replete with rhetorical devices. For example, in one particularly impressive style of *qaṣīdah*, he begins each half verse with the next successive letter of the alphabet. Al-Ṣāḥib was equally adept at writing prose. His rhymed prose, due to the sheer quantity of rhetorical devices employed, tends toward the ostentatious. Unfortunately, his style does not translate well. Nevertheless, it should be clear that this description of a *majlis* is florid (al-Thaʿālibī *Yatīmat,* 3:286):

> …the narcissus's eye opened in it [the assembly], and the violet's cheeks flushed, the scent of citron was diffused, and the streams of orange were released, and the tongues of trees were loosened, and the preachers of music stood up, and the breezes of goblets wafted, and the trade of sociability found its market…

Al-Ṣāḥib also wrote a work on Arabic prosody, *al-Iqnāʿ fī 'l-ʿarūd wa-takhrīj al-qawāfī*, which displayed the depth of knowledge behind his display of literary skills. Al-Ṣāḥib was also a literary critic. He criticized poets who had already achieved a high reputation, such as al-Mutanabbī. Although al-Ṣāḥib's comments sometimes seem severe, they do reflect contemporary standards. For example, in *al-Kashf ʿan masāwī shiʿr al-Mutanabbī*, he complains that Mutanabbī's expression of emotion obscures truth and that his expression of desire obscures sincerity. Nevertheless, al-Ṣāḥib borrowed freely from al-Mutanabbī's poetry.

Al-Ṣāḥib's exceedingly high level of political and literary achievements did not relieve whatever stresses caused his contradictory behaviors. Al-Tawḥīdī, who left al-Ṣāḥib's service empty-handed and unhappy after three years, nevertheless found much to admire about him: his memory was exceptional, he was educated in all branches of literature, he had thoroughly assimilated Muʿtazilite scholarship, and he was a master of meter and rhetoric devices and composed a large amount of extempore poetry. On the other hand, al-Tawḥīdī also represented him as bold, foul-mouthed, and unscrupulous in his use of power and as a man who meted out severe punishments, stinted on rewards, and was assiduous with his reproofs. In addition, he was shown by his contemporaries to be hot tempered, superstitious, spiteful, and envious of those who were competent. He could be arbitrary in his treatment of people and was highly susceptible to flattery, whether the flatterer was credible or not. Abū Bakr al-Khwārizmī wrote that al-Ṣāḥib had impressive abilities, but that his chamber was usually empty due to his unpleasant temperament.

Al-Ṣāḥib's unpleasant nature carried over into his patronage and his writings. He was described as adamantly opposed to men who studied philosophy, and loosely, the natural sciences, such as mathematics, logic, statistics, and astrology. This too was contradictory, since Muʿtazilism, in which he was thoroughly trained, was strongly grounded in philosophy and logic. He is also known for sending a few derogatory stanzas of poetry when someone died, instead of the more normal poem in praise of the person and their accomplishments. For example, when he heard that Abū Bakr al-Khwārizmī had died, he recited these lines (*Dīwān*, ed. Āl Yāsīn, 285):

I said to the rider traveling from Khurāsān
Has your Khwārizmī died? He said to me, Yes
So I said, Write on the plaster over his gravestone
Indeed, the Merciful [God] punishes the one ungrateful for favors.

Although al-Ṣāḥib was highly cultured and wrote literature in traditional, formal styles, he was highly fascinated with the jargon and habits of the mendicant classes. Although this might seem to be another example of the opposites found in al-Ṣāḥib's nature, an interest in the mendicant classes was not unique to him. Instead, it seems to derive from the close juxtaposition of disparate economic classes that developed along with urbanization of the Islamic Empire. To satisfy his interest, al-Ṣāḥib hosted Abū Dulaf, a vagrant, on a regular basis. Abū Dulaf lived to nearly 90 and spent much of his time traveling as a beggar. His visits to al-Ṣāḥib satisfied his daily needs. They also allowed Abū Dulaf to obtain letters and financial drafts to support his journeys. The two men would spend time together exchanging comments in mendicant jargon. Abū Dulaf wrote the *Qaṣīdat Banī Sāsāniyyah* (The Poem of the Banī Sāsāniyyah) for al-Ṣāḥib, and in it described different categories of beggars and their practices. Two other such poets are mentioned in connection with al-Ṣāḥib: Ibn Fashīshā and al-Aqtāʿ al-Munshid al-Kūfī, a vagabond and thief who freely admitted his immorality. The latter was such a good informant on mendicants and their language that al-Ṣāḥib housed him at court, refusing to let him go home for long periods.

Al-Ṣāḥib also openly exhibited a fascination with pornography. Without further study, it is not clear whether this was truly an interest in pornography or whether it was an interest in *sukhf*, a style of literature that emphasizes the opposites of social values and which was in vogue during this period. His attitude is typically contradictory. Al-Tawḥīdī attributes verses to al-Ṣāḥib that open express his enjoyment of homosexual activities and that even combine affirmation of his espousal of Muʿtazilism with affirmation of his enjoyment of homosexual practices. At other times, al-Ṣāḥib denied these declarations. Nevertheless, al-Ṣāḥib exhibited a consistent interest in famous *mukhannath*, or men who entertained in female clothing, and in writers of *mujūn* literature who open subscribed to homosexuality. *Mujūn*, a term which has yet been only roughly defined, means "jesting" as opposed to "seriousness," but specifically it seems to mean types of jesting depicting without shame activities that are generally socially inappropriate, i.e. debauchery, vulgarity, bad manners, and the use of obscenity. Al-Ṣāḥib approved of and could quote the poetry of Ibn al-Ḥajjāj, a poet known for using the language of the lowest inhabitants of Baghdad and for the unremitting obscenity and pornographic aspects of his work. Ibn al-Ḥajjāj wrote poems in praise of al-Ṣāḥib.

Al-Ṣāḥib's career had its first and last major failure in 989, when he attempted to take Baghdad from Ṣamṣām al-Dawlah. Although he initially succeeded, a flood took place and eliminated his success. Despite Fakhr al-Dawlah's displeasure at al-Ṣāḥib's failure, he was not dismissed. When al-Ṣāḥib was suffering his last illness, Fakhr al-Dawlah even visited him. Al-Ṣāḥib died on Mar. 30, 996. Fakhr al-Dawlah greatly esteemed him and he and his court officials observed a very long period of mourning. The populace also mourned deeply. Nevertheless, Fakhr al-Dawlah was still sufficiently displeased to confiscate al-Ṣāḥib's property shortly thereafter. But at the time at least 500 poets wrote elegies to commemorate him. The poet Sharīf al-Raḍī (d. 1015) wrote a particularly noteworthy *qaṣīdah*.

REFERENCES

Muḥammad Ḥasan Āl Yāsīn, *al-Ṣāḥib Ibn 'Abbād: hayātuhu wa adabuhu* (Baghdad: Maṭba'at al-Ma'ārif, 1957);

Clifford Edmund Bosworth, *The Mediaeval Islamic Underworld: the Banū Sāsān in Arabic Society and Literature*, 2 vols. (Leiden: Brill, 1976);

Mafizullah Kabir, "The Sahib Isma'il ibn 'Abbad (326 A.H./938 A.D.-385 A.H./996 A.D.)," *Islamic Culture*, no. 30 (1956): 190-198;

Mafizullah Kabir, "As-Sahib ibn 'Abbad as a Writer and Poet," *Islamic Culture*, no. 17 (1943): 176-205;

Ibn Khallikān, *Wafayāt al-a'yān*, ed. Iḥsān 'Abbās (Beirut: Dar Assakafa, 1968-1972);

Joel L. Kraemer, *Humanism in the Renaissance of Islam: a Preliminary Study: the Cultural Revival during the Buyid Age*, 2d. ed. (Leiden: E.J. Brill, 1992), 259-271;

al-Mufaḍḍal ibn Sa'd Māfarrūkhī, *Kitāb maḥāsin Iṣfahān* (Tehran: Maṭba'at Majlis al-Millī, 1933);

Zaki Mubarak, *La Prose Arabe au IVe siècle de l'Hégire (Xe siècle)* (Paris: Maisonneuve, 1931);

Charles Pellat, "al-Ṣāḥib Ibn 'Abbād," in *'Abbasid Belles-Lettres*, ed. Julia Ashtiany et al. The Cambridge history of Arabic literature (Cambridge: Cambridge University Press, 1990), 96-111;

Abū Ḥayyān al-Tawḥīdī, *Akhlāq al-wazīrayn, mathālib al-wazīrayn al-Ṣāḥib Ibn 'Abbād wa-Ibn al-'Amīd* (Damascus: Maṭbū'āt al-Majma' al-'Ilmī 'l-'Arabī bi-Dimashq, 1965);

Badawī Aḥmad Ṭabānah, *al-Ṣāḥib Ibn 'Abbād: al-wazīr, al-adīb, al-'ālim* (Cairo: al-Mu'assasah al-Miṣriyyah al-'Āmmah li 'l-Ta'līf wa 'l-Tarjamah wa 'l-Ṭibā'ah wa 'l-Nashr, 1964);

Abū Manṣūr al-Malik al-Tha'ālibī, *Yatīmat al-dahr fī maḥāsin ahl al-'aṣr*, ed. Muḥammad Qumayḥah, 5 vols. (Beirut: Dār al-Kutub al-'Ilmiyyah, 1983), 3:225-337;

Yāqūt al-Ḥamawī, *Irshād al-arīb ilā ma'rifat al-adīb*, ed. D.S. Margoliouth, 7 vols. E.J.W. Gibb Memorial Series (Leiden: E.J. Brill, 1907-1931), 2:273-343.

Aḥmad ibn Muḥammad al-Sanawbarī

(886?—945)

JOCELYN SHARLET

University of California at Davis

WORKS

Dīwān.

Editions

Tatimmat dīwān al-Sanawbarī, ed. Luṭfī 'l-Ṣaqqāl and Durriyyah al-Khaṭīb (Aleppo: Dār al-Kitāb al-'Arabī bi-Halab, 1971);

Sharḥ dīwān Bā'iyyat Dhī 'l-Rummah, ed. Maḥmūd Muṣṭafā Ḥalāwī (Beirut: Mu'assasat al-Risālah, 1985);

Dīwān al-Sanawbarī, ed. Iḥsān 'Abbās (Beirut: Dār Ṣādir, 1998).

Aḥmad ibn Muḥammad ibn al-Ḥasan ibn Murad Abū Bakr al-Sanawbarī al-Ḍabbī 'l-Ḥalabī was a poet and writer who lived in the ninth and tenth centuries, praised elites of Aleppo, and became affiliated with the major regional ruler Sayf al-Dawlah (915 or 916-967) before the latter became established in Aleppo in 333/944, and continued to be affiliated with him there. Al-Sanawbarī is best known as a highly skilled and innovative descriptive poet, especially in descriptions of the natural world. In his name, al-Ḍabbī indicates his tribe and al-Ḥalabī indicates his residence in Aleppo. Some sources identify the name al-Sanawbarī not with someone who makes a living selling pine nuts, the literal meaning of the word, but with an event that occurred in the life of al-Sanawbarī's paternal grandfather. It is said that the grandfather, while he was the head of one of the Caliph al-Ma'mūn's academies, pleased the caliph with his performance in a debate, so that the caliph described him in an idiomatic expression that contained the word "sanawbarī" referring to his cleverness and wit. Al-Sanawbarī may have been born around 273 /886 and he died in 334/945.

Al-Sanawbarī was probably born in Antakya, a city that is located in present-day Turkey but claimed by Syria as well, and raised in Aleppo. His collected poems include elegies for a daughter and he is said to have inscribed poetry upon the sides of her tomb. It is said that when he found his son distraught as a child because he had just been weaned, al-Sanawbarī inscribed poetry upon his cradle. Al-Sanawbarī studied with the scholar ʿAlī ibn Sulaymān al-Akhfash (d. 927) and his closest professional connection was with the poet Maḥmūd ibn al-Ḥusayn Kushājim, who was also known for his descriptive poetry, but was less distinguished as a poet of nature than al-Sanawbarī. His most powerful patron was the regional ruler Sayf al-Dawlah, for whom he worked as a poet and librarian. He worked for Sayf al-Dawlah in Mosul and then in Aleppo. Sayf al-Dawlah presided over a region that included what is now northern Iraq, southeastern Turkey, and northern Syria. Sayf al-Dawlah was known for his military prowess, especially in conflicts with the Byzantines, and he was also known for his cultivation of poetry and writers at his court. Al-Sanawbarī owned a garden in Aleppo, perhaps one source of his nature poetry. He also spent time in Damascus, al-Raqqah, and Baghdad, a fairly typical pattern of travel and residence in different locations for poets at this time. This type of travel often involved the need to seek patronage from diverse sources as well as an interest in connections with other poets and writers. Panegyric was an important part of al-Sanawbarī's career, but he is also well-known for his poetry addressed to friends and peers. His collected poems include poems dedicated to the Prophet and his family, so that he is referred to as aligning himself with the ʿAlids, or the community that developed into the Shiite sect. The main source for al-Sanawbarī's biography is Ibn ʿAsākir's *Tārīkh Dimashq* ([Biographical] History of Damascus), and the editor of al-Sanawbarī's collected poems points out that almost all other notices are derived from this one. In addition to notices about him, al-Sanawbarī appears in notices about other poets and writers in medieval Arabic biographical dictionaries.

Al-Sanawbarī's poetry was transmitted by several transmitters, including Muḥammad ibn Aḥmad ibn Jumayʿ al-Ghassānī (917 or 918-1011 or 1012), who also composed an early biography of him, Abū 'l-Ḥasan al-Maʿnāwī, al-Shaykh al-Ṣāliḥ, Abū 'l-Faḍl Naṣr ibn Muḥammad al-Ṭūsī, Ibn Kujak al-Ḥusayn ibn ʿAlī (who was a contemporary and friend of al-Sanawbarī), and Abū 'l-Ḥasan Aḥmad ibn Muḥammad ibn Muḥammad ibn Abū Qadūmah. The well-known writer Muḥammad ibn Yaḥyā 'l-Ṣūlī (d. ca. 947) compiled al-Sanawbarī's collected poems during his lifetime. The collection was circulating in Andalusia, in what is now southern Spain, twenty years after his death. The circulation of his poetry, the biographical notices about al-Sanawbarī in a number of major medieval Arabic biographical dictionaries, and the appearance of his poetry in medieval Arabic poetry anthologies and other prosimetrical works are testimony to his reputation as a poet. The selection of poems that has survived and been published, edited by the esteemed scholar Iḥsān ʿAbbās, is large but is not the complete collection. Readers of Arabic with access to an extensive Arabic library may wish to consult some of the pre-modern biographical entries listed in the introduction to this edition, since they contain significant quantities of his poetry as illustrations of his life. In addition, other scholars have gathered more poetry by al-Sanawbarī from a range of sources and compiled it as a complement to the collected poetry. Some scholars have speculated that the incomplete transmission of al-Sanawbarī's collected poems is in part due to the fact that he fell between the periods of two major biographers, Abū 'l-Faraj al-Iṣbahānī (897–ca. 972) in the ninth century and ʿAbd al-Malik ibn Muḥammad al-Thaʿālibī (961 or 962-1037 or 1038) in the tenth. The omission of al-

Sanawbarī by these two biographers also helps to explain the relative dearth of biographical information about him. The translation of his poetry by Arthur Wormhoudt appears in a series that emphasizes quantity of translations rather than reliability, so is not recommended here.

Al-Sanawbarī worked in an environment where connections with other poets and writers were often made either in gatherings with patrons or in gatherings among peers. The appreciation and description of nature in such gatherings was an indication of refinement. Nature in al-Sanawbarī's poems is not something separate from the human sphere, but rather is a kind of extension of the human sphere. What matters about nature is people's appreciation of it. Such descriptions of nature refers to manmade luxuries, human bodies, human interaction, and ideas from the human sphere. The poems are about human life refracted through the natural world. The Arabic introduction of some types of the long poetic genre known as the *qaṣīdah* contains a more established tradition of nature description, i.e., nature description focused on the desert in conjunction with loss of a lover, including garden imagery representing beloved women who had become inaccessible to the lover due to tribal migrations. In the ninth century, in some *qaṣīdah* introductions, these ancient uses of nature imagery began to give way to the description of the gardens of what is now Syria and Iraq by poets such as Abū Tammām (796 or 804-842/843 or 845/846) and al-Walīd ibn ʿUbayd al-Buḥturī (821-897 or 898). However, it was only in the work of descriptive poets, especially al-Sanawbarī, that nature description as an expression of pleasure and fertility became widespread and began to appear as an independent genre. This evolving use of nature description to express pleasure and fertility also became important in Andalusia, where it was cultivated by poets such as Ibrāhīm ibn Abī 'l-Fatḥ Ibn al-Khafājah (1058 or 1059-1138 or 1139). The following examples should give a general idea of the importance of fertility and the human sphere in al-Sanawbarī's nature poetry, including human social and ethical practices, emotional and intellectual life, and material culture.

And he said about rain (*Dīwān*, 25, poem 15):

A flow that remained all night long,
pouring down until dawn broke brightly,
Continued to rain down until morning
from the ceiling of a house that was like a tomb
That, when the flash of lightning bolts made it laugh,
cried with an eye whose tears are raindrops
As if its ceiling were the clouds when
clouds pour out benefit, and its floor were the sea

And he said about flowers (*Dīwān*, 42-43:34):

...And the earth is a ruby, the air a pearl
the vegetation turquoise and the water crystal
The vegetation does not go without a cup from its [spring's] clouds
so that it is of two kinds: drunk and hung over
Spring in which roses are piled up [like fine fabrics] for us, covering [like a garment] what is between gatherings
and the poppies are scattered [like pearls or coins]
And narcissi with enchanting eyes are not
like eyes blinded and enchanted
This violet, this jasmine, and that
daffodil, that lily, famous for their beauty,
Spring in which the clouds continue to scatter their pearls
so that the earth is laughing and the birds are joyful
And in which, wherever you look, you find a turtledove and a ring dove
singing, and a pigeon and a lark
And in which, when two nightingales sing, they are
a flute and a piccolo, or rather a lute and a mandolin...

In addition to his well-known nature descriptions, some of al-Sanawbarī's descriptive poems focus on manmade objects related to the pleasures of social life in such gatherings, especially in poems that are identified with the exchange of gifts or invitations. In addition, gift poems may take the form of requests for things, and so bear a resemblance to the use of formal panegyric to secure payment and sometimes a gift of high value. In general the gifts are quite modest, emphasizing their use in relationships rather than their value in themselves. For example, gifts may be flowers, wine, perfume, candles, shoes and sandals, or oil. In poems about a gift, the ethical and social dimensions of friendships are implied. The following gift poems demonstrate the way relationships become intertwined with the description of gifts.

Abū Bakr Aḥmad ibn Muḥammad al-Sanawbarī said about candles that he gave as a gift (*Dīwān*, 15:1):

O Abū Hafs, I have chosen
  and I have not fallen short in my choice
And I have considered gifts
  great and small
I did not find anything like that which
  turns night to day
So look closely
  at a tree that bears fire
And drape it in an honorary robe of acceptance
  so that you drape its giver in an honorary robe of pride

And he said to a man who gave him wine and asked for his pardon (75:78):

The goodness of that request for pardon increased
  my pleasure when I drank this wine
And we drank that which reminded us of your face when
  the perfection of joy was in the reminder
And we saw you in our hearts, Abū Bakr,
  as if we had seen you with our eyes
And it was as if, due to the good memory of you, we were in
  a garden of anemones, narcissi, and daisies

Poems about things by al-Sanawbarī and others like him often deal with things that are used and that provide sensual pleasure or comfort, but they are not exactly essential things. This slight luxury of a little extra comfort is an important way of emphasizing the refinement of the people who enjoy these things and especially the poetry about them. Poems about modest objects may echo the lofty ethical themes of formal panegyric, both paying homage to and parodying this more established use of poetry. In addition, poems about objects may echo more formal uses of poetry when they are about the praise or blame of a particular object, or even elegies for things. In conjunction with this description of things in ways that imply human relationships, al-Sanawbarī and other descriptive poets of this period are distinguished by their emphasis on using the description of things to explore the subjectivity of the observer and the audience. In other words, al-Sanawbarī's poems about things are at least as much about the emotional, intellectual, spiritual, and social life of people as they are about the things themselves.

While earlier poets had used the description of nature and sometimes manmade things in the context of other genres of poetry, al-Sanawbarī and other descriptive poets of this period are distinguished by their frequent focus on description as a genre in its own right. In these descriptive poems, the ethical framework of longer genres has been channeled into allusive imagery in the description of things. While the power of the observer's gaze is important in this poetry, the impact of that which is observed upon the observer, a central feature of medieval ideas about vision and observation, also plays a major role. Poems about things, both natural and manmade, become occasions for the observer to investigate his identity and relationships with other people.

Some gatherings of al-Sanawbarī and other literary types occurred in conjunction with the emerging importance of booksellers. The increasing role of writing in cultural production complemented the development of the ornate rhetoric of descriptive poetry. While poetry often circulated orally, it also began to be circulated in writing, and several descriptive poets were copyists of their own or other poetry. The increasing role of writing made it possible for literary types to produce and consume poetry in conjunction with written genres such as biographical dictionaries, anthologies, and collections of anecdotes. For example, the compilation about gift exchange by the two Khālidī brothers, who were also descriptive poets, includes two poems that al-Sanawbarī wrote to accompany gifts of candles, another that he wrote to thank the Khālidī brothers for a gift of roses and wine, and another in which he requests sandals. The anthology of poetry about the lover, the beloved, fragrances, and wine by the descriptive poet Abū 'l-Ḥasan ibn Aḥmad al-Sarī 'l-Raffā' includes dozens of selections by al-Sanawbarī.

While formal panegyric exchange worked well only if it involved an original work by one poet given to one patron in exchange for a payment or large gift, some short descriptive poems that focused on nature or things were less specific and could work well while circulating more freely. This kind of circulation appears in positive ways, such as in two versions of the same poem about a ring by al-Sanawbarī and Kushājim. Al-Sanawbarī's version is described as being composed to accompany a ring that he gave Kushājim, and Kushājim's version is described as being composed to accompany a ring that Kushājim gave to al-Sanawbarī. This overlap complements the praise and mild censure that was exchanged by the poets. Free circulation of verse also appears in negative ways, such as the ongoing rivalry between al-Sarī 'l-Raffā' and the two Khālidī brothers over the attribution of their poetry. Extensive discussions on borrowings in medieval Arabic literary criticism and other sources show that the distinction between intertextuality and plagiarism was far from settled.

Al-Sanawbarī was known for his familiarity with and use of strange words in Arabic, and Persian words. Both types of expression contributed to the elaborate rhetoric of his descriptive poetry. While strange words in Arabic were associated with the legacy of the poetry attributed to Preislamic Arabic poets and an assertion of identity that revolved around Arabic, Persian words were associated with the rapid expansion of Persian culture and influence in the Arabic-language cultural production of this region in the ninth and tenth centuries. By using both types of expression, al-Sanawbarī suggests an emphasis on rhetorical skill, drawing on all available sources for elaborate description, rather than affiliation with his own Arab identity or Persian cultural influence. The interest in elaborate rhetoric, which emerged as a crucial issue in cultural production of the ninth century in other genres of poetry, continued in the descriptive poetry of the late ninth and tenth centuries. This interest in elaborate rhetoric was related to a way for people from diverse backgrounds to assert their position in an expanding cultural elite that revolved around literacy in Arabic. Elaborate rhetoric focuses not on what is described, but on the intellectual capacities of the poet and audience to analyze what is observed. The interest in elaborate rhetoric in descriptive poetry emerged out of the earlier emphasis on elaborate rhetoric in the more formal genre of court panegyric by poets such as Abū Tammām, who was known for his ornate use of rhetorical devices and imagery.

The importance of this kind of elaborate rhetoric in descriptive poetry is more than just ornamentation. Al-Sanawbarī's use of this kind of expression in descriptive poetry allows him to link the inanimate with the animate, offer multiple perspectives on the experience of observation and the impact of that which is observed upon the observer, and experiment with ways to use the description of objects as indirect articulations of human emotions, ideas, relationships, status, and conflict. Like the description of the experience of time and fate in the short genre of wisdom poetry, of which al-Sanawbarī's collected poems includes examples, the description of things also offers perspectives on the human experience of time and fate. The appreciation of things is not simply an interaction between people and the world. It is important that this significance of things is mediated by artful description. Anybody can enjoy flowers and candles; only the literate and expanding cultural elite can demonstrate true refinement by producing, consuming, and circulating poetry about flowers and candles.

While al-Sanawbarī and other descriptive poets played a big role in the expansion of the literary sphere beyond the courts of rulers, none of them were completely cut off from or in opposition to these courts. In addition to descriptive poetry, al-Sanawbarī and most poets like him also worked in the genre of panegyric dedicated to political and military elites, a major source of literary patronage in medieval Arabic culture. In addition, the genre of descriptive poetry emerged in conjunction with the widespread interest in poetry and rhetoric among the administrators who worked for the courts of rulers. For these administrators, skills in producing, consuming, and discussing descriptive poetry were a part of their formal professional development as writers of court documents as well as their informal professional advancement as men of refinement. While al-Sanawbarī and poets like him sometimes addressed panegyric to elites of lower status and peers, they also addressed panegyric to major elites of the court, such as the panegyric for Sayf al-Dawlah by al-Sanawbarī and al-Sarī 'l-Raffā'. Moreover, al-Sanawbarī and poets like him, who became known for their descriptive poetry and their role in literary culture beyond the court, did not dominate literary activity of the period. While al-Sanawbarī and poets like him were exchanging poems describing gifts in informal gatherings, the towering figure of Abū 'l-Ṭayyib al-Mutanabbī (915-965) and other court poets continued to develop the role of formal, courtly panegyric and related genres in this period. However, medieval and modern observers have noticed one way in which his formal court panegyric incorporates a more informal dimension. He sometimes addresses his patron with terms of affection that complement the expanding use of poetry among friends by poets like al-Sanawbarī. It should not be concluded that al-Mutanabbī in some way represented the past and al-Sanawbarī and poets like him represented a completely new movement. Both formal court panegyric and less formal descriptive poetry drew on Arabic poetry of earlier centuries of the pre-Islamic and Islamic eras. In this context, it is important to note that ʿAlī ibn al-ʿAbbās Ibn al-Rūmī (836-896) became well-known for both descriptive poetry and the more formal use of court panegyric for political elites. Likewise, al-Buḥturī, who was known as a major court panegyrist, also has a number of short descriptive poems that have received less scholarly attention. Al-Buḥturī also used the material description of buildings as an approach to portraying patrons in panegyric, rather than focusing exclusively on the description of ethical qualities and events in battle and at court that dominate the genre.

In addition to courtly panegyric, al-Sanawbarī's poems dedicated to people include many poems that simply express affection for the person and admiration of his qualities, sometimes echoing the description of love in the introduction to a *qaṣīdah*, rather than formally praising him.

And he said, expressing affection for ʿAbd al-Raḥmān ibn Muḥammad al-Julābī (150:161):

You have gone and left me behind to grief
  lacking consolation and at a loss for patience
I consider friends enemies and I do not
  take pleasure in companions or gatherings
O Abū Qāsim, did distance tear you away by force
  or did you choose to don it as a garment?
For you went away and left destitute one for whom you did not cease
  to bring cheer in spite of his loneliness...

Invitation poems are also informal poems that are dedicated to people, although they focus on the prospect of the gathering and often describe the delights to be enjoyed there by guests. In this sense, invitation poems combine elements of poems about affection for friends and poems about gifts. The porous boundary between formal panegyric and informal poems of affection appears in the use of both types of poetry for the same person.

Al-Sanawbarī and poets like him were part of a movement in literary culture that involved using descriptive poetry in less formal settings as part of social life for the cultural elite of literate people, but they also built on several short genres of poetry that include the description of nature, bodies, and manmade things, and that were already well-established in Arabic in the eighth and early ninth centuries. These earlier genres included short poems about love, wine drinking, and hunting. Short love poetry sometimes focused on the lover's desire more than on the beloved, but also included descriptions of the beloved person. It complemented the love introduction to panegyric, in which the description of love, including the beloved, was cultivated by poets like the early Islamic poet Jarīr ibn ʿAṭiyyah, d. 728 and the ninth century poet al-Buḥturī. In short love poetry by the early Islamic poet ʿUmar Ibn Abī Rabīʿah (643 or 644-711 or 712), love and the beloved became the focus. Similarly, the wine and hunting poetry of poets like the early Abbasid poet Abū Nuwās (ca. 756-ca. 810) combine the description of things with an explicit presence of people and development of scenes. These short genres developed in conjunction with the role of hunting and wine drinking in earlier longer genres of Arabic poetry such as boasts and panegyric. There is an important difference between earlier love, wine, and hunting poetry and later descriptive poetry. In the descriptive poetry of al-Sanawbarī and poets like him, the presence of people is more marginalized or completely absorbed into the imagery used to describe things. However, as portrayals of elite refinement, love, hunting, and wine poetry resemble this later descriptive poetry. Alongside his more famous poems that focus on the description of nature and manmade things, al-Sanawbarī has many poems that are love, wine, or hunting poems. An important feature of these earlier short genres and later short descriptive poetry is the use of short poems that are easier to share in informal settings. In the case of descriptive poetry, a poem may be no more than a couple of lines. It is likely that in the social circulation of poetry, even slightly longer poems were shared in the form of segments rather than whole poems.

Al-Sanawbarī and his friend Kushājim were among a fairly diverse group of poets of the late ninth and tenth centuries who cultivated refined skills in descriptive poetry, including ʿAbd Allāh Ibn al-Muʿtazz (862-908) from the caliphal family and al-Sarī 'l-Raffāʾ, who was the son of a tradesman. This group also included Ibn al-Rūmī, ʿAbd al-Wāḥid ibn Naṣr al-Babbaghāʾ (d. 1007 or 1008), the two Khālidī brothers, and ʿAbd al-Salām ibn al-Ḥusayn al-Maʾmūnī (d. 993) and this type of poetry was further cultivated by Andalusian poets such as Ibrāhīm ibn Abī 'l-Fatḥ Ibn al-Khafājah (1058 or 1059-1138 or 1139), who was also known as a poet of nature description. In addition to descriptive poetry, poets like Kushājim, al-Sanawbarī, al-Sarī 'l-Raffāʾ, the two Khālidī brothers, and Ibn al-Muʿtazz also wrote prosimetrical works (works combining prose and poetry in varying proportions) that related in different ways to the practice of descriptive poetry.

For example, al-Sanawbarī wrote a commentary on a famous poem by the early Islamic poet Dhū 'l-Rummah who, like al-Sanawbarī over two centuries later, was best known for his descriptions of nature. In his brief introductory remark, he explains that he read the poem with his teacher al-Akhfash, studied the scholarly commentaries on it, and then produced his own. This commentary can be understood as an approach to al-Sanawbarī's own interest in difficult language in poetry and his innovations in descriptions of nature. However, it is important to note that this connection between the work of Dhū 'l-Rummah and al-Sanawbarī is as much about al-Sanawbarī distinguishing himself from this earlier poet as it is about drawing on his work. In Dhū 'l-Rummah's time, the description of nature was still firmly rooted in the significance of the desert as a setting for the love introduction, the journey section that sometimes appeared in older poems between the introduction and the main topic of the poem, and the portrayal of nature in the main section of the poem. By al-Sanawbarī's time, pleasure in the natural world of what is now Syria and Iraq had come to play an important role in the description of nature, which became more extensive as an independent genre of poetry. In addition, while the description of nature in Dhu 'l-Rummah's time often focused on hardship or lost pleasures of the past, the description of nature in al-Sanawbarī's time had become an important way to express refined pleasure in gatherings, with poetry displaying the appreciation of gardens.

Similarly, al-Sanawbarī's friend Kushājim has a book on the drinking companion and a book on the hunt that offer a context for the kinds of gatherings in which descriptive poetry was circulated. Ibn al-Muʿtazz also has a book on wine. The two Khālidī brothers have an anthology of short selections of poetry as well as a prosimetrical compilation on the topic of gift exchange. Finally, al-Sarī 'l-Raffāʾ has a long anthology of short segments of poetry, mostly contemporary, on the topics of the lover, the beloved, fragrances, and wine. Al-Sanawbarī's work as an innovative descriptive poet can best be understood in the context of the work of these other poets, and in the context of the related phenomena of the expanding cultural sphere, the use of elaborate rhetoric, the genre formal court panegyric, older short genres, and the increasing importance of writing in cultural production.

REFERENCES

ʿAlī Ibrāhīm Abū Zayd, *Fanniyyāt al-taṣwīr fī shi'r al-Ṣanawbarī* (Cairo: Dār al-Maʿārif, 2000);

Carl Brockelmann, *Tārīkh al-adab al-'Arabī*, 10 vols., tr. Maḥmūd Fahmī Ḥijāzī (Cairo: al-Ḥay'ah al-Miṣriyyah al-ʿĀmmah li 'l-Kitāb, 1993), 1:417-418;

Alma Giese, *Waṣf bei Kušājīm: eine Studie zur beschreibenden Dichtkunst der Abbasidenzeit*, Islamkundliche Untersuchungen, Bd. 62 (Berlin: Klaus Schwarz Verlag, 1981);

Andras Hamori, "Two Views of Time," in *On the Art of Medieval Arabic Literature* (Princeton, New Jersey: Princeton University Press, 1974);

Ḥabīb Ḥusayn al-Ḥasanī, *al-Sarī 'l-Raffā', ḥayātuhu wa-shi'ruh* (Baghdad: Maṭbaʿat Dār al-Salām, 1976);

Īlīyā Salīm al-Ḥāwī, *Fann al-waṣf wa taṭawwirahu fī 'l-shi'r al-'arabī* (Bayrut: Dār al-Kitāb al-Lubnānī, 1987);

ʿAlī ibn al-Ḥasan ibn Hibat Allāh Ibn ʿAsākir, *Tārīkh Dimashq al-kabīr*, 74 vols. in 37 vols., ed. ʿAbd Allāh ʿAlī ʿĀshūr al-Janūbī (Beirut: Dār Iḥyā''al-Turāth al-ʿArabī, 2001), 5(3), 275-80;

Philip F. Kennedy, *The Wine Song in Classical Arabic Poetry: Abu Nuwas and the Literary Tradition* (Oxford: Clarendon Press, 1997);

Maḥmūd ibn al-Ḥusayn Kushājim, *Dīwān Kushājim*, ed. al-Nabawī ʿAbd al-Wāḥid Shalān (Cairo: Maktabat al-Khānjī, 1996);

J. E. Montgomery, "Ṣanawbarī" in *Encyclopaedia of Islam, Second Edition*, ed. P. Bearman, Th. Bianquis, C.E. Bosworth, E. van Donzel and W.P. Heinrichs (Brill, 2008, Brill Online) http://www.brillonline.nl/entry?entry=islam_SIM-6599;

Magda M. al-Nowaihi, *The Poetry of Ibn Khafajah: a Literary Analysis* (Leiden: E. J. Brill, 1993);

Ṣālaḥ al-Dīn Khalīl ibn Aybak al-Ṣafadī, *Kitāb al-wāfī bi 'l-wafayāt*, 29 vols., ed. Iḥsān ʿAbbās (Stuttgart: Franz Steiner, 1992), 7:379-383;

Abū 'l-Ḥasan ibn Aḥmad al-Sarī 'l-Raffā', *al-Muḥibb wa 'l-maḥbūb wa 'l-mashmūn wa 'l-mashrūb*, 4 vols., vols. 1-3 ed. Miṣbāḥ Ghalāwinjī, vol. 4 ed. Mājid Ḥasan al-Dhababī (Damascus: Majmaʿ al-Lughah al-ʿArabiyyah, 1986-1987);

Gregor Schoeler, *Arabische Naturdichtung: die Zahriyyāt, Rabī'iyyāt und Rauḍiyyāt von ihren Anfängen bis aṣ-Ṣanaubarī, eine gattungs-, motiv- und stilgeschichtliche Untersuchung* (Beirut: Orient-Institut der Deutschen Morgenländischen Gesellschaft; Wiesbaden: Franz Steiner Verlag, 1974);

Akiko Motoyoshi Sumi, *Description in Classical Arabic Poetry: Wasf, Ekphrasis, and Interarts Theory* (Leiden: Brill, 2004).

Muḥammad ibn Yūsuf Ibn al-Ashtarkūnī, known as al-Saraquṣṭī

(second half of the eleventh century – 8 December 1143)

IGNACIO FERRANDO

University of Cádiz, Spain

WORKS

Kitāb al-Musalsal fī 'l gharīb lughat al-'arab (The book of Concatenation, on Rare Words in the Language of the Arabs);

al-Maqāmāt al-Luzūmiyyah.

Editions

Kitāb al-Musalsal fī 'l gharīb lughat al-'arab ed. by Muḥammad ʿAb al-Jawād and Ibrāhīm al-

Dasūqī 'l-Bāssāṭī (Cairo: Maktabat al-Khānjī, 1981);

al-Maqāmāt al-Luzūmiyyah, ed. Ibrāhīm Badr Aḥmad Ḍayf (Alexandria: al-Hay'ah al-Miṣriyyah al-'Āmmah li'l-Kitāb, 1982);

al-Maqāmāt al-luzūmiyyah, ed. Ḥasan al-Warāgilī (Rabat: Manshūrāt 'Ukāẓ, 1995).

Translations

Las sesiones del Zaragocí: relatos picarescos (maqāmāt) del siglo XII, trans. Ignacio Ferrando (Zaragoza, España: Prensas Universitarias de Zaragoza, 1999);

al-Maqāmāt al-Luzūmiyyah, trans. with a preliminary study by James T. Monroe. Studies in Arabic literature, v. 22 (Leiden; Boston: Brill, 2002).

Abū'l-Ṭāhir Muḥammad ibn Yūsuf ibn 'Abd Allāh ibn Yūsuf ibn 'Abd Allāh ibn Ibrāhīm al-Tamīmī Jamāl al-Dīn al-Māzinī'l-Saraqusṭī'l-Andalusī Ibn al-Ashtarkūnī is a famous Arab Andalusian writer, an outstanding example of the typical Arab polygraph, author of poetry, rhymed prose and linguistic treatises. His renown is due to the fact that he wrote a masterpiece belonging to the *maqāmah* genre, an ornate narrative literary genre couched in rhymed prose and containing passages of poetry. This genre represents a counter-genre to noble literary genres such as epics, romances of chivalry, sermons, holy scripts, etc. and may be considered as an ancestor to further picaresque literature. The title of this master piece is *al-Maqāmāt al-Luzūmiyyah*. Although the name of the author, together with the title of his outstanding work are frequently cited by biographers and reference books from the period of his life, it was not until 1982 that the first edition of this work appeared in Egypt, providing readers with access to the source material that had until then been preserved only in a large number of manuscripts all around the Islamic and Western Europe libraries. Another Moroccan edition was published in 1995, which improves many readings of the intricate Arabic text, together with a complete Spanish translation in 1999 and, finally, an English version by James T. Monroe in 2002, all of which allows scholars and readers the task of analyzing and appreciating the value of this work, which has been celebrated as one of the most important examples of the Andalusian ornate prose literature.

It may be inferred from his most commonly cited *nisbah*, *al-Saraqusṭī*, which is the name indicating his place of origin, that he was born in the city of Saraqusṭah (Spanish Zaragoza, English Saragossa) into a family from the distinguished Arab tribe of the Banū Tamīm, of which numerous members had settled in al-Andalus, from the period of the conquest in the eighth century. The other *nisbah*, *al-Aṣtarkūnī*, suggests that he or his family were associated with the now abandoned fortress town of Estercuel de Ribaforada, in the province of Navarra, just a few kilometers from the city of Tudela, by the river Ebro, about 65 kilometers northwest of Saragossa. The name of this small village probably stems from the Old Spanish '*estercuelo* or *estercol*,' both meaning the place where the manure is left, thus suggesting that it was not an important settlement. Biographers do not specify approximately when al-Saraqusṭī or his ancestors settled down in Saragossa. However, based on the words of most of his biographers, who state that he achieved a reputed and honored place in the court of the Banū Hūd, the Arab dynasty of Saragossa whose most important rulers reigned from 1046 to 1110, it is quite safe to assume that he received his early education in that city.

At that time, the city of Saragossa was the main center of the Northern Province of al-Andalus, and therefore attracted a significant number of poets and cultivated individuals from all over the Iberian Peninsula. It was under the rule of the famous Banū Hūd that the "taifa" of Saragossa experienced its most brilliant period of culture, which occurred together with a relatively stable political situation. In this milieu, al-Saraqusṭī received his first instruction and developed his early career. A detailed list of the teachers from whom al-Saraqusṭi learned, not only in his native land, but also in other Andalusian towns, may be consulted in the introduction written by Ḍayf in his edition of the *al-Maqāmāt al-Luzūmiyyah* (1982, 15-23), where he lists more than fifteen teachers, including such famous individuals as 'Abd Allāh ibn Muḥammad Baṭalyawsī (1052-1127), also known as Ibn Sīd of Badajoz, and Muḥammad ibn ʿAbd Allāh Ibn al-ʿArabī (1076-1148) of Seville.

Information provided by the original sources about his life and career is very scanty, as stated by all modern sources which deal with the figure of al-Saraqusṭī. It seems that he spent most of his life traveling all around al-Andalus where he visited the most renowned cities in order to attend the classes of the great teachers of that time, especially in Cordoba, Granada and Seville. This is the "search of knowledge," the way Andalusians and Arabs used to build up their scientific or literary education. At a non-specified stage, once he had gained a solid reputation among his colleagues, based on guidelines for obtaining knowledge of Islamic civilization, the student became the teacher and began offering his own classes on linguistic, literary and religious matters to other students who came to him. We are not informed by sources about any travel on his part to the Eastern Islamic countries, unlike many other Andalusian authors, who profitted from the pilgrimage by attending the classes of prestigious Eastern teachers and bringing back to al-Andalus the new ideas and trends from the Islamic heartland. However, it is clear from considering the teachers he studied with (see Monroe 1997, 8 and Ḍayf 1982, 15-23) that he was well aware of the innovations occurring in the East, even the most progressive and revolutionary ones, in contrast to the traditional conservative education of Andalusian cultivated people of his time. Some of the available sources (see details in Monroe, 1997, 3-5) tell us that our author was observed on the road, traveling on his camel across the deserts that stretch between Granada and Almería, on his way to visit Rafīʿ al-Dawlah, the governor of the latter city, himself a poet, to whom al-Saraqusṭī dedicated some odes. This travel must have taken place, at very latest, before the year 1091. It seems also, in accordance with the sources, that al-Saraqusṭī corresponded with Muḥammad ibn ʿAbd Allāh Ibn al-ʿArabī, when this latter famous philosopher and Sufi returned from the Middle East and settled down in Seville, someimte after the year 1099. Al-Saraqustī studied in the cities of Valencia and Cordoba at an unspecified date with the grammarian and philosopher ʿAbd Allāh ibn Muḥammad Baṭalyawsī, probably not later than the year 1106. It is reported that during 1114 and 1115, al-Saraqusṭī attended the lectures on Islamic tradition (*ḥadīth*) of Ḥusayn ibn Muḥammad Ibn Sukkarah (d. 1120 or 1121), with "an extreme care in learning everything the teacher transmitted." In the year 1118 a man named Ayyūb ibn Muḥammad ibn Wahb ibn Muḥammad Bakr ibn Sahl ibn Ayyūb (d. 1180), himself from Saragossa, claims to have met and studied with our author in Granada. In this year, 1118, the Saragossa fell to the Christians. This historic fact prevented al-Saraqusṭī from returning to his home-land and forced him to make Cordoba his base, from which he continued to visit the major Andalusian centers of knowledge. In the city of Cordoba, al-Saraqusṭī met one of his most brilliant disciples (together with Aḥmad ibn Muḥammad ibn Ibrāhīm ibn Yaḥyā ibn Ibrāhīm ibn Khalaṣah al-Ḥimyarī (1129-1213), also called Abū Jaʿfar), namely Aḥmad ibn ʿAbd al-Raḥmān Ibn Maḍā' (1119-1195 or 1196), one of the greatest grammarians of the Almohad age. He studied with al-Saraqusṭī around the years 1130-1140. In that year, al-Saraqusṭī began suffered from a chronic illness and finally died in Cordoba at noon on Wednesday the 21st of Jumādà I, in the year 538, that is to say, December 8, 1143. Thus, we can establish that his literary production came to an end at about 1140.

The information collected by the sources provides us with a sketchy insight into the life and career of al-Saraqusṭī, a prestigious writer capable of writing more than one literary genre, as was the not-infrequently the case in Andalusian civilization. According to our records, he did not hold any official position such as secretary, nor did he hold an administrative position under any of the governors to whom he dedicated some of his odes. It seems, as we suggested before, that thoroughout his life he remained interested in the renewal of political ideas and the new philosophic developments taking place in other Islamic lands. This notwithstanding, it is quite difficult to detect in his works the trends and ideas he adopted during his educational years, because the works of al-Saraqusṭī are highly formal and this prevents them from giving a clear picture of his own thinking. Even if his works do not cast much light into the individual, it is interesting to examine his writings to gain a broader view of al-Saraqusṭī.

To begin with, his poetry can be divided into two groups. The first group is the large number of verses included in the text of the *Maqāmāt* which will be treated below. The second consists of verses collected by his biographers or scattered in reference works on Andalusian literature. The few verses that have reached us constitute a brief *diwān*. To be sure, it is only a minor part of his actual poetic production. The exact contents are five pieces of love-poetry in a lyric style, which includes topics related to Bacchic themes, subjects which were highly esteemed by the readers of Andalusian poetry. On the other hand, five separate pieces of panegyric style are preserved. They are dedicated primarily to the governor of the city of Almería, the famous and cited *supra Rafī' al-Dawlah de Almería.* An attentive reading of these selections, completely different from those included in the text of the *Maqāmāt* shows clearly that al-Saraqusṭī was a talented poet, capable of composing love poetry in a fine, ornate style, utilizing two different poetic patterns. One type is love-poetry as characterized by the *'udhrī* style of love which is a type of platonic courtly love, in which the relationships are always chaste and the beloved does not respond with physical actions to the feelings of the lover and narrator of the poem. Thus, the poem produces a suffering which could be labeled as a kind of masochism. On the other hand, al-Saraqusṭī wrote some love poems with much more modern qualities. These, in fact, represent the topics and themes of hedonism and the spirit represented by the Latin adage *carpe diem.* Both types of poetic excerpts may be found in original Arabic texts in some of the anthologies which discuss al-Saraqusṭī. A complete English version of these poems was produced by James T. Monroe (1997:31-7). A partial Spanish translation of some of the most distinguished pieces was presented by Ferrando (1999: XIV-XVI).

The *Kitāb al-Musalsal fi 'l-gharīb lughat al-'arab* (The book of Concatenation, on Rare Words in the Language of the Arabs) is one of the works by al-Saraqusṭī that has survived. It is a linguistic treatise consisting of fifty chapters. Each chapter begins with a poetic quotation including a rare or obscure word from a well-known line of poetry. Starting from this word, the author provides another word, a synonym of the first one, but with a double meaning. The third word is another synonym of the second, also with a double meaning. This chain of related words stretches through the entire chapter, concluding with a last word illustrated with another example of a line of poetry famous in the Arabic literature. Al-Saraqusṭī appears in this work as a powerful lexicographer, capable of distinguishing most of the subtleties of the Arabic language, soaring from one meaning of obscure, rare and ambivalent words to another. Even if we, from our modern perspectives, cannot appreciate the value of this kind of intricate and highly erudite work, there is no doubt that this linguistic treatise justifies al-Saraqusṭī's fame as an outstanding lexicographer. According to Monroe (1997:13-14), this book is not a frivolous enterprise, as it might appear at first sight. Instead, it was an essential feature of allegorical interpretation, and provides a device whereby scholars could memorize the multiple meanings of Arabic words they needed to know in order to interpret holy text allegorically. This way of presenting linguistic material connects our author with Muʿtazilite methodology and schools.

According to one of his biographers (Ibn al-Abbār, Ḥullah I, 204), al-Saraqusṭī worked on the compilation an edition of the *dīwān* of the famous Andalusian Muḥammad Ibn ʿAmmār (1031-1084 or 1085) of Silves (now Portugal)' a governor and poet who visited the city of Saragossa several times. The compilation of this *dīwān* should have taken place before the death of the poet, that is to say, before 1083, seemingly in the youth of al-Saraqusṭī. However, there is not enough evidence to assure that this information, provided by only one source, is reliable. Nothing more is known to us about this alleged work.

The most important and renowned work by al-Saraqusṭī is his major literary work, a collection of fifty nine tales which are essentially picaresque in nature. These tales are written in a combination of rhymed prose and poetry, and are known to us as *al-Maqāmāt al-Luzūmiyyah,* because the author follows strictly a kind of rhymed prose created by the blind poet Abū'l-ʿAlā' al-Maʿarrī (973-1058), labeled as *luzūm mā lā yalzam*, which means, "to observe [a rule] that is not compulsory." This is a technique of inserting one or more unrequired rhyming consonants before the single rhyming consonant that is required in Arabic prosody. This innovation is applied by our author both to the rhymed prose as well as to the poetry contained in the *Maqāmāt*. Other names applied to this collection of picaresque tales are *al-Maqāmāt al-Saraqusṭiyyah*, referring to the home land of the author and *al-Maqāmāt al*-Qurṭubihyyah, referring to the fact that al-Saraqusṭī probably composed and finished his major work in that city, surely after the Christian conquest of Saragoss (1188).

The two available Arabic editions of *al-Maqāmāt al-Luzūmiyyah* differ in the arrangement of the stories and include a different number of *maqāmāt*. The Moroccan edition by al-Warāglī (1995) contains 59 *maqāmāt* whereas the Egyptian editor, Ḍayf (1982) includes only 50 *maqāmāt*. In both English and Spanish translations the plan of the work of al-Warāglī has been preferred over the Egyptian edition, because the first one consulted a larger number of manuscripts, esspecially the oldest ones, thus producing a more complete and detailed edition than Ḍayf. In some instances, however, the translation or interpretation of Ḍayf seems to be more accurate. Al-Warāglī edits the last nine *maqāmāt* as an appendix to the main body of the book, which must be equivalent to the magic number fifty, like the earlier *Maqāmāt* by Abū Muḥammad al-Ḥarīrī (1054-1122). In any case, some scholars have postulated that these nine *maqāmāt* are simply an addition to the main text, and were not authored by al-Saraqusṭī himself, but by some of his disciples.

The work is arranged as a reflexion of the collection of *Maqāmāt* authored by al-Ḥarīrī of Basra. Al-Ḥarīrī's work, written in the Eastern part of the Islamic Empire, arrived in al-Andalus very quickly and was al-Saraqusṭī's main inspiration. In fact, all the elements of the Saragossa work mirror the source which was used by al-Saraqusṭī. Not only do both works agree in the linguistic virtuosity exhibited by the authors, but also in the regular narrative patterns and scenarios, together with the duration of each tale. More than that, the roles played by the characters are almost the same. Also, the extent and size of the poetry sections inserted in each *maqāmah* are once again the same in both collections. All these elements point to the fact that al-Saraqusṭī effectively took al-Ḥarīrī as his model and produced a faithful reflexion of his much esteemed work. This notwithstanding, there are a number of particular points in the *Maqāmāt* by al-Saraqusṭī that deserve a detailed examination to show that *al-Maqāmāt al-Luzūmiyyah* is more than a simple copy of its Eastern predecessor. The first point is the total number of the tales in the collection. In the introduction by the author (or the original editor), it is clearly indicated that the number of the tales is fifty, a round figure which is precisely the number used by al-Ḥarīrī. This is the number of tales included in Ḍayf's Egyptian edition. However, the other edition by al-Warāglī includes 59 tales. This disagreement between the editors comes from the fact that each one of them used a different manuscript as the basis of their edition. While Ḍayf preferred the manuscript known as Vaticano 372 Arabo (V), the Moroccan editor, al-Warāglī, based his edition on the manuscript known as Fayḍ Allāh Afandī 1761 (F). Although both manuscripts do contain the same number of *maqāmat*, namely 50, nine of the *maqāmāt* included in the F manuscript are not found in the V manuscript (namely the numbers 27, 28, 38, 44, 45, 47, 48, 49, and 50). In turn, nine of the *maqāmāt* included in the V manuscript are not recorded in the F manuscript. The way al-Warāglī chooses to solve this disagreement is to add an appendix containing the text of the nine *maqāmāt* that do not appear in his primary manuscript. On the other hand, it seems that the Egyptian editor, Ḍayf, considers that the nine *maqāmāt* not included in his base manuscript were not authored by al-Saraqusṭī and must be seen as false texts. This very point is dealt with by another Egyptian scholar, Iḥsān ʿAbbās, in his work *Fann al-maqāmah fī'l-qarn al-sādis* (Alexandria: Dār al-Maʿārif), 54-58, where it is proposed that the nine tales not included in the V manuscript are either false texts, or the work of some of al-Saraqusṭī's disciples or readers, or even nothing but tentative essays by al-Saraqusṭī that were finally rejected and not included in the ultimate form of his major literary piece as it was transmitted to his disciples.

Only some of the *Maqāmāt* bear a specific title, namely numbers 12, 16, 17, 20, 25, 26, 30, 31, 34-41, 43, 46, and 51-59. This title may refer to a character appearing in the tale, or to a given event. For instance, we have the *maqāmah of the bear* (35), the *maqāmah of the wine* (20), the *maqāmah of the lion* (39), the *maqāmah of the horse* (34), and so on. Several of the titles allude to a geographical or cultural reference, that is to say, the place in which the story takes place or the human atmosphere: the *maqāmah of Tarifa* (43) and the *maqāmah of the Berbers* (41). Some other titles refer to a stylistic or technical feature that distinguish a given *maqāmah* from the rest of the series. This is the case with the *maqāmah* number 16, named as *the triple'* because of the fact that it presents the rhyme organized by trios instead of the usual couples of rhymes in the other *maqāmāt*. Number 17 is called the *inlayed maqāmah'* for it includes an additional non required rhymed word before the typical rhymed ending word of each segment of the rhymed prose. *Maqāmāt* 51 to 55 bear the name of the rhyming consonant, which stands the same all through the *maqāmah*. Finally, *maqāmāt* 56 to 59 include a subtitle indicating that the rhymes are arranged in alphabetical order, from *alif* to *yā*. In this point, al-Saraqusṭī differs from his outstanding predecessors, both Badīʿ al-Zamān Aḥmad ibn al-Ḥusayn al-Hamadhānī (circa 358/969–398/1008) and al-Ḥarīrī, because they included geographical or thematic titles, at least in the manuscripts that have survived, in all of their *Maqāmāt*. The lack of titles for a large part of the *al-Maqāmāt al-Luzūmiyyah*, together with the fact that the extant manuscripts seemingly go back to two different archetypes, suggest to us that the author, al-Saraqusṭī, did not transmit to his disciples a definite, complete version of his master piece, unlike many other authors, who usually approved an "official" version of their works together with the permission for transmitting it to other disciples. The divergences attested in the manuscripts were thus the result of emendations or variants made by the author himself, or, less probably, to textual corruptions originating from the process of transmission from one disciple to another.

There is another interesting aspect in the work of al-Saraqusṭī that we cannot fail to observe and discuss. It is remarkable that, throughout the series of *Maqāmāt*, references to the Islamic West, and even to al-Andalus, the homeland of the author, are very few. Only three of the *maqāmāt* take place outside of the Eastern lands. They are the *maqāmah* number 41, that of the Berbers, which takes place in the vicinity of Tangier, close to the Straits of Gibraltar, the *maqāmah* number 43, that of Ṭarīf or Ṭarīfa, situated in the town of Tarifa, close to Gibraltar, and the *maqāmah* number 29, that of Qayrawān, which takes place in that Tunisian city. In addition to that, there are no references, or only very few, to Andalusian celebrities nor to events related to the history of al-Andalus. As a result of this, the work, seen in its entirety, could well be perceived as the work of an eastern Arab author. The reason for that is probably an intentional *orientalism* or exotism that invited the author to place the events of his *Maqāmāt* in the lands of the Eastern Islam, preferably in the Arabian Peninsula and the regions of Persia (nowadays Iran), but also in some more exotic lands, such as the Indian Peninsula, China, and even some other more obscure places. It would be exceedingly simple, in order to explain this peculiarity, to consider that a desire to imitate eastern models led our author to borrow all the place names of towns and lands used in eastern sources and in the works of his predecessors, esspecially those found in the greatly admired *Maqāmāt* by al-Ḥarīrī, whom al-Saraqusṭī undoubtedly wanted to emulate. It would then be another of al-Saraqusṭī's "lack of originality," as we have previously indicated in other aspects of his work. Instead, we are prone to consider that this lack of Eastern and Andalusian references may be connected to al-Saraqusṭī's feeling of pessimism and even resignation in the face of the historical occurring during his times in Andalusian society, starting with the disintegration of Islamic central power, through the formation of the kingdoms of *taifas* and then the new dominance of the Almoravids, the Berber dynasty that came to regain Islamic dominance over most of the Iberian Peninsula as a way to stop the progress of the Christian Reconquista. It was much like looking back to the eastern Islamic empire, where the most brilliant and glorious pages of the history of the Arab peoples and Arab Islamic civilization were once written. Eastern Islamic culture was always the mirror Andalusians tended to look at thoroughout its history. It is not necessary, in our opinion, to identify the lack of Western references with a lack of interest in al-Saraqusṭī's own society or with a feeling of detachment from the course of Andalusian history. This apect would better be interpreted as irony, creating a sharp criticism of a decadent society in which the purity of races and moral values were in trouble. It was a desperate call to recover the very essence of Islamic culture and way of life.

The narrative structure and arrangement adopted in the *Maqāmāt* follow the broad lines of that adopted by the predecessor of al-Saraqusṭī, al-Ḥarīrī, in his fifty *maqāmāt.*Each *maqāmah* begins with the so-called *isnād* or chain of transmission, which is the procedure used in *ḥadīth* in order to demonstrate the authenticity of the contents. In the *maqāmah*, the same device is used ironically (the chain shown in the *maqāmah* is very brief, only two transmitters, and there is no way to verify it)' to indicate from the very beginning the fictional nature of the genre, as well as its subversive spirit. After that, the narrator informs the reader about the arrival of the second narrator, called al-Sā'ib ibn Tammām, during one of his numerous travels throughout the world, at a given city or place within the Islamic regions. It may be observed, in general terms, that the character of the narrator goes from one place to another, at the whim of destiny, and not by his own choice. This is a sort of inexorable determinism, very well represented in many branches of Arabic literature. Once the narrator reaches his destination, he finds, in many diverse places and contexts, and under many different aspects and guises, the central character, that is to say, the rogue called Abū Ḥabīb al-Sadūsī, an Omani. This rogue usually attracts the attention of an audience with a very elegant and brilliant speech. After persuading people that his words are true, Abū Ḥabīb manages to benefit from the situation, exploiting the innocence of his listeners, whom he asks for money on the basis of many different pretexts, consistently acting like a con man. Sometimes he steals out during the night or makes unfair use of their carelessness. Then the rogue, Abū Ḥabīb, proceeds to run away from the scene with the money in his pocket. It is only after this exhibition of rhetorical brilliance or after his deceptive performance, that al-Sā'ib ibn Tammām' persecutes him, identifies him and criticizes him for his immoral behavior during the *maqāmah*. In some cases, the narrator himself is one of the people damaged by the tricks performed by the rogue. In other *maqāmat*, he is only a witness of the facts, and in other cases he acts as a silent accomplice. Abū Ḥabīb's reaction in this situation, as in most of the *maqāmāt* is to ask al-Sā'ib to leave and to remain silent. In some of the tales we witness some confrontation between the two characters, at times very sharp, at times less. In order to justify his wicked behavior, Abū Ḥabīb ends the *maqāmah* by reciting a few "wisdom" verses. In these pieces of poetry the rogue develops his main ideas, which lie somewhere between pure materialism, in which he is almost insensitive to human misery, and the respect and admiration for the code of honor which was allegedly current among traditional Arab nobles and gentlemen. After this moral episode, the *maqāmah* concludes with the departure of Abū Ḥabīb, who is at this stage ready for a new adventure in other lands among another audience, which will begin in the next *maqāmah*. We are faced with a cyclical structure without any hierarchical order, and without any chronological or spatial limits. A summary of the narrative structure applied to most *maqāmāt* could resemble the following, based on the words of Douglas Young, in his review article of the Spanish translation of the *Maqāmāt*, (2001, 76):

1. Travel and arrival at a destination
2. Encounter with an unidentified orator
3. Orator's speech soliciting gifts (variant: ruse of the orator)
4. Orator obtains goods or money
5. Attempt to flee
6. Narrator's recognition of the rogue
7. Farewell and departure

This narrative structure means that the main character, that of the rogue, is generally exposed to two tests. The first one is obtaining money or goods (number 4)' which may be solved within the text of the tales in two different ways, depending on the preferred variant. The second test faced by the rogue is that of the fleeing from the audience whom he had deceived or even robbed. This flight is not only away from the audience, but also from the narrator, al-Sā'ib, who, in many of the *maqāmāt* represents another obstacle. After passing both tests, a new development takes place at the beginning of a new *maqāmah*, where the rogue arrives at a new place, but behaves in the same manner. As a result of this structure' we do have a narrative continuum, a consistent link between particular episodes. It should be indicated, however, that not all *maqāmat* fit well into the same structure, which is, without doubt, clearly a simple one. Some deviations from this general structure occur. For example, in some *maqāmāt* we witness the introduction of love episodes, although in a quiet superficial manner (numbers 10 and 43). Two *maqāmāt* deal with aspects of literary criticism: *maqāmah* number 30, the *maqāmah* of the poets, and *maqāmah* number 40, the *maqāmah* of the prose and the poetry. In *maqāmah* number 50, the death of the rogue Abū Ḥabīb is described, as well as the other character, al-Sā'ib visiting his grave. Other characters who appear occasionally in some of the *Maqāmāt* are the two sons of the rogue Abū Ḥabīb, who are called Ḥabīb and Gharīb, or his daughter. These secondary characters usually play the role of assistants to their father during one of his tricks or traps.

The ambiance, the story, the secondary characters and even the action are nothing but subordinate elements that may vary, but integrate themselves into a stable, rigid structure. We are faced with a fictional tale which is constructed around the character of the rogue, a very controversial figure not only because of its changeable ideas and moral values, but also because of the fact that someone who is not well established in the society, who is not a rich man or a member of the cultivated elite, is capable of of defeating many a wise individual in many a field of knowledge, such as literature, astronomy, medicine, etc. by means of the richness and brilliance of his oratory. The point of irony lies in the fact that the protagonist of the tales is nothing but an antihero, a wandering individual completely devoid of scruples, who acts in a very wicked manner but who speaks in a highly formal way, expressing many irreproachable ideas and principles. This character finally obtains everything he was looking for, deceiving many virtuous and decent people to benefit himself, without disregard for the troubles caused his victims.

Such a contradiction between words and deeds is not devoid of a component of criticism for Andalusian society of the late eleventh and the first half of the twelfth century, and even towards the whole of the Arab world and its civilization. It is a criticism dominated in some respect by a strong feeling of pessimism in anticipation of events which were taking place in the Iberian Peninsula at that time. We should remember at this point that during al-Saraqusṭī's life, a war atmosphere pervaded the Iberian Peninsula. The ideal of an Arab society full of purity, honor and spirit of chivalry was only loosely held, even disregarded due to the course of events. The fall of this model caused some decay in time-honored social behavior' that is to say, a real crisis of traditional values and models of life. It seems to us that the character of the antihero represents those individuals who were set apart from the typical virtues and values of the Bedouin Arab world. This antihero secures personal benefit from two of the most outstanding virtues of that ancient society: generosity and hospitality. By presenting such facts, the author criticizes the abandonment of traditional values and behavior. In summary, the *maqāmāt* are far more than a mere pretext to exhibit an author's eloquence and his linguistic virtuosity, as some scholars have proposed. The *maqāmāt* represents a sharp criticism of the decadence of the Andalusian society. It is certainly not a beautiful package with nothing inside.

The *Maqāmāt* are written, in *saj'*, or rhymed prose. In addition, a large number of poetic fragments are inserted in the narrative context of every *maqāmah*, giving it its particular flavor. Poetry is not just a complement but an important part of the narrative structure. It is employed to bring a close to the story, to summarize some facts, to present the views of the characters, mostly the rogue, Abū Ḥabīb, and so on. In this respect, al-Saraqusṭī is indebted to his predecessor, al-Ḥarīrī, who also employed abundant selections of poetry within the text of his *maqāmāt*. Based on the role played by these selections of poetry and on the style and technique, they can be divided in two types. The first type consists of descriptive and narrative verses, including some selections related to love and wine odes. They act as a sort of secondary elements within the frame of the story. The second type, represented by most of the included pieces of poetry, is that of wisdom and exemplary poetry. Abū Ḥabīb, the rogue, makes use of this kind of poetry to present his views and attitudes towards life. By doing this, he reveals all the ideas and motifs which move him and control his apparently inexplicable acts. This second type of poetry deals mainly with the question of the power of destiny seen as something immutable and powerful as opposed to the capacity of human beings to handle their lives and to guide their acts in a free way, that is to say, according to free will. In some of the "wisdom" pieces, a strong feeling of bitterness towards the vicissitudes of destiny may be clearly observed. Destiny is presented as the sole factor controlling human beings. It is not the narrator, in fact, who freely chooses the development of his movements. On the contrary, fate controls all things and move human beings wherever it wants. A certain feeling of resignation in regard to the brevity of life is detected. This feeling is usually expressed, and not only in the poetic pieces, by means of the motif ubi sunt, that is to say, to wonder where the past glories of man are' since all of them perished without exception in spite of their fame, power or glory. The inevitability of death is another repeated topic dealt with in this context. Since it is absolutely clear that destiny is a powerful enemy, the most direct response is an invitation to enjoy the moment, the delightfulness of life. This is the ancient literary *topos* called *carpe diem*, in other words, enjoy the moment, which is alluded in the text of the *maqāmāt* many times. One can interpret this answer in terms of irony, or at least as the logical result of the subversive values represented by the picaresque character of the rogue. This notwithstanding, it seems that the author does not propose engrossing oneself in delights from resignation and desperation. It is rather a kind of revenge taken on destiny' a fight in which the sign of victory is the attainment of benefit and delight, always from the perspective of pride and arrogance, much as was the custom of Bedouin Arab chevaliers. It is, no doubt, an ephemeral victory. On this basis, the poet often invites the reader, through the narrator's words, to face destiny and not remain silent and immovable before the vicissitudes of the fate. According to this way of presenting the facts, those who emerge victorious are only those who face the bitterness of fate with a good deal of firmness and determination. However, if we take into account that the rogue is a very contradictory character, who trifles with the others by hiding his thoughts and deceiving them, it is not unusual to hear invitations to the good path and piety in his own voice. It is indeed a double standard. The contradiction lies in the fact that, on the one hand, everything is acceptable when looking for personal benefit. On the other hand, the values and virtues of nobility, honesty and generosity are often praised and recommended. A fine game of irony against sincerity is presented throughout the *maqāmāt*. At the end of the work, it is not clear whether Abū Ḥabīb repents of his sins, when, in *maqāmah* number 50, he seems to give up committing them and chooses a life of contrition and asceticism according to the content of the following verses˙ "I comitted a lot of sins, my God; you are well aware of that. Please, forgive me and be generous in your compassion, my God, the owner of destiny." Given the usual hypocrisy in the figure of the rogue, we do not know precisely whether this repentance is true, followed by a new path opening towards moral propriety, or, whether, to the contrary, it is one more of the tricks played by the author, who would close his trick in that way, with an official conversion of the rogue into an ascetic pious man, just to conform to social rules, or only as an ironic finishing touch. In conclusion, it is significant to propose that the intention of the author is to move the reader towards a critical attitude. Since al-Saraqusṭī had a rather negative and pessimistic view of the course of events taking place in his time. He was propounding an active, combative position, instead of the passivity in the face of events, especially before the progress of the Christian Reconquista and the break up of the Islamic power, i.e., the state of al-Andalus in the Iberian Peninsula.

Some of the most outstanding features in the work by al-Saraqusṭī belong to the domain of form and aesthetics. The use of rhymed prose, for instance, does not consist only of arranging the narrative material into rhymed couples. The question goes much further. The practitioners of the *maqāmah* gender usually include many morphophonemic parallel elements, in an almost systematic way. This parallelism, which benefits from the regularity of morphological shape of Arabic words, conforms, together with the disposition of rhymes, to the rhythmical basis of the *maqāmah*. But the most remarkable feature of the type of prose used by al-Saraqusṭī is the rhyme chosen by the author, for both prose and poetry sections of the *maqāmāt*. It consists of using a stricter system of rhyme, that is, using an additional rhymed consonant instead of the usual single consonant, following the innovation begun by the eastern blind poet al-Maʿarrī, who called his collection of poems *al-Luzūmiyyāt* a name later borrowed by al-Saraqusṭī or his own *Maqāmāt*. It seems *a priori* that this added difficulty, together with the linguistic virtuosity reflected in the use of a plethora of rhetorical figures and obscure and rare words, could mean a decrease of the literary value of the work. But, according to the opinion of some critics, and to a great extent according to our own opinion, it is remarkable that the literary style of the *maqāmāt* written by al-Saraqusṭī does not sound very artificial. Within natural limitations, it is a quite fluent and elegant prose. It could be safely affirmed, without any exaggeration, that the *al-Maqāmāt al-Luzūmiyyāh*, by al-Saraqusṭī are a major piece of literature, the only truly representative of the eastern genre in the lands of al-Andalus, a genre that, in its classical shape, reapidly acquired fame and prestige, to the point that it was admired throughout the Arab speaking lands, both in ancient and modern times. It is true that, for the Western reader, this work lacks action and is more ornate than current literature. One should note, as some of the orientalist critics have done, that formal aspects play an important, even dominant role in this work. But it is not legitimate to state that the content is insignificant and the form everything. We have seen earlier that the text of the *maqāmāt* does contain a considerable amount of social criticism. The *maqāmāt* by al-Saraqusṭī represents a new attitude towards life, an innovative ideology in the social and historical context of the Almoravid period of al-Andalus.

REFERENCES

Ignacio Ferrando Frutos, "La Maqama barbariyya de al-Saraqusti," *Anaquel de Estudios Arabes* 2 (1991): 119-129;

Ignacio Ferrando Frutos, "La maqāma de Ṭarīfa de al-Saraqusṭī," al-Qanṭara 18 (1997): 137-151;

Ignacio Ferrando Frutos, "Un poema estrófico (*musammaṭ*) en las *Maqāmāt Luzūmiyya* de as-Saraqusṭī," *Anaquel de Estudios Arabes* 7 (1996): 119-128;

Muḥammad ibn ʿAbd Allah Ibn al-Abbār, *Kitāb al-Ḥullah al-siyarā'*, 2nd ed., ed. Ḥusayn Mu'nis (Cairo: Dār al-Maʿārif, 1985);

Hugh Kennedy, *Muslim Spain and Portugal: a Political History of al-Andalus* (London: Longman, 1996);

James T. Monroe, "al-Saraqusti, Ibn al-Aštarkūwī: Andalusī Lexicographer, Poet and Author of al- *Maqāmāt al-luzūmiyya*," *Journal of Arabic Literature* 29 (1998): 31-58;

James T. Monroe, *The Art of Badī' al-Zamān al-Hamadhānī as Picaresque Narrative* (Beirut: Beirut Center for Arab and Middle East Studies, American University of Beirut, 1983);

Ismail El-Outmane, "La *Maqāmah* en al-Andalus," *Foro Hispánico: la sociedad andalus y sus tradiciones literarias*, ed. Otto Zwartjes (Amsterdam: Rhodopi, 1994): 105-125;

Douglas Young, "Review article: Las sessiones del Zaragocí," *Journal of Arabic Literature* 32:1 (2001): 74-83.

al-Sharīf al-Raḍī

(969–27 June 1015)

TERRI DEYOUNG
University of Washington

WORKS

Dīwān (Collected poems);
Khasā'is al-Imām 'Alī (Special Characteristics of the Imam ʿAlī);
al-Rasā'il al-mutabādalah bayna 'l-Ṣābi wa 'l-Sharīf al-Raḍī (Letters Exchanged between [Abū Isḥāq] al-Ṣābī and al-Sharīf al-Raḍī);
Ḥaqā'iq al-ta'wīl fī mutashābih al-tanzīl (Truths of Interpretation in the Unclear Verses of the Revelation);
Nahj al-balāghah (The Path of Eloquence);
Talkhīs al-bayān fī majāzāt al-Qur'ān (The Summary of Clarity in the Figurative Language of the *Qur'ān*);
al-Majāzāt al-Nabawiyyah (The Prophet's Figurative Language).

Editions

Dīwān al-Sayyid al-Raḍī 'l-mūsawī 'l-'alawī (Bombay: Maṭbaʿat Nukhbat al-Akhbār, 1889);
Dīwān al-Sharīf al-Raḍī, ed. Aḥmad ʿAbbās al-Azharī and Muḥammad Salīm al-Labābīdī (Beirut: Dār Ṣādir, 1961);
Dīwān al-Sharīf al-Raḍī, ed. ʿAbd al-Fattāḥ Muḥammad al-Ḥulw (Giza: Hajr, 1992);
Dīwān al-Sharīf al-Raḍī, ed. Yūsuf Shukrī Faraḥāt (Beirut: Dār al-Jīl, 1995);
Khasā'is *amīr al-mu'minīn* al-Imām ʿAlī (Najaf: n.p., 1948-1949);
Khasā'is amīr al-mu'minīn 'Alī ibn Abī Ṭālib (Beirut: Mu'assasat al-Aʿlamī li 'l-Maṭbūʿāt, 1986);
al-Rasā'il al-mutabādalah bayna 'l-Ṣābī wa 'l-Sharīf al-Raḍī, ed. Muḥammad Yūsuf Nijm (Kuwait: Dā'irat al-Maṭbūʿāt wa 'l-Nashr, 1961);
Ḥaqā'iq al-ta'wīl fī mutashābih al-tanzīl, ed. Muḥammad al-Riḍā Āl Kāshif al-Ghitā' with an introduction by ʿAbd al-Ḥusayn al-Ḥillī 'l-Najafī (Baghdad: al-Lajnah al-ʿIlmiyyah min Aʿdā' Muntadā 'l-Nashr, 1936);
Haqā'iq al-ta'wīl fī mutashābih al-tanzīl, ed. Muḥammad al-Riḍā Āl-Kāshif al-Ghitā' (Beirut: Dār al-Adwā', 1986);
Nahj al-balāghah, 1 vol. in 4 parts, ed. Muḥammad ʿAbduh (Beirut: Dār Ihyā' al-Turāth al-ʿArabī. n.d.);
Sharḥ nahj al-balāghah, ed. Ibn Abī 'l-Ḥadīd and Abū Ḥamīd ibn Hibat Allāh (Cairo: Maṭbaʿat ʿĪsā 'l-Bābī 'l-Halabī, 1959-1964);
Talkhīs al-bayān fī majāzāt al-Qur'ān, ed. Muḥammad ʿAbd al-Ghanī Ḥasan (Cairo: Dār Ihyā' al-Kutub al-ʿArabī, 1955);
al-Majāzāt al-Nabawiyyah (Baghdad: Maṭbaʿat al-Ādāb, 1910); ed. with an introduction by Maḥmūd Muṣṭafā (Cairo: Maṭbaʿat Muṣṭafā 'l-Bābī 'l-Ḥalabī, 1938).

Translations

A.J. Arberry, *Arabic Poetry: a Primer for Students* (Cambridge: Cambridge University Press, 1965), 98-106;
ʿAlī ibn Abī Ṭālib, *Nahjul Balagha: Peak of Eloquence* compiled by Syed Razi, translated by Sayed Ali Reza with an introduction by Syed Mohamed Askari Jafery (Elmhurst, New York: Tahrike Tarsile Qur'an, 1978).

Al-Sharīf Ismāʿīl al-Raḍī was one of the most important intellectual figures in late tenth-century and early eleventh-century Iraq. He inspired a group of individuals who fostered a new, strong Shiite identity in this era, but over the centuries Sunnis have also read and been influenced by his work. An accomplished poet, highly admired during his lifetime, he inherited from Abū 'l-Ṭayyib al-Mutanabbī (915-965) and

Abū Firās ibn Sa'īd ibn Aḥmad ibn Ḥamdān al-Ḥamdānī (932-968) the mantle of leadership for a trend that emphasized classicizing tendencies in Arabic literature, celebrating the traditions of the formal three-part poem, the *qaṣīdah*. He also explored the intricacies of the *Qur'ān*, and he was deeply interested in the rhetorical tradition of the Arabic language. Combining both his rhetorical and religious interests, he compiled one of the most important formative texts of the Shiite Muslim tradition, a collection of speeches, letters, and sermons attributed to the Imam 'Alī ibn Abī Ṭālib (ca. 600-660), called *Nahj al-balāghah* (*The Peak of Eloquence*), which has never ceased to be a model for educating students of the Arabic language. In a society lacking an entrenched aristocracy, he was the closest in his age to a "poet-prince."

Abū 'l-Ḥasan Muḥammad ibn Abī Aḥmad al-Ḥusayn al-Mūsawī, later given the title of al-Sharīf al-Raḍī ("the Noble Content One"), was born in Baghdad in 970 to a life of wealth and privilege. But his family's high position was of relatively recent vintage. His father, Abū Aḥmad al-Ḥusayn, was appointed as marshal (*naqīb*) of the Shiite community in Baghdad only five years before his son's birth. Before that time, he had lived quietly in Basra. The family was descended from Mūsā 'l-Kāẓim (ca. 745–ca. 800), the seventh Shiite Imam, but they did not play a prominent role in public life before the rise of the Buwayhid dynasty, who occupied Baghdad and wrested control of the surrounding territories from the Abbasid dynasty in 945. The Buwayhids divided Iraq into smaller units, essentially city-states, each one ruled by a member of their family. At first, the Buwayhid ruler of Baghdad, Mu'izz al-Dawlah (915 or 916-967), appointed marshals from the Zaydī sect of Shiism, but when the marshal in 964, Ibn al-Dā'ī, fled eastward in an unsuccessful attempt to proclaim himself Imam (divinely sanctioned leader of the Muslim community), Mu'izz al-Dawlah appointed the deputy marshal in Basra, al-Raḍī's father, head of the community in Baghdad. Abū Aḥmad has already proved himself a master mediator, having served as emissary for Mu'izz al-Dawlah in delicate negotiations on several occasions. He was also married to Fātimah bint al-Ḥusayn (660 or 661-728 or 729), granddaughter of the former ruler of Daylam (on the southern Caspian sea) who had converted the tribesmen there to Shiite Islam. She further had a claim on Mu'izz al-Dawlah's family because she was niece to his chief wife. These connections, as well as his own demonstrated abilities, undoubtedly made Abū Aḥmad seem a natural choice for the office of Marshal (which had been instituted by the Buwayhids as a counterbalance to the power of the Abbasid caliphs in Baghdad).

Abū Aḥmad's hold over the office of marshal remained strong until his death in 1009, at the advanced age of 97. But his tenure did not always go smoothly. The most difficult period of his career began in 980, when 'Aḍud al-Dawlah (936-983), who had taken over from Mu'izz al-Dawlah's incompetent son 'Izz al-Dawlah in 977, imprisoned Abū Aḥmad and several other prominent members of his government in a castle in Fāris (southwestern Iran). The reasons given for this action are not entirely clear or consistent, but Abū Aḥmad remained confined for seven years. He was only released in early 987, four years after 'Aḍud al-Dawlah's death in 983. His father's disgrace was traumatic for the young al-Raḍī and occasioned some of his earliest poetry, including a 78-line poem, composed when he was in his teens, glorifying his family and his ancestors, in reply to aspersions cast by 'Aḍud al-Dawlah's chief vizier, who had remarked that the family spent too much time vaunting their noble lineage, rather than seeking to impress others by their accomplishments.

Even more salient was the poem he sent to his father upon hearing of 'Aḍud al-Dawlah's death (*Dīwān*, ed. Faraḥāt, 254):

Convey—you two—a message from me to [my father] Ḥusayn:
"The one who stood on the high mountain, looking down on you, has himself been swallowed up in the mud.
And that shooting star at whose flame you could warm yourself—
circumstances have reversed its light, now it's faded away.
And the stallion that wore its armor to the ends of the earth,

destruction has stretched him out, and made him kneel down."

Although the poem was revised later—according to the notation in the *Dīwān*—if it has not strayed too far from the original, it is actually notable for its restraint in an age when biting invective was much more the norm, limiting itself to pointing out the inevitability of death or misfortune while paying due attention to ʿAḍud al-Dawlah's undoubted gifts as a leader of men. This self-control, moderation, and absence of direct accusation against a family enemy can be seen as characteristic of al-Sharīf al-Raḍī's later work as well.

Because al-Raḍī's family was unusually prominent for a long period of time, the relationships between them are copiously documented for an age when such information was by no means routinely preserved. His relationship with his mother, for example, appears to have been an important formative influence on his life. When her husband was jailed and his own personal wealth sequestered, Fāṭimah bint al-Ḥusayn took charge of the family's welfare and her children's education, paying for their upkeep out of her own fortune. In a story—not necessarily apocryphal—related by one of al-Raḍī's Shiite biographers, the leading Shiite theologian of the time, Shaykh Muḥammad ibn Muḥammad al-Mufīd (d. 1022), had a dream one night in which Fāṭimah (d. 632 or 633), the Prophet Muḥammad's (d. 632) daughter (long dead), came to him, flanked by her sons al-Ḥasan and al-Ḥusayn (martyred by the Umayyads). In what seemed to him a strange request, she asked him to take charge of their education. The next morning, her namesake, Fāṭimah bint al-Ḥusayn, visited the Shaykh accompanied by al-Raḍī and his slightly older brother al-Murtaḍā and made the exact same plea. At what was no doubt considerable risk to himself (since it would have been dangerous to associate too closely with the family of a disgraced courtier), the surprised al-Mufīd immediately agreed and personally took charge of the boys' religious instruction, thus establishing a relationship that would endure throughout al-Raḍī's life.

Al-Raḍī's affection for his mother and his gratitude for her care and guidance during his unsettled adolescence never seems to have waned. When she died in 995, he mourned her with an elegy that, while being a model of restrained filial piety, nevertheless reflects genuine emotional turmoil and pain, as is shown in the following excerpt (*Dīwān*, ed. Faraḥāt, 27):

I would weep openly for you if such tears would slake my burning grief
 and I would speak, if such would heal my diseased body.
Or I would take refuge in sublime fortitude as a consolation,
 if such would actually console me.
But at times my tears lie in wait and gang up on me, while at others
 I can seek shelter in remembrance of my noble character and and my wish to restrain myself before others.

Obviously the strength of his feelings, and his inability to control them in these trying circumstances (as his social position dictated he should), constitute the dramatic tension in these lines. But here, and at the end of the poem, al-Raḍī also breaks the bonds of convention by speaking directly to his mother. These two asides sandwich a more conventional enumeration of his mother's ancestry and virtues in the third person that comprise the bulk of the poem, which gives these interludes even more force.

Al-Raḍī also had two sisters, Zaynab and Khadījah, who are much more shadowy figures in his life than his mother. But one of them (we do not know which) predeceased her brother, and the elegy he penned for her reveals the depth of his feelings, but in a very different style from that of his lament for his mother. The entire poem has been translated in A.J. Arberry's *Arabic Poetry*, where it is obvious that its central conceit casts al-Raḍī's sister in the role of the cruel beloved of the *naṣīb*, or prelude, of the conventional *qaṣīdah*, who always abandons the poet to follow her kin to new pastures where they may find sustenance for their camels. Normally, elegies in the Arabic tradition do not incorporate *naṣīb*s, since to speak of a love affair, no matter how sad the outcome, would be inappropriate on an occasion of mourning someone deceased. But in this case, the intensity of emotion generated by combining the forms serves al-Raḍī's purpose well in dramatizing the importance to him of his sister's death, as she assumes the place of the lost beloved forever beyond his reach. This literary maneuver, of course, differs considerably from his handling of his mother's commemoration but both in their way are equally effective. This adroit ability to adapt the form to particular circumstances while still respecting its conventions and traditions is probably why al-Raḍī became known to subsequent generations as the "prince of the elegy." The ability to highlight the personal and individual while never losing sight of the requirements of a very public form carries over into his later elegies for important male figures in his life, like his father and Shaykh al-Mufīd.

After his father, probably the member of his family with whom al-Raḍī had the most complex and emotionally sustaining relationship was his elder (by five years) brother, al-Sharīf al-Murtaḍā. The brothers seem to have had genuine respect for one another, and frequently worked together to support their father as representatives of the Shiite community. But al-Murtaḍā appears to have had a retiring nature, sustained by a deep interest in Shiite theology, and willingly left the role of public spokesperson for the most part to his more charismatic younger brother. Their relationship had its ups and downs over the years—probably enhanced by the fact that al-Murtaḍā, as the older brother, seems to have had better access to his parents' wealth—and there were times when they came close to being estranged. But they shared an interest in poetry, and history records at least one instance when literature was the avenue to their communication and reconciliation.

On this occasion, al-Murtaḍā decided to break the ice after a quarrel by sending his brother a *Dāliyyah* (a poem rhyming in the consonant "d") in the meter of *ṭawīl*, which begins:

The errant path of censure has laid bare fine lineaments of [old] pacts
and hastened the imminence of our reunion after distance.
Let us return the serenity of amity as it used to show
as one would do who never found escape from this.
And like you, I would be guided to return to guidance
and led aright to shun the path of self-righteousness.

Reportedly, al-Raḍī's heart softened upon hearing his brother's words, and he replied in a poem using the same meter and rhyme (*Dīwān*, ed. Faraḥāt, 299):

I wonder at the days, how they carry out my promises,
and how they bring close what had been distant to me.
I gave you my aversion publicly
but all my inner thought was fixed on how I might continue amity.

This poem is a graceful homage (and subtle challenge) to his brother's verse, full of word play and verbal echoes of its model in the original Arabic. It certainly did its work in reconciling the brothers and illustrates well the important role played by literary exchange in smoothing personal—as well as public—interactions among the Arab elite at this time. This practice, known as *mu'āraḍah*, or contrafaction, would become an entrenched part of Arabic literary culture in succeeding centuries, lasting into even early modern times.

We have already seen how al-Raḍī, along with his brother, came to receive his religious instruction at the hands of one of the most important Shiite theologians of the age, Shaykh al-Mufīd, whose understanding of Islam was profoundly affected by Muʿtazilī rationalistic speculation prevalent in Baghdad at the time. But he was to receive first-rate instruction under the tutelage of other masters in their fields as well. Most notable of these was Ibn Jinnī (d. 1002), the most important grammatical theoretician of the age, whose masterwork, *al-Khasā'is* (The Attributes) is a profound exploration of the nature of language whose insights continue to be relevant in modern times.

In addition, Ibn Jinnī had been an admirer and sometime companion of the greatest poet of the preceding generation, al-Mutanabbī, visiting him at the court in Aleppo, when the latter had been employed as chief panegyrist for the Ḥamdānid prince Sayf al-Dawlah (915 or 916-967). Al-Mutanabbī had also visited Iraq, praising the Buwayhid ruler 'Aḍud al-Dawla in his heyday. Ibn Jinnī had written two volumes of commentary on al-Mutanabbī's poetry, which he undoubtedly shared with his young pupil of rising literary ambitions. Al-Mutanabbī himself is reputed to have said of Ibn Jinnī, "he knows my poetry better than I do."

There were also other mentors who supervised the education of al-Raḍī and his brother al-Murtaḍā. Some of these were, formally, teachers of theirs. Such included many scholars of ḥadīth, who were later explicitly mentioned in al-Raḍī's prose works. Probably the most famous of them, after al-Mufīd, was 'Abd al-Jabbār ibn Aḥmad al-Asadābādī (d. 1024), a Shafi'i scholar and the leading Mu'tazilī theologian of his time, and who later became chief qāḍī (Islamic judge) for the Buwayhids. It was from him that al-Raḍī learned the principles of Mu'tazilism. He also studied Ḥanafī and Shafi'i law with Abū Muḥammad 'Abd Allāh al-Asadī 'l-Akfānī (d. 1014), a well-known judge in Baghdad. Later, he studied the Qur'ān (and probably Mālikī law) under the Sunni Mālikī jurist Ibrāhīm ibn Aḥmad al-Ṭabarī (d. 1002). Ibn Aḥmad developed a close relationship to both brothers, living with them in their house, and eventually became keeper of their Dār al-'Ilm (House of Knowledge), the library (containing, some say, as many as 80,000 volumes) and study institute founded by the brothers (perhaps in imitation of similar Fatimid initiatives in Cairo) after the family fortunes were restored in the 990s.

Linguistic study of Arabic also played a central role in al-Raḍī's early education. His earliest teacher of Arabic grammar was Abū Saʿīd al-Ḥasan ibn Baḥzād 'Abd Allāh al-Marzubān al-Ṣayrafī, who was known as the leading authority on the Basran school of grammar in Baghdad at the time, as well as being an expert in Ḥanafī law. But al-Ṣayrafī died early, in 979, and thus could not have

taught al-Raḍī for very long. Nevertheless, al-Raḍī's elegy (composed in 995) for al-Ṣayrafī's son Yūsuf—also a grammarian—contains reminiscences showing his regard for Yūsuf's father and gives evidence of his long closeness to the family (Dīwān, ed. Faraḥāt, 586-587). Probably of more lasting importance to al-Raḍī's grammatical education were the lessons he received from 'Alī ibn 'Īsā Abū 'l-Ḥasan al-Rabaʿī (939 or 940-1029), who was a pupil both of al-Ṣayrafī and Ibn Jinnī's mentor al-Ḥasan ibn Aḥmad Abū 'Alī 'l-Fārisī (901 or 902-987). Al-Rabaʿī was famous to later generations, mentioned by major figures like al-Suyūṭī (1445-1505), for his commentaries on the master treatise on Arabic grammar by 'Amr ibn 'Uthmān al-Sibawayh and his work on al-Fārisī's Kitāb al-Idāḥ (Book of Clarification). Al-Raḍī himself tells us that he read al-Idāḥ with al-Rabaʿī and that he was his teacher before Ibn Jinnī. The combined influence of al-Rabaʿī and Ibn Jinnī may be seen in the fact that al-Raḍī composed an elegy for their master al-Fārisī upon his death in 987, even though the latter had never been formally his teacher.

Once Ibn Jinnī became his teacher (probably by the mid-980s), he undoubtedly had an enormous impact on al-Raḍī's literary education as well as his study of Arabic. But there were others who also had the opportunity to shape his literary taste. Among his formal teachers, such would have included Abū 'Abd Allāh Muḥammad ibn 'Imrān ibn Mūsā, ibn Saʿīd ibn 'Abd Allāh al-Marzubānī (d. 994), who—besides his expertise on Mu'tazilism, which was widely respected—wrote an two influential descriptive works on the poetry and poets of his time, Mu'jam al-shu'arā' and al-Muwashshah fī ma'ākhidh al-'ulamā' 'alā 'l-shu'arā'. Al-Marzubānī was older than his two charges, dying without being memorialized by either brother, so we know little about the specific nature of his influence on his pupils in literary matters, though al-Murtaḍā cites him frequently in his theological works. With reference to the training al-Raḍī received in poetic composition, mention should also be made of a much younger man, Abū 'l-Ḥasan Muḥammad ibn Ja'far Muḥammad ibn Abū 'l-Ḥasan al-Jarrār, who taught the brothers about the Arab tribal genealogies, and probably in the process about desert life—subjects of great importance for poets who, like al-Raḍī and al-Murtaḍā, cultivated an atmosphere in their works that deliberately harked back to the early Islamic tribal past of their illustrious ancestors. Al-Raḍī may have also garnered valuable information about these subjects through the friendships he cultivated with the leaders of the great tribal confederations of the time (in whose praise he wrote a certain number of panegyric and elegiac poems), especially that of the ʿUqaylids, who controlled much of northern Iraq during the period.

Al-Raḍī's literary expertise may also have been enhanced by less formal relationships he developed in his adolescence during the 980s. The most immediately important of these would have been Abū Isḥāq Ibrāhīm al-Ṣābī (925-994), formerly chief clerk for Muʿizz al-Dawlah's influential and highly cultivated vizier, Abū Muḥammad al-Ḥasan ibn Muḥammad al-Muhallabī (903-963). Al-Ṣābī belonged to an established family of doctors who originally hailed from the Sabaean (pagan) community in the city of Harran, and he retained a lifelong interest in science and especially astronomy. But al-Ṣābī's skills in Arabic rhetoric and poetic composition so impressed his father that, according to anecdote, he gave his son permission to abandon medical study and try instead to enter the government bureaucracy. With time, he became the right-hand man of al-Muhallabī, and survived the latter's disgrace and dismissal in 963. But he eventually ran afoul of ʿAḍud al-Dawlah—like al-Raḍī's father—and ended up in prison (though not the same one as Abū Aḥmad). During al-Ṣābī's long incarceration (like Abū Aḥmad, he was only released after the death of ʿAḍud al-Dawlah), and until his death in 994, he and al-Raḍī carried on a regular correspondence, a part of which recently came to light and was published in Kuwait in 1961. These letters show how al-Raḍī may have learned the craft of producing elegant rhymed prose in chancery style from his mentor, who also imparted to him sage advice on proper conduct for a person of his station.

Along with the sound guidance of al-Ṣābī, al-Raḍī also received literary input from what was a far more questionable source. He seems to have formed a close bond during this period with the unconventional Shiite poet Abū ʿAbd Allāh al-Ḥusayn ibn Aḥmad Ibn al-Ḥajjāj (ca. 931–24 May 1001), whose scurrilous verse delighted many in the salons of Buwayhid society and outraged more conventional citizens. In terms of the style of their poetry, it is difficult to imagine a greater contrast than the work of the two poets. But in some of his early poems, al-Raḍī talks of his disinclination to be bound in by social convention, and this may reflect an influence of Ibn al-Ḥajjāj. At any rate, the bond between the two does not seem to have waned, for, when Ibn al-Ḥajjaj passed away in 1001, al-Radi elegized him and compiled a selection of his poetry in writing

Probably more congenial to al-Raḍī as a poet (or at least to his teacher Ibn Jinnī) would have been the model of the greatest panegyric poet working in Iraq during that period, ʿAbd al-ʿAzīz ibn ʿUmar Ibn Nubātah (939-1015). His poetry was of the kind that would have formed a better prototype for al-Raḍī's training. His work consists largely of panegyrics, many addressed to members of the Buwayhid family, so much so that he has been called the official court poet of Sharaf al-Dawlah (d. 989), eldest son of ʿAḍud al-Dawlah. Al-Raḍī, interestingly, would later compose an impressive twenty-six panegyrics to Sharaf al-Dawlah's younger brother, Bahā' al-Dawlah (d. 1012), who supplanted his elder brother in Baghdad in 989. Because Ibn Nubātah was a name also borne by a famous orator at the court of the Ḥamdānid ruler Sayf al-Dawlah in Aleppo, there is some confusion in the sources which of the two was formally engaged as a teacher for the brothers. Nevertheless, the closeness of al-Raḍī to ʿAbd al-ʿAzīz ibn ʿUmar Ibn Nubātah can be inferred by the fact that Abū 'l-Ḥusayn Mihyār ibn Marzawayh al-Daylamī (ca. 977–1037)—al-Sharīf al-Raḍī's best known pupil—composed a long and detailed elegy for Ibn Nubātah the poet when the latter died in 1015, the same year al-Raḍī passed away. Because of the strong affinities between their poems, al-Raḍī and Ibn Nubātah can be considered as belonging to the same literary school—unlike al-Raḍī and Ibn Ḥājjāj—although it is not entirely clear who should be considered the leader and who the follower.

The seven years of his father's imprisonment, then, should be considered the decisive time of al-Sharīf al-Raḍī's educational formation. They were also the years of his poetic apprenticeship, whether under the tutelage of Ibn Jinnī or Ibn Nubātah, or both. Most of the works that survive from these years in al-Raḍī's *Dīwān* are panegyrics, sent either to his father or recited before the Abbasid caliph reigning during that decade, al-Ṭā'ī' li-Allāh, who had been close to al-Raḍī's father and seems to have kept an eye out for his son. By al-Raḍī's youth it had become common practice to send poems (instead of reciting them in person) to patrons or other respected senior figures in society for the Persian holidays of Nawruz (in late March) and Mihrajan (in the autumn), as well as on the Islamic holidays, which, based on a lunar calendar, cycled throughout the year.

The earliest of al-Raḍī's poems are clearly novice pieces. They occasionally exhibit brilliant individual lines, but overall the design of the works should be regarded as weak. By the middle of the decade, however, the poems display a more assured architectonic quality. They also show an increasing interest in foregrounding the *naṣīb*, which, as Arab poets and their patrons moved away from the desert environment, had come to play a less central role in the formal Arabic panegyric *qaṣīdah*. Following the precedent of al-Mutanabbī—who had highlighted this practice in his panegyrics to Sayf al-Dawlah—al-Raḍī began to use the depiction of the relationship between the poet and his beloved in the *naṣīb* as a way to explore indirectly the frustrations experienced by the poet when the patron refused to satisfy his desires (for money, of course, rather than kisses or trysts) or otherwise did not live up to his expectations.

An interesting example of this growing assurance can be seen in the panegyric al-Raḍī sent to his father in 984. This was when the family's fortunes were at perhaps the lowest point. ʿAḍud al-Dawlah had been dead for a nearly a year, yet there had been no movement to release Abū Aḥmad, and he languished in the fortress at Fāris. Al-Raḍī himself, midway through the poem makes allusion to an unspecified desire to seek his fortune elsewhere, presumably in greener pastures, in foreign courts (*Dīwān*, ed. Faraḥāt, 279):

What is wrong with me that I do not shun a land
that is so full of those who envy me?
Ways to make a living do not reside [exclusively] in Karkh, nor do
the jeweled collars of the heights lie upon the white necks of Baghdad.
In every land—if I could reach one of them—there are dwellings similar [to
these] and ones that are exactly the opposite.
The pursuit of the heights has wasted my flesh
and that is my glory among my peers.

This passage comes after a long (nine-line) intricate *naṣīb* that describes in detail the lush and inviting landscape of a pool in the desert, which the poet shuns because he "seeks the heights," even though it means he may perish from thirst. In the section quoted above, he then clarifies that it is not a simple physical journey to the highlands he is contemplating but leaving what is familiar and pleasant in order to seek glory and renown. This is a journey his father has preceded him on, which is made clearer as he turns to address his parent directly:

I have left behind the one who has no high aspirations,
who is absorbed in [finding] water and provisions.
You have followed Mūsā ['l-Kāẓim] with a [true] son upon the heights
[one] who has the virtue (*faḍl*) of fathers and forefathers.
You give the boon of armor's protection for the day of tumult
and are the shepherd of forbearance in the meeting house.
If we encounter the onrush of [the enemy's] arm extended,
you clasp him in a robe dyed mulberry red.

Before moving into the kind of praise for his father that is typical of Abbasid *qaṣīdah*s, which combines a catalogue of martial virtues with qualities of forbearance and tolerance more suited to the councils of government, al-Raḍī makes an observation about himself (as the son in the lineage of Mūsā 'l-Kāẓim, the seventh Imam) that emphasizes the notion that virtue and prowess is something inherited from one's ancestors, qualities that he has in ample measure.

Thus al-Raḍī neatly deflects the question of desire in his poem. He may be praising his father, but he needs nothing further from him than what he has already given: the example of virtue and restraint where possible, and decisiveness and retribution where necessary. The source of the poet's longing and frustration—as he delineates it—lie elsewhere, in the circumstances of the time and the envy of those around him. In what may be a direct riposte to ʿAḍud al-Dawlah's vizier's jibe about his family's unproductive concern with their lineage, al-Raḍī uses his ancestry—as personified in his father's character—to fortify himself to endure his current difficult circumstances and even to contemplate his own death fighting for his rights, as he describes toward the end of the poem:

It is the same [to me] whether I travel upon a swift courser
or a bier, my striped robes flutter [in the same way].
Why should a freeborn man cling to life,
since life is full of troubles lying in ambush?
[Evil] tongues offer up the bold young man for sacrifice during his lifetime
and when death visits him no substitute may be offered.

Here, besides the obvious crescendo in intensity and the shift from his description of himself (earlier in the poem) as a mere aspirant to glory to full-blown warrior willing to risk death, we also can discern evidence of his greater attention to issues of structural cohesiveness in this poem. He tells us that there is no difference between how his striped robes flutter on a bier being carried through the streets to the grave (presumably following a heroic death) or when he is mounted upon his war horse (presumably ready to lead a battle charge). "Striped robes"—which are more difficult to weave than plain ones—are a metonymy used in Arabic literature to signify daring and courage as well as wealth, since they were worn primarily by young members of the warrior class. At the beginning (line 2) of his poem, al-Raḍī had metaphorically described the cloud bringing rain to the pool in the desert as wearing "striped robes." Now, in using the same imagery to describe his own attire, he indirectly transfers the life-giving powers of the cloud to himself, and significantly enhances the underlying unity of the poem on the level of language. He immediately follows this up by employing a similar instance of linguistic echo in the last line of the poem:

And if I were to be envious of virtue (*faḍl*) among those who possess it
then my envy would be directed at my fathers and forefathers.

Earlier, in line 13 of the poem, complimenting his father on having produced such a noble son, al-Raḍī had described himself as possessing "the virtue (*faḍl*) of [having] fathers and forefathers." Now he brings the poem to closure by returning to the earlier statement and gracefully rephrasing it to acknowledge how much he owes to the example of those ancestors, including, of course, his own father. Thus, he turns what might have been an unseemly emphasis on boasting about himself back into the more conventional impetus for panegyric, singing the praises of another.

In the spring of 987, ʿAḍud al-Dawlah's eldest son, Sharaf al-Dawlah ((961–989, who had been passed over in the succession) entered Baghdad in triumph after having peacefully negotiated the removal of his younger brother from the scene. He brought with him ʿAḍud al-Dawlah's former political prisoners, including al-Sharīf al-Raḍī's father. Al-Radi recited a panegyric to him, thanking him for releasing his father. It is much more the conventional sort of panegyric, unproblematically praising the recipient, that is typical of the sort of poems al-Raḍī wrote to dignitaries in the state administration, whether they came from the Buwayhid family or the Abbasids (*Dīwān*, ed. al-Ḥulw, 526):

He is the most favored of kings among times and nations,
one who takes no comrades but among white [swords] and [spear] points,
And the most noble of people, ever occupied with his aspirations

held in high regard among the tips of slender lances.
His scruples overwhelm the rapiers of [other] heroes
and he is the wielder of a sword pledged to the heights.

This sort of unqualified acclaim is also typical of the many panegyrics he addressed to the Abbasid caliph al-Ṭā'iʿ during this period, and is also characteristic of the elegy he composed upon the caliph's death in 1002.

For the remainder of the decade, al-Sharīf al-Raḍī and his family were in the ascendant. Although Sharaf al-Dawlah died in 989, Abū Aḥmad and his sons were initially held in even higher regard by his successor Bahā' al-Dawlah. But Bahā' al-Dawlah's brother, Ṣamṣam al-Dawlah (964–998), had escaped from captivity and set himself up in Shirāz as a rival ruler. This threat, coupled with various military reverses to the north and south, seems to have strained Bahā' al-Dawlah's financial resources. Perhaps coveting the Abbasid caliph al-Ṭā'iʿ's riches, he removed the longtime friend of Abū Aḥmad from power, plundered his palace, and replaced him with al-Ṭā'iʿ's paternal cousin al-Qādir. At first, relations with al-Qādir were friendly and al-Sharif al-Raḍī wrote one of his formulaic panegyrics for him to celebrate Ramadan at the end of 991. But for his second panegyric for al-Qādir, al-Raḍī composed a very different sort of poem, one that incensed many who heard it, including the Caliph himself, and provoked a scandal that received ample coverage in the literary annals of the time, like ʿAbd al-Malik ibn Muḥammad Thaʿālibī's (961 or 962-1037 or 1038) *Yatīmat al-Dahr*. Although it seems to have had no immediate political fallout, the episode was no doubt remembered when al-Qādir and the Mūsawī family came to represent more clearly the opposing camps, respectively, of Sunni and Shiite following the re-appointment of Abū Aḥmad as marshal in 1003 and the unsuccessful attempt to install him as Chief Judge of Baghdad, which was thwarted by al-Qādir.

Even as early as 990, al-Raḍī had begun to assume some of the duties attached to the marshal's office, since his father, already 75, was by this time unable or unwilling to carry them out. In particular, he became the supervisor and organizer of the annual pilgrimage caravan from Baghdad to Mecca. In 992, he presented the pilgrims coming from Khūrasān to al-Qādir, who granted them an audience in his palace. Al-Qādir seems to have conceived this and similar occasions as an opportunity to exhort the pilgrims to urge their rulers (the Samanid and Ghaznawid dynasties) to recognize him as caliph instead of the deposed al-Ṭā'iʿ (which they would not do until the year 1000).

In this politically charged atmosphere, al-Raḍī arose to deliver a panegyric that, instead of launching into an enumeration of al-Qādir's virtues, begins with a long *naṣīb* describing the sort of an arduous desert journey—very much, no doubt, on the pilgrim's minds—where the poet also speaks in detail of his longing for and loyalty to a lost love who haunts his dreams at night only to abandon him with the coming of day. He finds relief only when he comes into the presence of the Commander of the Faithful, al-Qādir, whom he begins to praise in the expected way as "the morning light," and "a superintendent of justice." But no sooner has al-Raḍī begun this transition from the *naṣīb* than he forestalls it by shifting the addressee of his praise from the masculine singular form of "you" in Arabic to the masculine plural. In other words, he moves away from praising al-Qādir the individual to praising the entire Abbasid family (*Dīwān*, ed. Ḥulw, 476):

All of you are garments [to spread over] any mishap that might be feared
and in all of you every door is cracked and opened.
And your father al-ʿAbbās: no tribes ever asked for succor
after despairing, without receiving it.
He would slit open the clouds because of a call heard
and a spot brightened with twinkling beams, pouring forth rain, would respond.

But he did not content himself with simply diminishing al-Qādir as the patron by submerging into the commonalty of the family and moving backwards in time to praise instead al-ʿAbbās, the founder of the dynasty. Toward the end of the poem he returns briefly to acknowledge and praise al-Qādir, saying that he has "planted the seeds of love men's hearts, that will grow with the passage of time and put forth leaves." But then he follows this in the concluding lines with an unexpected invitation:

Bend close, O Commander of the Faithful, for we are
in a shade tree of the heights that we may not be parted from.
There is no dissimilarity between us, ever,
for both of us are deeply rooted in nobility.
Except the caliphate has distinguished you:
I am devoid of it, and you are necklaced by it.

Here, al-Raḍī—at this time barely 22 years old—places himself on an equal footing with the far more seasoned al-Qādir, at this time in his mid-forties and veteran of many upheavals and palace intrigues. But, beyond this effrontery, he suggests in the final line that the only thing separating him from the caliphate is the accident that it has graced al-Qādir like a necklace he has done nothing to deserve. It is no wonder that, given the audience and the public nature of the occasion, that the caliph was offended, and al-Raḍī never had the opportunity to hold the stage in such a way again. He only recited one more panegyric before al-Qādir, the following year, and this was a brief three-line poem apparently delivered in an ordinary public audience, which did nothing to lessen the estrangement between the two.

The whole episode nevertheless did undoubtedly enhance al-Raḍī's growing reputation as a poet able to masterfully manipulate the traditional form of the Arabic poem as a tool expressive of his own ends. At least his reputation began to spread far beyond Baghdad itself, and reached the ears of the most powerful of Buwayhid viziers, al-Ṣāḥib ibn ʿAbbād (d. 995) in distant Rayy (near modern Tehran), where he served the senior prince of the Buwayhid house, Fakhr al-Dawlah (d. 997). Al-Ṣāḥib ibn ʿAbbād was known as a great connoisseur of literature, and it was thus a great compliment when he sent a copyist to Baghdad, shortly before his death, expressly to transcribe all of al-Raḍī's poems for his own perusal. Al-Raḍī forwarded the document with a graceful poems of thanks attached to it. It was perhaps a great satisfaction to him to receive such recognition in what was rapidly becoming a very troubled time. A decade earlier, when his family was in disgrace, he had composed a panegyric to the legendary vizier, but never dared send it.

By 994, Bahā' al-Dawlah had left Baghdad to establish his court in southern Iraq, and that very year his deputy in Baghdad would dismiss Abū Aḥmad from his position. It is perhaps no coincidence that al-Raḍī began at this time to devote more of his time to writing prose and a diversity of intellectual pursuits. At some point in this period, he conceived a project to write a history of the lives of the ʿAlid *imāms*, the leaders of the Shiite community since the time of the Prophet. The first fruit of this was a book about the Imam ʿAli, detailing his claims to the caliphate, his talents as a judge and political leader, and his deep, abiding religious piety. This book al-Raḍī called *Khaṣā'is Amīr al-Mu'minīn* (Special Attributes of the Commander of the Faithful)—"Commander of the Faithful" being in Shiite tradition a title specific to ʿAlī, and not a general appellation of the caliph. He mentions having composed it in the early 990s, during the course of his introduction to the later work *Nahj al-Balāghah* (The Peak of Eloquence). A text by this name, attributed to al-Raḍī, was published in Iraq in the mid-1940s (and recently republished), but some scholars have cast doubts on its authenticity on stylistic grounds. Whatever truth there may be to these reservations, the fact that al-Raḍī did compose a work on this subject indicates his interest in participating in the general movement to create a sound textual and documentary basis for Shiite belief that is consistent with other developments during this decade, like Shaykh al-Mufīd's project to systematize the Shiite legal tradition.

Interestingly, this new focus on Shiism did not extend into the poetic arena. Unlike other Shiite poets, al-Sharīf al-Raḍī never turned his hand to producing poems solely dedicated to the enumerating the virtues of the descendants of the Prophet Muḥammad through ʿAlī and Fātimah (known in Arabic as the Āl al-Bayt or "Family of the House"). Nor did he direct his talents to writing extensively about the tragic death of al-Ḥusayn—ʿAlī and Fātimah's younger son—in

680, following his gallant but futile rebellion against the Ummayads on the plains outside Karbala in Iraq. Of the more than 400 poems in his *Dīwān*, only four—the first composed in 987, the second ten years later in 997, the third in 1000 and the fourth in 1004—are identifiably mourning poems for al-Ḥusayn. This would be an usually low number for a later Shiite poet. While it is true that praise for the Āl al-Bayt is found throughout al-Raḍī's panegyric poems to his father and those that praise his ancestry, it is also the case that, in order to gauge his engagement with Shiism, one must turn to his prose, which became his more favored means of expression in his later years.

The most notable innovation in his poems that can perhaps be traced to the last decade of his life were the short verses called the *Ḥijāziyyāt*. These are short poems about unrequited love, ranging in length from nine to thirty lines, which are set in the desert, often in the context of making the pilgrimage to Mecca. From the time of the rise of Islam, love poets had written of the opportunities the pilgrimage offered to see the faces of their beloveds (since women must unveil when performing the ceremonies), and al-Raḍī built his poems upon this convention. But his passion is chaste, and the poems become opportunities for exploring the psychology of obsession in the lover's mind much more than celebrations of the beauties he is able to glimpse. Their metaphorical tone, often verging on the allegorical, sometimes seem to anticipate the kind of spiritualized hyperbole associated with the mystical Sufi verse that had already begun to develop at this time, but there is nothing in these vignettes that requires they be religiously interpreted and thus it would be premature to do so in the absence of more compelling evidence.

Modern editions of the *Dīwān* simply incorporate the *Ḥijāziyyāt* with al-Raḍī's other poems, but medieval recensions do exist that preserve them as a separate group. They are undated, so it is impossible to assign them all to a particular time. Al-Sharīf al-Raḍī would have had many opportunities to accompany the pilgrimage caravan, but it was not required that the official in charge of organizing and overseeing it—as he did for his father in the early 990s—had to actually lead it to Mecca, and the historical chronicles list many occasions in those years when the leader was someone else. In fact, it is only possible to pinpoint two years when al-Raḍī did make the pilgrimage—998 and 1002—and in neither year was he officially in charge of organizing it. The style of the *Ḥijāziyyāt*, however, are very similar to three poems he composed about his feelings on turning thirty years old and seeing his first white hairs (they too have a desert setting), which can plausibly be connected to the 998 journey. So it is more likely than not that at least some of the *Ḥijāziyyāt* also belong to this period and should be considered among al-Raḍī's later poems, rather than included in his early work.

When Abū Aḥmad, having worked hard to place himself back in the good graces of Bahā' al-Dawlah, was restored to his offices in 1003, al-Raḍī was perforce required to devote more time to public affairs. But this did not mean that he entirely abandoned literary pursuits, either in prose or poetry. He had by this time attracted a serious circle of like-minded disciples, among whom probably the most famous was Mihyār al-Daylamī, who would carry his master's style into the next generation. His reputation also continued to spread on an international level. In 1008, the daughter of the Ḥamdānid ruler Sayf al-Dawlah, now living in Egypt, would send a copyist to transcribe al-Raḍī's *dīwān*, just as al-Ṣāḥib ibn ʿAbbād had done more than a decade before. Then, in 1009, the famous Syrian poet Abū 'l-ʿAlā' al-Maʿarrī visited Baghdad and stayed for several months with al-Raḍī, engaging him and his brother in many spirited discussions about poetry and intellectual issues. When al-Raḍī's father passed away in that year, al-Maʿarrī commemorated him with an elegy, in the company of Mihyār and al-Sharīf himself.

The following year, 1010, is when we see the culmination of al-Sharīf al-Raḍī's decade-long interest in fixing the basis of Shiite beliefs in textual form. He finished the book known as *Nahj al-balāghah* (*The Peak of Eloquence*) a collection of over 300 short sermons, speeches and letters attributed to the Imam ʿAlī, followed by a separate listing of nearly 500 shorter maxims and instructions (both with extensive linguistic commentary by al-Raḍī himself). This, as he tells us in the introduction, comprised a virtually comprehensive collection of all he could find in written or oral form that had been uttered by ʿAlī in his lifetime. Even more than the Prophet Muḥammad himself, ʿAlī had been increasingly recognized by Muslims over the centuries as a superb master of the rhetorical resources of the Arabic language, and this compilation by al-Raḍī cemented that reputation. The work itself, with all its attendant critical apparatus, is a formidable piece of scholarship and a testimony to al-Raḍī's superb education in the crystallizing Shiite traditions of his time. But, because it appears to rely on oral as written sources, and it comes out of a branch of Muslim religious tradition prone to controversy, it has attracted its share of criticism—both polemical and not—over the centuries. Ibn Khallikān (1211-1282), author of the most comprehensive medieval biographical dictionary, accused al-Raḍī of personally fabricating at least some of the material in *Nahj al-balāghah*. It should be noted, of course, that most of the material had already been reproduced in written form, some at least several centuries before al-Raḍī's lifetime. But because part was also derived apparently derived from oral reports, it is virtually impossible to prove that al-Raḍī would not have had the opportunity to embellish. Nor would this necessarily detract from the use to which the book has been put by Shiites and Sunnis alike: as a compendium for training students in finest traditions of Arabic rhetoric.

It is probably not surprising to find that al-Raḍī, as a student of Ibn Jinnī, was also deeply interested in questions of linguistic meaning. Along with *Nahj al-balāghah*, he spent most of the decade of the 990s and beyond composing a work dealing with the language of the *Qur'ān*, since this text—according to Muslim belief the literal words of God—was considered the most perfect example of linguistic speech. The *Qur'ān* itself tells us (Sūrat Āl ʿImrān (3:7) that it contains verses that are clear and precise (*muḥkam)*, while others in the Book are capable of more than one interpretation (*mutāshabih*). Like other Muslim scholars before and after him, al-Raḍī took upon himself the challenging task of writing commentary on the *mutashābih* verses. The result was a work, *Ḥaqā'iq al-ta'wīl fī mutashābih al-tanzīl*, that stretched to five volumes in its original version (though only the fifth volume survives), of which Ibn Jinnī himself said "Al-Raḍī has compiled a book on the meanings of the *Qur'ān* that requires no supplementation." Although it never quite gained the currency of other *Qur'ānic* commentaries, like al-Ṭabarī's or al-Badāwī's, it nevertheless continued to be used and referenced through several centuries after the author's death.

At least a substantial portion of this work must have been completed by Ibn Jinnī's death in 1002, but al-Raḍī continued to study the figurative language used in the *Qur'ān* in the subsequent decade, and in 1011 he produced a work devoted to that subject, *Talkhīs al-bayān fī majāzāt al-Qur'ān*. The manuscript was lost, however, for many centuries and it was only re-discovered in the twentieth century and published in the mid-1950s. Nevertheless, at least one major modern literary critic (Kamal Abu Deeb) has praised it for "its revealing insights" into Arabic as it is used in the *Qur'ān* and literature more generally. The same spirit animated a companion volume composed at approximately the same time, *al-Majāzāt al-Nabawiyyah* (The Prophet's figurative language). It contains nearly four hundred narratives and sayings (*ḥadīth*s) from Muḥammad, with commentary by al-Raḍī discussing the circumstances of their origin and the varieties of figurative language used therein.

It might seem as though al-Raḍī was working feverishly toward the end of his life to finish these various scholarly projects because he had a sense of impending death. But the facts do not necessarily bear this out. His final illness seems to have come on him very suddenly, since he was engaged in his normal activities until shortly before his death and even sent a poem to Bahā' al-Dawlah's son Sulṭān al-Dawlah in Arrajān a few months before it happened. That the death was swift and shocking can be inferred from the fact that his brother al-Murtaḍā was so prostrate with grief he could not attend the funeral and Fakhr al-Mulk (d. 1016), the current vizier and a family friend, officiated at the ceremony. He was only 47 when he died.

REFERENCES

Iḥsān 'Abbās, *al-Sharīf al-Raḍī* (Beirut: Dār Ṣādir, 1959);

Kamal Abu Deeb, "Literary Criticism" in *Abbasid Belles-Lettres*, ed. Julia Ashtiany et al. (Cambridge: Cambridge University Press, 1990), 339-387;

Ḥasan Maḥmūd Abū 'Alīwī, *al-Sharīf al-Raḍī: dirāsah fī 'aṣrih wa-adabih* (Beirut: Mu'assasat al-Wafā', 1986);

John J. Donohue, *The Buwayhid Dynasty in Iraq 334 H./945 to 403H./1012* (Leiden: E.J. Brill, 2003);

Muḥammad 'Abd al-Ghanī Ḥasan, *al-Sharīf al-Raḍī* (Cairo: Dār al-Ma'ārif, 1970);

Joel L. Kraemer, *Humanism in the Renaissance of Islam: the Cultural Revival during the Buyid Age*, 2d ed. (Leiden: E.J. Brill, 1992);

Zakī Mubārak, *'Abqariyyat al-Sharīf al-Raḍī* (Beirut: al-Maktabah al-'Asriyyah, 1941);

'Abd al-Laṭīf 'Umrān, *Shi'r al-Sharīf al-Raḍī* (Damascus: Dār al-Yanābī', 2000).

Ṭalā'i' ibn Ruzzīk

(1101 or1102-September 1161)

TERRI DEYOUNG

University of Washington

WORKS

Dīwān.

Editions

Dīwān al-Wazīr al-Miṣrī Ṭalā'i' ibn Ruzzīk, ed. Aḥmad Aḥmad Badawī (Cairo: Maktabat Nahḍat Miṣr, 1958);

Dīwān Ṭalā'i' ibn Ruzzīk al-Malik al-Ṣāliḥ, ed. Muḥammad Hādī Amīnī (Najaf: Dār Manshūrāt al-Maktabah al-Ahliyyah, 1964).

Al-Malik al-Ṣāliḥ Abū 'l-Ghārāt Ṭalā'i' ibn Ruzzīk has been famous to history mainly as the vizier who presided over the functional end of the Fatimid caliphate in Egypt. But he was also an accomplished and prolific poet, who should be remembered for two things. First, he conducted an extensive poetic correspondence with the most famous literary figure of the age, Usāmah ibn Munqidh. His exchanges with Usāmah, which continued for over a decade, provide instructive insight into the nature of the poetic genre of *ikhwāniyyāt* (fraternal poems), a kind of verse epistle that was very popular in the later Abbasid period of Arabic literature.

Second, his *dīwān* preserves many poems mourning the tragic death of al-Ḥusayn, the grandson of the Prophet, and enumerating the virtues of the Āl al-Bayt, Muḥammad's (d. 632) family. Ṭalā'i' ibn Ruzzīk was a lifelong Shiite, and probably because of his official position with the Fatimid state, governed by a Shiite dynasty that based its claims to rule on descent from the Āl al-Bayt, he cultivated poetry based on this theme. Both these forms of poetry are important in understanding the literary climate of the time and subsequent developments in Arabic literature, but have been vastly understudied. Thus, Ibn Ruzzīq's poetry is well worth greater attention that it has hitherto received.

The standard historical narrative has it that al-Ṭalā'i' ibn Ruzzīk was born in 1101 or 1102 in the area of Armenia, to a family of solid background that had suffered reverses and was at the time undergoing great hardships. He did, however, receive a thorough Islamic education for the time. Due to his family's circumstances, it appears that he was compelled to leave home at an early age. He ended up in the Iraqi city of Najaf, even then a holy center of Shiite pilgrimage.

According to later historians, during Ibn Ruzzīk's stay there, the custodian of the shrine there, Sayyid al-Maʿsūm had a dream in which he saw a vision of ʿAlī ibn abi Ṭālib (ca. 600-660). ʿAlī told the Sayyid to inform Ibn Ruzzīk to travel to Egypt, where he would be made a ruler among men. Whether or not this tale was historically true, by the 1140s Ṭalā'iʿ had attached himself to the Fatimid court and risen to a high position there. It was during this time that he met and befriended Usāmah ibn Munqidh, who came to Cairo in 1144.

Despite—or perhaps because of—the dissensions within the Fatimid court under the insecure rule of the Caliph al-Ḥāfiẓ (who held the office until he died in 1149), it gave many opportunities for advancement to men of demonstrated competence even if they did not subscribe to the religious beliefs of the Fatimid form of Shiism. This can be seen in the fact that many members of the Fatimid army at the time were Christian Armenians (thus fellow countrymen of Ṭalā'iʿ). Even in the case of Ibn Ruzzīk himself, historians close to the period always emphasize that he was an Imami or Twelver Shiite, and thus did not ascribe to the Ismaili-influenced Shiism of the Fatimid inner circle. We can also observe a similar, personal broad-mindedness in Ibn Ruzzīk's close relationship with Usāmah ibn Munqidh, who was Sunnī.

Such inclusiveness also carries over into Ibn Ruzzīq's poetry. Alongside the more usual poems in the genres of love poetry, self-praise, and panegyric (constituting, surely, the earlier portion of his work), one also finds a long series of poems praising ʿAlī ibn Abī Ṭālib and (even more consistently) al-Ḥusayn, ʿAlī's son, who had died tragically at the hands of troops sent by the Umayyad caliph Yazīd ibn Abī Sufyān (d. 640), and had thus become a heroic figure to the Shiah. They felt that al-Ḥusayn represented a principled opposition to injustice in the world, regarding the Umayyads as unscrupulous usurpers of the rule that belonged legitimately to ʿAlī and his sons by Muḥammad's (d. 632) daughter Fātimah (d. 632 or 633). For Ṭalā'iʿ ibn Ruzzīq a focus on the particular sufferings of al-Ḥusayn in these poems is often preceded by general reflections on the transience of worldly success and the pervasiveness of the failure of ideals (*Dīwān*, ed. Amīnī, 76):

Heart of mine, how frequent is this deception,
  lies and untruth can mislead any desire.
Or hopes held too long
  will show [only] the shortness of life.
And one who looks beyond the surface will see a lesson
  in what we have become now.

From these almost epigrammatic generalities, Ibn Ruzzīq proceeds to focus on the tragic example of al-Ḥusayn as an illustration of his verdict on the uncertainties of life (*Dīwān*, ed. Amīnī, 76-77):

See you al-Ḥusayn, penned down at Karbala
  with no one to help him.
Both before and after the deceit,
  there was the people's betrayal of his cause.
So it happened that the generous young men with him,
  came to their downfall,
Which met them near al-Taff
  on a very dusky day.
The broth of their blood became
  a pool of water where it swirled.

Some of Ibn Ruzzīk's poems describing the killing of al-Ḥusayn in vivid images like these are specifically labeled as having been produced for recitation at the ceremonies held during the commemoration of his death on the tenth of the Muslim month of Muḥarram, a commemoration that was encouraged by the Shiite Fatimids. It is likely that most, if not all, of these poems were composed for this occasion, which helps to explain their very great number.

By the end of the 1140s, however, Ṭalā'iʿ would not have been participating personally in these ceremonies, as al-Ḥāfiẓ had appointed him governor of the provinces surrounding Aswan in Upper Egypt. In 1149, al-Ḥāfiẓ died and this precipitated a crisis among the governing elite of the state.

The new ruler, al-Ḥāfiẓ's son al-Ẓāfir (d. 1154), was only seventeen upon his accession and in an extremely tenuous position. If we can believe Usāmah ibn Munqidh, al-Ẓāfir was forced to appoint one of his governors, Ibn Sallār, vizier in the year he came to the throne (after the latter had arranged for the death of the preceding vizier). Perhaps aware that Egypt was growing increasingly unstable, the Crusaders stepped up their raids over the borders, so Ibn Sallār sent Usāmah to ask the powerful ruler of Damascus, Nūr al-Dīn (1118-1174), to aid him in fighting the Crusaders. When this scheme went awry, Ibn Sallār—already unpopular in Egypt—was killed by al-Ẓāfir's favorite, Naṣr, and the latter's father ʿAbbās (Ibn Sallār's adopted son) became vizier. In 1154, as the situation in Egypt worsened, ʿAbbās and Naṣr reacted by killing the young caliph, putting al-Ẓāfir's six-year-old son, al-Fā'iz (d. 1160), on the throne. Usāmah (who by this time had returned from Syria) played a role that some saw as unsavory in these last events, but—according to Usāmah's account—it was because he feared for his family's safety, since they were living under ʿAbbās' control.

The murdered caliph's relatives and retainers sent for Ṭalā'iʿ ibn Ruzzīk, who marched on Cairo with a large contingent of troops. Ṭalā'iʿ restored order and was rewarded with the position of vizier and the title of al-Malik al-Ṣāliḥ (just as Ibn Sallār had been al-Malik al-ʿĀdil, the "just king"). ʿAbbās and Naṣr now fled the city, with Usāmah in tow. They were captured by the Crusaders (while Usāmah escaped). They killed ʿAbbās and sent Naṣr back to Ibn Ruzzīk, who promptly had him executed. Usāmah sought refuge at Nūr al-Dīn's court in Damascus, where he entered that prince's service.

This was when Ṭalā'iʿ and Usāmah began their lengthy poetic correspondence, examples of which are preserved in the historians ʿIzz al-Dīn Ibn al-Athir's (1160-1233) *al-Kāmil fī 'l-Tārīkh* (The Perfection of History), and Abū Shāmah's *Kitāb al-Rawḍatayn*. Ṭalā'iʿ, apparently convinced from the first that Usāmah had been forced into cooperation with ʿAbbās, at first urged him insistently to return, as can be seen in one of their earliest exchanges. Usāmah sent a letter to Ṭalā'iʿ containing a poem that began (*Dīwān*, ed. Amīnī, 59):

My soul cannot be quieted with patient resolve to renounce you,
nor can it be content after [sharing your] houses, with [mere] proximity.

Once Ṭalā'iʿ read the poem, he replied with another—contrafacting Usāmah's—:

From this day, as long as I live, I will not be deluded by love,
nor will I seek a favor from a friend, by [resorting to] complaint.
I will not be satisfied with distance from someone I feel affection for,
nor will I be content with missives and letters from him.
And especially if he says to me, in an affected tone:
"My body is far from you, but my heart will remain your neighbor."

This last line is a direct quotation from Usāmah's original poem. In this, we can see how intimately intertwined these poems are, reflective of the general nature of *ikhwāniyyāt* poems, whose effect often cannot be gauged without access to both sides of the correspondence. Clearly, Ibn Ruzzīk is questioning—by quoting this line in the context he does—what he sees as Usāmah's too easy repetition of a polite expression of regret at their parting, which he wishes to contrast with his own, more heartfelt, sorrow.

Very often, both Usāmah's and Ṭalā'iʿ's poems use a combination of direct quotation, formal contrafaction of meter and rhyme, and the repetition of key words and concepts to convey either their points of agreement or to challenge each other's worldview. For example, when Ṭalā'iʿ begins a poem by saying

God has made fate our lot, but glory and victory
will be our servants during our [time of] rule,

he is suggesting that fate—whatever it may be—will have the upper hand in the conduct of life, likely frustrating the designs of human beings. People can only rely upon their deeds to enhance their reputation for the short time that they are allowed to rule or otherwise control their affairs (a viewpoint that tragically foreshadows his own violent end). Usāmah takes this notion (the power of fate to overturn man's dearest ambitions) and endeavors to show its inadequacy at the beginning of his poem (*Dīwān*, ed. Amīnī, 81):

God has made victory our lot, so that the world
will live
through us and the age will have something
worth boasting about.
Then the days will serve us as we wish, and fate
will be led in chains during our lifetime.

Here, Usāmah turns the phraseology of Ṭalā'iʿ by substituting "victory" for Ṭalā'iʿ's "fate," in the first hemistich, making it the keyword of his line (highlighting it by leaving every other element in the line undisturbed). The power of human endeavor—summed up in the idea of "victory"—becomes the central concept of his exposition (just as "fate" was in his friend's line), and this more optimistic view allows him to assert that fate will be his captive for as long as he lives.

Probably the one point in this correspondence where we can see a break from the atmosphere of intense intellectual engagement that runs through their poems was in 1157, when an earthquake destroyed Usāmah's family stronghold of Shayzar (claiming the lives of many of his relatives). When Ṭalā'iʿ heard of the disaster, he wrote to his friend (*Dīwān*, ed. Amīnī, 61):

By my father, your person is never absent
from my eyes, whether [you be] near or far,
Dear friend in Syria, even though you be absent
[from me],
my desire for you is not absent.
The days have robbed us of your presence,
a violation that never stops.
Syria hates its people, so it is worthy of never
having someone wise live there—
When wars lifted their clouds awhile there,
they were followed by calamities and
earthquakes.

It would seem that Ṭalā'iʿ cannot resist pausing momentarily in these lines to compare Syria (by implication) unfavorably with Egypt, which he depicts as a more hospitable environment in many poems. But in the remaining verses he much more straightforwardly, and without his usual literary flourishes, offers Usāmah comfort and condolences for his great loss.

Unfortunately, Ṭalā'iʿ himself would soon be confronted with a crisis stemming from the rising discontent at this rule in Egypt. A conspiracy was set in motion by the Caliph's relatives with the cooperation of one of Ibn Ruzzīk's own governors, Shawār. In 1161 Ṭalā'iʿ was assassinated on his way back home from the caliphal palace. He left a mixed legacy. On the one hand, he was a great sponsor of the arts, and himself a proficient poet. But his patronage was paid for by harsh taxation and frequent confiscation of properties belonging to members of the court. Nor did he do enough to defend Egypt and its people from raids by the Crusaders. The country only regained a strong military and economic footing when Ṣalāḥ al-Dīn (with Usāmah as part of his entourage) took over its governance in 1174.

REFERENCES

'Abd al-Raḥmān ibn Ismā'īl Abū Shāmah, *Kitāb al-rawḍatayn fī akhbār al-dawlatayn*, vol. 1, ed. Ibrāhīm al-Zaybaq (Beirut: Mu'assasat al-Risālah, 1997) *passim*;

Hadia Dajani-Shakeel, "Jihad in Twelfth-Century Arabic Poetry: a Moral and Religious Force to Counter the Crusades," *Muslim World* 66:2 (April 1976): 96-113;

Muḥammad Kāmil Ḥusayn, *Fī adab Miṣr al-fāṭimīyah* (Cairo: Dār al-Fikr al-ʿArabī, 1963), 193-203;

ʿIzz al-Dīn Ibn al-Athīr, *al-Kāmil fī 'l-tārīkh*, vol. 11 (Beirut: Dār Ṣādir, 1967),193-194, 218-220, and 274-276;

Taqī al-Dīn Aḥmad al-Maqrīzī, *Itti'āẓ al-ḥunafā'' bi-akhbār al-a'immah al-Fāṭimīyīn al-khulafā'*, vol. 2, ed. Jamāl al-Dīn al-Shayyāl (Cairo: al-Majlis al-Aʿlā li 'l-Shu'ūn al-Islāmīyah), 216-220.

Abū Ḥayyān al-Tawḥīdī

(ca. 922-ca. 1014)

MARY ST. GERMAIN
University of Washington

WORKS

Akhlāq al-wazīrayn (The Characters of the Two Viziers) also known as *Dhamm al-wazīrayn*;

al-Baṣā'ir wa 'l-dhakhā'ir (Insights and Treasures) also known as *Baṣā'ir al-qudamā' wa-sarā'ir al-ḥukamā'*;

al-Hawāmil wa 'l-shawāmil (Searching [Questions] and Compendious Answers) written jointly with Aḥmad ibn Muḥammad Ibn Miskawayh (d. 1030);

al-Imtā' wa 'l-mu'ānasah (Delight and Entertainment);

al-Ishārāt al-ilāhiyyah (Divine Intimations);

al-Muqābasāt (Conversations);

Risālah fī 'l-'ulūm (Epistle on the Branches of Knowledge) also known as *Thamarāt al-'ulūm*;

Risālah fī 'ilm al-kitābah (Epistle on Penmanship);

Risālah ilā 'l-qāḍī Abī Sahl (Epistle to the Qāḍī Abū Sahl);

Risālat al-ṣadāqah wa 'l-ṣadīq (Epistle on Friendship and Friends);

Riwāyat al-Saqīfah (Recitation of al-Saqīfah) also known as *Risālat al-Imāmah* (Epistle on the Imamate);

Thamarāt al-'ulūm (The Fruits of Sciences).

Editions

Akhlāq al-wazīrayn: mathālib al-wazīrayn al-Ṣāḥib ibn 'Abbād wa-Ibn al-'Amīd, ed. Muḥammad ibn Tāwīt al-Ṭanjī (Damascus: Maṭbū'āt al-Majma' al-'Ilmī 'l-'Arabī, 1965);

al-Baṣā'ir wa 'l-dahkhā'ir, ed. Aḥmad Amīn and Aḥmad Ṣaqr (Cairo: Maṭba'at Lajnat al-Ta'līf wa 'l-Tarjamah wa 'l-Nashr, 1953); ed. Ibrāhīm al-Kīlānī, 2 vols. (Damascus: Maktabat Atlas, 1964); ed. Wadād al-Qāḍī, 6 vols. (Beirut: Dār Ṣādir, 1988);

al-Hawāmil wa 'l-shawāmil, ed. Aḥmad Amīn and Aḥmad Ṣaqr (Cairo: Lajnat al-Ta'līf wa 'l-Tarjamah wa 'l-Nashr, 1951);

al-Hawāmil wa 'l-shawāmil: su'ālāt Abī Ḥayyān al-Tawḥīdī li-Abī 'Alī Miskawayh, ed. Sayyid Kasrawī Ḥasan (Beirut: Dār al-Kutub al-'Ilmiyyah, 2001);

al-Ishārāt al-ilāhiyyah, ed. 'Abd al-Raḥmān Badawī (Cairo: Maṭba'at Jami'at Fu'ad al-Awwal, 1950); ed. Wadād al-Qāḍī (Beirut: Dār al-Thaqāfah, 1973);

Kitāb al-imtā' wa 'l-mu'ānasah, ed. Aḥmad Amīn and Aḥmad al-Zayn, 3 vols. (Cairo: Lajnat al-Ta'līf wa 'l-Tarjamah wa 'l-Nashr, 1939-1942); ed. Khalīl Manṣūr (Beirut: Dār al-Kutub al-'Ilmiyyah, 1997);

Kitāb al-muqābasāt, ed. Muḥammad Malik al-Kuttāb al-Shīrāzī (Bombay, C.P. Press, 1887-1888); ed. Ḥasan al-Sandūbī (Cairo: al-Maṭba'ah al-Raḥmāniyyah, 1929); ed. Muḥammad Tawfīq Ḥusayn (Baghdad: Maṭba'at al-Irshād, 1970);

Mathālib al-wazīrayn: akhlāq al-Ṣāḥib ibn 'Abbād wa-Ibn al-'Amīd, ed. Ibrāhīm al-Kīlānī (Damascus: Dār al-Fikr, 1961);

Risālatān li-Abī Ḥayyān al-Tawḥīdī: al-risālah al-ulā fī 'l-ṣadāqah wa 'l-ṣadīq, wa 'l-risālah al-thāniyyah fī 'l-'ulūm (Constaninople: Maṭba'at al-Jawā'ib, 1884);

Risālah fī 'ilm al-kitābah, ed. Franz Rosenthal, *Ars Islamica*, 13-14 (1948): 21-27;

Risālah fī 'ilm al-kitābah (al-Ẓāhir, Cairo: Maktabat al-Thaqāfah al-Dīniyyah, 2001);

Risālat al-ṣadāqah wa 'l-ṣadīq (includes "Risālah ilā 'l-Qāḍī Abī Sahl," and "Risālah fī 'l-'Ulūm"), ed. Ibrāhīm al-Kīlānī (Dimashq: Dār al-Fikr, 1964);

Riwāyat al-Saqīfah, in Aḥmad ibn 'Abd al-Wahhāb Nuwayrī, *Nihāyat al-'arab fī funūn al-adab*, ed. Saʿīd ʿAbd al-Fattāḥ ʿĀshūr (Cairo: al-Mu'assasah al-Miṣriyyah al-ʿĀmmah li 'l-Ta'līf wa 'l-Tarjamah wa 'l-Ṭibāʿah wa 'l-Nashr, 1964-);

Riwāyat al-Saqīfah, in Aḥmad ibn ʿAlī Qalqashandī, *Subḥ al-aʿshā fī ṣināʿat al-inshā'*, 16 vols. (Cairo: al-Muʾassasah al-Miṣriyyah al-ʿĀmmah li 'l-Ta'līf wa 'l-Tarjamah wa 'l-Ṭibāʿah wa 'l-Nashr, 1964);

Riwāyat al-Saqīfah, in Ibn al-ʿArabī, *Kitāb muḥāḍarat al-abrār wa-musāmarat al-akhyār fī 'l-adībāt wa 'l-nawādir wa 'l-akhbār*, 2 vols. (Damascus: Dār al-Yaqẓah al-ʿArabiyyah, 1968);

Riwāyat al-Saqīfah, in Ibn Abī 'l-Ḥadīd, *Sharḥ nahj al-balāghah*, 20 vols. (Cairo: ʿĪsā 'l-Bābī 'l-Ḥalabī, 1959-1964).

Translations

Abū Haiyān al-Tawḥīdī on Penmanship, trans. by Franz Rosenthal, *Ars Islamica*, 13-14 (1948): 1-29;

La satire des deux vizirs, transl. by Frédéric Lagrange (Arles: Actes Sud; Paris: Sindbad, 2004);

De l'amitié, transl. by Evelyne Larguèche and Françoise Neyrod (Arles: Actes sud, 2006).

Abū Ḥayyān al-Tawḥīdī was an extremely skilled writer of prose literature and a philosopher who worked under the second and third generations of Buwayhid rulers, specifically ʿAḍūd al-Dawlah (936–983), Mu'ayyid al-Dawlah (d. 984), Fakhr al-Dawlah, (952–997) and Ṣamṣām al-Dawlah (964–998). He spent many years as a scribe in Baghdad and simultaneously participated in philosophical circles. Following financial reversals, he attempted, with varying success, to find and keep employment as a secretary and a courtier. He moved from Baghdad to Rayy twice in pursuit of patronage, but each time returned to Baghdad unsuccessful. When an enemy of his became vizier in Baghdad in 984, he soon left for Shiraz and remained there the rest of his life. He never again held a court position nor did he find a new patron. He wrote very productively from around 996 until 1010 and then renounced writing altogether.

Al-Tawḥīdī was extremely witty, was always exceptionally well-informed about current intellectual and political activities and knew all the latest gossip. These qualities made him attractive to the kind of powerful men who offered patronage. Unfortunately, al-Tawḥīdī's sharp tongue, a tendency to criticize the rich and powerful, and manners insufficiently polished for life at court usually ruined his chances of obtaining a stable position. Al-Tawḥīdī's excellent prose style emulated that of Abū ʿUthman ʿAmr ibn Baḥr al-Jāḥiẓ (d. 868 or 869), whom he greatly admired. He was distinguished for encyclopedic knowledge rather than for a deep specialization in any single field. Al-Tawḥīdī was an unusually keen observer and therefore his works are extremely important because they present an unvarnished, exceptionally complete and detailed picture of the leading figures, intellectual thought, society, and culture of the Buwayhid period.

A biography of al-Tawḥīdī was not written until nearly two hundred years after his death. The biographers who presented him at the very end of Abbasid rule were Yāqūt ibn ʿAbd Allāh al-Ḥamawī (1179?–1229), and Muḥammad ibn Aḥmad al-Dhahabī (1274–1348). Even at that time, Yāqūt complained that information about al-Tawḥīdī was quite incomplete. Later research has not found substantially more information. One reason contemporary writers may not have recorded biographical information about al-Tawḥīdī, is that his religious beliefs, as expressed in his *al-Ḥajj al-ʿaqlī idhā dāqa 'l-faḍā' ʿan al-ḥajj al-sharʿi* (The Intellectual Pilgrimage If the Environment is Inhospitable for the Lawful Pilgrimage) and his *Risālat al-Imāmah*, tended towards what would have been thought of as heresy in the tenth century and afterwards. Both of these works will be discussed later.

Abū Ḥayyān ʿAlī ibn Muḥammad Ibn al-ʿAbbās al-Tawḥīdī was born sometime between 922 and 932. His place of birth is variously given as Baghdad, Shiraz, Nishapur, and Wāsiṭ. It is unclear whether he was of Arabic or Persian descent. His father is said to have been a poor date seller and the name "al-Tawḥīdī," is assumed to be derived from a type of date, the "tawḥīd." Al-Tawḥīdī's silence about his parentage corroborates his lowly origins.

Nothing is known about al-Tawḥīdī's early life. However, the period of his youth was a period of substantial cultural and political ferment in Baghdad. The Buwayhids, a Shiite Daylamī family, were the predominant rulers of the region of Fārs in Iran and of much of Iraq. From 944, they were the true rulers of Baghdad, although, to promote political stability, they preferred that the caliph remain the nominal ruler. The Sunni populations, who looked to the caliph for support, and the Shiite populations, who looked to the Buwayhids for support, frequently clashed violently as they publicly expressed their devotion to their beliefs. During the Abbasid period, a variety of sects and movements such as Ismailism, Mu'tazilism, Sufism, and Ash'arism, had developed within Islam and adherents of all of them were active in Baghdad.

During the same period, Greek philosophical works had been translated and were widely studied. By the Buwayhid period, Greek philosophy was an important influence in intellectual life, even though it was not always regarded as compatible with the beliefs of Islam. Decades of economic instability had caused population displacements and internal migrations. Although the Buwayhids' native language was Persian, which was resurfacing as a literary language in the second half of the 10th century, Arabic remained the dominant language of scholarship, culture and administration. The period's reshuffling of society and its resulting cultural pluralism stimulated intellectual interactions between individuals from widely varying backgrounds and beliefs. The resulting juxtaposition and open discussion of different ideas, philosophies and beliefs led to a renaissance of Islamic culture.

Al-Tawḥīdī was very much a product of the diverse and volatile conditions of his time. He studied in Baghdad with a selection of the most notable teachers of the time, men who reflected the city's diversity. The foremost of his teachers was Abū Sa'īd al-Sīrāfī (d. 979), a grammarian and logician. He served as a Ḥanafī judge, taught a wide range of subjects, and worked as a copyist. He was also a Mu'tazilī, or member of an Islamic movement that believed the examination of topics by reasoning was necessary to attain knowledge of God, and a Sufi, or mystic who devoted himself to serve God, which required eliminating the self and renouncing the world. Mu'tazilī discussions engaged in to investigate Islam fell within the field of theology. Over time, Mu'tazilī methods of discussion proved applicable in many fields. Al-Tawḥīdī studied grammar with him and records some of the activities of his *majlis*. For example, in *al-Imtā' wa 'l-mu'ānasah*, al-Tawḥīdī recorded the debate between al-Sīrāfī and the logician Mattā ibn Yūnus on the similarities between Greek logic and Arabic grammar. Mattā's argument was that only through logic was it possible to know the difference between correct and incorrect, including the difference between correct and incorrect meanings. He also promoted the idea that meaning and utterance were separate entities. Meaning could only be investigated through logic and utterance could only be investigated by grammar. Al-Sīrāfī's influence on al-Tawḥīdī was strongest in the fields of logic and mysticism. For example, their ideas about mysticism and Sufism are very similar. The works of both men show a belief in determinism based more in religion than in philosophy, and an absolute confidence in God.

Another teacher who clearly influenced al-Tawḥīdī was 'Alī ibn 'Īsā 'l-Rummānī (908-994). Although, like al-Sīrāfī, he had encyclopedic knowledge, he was primarily a grammarian. Another philologian, 'Abd al-Raḥmān ibn Muḥammad Ibn al-Anbārī (1119-1181), reported that al-Rummānī had a habit of integrating logic and grammar, a unique approach that was hard for others to follow. He was particularly influential in the early development of Arabic literary theory. Rummānī broke new ground in discussions of the bases of meaning and definitions of rhetorical devices. In his *Nukat fī i'jaz al-Qur'ān* (Epitome Concerning the Inimitability of the *Qur'ān*), he defines eloquence as the conveying of a given idea to the heart in the most beautiful form of wording, whereas earlier grammarians had defined it in terms of making an idea understood. He also introduced the concept of "*aṣl al-lughah*" ("the basic meaning of a phrase"), a concept that would become widely used in later literary theory. Al-Rummānī was a Mu'tazilī and an expert in *kalām*, or theology analyzed and defended by discursive arguments. He conveyed grammar, *kalām* and a tendency to asceticism to al-Tawḥīdī.

Al-Tawḥīdī studied philosophy with two very important philosophers. One, Yaḥyā ibn 'Adī (ca. 893-974) translated Aristotle from Syriac. He, like some of al-Tawḥīdī's other teachers, discussed the relationship of logic and grammar, using the terms that are the basics of modern linguistics: utterance, meaning and signified. He was Christian and earned his living as a copyist and book seller. Both Yaḥyā ibn 'Adī and al-Tawḥīdī expressed themselves in a very pure style with rich vocabulary and expressed their arguments in a particularly clear and precise manner.

The other of the philosophers with whom al-Tawḥīdī studied, Muḥammad ibn Ṭāhir al-Sijistānī (ca. 912-ca. 985), was considered the best logician and philosopher of his time. Unlike those of al-Tawḥīdī's teachers mentioned above, he was not interested in philology. His circle discussed general philosophical topics, in which discussions they frequently referred to Greek philosophy. One of their topics that generated interest beyond al-Sijistānī's circle was the art of governance and the concept of the state. Al-Tawḥīdī attended al-Sijistānī's circles from around 980 to 985.

Al-Tawḥīdī studied Shafi'i law with Abū Ḥamīd al-Marwarūzī (d. 972) and Abū Bakr al-Shāshī (903-975). The latter was one of the most renowned Shafi'i legalists and also an expert in *ḥadīth*, grammar and poetry. He was a Mu'tazili and dabbled in Ash'arism. Another of his teachers was Abū 'l-Faraj al-Mu'āfā ibn Zakariyyā 'l-Jarīrī 'l-Nahrawānī (ca. 917-1000), who specialized in jurisprudence, poetry and generally had encyclopedic knowledge. Al-Tawḥīdī studied eloquence with Abū 'l-Ḥusayn ibn Sham'ū (d. 997) and mysticism with Abū Muḥammad Ja'far al-Khuldī.

Exactly when al-Tawḥīdī moved beyond studying to writing is not known. For many years, he made a living as a copyist, as did many of his teachers. The first report of a specific event in his life involves Abū Muḥammad al-Ḥasan ibn Muḥammad al-Muhallabī (903-963), vizier of the Buwayhid *amīr* Mu'izz al-Dawlah (915 or 916-967). Al-Muhallabī became vizier in Baghdad in 959 and was responsible for preventing riots between the Sunni's and Shiites in Baghdad. Mu'izz al-Dawlah, among the Buwayhids was a particularly strong supporter of the Shiite orientation and required al-Muhallabī to enforce public celebration of some Shiite celebrations. Measures were taken against Sufis, who tended to ignore standard public forms of religious observation. It is reported that al-Muhallabī exiled al-Tawḥīdī from Baghdad on the basis of heretical ideas found in the latter's *al-Ḥajj al-'aqlī idhā dāqa 'l-faḍā' 'an al-ḥajj al-shar'i*. There is some doubt as to the veracity of the story because there is no other record of any relationship between al-Muhallabī and al-Tawḥīdī. The work clearly shows the influence, in its discussion of a union between the soul and God, of the teachings of al-Ḥusayn ibn Manṣūr al-Ḥallāj (857-922), a Sufi who practiced his Sufism very publicly and who was eventually convicted of heresy for claiming his soul had united mystically with God's. Whether or not al-Tawḥīdī was exiled, he left Baghdad in 959 or 960, relatively soon after al-Muhallabī came to power. The story does suggest that *al-Ḥajj al-'aqlī idhā dāqa 'l-fadā' 'an al-ḥajj al-shar'i* must have been written by 959.

Al-Tawḥīdī also writes about the first caliphs, Abū Bakr (d. 634), 'Umar ibn al-Khaṭṭāb (d. 644), 'Uthman ibn 'Affān (d. 656) and 'Alī ibn Abī Ṭālib (ca. 600-660), Muḥammad's nephew, and their relationships with each other in his *Riwāyat al-Saqīfah*, also known as *Risālat al-Imāmah*. It is not known when in his career this work was written, but it too linked him with heresy. The "Imamate" refers to the decision as to who would lead the Muslims after Muḥammad's death. The contenders were Abū Bakr, 'Umar, 'Uthman and 'Alī, Muḥammad's nephew. The greatest contention concerned whether or not Muḥammad considered that 'Alī had a special position in relation to the Muslim community and whether he should become Imam on the basis of that relationship. Sunnis and Shiites had established their views on the subject at the time of the original discussions. Instead of simply accepting existing arguments, the Mu'tazilis considered that the original decisions about the Imamate and the men who made them could be investigated rationally. At a philosophical circle, al-Tawḥīdī heard arguments made in favor of 'Alī that he considered excessively biased. He wrote his *Riwāyat al-Saqīfah* to refute those arguments and in it refers to a letter written by Muḥammad's companions. Al-Tawḥīdī's contemporaries considered that he forged that letter, which was equivalent to the heretical act of falsifying *ḥadīth*.

In 961, al-Tawḥīdī decided to become a prose writer. He began writing *al-Baṣā'ir wa 'l-dhakhā'ir* that year, but did not complete it until 986. It was originally intended to be a work illustrating *adab*, or a combination of literary erudition and social graces required of educated, cultured men. In *al-Baṣā'ir wa 'l-Dhakhā'ir* al-Tawḥīdī records what he saw and studied during the approximately twenty five years that he spent writing the nine-volume work, specifically anecdotes and sayings drawn from al-Tawḥīdī's readings and interactions with other intellectuals. In essence, it is the summation of his experience. This is an example of an amusing anecdote featuring a well known joker (*al-Baṣā'ir*, ed. al-Qāḍī, 1:186, anecdote 572).

> Al-Jummāz entered [the home] of the owner of a singing girl who was his lover. The man said to him, "Would you like something to eat?" He responded, "I have [already] eaten. He poured him honeyed date wine. When he drank it, he began to eat the rose petals, as though he was transported by it. The slave girl perceived [what was up] and said to her master, "Give this man something to eat, or his feces will come out as honeyed rose jam."

Al-Tawḥīdī greatly admired Abū ʿUthman ʿAmr ibn Baḥr al-Jāḥiẓ (d. 868 or 869), an extremely famous Arab prose writer particularly famous for his style of writing, and imitates him faithfully in *al-Baṣā'ir wa 'l-dhakhā'ir*. In particular, he employs al-Jāḥiẓ's technique of collecting material on many subjects and juxtaposing the different topics, as well as serious and amusing selections, in a way intended to prevent boredom. The anecdotes and saying stand independently; there is no dialogue to connect them. While he was writing this work, al-Tawḥīdī spent time in Iraq, Iran and the Ḥijaz, in a variety of situations, all or which enabled him to depict a broad panorama of the Buwayhid period.

In 963, al-Tawḥīdī made a pilgrimage to Mecca. He walked, which indicates he was too poor to own a riding beast. In Mecca, he spent his time with a group of Sufis. Although Sufism as a way of life was becoming more widespread during this period, Sufis, because they had renounced materials goods and sometimes even failed to observe customary Muslim manners, were considered far below the notice of the classes who might provide employment or patronage for a writer. After completing the pilgrimage, al-Tawḥīdī returned to Baghdad and remained there until 968. During this period, he made a short trip to Arrajān, where he visited the mathematician al-Wafā' al-Būjazānī (940-998), who would be of help to al-Tawḥīdī later in his life.

In 968, al-Tawḥīdī went to Rayy, a city near Isfahan, to the court of Abū 'l-Faḍl Ibn al-ʿAmīd (d. 970), the vizier of the Buwayhid *amīr* Rukn al-Dawlah (d. 976). Under the Buwayhids, the caliph had been reduced to a figurehead and his court was no longer set cultural standards. Instead, an increased number of smaller courts developed, particularly in Basrah, Kufa, Rayy, Isfahan, Shiraz and Aleppo, generally ruled by a member of the Buwayhid family and presided over by a powerful vizier, each with varying levels of prosperity at different times. Abū 'l-Faḍl Ibn al-ʿAmīd was a good administrator and therefore had one of the more prosperous courts. Al-Tawḥīdī addressed an epistle to Ibn al-ʿAmīd in hopes of being retained as a member of the court, but he was not successful. Ibn al-ʿAmīd was displeased by al-Tawḥīdī's fascination with Sufism, his unsightly appearance and his shabby clothing. However, his sojourn in Rayy enabled al-Tawḥīdī to develop a relationship with Aḥmad ibn Muḥammad Ibn Miskawayh (d. 1030), one of the most important classical Arab historians and a philosopher, who was employed as Ibn al-ʿAmīd's librarian.

In 971, al-Tawḥīdī was living in Karkh, the neighborhood of Baghdad to the southwest of the central "Round City," which had been built as the new capital city of the Abbasid dynasty. Under the Buwayhids, the western half of Baghdad generally declined. Karkh had become the most successful of the western neighborhoods because Baghdad's merchants lived and conducted business there. Karkh had a large Shiite population and was the location of frequent altercations and rioting between Sunnis and Shiites and of the accompanying looting and general destruction. It was also home to many singing girls and to the entertainment industry of the times. During this period, al-Tawḥīdī attended the meetings the circle of Yaḥyā ibn 'Adī, one of the philosophers with whom he studied regularly.

At about this time, al-Tawḥīdī began writing *al-Muqābasāt*. He did not finish it until 1001. *Al-Muqābasāt* is organized in the form of one hundred and six conversations, each on a different topic. They vary in length and are a record of the discussions that took place at circles al-Tawḥīdī attended, mostly those of Yaḥyā ibn 'Adī and of al-Sijistānī, the other philosopher with whom al-Tawḥīdī was closely associated. In general, the conversations begin with one of al-Sijistānī's students asking him a question which will the topic of the ensuing discussion. Al-Sijistānī's response stands out for its appropriateness and clear expression. The topics predictably include many aspects of philosophy, but also cover Greek logic, Arabic grammar, ethics, rhetoric, literary theory, agriculture and even some current events. The text is a particularly valuable record of the period because it depicts its intense intellectual inquiries and the variety of the beliefs and sects of the intellectuals who participated. A short list of the more common options includes: Jacobite Christians, Nestorian Christians, Melchite Christians, Sabaeans, Sunnis, Shiites, Zaydī Shiites, Ismailis, Mu'tazilis, Sufis, Ash'arīs, and Ḥanbalīs.

In 972, al-Tawḥīdī lived in the Bayn al-Sūrayn, one of the best areas of Karkh. The Byzantines invaded Syria and northern Mesopotamia in that year. Bakhtiyār (d. 967 or 968), the Buwayhid ruler in Iraq, sent to Baghdad for recruits to fight them. The populace gathered, but the Sunnis and Shiites began fighting each other. The rioting progressed to pillaging neighborhoods. Before the mayhem was quelled, al-Tawḥīdī's house was pillaged, all his possessions and money were stolen and his slave girl was killed. By this time, he was middle aged. Work as a copyist did not pay well enough for him to have expectations of recouping his losses.

Following this loss, al-Tawḥīdī sought patronage from Abū 'l-Faḍl Ibn al-ʿAmīd. Abū 'l-Fatḥ ʿAlī ibn Muḥammad Ibn al-ʿAmīd, (948 or 949–ca. 977) had succeeded his father, Abū 'l-Faḍl Ibn al-ʿAmīd, as Rukn al-Dawlah's vizier. When Rukn al-Dawlah sent his son 'Aḍūd al-Dawlah, who would soon become the greatest *amīr* of the Buwayhid dynasty, to Iraq in 974-975 to support the rule of another Buwayhid prince, Bakhtiyār, Abū 'l-Fatḥ Ibn al-ʿAmīd participated in the campaign and remained in Baghdad after it ended. Al-Tawḥīdī attended Abū 'l-Fatḥ's salons in hopes of obtaining a position, but was not offered employment. Although al-Tawḥīdī considered Abū 'l-Fatḥ to have a very promising career, the latter quarreled with older, better established administrators. He was arrested and executed. Al-Tawḥīdī had gained an excellent reputation from his participation in his salons, but he still failed to achieve the profitable position he so desired among a powerful man's closest advisors.

In 977, al-Tawḥīdī again left Baghdad for Rayy. This time he sought the patronage of al-Ṣāḥib Ibn 'Abbād (938-995), the vizier of two Buwayhid princes of the second generation of the dynasty, Mu'ayyid al-Dawlah (d. 984)—who ruled in Isfahan and Rayy—and Fakhr al-Dawlah (ca. 952–997)—who first ruled in Hamadān and Dīnawar and later in Isfahan and Rayy. Al-Tawḥīdī did not find the sort of position he hoped for. Instead of being employed as a scholar or close companion, he was employed as a copyist, a profession he wished to abandon. Al-Ṣāḥib Ibn 'Abbād did not hesitate to point out the lowly position of his employees in relation to his own, which made life even less tolerable. In addition, he was lax about paying them. Al-Ṣāḥib Ibn 'Abbād disliked philosophers and by extension, disliked al-Tawḥīdī's skill as a *mutakallim*. He also disliked al-Tawḥīdī's praise of Abū 'l-Fatḥ Ibn al-ʿAmīd. The final insult was when al-Ṣāḥib Ibn 'Abbād assigned the job of copying all thirty volumes of his writings to al-Tawḥīdī, who offered to copy a selection of them. After three years, in 980, al-Tawḥīdī returned to Baghdad, still impoverished. As a result of his experience, al-Tawḥīdī wrote *Akhlāq al-wazīrayn*. The work satirizes two of his former employers whom he felt had treated him badly: Abū 'l-Fatḥ Ibn al-ʿAmīd and al-Ṣāḥib Ibn 'Abbād.

Upon his return to Baghdad in 980, al-Tawḥīdī consulted an old friend, al-Wafā' al-Būjazānī, who in addition to being a renowned mathematician, had twenty-two years experience in working with politics and the wealthy, powerful men who set policies and ruled. Al-Būjazānī arranged a position for al-Tawḥīdī at the hospital in Baghdad. The pay was not sufficient. Al-Būjazānī then introduced him to Abū ʿAbd Allāh al-Ḥusayn ibn Aḥmad Ibn Saʿdān (d. 984 or 985), who was an official in Baghdad and later vizier under the Buwayhid *amīr* Ṣamṣām al-Dawlah (964–998).

Ibn Sa'dān first employed al-Tawḥīdī to copy al-Jāḥiẓ's *Kitāb al-ḥayawān* (The Book of Animals), a book of moral anecdotes featuring animals. Al-Tawḥīdī soon rose to the kind of position he had always sought. He was a constant companion to Ibn Sa'dān at his salons and was allowed to call him by his first name. He wrote *al-Imtā' wa 'l-mu'ānasah* to record conversations between himself and Ibn Sa'dān. The work gives two explanations for why it was written. One explanation is that al-Wafā' al-Būjazānī reminds al-Tawḥīdī that he is behaving inappropriately, that is, he prattles, forgets his place, is tactless and does not wear the right sort of clothes. Al-Wafā' al-Būjazānī requires him to report all his talks with Ibn Sa'dān and explains how he must write them. The other variant depicts Ibn Sa'dān desiring al-Tawḥīdī's company in order to learn from him.

Al-Imtā' wa 'l-mu'ānasah is divided into three books, with the forty nights it depicts numbered sequentially across them. Each night, Ibn Sa'dān proposes a topic and al-Tawḥīdī expands on it. The evening ends with an admonition to al-Tawḥīdī to continue the discussion the next night—a technique also used in popular literature like the *Thousand and One Nights*. In *al-Imtā' wa 'l-mu'ānasah*, al-Tawḥīdī criticizes the important men of his times. Like most of his works, it provides a good deal of information on the intellectual and social conditions of the Buwayhid period. Besides the description of the debate between Abū Sa'īd al-Sīrāfī and Mattā ibn Yūnus described above, the work also includes another work that has not survived elsewhere: a chapter from the *Ikhwān al-ṣafā'* (Brethren of Purity), an Ismaili work describing fifty-one sciences so that individuals may use them to purify their souls. In terms of style, al-Tawḥīdī strove to write clearly, to balance meaning and elegance of expression, and to instruct and entertain readers. A wide variety of types of material appear in *al-Imtā' wa 'l-mu'ānasah*. This is one short selection (*Kitāb al-imtā'*, ed. Amīn, 2:172)

> . . . the ecstasy of Ibn Ma'rūf, the Chief Judge, over the singing of 'Ulayyah when she sings the poetry of Ibn Abī Rabī'ah, her melody vibrating with feeling through her sweet throat:

Shine out in place of the moon if the moon sets
And take the place of the sun when dawn is delayed
For you have from the brilliant sun, its light
But it does not have your eyes and teeth.

Beginning in 981, al-Tawḥīdī expanded his activities and began to attend al-Sijistānī's salons. In 984, political rivals succeeded in having Ibn Sa'dān dismissed from his position as vizier. He was arrested and executed. He was succeeded as vizier by 'Abd al-'Azīz ibn Yūsuf Abū 'l-Qāsim al-Jakkār (d. 998), who was an enemy of al-Tawḥīdī. Since the next known mention of al-Tawḥīdī refers to 992 or 993, it seems safe to assume he was again without a patron. It is likely that he left Baghdad. It is possible that al-Tawḥīdī began *al-Ṣadāqah wa 'l-ṣadīq*, which will be discussed below, during his time with Ibn Sa'dān, but he certainly did not finish it before the latter died.

In 992 or 993, al-Tawḥīdī appeared in Shiraz. He was seeking patronage from al-Dalajī, a vizier under the still ruling Ṣamṣām al-Dawlah. He did not find a patron and so remained in

Shiraz, living in poverty. Despite the difficulty of his life, the period from around 996 until 1010 was very productive in term of his writings. He completed *al-Muqābasāt*, which was discussed above. *Al-Ishārāt al-ilāhiyyah*, al-Tawḥīdī's only work entirely on mysticism, was also written during this period. He finished writing *al-Ṣadāqah wa 'l-ṣadīq*, a work which was suggested by Ibn Sa'dān. Al-Tawḥīdī states in the work that he asked him to write a work on friends and friendship reminiscent of classical Latin or Greek works on the same topic. It is a collection of literary excerpts about all aspects of friendship. The excerpts are drawn from both prose and poetry written from Preislamic times through the tenth century. The authors include famous men whose works still exist and writers whose works have since been lost. Although al-Tawḥīdī writes about the positive aspects of friendship, he complains in his introduction that he never found the kind of sincere friend who would value him despite his shortcomings.

In 1010, with no outward sign of a developing change in attitude, al-Tawḥīdī seems to have experienced an inward spiritual crisis. He burned all of his books. Yāqūt ibn ʿAbd Allāh al-Ḥamawī relates that he complained that his earlier fame had been forgotten and that he had no respite from poverty and the struggle to survive, even to the point where he had to violate his standards of piety and virtue. He grieved over no longer having family or friends who would look on his works with forbearance. He particularly deplored his illness and poverty. It is apparent that he was beginning to look towards death. He compared his action to other notable pious men who had set aside their books in old age to concentrate on good works, piety and asceticism. He died in 1023 and was buried in Shiraz.

At the end of the nineteenth century, a work given the title *al-Risālah al-baghdādiyyah* came to be written about in association with al-Tawḥīdī. No information contemporary with al-Tawḥīdī describes the work. ʿAbbūd al-Shāljī links the title with a manuscript on whose first leaf is noted the title "*Ḥikāyat Abī 'l-Qāsim al-Baghdādī min al-'ajāyib wa 'l-gharāyib 'alā mājumi'at min al-ḥikāyāt*" (The Improvisation of Abū 'l-Qāsim al-Baghdādī from among the Wonders and the Novelties collected from the Improvisations). The beginning of the text specifies the author as Abū 'l-Muṭahhar Muḥammad ibn Aḥmad al-Azdī, who is not identifiable. The *Ḥikāyah min al-'ajāyib wa 'l-gharāyib 'alā mājumi'at min al-ḥikāyāt* quotes al-Tawḥīdī extensively, but it also quotes Abū ʿAbd Allāh al-Ḥusayn ibn Aḥmad Ibn al-Ḥajjāj (ca. 931–24 May 1001), a poet known for composing obscene poetry, equally extensively. Al-Shāljī additionally supports his argument by fallaciously conflating Abū 'l-Qāsim's personality with that of al-Tawḥīdī. Although the *Ḥikāyah* depicts a salon and a mendicant—a setting and a social class dear to al-Tawḥīdī—it is also unlike Tawḥīdī's other works in that it has a continuous narrative, plays extensively with literary genre, and includes almost no philosophical content. At best, attaching a title mentioned in passing to a work with no provenance is a questionable activity, and one should proceed cautiously in ascribing this particular work to al-Tawḥīdī.

REFERENCES

Aḥmad ʿAbd al-Ḥādī, *Abū Ḥayyān al-Tawḥīdī: faylasūf al-udabā' wa-adīb al-falsafah* (Cairo: Dār al-Thaqāfah, 1997);

Mohammed Arkoun, "L'Humanisme arabe au IVe/Xe siècle, d'après le Kitâb al-Hawâmil wa 'l-Šawâmil," *Studia Islamica*, No. 14 (1961): 73-108;

Mohammed Arkoun and Ḥāshim Ṣāliḥ, *Naz'at al-ansinah fī 'l-fikr al-'arabī: jīl Miskawayh wa 'l-Tawḥīdī* (Beirut: Dār al-Ṣāqī, 1997);

ʿAbd al-Amīr al-A'sam, *Abū Ḥayyān al-Tawḥīdī fī kitāb "al-Muqābasāt"* (Beirut: Dār al-Andalus li 'l-Ṭibā'ah wa 'l-Nashr wa 'l-Tawzī', 1980);

Afīf Bahnassī, *Falsafat al-fann 'inda 'l-Tawḥīdī* (Damascus: Dār al-Fikr, 1987);

Afīf Bahnassī, *al-Fikr al-jamālī 'inda 'l-Tawḥīdī* (Cairo: al-Majlis al-'Alā li 'l-Thaqāfah, 1997);

Marc Bergé, "Épitre sur les Sciences (Risāla fī 'l-'Ulūm) d'Abū Ḥayyān al-Tawḥīdī 310/922 (?)-414/1023): glossaire et index analytique," *Bulletin d'études orientales*, no. 21 (1968): 313-346;

Marc Bergé, *Essai sur la personnalité morale et intellectuelle d'Abū Hayyān al-Tawḥīdī*, 2 vols. (Lille: Service de reproduction des thèses, Université de Lille III, 1974);

Marc Bergé, *Pour un humanisme vécu: Abū Ḥayyan al-Tawḥīdī: essai sur la personnalité morale, intellectuelle et littéraire d'un grand prosateur et humaniste arabe engagé dans la société de l'époque bouyide, à Bagdad, Rayy et Chiraz, au IVe/Xe siècle (entre 310/922 et 320/932-414/1023)* (Damascus: Institut français de Damas, 1980);

Muḥammad ibn Aḥmad al-Dhahabī, *Mīzān al-i'tidāl fī naqd al-rijāl*, 4 vols. (Cairo: 'Īsā 'l-Bābī 'l-Ḥalabī, 1963-1964);

Abbas Hamdani, "Abū Ḥayyan al-Tawḥīdī and the Brethren of Purity," *International Journal of Middle East Studies*, 9, no. 3 (Oct., 1978): 345-353;

Zakariyyā Ibrāhīm, *Abū Ḥayyān al-Tawḥīdī: adīb al-falāsifah wa-faylasūf al-udabā'* (Cairo: al-Mu'assasah al-Miṣriyyah al-'Āmmah li 'l-Ta'līf wa 'l-Anbā' wa 'l-Nashr, 1964);

Ma'mūn ibn Muḥyī 'l-Dīn al-Jannān, *Abū Ḥayyān al-andalusī: manhajuhu al-tafsīrī* (Beirut: Dār al-Kutub al-'Ilmiyyah, 1993);

Mahā Maẓlūm Khidr, *Abū Ḥayyān al-Tawḥīdī: bibliyūjrāfiyyah mukhtārah* (Cairo: al-Hay'ah al-'Āmmah li-Dār al-Kutub wa 'l-Wathā'iq al-Qawmiyyah bi 'l-Ta'āwun ma'a 'l-Majlis al-'Alā li 'l-Thaqāfah, 1995);

Ibrāhīm Kīlānī, *Abū Ḥayyān al-Tawḥīdī* (Cairo, Dār al-Ma'ārif, 1971?);

Ibrāhīm Kīlānī, *Abū Ḥayyān at-Tawḥīdī: essayiste arabe du IVes de l'Hégire (Xes): introduction a son oeuvre* (Beirut: Institut français de Damas, 1950);

Ibrāhīm Kīlānī, *Rasā'il Abī Ḥayyān al-Tawḥīdī: muṣaddarah bi-dirāsah 'an hayātihi wa-āthārihi wa-adabih* (Damascus: Dār Ṭalās, 1990-1994);

Joel L. Kraemer, *Humanism in the Renaissance of Islam: a Preliminary Study: the Cultural Revival during the Buyid Age*, 2nd ed. (Leiden: E.J. Brill, 1992), 212-222;

Muḥyī 'l-Dīn Lādhiqānī, *Ābā' al-ḥadāthah al-'arabiyyah: madkhal ilā 'awālim al-Jāḥiẓ wa 'l-Ḥallāj wa 'l-Tawḥīdī* (Cairo: al-Hay'ah al-Miṣriyyah al-'Āmmah li 'l-Kitāb, 1998);

Ḥasan al-Maltāwī, *Allāh wa 'l-insān fī falsafat Abī Ḥayyān al-Tawḥīdī* (Cairo: Maktabat Madbūlī, 1989);

Everett K. Rowson, "The Philosopher as Litterateur: al-Tawḥīdī and his Predecessors," *Zeitschrift für Geschichte der arabisch-islamischen Wissenschaften*, 6 (1990): 50;

Khayrī Shalabī, *Abū Ḥayyān al-Tawḥīdī: rabī' al-thaqāfah al-'arabiyyah* (Cairo: Mu'assasat al-'Urūbah li 'l-Ṭibā'ah wa 'l-Nashr, 1990);

'Alī Shalaq, *Abū Ḥayyān al-Tawḥīdī wa 'l-qarn al-rābi' al-hijrī* (Beirut: al-Dār al-'Arabiyyah li 'l-'Ulūm: Dār al-Ijtihād, 2003);

'Abd al-Wāḥid Ḥasan al-Shaykh, *Abū Ḥayyān al-Tawḥīdī wa-wujūduhu 'l-adabiyyah wa 'l-fanniyyah* (Alexandria: al-Hay'ah al-Miṣriyyah al-'Āmmah li 'l-Kitāb, 1980);

al-Ḥabīb Shubayl, *al-Mujtama' wa 'l-ru'uyah: qirā'ah naṣṣiyyah fī 'l-imtā' wa 'l-mu'ānasah li-Abī Ḥayyān al-Tawḥīdī* (Beirut: al-Mu'assasah al-Jāmi'iyyah li 'l-Dirāsāt wa 'l-Nashr wa 'l-Tawzī', 1993);

Fā'iz Ṭāhā 'Umar, *al-Nathr al-fannī 'inda Abī Ḥayyān al-Tawḥīdī* (Baghdad: Dār al-Shu'ūn al-Thaqāfiyyah al-'Āmmah, Āfāq 'Arabiyyah, 2000);

Yāqūt ibn 'Abd Allāh al-Ḥamawī, *Irshād al-arīb ilā ma'rifat al-adīb*, ed. D.S. Margoliouth, 7 vols. E.J.W. Gibb Memorial Series, (Leiden: E.J. Brill, 1907-1931).

ʿUbādah Ibn Māʾ al-Samāʾ

(d. 1028 or 1030)

TERRI DEYOUNG
University of Washington

WORKS

Abū ʾl-Ḥasan ʿAlī Ibn Bassām al-Shantarinī, "Faṣl fī dhikr al-adīb Abī Bakr ʿUbādah ibn Māʾ al-Samāʾ wa-ithbāt jumlah min shiʿrih maʿa mā yataʿallaq bih min dhikrih" (Chapter concerning the Mention of the Literary Figure ʿUbādah Ibn Māʾ al-Samāʾ and the Listing of a Collection of His Poetry, together with What is Associated with the Mention of Him), in *al-Dhakīrah fī maḥāsin ahl al-Jazīrah* (The Treasury Containing the Virtues of the People of the [Iberian] Peninsula);

Muḥammad ibn Shakir al-Kutubī, "Ubādah ibn ʿAbd Allāh Ibn Māʾ al-Samāʾ al-Shāʿir al-Andalusī" (ʿUbādah Ibn Māʾ al-Samāʾ the Andalusian Poet), in *Fawāt al-wafayāt* (The Passing of the Deceased).

Editions

Abū ʾl-Ḥasan ʿAlī Ibn Bassām al-Shantarinī, *al-Dhakīrah fī maḥāsin ahl al-Jazīrah*, ed. Iḥsān ʿAbbās, vol. 1 pt. 1 (Beirut: Dār al-Thaqāfah, 1975), 468-480;

Muḥammad ibn Shakir al-Kutubī, *Fawāt al-wafayāt*, ed. Iḥsān ʿAbbās, vol. 2 (Beirut: Dār al-Thaqāfah, 1974), 149-153;

Sayyid Ghāzī, *Dīwān al-muwashshaḥāt al-Andalusiyyah*, vol. 1 (Alexandria: Munshaʾat al-Maʿārif, 1979), 5-10.

Abū Bakr ʿUbādah ibn ʿAbd Allāh Ibn Māʾ al-Samāʾ was an accomplished and versatile courtier, poet and teacher of literature who achieved a notable measure of success in his time. He lived during the waning days of the Umayyad caliphate in Cordoba and on into the days of civil strife when central power disintegrated in al-Andalus. He was insulated from these upheavals to a certain degree by his association with the Ḥammūdid dynasty, and when Yaḥyā, the last member of the family to reign in Cordoba, left that city for his base of power in the southern town of Malaga, ʿUbādah accompanied him, dying there in the late 1020s or early 1030s.

What ʿUbādah has been best known for, however, is as being one of the earliest poets to compose in the strophic poetic form known as the *muwashshaḥ*. He was long believed to have been the first of these whose work has come down to us. Recently this claim has been modified due to the discovery that one of the *muwashshaḥa*s included in the anthology called *ʿUddat al-Jalīs* (50-52) was by Abū ʾl-Qāsim ibn al-ʿAttār, an Andalusian poet born early in the tenth century. But ʿUbādah still remains, as Samuel Stern has said, "the first *washshāḥ* [writer of *muwashshaḥa*s] who is more than a name to us" (63).

Although there is no evidence that ʿUbādah's poetry was ever collected in a *dīwān*—either in his lifetime or later—his works were well-known to his contemporaries and continued to be so on into the succeeding century, when the great anthologist Abū ʾl-Ḥasan ibn ʿAlī Ibn al-Bassām al-Shantarinī (d. 1147) devoted a dozen or so pages to discussing Ibn Māʾ al-Samāʾ's poems in classical Arabic, including several panegyrics to the Ḥammūdid family. Ibn Bassām also connects Ibn Māʿ al-Samāʾ to the production of *muwashshaḥa*s, saying "it was as though no [*muwashshaḥa*s] were heard in Andalus, except his, and none were taken except from him" (469). Although Ibn Bassām then goes on to tell us that he has decided not include any *muwashshaḥa*s by Ibn Māʾ al-Samāʾ because they do not fit into his criteria for his anthology, not "being in meters used by the

Arabs," he does, in the course of describing Ibn Māʾ al-Samāʾ's fame, give us the first extensive description of what the *muwashshaḥ* was like. The actual texts of two *muwashshaḥa*s by him were preserved in other anthologies, like the twelfth-century biographical dictionary *Fawāt al-wafayāt* by Muḥammad Ibn Shākir al-Kutubī (d. 1363).

These sources, however, give relatively little information about Ibn Māʾ al-Samāʾ's background. He has a lengthy genealogy (given in the entry on him, for example, by Khalaf ibn ʿAbd al-Malik Ibn Bashkuwāl (1101-1183)) tracing his ancestry back to the head of the Khazraj tribe in Muḥammad's (d. 632) time, Saʿd ibn ʿUbādah, though how or why his ancestors emigrated to Andalus is not mentioned. Similarly, we do not know if he grew up in Cordoba or came there, as an aspiring courtier, seeking an education. Nor do we have exact information on when he was born. Given the fact, however, that his most important teacher, the grammarian Abū Bakr Muḥammad al-Zubaydī died around the year 1000, it is most likely he was born sometime around 980, perhaps as late as 985.

Such a birth date would be in keeping with the fact that he is recorded as composing one (but only one) panegyric (Ibn Bassām, 475) in honor of the chamberlain al-Manṣūr (d. 1002):

We have a chamberlain who has seized the heights entirely
becoming in his varied character of one nature,
But let the ignorant one not be deceived by his apparent pleasantness
for most of the terror in thunder follows upon the lightning flash.

Such a slight product has all the hallmarks of youthful experimentation and does not suggest any close relationship between the poet and the shrewd politician.

But, early in life, Ibn Māʾ al-Samāʾ was already showing a predilection for the kind of love and wine poetry, inherited from past generations, that was an integral part of the social fabric of Cordoba at its height. As Ibn Bassām tells us, ʿUbādah recounted more than once the story of his first composition that gives something of the flavor of that period. He had decided to while away an afternoon watching the archery contests taking place among the soldiers on the banks of the Guadalquiver river outside the city of Cordoba. While there ʿUbādah fell instantly in love with one of the soldiers at practice, and he was moved to compose the following lines (475):

Nothing frightens me but arrows pelting
toward a target, shot by the two [firm] hands of a gazelle.
They stand up tall to shoot at it, but they have no goal
save my heart in shooting.

This a simple excursion turns into an occasion charged with aesthetic power and erotic tension, brought about through the mediation of poetry.

Similarly, probably his most famous lyric was a short poem describing a night of drinking in a wine shop (473):

Have you seen anything more beautiful than cups
kissed by parted lips, cradled in [open] hands?
He says to the cupbearer: "Help me to it,
take some silver and give it back to me as gold."
Care can drown there, while bubbles
float atop it, in a frothy foam.
A mustache can turn white there
while he takes it in his hand eternally.

The notion that wine can be transformative—foreshadowing the positive effects of change through the lens of its intoxicating power—is very old in Islamic culture, going back at least to the work of the early Abbasid court poet Abū Nuwas (ca. 756-ca. 810). Ibn Māʾ al-Samāʾ's metaphor comparing the golden color of the wine with money (the medium for which it is exchanged) however, was seen by critics like Ibn Bassām as a satisfyingly original variation on this venerable theme.

ʿUbādah's facility with this kind of poetry may have fed his interest in the *muwashshaḥ* form, which early on and through most of its history has been associated with music and revelry. Certainly one of the two *muwashshaḥa*s associated with Ibn Māʾ al-Samāʾ's name is of this type. It describes in exquisite detail a young woman with whom 'Ubādah has fallen in love (Ghāzī, 5-7):

The love of the doe is an act of devotion
from every smiling bracelet a full moon rises.
In all the goodness of the lands of perfection
its goodness is the most original.

What is most immediately arresting about these lines in the original—besides their affinity with the rest of the Arabic lyric love tradition extending back for several centuries—is their novel rhyme scheme. 'Ubādah successfully uses rhyme as a stylistic device to highlight the affinities between separate images in a skillful way, but more than that he focuses on variation in rhyme (rather than the reinforcement resulting from monorhyme) to achieve this effect.

Arabic had been the first great literary tradition to emerge from the lands bordering the Mediterranean to employ rhyme. Neither Greek nor Latin verse, nor the Semitic languages Hebrew and Syriac, all of which had given rise to sophisticated poetry, had ever regularly resorted to this device. One can discern certain rhyme effects, especially assonance, in individual poems from these traditions, but they are the exception and not the norm. This ancient aversion to rhyme was already beginning to break down in Late Antiquity, possibly through the intervention of choral music in church and synagogue and the rise of popular forms of poetry (which may have been more receptive to such an oral, rhythmic feature). So it is perhaps not surprising to find in the first great poetic tradition to emerge in the wake of the transformations taking place as Antiquity evolved toward the medieval world—Arabic—not only consistent rhyming of poems but a kind of hyper-rhyme (monorhyme) where every line concluded with a word ending in the same consonant.

The *muwashshaḥ* represents one of several forms in Arabic poetry that had begun to appear in written sources in the tenth and eleventh centuries taking the convention of monorhyme to the next level by varying the rhyme scheme. In 'Ubādah's *muwashshaḥ*, for example, the rhyme scheme of the *qufl* (initial stanza) is:

a b c
d c

where both lines end in the same rhyme (the monorhyme), while varied rhymes are used within each line (the second line being one foot shorter than the first). Based on contemporary descriptions of how the *muwashshaḥ* was sung (as well as modern parallels and parallel forms in other languages), scholarly consensus is now that these initial lines (the first *qufl*) most likely comprise a sort of refrain that was repeated at the end of every succeeding stanza. Indeed, the last two lines of the five stanzas that make up the body of the poem repeat exactly the entire rhyme scheme of the *qufl*, thus creating a smooth transition to choral repetition of the initial *qufl* as a refrain. The last set of lines rhyming with the *qufl* pattern—often in colloquial Arabic or Romance (though not always)—was given a special name, the *kharjah*.

The first three lines in each of the five stanzas (preceding the two lines following the *qufl* rhyme scheme) are called the *ghusn*, the Arabic word for "bough." Each line is endstopped with monorhyme, and in addition has another rhyme, repeated throughout the *ghusn*, in the middle of the line, yielding the following pattern:

ab
ab
ab

This is the innovation that 'Ubādah created, according to Ibn Bassām's account (469):

> The first to compose the rhythms of these *muwashshaḥa*s in our country, and to invent their method of composition—as far as I have determined—was Muḥammad ibn Maḥmūd al-Qabrī, the Blind. He used to compose them according to the hemistiches of poems [in Arabic]. He composed most of them, however, according to meters that do not follow the accustomed system of metrics and are not used. He used to take colloquial expressions, not in good Arabic, and he called them the *markaz* [equivalent to the term *kharjah*]. He built the *muwashshaḥ* on them, not using internal rhyme or *ghusns*. It is said that

> Ibn ʿAbd Rabbih, the author of *al-ʿIqd al-farīd* (The Unique Necklace) was the first to compose this type of *muwashshaḥ* among us. Then Yūsuf ibn Hārūn al-Ramādī arose, and he was the first one who frequently used internal rhyme in the *markaz*. He would particularly use internal rhyme at every place where a foot came to an end. The poets of our age have continued in this way, like Mukarram ibn Saʿīd and the two sons of Abū ʾl-Ḥasan. Then ʿUbādah [Ibn Māʾal-Samāʾ] arose, and he originated [the technique of] *tadfīr*, that is, he emphasized the places where the *ghusn* paused internally with rhymes, as al-Ramādī had done with the *markaz*.

This passage is the earliest discussion of the historical development of the *muwashshaḥ* (even though coming from as late as the beginning of the twelfth century). It has thus greatly influenced writing about the history of the form, despite its occasional contradictions and omissions. There has been, however, no way of independently verifying the account Ibn Bassām provides here, because ʿUbādah's *muwashshaḥa*s have always been the earliest examples that have come down to modern times. Certainly, the formal description he gives conforms well to the structural features we see in both of ʿUbādah's poems. Unfortunately, Ibn al-ʿAttār's poem—tentatively dated to the beginning of the tenth century—exhibits exactly the same rhyme structure we see in Ibn Māʾ al-Samāʾ's work. So whether he actually did invent the technique of *tadfīr* is open to question. We may never be able to provide a definitive answer to this issue, because of the paucity of evidence at our command.

There are other aspects of ʿUbādah's *muwashshaḥa*s—and the form in general—that are equally problematic. Chief among these is the question of the meter(s) used to compose these poems. It certainly is true, as Ibn Bassām said, that the meters do not follow the usual patterns found in Arabic poems. Some scholars have said that these unusual metrical patterns are simply minor variations on the traditional system of Arabic prosody and they may thus be scanned using this system of long and short syllables. Others have proposed that it would be actually more faithful to the real rhythms of the poems to scan them according to a system of accentual stress. Since many of these poems are in colloquial Arabic (and some use Spanish Romance elements), and Hispano-Arabic colloquial is no longer a living language, it may be impossible to answer the question with precision. Certainly, a system of scansion may simply be an imposition of convenience, having virtually nothing to do with the actual rhythm of the poem, as can be seen in the English Renaissance author George Gascoigne's (d. 1577) attempts (in his *Certayne notes of Instruction*) to scan English verse using a quantitative model, presumably because of the greater prestige attached to (quantitative) Greek and Latin verse.

A similar problem occurs when we try to harmonize Ibn Bassām's discussion of the *kharjah* (he uses the term *markaz* for both the *kharjah* and the *qufl* in general) with the practice ʿUbādah followed in composing both of his *muwashshaḥa*s. Although Ibn Bassām specifically states that this section of the poem should be in colloquial Arabic or Romance, in both examples attributed to ʿUbadah, the relevant section is in perfectly acceptable standard Arabic. Even in Ibn al-ʿAttār's poem—where the *kharjah* is closer to colloquial than in either of Ibn Māʾ al-Samāʾ's *muwashshaḥa*s—it could still be considered standard Arabic. There are poems that clearly have *kharjah*s in Romance or Arabic colloquial, but they are later than these early examples. Clearly, the course of development in these poems is not a straightforward evolution from a popular form to a more learned one. Further, it was worth asking what relevance these features of ʿUbādah's *muwashshaḥa*s might have to the broader question of the relationship between the *muwashshaḥ* and the *zajal*, which is a strophic poem produced entirely in colloquial (Abū Bakr ibn ʿAbd al-Malik Ibn Quzmān (1078 or 1080-1160) provides us with our most comprehensive examples of this genre in his *dīwān*), and with a less complex structure? Although it would seem to be common sense that the *muwashshaḥ* evolved from the *zajal* form—and not the other way around—the evidence currently available has not compelled all scholars to draw that conclusion, and each interpretation has its proponents.

To return to the question of the content in Ibn Mā' al-Samā's first *muwashshaḥ*, the first stanza (*ghusn* plus *qufl*) creates an almost pointillist portrait of the poet's beloved, concentrating serially on different aspects of her form and appearance, virtually anticipating the cinematic technique of successive close-ups:

To God belongs that good one
with a saucy face,
She has the stature of a swaying bough
and her earring is the Pleiades,
Parted lips, droplets from a rain cloud,
moistened with wine.
Sipping it is happiness, as though it were
the purest claret, jewels faceted.
From there you drink fresh flowing water,
the watering place unsullied and sweet.

The comparisons—her long back like a swaying bough, her earring resembling the constellation of stars known as the Pleiades—are conventional in Arabic love poetry, and do not involve particular innovations. Even the technique used here so extensively by Ibn Mā' al-Samā', of bringing one feature into focus, then abruptly moving to another, can typically be found in earlier verse. Taken together, the inventory of her characteristics here at the beginning of the poem is just that: a list of items that do not coalesce to create a whole, and certainly do not give the impression of a living, breathing woman (and the pronoun referents—unlike in 'Ubādah's first poem—are clearly female in gender here).

This emphasis on visual presentation of the poem's subject—and its attendant dissolution of her human integrity—is indirectly challenged in the last stanza of the poem where the power of the poet's visual sensory input is shown to be limited, especially in the *kharjah*:

With modest robes trailing,
her garments immaculate,
Ravisher of minds,
more delicate [in her effect] than drink,
My emaciation from love is blood sacrifice to
her,
in my torment.
In sleep I might have escape,
but her rule is potent: whenever I withdraw
From her, then the dream
phantom visits me while I am asleep.

The poet at first seems to believe that, if he stops looking at her and takes refuge in sleep, he will be able to overcome the impasse between visual possession and actual possession: (the first of which he has but the other he does not, leading to his eternal frustration). What happens in the poem instead is that the dynamics of control are reversed. Now the beloved is able to visit the poet in sleep and disturb his slumber with dreams of her, while the power formerly provided by his ability to hold her in place and dissect her with his eyes has vanished. Even were this not a *muwashshaḥ*, it would be an effective poem, and the motive behind its preservation is easy to understand.

We cannot date this *muwashshaḥ* with any precision, but it is certainly likely that it was an early composition by 'Ubādah. Once the Umayyad caliphate in Cordoba began to disintegrate, and new rulers began to replace each other with astonishing frequency, the panegyric form—praising the qualities of an ideal leader—began probably to take on greater urgency, and this is certainly true of 'Ubādah's poetic output. He seems to have reached his peak as a poet in panegyrics for the Ḥammūdid dynasty that held power (with some interruptions) between 1016 and 1024. Ibn Bassām includes a number of poems by Ibn Mā' al-Samā' praising in equally enthusiastic terms all three members of the dynasty: 'Alī (d. 1018), his brother Qāsim (d. 1039-1040), and 'Alī's son Yaḥyā (d. 1035).

'Alī had been the governor of Algeciras and Ceuta in the previous regime, who had rallied a large army from that area to rescue the last legitimate Umayyad caliph, Hishām al-Mu'ayyad (d. ca. 1013). This individual had been used by as a figurehead by the 'Āmirids during their tenure, and had been imprisoned by his cousin Sulaymān (d. 1016) when the latter had secured a precarious hold on the office of caliph in 1013. 'Alī now swore to liberate Hishām and return him to the throne.

In addition to the authority provided by his proclaimed mission to deliver Hishām, ʿAlī (though he had grown up among the Berber tribes of North Africa) could claim an illustrious lineage of his own, stretching back to the Prophet Muḥammad (through his daughter Fāṭimah (d. 632 or 633) and son-in-law ʿAlī ibn Abī Ṭālib (ca. 600-660)). This image undoubtedly strengthened his standing among the troops he commanded. But his plans seem to have changed substantially when, after capturing the city, the now-captive Sulaymān told him that Hishām had been murdered. ʿAlī had already proclaimed to his allies that Hishām had appeared to him in a dream and foretold that, were the Umayyad line to fail, a man whose name began with the letter *ʿayn* (as ʿAlī does) would become the ruler of al-Andalus. This prophetic vision was now used to give him a pretext to seize power in his own name.

Among those who welcomed ʿAlī to Cordoba was ʿUbādah Ibn Māʾ al-Samāʾ, who composed a long panegyric to honor him at his accession. The poem begins with lines that allude to ʿAlī's noble background and the providential inevitability of his assumption of sovereignty (Ibn Bassām, 478):

Hearts have become obedient to you, so too the one who has been rebellious,
and the party of God is your party, ʿAlī!
All who have claimed a right to stand on the heights with you
is given to lies, as was the Pretender. . .
If someone seeking to boast says: "So-and-so is my ancestor"
you have only to say: "My ancestor is the Prophet."

It was the intensity of this adulation that probably caused Ibn Bassām to label ʿUbādah a "partisan" of the Ḥammūdids. The word he uses (*tashayyuʿ*) is related to the root from which the term "Shiite" is derived, and certainly the kind of veneration some Shiite groups gave to their leaders would have been familiar in the area ever since the Fatimid movement had arisen in North Africa a century earlier. This has led some scholars to consider the Ḥammūdids a Shiite dynasty and ʿUbādah a believer in Shiite doctrines. While the language used in this panegyric—like the "party of God," or the explicit connection made between ʿAlī and the Prophet's family—is suggestive, it should be remembered that Ibn Bassām also describes Abū Muḥammad ʿAlī ibn Aḥmad Ibn Ḥazm's (994-1064) regard for the Umayyads as "partisanship" (*tashayyuʿ*) and there is no hint of Shiism in that relationship, since Ibn Ḥazm's entire career was built on a rejection of Shiism.

It was probably during this period (ʿAlī's investiture) that the second *muwashshaḥah* we have from ʿUbādah was composed. It differs from the first in being a panegyric. The praise is addressed to an individual named ʿAlī, who may very well be ʿAlī ibn Ḥammūd (d. 1018).

At any rate, it mixes motifs familiar in Arabic love poetry with the language of power and dominance, as is clear from the first *qufl* (Ghāzī, 8):

One who been given command
in a nation, and not behaved with justice,
Will be censured, except by the glances of fawn with dark eyes.

Here, the idiom of love poetry clearly mixes with the language of authority and power. The beloved is characterized as an unjust prince, who is censured by all his subjects, except the beloved (poet), the "fawn with dark eyes."

The poet's oscillation between the vision of the patron as beloved and as king (source of favors) continues throughout the poem, neither characterization being allowed to dominate over the other. This view of the person being addressed in the poem as a sort of divine figure who should be adored in a way mere humans cannot, has seemed to some as further evidence of ʿUbādah's Shiite leanings. But it is also worth noting that he seems to have been greatly influenced in much of his work by the Eastern poet Abū al-Ṭayyib al-Mutanabbī (915-965). Ibn Bassām gives many examples of how Ibn Māʾ al-Samāʾ quotes al-Mutanabbī, or alludes to lines by him. Mutanabbī was well-known for using imagery taken from love poetry in addressing his patron, Sayf al-Dawlah (915 or 916-967), in his *qaṣīdah*s. So we may have here more of a borrowing from literary convention, and not so much an imposition of specifically Shiite religious attitudes.

We certainly see the same admixture of martial and autocratic imagery with erotic desire in another, more formal poem that likely comes from the end of Ibn Mā' al-Samā''s life (because it interweaves with the idyllic moment nostalgic references to his youth) (Ibn Bassām, 472):

Drink, for the age of youth should be taken advantage of,
[it is] an opportunity that, after it passes, [leaves behind only] regret.
Give [the wine] to me with a delicate hand,
[your] glances into people's souls are commanding.
They are like the prince's sword
whose edges are dipped in the blood of his enemies.
Give the cups as a remembrance
for no dessert is sweet unless a mouth enfolds it.

Even at the moment of the poet's greatest enjoyment of the present moment, he is reminded that death is not far, but lies at the edge of the prince's sword.

The Ḥammūdids gave up their attempts to control Cordoba at the end of 1025, so it is likely that 'Ubādah never returned there after that date, but lived out the remainder of his life in Malaga, which had become the seat of power for the dynasty. It may have been during this time that he became more involved in teaching, and may have put the finishing touches on his masterwork, *Ṭabaqāt al-shu'arā' al-Andalus* (Ranking of the Poets of Andalus), which survives only in fragmentary quotations. This work was singled out, however, by 'Ubādah's contemporary Ibn Ḥazm (in his treatise *Faḍl al-Andalus wa-dhikr rijālih* (The Virtues of Andalus and the Mention of its Great Men)) as an important contribution to the vigorous cultural life emerging in Andalus at the time despite the surrounding political upheavals.

There is some difference of opinion as to exactly when 'Ubādah died. Both the historian Abū Marwān Ḥayyān ibn Khalaf Ibn Ḥayyān (987 or 988-1076) and the rhetorician Abū 'Āmir Aḥmad Ibn Shuhayd (992-1035) say he died in 1028. On the other hand, Ibn Ḥazm—the source of so much biographical material about this period—states that Ibn Mā' al-Samā' must have lived at least until early 1030, because he is credited with composing a short poem about a remarkable hail storm that occurred during that year. It is perhaps fitting that even the resolution of something so mundane as the date of 'Ubādah's death is put down to the evidence offered by one of his poems, and that—as seems to be so often the case with this very real yet very mysterious poet, his work raises more questions than it answers.

REFERENCES

Iḥsān 'Abbās, *Tārīkh al-adab al-Andalusī*, rev. ed., vol. 1 (Beirut: Dār al-Thaqāfah, 1969), 303-322;

'Alī ibn Bishrī, *'Uddat al-jalīs*, ed. Alan Jones (Cambridge: E.J.W. Gibb Memorial Trust, 1992);

George Gascoigne, *Certayne notes of Instruction in English Verse; The Steele Glasse; The Complaynt of Philomene*, ed. Edward Arber (Westminster: A. Constable, 1895);

Khalaf ibn 'Abd al-Malik Ibn Bashkuwāl, *Kitāb al-ṣilah* (Cairo: al-Dār al-Miṣriyyah li 'l-Ta'lif wa 'l-Tarjamah, 1966);

Abū Muḥammad 'Alī ibn Aḥmad Ibn Ḥazm, *Rasā'il*, 2 vols., ed. Iḥsan 'Abbās (Cairo: Maktabat al-Khanī, 1954);

James T. Monroe, "*Zajal* and *Muwashshaḥa*: Hispano-Arabic Poetry and the Romance Tradition," in *The Legacy of Muslim Spain*, ed. Salma Khadra Jayyusi (Leiden: E.J. Brill, 1994), 398-419;

Samuel M. Stern, *Hispano-Arabic Strophic Poetry: Studies by Samuel Miklos Stern*, ed. L.P. Harvey (Oxford: The Clarendon Press, 1974), *passim*.

Usāmah ibn Munqidh

(4 July 1095-15 November 1188)

TERRI DEYOUNG
University of Washington

WORKS

Dīwān (Collected Poems);
al-Manāzil wa 'l-diyār (Dwellings and Abodes);
Kitāb al-'asā (Book of the Staff);
Lubāb al-ādāb (Kernals of Refinement);
al-Badī' fī 'l-badī' fī naqd al-shi'r (Marvels in the Art of Rhetoric in the Criticism of Poetry);
Kitāb al-i'tibār (The Book of Moral Lessons).

Editions

Dīwān, ed. by Aḥmad Aḥmad Badawī (Cairo: al-Maṭbā'ah al-'Amiriyyah, 1953);
al-Manāzil wa 'l-diyār, ed. by Muṣṭafā Ḥijāzī (Cairo: Dār al-Taḥrīr li 'l-Ṭab' wa 'l-Nashr, 1968);
Kitāb al-'aṣā, ed. by 'Abd al-Salām Hārūn (Cairo: n.p., 1953);
Lubāb al-ādāb, ed. by Aḥmad Muḥammad Shākir (Cairo:Maktabat Luwīs Sarkīs, 1935);
al-Badī' fī 'l-badī' fī naqd al-shi'r, ed. by 'Abd Allāh 'Alī Muhannā (Beirut: Dār al-Kutub al-'Ilmiyyah, 1987);
Kitāb al-i'tibār, ed. Philip K. Hitti (Princeton: Princeton University Press, 1930).

Translations

Usamah ibn Munqidh, *An Arab-Syrian Gentleman and Warrior in the Period of the Crusades: Memoirs of Usamah ibn Munqidh*, transl. by Philip K. Hitti (Princeton: Princeton University Press, 1929);
Paul M. Cobb, "Usama ibn Munqidh's *Book of the Staff* (*Kitāb al-'Asa*): Autobiographical and Historical Excerpts," *al-Masaq: Islam and the Medieval Mediterranean* 17, 1 (2005): 109-123;
Paul M. Cobb, "Usama ibn Munqidh's *Kernals of Refinement* (*Lubāb al-ādāb*): Autobiographical and Historical Excerpts," *al-Masaq: Islam and the Medieval Mediterranean* 18, 1 (2006): 67-78.

Usāmah ibn Munqidh was part of an influential circle of literary figures who eventually coalesced around the court of Ṣalāḥ al-Dīn, founder of the Ayyubid dynasty and foe of the Crusaders, in the late twelfth century C.E. Usāmah was the most noted poet of the group, becoming the favorite of Ṣalāḥ al-Dīn al-Ayyūbī (1137-1193) himself, who is known in Europe as Saladin. The others, like 'Imād al-Dīn Muḥammad ibn Muḥammad Kātib al-Iṣfahānī (1125-1201), 'Abd al-Raḥīm ibn 'Alī 'l-Qāḍī 'l-Fāḍil (1135-1200), and Usāmah's special friend Ṭalā'i' ibn Ruzzīk (1101 or1102-September 1161), were by profession chancery clerks (*kātibs*) and more noted for their prose. So it is a historical irony that Usāmah became the best-remembered of the group for a prose work that survived in a single manuscript, but nevertheless has been translated into English and several other European languages, and is considered to give the liveliest and most compelling account of the experience of the Crusades from a Muslim perspective. This book, *Kitāb al-i'tibār*, in its English version (entitled by its translator, Philip K. Hitti, *An Arab-Syrian Gentleman and Warrior in the Period of the Crusades: Memoirs of Usāmah ibn Munqidh*) has never been out of print since it was published in 1929, a distinction few other Arabic books can claim.

The situation was quite the reverse in the medieval period. Then, Usāmah's poetry was well-known, as were his anthologies *al-Manāzil wa 'l-diyār, Kitāb al-'aṣā*, and *Lubāb al-ādāb*, and his rhetoric manual *al-Badī' fī 'l-badī'*, while *Kitāb al-i'tibār* was virtually unknown.

He and his circle even enjoyed a short-lived popularity among the bureaucratic administrators and court poets of the Egyptian ruler Muḥammad ʿAlī Bāshā (1769-1849) in the early nineteenth-century for their epistles and poetry. After that, Usāmah's reputation languished for several decades. But when *Kitāb al-i'tibār* was discovered among a cache of manuscripts at the Escorial Library in Spain by the French orientalist Hartwig Derenbourg in 1889 and translated into French, matters changed significantly. The book became an object of interest in Arabic as well, and led eventually to the publication of his other works in modern editions. With the inclusion of selections from *Kitāb al-i'tibār* in primary and secondary curricula, Usāmah became famous even to schoolchildren in the Arab world, while his friends and compatriots receded into the background, their work solely the province of specialists in a relatively neglected era of Arabic literature.

Usāmah was born in a fortress that is today near the eastern coast of Syria, about twenty-five miles from the urban center of Homs. At the time of his birth, this castle, Shayzar, had recently been recaptured from the Byzantines, though his family had been granted lands in the neighborhood as early as 1025 by the ruler of Aleppo at the time, the founder of the Mirdāsid dynasty. The Banū Munqidh could trace their ancestry back to Arab tribes of the Preislamic period, so Usāmah could claim to have a noble heritage. Philip Hitti's characterization of him, however, as a "gentleman"—and not a prince—should be given its due. His was not one of the greatest families in the history of Islam, but they had been an integral part of the warrior class who formed the backbone of the armies of the early Arab conquests, and they were well respected by their peers.

Kitāb al-i'tibār gives us much information about the early period of Usāmah's life. But, despite the fact that its translator characterized it as a "memoir," it is not a straightforward account of the author's life, and should be used with caution as a biography. Its title in Arabic means "Book of Moral Lessons," but even that is not necessarily an informative description of its purpose. It is akin to a sort of composition that was very popular in medieval Arabic literature, *'ajā'ib al-makhlūqāt* (the wonders of creation) that could be considered to have a counterpart in the medieval Latin *mirabilia* genre. In other words, most of the book concerns instances that Usāmah has encountered in his life that revealed to him the unfathomable power of God because these events run counter to the expectations of a rational, educated person. Usāmah's plan is probably more obscure, to modern readers especially, than it would have been otherwise by the fact the first forty-two pages of the manuscript have been lost. But it becomes clearer as one proceeds past the introductory section (which does follow a rough chronological order) to the following ones that recount, not a sequence of events, but a selection of amazing incidents from Usāmah's life, frequently prefaced by the phrase "one of the amazing things I witnessed was. . ." (Hitti, 33). So, Usāmah's references to unusual cures (87 and 213ff.) the bravery of women (152-53), or one Crusader knight routing four Muslim warriors (96) should not be taken as stories of what were usual and normal events in his life, but illustrations of those moments when God seemed to intervene and reveal to him how little his rational faculties were up to the task of explaining the world around him. It reflects the change in the orientation of Muslim intellectuals over the preceding century. In the late 900s and early 1000s, thoughtful men were still very much influenced by the doctrines of Muʿtazilism, a school of Islamic theology that stressed the idea that all creation was capable of rational explanation For Usāmah and his contemporaries, this approach to phenomena was no longer considered viable.

Usāmah's long lifetime contained many reversals of fortune whose explanation would have challenged even the most skeptical and worldly of men. He was born in the midsummer of a year when the lords of Shayzar were enjoying the end of a period of peace and prosperity for the family and their subjects. Usāmah's grandfather had been able to annex the fortress—which guarded a strategic crossroads inland from the coast—a decade before, in 1081. Prior to that time, the castle and the area as far as the coastal port of Latakia had been for eighty years under the control of the Byzantines. But their troops had withdrawn to Constantinople in the wake of the disastrous Byzantine defeat at Manzikert (far away on the eastern marches of the Empire), where the Seljuk Turks had destroyed most of the army and taken the Emperor prisoner. In the intervening decade, however, Seljuk power had also begun to decline, and the small principalities—like that of the Banū Munqidh—grew proportionately stronger.

In the same year that Usāmah was born another event took place in distant Europe that would have an incalculable impact on his entire life. In November 1095, the new Pope, Urban II (ca. 1042-1099), had been approached by envoys from the recently installed Byzantine emperor Alexius I Comnenus (1048-1118). Alexius was asking for troops to help him re-conquer some of his lost territories, most especially the major port of Antioch, located to the northeast of Shayzar. Urban was receptive to the idea and, at the end of the month, he preached a sermon at the small southern French town of Clermont where he had summoned all the leaders of the Church for the first great council of his reign. We do not know exactly what he said (the surviving accounts of the sermon differ quite significantly from one another), but he was able to persuade several great lords of Europe to travel to the East with their armies and join with Alexius, with the ultimate goal of retaking the city of Jerusalem from Muslim control.

At this time, Jerusalem was no longer under Turkish suzerainty, but had been restored to the Egyptian Fatimid caliphs, the last of the great imperial states (the Buwayhids in Iraq and the Umayyads in Spain being the others) ruling at the beginning of the eleventh century that were still in power. The Fatimids had always been (with the notable exception of the Caliph Ḥākim bi-Amr Allāh, who had disappeared mysteriously in 1021, and was thereafter presumed dead) tolerant to non-Muslims, and had encouraged and protected Christian pilgrims to Jerusalem. But now the Fatimid dynasty was on its last legs, as the adult Usāmah would find to his cost when he became embroiled in the intrigues rampant during its dying days. All this set the stage for Usāmah having to navigate a world that his training and upbringing did not prepare him for, and that frequently frustrated his expectations.

The upheavals generated by the Crusaders' march down the coast in 1097 and 1098, and the generally insecure situation for Muslims in the towns they occupied in the ensuing years ironically meant that Usāmah enjoyed a more brilliant education at Shayzar than he might otherwise have had. A number of locally important intellectuals and literary figures took refuge in the castle over the years, for Usāmah's grandfather and uncle Sultan purchased their security by lavish presents to the leaders of the armies (both Muslim and Christian) that sought to invest and capture Shayzar on several occasions during Usāmah's childhood and youth. We know, for example, the two locally famous poets, Aḥmad ibn Munīr al-Trabulsī (from Tripoli) and Abū 'l-Muʿafā Sālim (from Maʿarrat al-Nuʿmān, the hometown of the leading poet of the preceding period, Abū 'l-ʿAlā' al-Maʿarrī (973-1058)) spent considerable time at Shayzar in Usāmah's early years. He studied literature more formally (for a long time) with Abū ʿAbd Allāh ibn Munīrah, who was also a refugee at Shayzar.

It was, however, his grammar teacher, Abū ʿAbd Allāh al-Tulaytilī (former head of Dār al-ʿIlm—the Center for Advanced Studies—in Tripoli) who seems to have made the greatest impression on him. He tells us in *Kitāb al-iʿtibār* of a time when he went to his teacher's room and found all the great grammar textbooks—including ʿAmr ibn ʿUthmān Sibawayh's *Kitāb*, Ibn Jinnī's (d. 1002) *Khasā'is*, and Abū ʿAlī 'l-Fārisī's (900-987) *Īḍāh*—laid out before Abū ʿAbd Allah. He asked him if he had read all these and his master replied that, yes, he had read them. But not just that, he had them all completely memorized. To prove it, he had Usāmah open the books at random and start to read a passage. In each case Abū ʿAbd Allāh was able to complete the passage and continue on with the rest of the page. This feat impressed Usāmah so much that he worked hard to cultivate his own powers of memorization. So much so that a later biographer recorded (probably with some exaggeration) that Usāmah knew by heart 20,000 lines of poetry composed by the great Preislamic poets. Certainly, this ability would have stood him in good stead when he lost his entire library (said to have contained 4,000 volumes) at sea during his family's escape from Egypt in 1154. The wreck was said to have washed up on the shores of Crusader-held Palestine, and Usāmah's volumes to have been presented to William of Tyre, at that time hard at work on the early stages of his monumental history of the Crusader state. Later, living in the backwater town of Diyarbakr on the upper Euphrates (where most of his non-poetic works were composed), this near-photographic memory would undoubtedly have made it easier for Usāmah to range widely through a number of fields, including *ḥadīth*, poetry and various grammatical citations, as is seen in encyclopedic works like *Kitāb al-'asā* (The Book of the Staff) and *Lubāb al-ādāb* (Kernals of Refinement).

It is most likely that Usāmah began his literary career by composing poetry but very little of that, if any, survives. His *dīwān* (collected poems), compiled during his lifetime, shows signs of extreme selectivity (probably done by the poet himself). No doubt his juvenalia was either extensively edited or simply omitted from the text.

Usāmah also seems to have kept a rather strict division between the subjects he wrote about in prose and those he tackled in his poetry. He includes extensive reminiscences about hunting, for example, in *Kitāb al-i'tibār*. He devotes a whole section to lion hunting, not only because they were still common in the Levantine plains during his lifetime, but because his own name means in Arabic "lion." Hunting poetry was a relatively common genre in medieval Arabic literature but, somewhat surprisingly, Usāmah does not favor it in his surviving compositions.

Similarly, *Kitāb al-i'tibār* has many passages where the Frankish knights are depicted as friends and even comrades. This is especially true of vignettes, found in *Kitāb al-i'tibār,* from the two embassies Usāmah made to the court of King Fulk (d. 1143) in the late 1030s and early 1040s on behalf of his friend and new employer, Unur, the regent of Damascus. Usāmah had been exiled from Shayzar by his uncle Sultan in 1138 and had gone to Damascus to revive his fortunes. According to Usāmah himself, Sultan had grown jealous of his nephew, now that Sultan had a young son, and he no longer wanted him or his brothers within the castle walls. But it was also true that the same year, in the spring of 1138, the new emperor of Byzantium, John, invaded the area around Antioch with the assistance of the Crusaders, to re-establish his authority there. Shayzar was nearly lost by siege to the Christian forces, and Usāmah's move may have reflected the new realities of the situation, where his old home seemed much less safe and secure than it had in the past.

Some of Usāmah's poetry from this period gives a very different picture of relations with the Christians than in *Kitāb al-i'tibār*. In one poem looking back at this difficult time and celebrating the victories that had occurred since, for instance, he says while describing the capture of Baldwin of Marash (Kīlānī, 379):

As we advanced he grew fearful of meeting us,
  then evil and misery were banished because of our prowess.
He turned back, contesting the road with our arrows,
  while his ears were weighted down with the sound of our swords striking flesh and bone,
Then he abandoned his knights and his household to us:
  half of them killed and half taken prisoner.
The horses [set out after him] and the reins were not able to
  to hold them back, even had an eagle flown off with him through the heavens.
Until now he is [captured], visiting with [Count] Jocelyn [in prison]
  sharing with him a night whose darkness has no dawn.
And we will redeem Jerusalem the pure from them,
  not one inch of it will remain their territory.
If the fortresses there are like labyrinths, we have
  keys to open them which are white, with reddened notches.

These lines have a seriousness of tone and an uncompromising intensity that are a far cry from the sometimes almost comical encounters that

Usāmah records in *Kitāb al-iʿtibār*, as when the Templar knights apologize profusely for the behavior of a newly arrived member of their order, who tries to force Usāmah to pray eastwards on one occasion, rather than more properly in the direction of Mecca, which is to the south of Jerusalem (*Arab-Syrian Gentleman*, 163-164).

This poem is also notable in that it forms part of a group that was exchanged between Usāmah and a new friend he had made, the Egyptian *kātib*, and eventually chief vizier of the Fatimid state, Ṭalāʾiʿ ibn Ruzzīk (or Ruzzayk). Ibn Ruzzīk was a committed Ismaili Shiite, as was appropriate to a high official of the Fatimids, and most of his poetry—aside from that he exchanged with Usāmah—was composed to celebrate the virtues of the Ahl al-Bayt (the family of the Prophet Muḥammad's (d. 632) cousin and son-in-law ʿAlī ibn Abī Ṭālib (ca. 600-660) and to mourn their tragic deaths at Shiite festivals like ʿAshūra. Usāmah, on the other hand, was a staunch Sunni, and even produced summaries of two works by Abū ʾl-Faraj ʿAbd al-Raḥmān ibn ʿAlī Ibn al-Jawzī (ca. 1116-1201) celebrating heroes of that tradition, the second Caliph, ʿUmar ibn al-Khattāb (d. 644), and ʿUmar II (d. 720) of the Umayyad Dynasty (the latter is lost, but the former is still extant in manuscript). Despite their different religious orientation, when Usāmah went to Egypt from Damascus in 1144, he and Ibn Ruzzīk became inseparable. Their poetic correspondence is notable for its volume and long persistence but also for the cultivation of a lively spirit of (good-natured) competition designed to show the dexterity and polish of the two devotees of the art of literature.

Once Usāmah arrived in Cairo, he took service with the caliph as a soldier and man-at-arms, eventually becoming an ambassador sent to Nūr al-Dīn (1118-1174), at that time ruler of Aleppo (with designs on Damascus) and son of the first effective leader against the power of the Crusaders to arise among the Muslims of northern Syria, Imād al-Dīn Zanjī (d. 1146). The vizier at the time, al-Malik al-ʿĀdil Ibn al-Sallar, had hoped that Usāmah, with his Syrian ties, would be able to persuade Nūr al-Dīn to attack the Crusader city of Tiberias as a diversion, while the Fatimid army launched its own assault against the southern Crusader stronghold of Ascalon, on the border between Palestine and Egypt. Usāmah was unsuccessful in his mission and eventually returned to Egypt in 1152. He quickly became enmeshed in a plot to kill Ibn al-Sallar, instigated by his step-son, Rukn al-Dīn al-ʿAbbās, who sought to become chief vizier himself. When Ibn al-Sallar was assassinated, on April 3, 1153, Usāmah joined the household of al-ʿAbbās (*Arab-Syrian Gentleman*, 43-53). Relations between al-ʿAbbās and the caliph al-Ẓāfir worsened and after slightly more than a year, al-Ẓāfir was murdered in an attack in which Usāmah was deeply implicated. The remaining members of al-Ẓāfir's family appealed to Usāmah's friend, Ṭalāʾiʿ ibn Ruzzīk (at this time provincial governor in Aswan, in upper Egypt) for protection and vengeance. Ibn Ruzzīk assembled an army, and set out against al-ʿAbbās. Al-ʿAbbās tried to muster his own troops, but they mutinied and in the ensuing chaos he ordered Usāmah to set out with him for Syria. Usāmah, perhaps believing that he might forfeit his life if he stayed, and perhaps thinking he could return to Shayzar, agreed to go, taking his household with him. But their escape route proved so difficult he eventually sent his family back to Cairo, where they were treated well by Ibn Ruzzīk

Nūr al-Dīn, having just taken Damascus for good, welcomed the fugitive warmly and Usāmah quickly entered his service (al-ʿAbbās having been killed by a raiding party of Frankish soldiers as they tried to cross the border between Egypt and Palestine). There, Usāmah renewed his acquaintance with one of Nūr al-Dīn's generals, Shirkuh, uncle of a young Ṣalāḥ al-Dīn.

Finally, in 1156, Usāmah was able to enlist Nūr al-Dīn's help in bringing his family from Egypt to Damascus by boat. The boat, however, was attacked by sailors loyal to the Crusader king, and Usāmah lost all his possessions, including his books (*Arab-Syrian Gentleman*, 60-61). His family was sent on to Damascus with barely the clothes on their backs.

The next year, further tragedy awaited Usāmah. His uncle Sultān had died three years before, in 1154, and Usāmah had gingerly begun to try to re-establish communication with his cousin Tāj al-Dawlah Muḥammad, even sending him a long conciliatory poem. But in August 1157, a powerful earthquake struck northern Syria. Most of the large cities were devastated, and Shayzar was completely destroyed. Virtually all of Tāj al-Dawlah's extended family (with the exception of Usāmah and his kin) had been present inside the castle, celebrating the circumcision ceremony of his young son. Only Tāj al-Dawlah's wife and a servant survived. Such a loss in a single day naturally was a bitter blow to Usāmah, and he felt it keenly. Only after a considerable time had passed was he able to assuage his grief somewhat through the composition of his encyclopedic work *al-Manāzil wa 'l-Diyār*, an examination of all the different ways poets have begun their *qaṣīdah* poems by weeping over abandoned campsites or deserted dwellings. He immediately personalizes the work by telling us at the beginning of the introduction that he was motivated to gather all this material together because of "the destruction visited on my land and my birthplace."

Usāmah, however, would not be able to embark on this project—or the other works that would make his literary reputation—for a number of years to come. It would take several years of hard work by everyone—Muslim, Christian and Jew alike—to repair the damage wreaked by the earthquake. Ibn Ruzzīk, concerned that the Crusaders might be contemplating an invasion of Egypt and eager to follow up on a victory at Ascalon, urged Usāmah to help him arrange an alliance with Nūr al-Dīn. But Usāmah, perhaps more aware of his advancing age, elected instead to carry out his religious duty in 1160 and perform the pilgrimage. Shortly after his return, in 1161, he heard that Ibn Ruzzīk had been stabbed to death by his lieutenants, at the instigation of the Caliph's aunt. Thus ended Usāmah's interest in Egypt.

Nūr al-Dīn then embarked on a series of inconclusive engagements with the Crusaders and Byzantines in northern Syria, around Antioch, and Usāmah was included among his generals. During this time, he became acquainted with Qarā Arslān, also serving in the army. Qarā Arslān was ruler of the fortress of Hisn Kayfā, far away in the remote province of Diyarbakr in northern Iraq. For reasons that are not entirely clear today, Usāmah agree to take service with Qarā Arslān at Ḥiṣn Kayfā in 1164, and it was there that he would spend the next few years in quiet retirement, spending a good deal of his time mapping out the plan for the works (including *Kitāb al-i'tibār*) that would bring him his lasting fame.

Al-*Manāzil wa 'l-Diyār* was probably the first of these works to be finished, and it is easy to understand—given Usāmah's experience in the earthquake—why this subject (deserted dwellings and campsites as places of mourning) would have resonated for him But this was also a topic that had interested others before him, as can be seen with the anonymous work known as *Adab al-Ghurabā'*, probably from the century before Usāmah was born, which has been recently translated into English and published as *The Book of Strangers*.

Similarly, his next composition, *Kitāb al-'asā* (The Book of the Staff), apparently owes its existence to both a personal incident in Usāmah's life and to literary precedent. He tells us in the introduction to this work that he was inspired to compose it because of a tantalizing story had been told of as a child about a mysterious book called *Kitāb al-'asā* that he had searched for as an adult and never been able to find. So he decided to compose it himself. But the structure of *Kitāb al-'asā* owes a great deal to literary precedent in the treatises of the early masters of prose like al-Jāḥiẓ. Nor should it be considered a coincidence that there is a section in al-Jaḥiẓ's masterwork, *Kitāb al-bayān wa 'l-tabyīn* (The Book of Elegant Expression and Clarity of Exposition) on the classification and varieties of staffs and sticks, and their uses.

Taking as its starting point a humble, everyday object—that would seem to present a challenge to elevated literary treatment—the book moves freely between citation of authoritative source material like the *Qur'ān* and *ḥadīth*, traditional stories, personal reminiscence, and poetic quotation. Some of the poems are Usāmah's own, and reflect his lifelong interest in staffs and walking sticks of various sorts, of which he seems to have been something of a connoisseur. But advancing age and the growing importance of the staff or stick to someone who cannot walk as nimbly as he once did, have clearly affected his perception in the humble prop. In one short poem included in the work (442) one can see how the staff becomes for Usāmah the visible reminder of aging:

Time has encompassed me,
and the nights and change have handed me over to destruction.
I have become like a bow—bent over—and my (walking) stick
is the string upon the bow.
I shamble as I walk, and my steps
are too short to take me where I want to go.

Here, an almost unbearable reality is distanced and aestheticized by the artful use of simile, a strategy much cultivated in Arabic poetry.

In 1167 Qarā Arslān died, and Usāmah does not seem to have gotten along as well with his friend's heir, so he spent the next few years shuttling restlessly about from place to place within the province. Finally, in 1174 Ṣalāḥ al-Dīn, now well advanced in his formidable career as a warrior and stateman, returned to Damascus from Egypt, where he had ruled since 1169 on behalf of his old commander Nūr al-Dīn. When Nūr al-Dīn died in May of 1174, Ṣalāḥ al-Dīn came back to his old haunts and eventually would supplant Nūr al-Dīn's heirs as head of the principality. But even before he succeeded, he called Usāmah to his side, a summons that was reputed to have been suggested by Usāmah's son Murhaf, who had become a trusted advisor by Ṣalāḥ al-Dīn.

Since Ṭalā'iʿ ibn Ruzzīk's death, Ṣalāḥ al-Dīn had to a certain extent supplanted as Usāmah's most frequent correspondent. The relationship between the two was different, to be sure. Despite his seniority in age, Usāmah was always the respectful courtier, as can be seen in the following excerpt from a panegyric he enclosed in a letter to Ṣalāḥ al-Dīn in 1176:

You are always surrounded, O King of Islam, by blessing
whose consorts would be the two fortunate ones: victory and triumph.
You destroy enemies and you confiscate their kingdoms
and your helpers are the two sharp ones: the sword and fate.
You are the Alexander of this world: in your light, the two darknesses—
—tyranny and destruction—have faded away.

This is not the bantering tone of equals that we so often encounter in Usāmah's poems for Ṭalā'iʿ ibn Ruzzīk. It is the respectful homage of a subject for his overlord, which continues on throughout the entire poem. Its tone is consistent with the long encomium that concludes *Kitāb al-i'tibār*. But the placement of this praise for Ṣalāḥ al-Dīn at the end Usāmah's prose work suggests that it may have been produced at his behest and financially sponsored by him as well. At the very least, he would not have been unaware of it.

Usāmah, however, did not just rely on the patronage of Ṣalāḥ al-Dīn for his support in the concluding years of his life. Certainly, the ruler took care of his immediate needs, but he had a wide circle of acquaintances who were interested in his hearing about his moral ideas, the fruits of his experiences in government for many decades, and his thoughts on literature. It is in this context that we should view the composition of his last works. Besides *Kitāb al-i'tibār*, these would have included *Kitāb lubāb al-ādāb* (Kernels of Refinement) and *al-Badī' fī 'l-Badī' fī naqd al-shi'r* (Marvels in the Art of Rhetoric in the Criticism of Poetry). These latter two works are highly didactic in their format and would have been most useful in an educational context. Even though by the time of their composition he was nearly ninety, it was possible that Usāmah was working formally as a teacher in these years. Certainly, many prominent later scholars proudly referred to him as their instructor in a variety of fields of learning.

Though he remained active well into his nineties, Usāmah finally succumbed to old age in 1188. The year before, his friend and overlord Ṣalāḥ al-Dīn had finally achieved Usāmah's lifelong wish and conquered Jerusalem, thus inaugurating the end of the Crusader state. Thus, more any other individual of his time, Usāmah was a witness to the first period when the West and the Arab world became aware of one another and found themselves living side by side in a—frequently strained and uneasy—state of engagement whose effects resonate to this day.

REFERENCES

Paul M. Cobb, *Usama ibn Munqidh: Warrior Poet of the Age of the Crusades* (Oxford: Oneworld Publications, 2005);

ʿImād al-Dīn al-Isfahānī, *Kharīdat al-qaṣr wa-jarīdat al-ʿaṣr*, 4 vols., ed. by Shukrī Fayṣal (Damascus: al-Maṭbaʿah al-Hāshimiyyah, 1955-1968);

Robert Irwin, "Usamah ibn Munqidh: an Arab-Syrian Gentleman and Warrior in the Period of the Crusades Reconsidered," in *The Crusades and Their Sources: Essays Presented to Bernard Hamilton*, ed, by J. France and W.G. Zajac (Aldershot: Ashgate Publications, 1998), 71-87;

Attributed to Abū 'l-Faraj al-Iṣfahānī, *The Book of Strangers: Medieval Arabic Graffiti on the Theme of Nostalgia*, trans. by Patricia Crone and Shmuel Moreh (Princeton: Markus Wiener Publishers, 2000);

Aḥmad Qadrī 'l-Kīlānī, *Usāmah ibn Munqidh* (Damascus: al-Maṭbāʿah al-ʿIlmiyyah, 1997);

David W. Morray, *The Genius of Usama ibn Munqid: Aspects of* Kitāb al-Iʿtibār (Durham: Centre for Middle Eastern and Islamic Studies, University of Durham, 1987);

Steven Runciman, *A History of the Crusades*, vols. 1 and 2 (Cambridge: Cambridge University Press, 1951).